The Cult Film Reader

The Cult Film Reader

Edited by Ernest Mathijs and Xavier Mendik

Open University Press

Open University Press
McGraw-Hill Education
McGraw-Hill House
Shoppenhangers Road
Maidenhead
Berkshire
England
SL6 2QL

PN
1995.9
. C84
C85
2008

email: enquiries@openup.co.uk
world wide web: www.openup.co.uk

and Two Penn Plaza, New York, NY 10121-2289, USA

First published 2008

A catalogue record of this book is available from the British Library

ISBN10: 0 335 21923 3 (pb)   0 335 21924 1 (hb)
ISBN13: 978 0 335 21923 0 (pb)   978 0 335 21924 7 (hb)

Library of Congress Cataloging-in-Publication Data
CIP data applied for

Typeset by RefineCatch Limited, Bungay, Suffolk
Printed in Great Britain by Bell and Bain Ltd, Glasgow

The McGraw-Hill Companies

Contents

SECTION 4
Cult consumption

Contributors

Jinsoo An has recently completed his Ph.D. on Korean melodramatic films at the University of California, Los Angeles. He has written widely on East Asian cinema in Korean and English journals, and is a regular curator for screenings of Hong Kong and Korean cinema.

Jane Arthurs is Principal Lecturer and Head of the School of Cultural Studies at the University of the West of England. She is co-editor of *The Crash Controversy* (2001), *Crash Cultures* (2002), and author of *Television and Sexuality* (2004). Her essays appeared in *Feminist Media Studies*, *Screen*, and the collection *Feminism in Popular Culture* (2006).

Bruce A. Austin is Professor of Communication Studies at the Rochester Institute of Technology. His articles on cult and art-house audiences have appeared in the *Journal of Communication*, and the *Canadian Journal of Communication*. His books include *Immediate Seating: A Look at Movie Audiences* (1989), and *The Film Audience* (1995). For years, he was the editor of *Current Research in Film* (1984–90).

Martin Barker is Professor of Film Studies at the University of Wales, Aberystwyth, where he directs the Centre for Audiences and Reception Studies (CARS). He has written on controversial, cult and popular cinema, and is the author of *Haunts of Fear* (1984), *Knowing Audiences* (with Kate Brooks, 1998), *From Antz to Titanic* (with Thomas Austin, 2000), and *The Crash Controversy* (with Ramaswami Harindranath and Jane Arthurs, 2001). His essays have appeared in *Media, Culture and Society*, *Screen, Sight and Sound*, and the *European Journal of Cultural Studies*. He directed the *International Lord of the Rings Research Project* (published in *Watching the Lord of the Rings*, 2007).

Walter Benjamin was a leading member of the Marxist school of critical theory in Germany in the 1930s. His work concentrated on the tensions between high art (literature) and 'art for the masses' (on which he wrote *The Work of Art in the Age of Mechanical Reproduction*). Selections of his writings are published by Harvard University Press (*Selected Writings*), and Pimlico (*Illuminations*). His correspondence with Siegfried Kracauer and Theodor Adorno is also published. Benjamin died in 1940 while trying to escape from Germany via France to Spain.

Harry Benshoff is Associate Professor in film at the University of North Texas. He has taught widely on the horror film, the Western, American film history, international film, television history and lesbian, gay and queer film and video. His publications include his book *Monsters in the Closet: Homosexuality and the Horror Film* (1997) as well as essays on blaxploitation horror films, Dark Shadows fan cultures, and Walt Disney's Silly Symphonies. Most recently he published *America on Film* (2003, with Sean Griffin).

Pierre Bourdieu was a French sociologist at the Ecole des Hautes Etudes en Sciences Sociales and the Collège de France. He was also director of the Centre de sociologie Européenne, and founder of the journal *Actes de la Recherche en Sciences Sociales*. Among his best-known books are *Outline of a Theory of Practice* (1977), *Distinction: A Social Critique of the Judgment of Taste* (1979/1984), *Homo Academicus* (1990), *Language and Symbolic Power* (1991), *Practical Reason* (1998), and *On Television* (1999).

Noel Carroll is Andrew W. Mellon Term Professor in the Humanities at Temple University. He has written widely on horror, popular cinema and avant-garde film. His books include *The Philosophy of Horror or Paradoxes of the Heart* (1990), *Interpreting the Moving Image* (1998), *Theorizing the Moving Image* (1998) and *A Philosophy of Mass Art* (1999). He is a regular contributor to the *Journal of Aesthetics and Art Criticism*.

Steve Chibnall is Professor of British Cinema at De Montfort University and Coordinator of the British Cinema and Television Research Group. He is a founding member of the *Journal of British Cinema and Television*, and co-editor of Routledge's British Popular Cinema series. He has recently published books on *British Crime Cinema*, *British Horror Cinema* (1999, 2001), *Get Carter* and *Brighton Rock* (2003, 2004), *J. Lee Thompson* (2000), and the cult film director *Peter Walker* (1998).

Umberto Eco is Professor of Semiotics and President of the Scuola Superiore di Studi Umanistici at the University of Bologna. He holds a keen interest in the semiotic structures of popular culture, on which he has published numerous books and essays. His books include *The Open Work* (1962), *Theory of Semiotics* (1976), *A Semiotic Landscape* (1979), *Semiotics and the Philosophy of Language* (1985), *Meaning and Mental Representations* (with Marco Santambrogio and Patrizia Violi, 1988), *The Limits of Interpretation* (1990), and *Travels in Hyperreality* (1995). He has also written several novels, including *The Name of the Rose* (1980) and *Foucault's Pendulum* (1988).

Nezih Erdoğan is Professor of Film and TV Studies at the University of Istanbul. His publications and presentations in English and in Turkish include 'Mute bodies, disembodied voices: notes on sound in Turkish popular cinema' in *Screen*, 'The making of our America: Hollywood in a Turkish context' in *Hollywood's Abroad* (Richard Maltby and Melvyn Stokes, eds, 2005) and 'Powerless signs: hybridity and the logic of Turkish excess' in *Mapping the Margins: Identity Politics and the Media* (Karen Ross, Brenda Dervin, Deniz Derman, eds, 2003).

Welch Everman was Professor of English at the University of Maine from 1987 until his death in 2004. He was the author of *Cult Horror Films* (1993), *Cult Science-Fiction Films* (1995), and *Who Says This?: The Authority of the Author, the Discourse, and the Reader* (1988). He also wrote literary criticism, and taught courses on comic books and Samuel Beckett.

John Fiske is Professor Emeritus in Communication and Cultural Studies at the University of Wisconsin-Madison. He is the author of *Reading Television* (1978, with John Hartley), *Television Culture* (1988), *Understanding Popular Culture* (1989), *Reading the Popular* (1989) and *Media Matters: Race and Gender in US Politics* (1996). He was the general editor of *Cultural Studies* during the 1980s to the early 1990s.

Barry K. Grant is Professor of Film and Cultural Studies at Brock University, Ontario. He is the author of *Documenting the Documentary* (1998, with Jeannette Sloniowski), *The Dread of Difference: Gender and the Horror Film* (1996), *Film Genre Reader II* (1995), and *Voyages of Discovery* (1992). His writings have appeared in *The Cult Film Experience* (1991, J.P. Telotte, ed.), *Post Script, Film Quarterly, Journal of Film and Video, Wide Angle* and *Literature/Film Quarterly*.

Ramaswami Harindranath is Senior Lecturer in the department of Culture and Communication at the University of Melbourne. He is the author of *Perspectives on Global Culture* (2006), co-editor of *The Crash Controversy* (2001) and edited a special issue on 'International audience research: continuing concerns and novel developments' for the online journal *Participations* (2006). He has also published essays in the *International Journal of Media and Cultural Politics*, and *Qualitative Sociology Review*.

Joan Hawkins is Professor in Comparative Literature at Indiana University in Bloomington. She has published widely on cult, most notably in *Cutting Edge: Art-Horror and the Horrific Avant-garde* (2000). She has also published 'The anxiety of influence: Georges Franju and the medical horrorshows of Jess Franco', 'Sleaze mania, Euro-trash and high art: the place of European art films in American low culture' and 'One of us: Tod Browning's freaks'.

Gary Hentzi is an Associate Professor of English at the City University of New York. He is co-editor and co-author of *The Columbia Dictionary of Modern Literary and Cultural Criticism* (1995). In addition to his work on criticism, he is a specialist in eighteenth-century English literature and has published several articles on the novels of Daniel Defoe, as well as a number of essays on contemporary film in *Film Quarterly*. He has been an editor of the journal *Critical Texts*.

Matt Hills is Senior Lecturer in Media and Cultural Studies in the School of Journalism at Cardiff University. He has published widely on fandom and cult cinema, including *Fan Cultures* (2002), *How To Do Things with Cultural Theory* (2005) and *Pleasures of Horror* (2005), and contributed essays to *New Media and Society* and *Velvet Light Trap*. He was the founder of the online journal *Intensities*.

J. Hoberman is the senior film critic for *The Village Voice*, for which he has been writing for more than 20 years. He is the author of *Bridge of Light: Yiddish Film Between Two Worlds* (1991), and *Entertaining America: Jews, Movies, and Broadcasting* (with Jeffrey

xii   THE CULT FILM READER

Shandler, 2003), and has also written on Jack Smith (*Jack Smith: Flaming Creatures and Wait for me at the Bottom of the Pool*). Many of his essays are collected in *Vulgar Modernism* (1991). With Jonathan Rosenbaum he wrote *Midnight Movies* (1983).

Leon Hunt is Senior Lecturer in Film and TV Studies at Brunel University. He is the author of *British Low Culture: From Safari Suits to Sexploitation* (1998) and *Kung Fu Cult Masters: From Bruce Lee to Crouching Tiger* (2003), and he has written about a variety of cult genres (in *Unruly Pleasures*, Xavier Mendik, ed., 2000; and *Alternative Europe*, Ernest Mathijs and Xavier Mendik, eds, 2004).

I.Q. Hunter is Head of Film Studies at De Montfort University, Leicester. He is co-editor of Routledge's British Popular Cinema series, for which he edited *British Science Fiction Cinema* (1999) and *British Spy Cinema* (forthcoming). Among his other publications are the co-edited books *Pulping Fictions* (1996), *Trash Aesthetics* (1997), and *Retrovisions* (2001). His recent work has focused on Paul Verhoeven, British exploitation cinema, and Hammer's science fiction and fantasy films, on which he is writing a book.

Mark Jancovich is Professor of Film Studies at the University of East Anglia. He has written on horror, fans and cult cinema, and is the author of *Horror* (1992), *Approaches to Popular Film* (with Joanne Hollows, 1995), *The Film Studies Reader* (with Joanne Hollows and Peter Hutchings, 2000), *Horror the Film Reader* (2002), *Defining Cult Movies* (2003), *The Place of the Audience* (with Lucy Faire and Sarah Stubbings, 2003), and was for years the general editor of *Scope*. His essays have appeared in *Cinema Journal*, *Scope* and *Cultural Studies*.

Henry Jenkins is Professor of Literature and Director of the Comparative Media Studies Program, Massachusetts Institute of Technology. He has published on media fandom and new media. His books include *Textual Poachers* (1992) and his (co-)edited collections include *Science-Fiction Audiences* (1995), *From Barbie to Mortal Kombat: Gender and Computer Games* (1998), *Hop on Pop: the Politics and Pleasures of Popular Culture* (2003), *Democracy and New Media* (2003) and *Rethinking Media Change* (2003). He is a regular contributor to *Computer Games Magazine*, *Flow* and *Technology Review*.

Anne Jerslev is Professor at the Institute of Film and Media at the University of Copenhagen. She was a visiting Professor at the University of California in Los Angeles in 1995. Her research focuses on the semiotic and public reception of cult and horror film (with a special interest in David Lynch, on whom she wrote *David Lynch in Our Eyes*, 1991). She has published on these issues in *Media Cultures* (1992), *Young. Nordic Journal of Youth Research* (1996), and *Kritik* (2001), and has edited (with Ib Bondebjerg) *Realism and Reality in Film and Media* (2002).

Siegfried Kracauer earned a doctorate in engineering and worked as an architect before becoming the literature and film editor for the *Frankfurter Zeitung*. His work on contemporaty culture is published as *The Mass Ornament* (1927). After fleeing from the Nazis, first to Paris, then to the USA, Kracauer worked at the Museum of Modern Art and Columbia University, and wrote *From Caligari to Hitler* (1947) and *Theory of Film* (1960). He died in 1966.

Gina Marchetti is Lecturer in the Department of Comparative Literature at the University of Hong Kong. She is the author of *Romance and the 'Yellow Peril': Race, Sex, and Discursive Strategies in Hollywood Fiction* (1994), and co-editor of the forthcoming anthology *Chinese Connections: Critical Perspectives on Film, Identity, and Diaspora*. Her essays have appeared in *Current Research in Film, Film Quarterly* and *Asian/Pacific Cinemas* (Yau and Hyun Kim, eds, 2001).

Ernest Mathijs is Assistant Professor of Film and Theatre Studies at the University of British Columbia, Vancouver. He is the (co-)editor of *Alternative Europe, The Cinema of the Low Countries, From Hobbits to Hollywood* and *Watching The Lord of the Rings*, and the author of *The Cinema of David Cronenberg*. He is co-editor of the book series Cultographies (Wallflower Press) and Contemporary Cinema (Rodopi).

Xavier Mendik is director of the Cult Film Archive, and convener of the main cult film and TV at Brunel University. He is the author of *Tenebrae* (2000) and the (co-)editor of *Underground USA* (2002), *Alternative Europe* (2004) and *Shocking Cinema of the Seventies* (2004). He is also a documentary filmmaker on horror cinema, as well as Director of the Cine-Excess Film Festival.

Tom Mes is the founder and co-editor of *MidnightEye.com*, the world's leading English-language publication on contemporary Japanese cinema. His work has appeared in such magazines as *Fangoria, Impact, Japan Magazine* and *Skrien*, and in *The Cinema of Japan and Korea* (2004). Recently, he has written *Agitator, the Cinema of Takashi Miike* (2003).

Sheila J. Nayar is Assistant Professor of English and Communication Studies at Greensboro College. She performs scholarly research on orality and literacy in world cinema and Indian popular film in particular. Her publications include essays in the *Journal of Popular Culture, Visual Anthropology, Film Quarterly* and the *Journal of Popular Film and Television*. She also co-wrote the screenplay for *Drowning on Dry Land*.

Gary Needham is Lecturer in media and cultural studies, Nottingham Trent University. He specializes in Italian and Asian cult and horror cinema, on which he has published in *Kinoeye*, and collections such as *Sound in Hong-Kong Cinema* and *Perspectives on Transnational East-Asian Cinema*. He is the co-editor of the *Asian Cinemas Reader* (2006) and he is currently working on an edited collection on queer television, *Pleasures of the Tube*.

Annalee Newitz is Knight Science Fellow at the Massachussets Institute of Technology, where she is researching the history of sex machines and the invention of cyberwarfare. She writes about technology, pop culture and sex in *Wired, Salon* and the *San Francisco Bay Guardian*. She is the editor of *White Trash: Race and Class in America* (1996) and *The Bad Subjects Anthology* (1997). Currently, she is at work on two books on monster movies, capitalism, sex and machines.

Lawrence O'Toole is a literary and cultural critic for numerous North American publications, most notably *Maclean's* from Toronto, for which he was also a staff film critic. He has written extensively on subcultures in film and music, especially in the 1980s.

Harry Allan Potamkin was a film critic for *The New Masses*, *Close-Up*, *The National Board of Review Magazine* and *Variety*. He also wrote poetry, children's literature, and literary criticism. He died in 1933.

Jonathan Rosenbaum is film critic for the *Chicago Reader*, and author of many books on alternative and independent cinema: *Placing Movies: The Practice of Film Criticism* (1995), *Moving Places: A Life at the Movies* (1980; reprint 1995), *Movies as Politics* (1997) and *Essential Cinema* (2004). His most popular work is *Movie Wars: How Hollywood and the Media Limit What Movies We Can See* (2002). He wrote the Modern BFI Classic for *Dead Man*. With J. Hoberman he wrote *Midnight Movies*.

Andrew Ross is Professor in American Studies at New York University. His main research concentrates on labour and work, urban and suburban studies, intellectual history, social and political theory, science, ecology and technology, and cultural studies. He has written *No Respect: Intellectuals and Popular Culture* (1989), *Technoculture* (1991, co-ed.), *Science Wars* (1996, ed.), *The Celebration Chronicles: Life, Liberty, and the Pursuit of Property Value in Disney's New Town* (1999) and *No-Collar: The Humane Workplace and its Hidden Costs* (2002).

David Sanjek is director of the BMI archives in New York City. He has published work on fandom, horror films, and contemporary cinema in *Spectator*, *Post Script*, *Literature/Film Quarterly*, *Film Criticism*, *Cineaste* and *Cinema Journal*, and has chapters in *Sights on the Sixties* (1992), *The Films of Oliver Stone* (1997), *CINESONIC: The World of Sound on Film* (1999), *Film Genre 2000: New Critical Essays* (2000), and *The Trash Film Reader* (2001). He is at work on a collection of essays and a study of musical copyright.

Eric Schaefer is Associate Professor at Emerson College, Boston. He is the author of the award-winning book, '*Bold! Daring! Shocking! True!': A History of Exploitation Film, 1919–1959* (1999) and is working on *Massacre of Pleasure: A History of Sexploitation Films, 1960–1979*. He has also written several essays on related material, published in *Film Quarterly* and *Cinema Journal* (where he also co-edits the archival notes).

Steven Jay Schneider is a producer of horror films, and the author and editor of numerous collections on cinema. He is the author of *Designing Fear: An Aesthetics of Cinematic Horror*, editor of *New Hollywood Violence*, *Fear without Frontiers: Horror Cinema Across the Globe* (2004), and *100 European Horror Films* (2007), and co-editor of *Horror International* (2005). He is the general editor of *1001 Movies You Must See Before You Die* (2003), *501 Movie Directors* (2007) and *501 Movie Stars* (2007). With Xavier Mendik he edited *Underground U.S.A.: Filmmaking Beyond the Hollywood Canon* (2002) and he co-edits the book series Contemporary Cinema with Ernest Mathijs.

Jeffrey Sconce is Associate Professor in the School of Communication at Northwestern University. His research focuses on horror cinema, trash cinema and portrayals of technology in cinema. He is the editor of *Sleaze Artists: Cinema at the Margins of Taste, Style and Politics* (2007), and author of *Haunted Media: Electronic Presence from Telegraphy to Television* (2000). He has also published in *Defining Cult*

Movies (2003), *Screen* (1995, 2002), *Film Quarterly, Science as Culture* and *Film Theory Goes to the Movies* (1993).

Susan Sontag was until her death in 2004 an international figure of fiction and theory as well as a leading human rights activist. Her published fiction includes *The Benefactor, Death Kit, The Volcano Lover* and *In America*, while her theoretical and interpretive publications include *Against Interpretation, On Photography, Illness as Metaphor, Where the Stress Falls* and *Regarding the Pain of Others*.

Janet Staiger is William P. Hobby Centennial Professor at the University of Texas in Austin, where she is also Director of the Center for Women's Studies. She has published mainly on film reception and postfeminist/queer approaches to authorial studies. Her publications include *The Classical Hollywood Cinema* (with David Bordwell and Kristin Thompson, 1985), *Interpreting Films* (1992), *Perverse Spectators* (2000) and *Media Reception Studies* (2005).

J.P. Telotte is Professor in the School of Literature, Communication and Culture at Georgia Tech Ivan Allen College. His research interests revolve around cult cinema, the interface between film and technology and the films of Paul Verhoeven. He has published on this, and related topics, in *Film Quarterly* and *Literature/Film Quarterly*, and his books include *The Cult Film Experience* (1991), *Disney TV* (2004), *Voices in the Dark* (1989), *Science Fiction Film* (with Barry Keith Grant, 2001, eds), *A Distant Technology* (1999) and *Replications: A Robotic History of the Science Fiction Film* (1995).

Parker Tyler was a film critic for *Film Culture*, and the author of several collections of film criticism, such as *The Hollywood Hallucination* (1944), *Magic and Myth of the Movies* (1947), *Underground Film* (1969) and *Screening the Sexes* (1972) – one of the first studies of homosexuality on screen. He wrote the experimental novel *The Young and Evil* (1933), and became a character in Gore Vidal's *Myra Breckenridge*.

Jean Vigo was a French filmmaker and critic. His most famous films are *Zero de Conduite* (1933) and, released posthumously, *L'Atalante* (1934). He is considered a leading figure in surrealist, anarchist, and realist cinema.

Harmony Wu holds a Ph.D. in philosophy from the University of Southern California, and currently teaches at Emerson College, Boston. She has published widely on horror and gay and lesbian cinema and is the editor of *Axes to Grind: Re-Imagining the Horrific in Visual Media and Culture* (a special issue of *Spectator*). She also contributed to *Defining Cult Movies* (Mark Jancovich *et al.*, eds, 2003), and *Visible Nations* (Chon Noriega, ed., 2001).

Foreword
From countercultural to cult:
an introduction by Roger Corman

I am always excited and invigorated when a book like *The Cult Film Reader* comes across my desk. It is becoming ever more important in this era of transient technologies to maintain the essential links between the creative processes of filmmakers like myself and the academic study and appreciation of our work. What is written on a web page today may be deleted tomorrow, however with a book like *The Cult Film Reader* you can capture a moment in time and suspend ideas and concepts for eternal future generations of scholars to study. They really will be able to see the whole picture and not just what's left on the hard drive.

While we are all personally familiar with great movie masters such as Ford, Hitch-cock, Fellini, Bergman, Godard and Kurosowa, we know less about those directors and producers like Tobe Hooper, Richard Kelly, Jess Franco, Jack Hill and Takashi Miike, whose creativity lies outside the accepted canon of film interpretation. I hope that this new volume will offer a fresh outlook on those individuals who have devoted their careers to creating cult and so-called 'exploitation' cinema.

In my roles as director, producer, studio head and mentor I have consistently cre-ated films that have been defined as 'cult', be they gothic horror or gangster film, biker movie or blaxploitation, women in peril movies or women in prison flicks. What attracts me about these types of movie is the fact that they can be more experimental and more daring than the big budget studio films, which are so often constrained by narrow economic interests, business dictates and ideological agendas.

It is precisely these narrow kinds of viewpoint that the cult film seeks to expose, belittle and overthrow. If this means that the cult film has to be defined as a rebellious format I can only say that my own films have always been inspired by countercultural ideals and have tried to combine entertainment with a more subversive message. During the late 1960s when I was making films such as *The Wild Angels* (1966) and *The Trip* (1967), I was very much aware of the ability of cult movies to be both political and popular. Whereas previous 'message' movies failed to make an impact on the young and discontented, the use of exploitation imagery allowed these films to act as a rallying point for the wave of anti-authoritarianism which was sweeping Europe and America at that time. With what is happening in the USA and the UK today I think there is even a greater need to artistically rebel against authority, which is why this new volume is so timely and appropriate. I hope it will inspire at least one person to pick up a camera and start shooting.

What is fascinating about current movie trends is the way in which mainstream cinema is increasingly interested in the cult creator. This is because the cult producer, writer and director is always taking chances, disobeying rules and breaking new and dangerous ground. The cult creator remains more in tune with the audience and setting new trends. Despite our limitations of budget, distribution and marketing machines, the cult creator remains in front of the big budget mainstream movie and they always learn new tricks from us, whether they acknowledge this or not. The cult creator is often young and idealistic because they realize that they have the ability to influence a new generation of moviegoers. Although I'm not that young any more, I am proud to have worked, and to continue to work, in the exciting and unconventional field of cult cinema.

I personally believe that we are now entering a new era of film production and distribution and in this period it is the responsibility of both film academics and filmmakers to produce and theorize those movies which retain this rebellious edge. Having lost the drive-in and video store, technology such as the internet and video on demand are now the new battle grounds between cult and conventional cinema. By charting the changes from grindhouse and midnight movie to contemporary forms of cult exhibition such as the internet, this book captures the important transitions that have occurred in this unorthodox arena of moviemaking. By also comparing past American and European exploitation traditions with contemporary cult cycles emerging from the Far East and the developing world, this book will remain a relevant guide to current countercultural trends. I look forward to *The Cult Film Reader* being required reading for moviemakers and grad students for many years to come.

Roger Corman
July 2007

Cult corner: acknowledgements

From idea to publication, this project has completed a journey not unlike that of many a revered cult film: it started as a wild ambition, then took a few years before the initial plan was executed, and it underwent many changes before we arrived at a final cut – one which like all cult films is but a stage in the longer reception trajectory of the study of cult. Those who know film cults will not be surprised to hear that the most fruitful stages of the entire process, the moments when bursts of inspiration pushed us forward, took place during festivals, in the fringes of which a project like this one is bound to blossom.

Our first and foremost thanks must go to the contributors whose writings on cult cinema have given this book its impetus. Thanks for your kind permissions to reproduce your works. We thank the original publishers of the works included in this reader for their permissions to reprint and redistribute these works. We explored every possible avenue to obtain rights to reprint, but in the few cases where we have not received an answer we hope any forthcoming rights owners will recognize the spirit of appreciation within which all essays are reprinted. All new information will be included in subsequent editions of this reader.

Like all cult films, the inspiration for this book is of a collaborative nature, and we owe gratitude to a number of fellow travellers for their support, enthusiasm and comments, especially Martin Barker, Ethan De Seife, Steve Dixon, Leon Hunt, Russ Hunter, Gérard Kraus, Howard Martin, Tereza Mendik, Tamao Nakahara, Julian Petley, Julian Savage, Jamie Sexton, Rebekah Smith and Dirk Van Extergem. We thank Roger Corman, Harry Kümel, John Landis, Brett Sullivan, Emily Perkins and Brian Yuzna for their heartfelt endorsements of the reader, and for their useful comments. Thanks too, to the staff of the Brussels International Festival of Fantastic Film (BIFFF), and the Cine-Excess/Sci-Fi London Film Festival for allowing us to roam freely and cheaply in their midst.

Eve Bennett laboured hard, in the darkest, most cultish corners, to compile essential parts of the bibliography, and we owe her gratitude for her work.

We are indebted to the editors at Open University Press and McGraw-Hill, especially Chris Cudmore, who instigated this project, and oversaw it from beginning to end, and Jack Fray, whose dedication ensured no single aspect of this endeavour was overlooked.

Thanks too to the Department of Theatre, Film, and Creative Writing of the University of British Columbia, and the School of Arts at Brunel University, for grants and logistic support that made the execution of our plans possible.

London, Vancouver, September 2007

Publisher's acknowledgements

The editors and publisher wish to thank the following for permission to use copyright material.

Potamkin, H. 'Film cults' in Jacobs, L. (ed.) *The Compound Cinema: The Writings of Harry Allan Potamkin* (New York: Teachers College Press, 1977). Reproduced with kind permission of Lillian Jacobs.

Benjamin, W. 'The Work of Art in the Age of Mechanical Reproduction' in *Illuminations* (1936). Reproduced with permission of Harcourt, Inc.

Sontag, S. 'Notes on Camp' in *Against Interpretation and Other Essays* (New York: Farrar, Strauss and Giroux) 1964. © 2001 The Estate of Susan Sontag, reprinted with permission of the Wylie Agency Inc.

Ross, A. 'Uses of camp' in *No Respect: Intellectuals and Popular Culture* (New York: Routledge, 1989). Reproduced by permission of Routledge, a division of Taylor & Francis Group.

Grant, B.K. 'Science fiction double feature: Ideology in the cult Film' in Telotte, J.P. (ed.) *The Cult Film Experience* (Austin: University of Texas Press, 1991).

Jerslev, A. 'Semiotics by instinct: "Cult film" as a signifying practice between film and audience' in Skovmond, M. and Schroder, K. (eds) *Media Cultures: Reappraising Transnational Media* (London: Routledge, 1992). Reproduced by permission of Routledge, a division of Taylor & Francis Group.

Sconce, J. 'Trashing the academy: Taste, excess and an emerging politics of cinematic style' in *Screen*, 36(4). Reproduced by permission of Oxford University Press.

Hills, M. 'Media fandom, neoreligiosity and cult(ural) studies' in *The Velvet Light Trap*, 46 (Austin: University of Texas Press, 2002).

Jancovich, M. 'Cult fictions: Cult movies, subcultural capital and the production of cultural distinctions' in *Cultural Studies*, 16(2). Reproduced by permission of Taylor & Francis Group.

Hawkins, J. 'The anxiety of influence: Georges Franju and the medical horrorshows of Jess Franco' in *Cutting Edge: Art Horror and the Horrific Avant-Garde* (Minneapolis: University of Minnesota Press, 2000).

Schaefer, E. 'The obscene seen: Spectacle and transgression in postwar burlesque films' in *Cinema Journal*, 36(2). Reproduced by permission of the University of Texas Press.

Benshoff, H. 'Blaxploitation horror films: Generic reappropriation or reinscription?' in *Cinema Journal*, 39(2). Reproduced by permission of the University of Texas Press.

Chibnall, S. '*Carter* in context' in *Get Carter* (London: IB Tauris, 2003).

Staiger, J. 'Hitchcock in Texas: Intertextuality in the face of blood and gore' in Iversen, G., Kulset, S. and Skretting, K. (eds) *As Time Goes By: Festskrift I anledning Bjorn Sorenssens 50-arsday* (Trondheim: Tapir, 1996).

Schneider, S.J. 'The essential evil in/of *Eraserhead*' (or, Lynch to the contrary) in Sheen, E. and Davison, A. (eds) *The Cinema of David Lynch: American Dreams, Nightmare Visions* (London: Wallflower Press, 2004).

Needham, G. 'Playing with genre: An introduction to the Italian *giallo*' in *Kinoeye*, 2(11), www.kinoeye.org/02/11/needham 11.php.

Hunt, L. 'Han's Island revisited: *Enter the Dragon* as transnational cult film' in Mendik, X. and Harper, G. (eds) *Unruly Pleasures: The Cult Film and its Critics* (Guildford: FAB Press, 2000). Originally published by FAB Press. www.fabpress.com.

An, J. '*The killer*: Cult film and transcultural (mis)reading' in Yau, E. (ed.) *At Full Speed: Hong Kong Cinema in a Borderless World* (Minneapolis: University of Minnesota Press, 2001).

Erdogan, N. 'Mute bodies, disembodied voices: Notes on sound in Turkish popular cinema' in *Screen*, 43(3). Reproduced by permission of Oxford University Press.

Mes, T. '*Ichi the Killer*' in *Agitator: The Cinema of Miike Takashi* (London: FAB Press, www.fabpress.com.

Kracauer, S. 'Cult of distraction: On Berlin's Picture palaces' reprinted with kind permission of the publisher from *The Mass Ornament*: *Weimar Essays* by Siegfried Kracauer, translated and edited by Thomas Y. Levin, pp. 323–8, Cambridge, MA: Harvard University Press, Copyright © 1995 by the President and Fellows of Harvard College.

Bourdieu, P. 'Introduction' in *Distinction: A Social Critique of the Judgement of Taste* (London: Routledge, 1984).

Jenkins, H. ' "Get a life!": fans, poachers, nomads' in *Textual Poachers* (New York: Routledge, 1992). Reproduced by permission of Routledge, a division of Taylor & Francis Group.

Fiske, J. 'The cultural economy of fandom' in Lewis, L. (ed.) *Adoring Audiences* (London: Routledge, 1992). Reproduced by permission of Routledge, a division of Taylor & Francis Group.

Hunter, I.Q. 'Beaver Las Vegas! A fan boy's defence of *showgirls*' in Mendik, X. and Harper, C. (eds) *Unruly Pleasures: The Cult Film and its Critics* (Guildford: FAB Press, 2000). Originally published by FAB Press. www.fabpress.com.

Barker, M., Arthurs, J. and Harindranath, R. 'The *Crash* controversy: Reviewing the press' in *The Crash Controversy: Censorship Campaigns and Film Reception* (London: Wallflower Press, 2001).

Every effort has been made to trace the copyright holders but if any have been inadvertently overlooked the publisher will be pleased to make the necessary arrangement at the first opportunity.

Editorial Introduction: What is cult film?

The necessity of a definition of cult film

It seems cult is everywhere. *Rough Guides* and *Sixty Second* pocket books on cult films are available in practically every bookshop. In recent years, major television networks as diverse as MTV, TMF, A-Channel, Channel 4 and Channel 5 have devoted special shows to cult cinema. On a more academic level, the online journal *Intensities* and book series on cult and exploitation films like *Cultographies* and *Alterimage*, and research initiatives like the Cult Film Archive testify to how firmly entrenched the topic is becoming within academia. There is an important cultural and economical significance to this wide spread of cult. It is part of a more general widening of popular and alternative tastes, de facto creating more interest, and more cults. This leads to 'countless niches', undermining taste regimes, canons, and challenging business plans – a cult film is quickly becoming as powerful a business force as a blockbuster. A definition of cult cinema is surely timely then. Everyone is waiting for it, and the high number of offhand definitions given on the internet almost scream for an academic attempt. Capturing the topic, isolating and determining the species through a definition, now is urgent.

It is essential to carve out the elements that surround cult cinema. Typically, a cult film is defined through a variety of combinations that include four major elements:

1 *Anatomy*: the film itself – its features: content, style, format and generic modes.
2 *Consumption*: the ways in which it is received – the audience reactions, fan celebrations and critical receptions.
3 *Political economy*: the financial and physical conditions of presence of the film – its ownerships, intentions, promotions, channels of presentation, and the spaces and times of its exhibition.
4 *Cultural status*: the way in which a cult film fits a time or region – how it comments on its surroundings, by complying, exploiting, critiquing or offending.

We do not propose that all of these elements need to be fulfilled together in order to speak of a film as a cult film. But we do suggest that each of them is of high significance in what *makes* a film cult.

The anatomy of cult film

There are some features that tend to be associated with cult films more than others. The first two of these features are pretty basic, relating to the extremes of quality. But it is their combination with the other features that gives them credence.

(1) *Innovation*: cult films contain an element of innovation, aesthetically or thematically. There is a curious overlap (though far from a total one) between regular canons of cinema and cult cinema. Often this is the result of the way art cinema challenges conventions and instigates new techniques. Cult films also innovate film history. In fact, they are the shocks to the system. As a result, many 'art house' films have gained a status as being of particular cult quality, and have crossed over. Examples include *Un chien andalou* (1928), *Salo* (1975) *Le weekend* (1967) or *In the Realm of the Senses* (1976).

(2) *Badness*: conversely, cult films are also, and often at the same time, considered bad, aesthetically or morally. Of particular interest are those films being valued for their 'ineptness' or poor cinematic achievement, often placing them in some kind of opposition to the 'norm' or mainstream in that they attain a status of 'otherness'. Such 'bad' films quickly gain a status as cult (though far from all 'bad' films achieve that status). Examples include *Reefer Madness* (1934), *Plan 9 From Outer Space* (1959) or *Showgirls* (1995).

(3) *Transgression*: beyond the basic poles of good and bad, a lot of the competence of a cult film lies in its ability to transgress the barriers of good and bad; to obliterate them. A common way of achieving this is through the challenging of one or more 'conventions' of filmmaking, which may include stylistic, moral or political qualities. It allows for the employment of far-reaching techniques that violate traditions, either through their crudeness (*Thundercrack*, 1975) or their inventiveness (*Eraserhead*, 1977), and it invites a wide arsenal of critical connections and references to be used within one story-framework, often defying more consensual logistics of narrative construction. This aesthetic is often described as a connection with US avant-garde cinemas, like Kenneth Anger, Jack Smith and the Kuchar Brothers, but it also relates to unusual films like *El Topo* (1970) or *The Rocky Horror Picture Show* (1975).

(4) *Genre*: cult films are often made within the constraints and possibilities of genres, and as such they adhere to generic regimes of production. Yet, as a rule, they blur and push the generic conventions they are supposed to respect. They do this by mixing genres (*Alien*, 1979), exposing and/or mocking a genre's unwritten rules satirically (*Blazing Saddles*, 1974) or hyperbolically exaggerating those rules (*Barbarella*, 1968). As such, the treatment of genre by cult movies is either premodernist in that instead of taking culture seriously, it carnivalizes it; or postmodernist in that it endlessly and relentlessly reflects on culture. The most popular genres that lend themselves to these treatments are horror, science fiction and fantasy because of their utopian and dystopian opportunities (*Blade Runner*, 1982; *Labyrinth*, 1984); and melodrama and musical because of their overplaying of the emotional states of characters and situations (*Gone With the Wind*, 1939; *The Sound of Music*, 1965). Often, generic styles are upset by the use of decidedly artificial motifs, such as surrealist imagery, and deadpan existentialist performances are favourite techniques (*The Blues Brothers*, 1980; *The Big Lebowski*, 1998).

(5) *Intertextuality*: how a film invites comparison, connections and linkages with other films and other parts of culture is crucial in determining a film as cult. This involves not only the inclusion of references to other film texts in the form of quotes or cameos but also the calling into reflection of cultural myths, historical backgrounds and archetypes. At its most subtle, intertextuality offers playful inside jokes for avid audiences. Good examples are the layers of references in *From Dusk 'till Dawn* (1995) or *Ginger Snaps* (2000). It puts cult films at the centre of a cultural era, and sometimes of fashion, such as hippiedom in *Easy Rider* (1969) or Generation X in *Slacker* (1993). At their widest these uses enable a cult film to be so indicative of its contemporality that it becomes a true 'sign of the times'. At its extreme, intertextuality forms the basis of the narrative, turning the story into a direct address of films or media, as in *Videodrome* (1983).

(6) *Loose ends*: many cult films leave room for narrative and stylistic loose ends. In most cases, this shows itself in abrupt, insultingly conformist or problematic endings, often dissatisfying or puzzling. The openness is also typically a feature of scenes that show obvious signs of inclusion at a later stage, violating continuity, disrespecting narrative cohesion (either a sign of integrity, incompetence or of selling out), or of a clear intervention that resulted in deleted scenes (caused by censorship, malpractice, wear or *force majeure*) Ironically, these interventions offer viewers the freedom of speculating on the story, and polishing or radicalizing the style on the film's behalf. It puts hilariously bad movies (*Maniac*, 1934) shoulder to shoulder with films that received harsh censorship treatments (*Last House on the Left*, 1972), and films whose story is simply too complex or convoluted for a straightforward narrative (*2001, A Space Odyssey*, 1968). These films often exist in different formats, with director's cuts and uncensored versions adding to their cult reputations.

(7) *Nostalgia*: a core feature of many cult films is their ability to trigger a sense of nostalgia, a yearning for an idealized past. The nostalgia can be part of the film's story. Humphrey Bogart's assertion, in *Casablanca* (1942), that he and Ingrid Bergman will 'always have Paris' is perhaps the best example. But most likely it is an emotional impression. Much of the cult reputation of *Sissi* (1955–7) and *The Sound of Music* (1965) relies on their ability to evoke nostalgia for the glamour and picturesque scenery of traditional Austria, encapsulated in the cities of Vienna and Salzburg (which have since becomes sites of pilgrimage for fans). Cities oozing nostalgia, such as Rome (*Roman Holiday*, 1953) or Venice (*Don't Look Now*, 1973) add to films' cult appeal. Painstakingly authentic historical epics, such as *Das Boot* (1981), while not evoking nostalgia in the same way, also draw a lot of their cult appeal through their ability to submerge audiences in a 'past world'. A trope often appearing in combination with nostalgia is time-travel. It allows for visualizations of past, future, or a parallel present, and it is a guaranteed way of generating speculation on how to interpret the story, and where (and when) it belongs, as evidenced by the cult followings for *Donnie Darko* (2001), *Back to the Future* (1985) and *It's a Wonderful Life* (1946).

(8) *Gore*: 'yukkie stuff' is a sure way to grant films a cult status. This not only relates to films that transgress on the level of explicit violence or presentation of uncomfortable material. Often these will be horror films, though not necessarily exclusively so. It also relates to films whose content and style invokes a sense of 'impurity' or 'endangerment' of the human body's physical integrity, in the sense that they contain explicit

violence, decay, mutilation or cannibalism. Examples are *The Act of Seeing With One's Own Eyes* (1971), and *The Texas Chain Saw Massacre* (1974). Tied into this, a film's appeal as a cult film lies in its ability to convincingly use special effects in simulating gore. Much of the reputation of *Evil Dead* (1982), *The Thing* (1982), and *Scanners* (1981) relies on their make-up and explosion effects.

The consumption of cult film

The way cult films are received differs radically from mainstream cinema. The emphasis of their reception is not on box office figures and mass audiences. Nor do cult films rely too heavily on the critical acclaim so essential for art-house and independent cinema. Their reception does not typically end at the vaults of a bank or the archives of a museum of heritage. Instead, the consumption of cult cinema relies on continuous, intense participation and persistence, on the commitment of an active audience that celebrates films they see as standing out from the mainstream of 'normal and dull' cinema. That audience aligns itself fully with what they perceive to be an attitude of rebellion or a sense of shared belonging. Both indicate a radical refusal to become associated with the anonymous mainstream, and they result in a strong desire to champion films that embody that refusal. Let us explore these receptions.

(1) *Active celebration*: the activeness of the celebration is to be taken literally here, and comes indeed close to the organized forms of religious or spiritual worshipping of the original meaning of the term 'cult' (see Section one). A key term here is *ritual*: as with traditional cultism, cult cinema reception relies on ritualized manners of celebration, sometimes with hierarchical orders imposed on the activities, and with fairly strict delineations for roles in the ceremonies. As with most rituals in society, aspects of purity, initiation and infection play a crucial role in this celebration.

(2) *Communion and community*: cult reception is, however, not as easily described as 'organized' in the same sense as many cults. The sense of communion and community to be experienced at such events might be described as pre-programmed, and sometimes even semi-automatic, as reports on *The Rocky Horror Picture Show* stagings and *The Sound of Music* singalongs indicate, but it is equally possible to see it as more spontaneous, as an unplanned or even imagined sense of camaraderie and fellowship before, during, or after a screening. The way audiences have described their sense of belonging to a group after having seen the avant-premiere of *The Lord of the Rings* (2001–3), or a rare screening of *One Second in Montreal* (1969), are good examples of this.

(3) *Liveness*: what all cult film consumptions have in common is that they are 'lived' experiences, either physically or by proxy. Many celebrations of cult movies are in fact live-events, within an atmosphere akin to theatrical performance, in which 'being there' and 'being part' become important, and technological accidents (like a screening being interrupted) enhance the 'lived' aspect of the screening. The element of physical endurance of some cult celebrations, like full-length screenings of *Empire* (1964), marathons of the *Heimat* series (1984), the timing of the original 'midnight movies' (literally at midnight), festivals' all-nighters, or intimate 'sleepover' viewings, enhances films' status to the level of cult, as a rite involving debutantes, survivors and veterans. The liveliness and outrageousness of such lived experiences emphasize cult

consumption's refusal to be dull and 'normal'. Cult audiences seek for films, and seek to enjoy films in ways that stand away from regular or mainstream reception. There is a tendency to search rare and extreme occasions, in the margins of legality. The most notorious example of this is the search for 'snuff movies' (films in which actual people are killed) – a search that has so far proven them to be an urban myth.

(4) *Commitment*: the consumption of cult cinema also demonstrates a continuous commitment. It is not a fad or craze. Once bitten, the bug stays. The most commonly known commitment is *fandom*. Fans are publicly declared dedicated followers of a film. There is some ambiguity as to whether cult films typically attract fandom, and if they do, whether that fandom is of an atypical, extreme kind. Cult films do have fans, and the many fan conventions, associations and formations involving cult movies, from the highly organized *Star Wars* fans, over the loosely organized *Exorcist* devotees, to the private fandoms of erotic thrillers testify of this. But at the same time there is a sense that the term fandom is too generalist and tame to actually capture the particular kinds of persistence and dedication involved in cult. Perhaps the difficulty of cult fandom is that it always needs to be of an offbeat kind. So, it is not the huge numbers of fans that might make *Titanic* (1997) cult but rather the way in which it was celebrated through all-girl repeat viewings. Traditional fandom remains largely respectful towards the film's interpretive integrity but other ways of commitment involve challenges to its interpretations, either by robbing it of its meaning, or by replacing it with one that might counter its intentions. The processes through which this happens vary, but *bricolage* (the use of bits from different films in fandom), *sampling* (the copying of bits into a new textual unity) and *poaching* (often equal to fan fiction – the construction of a new text based on the raw materials of the original) are often mentioned as ways in which fans appropriate, and come to own, the meaning of a film – a sign of high commitment. The 'outing' of *Top Gun* (1986) as a reportedly closeted gay film is a good example of how this appropriation can fulfil political purposes; in this case unmasking the homo-erotic subtexts in an otherwise very macho film. The more such appropriation happens for one film, the more likely it will be a cult film.

(5) *Rebellion*: audiences of cult movies stress their rebellious attitude, and they frequently consider themselves outsiders, renegades roaming the borders of what is morally acceptable. Often this attitude exhibits itself in a fierce and radical refusal to condone regular movie-going, and in a penchant desire to disrupt such practices, for instance by inappropriate behaviour, such as disturbing sounds or 'call and response' reactions. A most peculiar example of this is the Brussels International Festival of Fantastic Film, where premieres, award ceremonies and revivals alike are greeted with boisterous audience behaviour. Among the rebellious attitudes, *cinephilia* is the best known. It is a righteous, eclectic and often pretentious form of aesthetic judgement of films that mercilessly condemns 'mainstream' taste and supports only esoteric networks of appreciation. Cinephiles are viewers who pride themselves on expert opinions on the topic of cinema. They have a preference for films that 'challenge' and/or contain 'philosophical journeys' – an appreciation for films that are 'demanding'. Examples of films that are known to attract cinephiles are *A Clockwork Orange* (1971), *Crash* (1996), and *Fight Club* (1999). *Buffs* are the extreme opposite of cinephiles, revelling in their appreciation of, and trivial knowledge of, literally every single film, loving it simply because

it is part of the medium, and loving film facts simply because they are film related facts. Cinephilia and buffery come close to cultist consumption because of the way their extreme nature of appreciation challenges traditional forms of liking or disliking films. In between, many other rebellious attitudes are possible, two of which deserve particular attention: avid audiences and slash fiction. *Avid* or *smart audiences* combine in-depth factual and theoretical knowledge about films with an informed understanding of narrative and stylistic sophistication. They revel in the number of references, interpretations and connections their knowledge allows them to make and by doing so they equip films with multiple subtexts. They do not usually make the harsh and detached aesthetic judgements cinephiles make. *Kill Bill* (2003–4), *Ginger Snaps* (2000) and Japanese manga films have attracted such consumption; and manga's punk-like fans (the 'otaku'), or *Ginger Snaps'* feminist Gothic following are good examples of avid audiences – in a sense that these are relentlessly reflexive audiences for relentlessly reflexive films, often identified as 'nerdish'. Finally, *slash fiction* is the superlative step in the rebellious attitude of the consumption of cinema, rendering films a cult status through their particularly obnoxious and disrespectful rejection of any cultural value. While similar to fan fiction, slash fiction is typically very rude and nihilistic. It lacks any reverence for the original, as is evidenced by a community like *Smartania*, which opposes, and mocks, anything whatsoever.

(6) *Alternative canonization*: the final step in cult movie consumption is the construction of an alternative canon of cinema, pitched against the 'official' canon. Cult moviegoers do not just consume but also champion a particular kind of film. This championing demonstrates itself in a variety of ways, but lists ('top-100s', 'best ever'. 'most bloody') are a typical characteristic of this. The *Psychotronic Movieguide* and numerous *Cult Movies* collections are key examples, as is the way in which a magazine like *Fangoria* established a canon in the 1980s. List-mania, to be found on virtually all websites devoted to cult cinema (and now in rapid adoption by online retailers) is the most visible feature of the alternative canon and partisanship of taste typical of cult cinema reception. Significantly, a lot of the canonizing is done amateurishly: in semi-communal circles (nerd circles, governed by rituals and exclusion), in customer reviews, blogs, fanzines, or on discussion lists, with a lot of respect for freelance, non-aligned, film criticism. Cult film takes a prominent place as a catalyser of this form of consumption. Since the mid-1990s, this process has become known as *paracinematic* consumption, and the resulting canon as *paracinema*. The term describes the complexity of the alternative canon constructed. The paracinematic attitude is one that finds 'different reasons' for enjoyment of cinema, outside accepted 'good tastes'. So, a film also appearing in the official canon of cinema, such as *Citizen Kane* (1941) or *Battleship Potemkin* (1926) can also appear in the alternative, cult canon, but judged by 'differing' standards. These standards usually involve the blurring of numerous categories, making the organizing principles of the ranking and listing almost invisible and/or intangible. This obfuscation is exactly what paracinema aims for.

The political economy of cult film

In a landscape that is characterized by niche consumption, the cultures that enable and regulate cult receptions are of prime importance. Cult films rely on reputations, and reputations are the result of specific types of presence in a public sphere (in other words: a cult film needs to be noted). Like other types of cinema, cult films are part of an economic premise: a lot of them are produced for profit, through the routines of production of their genre, region or period (or willingly violating those routines), and released to maximize exposure and, hence, revenue. At least in theory. In practice, cult films typically fall foul of a full routine run through these mechanisms. Something always goes wrong with cult films – there is always something unplanned intervening in one of the levels of production, promotion or reception.

(1) *Production – legends and accidents*: next to an auteurist intention, each film also has an entrepreneurial aim – be it to produce entertainment, make money or achieve cultural gain. Yet cult films are more likely to be the result of 'accidents'. They invariably have complex, confused, controversial or bumpy origins, wrought with smaller or bigger narratives ('legends', 'myths'). They seem to happen, more than to be planned, even in the cases of generic cult movies, like Roger Corman's exploitation movies shot on the fly, such as *Caged Heat* (1974) or *The Terror* (1963). The murky and bizarre legends of their origin help form a basis for their cult(ural) presence. Even legendary auteurs whose work is seen as very consistent or planned seem to have the odd one out, and that is most likely to be a cult favourite (like Hitchcock's *Psycho*, 1960; or *Rope*, 1948). Filmmakers whose careers are littered with such accidents, and their accompanying legends, like Orson Welles (*The Magnificent Ambersons*, 1942) or Terry Gilliam (*Brazil*, 1984), are likely to be celebrated as cult figures. Brilliant failures and initially 'tanking' films have a good chance of picking up cult credentials. Likewise, cult stardom differs from regular celebrity culture. Cult stars often suffer major setbacks (personally as well as professionally) and their careers and lives are surrounded by mystery and tragedy. The sudden death of Rudolph Valentino, Bela Lugosi's sad demise, the closet sexuality of Rock Hudson, the self-destruction of Judy Garland and the excesses of Elvis Presley are key to their cult legend – leading to dedicated followings sympathizing with plights marked by addiction, abuse or suicide. Such followings are not always free from campy or ironic irreverence. A quite separate category is the cult star known for one role only, most likely monsters, like Gunnar Hansen's Leatherface from *The Texas Chainsaw Massacre*, a frequent feature at monster conventions, or self-aware sex symbols, like Raquel Welch in *Myra Breckinridge* (1969).

(2) *Promotion – specialist events and limited access*: often, promotion campaigns even try to present a film as 'cult' before it has reached an audience – packaging it as cult to fit into a niche market segment, or using opportunist showmanship, from Barnum-like stunts to William Castle-type gimmicks. Still, in most cases a film becomes cult through a failure in effectiveness or containment of tested techniques (missed opportunities, messed up openings, unintended scandals). A good example is the 'freak' programming of *The Texas Chainsaw Massacre* as a 1970s children's matinee movie. It provides them with a unique presence, undeniably original. Among these presences, specialist events such as festivals and screenings play an important role. The 1970s circuit of midnight screenings that led to the cult reputations of *El Topo*,

Eraserhead or *The Rocky Horror Picture Show* is one example; the circuit of specialist festivals is another. Exploitation cineastes like Lucio Fulci and Jean Rollin, and the more edgy work of iconoclastic directors like Guy Maddin or Gregg Araki thrive on such circuits. Ironically, the lack of availability often determines a film's cult. The cult reputation of the 'video nasties' in the 1980s was directly connected to their unavailability in the UK. Other 'inaccessible' films that have attracted a certain following because they were, temporarily or permanently, hidden from public view include *Vampyr* (1932, no finished version survives), *Zéro de conduite* (1933, banned for decades) or *Superstar: the Karen Carpenter Story* (1987, blocked by courts). In some cases, this inaccessibility is alleviated by access to ancillary materials, and those materials then become subject of a proxy cult, or even overshadow the film's original presence. *Koyaanisqatsi* (1982), for instance, is a film to which one had, for a long time, only access via its soundtrack. Even so-called blockbuster cults, such as *Pirates of the Caribbean* (2003–7) or *The Lord of the Rings* (2001–3), which are available in abundance, operate according to this mechanism of limited access – in this case the element of 'rarity' shifts back to specialist events like dress-up screenings or red carpet premieres.

(3) *Reception – tales and tails*: though they often exist in the margins of cultural radars, cult films typically enjoy a long period of public presence – they sediment in niches and fetish markets where they remain in demand. One important characteristic of this long tail reception is the constant stream of tales around a film. *Scanners* (1981) for instance remained a hotly debated film for years after its release, becoming associated by proxy with several kinds of scandal (video nasties, school shootings) and debates (over the special effects). Such continuous presence often convinces producers there is room for serialization of franchises through sequels and remakes, all of which of course add to the attention the original receives. The numerous sequels to *Friday the 13th* (1980), including tie-ins with that other franchise *Nightmare on Elm Street* (1984), and the stream of Hollywood remakes of Japanese horror films, like *Ring* (1999) or *Dark Water* (2003) have given the originals an almost endless reception tail. In addition, retrospectives, restorations, revivals, re-releases, director's cuts, spin-offs, rip-offs and spoofs solidify their reception presence, making cult reception one of the most sought after reception conditions in filmmaking.

The cultural status of cult film

The cultural context within which films exist plays a prominent role in how films come to be labelled cult. Such contexts depend heavily on ethical and political customs, both in their applied forms, as laws and regulations, and their implied shapes, as routines and practices. The way many films travel, often accompanied only by limited publicity campaigns, can cause audiences to be unprepared for their themes and imageries, and unaware of their intentions. Cult films often seem to represent topics deemed unusual or inappropriate. At its least extreme, this simply leads to vague perceptions of 'strangeness', but in some cases they might upset cultural sensitivities, causing condemnation or even persecution.

(1) *Strangeness*: some films may seem 'normal' to their home cultures, but become objects of curiosity once they leave that context. The reception of a film outside its initial cultural surrounding may easily evoke celebration, devotion or even hostility of a cultist

kind. Hong Kong's police thrillers (*The Killer*, 1988), Japanese manga films (*Akira*, 1988), Belgian realist horror (*Man Bites Dog*, 1992), blaxploitation (*Shaft*, 1971) or Bollywood films (*Surakksha*, 1979) are obvious examples of this. Films depicting, or set in, rarely viewed locations, such as rainforests or the poles, also attract curiosity. Werner Herzog's Amazon films (*Aguirre*, 1972; *Fitzcarraldo*, 1981) make them stand out among other stories of exploration, an important explanation for their cult appeal. And while a topic may have been deemed acceptable and even mundane during its making, it can become eyebrow-raising material in another day and age (or the other way around), such as depictions of sexuality in Hollywood films before the Hays code, like in *Tarzan and his Mate* (1934). When this happens, it adds to a film's cultist credentials. In a few cases, films also find timely, often unintended, fits with issues high on the cultural agenda, giving them a pressing topicality. *The Fly*'s (1986) metaphors of sex and disease rang parallel to concerns about AIDS at the time, augmenting its cult status.

(2) *Allegory*: film stories set in imaginary times and places carry a high potential for cultdom. Regardless of the aesthetic accomplishment of such films, they frequently manage to elicit speculation about what the times and locations stand for. Fantasy films are the prime example here. In the case of *The Lord of the Rings* (2001–3) discussions of its allegorical meanings as a metaphor for global conflict, or a call to question authority, have been of huge importance in the development of its cult status. Similarly, *Planet of the Apes* (1968) and *Edward Scissorhands* (1991) are often seen as metaphors for 1960s and 1950s race relations. And *The Wizard of Oz*'s (1939) openness to multiple allegorical interpretations has given it cultural weight and a cult reputation. Adaptations of comic books, themselves often already equipped with a cult following, also seem to attract such interpretations, especially when the allegorical themes are contentious, and clouded by less than fully accomplished storytelling with stylistic limitations, as the cases of *Flash Gordon* (1980), *Judge Dredd* (1994), *Tank Girl* (1995), *Blade* (1998) or *Hellboy* (2004) indicate. In all of these films colour-coding is a key instrument to suggest metaphorical meaning.

(3) *Cultural sensitivities*: the status of a film as a cultural representation is related to its cult reputation. In fact, that reputation increases the more dubious or ambiguous its status as a culturally acceptable representation is, especially in its treatment of cultural sensitivities. Cult films often walk a blurry line between exposing and capitalizing on these sensitivities, regularly giving the impression that they problematize as well as reinforce prejudices. It is a core reason for their appeal, and of course a point of contention. The most hotly debated sensitivities are representations of animal cruelty, misogyny, non-western ethnicities, small-town mentality and the Holocaust. Films containing animal cruelty are prone to bans in most countries, and as a result many only have a restricted availability. *Le sang des bêtes* (1949) is usually seen as an example that exposes animal cruelty while showing it, while *Cannibal Holocaust* (1980) was persecuted in several countries for exploiting it – hence it is more of a cult film. Claims of misogyny are often made against rape-revenge films, like *Straw Dogs* (1971), *I Spit on Your Grave* (1978), *Baise-moi* (2000) or *Ichi the Killer* (2001), with the films receiving praise for their boldness as well as criticism for their objectification of women. Similarly, the films of David Cronenberg (such as *Shivers*, 1975) and Dario Argento (like *Tenebrae*, 1982) are often perceived as insensitive in their representations of women – in most cases they are victims of gruesome acts of violence. The representation of non-western

ethnicities as stereotypically mysterious, seductive, immoral, deceptive, barbaric or savage is also a prominent feature of cult cinema's cultural status, with mondo cinema (*Mondo Cane*, 1962) and exotic soft-porn (*Emmanuelle*, 1972) as prototypical examples. While such films are often criticized as racist, it is remarkable how they also exhibit a liberal attitude towards the breaking of cultural taboos, especially those surrounding sexuality, promoting 'forbidden desires' and fetishes. In this sense, cult cinema becomes a meeting point for anthropological documentaries such as *Les maîtres fous* (1954) or exploitation fare such as *Black Emannuelle* (1975). In much the same vein, films that mock, or brutally expose, the life in 'backward' rural communities within western culture often receive cult reputations. *The Texas Chainsaw Massacre* (1974) is an iconic example, as are *Deliverance* (1972) or *The Wisconsin Death Trip* (2000). Again, while these films receive criticism for their unsalted depiction of such communities, they also attract praise for exposing the issues of class that underpin many considerations of rural life as brutal, cruel, simple, simplistic or incestuous. *House on the Edge of the Park* (1980) is one cult film in which such class issues come to the fore. Finally, representations of the Holocaust frequently receive a cult reputation simply because they attempt to represent the unrepresentable: the biggest atrocity since the invention of cinema. Here, the cult status is the result of an unintentional ambiguity: the fact that they struggle to find a means to represent the horror makes them 'curiosities'. Educational purposes aside, audiences sense the tension behind and underneath the imagery used, and because of that discomfort representations of the Holocaust do not fit in with other films – they always stand on the margins of culture, too radical for anything else. Films like *Shoah* (1985) or *Nuit et Brouillard* (1955) do not attract fandom, but they do have a magnetic appeal for audiences looking to have their sensitivities challenged.

(4) *Politics*: whenever a film's strangeness, allegorical powers or representations of cultural sensitivities contain a strong ideological component, it is likely to become a politically inspired pamphlet. If the alignment is with a subculture perceived as 'dangerous' or 'subversive' such films are more likely to become objects of cult themselves. The 1960's counterculture is a favourite topic. *The Trip* (1967), *Le weekend* (1967), *Easy Rider* (1969) and *Zabriskie Point* (1970), for instance, all share a positive representation of that decade's counterculture, often depicting drug taking, 'deviant' behaviour, alternative rock music and political protest. British punk cinema, such as *Jubilee* (1978) and *Rude Boy* (1980), is another example of ideologically inspired cult film. A common tool in the politically inspired cult film is that of deconstruction, of breaking down the cohesiveness of official culture by exposing its incoherencies and prejudices, and by celebrating 'lapses, breaks and gaps' in its discourse. The tool has helped make the feminist genre films of Stephanie Rothman such as *Terminal Island* (1973) or *The Working Girls* (1974), and several adaptations of David Mamet's attacks against political correctness, such as *Oleanna* (1994), or *Edmond* (2005), into cult films.

Conclusion: the definition of cult film

A cult film is a film with an active and lively communal following. Highly committed and rebellious in its appreciation, its audience regularly finds itself at odds with the prevailing cultural mores, displaying a preference for strange topics and allegorical themes that rub against cultural sensitivities and resist dominant politics. Cult films transgress common notions of good and bad taste, and they challenge genre conventions and coherent storytelling, often using intertextual references, gore, leaving loose ends or creating a sense of nostalgia. They frequently have troublesome production histories, coloured by accidents, failures, legends and mysteries that involve their stars and directors, and in spite of often-limited accessibility, they have a continuous market value and a long-lasting public presence.

A note on the organization of the materials

This reader consists of four sections, encapsulating four major ways of studying cult cinema. The first section addresses theoretical issues in the study of cult cinema; the second offers case studies of key cult films; the third one discusses cult cinema in its cultural contexts; and the fourth one focuses on practices of reception of cult cinema.

Each excerpted essay is preceded by a brief abstract in which we have situated the origin of the approach (where it situates itself within the broad framework of the study of culture, to which philosophical paradigms it links itself), the institutional background from which it came (which 'schools of thought' and 'invisible colleges' have influenced it), the core beliefs and assertions of the arguments (and how they relate to previous and subsequent conceptualizations of cult), the exemplars and examples it employs to demonstrate its ideas (and to which aspects of cinema history these primarily relate), and its place in the emergent field of the study of cult cinema (and how it has been received by the academic community).

Each excerpt is also preceded by a brief note on the source material, including information on its initial place of publication, the existence of (and relation to) alternative versions of the source, and (if applicable) a rationale for the editing of the essay (why we have emphasized certain arguments and deleted certain passages).

SECTION 1

The concepts of cult

Introduction

This section introduces the reader to the ways in which cult film is studied and framed theoretically. As such it emphasizes the perspectives, terms and concepts used to define cult cinema. It also stresses the reasons for, and the ways in which, scholars have arrived at seeing cult cinema as a topic worthy of academic investigation. Finally, it asks attention for the institutional history of the study of cult cinema within academia, in its rise to become a legitimate field of inquiry.

Philosophy of the cult film

There are, by and large, two major philosophical perspectives on cult cinema, an ontological and a phenomenological. Ontological approaches to cult cinema are usually essentialist: they try to determine what makes 'cult cinema' a certain type of movie. Attempts to do so typically try to describe cult cinema through formal features like a genre or a style, or through recurrent themes embedded in the use of metaphors, tropes and motives. The genres that cult cinema is mostly associated with are popular ones, like the horror film, science fiction, and fantasy – three genres that rely heavily upon formalized story worlds hugely different from reality, but which are also extremely coherent internally – as such they provide worlds one can get lost in or expand upon. But cult is also closely linked to genres that depend on the illogical transgression between story world and real world – like absurd comedy, surrealism, pastiche and satire or the musical. Ontological approaches stress how these features connect to each other, offering a coherent (or in the case of cult cinema a typically incoherent) whole. In terms of methodology, ontological approaches are objectivist: they are likely to rely upon formalism and semiotics to generate evidence of how what is present *inside* the text regulates its meaning.

Phenomenological approaches shift the attention from the text to its appearance in the cultural contexts in which it is produced and received. Such attempts usually see cult cinema as a mode of reception, a way of seeing films. In their least radical form, phenomenological approaches still rely on the analysis of the text, but stress those features of a film that are likely to be attractors (or detractors) to anyone perceiving that text – like the way in which a cult film refers to other films, or the way it creates shock, generates upheaval and elicits controversy. At their most radical, phenomenological approaches refuse to believe a film has any properties at all, and instead posit that all features of a film are attributed by audiences and receptions – results of the ways in which the film has positioned itself within a cultural context. In terms of methodology, phenomenological approaches are subjectivist: they rely upon reception or audience research to generate evidence about how conditions *outside* the text regulate its meaning.

The ontological and phenomenological approaches share an interest in the ideas of enlightenment philosopher Immanuel Kant, whose attempts to combine an ontology of knowledge in the forms of reason and judgement with a consideration of its practices and appearances underlie practically every treatment of cult cinema, though mostly implicitly.[1] In a sense, if one can use a stretched comparison, Kant's difficulties in finding a rational foundation for the highest category of aesthetics, the sublime, are not dissimilar to those of the study of cult cinema. In order to find ways to describe the faculty of the sublime, Kant had to resort to obfuscated aspects of phenomenology (how the sublime shows itself) and perception (how one recognizes the sublime), ending up with an elegant compromise: the sublime is the category of aesthetic achievement which can only be known by proxy – like a storm at sea one watches from a cliff. Kantian aesthete Jerome Stolnitz, in discussing the philosophy of art criticism in a way not too dissimilar from how scholars usually study cult cinema, found himself confronted with the same problem, and resorted to a 'third way': he called it 'relative objectivism'. It is a perspective that holds that knowledge about a work of art's properties, which are believed to exist beyond doubt, can be achieved via its perception by the 'trained eye' – one that recognizes the task at hand, puts in the effort and engagement, and knows what to look for.[2] For cult cinema study, this relative objectivism holds the theoretical key to understanding the double bind between a film's properties and its appearance and appeal.[3]

Terms and concepts

The terms and concepts that play a role of importance in the theoretical study of cult cinema are incredibly diverse. Cult cinema study borrows from terminologies in film studies, cultural studies, media studies, sociology, philosophy, literary studies, anthropology and several other disciplines. It is not the intention of this introduction to provide an exhaustive dictionary. Rather we will point to the most recurrent and significant terms and concepts that are not explicitly explained in the essays excerpted below.

(1) *Cult*: at the core of it all lies the term 'cult'. Literally, a cult denotes the worship of a religious belief or worldview. The term cult was most notably employed by French sociologist Emile Durkheim, in his exploration of the elementary forms of religious life. Durkheim saw cults play an essential role in the ritual conduct associated with religion. He distinguished between 'negative' and 'positive' cults, the former based on rituals of prohibition (such as exclusion or asceticism), and the latter on rituals of exhibition (such as sacrificing or mourning). Later scholars placed Durkheim's analysis of religion against his ideas on contemporary society, in which he observed a worldview that, from the end of the nineteenth century onwards, seemed to replace collective ideas of aspiration with individual ones (the 'cult of the individual'). Film cults, as the readings below

demonstrate, hover between negative and positive cults, sometimes referring to strategies of exhibition (celebrating fan behaviour), and sometimes to strategies of exclusion (guarding niche tastes). They also oscillate between perspectives of collectivity and individuality, sometimes referring to the quantities of people that make up a cult following, and sometimes to the qualities of the kind of worship that characterize it. In most modern views, cults are seen as situated outside the mainstream – at odds with the dominant, ruling systems of belief or worldviews. A cult will often find itself in a state of persecution, and its followers use that state to define for themselves a *raison d'être*, in reference to the rest of the world.[4]

(2) *Deviance*: because of the way cults are at odds with hegemonic, dominant systems of culture, they are seen as deviant. When, since the 1950s, research into youth cultures became more common, comparisons were made between cults and the operations and beliefs of teenagers (especially, need it be mentioned, in relation to the kinds of idolatry youths are seen to be susceptible to). Most of these studies emphasized how these deviances were morally unacceptable and tended to lead to crime (it will not surprise anyone that this strand of thought still carries some prevalence in the study of law and criminology). It also became attached to certain examples of youth culture and subculture, especially the ones who found themselves broaching illegality (like the Hell's Angels) or what is perceived as subversion (like the rockers/ mods, teddies, punks, rasta's, goths, etc.). A lot of these 'deviating' cultural niches have been characterized by outspoken and totemic tastes in appreciation, and occasionally they have become identified through them – in which case film cults and cult film become virtually synonymous.[5]

(3) *Taste*: in the study of aesthetics, of the beauty, meaning, and judgement of art, taste is a faculty of the perceiver of good art. When one is able to discern between false and true art, one has taste. As such, taste requires training – an education in distinguishing between the categories and hierarchies of kinds of art (the 'relative objectivism' of Stolnitz). It also requires a moral basis: taste is not just a judgement of the object of art, it is also a judgement of one's self – a positioning within culture of one's capability to succeed in such tests of distinction between 'good' and 'bad', or of one's decision to refute compliance (deviance). And since the meanings of what is good and what is bad depend on specific cultural contexts, they shift constantly. This means that taste is a social construct, and can be 'faked' (snobbery, faddism, hypes, 'cool', 'hip', 'hot'). According to Pierre Bourdieu and Terry Eagleton, taste is an invention of the bourgeoisie, designed to detect their own and exclude others (like a secret handshake). In the twentieth century, this has led to counter-taste movements, where 'bad' taste, as a voluntary resistance to adhere to bourgeois regimes, is seen as a positive act of opposition – a revolution against the oppressor. Cult taste, especially in the form of the appreciation of cinema that is not to be liked, is usually seen as an example of such resistance. It is thence seen as an example of the liberation from taste regimes, in favour of free choice. In time, 'bad taste' hierarchies have themselves come under similar attack, blamed for the same kind of strategies as they set out to oppose – leading to the study of cult cinema putting 'eclecticism', the seemingly un-positionable preferencing of certain films over others, central in its considerations of appreciation.[6]

(4) *High/low culture*: if cult is discussed in terms of aesthetics the distinction between high and low culture becomes inevitable. Cults are often, in fact almost always,

seen as existing at odds with the reigning judgements of art. In early considerations of film, cult cinema refers to types of cinema which are so out of the ordinary that they attracted a specific kind of elite, sophisticated appreciation (like *The Cabinet of Dr. Caligari* [1919] – for some the first cult film ever). This would be the cult of high culture. Another option, and one which would become increasingly dominant for later considerations, is that cult cinema is the kind that through its mass, popular appeal acquires a force (economical, cultural) that puts it outside the realm of proper taste (the films of Rudolph Valentino or Charles Chaplin are early examples). This would be the cult of low culture. Within this low culture appeal there is a separate category, that of exploitation. Often, films are produced for popular appeal, stressing those properties producers think will hit the lowest common denominator, like sex and violence. Films emphasizing these traits are called exploitation films, and they are always seen as part of low culture (even when they eventually become elevated into proper culture). There is a curious space in between high and low culture: the so-called midcult. This refers to a kind of mainstream appreciation that is high enough to not be ridiculed and yet popular enough to be widely accessible. Dwight MacDonald used the example of Ernest Hemingway – both acclaimed and popular – to indicate what midcults are.[7]

(5) *Value*: literally, value stands for the worth of a good within society. This is not just a matter of its intrinsic properties, but also of its status. If one takes a Marxist perspective towards value (and most approaches to cult cinema appear to do so in one way or another), then it is necessary to distinguish between a good's use value (its direct function in a society), and its exchange value. Use value is expressed in its application – a hammer is useful to hammer nails into wood and thus construct furniture. Exchange value is expressed in what one can get in return for the good (without even using it), like other goods or a commonly agreed currency (money). In trade, exchange values can be accumulated and lead to a surplus value (if a need of a certain good is perceived one may find that others are prepared to pay more for it than it is actually worth) – something which is usually the case for scarce goods or precious commodities. If the surplus value of a good/object exceeds the logic of its use and exchange value, as with a film that is adored outrageously by a devout following, then its symbolic value, or its *cult value*, as Walter Benjamin calls it, becomes a factor of importance. Seen this way, cult cinema is a precious commodity – it is desired and hence creates a demand, and a following. Because it has cult value, it is a cult object.[8]

(6) *Perception*: cult films challenge traditional means of watching films – either because they are weird, or because they evoke certain responses. Therefore the concept of perception (how one physically and psychologically perceives an object in its appearances) becomes pivotal for studying cult cinema. Among the many theories of perception, two are of importance for our purposes. On the one hand cult cinema can be seen to cause certain responses, to have effects with audiences. For such a perspective, a psychoanalytical theory of perception can be useful: it treats the perceiver as a subject who might not be aware of their own desires, impulses, fears and traumas – all of which can be activated by the film – and whose emotional attachment to the film can be the result of unconscious identifications and cultural dispositions (the belief that cult cinema sensationalizes 'women's bodies' and thus puts females in a passive position is an example). On the other hand cult cinema can be seen as a series of puzzles that require focused, directed activity from the audience in order to enjoy it. For

such a perspective, a cognitive theory of perception is useful: it sees the viewer as a puzzle-solver of the mysteries posed by the text, one whose awareness of cues, clues and references (all present in the film) can lead to enjoyment. In the study of cult cinema, both theories have their advocates and opponents, each one resisting the other.[9]

These terms and concepts make up the core of the terminology and concept-ology of cult cinema studies. They underpin terms like 'aura', 'camp', 'kitsch', 'intertextuality', 'transgression', 'excess', 'paracinema' or 'subculture', words that have come to form a jargon – a typical development for a discipline achieving its own independence. Since all of these terms are explained in detail in the essays extracted below we will leave it to the authors themselves to introduce them.

The history of cult film study

We have referred to the development of the theoretical study of cult cinema a few times now. The history of the study of cult cinema is short. After all, it only became a pressing topic in the last 20 years, and only in the last decade has there been a concerted effort to investigate it. But its seeds are sown much earlier, at the beginning of the twentieth century. Around that time, the issue of extreme appreciation, that did not seem to fit categories of taste and perception, appeared in literary studies, aesthetics and soci-ology. From the late 1920s onwards, this interest was extended into cinema, and film criticism started using the term 'cult'. Two 'movements' championed cults in cinema, each for different reasons (and each calling different types of films cult). The first is the Frankfurter School of critical theory, which saw cinema cults as an example of the negative influence of popular and mass culture upon the progressive development of a society as a force. While the Frankfurt critics, like Theodor Adorno, Siegfried Kracauer or Walter Benjamin did, at times, see film as not just a force of regression, they were quite clear that cult value stood in the way of aesthetic and social progress.[10] The second 'movement' is that of American film criticism. Since the 1930s and until the 1960s American critics used the term cult to champion art-house cinema (usually European) and cinema crossing the divide between high and low culture (like Chaplin's films). Examples are to be found in the writings of Harry Allan Potamkin (whose 'Film cults' opens the argument), James Agee, Robert Warshow, Manny Farber, Parker Tyler and Andrew Sarris (whose 'Confessions of a cultist' is a good example), and Susan Sontag (whose 'notes on camp' closes the argument). Unlike the Frankfurt School, the American critics usually resisted advancing their ideas as theory, but when grouped together they demonstrate an interest in cult as an aesthetic category that saw itself fall outside the mainstream – either by their aesthetic properties, or through their reception (James Agee for instance championed silent era slapstick comedy not just because he regretted it had moved out of the public's eye so quickly, but because it had had this exceptional appeal).[11] For the American critics, cult films stood out because they were exceptional, and had exceptional appeal; for the Frankfurt critics they stood out because they were utterly unexceptional but had exceptional appeal.

Parallel to this, but outside the realms of theory, from the late 1950s an interest arose in cult as a category of style and attitude, connected to the explosive growth in commercial youth culture. In the eyes of several French film critics for instance 'cult' became an indicator not just of exceptionality, but also of a certain rebellious attitude towards both high culture and mainstream culture, one shared by new generations of filmgoers who felt their appreciations and investments were unaccounted for in regular film criticism. In the USA this was mirrored by the way a fast growing fan press (especially since the early 1970s) started using cult as a concept of resistance against tediousness and repetition in genre cinema – this use was very eclectic and sometimes repetition didn't seem an issue at all.[12]

By the end of the 1970s, and at the beginning of the 1980s, the theorization of cult in film studies received a big boost from two angles. The increasing interest in the study of the horror film (many of which counted as cult films) provided the study of cult cinema with techniques and tools for analysing its generic (and extrageneric) features, and allowed it be framed in terms of its representations of gender, race, ideology and intertextuality.[13] Simultaneously, an increase in the study of the reception of popular arts and aesthetic subcultures and 'art worlds' in the sociology of the arts and in the developing fields of communication and cultural studies, especially in the wake of Pierre Bourdieu's monumental *Distinction*, offered tools for researching cult cinema's audiences and exceptional appeals.[14] By the end of the 1980s a large contingent of intellectuals and academics had accepted the legitimacy of studying popular culture (something which is noted and investigated by Andrew Ross) and as part of that, cult cinema study grew exponentially, leading to a first veritable wave of publications.[15]

It is necessary to note an accompanying development within cult cinema itself. From the 1980s onwards more films than ever before were labelled cult and received cultist receptions. The basis of this lies in the growth of popular genre cinema and the rapid boom of its ancillary industries (fan press, festivals, conventions, retrospectives, specialist distribution), whose circuits of reception were accelerated by video, television and other media. Underpinning these developments were activities like collecting, canon-creation, fan debates, nostalgia and postmodern 'topics' like time travel, parody and pastiche. For the first time cult cinema became self-aware of its status as cult, and, as a result, the ritualistic reception of cult cinema became institutionalized. It meant there were now more cult films than ever before, and more means to 'cultify' films.

By the 1990s the study of cult cinema as part of media studies (especially in the form of fandom studies), and film studies (in the form of formalist approaches) had found its way into several university programmes. It is a bit of a stretch to state that the study of cult cinema became entrenched at a handful of well-respected, mostly liberal universities, but if one has a look at where the theoretical study of cult cinema found its way into Ph.D. dissertations, publications and affiliations, then three American institutions stand out: the University of Texas, Austin, the University of California, Berkeley and the University of Wisconsin, Madison. Driven by a combination of perspectives, such as media studies, cultural studies, formalism and reception studies, the film studies programmes at these institutions often allowed room for discussions of popular cinema and cult cinema, powered of course by the research of the faculty. Next to large archive collections these locations also boasted typical college-towns opportunities (like midnight theatres, specialist video shops, small festivals), which created a general availability of, and sensibility towards, cult cinema. It enabled a first generation of scholars to graduate on the topic of cult-related cinema.[16] On the other side of the ocean, UK universities also opened up to the study of cult cinema, largely at the initiative of cultural studies scholars, leading to programmes, degrees and research centres at the universities of Sussex, Nottingham, Cardiff, Aberystwyth and Brunel.

Theory and practice: academia and the industry

By 2000 the increasing academic efforts in the theorization of cult cinema found their expression in the first *Cult Movies Conference*, in Nottingham. Since then several more international conferences have followed, and the professional societies of film and media studies have opened up to 'cult studies' panels and papers, leading to the overall visibility and acknowledgement of cult cinema study across academia. Two efforts in particular deserve mention: the *Born to be Bad Trash Cinema Conferences* in Berkeley (2002 and 2003), and the *Cine-Excess International Cult Film Conference* in London (2007). Their unique mix of academic and industry professionals displayed how the study of cult is never just confined to academia, but always, like its subject of study, transgresses boundaries between the academy and the industry. This is not just an observation. It is a unique characteristic that is helping to shape the kind of research done in cult cinema. It has created a situation in which academics and professionals demonstrate mutual respect, with noted filmmakers accepting, encouraging and facilitating investigations of cult cinema – even leading to unique endorsements and collaborations. *The Cine-Excess Conference* in particular celebrated this mixing as a quality not many similar subjects can tout, and in general it has created a landscape in which there is true interactivity between theory and practice, both informing each other.

Finally this. It is often mentioned that an emerging discipline needs to attach itself to well-respected, legitimate subjects of inquiry if it wants to achieve a similar recognition and respect. We are aware that that is what the introduction to this section may offer. But we also believe that the theoretical study of cult cinema, in all its diversities, does indeed connect to the inspirations and terms and conditions mentioned above. If that means it craves recognition, professionalization, tenure, then it probably does. For us, it means above all that its thinking does not pretend to exist in isolation.

The essays excerpted in this section represent this turbulent evolution. Their associations range from cult and trash, to exploitation and 'weird', but all of them have helped define this new area of study within the academy. With their emphasis on semiotic analysis, psychoanalysis and the cultural distinction of tastes, they construct the cult text as a set of oppositional frameworks, whose users interpret subcultural values in a manner contrary to mainstream readings. This section is organized chronologically (with one exception: we have grouped the two essays emphasizing 'camp' together) to allow for the study of the development of theoretical thought regarding the subject.

Notes

1 Kant, Immanuel (2000) *Critique of the Power of Judgment*, Cambridge: Cambridge University Press; Kant, Immanuel (1998) *Critique of Pure Reason*, London: Macmillan; Kant, Immanuel (1997) *Critique of Practical Reason*, Cambridge: Cambridge University Press.
2 Stolnitz, Jerome (1960) *Aesthetics and Philosophy of Art Criticism: a Critical Introduction*, Boston, MA: Riverside Press.

3   Beyond Kant, ontological and phenomenological approaches tend to champion ideas
    that combine textual exegesis with an acknowledgement for the context of perception.
    The semiology of V.N. Voloshinov, Mikhail Bakhtin, Roman Jakobson, Umberto Eco,
    Roland Barthes (the early Barthes is a favourite of ontologists, the later Barthes a hero of
    phenomenologists) or the postsemiotic writings of Jean Baudrillard have found welcome
    applications. See: Bakhtin, Mikhail and Pavel Medvedev ([1928] 1985) *The Formal
    Method in Literary Scholarship: a Critical Introduction to Sociological Poetics*, Cambridge,
    MA: Harvard University Press; Bakhtin, Mikhail (1981) *The Dialogic Imagination*, Austin,
    TX: University of Texas Press; Bakhtin, Mikhail (1984) *Rabelais and his World*, Blooming-
    ton, IN: Indiana University Press; Voloshinov, V.N. (1973) *Marxism and the Philosophy of
    Language*, New York: Seminar Press; Jakobson, Roman (1963) *Essais de linguistique
    générale*, Paris: Editions de minuit; Eco, Umberto (1989) *Open Work*, Cambridge, MA:
    Harvard University Press; Eco, Umberto (1990) *The Limits of Interpretation*, Bloomington
    & Indianapolis, IN: Indiana University Press; Barthes, Roland (1966) *Critique et vérité*,
    Paris: Seuil; Barthes, Roland (1974) *S/Z*, New York: Hill & Wang; Barthes, Roland (1977)
    Image/Music/Text, New York: Hill & Wang; Baudrillard, Jean (1996) *The System of
    Objects*, New York: Verso; Baudrillard, Jean (1995) *Simulacra and Simulation*, Ann Arbor,
    MI: Michigan University Press. To some extent, the ideas of the Russian Formalists like
    Victor Schklovsky, Yuri Tynjanov or Boris Eichenbaum, also found their way into theoriza-
    tions of cult cinema, often pitched against Marxist orthodoxy (see Bennett, Tony [1979]
    Formalism and Marxism, London: Methuen). Among the theoretical perspectives based
    on Marxism and Freudian and Lacanian psychoanalysis which have been prevalent in film
    studies for decades, especially in their poststructuralist formats, the writings of Michel
    Foucault have echoed through in the theorization of the study of cult cinema. See:
    Foucault, Michel (1988) *Madness and Civilisation*, New York: Vintage Books; Foucault,
    Michel (1979) *Discipline and Punish*, New York: Vintage Books; Foucault, Michel (1972),
    Archaeology of Knowledge, New York: Pantheon Books; Foucault, Michel (1971) *The Order
    of Things*, New York: Pantheon Books. It is interesting to note that in many cases these
    inspirations go unmentioned. But they reveal a wealth of information about the epistemo-
    logical grounding of the study of cult cinema.
4   Ideally, this reader would have included an excerpt from Durkheim's writings, but this was
    practically impossible. We refer readers to: Durkheim, Emile ([1915] 1995) *Elementary
    Forms of the Religious Life*, New York: Free Press; Chriss, James J. (1993) 'Durkheim's
    cult of the individual as civil religion: Its appropriation by Erving Goffman', *Sociological
    Spectrum*, 13(2), 251.
5   Cohen, Albert (1955) 'A theory of subculture', in Ronald Farrell and Victoria Lynn Swigert
    (eds) *Social Deviance*, Philadelphia, PA: Lippincott, 179–82; Becker, Howard (1963)
    Outsiders: Study in the Sociology of Deviance, New York: The Free Press; Cohen, Stanley
    ([1972, 1980] 2003) *Folk Devils and Moral Panics*, London: Routledge; Hebdige, Dick
    (1979) *Subculture and the Meaning of Style*, London: Routledge.
6   Bourdieu, Pierre (1984) *Distinction: A Social Critique of the Judgment of Taste*, London:
    Routledge; Eagleton, Terry (1984) *The Function of Criticism*, London: Verso; Sconce,
    Jeffrey (1995) 'Trashing the academy: Taste, excess and an emerging politics of
    cinematic style', *Screen*, 36(4), 371–93.
7   Macdonald, Dwight (1960) 'Masscult and midcult', *Partisan Review* (spring), reprinted in
    Dwight Macdonald (1962) *Against the American Grain*, New York: Random House, 3–75;
    Huyssen, Andreas (1986) *After the Great Divide: Modernism, Mass Culture, Postmodern-
    ism*, Bloomington & Indianapolis, IN: Indiana University Press.
8   Marx, Karl (1976) 'The fetishism of the commodity and its secret', in *Capital* (Vol. 1),
    London: Penguin, 163–77; Benjamin, Walter ([1969]1935) 'The work of art in the age of

mechanical reproduction', in Hannah Arendt (ed.) *Illuminations*, New York: Pimlico, 217–51. Although not operating from a Marxist point of view, Chris Anderson makes a similar point when he discusses why a band like My Chemical Romance did manage to attract good sales (thanks to its core cult following – similar to grassroots support), while another, equally talented, act failed to. See: Anderson, Chris (2006) 'The new tastemakers', in *The Long Tail: Why the Future of Business is Selling Less of More*, New York: Hyperion, 103–5.

9 The psychoanalytic take is exemplified by Zizek, Slavoj (1991) *Lookin Awry: An Introduction to Jacques Lacan through Popular Culture*, Cambridge, MA: MIT Press; and the cognitivist one is exemplified by Eco, Umberto (1986) 'Cult movies and intertextual collage', in *Travels in Hyperreality*, London: Picador, 197–211; see also Bordwell, David (1989) *Making Meaning; Inference and Rhetoric in the Interpretation of Cinema*, Cambridge, MA: Harvard University Press.

10 Kracauer, Siegfried (1926) 'The cult of distraction', from *The Mass Ornament*, Cambridge, MA: Harvard University Press, 323–8; Benjamin, Walter ([1969]1935) 'The work of art in the age of mechanical reproduction', in Hannah Arendt (ed.) *Illuminations*, New York: Pimlico, 217–51; Horkheimer, Max and Theodor Adorno (1976) *Dialectic of the Enlightenment*, London: Continuum; Adorno, Theodor (2001) *The Culture Industry*, London: Routledge.

11 Potamkin, Harry Allan (1977) 'Film cults' and 'Ritual of the movies', in Lewis Jacobs (ed.) *The Compound Cinema*, New York: Columbia University Press, 227–31; Agee, James (1949) 'Comedy's greatest era', *Life Magazine*, 3 September, reprinted in Gerald Mast and Marshall Cohen (eds) (1974) *Film Theory and Criticism* (1st edn), Oxford: Oxford University Press, 439; Sontag, Susan (1964) 'Notes on camp', in *Against Interpretation and Other Essays*, New York: Farrar, Strauss & Giroux, 275–92; Tyler, Parker (1969) *Underground Film*, London: Pelican Books; Sarris, Andrew (1970) *Confessions of a Cultist: on the Cinema (1955–1969)*, New York: Simon & Schuster; Taylor, Greg (1999) *Artists in the Audience: Cults, Camp, and American Film Criticism*, Princeton, NJ: Princeton University Press.

12 Sanjek, David (1990) 'Fans' notes: the horror film fanzine', *Literature/Film Quarterly*, 18(3), 150–60; Hawkins, Joan (2000) *Cutting Edge: Art Horror and the Horrific Avant-Garde*, Minneapolis, MN: University of Minnesota Press; Betz, Mark (2003) 'Art, exploitation, underground', in Mark Jancovich, Antonio Lazaro-Reboll, Julian Stringer and Andy Willis (eds) *Defining Cult Movies: the Cultural Politics of Oppositional Taste*, Manchester: Manchester University Press, 202–22.

13 Britton, Andrew, Robin Wood, Richard Lippe and Tony Williams (eds) (1979) *The American Nightmare: Essays on the Horror Film*, Toronto: Festival of Festivals; Barker, Martin (1983) *A Haunt of Fears: The Strange History of the British Horror Comics Campaign*, London: Pluto Press; Brophy, Philip (1986) 'Horrality: the textuality of contemporary horror films', *Screen*, 27(1), 2–13; Grant, Barry K. (1991) 'Science fiction double feature: Ideology in the cult film', in J.P. Telotte (ed.) *The Cult Movie Experience*, Austin, TX: University of Texas Press, 122–37.

14 Bourdieu, Pierre (1980) 'The aristocracy of culture', *Media, Culture and Society*, 2(3), 225–54; Bourdieu, Pierre (1984) *Distinction: A Social Critique of the Judgment of Taste*, London: Routledge; Becker, Howard (1984) *Art Worlds*, Berkeley, CA: University of California Press; Austin, Bruce (1981) 'Portrait of a cult film audience', *Journal of Communication*, 31 (spring), 43–54; Austin, Bruce (1981), 'Film attendance: Why college students chose to see their most recent film', *Journal of Popular Film and Television*, 9 (spring), 43–9; Austin, Bruce (1984) 'Portrait of an art film audience', *Journal of Communication*, 34 (winter), 74–87.

15   Corrigan, Timothy (1986) 'Film and the culture of cult', *Wide Angle,* 8(3–4), 91–9; Ross, Andrew (1989) 'The uses of camp', in *No Respect: Intellectuals and Popular Culture*, New York: Routledge, 135–70; Telotte, J.P. (ed.) (1991) *The Cult Film Experience: Beyond All Reason,* Austin, TX: University of Texas Press; Everman, Welch (1993) *Cult Horror Films*, New York: Citadel Press/Virgin Books; Jerslev, Anne (1992) 'Semiotics by instinct: "Cult film" as a signifying practice between film and audience', in Michael Skovmond and Kim Schroder (eds) *Media Cultures: Reappraising Transnational Media*, London: Routledge, 181–98; Jerslev, Anne (1993) *Kultfilm & Filmkultur*, Copenhagen: Amanda.

16   As the following short list of works on cult-related cinema with a common lineage from the University of Wisconsin, Madison, shows, it is no exaggeration to speak of genuine local sensibilities: Peary, Danny (1981, 1983, 1989) *Cult Movies I, II, and III*, New York: Delta Books; Bordwell, David (1989) *Making Meaning; Inference and Rhetoric in the Interpretation of Cinema*, Cambridge, MA: Harvard University Press; Fiske, John (1989) *Understanding Popular Culture*, Boston, MA: Unwin Hyman; Heffernan, Kevin (1989) Heterotextuality, unpublished paper, University of Wisconsin-Madison; Jenkins, Henry (1992) *Textual Poachers*, London: Routledge; McGilligan, Patrick (1992) *George Cukor: A Double Life*, New York: Griffin; Carroll, Noel (1998) *Interpreting the Moving Image*, Cambridge: Cambridge University Press; Taylor, Greg (1999) *Artists in the Audience: Cults, Camp, and American Film Criticism*, Princeton, NJ: Princeton University Press; De Seife, Ethan (2007) *This Is Spinal Tap*, London: Wallflower Press. Patrick McGilligan evokes this sensibility in the preface to *Film Crazy* when he reminisces on how exciting it was to gorge on cultist celebrations of film in Madison, Wisconsin: see McGilligan, Patrick (2000) 'Introduction', in *Film Crazy*, New York: St Martin's Griffin, 1–8.

1.1

Film cults
by Harry Allan Potamkin

Philadelphian Harry Allan Potamkin (1900–1933) became a film critic after his honeymoon trip to Europe, in 1925. Having spent numerous hours in Paris' Ciné-clubs, he became convinced of the power of the medium, and returned as a fierce proponent of cinema in the United States. As a left-wing liberal, Potamkin employed a Marxist view of film, judging them in the light of class struggles, and the bettering of human conditions. But it didn't lead him to abandon his sensitivity for aesthetics. Potamkin's criticism for specialist magazines like *Close-Up*, *The National Board of Review Magazine*, or *New Masses*, or for wide-circulation press, like *Vanity Fair*, combines an, at the time, unique blend of formalism and social consciousness. It allowed Potamkin to cross a divide which was insurmountable for other critics: that between high and low culture, between artistic quality and mass appeal, where so much of cult appreciation finds itself. Potamkin did not, as Lewis Jacobs writes, 'seek out the off-beat or experimental, but dealt with the so-called commercial productions'. In *Film Cults* (1932) he describes a wide range of films not usually grouped together: slapstick comedy (Chaplin and Langdon), German expressionism (the *Cabinet of Dr. Caligari*), avant-garde cinema (*Ballet Mécanique*), and cartoons (Mickey Mouse). For Potamkin, they belonged together because of the way they were received by audiences with high investments (the 'little cinema-goers', or the 'rebels', or the ones who will 'categorize certain materials as pre-eminently movie stuff'). Unlike so many of his contemporaries, Potamkin was far less denigrating towards popular taste and the masses. It gave him an acute sensibility for the taste-crossing appeal that is so typical for cult cinema.

A note on extracting: This essay is taken from Lewis Jacobs' selection of Potamkin's writings *The Compound Cinema* (Teachers College Press, Columbia University, New York, 1977, pp. 227–231). It originally appeared in *Modern Thinker and Author's Review* in November 1932.

The mass movie-fanatic is a part of a grand ritual. He does not specialize in the adulation of the rudimentary. That is left to the élite, the effete, the intelligentsia of cinema. As far back as 1910 a lone American crusader for movie as against theater based his defense of the former on its ability in melodrama, that agent of moral absolutes. Today, after a multitude of cults of single films, single personalities, products of certain studies, we find the aesthete raising movie melodrama to the summit of the movie's province. Actually the graph of enthusiasm has long ago reached its climax and now is about where it was at its point of origin. Film cultism had its inception in France. There it began, however, with more earnest zeal as dissent from the popular ritual. It might have materialized into actual guidance had it not deteriorated through propinquity to Dadaism, the cult of dissociations. The super-refined lads of the salons found their paradise in William S. Hart and Pearl White's smile, "that almost ferocious smile announcing the upheaval of the new world." Chaplin was the key cult, and although the brightness of his talent has dimmed, and he has never given us the quixotic film towards which his early pictures points, the cult still persists with a vengeance in Europe, and its echoes are dull but present in America.

About 1917 the echoes began to shout loud in America. We were propelled into cults of the slapstick or "churlish" comedy, especially of Mack Sennett, whose cult is still alive in France and in Gilbert Seldes. France had no experience of the American movie prior to 1917; she discovered it in that year (the year of America's entrance into the war) and Bill Hart, Pearl White, Charlie Chaplin became the tin gods of the aesthetes. The resonances motivated the American boys of delight. They began to write with seriousness, if not with critical insight, upon the rudimentary film, such as the serial *The Girl and the Game*, a railroad thriller, *The Exploits of Elaine*, with Pearl White. The most namby-pamby love-films were considered as exalted art. The boys were trying strenuously to reconcile the hostile environment with their sensibilities, and, in doing that, they became disproportionate populists. That was the era of machine-worship, to be followed by its equally hyperbolic reaction, machine-rancor. The aesthetes were thinking archaeologically, in terms of the major tool, and not, as contemplation of a social phenomenon demands, sociologically. Otherwise they might have seen the true nature of their object of worship. Or, had they been less academic, and looked into the film as a form of evolution, they might have been less content to idolize it at its primitive source.

And along came Charlie. "Charlie Chaplin has freed the moving pictures from the morons. This was easy for him because he is a poet. Poetry is a more violent acid than any other known acid. Its presence ruins the richest, the most powerful combinations, demands totally new beginnings." Chaplin did give a push to the comic film, but for the American comedy the push was a little off the right path, and Chaplin himself has trailed too far away from his original relevant mood. It is difficult to know today the point of his later works, with their overdose of maudlin pathos. He has developed much in aimlessness and directorial looseness. The enthusiasts have failed to see that in their eulogy of Chaplin the personality, the *raconteur*, they are actually offering a negative. A film is a whole, and the whole is greater than any of its parts, including Chaplin. Chaplin the personality has been up until lately generally successful, but the film of Chaplin has not always been realized. Eisenstein has said he likes most that Chaplin film where Charlie is everywhere yet nowhere, namely *A Woman of Paris*, one of the few American films expressive of a new principle of direction. In his last picture, *City Lights*, the first few moments are the peak. The remainder is an unleavened procession, now and then enlivened with a brief episode, a gag of quality. The film does not seem to proceed by its own motility. Its major motif, the relation between the millionaire and "the classic hobo," becomes subsidiary to the minor motif of the blind girl and Chaplin. The author-director-producer-star has weakened. He has fallen very far beneath the indications of *The Kid*, its social satire, its insistence on the major relationship, as against the formula romantic relationship. Reinhardt will continue to insist that Chaplin is the beginning and end of the cinema. What a "fixation!" The quasi-philosopher will find Chaplin the epitome of "the American Mind." Commentators will re-hash Chaplin's data. Popular writers will stress over and over again the nature of Chaplin as a man of moods. The muckraking columnist and pseudo-critic will take the opportunity to rush in a few doubts, mostly slander. But honest fundamental criticism of Chaplin as a digit of the motion picture, placing the motion picture above Chaplin, and society above the motion picture, will be disregarded.

In France, among the young *cinéastes*, looking for new fields to furrow, there has been an agitation to dethrone Chaplin. In order to do this a new tin god was to have been erected. Harry Langdon was to have been that fetish. But the American movie being less than its most gifted comedian, Langdon has found no film and no director to sustain him. No film-person has recognized in Harry's talkie-technique the only personal contribution to speech-as-sound made by an actor. Yet Langdon did, in his few shorts, introduce a verbal pattern paralleling his pantomime, a contribution which Chaplin has avoided. The French *cinéastes* have deserted Langdon for the four Marx Brothers, of whom only Groucho has a personal inventiveness. The *cinémas* of Paris specializing in American compounds are the new base for the Parisian cultism that looks to America for its fetishes.

That was in the days of the "little cinema," which began as an idealistic boycott of the shop-film. The cult *par excellence* of the little cinema was *The Cabinet of Dr. Caligari*, which still persists in the dreams of *arts-decoratifs*-minded "cinema-goers." Especially is this true in America, and even more especially in England, where the young men of Grub Street have only in the last few years discovered the cinema. They have followed the Old Lady of Threadneedle Street in her devotion to the lowly democratic art. Only gigolos follow old ladies. In 1927 the English critic was uncovering the western "horse opera" as "art," just ten years too late. And *Caligari*, long ago rightly called a date by the more conscientious French critics, is still pinnacle. *Caligari* may have hinted at a principle of integration, but it was certainly not an example to be followed. And it was not, save by the poseur reveling in banal fantasy.

The influence of a cult does not end with the cult itself. A residue may deposit itself in the recesses of an *atelier* to mingle with the dust and agitate less vivid senses to recreate the object of the cult. Years after France has given us the best of machine films, *Ballet Mécanique, Of What Are the Young Films Dreaming*, etc., and has shown us the best films where water is the subject-matter; after Soviet Russia has proven the validity of these instructions by incorporating them into human dramatic films (thereby invalidating them as forms in themselves) along come the American faddists presenting a program of machine and water films. And moreover, when the day of the separable musical accompaniment, the chamber concert, has passed; when even the little cinemas of Paris, that once encouraged the small unit orchestra playing to the film, have installed the mechanical medium, the faddists, too late, taking such a music-movie association unto themselves, applaud what they see and what they hear as achievement. And the films, mark you, have just been made here in the United States and stamped as "original." Fortunately, this inept stuffed-shirt affair can never be more than a family gathering, where the proud relatives inflate the precocious scion.

The main film cult, however, seeks identity (thereby comfort) with popular taste, and not with the recalcitrant or rebellious element in that taste beginning to make itself felt. Hence it builds melodrama to an ultimate category, and says that is what belongs most to the movie, that is what the movie does best. For "best" read "easiest." This melodramatic cult concentrates itself in some personality, a film or individual. It defends its position on the ground that in a movie it is the treatment and not the material that counts. This attitude must be fought as a form of intellectual selling-out. The movie is more than a "passing amusement." And deceptive platitudes limiting it to the snobbery or laziness of the cultists must be exploded. To explode it, the non-populist, non-cultist intellectual must join with the rebellious section of the popular audience in demanding a respect for a more substantial point of view.

The cultist mind abhors all discussion of theme, yet will categorize certain material as not movie stuff, and other as pre-eminently movie stuff. Anything in life is stuff to the film, given the mind that can handle it. And that includes literature. The Swedes made honorable pictures of Selma Lagerlöf's novels: that as expressing their life at its highest consciousness.

The most powerful of cults at the moment is the *Mickey Mouse*. I do not wish to be ungrateful: Mr. Disney has contributed a pleasurable bit to the screen, particularly at a time when the short film is moribund. But to exaggerate the repetitions and duplications of the Disney idiom as colossal or pace-setting is to thwart the progress of a form, the animated cartoon, which is still lisping. Indeed, it is this conception of the animated film as a "cartoon" in motion which refuses to see that Disney both in *Mickey Mouse* and *Silly Symphony* has only reiterated first statements. A comparison with the more varied Soviet animation or "multiplication" film will indicate the first statements as: a graphic that is not much more than a scrawl, line-contours with an occasional dull wash for setting, a lycanthropy with a bit of puerile sophistication, an absence of a pointed, developing narrative-idea, an unoriginal turkey-in-the-straw musical motif, "perpetual motion." On those rare occasions when the Disney cartoon emits a fresh yipe, we may get an inkling of the further possibilities of this medium. There is too much gag in the Disney film and not enough idea. Not to indicate this, but to say instead, as Diego Rivera has preposterously asserted, that Mickey Mouse will be the American personality of our generation to carry himself into our future national consciousness, is to be a foe to the very thing being eulogized.

This cartoon cult is not new. Seldes has continued his precious kowtowing before the newspaper strip. And several years ago, the British poet-novelist, Robert Nichols, advanced with great temerity – so he thought – the notion "that the theoretically ideal cinema-picture is of the type of the motion picture cartoons" (such as *Felix, the Cat*). This is a kind of cult of the child. The critic, knowing little or nothing of previous writings on the film, its cult-history, avoiding the contemplation of the intrinsic film, its future, retreating from any examinations of the basic evils frustrating the advance of the movie, and perishing to be at one with the easy-going movie fan, persists in the adoration of the infant cartoons. Cults are never self-critical. And being never self-critical, they are never objective. So that when they do turn on the idol of their creation, it is not a progressive act but an act of treachery.

Modern Thinker and Author's Review, *November, 1932*

1.2

The work of art in the age of mechanical reproduction
by Walter Benjamin

The writing of German philosopher Walter Benjamin (1892–1940) starts from a Marxist perspective, to establish a form of criticism of culture that recognizes the intricate connection between a text's appeal and its social position, deriving its meaning from the ways in which it dialectically negotiates class relationships. Benjamin usually wrote on literature (Charles Baudelaire), theatre (Berthold Brecht's epic theatre), and photography (August Sander), championing art, and aesthetic techniques such as alienation or politicization, which forced readers/ viewers into reading positions that made the economic and social aspects of art works explicit. In *The Work of Art in the Age of Mechanical Reproduction,* he discusses art history, literature, theatre, and cinema. For Benjamin, the technological means of art production and reproduction have repercussions on its status as a revered object in culture, an object of cult. They threaten its 'aura', its sense of uniqueness embodied in a work of art. The 'aura' is the main reason, according to Benjamin, for its canonization and ritual reverence. As such, it is also a category of perception. In an age in which the status of the 'original' is treated by the means of technology, a work of art's 'cult value' (its ability to evoke the sense of aura), shifts from the materialist properties of the object (its 'texture') to its psychological properties (the ways in which it can mobilize emotions), and to its exhibition and reception properties. Cinema's cult of stardom, carefully developed and maintained by Hollywood, is an example of such shift. Cult cinema, then, is for Benjamin one that mobilizes masses through its psychological presence (not its material one), leading to reading positions such as 'testing', shock' and 'distraction'. It also has the ability to exploit the 'aura' for political reasons, creating a new, revolutionary, sensitivity for audiences that allows a firm resistance against the domination of the mainstream aesthetic. Either that, or it complies with capitalist routines and loses all relevance.

A note on extracting: *The Work of Art in the Age of Mechanical Reproduction* originally appeared in German, in the *Zeitschrift für Sozialforschung,* 5(1), 1936 (page numbers unknown). It has since been reproduced many times, in readers of visual culture, media culture, film theory, art theory. Our extract is based on the version of the essay published in Hannah Arendt's edition of Benjamin's work, *Illuminations* (New York: Shocken Books, 1969, pp. 217–242), which is the most cited one. Our extract is different from those published or extracted in other readers in that it stresses the 'cult value' potential of technologically reproduced media (film first). We have therefore chosen to retain passages on cinema usually deleted in other extracts, and have omitted paragraphs that are more concerned with the political function of art (including Benjamin's endnotes), and historical theories of representation than with the cult value of film.

I

[. . .]

In principle a work of art has always been reproducible. Man-made artifacts could always be imitated by men. Replicas were made by pupils in practice of their craft, by masters for diffusing their works, and, finally, by third parties in the pursuit of gain. Mechanical reproduction of a work of art, however, represents something new. Historically, it advanced intermittently and in leaps at long intervals, but with accelerated intensity. The Greeks knew only two procedures of technically reproducing works of art: founding and stamping. Bronzes, terra cottas, and coins were the only art works which they could produce in quantity. All others were unique and could not be mechanically reproduced. With the woodcut graphic art became mechanically reproducible for the first time, long before script became reproducible by print. The enormous changes which printing, the mechanical reproduction of writing, has brought about in literature are a familiar story. However, within the phenomenon which we are here examining from the perspective of world history, print is merely a special, though particularly important, case. During the Middle Ages engraving and etching were added to the woodcut; at the beginning of the nineteenth century lithography made its appearance.

With lithography the technique of reproduction reached an essentially new stage. This much more direct process was distinguished by the tracing of the design on a stone rather than its incision on a block of wood or its etching on a copperplate and permitted graphic art for the first time to put its products on the market, not only in large numbers as hitherto, but also in daily changing forms. Lithography enabled graphic art to illustrate everyday life, and it began to keep pace with printing. But only a few decades after its invention, lithography was surpassed by photography. For the first time in the process of pictorial reproduction, photography freed the hand of the most important artistic functions which henceforth devolved only upon the eye looking into a lens. Since the eye perceives more swiftly than the hand can draw, the process of pictorial reproduction was accelerated so enormously that it could keep pace with speech. A film operator shooting a scene in the studio captures the images at the speed of an actor's speech. Just as lithography virtually implied the illustrated newspaper, so did photography foreshadow the sound film. The technical reproduction of sound was tackled at the end of the last century. These convergent endeavors made predictable a situation which Paul Valéry pointed up in this sentence: "Just as water, gas, and electricity are brought into our houses from far off to satisfy our needs in response to a minimal effort, so we shall be supplied with visual or auditory images, which will appear and disappear at a simple movement of the hand, hardly more than a sign." Around 1900 technical reproduction had reached a standard that not only permitted it to reproduce all transmitted works of art and thus to cause the most profound change in their impact upon the public; it also had captured a place of its own among the artistic processes. For the study of this standard nothing is more revealing than the nature of the repercussions that these two different manifestations—the reproduction of works of art and the art of the film—have had on art in its traditional form.

II

Even the most perfect reproduction of a work of art is lacking in one element: its presence in time and space, its unique existence at the place where it happens to be. This unique existence of the work of art determined the history to which it was subject throughout the time of its existence. This includes the changes which it may have suffered in physical condition over the years as well as the various changes in its ownership. The traces of the first can be revealed only by chemical or physical analyses which it is impossible to perform on a reproduction; changes of ownership are subject to a tradition which must be traced from the situation of the original.

The presence of the original is the prerequisite to the concept of authenticity. Chemical analyses of the patina of a bronze can help to establish this, as does the proof that a given manuscript of the Middle Ages stems from an archive of the fifteenth century. The whole sphere of authenticity is outside technical—and, of course, not only technical—reproducibility. Confronted with its manual reproduction, which was usually branded as a forgery, the original preserved all its authority; not so *vis à vis* technical reproduction. The reason is twofold. First, process reproduction is more independent of the original than manual reproduction. For example, in photography, process reproduction can bring out those aspects of the original that are unattainable to the naked eye yet accessible to the lens, which is adjustable and chooses its angle at will. And photographic reproduction, with the aid of certain processes, such as enlargement or slow motion, can capture images which escape natural vision. Secondly, technical reproduction can put the copy of the original into situations which would be out of reach for the original itself. Above all, it enables the original to meet the beholder halfway, be it in the form of a photograph or a phonograph record. The cathedral leaves its locale to be received in the studio of a lover of art; the choral production, performed in an auditorium or in the open air, resounds in the drawing room.

The situations into which the product of mechanical reproduction can be brought may not touch the actual work of art, yet the quality of its presence is always depreciated. This holds not only for the art work but also, for instance, for a landscape which passes in review before the spectator in a movie. In the case of the art object, a most sensitive nucleus—namely, its authenticity—is interfered with whereas no natural object is vulnerable on that score. The authenticity of a thing is the essence of all that is transmissible from its beginning, ranging from its substantive duration to its testimony to the history which it has experienced. Since the historical testimony rests on the authenticity, the former, too, is jeopardized by reproduction when substantive duration ceases to matter. And what is really jeopardized when the historical testimony is affected is the authority of the object.

One might subsume the eliminated element in the term "aura" and go on to say: that which withers in the age of mechanical reproduction is the aura of the work of art. This is a symptomatic process whose significance points beyond the realm of art. One might generalize by saying: the technique of reproduction detaches the reproduced object from the domain of tradition. By making many reproductions it substitutes a plurality of copies for a unique existence. And in permitting the reproduction to meet the beholder or listener in his own particular situation, it reactivates the object reproduced. These two processes lead to a tremendous shattering of tradition which is the obverse of the contemporary crisis and renewal of mankind. Both processes are intimately connected with the contemporary mass movements. Their most powerful agent is the film. Its social significance, particularly in its most positive form, is inconceivable without its destructive, cathartic aspect, that is, the liquidation of the traditional value of the cultural heritage. This phenomenon is most palpable in the great historical films. It extends to ever new positions. In 1927 Abel Gance exclaimed enthusiastically: "Shakespeare, Rembrandt, Beethoven will make films . . . all legends, all mythologies and all myths, all founders of religion, and the very religions . . . await their exposed resurrection, and the heroes crowd each other at the gate." Presumably without intending it, he issued an invitation to a far-reaching liquidation.

III

During long periods of history, the mode of human sense perception changes with humanity's entire mode of existence. The manner in which human sense perception is organized, the medium in which it is accomplished, is determined not only by nature but by historical circumstances as well. The fifth century, with its great shifts of population, saw the birth of the late Roman art industry and the Vienna Genesis, and there developed not only an art different from that of antiquity but also a new kind of perception. The scholars of the Viennese school, Riegl and Wickhoff, who resisted the weight of classical tradition under which these later art forms had been buried, were the first to draw conclusions from them concerning the organization of perception at the time. However far-reaching their insight, these scholars limited themselves to showing the significant, formal hallmark which characterized perception in late Roman times. They did not attempt—and, perhaps, saw no way—to show the social transformations expressed by these changes of perception. The conditions for an analogous insight are more favorable in the present. And if changes in the medium of contemporary perception can be comprehended as decay of the aura, it is possible to show its social causes.

The concept of aura which was proposed above with reference to historical objects may usefully be illustrated with reference to the aura of natural ones. We define the aura of the latter as the unique phenomenon of a distance, however close it may be. If, while resting on a summer afternoon, you follow with your eyes a mountain range on the horizon or a branch which casts its shadow over you, you experience the aura of those mountains, of that branch. This image makes it easy to comprehend the social bases of the contemporary decay of the aura. It rests on two circumstances, both of which are related to the increasing significance of the masses in contemporary life. Namely, the desire of contemporary masses to bring things "closer" spatially and humanly, which is just as ardent as their bent toward overcoming the uniqueness of every reality by accepting its reproduction. Every day the urge grows stronger to get hold of an object at very close range by way of its likeness, its reproduction. Unmistakably, reproduction as offered by picture magazines and newsreels differs from the image seen by the unarmed eye. Uniqueness and permanence are as closely linked in the latter as are transitoriness and reproducibility in the former. To pry an object from its shell, to destroy its aura, is the mark of a perception whose "sense of the universal equality of things" has increased to such a degree that it extracts it even from a unique object by means of reproduction. Thus is manifested in the field of perception what in the theoretical sphere is noticeable in the increasing importance of statistics. The adjustment of reality to the masses and of the masses to reality is a process of unlimited scope, as much for thinking as for perception.

IV

The uniqueness of a work of art is inseparable from its being imbedded in the fabric of tradition. This tradition itself is thoroughly alive and extremely changeable. An ancient statue of Venus, for example, stood in a different traditional context with the Greeks, who made it an object of veneration, than with the clerics of the Middle Ages, who viewed it as an ominous idol. Both of them, however, were equally confronted with its uniqueness, that is, its aura. Originally the contextual integration of art in tradition found its expression in the cult. We know that the earliest art works originated in the service of a ritual—first the magical, then the religious kind. It is significant that the existence of the work of art with reference to its aura is never entirely separated from its ritual function. In other words, the unique value of the "authentic" work of art has its basis in ritual, the location of its original use value. This ritualistic basis, however remote, is still recognizable as secularized ritual even in the most profane forms of the cult of beauty. The secular cult of beauty, developed during the Renaissance and prevailing for three centuries, clearly showed that ritualistic basis in its decline and the first deep crisis which befell it. With the advent of the first truly revolutionary means of reproduction, photography, simultaneously with the rise of socialism, art sensed the approaching crisis which has become evident a century later. At the time, art reacted with the doctrine of *l'art pour l'art*, that is, with a theology of art. This gave rise to what might be called a negative theology in the form of the idea of "pure" art, which not only denied any social function of art but also any categorizing by subject matter. (In poetry, Mallarmé was the first to take this position.)

An analysis of art in the age of mechanical reproduction must do justice to these relationships, for they lead us to an all-important insight: for the first time in world history, mechanical reproduction emancipates the work of art from its parasitical dependence on ritual. To an ever greater degree the work of art reproduced becomes the work of art designed for reproducibility. From a photographic negative, for example, one can make any number of prints; to ask for the "authentic" print makes no sense. But the instant the criterion of authenticity ceases to be applicable to artistic production, the total function of art is reversed. Instead of being based on ritual, it begins to be based on another practice—politics.

V

Works of art are received and valued on different planes. Two polar types stand out: with one, the accent is on the cult value; with the other, on the exhibition value of the work. Artistic production begins with ceremonial objects destined to serve in a cult. One may assume that what mattered was their existence, not their being on view. The elk portrayed by the man of the Stone Age on the walls of his cave was an instrument of magic. He did expose it to his fellow men, but in the main it was meant for the spirits. Today the cult value would seem to demand that the work of art remain hidden. Certain statues of gods are accessible only to the priest in the cella; certain Madonnas remain covered nearly all year round; certain sculptures on medieval cathedrals are invisible to the spectator on ground level. With the emancipation of the various art practices from ritual go increasing opportunities for the exhibition of their products. It is easier to exhibit a portrait bust that can be sent here and there than to exhibit the statue of a divinity that has its fixed place in the interior of a temple. The same holds for the painting as against the mosaic or fresco that preceded it. And even though the public presentability of a mass originally may have been just as great as that of a symphony, the latter originated at the moment when its public presentability promised to surpass that of the mass.

With the different methods of technical reproduction of a work of art, its fitness for exhibition increased to such an extent that the quantitative shift between its two poles turned into a qualitative transformation of its nature. This is comparable to the situation of the work of art in prehistoric times when, by the absolute emphasis on its cult value, it was, first and foremost, an instrument of magic. Only later did it come to be recognized as a work of art. In the same way today, by the absolute emphasis on its exhibition value the work of art become a creation with entirely new functions, among which the one we are conscious of, the artistic function, later may be recognized as incidental. This much is certain: today photography and the film are the most serviceable exemplifications of this new function.

VI

In photography, exhibition value begins to displace cult value all along the line. But cult value does not give way without resistance. It retires into an ultimate retrenchment: the human countenance. It is no accident that the portrait was the focal point of early photography. The cult of remembrance of loved ones, absent or dead, offers a last refuge for the cult value of the picture. For the last time the aura emanates from the early photographs in the fleeting expression of a human face. This is what constitutes their melancholy, incomparable beauty. But as man withdraws from the photographic image, the exhibition value for the first time shows its superiority to the ritual value. To have pinpointed this new stage constitutes the incomparable significance of Atget, who, around 1900, took photographs of deserted Paris streets. It has quite justly been said of him that he photographed them like scenes of crime. The scene of a crime, too, is deserted; it is photographed for the purpose of establishing evidence. With Atget, photographs become standard evidence for historical occurrences, and acquire a hidden political significance. They demand a specific kind of approach; free-floating contemplation is not appropriate to them. They stir the viewer; he feels challenged by them in a new way. At the same time picture magazines begin to put up signposts for him, right ones or wrong ones, no matter. For the first time, captions have become obligatory. And it is clear that they have an altogether different character than the title of a painting. The directives which the captions give to those looking at pictures in illustrated magazines soon become even more explicit and more imperative in the film where the meaning of each single picture appears to be prescribed by the sequence of all preceding ones.

VII

The nineteenth-century dispute as to the artistic value of painting versus photography today seems devious and confused. This does not diminish its importance, however; if anything, it underlines it. The dispute was in fact the symptom of a historical transformation the universal impact of which was not realized by either of the rivals. When the age of mechanical reproduction separated art from its basis in cult, the semblance of its autonomy disappeared forever. The resulting change in the function of art transcended the perspective of the century; for a long time it even escaped that of the twentieth century, which experienced the development of the film.

[. . .]

VIII

The artistic performance of a stage actor is definitely presented to the public by the actor in person; that of the screen actor, however, is presented by a camera, with a twofold consequence. The camera that presents the performance of the film actor to the public need not respect the performance as an integral whole. Guided by the cameraman, the camera continually changes its position with respect to the performance. The sequence of positional views which the editor composes from the material supplied him constitutes the completed film. It comprises certain factors of movement which are in reality those of the camera, not to mention special camera angles, close-ups, etc. Hence, the performance of the actor is subjected to a series of optical tests. This is the first consequence of the fact that the actor's performance is presented by means of a camera. Also, the film actor lacks the opportunity of the stage actor to adjust to the audience during his performance, since he does not present his performance to the audience in person. This permits the audience to take the position of a critic, without experiencing any personal contact with the actor. The audience's identification with the actor is really an identification with the camera. Consequently the audience takes the position of the camera; its approach is that of testing. This is not the approach to which cult values may be exposed.

IX

For the film, what matters primarily is that the actor represents himself to the public before the camera, rather than representing someone else. One of the first to sense the actor's metamorphosis by this form of testing was Pirandello.

[. . .]

X

The feeling of strangeness that overcomes the actor before the camera, as Pirandello describes it, is basically of the same kind as the estrangement felt before one's own image in the mirror. But now the reflected image has become separable, transportable. And where is it transported? Before the public. Never for a moment does the screen actor cease to be conscious of this fact. While facing the camera he knows that ultimately he will face the public, the consumers who constitute the market. This market, where he offers not only his labor but also his whole self, his heart and soul, is beyond his reach. During the shooting he has as little contact with it as any article made in a factory. This may contribute to that oppression, that new anxiety which, according to Pirandello, grips the actor before the camera. The film responds to the shriveling of the aura with an artificial build-up of the "personality" outside the studio. The cult of the movie star, fostered by the money of the film industry, preserves not the unique aura of the person but the "spell of the personality," the phony spell of a commodity. So long as the movie-makers' capital sets the fashion, as a rule no other revolutionary merit can be accredited to today's film than the promotion of a revolutionary criticism of traditional concepts of art. We do not deny that in some cases today's films can also promote revolutionary criticism of social conditions, even of the distribution of property. However, our present study is no more specifically concerned with this than is the film production of Western Europe.

It is inherent in the technique of the film as well as that of sports that everybody who witnesses its accomplishments is somewhat of an expert. This is obvious to anyone listening to a group of newspaper boys leaning on their bicycles and discussing the outcome of a bicycle race. It is not for nothing that newspaper publishers arrange races for their delivery boys. These arouse great interest among the participants, for the victor has an opportunity to rise from delivery boy to professional racer. Similarly, the newsreel offers everyone the opportunity to rise from passer-by to movie extra. In this way any man might even find himself part of a work of art, as witness Vertoff's *Three Songs About Lenin* or Ivens' *Borinage*. Any man today can lay claim to being filmed. This claim can best be elucidated by a comparative look at the historical situation of contemporary literature.

For centuries a small number of writers were confronted by many thousands of readers. This changed toward the end of the last century. With the increasing extension of the press, which kept placing new political, religious, scientific, professional, and local organs before the readers, an increasing number of readers became writers—at first, occasional ones. It began with the daily press opening to its readers space for "letters to the editor." And today there is hardly a gainfully employed European who could not, in principle, find an opportunity to publish somewhere or other comments on his work, grievances, documentary reports, or that sort of thing. Thus, the distinction between author and public is about to lose its basic character. The difference becomes merely functional; it may vary from case to case. At any moment the reader is ready to turn into a writer. As expert, which he had to become willy-nilly in an extremely specialized work process, even if only in some minor respect, the reader gains access to authorship. In the Soviet Union work itself is given a voice. To present it verbally is part of a man's ability to perform the work. Literary license is now founded on polytechnic rather than specialized training and thus becomes common property.

All this can easily be applied to the film, where transitions that in literature took centuries have come about in a decade. In cinematic practice, particularly in Russia, this change-over has partially become established reality. Some of the players whom we meet in Russian films are not actors in our sense but people who portray *themselves*— and primarily in their own work process. In Western Europe the capitalistic exploitation of the film denies consideration to modern man's legitimate claim to being reproduced. Under these circumstances the film industry is trying hard to spur the interest of the masses through illusion-promoting spectacles and dubious speculations.

[. . .]

XII

Mechanical reproduction of art changes the reaction of the masses toward art. The reactionary attitude toward a Picasso painting changes into the progressive reaction toward a Chaplin movie. The progressive reaction is characterized by the direct, intimate fusion of visual and emotional enjoyment with the orientation of the expert. Such fusion is of great social significance. The greater the decrease in the social significance of an art form, the sharper the distinction between criticism and enjoyment by the public. The conventional is uncritically enjoyed, and the truly new is criticized with aversion. With regard to the screen, the critical and the receptive attitudes of the public coincide. The decisive reason for this is that individual reactions are predetermined by the mass audience response they are about to produce, and this is nowhere more pronounced than in the film. The moment these responses become manifest they control each other. Again, the comparison with painting is fruitful. A painting has always had an excellent chance to be viewed by one person or by a few. The simultaneous contemplation of paintings by a large public, such as developed in the nineteenth century, is an early symptom of the crisis of painting, a crisis which was by no means occasioned exclusively by photography but rather in a relatively independent manner by the appeal of art works to the masses.

Painting simply is in no position to present an object for simultaneous collective experience, as it was possible for architecture at all times, for the epic poem in the past, and for the movie today. Although this circumstance in itself should not lead one to conclusions about the social role of painting, it does constitute a serious threat as soon as painting, under special conditions and, as it were, against its nature, is confronted directly by the masses. In the churches and monasteries of the Middle Ages and at the princely courts up to the end of the eighteenth century, a collective reception of paintings did not occur simultaneously, but by graduated and hierarchized mediation. The change that has come about is an expression of the particular conflict in which painting was implicated by the mechanical reproducibility of paintings. Although paintings began to be publicly exhibited in galleries and salons, there was no way for the masses to organize and control themselves in their reception. Thus the same public which responds in a progressive manner toward a grotesque film is bound to respond in a reactionary manner to surrealism.

[. . .]

XIV

One of the foremost tasks of art has always been the creation of a demand which could be fully satisfied only later. The history of every art form shows critical epochs in which a certain art form aspires to effects which could be fully obtained only with a changed technical standard, that is to say, in a new art form. The extravagances and crudities of art which thus appear, particularly in the so-called decadent epochs, actually arise from the nucleus of its richest historical energies. In recent years, such barbarisms were abundant in Dadaism. It is only now that its impulse becomes discernible: Dadaism attempted to create by pictorial—and literary—means the effects which the public today seeks in the film.

Every fundamentally new, pioneering creation of demands will carry beyond its goal. Dadaism did so to the extent that it sacrificed the market values which are so characteristic of the film in favor of higher ambitions—though of course it was not conscious of such intentions as here described. The Dadaists attached much less importance to the sales value of their work than to its uselessness for contemplative immersion. The studied degradation of their material was not the least of their means to achieve this uselessness. Their poems are "word salad" containing obscenities and every imaginable waste product of language. The same is true of their paintings, on which they mounted buttons and tickets. What they intended and achieved was a relentless destruction of the aura of their creations, which they branded as reproductions with the very means of production. Before a painting of Arp's or a poem by August Stramm it is impossible to take time for contemplation and evaluation as one would before a canvas of Derain's or a poem by Rilke. In the decline of middle-class society, contemplation became a school for asocial behavior; it was countered by distraction as a variant of social conduct. Dadaistic activities actually assured a rather vehement distraction by making works of art the center of scandal. One requirement was foremost: to outrage the public.

From an alluring appearance or persuasive structure of sound the work of art of the Dadaists became an instrument of ballistics. It hit the spectator like a bullet, it happened to him, thus acquiring a tactile quality. It promoted a demand for the film, the distracting element of which is also primarily tactile, being based on changes of place and focus which periodically assail the spectator. Let us compare the screen on which a film unfolds with the canvas of a painting. The painting invites the spectator to contemplation; before it the spectator can abandon himself to his associations. Before the movie frame he cannot do so. No sooner has his eye grasped a scene than it is already changed. It cannot be arrested. Duhamel, who detests the film and knows nothing of its significance, though something of its structure, notes this circumstance as follows: "I can no longer think what I want to think. My thoughts have been replaced by moving images." The spectator's process of association in view of these images is indeed interrupted by their constant, sudden change. This constitutes the shock effect of the film, which, like all shocks, should be cushioned by heightened presence of mind. By means of its technical structure, the film has taken the physical shock effect out of the wrappers in which Dadaism had, as it were, kept it inside the moral shock effect.

XV

The mass is a matrix from which all traditional behavior toward works of art issues today in a new form. Quantity has been transmuted into quality. The greatly increased mass of participants has produced a change in the mode of participation. The fact that the new mode of participation first appeared in a disreputable form must not confuse the spectator. Yet some people have launched spirited attacks against precisely this superficial aspect. Among these, Duhamel has expressed himself in the most radical manner. What he objects to most is the kind of participation which the movie elicits from the masses. Duhamel calls the movie "a pastime for helots, a diversion for uneducated, wretched, worn-out creatures who are consumed by their worries . . ., a spectacle which requires no concentration and presupposes no intelligence . . ., which kindles no light in the heart and awakens no hope other than the ridiculous one of someday becoming a 'star' in Los Angeles." Clearly, this is at bottom the same ancient lament that the masses seek distraction whereas art demands concentration from the spectator. That is a commonplace. The question remains whether it provides a platform for the analysis of the film. A closer look is needed here. Distraction and concentration form polar opposites which may be stated as follows: A man who concentrates before a work of art is absorbed by it. He enters into this work of art the way legend tells of the Chinese painter when he viewed his finished painting. In contrast, the distracted mass absorbs the work of art. This is most obvious with regard to buildings. Architecture has always represented the prototype of a work of art the reception of which is consummated by a collectivity in a state of distraction. The laws of its reception are most instructive.

Buildings have been man's companions since primeval times. Many art forms have developed and perished. Tragedy begins with the Greeks, is extinguished with them, and after centuries its "rules" only are revived. The epic poem, which had its origin in the youth of nations, expires in Europe at the end of the Renaissance. Panel painting is a creation of the Middle Ages, and nothing guarantees its uninterrupted existence. But the human need for shelter is lasting. Architecture has never been idle. Its history is more ancient than that of any other art, and its claim to being a living force has significance in every attempt to comprehend the relationship of the masses to art. Buildings are appropriated in a twofold manner: by use and by perception—or rather, by touch and sight. Such appropriation cannot be understood in terms of the attentive concentration of a tourist before a famous building. On the tactile side there is no counterpart to contemplation on the optical side. Tactile appropriation is accomplished not so much by attention as by habit. As regards architecture, habit determines to a large extent even optical reception. The latter, too, occurs much less through rapt attention than by noticing the object in incidental fashion. This mode of appropriation, developed with reference to architecture, in certain circumstances acquires canonical value. For the tasks which face the human apparatus of perception at the turning points of history cannot be solved by optical means, that is, by contemplation, alone. They are mastered gradually by habit, under the guidance of tactile appropriation.

The distracted person, too, can form habits. More, the ability to master certain tasks in a state of distraction proves that their solution has become a matter of habit.

Distraction as provided by art presents a covert control of the extent to which new tasks have become soluble by apperception. Since, moreover, individuals are tempted to avoid such tasks, art will tackle the most difficult and most important ones where it is able to mobilize the masses. Today it does so in the film. Reception in a state of distraction, which is increasing noticeably in all fields of art and is symptomatic of profound changes in apperception, finds in the film its true means of exercise. The film with its shock effect meets this mode of reception halfway. The film makes the cult value recede into the background not only by putting the public in the position of the critic, but also by the fact that at the movies this position requires no attention. The public is an examiner, but an absent-minded one.

[. . .]

1.3

Notes on 'camp'
by Susan Sontag

New York critic and intellectual Susan Sontag (1933–2004) made her name as essayist with the collection *Against Interpretation*, a series of writings on contemporary culture and art (twentieth century, and postwar mainly), with which she provided an alternative for the then prevailing modes of interpretation New Criticism, and Modernism. Calling attention to challenges to the canon of high art, Sontag wrote passionately about popular culture (movies, theatre, literature, fashion), arguing for it to be taken as seriously as high art. Her political activism penetrated her writings, giving them a pressing topicality, and demonstrating how popular culture embodies its times' ethos. 'Notes on "camp" is an attempt to tackle a very visible but nevertheless ignored fascination for forms of art that by all standards would be considered failures (sometimes close to achievement but never quite), but are nevertheless championed by patrons. Sontag claims that camp is an aesthetic sensibility that is characterized by a high degree of, and attention for stylization, artifice, travesty, *double entendre*, extravagance and unintentional badness. According to Sontag, we find this sensibility especially towards types of art that are closely associated with popular culture, like movies, fashion, design, or television. Sontag claims that in the twentieth century (since Oscar Wilde, she says) the appraisal of camp has taken the form of a cult, of a dedication that aims to challenge the distinctions between good and bad taste. Camp is 'good because it's awful'. Because, as Sontag writes, 'camp taste is, above all, a mode of enjoyment, of appreciation – not judgment' it can put itself in an outsider position. As such it can be the flea in the fur of proper taste – a form of buffery, dandyism, or snobbery free from responsibility. Camp is not limited to political and cultural boundaries – in fact it challenges these by pretending to be about pure aesthetics only. What distinguishes camp from true art is that it fails in its achievement of enlightenment (an argument similar to that of Benjamin). But instead it manages to hold up a mirror to the pretensions and prejudices of the art establishment. And in that sense it is very political.

A note on extracting: we have used the version of 'Notes on "Camp"' that was published on pages 275–292 in the essay collection *Against Interpretation*, published by Dell Publishing in 1966. This edition is an identical reprint from the original that was published by Farrar Straus & Giroux. 'Notes on "Camp"' contains 58 numbered paragraphs (the so-called notes). We have retained the original paragraph numbers.

Many things in the world have not been named; and many things, even if they have been named, have never been described. One of these is the sensibility—unmistakably modern, a variant of sophistication but hardly identical with it—that goes by the cult name of "Camp."

A sensibility (as distinct from an idea) is one of the hardest things to talk about; but there are special reasons why Camp, in particular, has never been discussed. It is not a natural mode of sensibility, if there be any such. Indeed the essence of Camp is its love—of the unnatural: of artifice and exaggeration. And Camp is esoteric—something of a private code, a badge of identity even, among small urban cliques. Apart from a lazy two-page sketch in Christopher Isherwood's novel *The World in the Evening* (1954), it has hardly broken into print. To talk about Camp is therefore to betray it. If the betrayal can be defended, it will be for the edification it provides, or the dignity of the conflict it resolves. For myself, I plead the goal of self-edification, and the goad of a sharp conflict in my own sensibility. I am strongly drawn to Camp, and almost as strongly offended by it. That is why I want to talk about it, and why I can. For no one who wholeheartedly shares in a given sensibility can analyze it; he can only, whatever his intention, exhibit it. To name a sensibility, to draw its contours and to recount its history, requires a deep sympathy modified by revulsion.

Though I am speaking about sensibility only—and about a sensibility that, among other things, converts the serious into the frivolous—these are grave matters. Most people think of sensibility or taste as the realm of purely subjective preferences, those mysterious attractions, mainly sensual, that have not been brought under the sovereignty of reason. They *allow* that considerations of taste play a part in their reactions to people and to works of art. But this attitude is naïve. And even worse. To patronize the faculty of taste is to patronize oneself. For taste governs every free—as opposed to rote—human response. Nothing is more decisive. There is taste in people, visual taste, taste in emotion—and there is taste in acts, taste in morality. Intelligence, as well, is really a kind of taste: taste in ideas. (One of the facts to be reckoned with is that taste tends to develop very unevenly. It's rare that the same person has good visual taste *and* good taste in people *and* taste in ideas.)

Taste has no system and no proofs. But there is something like a logic of taste: the consistent sensibility which underlies and gives rise to a certain taste. A sensibility is almost, but not quite, ineffable. Any sensibility which can be crammed into the mold of a system, or handled with the rough tools of proof, is no longer a sensibility at all. It has hardened into an idea. . . .

To snare a sensibility in words, especially one that is alive and powerful, one must be tentative and nimble. The form of jottings, rather than an essay (with its claim to a linear, consecutive argument), seemed more appropriate for getting down something of this particular fugitive sensibility. It's embarrassing to be solemn and treatise-like about Camp. One runs the risk of having, oneself, produced a very inferior piece of Camp.

These notes are for Oscar Wilde.

"One should either be a work of art, or wear a work of art."
                                        —*Phrases & Philosophies for the Use of the Young*

1. To start very generally: Camp is a certain mode of aestheticism. It is one way of seeing the world as an aesthetic phenomenon. That way, the way of Camp, is not in terms of beauty, but in terms of the degree of artifice, of stylization.

2. To emphasize style is to slight content, or to introduce an attitude which is neutral with respect to content. It goes without saying that the Camp sensibility is disengaged, depoliticized—or at least apolitical.

3. Not only is there a Camp vision, a Camp way of looking at things. Camp is as well a quality discoverable in objects and the behavior of persons. There are "campy" movies, clothes, furniture, popular songs, novels, people, buildings. . . . This distinction is important. True, the Camp eye has the power to transform experience. But not everything can be seen as Camp. It's not *all* in the eye of the beholder.

4. Random examples of items which are part of the canon of Camp:

Zuleika Dobson
Tiffany lamps
Scopitone films
The Brown Derby restaurant on Sunset Boulevard in LA
The Enquirer, headlines and stories
Aubrey Beardsley drawings
Swan Lake
Bellini's operas
Visconti's direction of *Salome* and *'Tis Pity She's a Whore*
certain turn-of-the-century picture postcards
Schoedsack's *King Kong*
the Cuban pop singer La Lupe
Lynn Ward's novel in woodcuts, *God's Man*
the old Flash Gordon comics
women's clothes of the twenties (feather boas, fringed and beaded dresses, etc.)
the novels of Ronald Firbank and Ivy Compton-Burnett
stag movies seen without lust

5. Camp taste has an affinity for certain arts rather than others. Clothes, furniture, all the elements of visual décor, for instance, make up a large part of Camp. For Camp art is often decorative art, emphasizing texture, sensuous surface, and style at the expense of content. Concert music, though, because it is contentless, is rarely Camp. It offers no opportunity, say, for a contrast between silly or extravagant content and rich form. . . . Sometimes whole art forms become saturated with Camp. Classical ballet, opera, movies have seemed so for a long time. In the last two years, popular music (post rock-'n'-roll, what the French call yé yé) has been annexed. And movie criticism (like lists of "The 10 Best Bad Movies I Have Seen") is probably the greatest popularizer of Camp taste today, because most people still go to the movies in a high-spirited and unpretentious way.

6. There is a sense in which it is correct to say: "It's too good to be Camp." Or "too important," not marginal enough. (More on this later.) Thus, the personality and many of the works of Jean Cocteau are Camp, but not those of André Gide; the operas of Richard Strauss, but not those of Wagner; concoctions of Tin Pan Alley and

Liverpool, but not jazz. Many examples of Camp are things which, from a "serious" point of view, are either bad art or kitsch. Not all, though. Not only is Camp not necessarily bad art, but some art which can be approached as Camp (example: the major films of Louis Feuillade) merits the most serious admiration and study.

"The more we study Art, the less we care for Nature."

—*The Decay of Lying*

7. All Camp objects, and persons, contain a large element of artifice. Nothing in nature can be campy. . . . Rural Camp is still man-made, and most campy objects are urban. (Yet, they often have a serenity—or a naïveté—which is the equivalent of pastoral. A great deal of Camp suggests Empson's phrase, "urban pastoral.")

8. Camp is a vision of the world in terms of style—but a particular kind of style. It is the love of the exaggerated, the "off," of things-being-what-they-are-not. The best example is in Art Nouveau, the most typical and fully developed Camp style. Art Nouveau objects, typically, convert one thing into something else: the lighting fixtures in the form of flowering plants, the living room which is really a grotto. A remarkable example: the Paris Métro entrances designed by Hector Guimard in the late 1890s in the shape of cast-iron orchid stalks.

9. As a taste in persons, Camp responds particularly to the markedly attenuated and to the strongly exaggerated. The androgyne is certainly one of the great images of Camp sensibility. Examples: the swooning, slim, sinuous figures of pre-Raphaelite painting and poetry; the thin, flowing, sexless bodies in Art Nouveau prints and posters, presented in relief on lamps and ashtrays; the haunting androgynous vacancy behind the perfect beauty of Greta Garbo. Here, Camp taste draws on a mostly unacknowledged truth of taste: the most refined form of sexual attractiveness (as well as the most refined form of sexual pleasure) consists in going against the grain of one's sex. What is most beautiful in virile men is something feminine; what is most beautiful in feminine women is something masculine. . . . Allied to the Camp taste for the androgynous is something that seems quite different but isn't: a relish for the exaggeration of sexual characteristics and personality mannerisms. For obvious reasons, the best examples that can be cited are movie stars. The corny flamboyant femaleness of Jayne Mansfield, Gina Lollobrigida, Jane Russell, Virginia Mayo; the exaggerated he-man-ness of Steve Reeves, Victor Mature. The great stylists of temperament and mannerism, like Bette Davis, Barbara Stanwyck, Tallulah Bankhead, Edwige Feuillière.

10. Camp sees everything in quotation marks. It's not a lamp, but a "lamp"; not a woman, but a "woman." To perceive Camp in objects and persons is to understand Being-as-Playing-a-Role. It is the farthest extension, in sensibility, of the metaphor of life as theater.

11. Camp is the triumph of the epicene style. (The convertibility of "man" and "woman," "person" and "thing.") But all style, that is, artifice, is, ultimately, epicene. Life is not stylish. Neither is nature.

12. The question isn't, "Why travesty, impersonation, theatricality?" The question is, rather, "When does travesty, impersonation, theatricality acquire the special flavor of Camp?" Why is the atmosphere of Shakespeare's comedies (*As You Like It*, etc.) not epicene, while that of *Der Rosenkavalier* is?

13. The dividing line seems to fall in the 18th century; there the origins of Camp taste are to be found (Gothic novels, Chinoiserie, caricature, artificial ruins, and so forth.) But the relation to nature was quite different then. In the 18th century, people of taste either patronized nature (Strawberry Hill) or attempted to remake it into something artificial (Versailles). They also indefatigably patronized the past. Today's Camp taste effaces nature, or else contradicts it outright. And the relation of Camp taste to the past is extremely sentimental.

14. A pocket history of Camp might, of course, begin farther back—with the mannerist artists like Pontormo, Rosso, and Caravaggio, or the extraordinarily theatrical painting of Georges de La Tour, or Euphuism (Lyly, etc.) in literature. Still, the soundest starting point seems to be the late 17th and early 18th century, because of that period's extraordinary feeling for artifice, for surface, for symmetry; its taste for the picturesque and the thrilling, its elegant conventions for representing instant feeling and the total presence of character—the epigram and the rhymed couplet (in words), the flourish (in gesture and in music). The late 17th and early 18th century is the great period of Camp: Pope, Congreve, Walpole, etc., but not Swift; les *précieux* in France; the rococo churches of Munich; Pergolesi. Somewhat later: much of Mozart. But in the 19th century, what had been distributed throughout all of high culture now becomes a special taste; it takes on overtones of the acute, the esoteric, the perverse. Confining the story to England alone, we see Camp continuing wanly through 19th century aestheticism (Burne-Jones, Pater, Ruskin, Tennyson), emerging full-blown with the Art Nouveau movement in the visual and decorative arts, and finding its conscious ideologists in such "wits" as Wilde and Firbank.

15. Of course, to say all these things are Camp is not to argue they are simply that. A full analysis of Art Nouveau, for instance, would scarcely equate it with Camp. But such an analysis cannot ignore what in Art Nouveau allows it to be experienced as Camp. Art Nouveau is full of "content," even of a political-moral sort; it was a revolutionary movement in the arts, spurred on by a utopian vision (somewhere between William Morris and the Bauhaus group) of an organic politics and taste. Yet there is also a feature of the Art Nouveau objects which suggests a disengaged, unserious, "aesthete's" vision. This tells us something important about Art Nouveau—and about what the lens of Camp, which blocks out content, is.

16. Thus, the Camp sensibility is one that is alive to a double sense in which some things can be taken. But this is not the familiar split-level construction of a literal meaning, on the one hand, and a symbolic meaning, on the other. It is the difference, rather, between the thing as meaning something, anything, and the thing as pure artifice.

17. This comes out clearly in the vulgar use of the word Camp as a verb, "to camp," something that people do. To camp is a mode of seduction—one which employs flamboyant mannerisms susceptible of a double interpretation: gestures full of duplicity, with a witty meaning for cognoscenti and another, more impersonal, for outsiders. Equally and by extension, when the word becomes a noun, when a person or a thing is "a camp," a duplicity is involved. Behind the "straight" public sense in which something can be taken, one has found a private zany experience of the thing.

"To be natural is such a very difficult pose to keep up."

—An Ideal Husband

18. One must distinguish between naïve and deliberate Camp. Pure Camp is always naïve. Camp which knows itself to be Camp ("camping") is usually less satisfying.

19. The pure examples of Camp are unintentional; they are dead serious. The Art Nouveau craftsman who makes a lamp with a snake coiled around it is not kidding, nor is he trying to be charming. He is saying, in all earnestness: Voilà! the Orient! Genuine Camp—for instance, the numbers devised for the Warner Brothers musicals of the early thirties (*42nd Street; The Golddiggers of 1933; . . . of 1935; . . . of 1937*; etc.) by Busby Berkeley—does not *mean* to be funny. Camping—say, the plays of Noel Coward—does. It seems unlikely that much of the traditional opera repertoire could be such satisfying Camp if the melodramatic absurdities of most opera plots had not been taken seriously by their composers. One doesn't need to know the artist's private intentions. The work tells all. (Compare a typical 19th century opera with Samuel Barber's *Vanessa*, a piece of manufactured, calculated Camp, and the difference is clear.)

20. Probably, intending to be campy is always harmful. The perfection of *Trouble in Paradise* and *The Maltese Falcon*, among the greatest Camp movies ever made, comes from the effortless smooth way in which tone is maintained. This is not so with such famous would-be Camp films of the fifties as *All About Eve* and *Beat the Devil*. These more recent movies have their fine moments, but the first is so slick and the second so hysterical; they want so badly to be campy that they're continually losing the beat. . . . Perhaps, though, it is not so much a question of the unintended effect versus the conscious intention, as of the delicate relation between parody and self-parody in Camp. The films of Hitchcock are a showcase for this problem. When self-parody lacks ebullience but instead reveals (even sporadically) a contempt for one's themes and one's materials—as in *To Catch a Thief, Rear Window, North by Northwest*—the results are forced and heavy-handed, rarely Camp. Successful Camp—a movie like Carné's *Drôle de Drame*; the film performances of Mae West and Edward Everett Horton; portions of the Goon Show—even when it reveals self-parody, reeks of self-love.

21. So, again, Camp rests on innocence. That means Camp discloses innocence, but also, when it can, corrupts it. Objects, being objects, don't change when they are singled out by the Camp vision. Persons, however, respond to their audiences. Persons begin "camping": Mae West, Bea Lillie, La Lupe, Tallulah Bankhead in *Lifeboat*, Bette Davis in *All About Eve*. (Persons can even be induced to camp without their knowing it. Consider the way Fellini got Anita Ekberg to parody herself in *La Dolce Vita*.)

22. Considered a little less strictly, Camp is either completely naïve or else wholly conscious (when one plays at being campy). An example of the latter: Wilde's epigrams themselves.

"It's absurd to divide people into good and bad. People are either charming or tedious."

—Lady Windemere's Fan

23. In naïve, or pure, Camp, the essential element is seriousness, a seriousness that fails. Of course, not all seriousness that fails can be redeemed as Camp. Only that which has the proper mixture of the exaggerated, the fantastic, the passionate, and the naïve.

24. When something is just bad (rather than Camp), it's often because it is too mediocre in its ambition. The artist hasn't attempted to do anything really outlandish. ("It's too much," "It's too fantastic," "It's not to be believed," are standard phrases of Camp enthusiasm.)

25. The hallmark of Camp is the spirit of extravagance. Camp is a woman walking around in a dress made of three million feathers. Camp is the paintings of Carlo Crivelli, with their real jewels and *trompe-l'oeil* insects and cracks in the masonry. Camp is the outrageous aestheticism of Sternberg's six American movies with Dietrich, all six, but especially the last, *The Devil Is a Woman*. . . . In Camp there is often something *démesuré* in the quality of the ambition, not only in the style of the work itself. Gaudí's lurid and beautiful buildings in Barcelona are Camp not only because of their style but because they reveal—most notably in the Cathedral of the Sagrada Familia—the ambition on the part of one man to do what it takes a generation, a whole culture to accomplish.

26. Camp is art that proposes itself seriously, but cannot be taken altogether seriously because it is "too much." *Titus Andronicus* and *Strange Interlude* are almost Camp, or could be played as Camp. The public manner and rhetoric of de Gaulle, often, are pure Camp.

27. A work can come close to Camp, but not make it, because it succeeds. Eisenstein's films are seldom Camp because, despite all exaggeration, they do succeed (dramatically) without surplus. If they were a little more "off," they could be great Camp—particularly *Ivan the Terrible I & II*. The same for Blake's drawings and paintings, weird and mannered as they are. They aren't Camp; though Art Nouveau, influenced by Blake, is.

What is extravagant in an inconsistent or an unpassionate way is not Camp. Neither can anything be Camp that does not seem to spring from an irrepressible, a virtually uncontrolled sensibility. Without passion, one gets pseudo-Camp—what is merely decorative, safe, in a word, chic. On the barren edge of Camp lie a number of attractive things: the sleek fantasies of Dali, the haute couture preciosity of Albicocco's *The Girl with the Golden Eyes*. But the two things—Camp and preciosity—must not be confused.

28. Again, Camp is the attempt to do something extraordinary. But extraordinary in the sense, often, of being special, glamorous. (The curved line, the extravagant gesture.) Not extraordinary merely in the sense of effort. Ripley's Believe-It-Or-Not items are rarely campy. These items, either natural oddities (the two-headed rooster, the eggplant in the shape of a cross) or else the products of immense labor (the man who walked from here to China on his hands, the woman who engraved the New Testament on the head of a pin), lack the visual reward—the glamour, the theatricality—that marks off certain extravagances as Camp.

29. The reason a movie like *On the Beach*, books like *Winesburg, Ohio* and *For Whom the Bell Tolls* are bad to the point of being laughable, but not bad to the point of being enjoyable, is that they are too dogged and pretentious. They lack fantasy. There

is Camp in such bad movies as *The Prodigal* and *Samson and Delilah*, the series of Italian color spectacles featuring the super-hero Maciste, numerous Japanese science fiction films (*Rodan, The Mysterians, The H-Man*) because, in their relative unpretentiousness and vulgarity, they are more extreme and irresponsible in their fantasy—and therefore touching and quite enjoyable.

30. Of course, the canon of Camp can change. Time has a great deal to do with it. Time may enhance what seems simply dogged or lacking in fantasy now because we are too close to it, because it resembles too closely our own everyday fantasies, the fantastic nature of which we don't perceive. We are better able to enjoy a fantasy as fantasy when it is not our own.

31. This is why so many of the objects prized by Camp taste are old-fashioned, out-of-date, *démodé*. It's not a love of the old as such. It's simply that the process of aging or deterioration provides the necessary detachment—or arouses a necessary sympathy. When the theme is important, and contemporary, the failure of a work of art may make us indignant. Time can change that. Time liberates the work of art from moral relevance, delivering it over to the Camp sensibility. . . . Another effect: time contracts the sphere of banality. (Banality is, strictly speaking, always a category of the contemporary.) What was banal can, with the passage of time, become fantastic. Many people who listen with delight to the style of Rudy Vallee revived by the English pop group, The Temperance Seven, would have been driven up the wall by Rudy Vallee in his heyday.

Thus, things are campy, not when they become old—but when we become less involved in them, and can enjoy, instead of be frustrated by, the failure of the attempt. But the effect of time is unpredictable. Maybe "method" acting (James Dean, Rod Steiger, Warren Beatty) will seem as Camp some day as Ruby Keeler's does now—or as Sarah Bernhardt's does, in the films she made at the end of her career. And maybe not.

32. Camp is the glorification of "character." The statement is of no importance except, of course, to the person (Loie Fuller, Gaudí, Cecil B. De Mille, Crivelli, de Gaulle, etc.) who makes it. What the Camp eye appreciates is the unity, the force of the person. In every move the aging Martha Graham makes she's being Martha Graham, etc., etc. . . . This is clear in the case of the great serious idol of Camp taste, Greta Garbo. Garbo's incompetence (at the least, lack of depth) as an actress enhances her beauty. She's always herself.

33. What Camp taste responds to is "instant character" (this is, of course, very 18th century); and, conversely, what it is not stirred by is the sense of the development of character. Character is understood as a state of continual incandescence—a person being one, very intense thing. This attitude toward character is a key element of the theatricalization of experience embodied in the Camp sensibility. And it helps account for the fact that opera and ballet are experienced as such rich treasures of Camp, for neither of these forms can easily do justice to the complexity of human nature. Wherever there is development of character, Camp is reduced. Among operas, for example, *La Traviata* (which has some small development of character) is less campy than *Il Trovatore* (which has none).

"Life is too important a thing ever to talk seriously about it."

—*Vera, or The Nihilists*

34. Camp taste turns its back on the good-bad axis of ordinary aesthetic judgment. Camp doesn't reverse things. It doesn't argue that the good is bad, or the bad is good. What it does is to offer for art (and life) a different—a supplementary—set of standards.

35. Ordinarily we value a work of art because of the seriousness and dignity of what it achieves. We value it because it succeeds—in being what it is and, presumably, in fulfilling the intention that lies behind it. We assume a proper, that is to say, straightforward relation between intention and performance. By such standards, we appraise. *The Iliad*, Aristophanes' plays, The Art of the Fugue, *Middlemarch*, the paintings of Rembrandt, Chartres, the poetry of Donne, *The Divine Comedy*, Beethoven's quartets, and—among people—Socrates, Jesus, St. Francis, Napoleon, Savonarola. In short, the pantheon of high culture: truth, beauty, and seriousness.

36. But there are other creative sensibilities besides the seriousness (both tragic and comic) of high culture and of the high style of evaluating people. And one cheats oneself, as a human being, if one has *respect* only for the style of high culture, whatever else one may do or feel on the sly.

For instance, there is the kind of seriousness whose trademark is anguish, cruelty, derangement. Here we do accept a disparity between intention and result. I am speaking, obviously, of a style of personal existence as well as of a style in art; but the examples had best come from art. Think of Bosch, Sade, Rimbaud, Jarry, Kafka, Artaud, think of most of the important works of art of the 20th century, that is, art whose goal is not that of creating harmonies but of overstraining the medium and introducing more and more violent, and unresolvable, subject-matter. This sensibility also insists on the principle that an *oeuvre* in the old sense (again, in art, but also in life) is not possible. Only "fragments" are possible. . . . Clearly, different standards apply here than to traditional high culture. Something is good not because it is achieved, but because another kind of truth about the human situation, another experience of what it is to be human—in short, another valid sensibility—is being revealed.

And third among the great creative sensibilities is Camp: the sensibility of failed seriousness, of the theatricalization of experience. Camp refuses both the harmonies of traditional seriousness, and the risks of fully identifying with extreme states of feeling.

37. The first sensibility, that of high culture, is basically moralistic. The second sensibility, that of extreme states of feeling, represented in much contemporary "avant-garde" art, gains power by a tension between moral and aesthetic passion. The third, Camp, is wholly aesthetic.

38. Camp is the consistently aesthetic experience of the world. It incarnates a victory of "style" over "content," "aesthetics" over "morality," of irony over tragedy.

39. Camp and tragedy are antitheses. There is seriousness in Camp (seriousness in the degree of the artist's involvement) and, often, pathos. The excruciating is also one of the tonalities of Camp; it is the quality of excruciation in much of Henry James (for instance, *The Europeans, The Awkward Age, The Wings of the Dove*) that is responsible for the large element of Camp in his writings. But there is never, never tragedy.

40. Style is everything. Genet's ideas, for instance, are very Camp. Genet's statement that "the only criterion of an act is its elegance" is virtually interchangeable, as a statement, with Wilde's "in matters of great importance, the vital element is not sincerity, but style." But what counts, finally, is the style in which ideas are held. The ideas about morality and politics in, say, *Lady Windermere's Fan* and in *Major Barbara* are Camp, but not just because of the nature of the ideas themselves. It is those ideas, held in a special playful way. The Camp ideas in *Our Lady of the Flowers* are maintained too grimly, and the writing itself is too successfully elevated and serious, for Genet's books to be Camp.

41. The whole point of Camp is to dethrone the serious. Camp is playful, anti-serious. More precisely, Camp involves a new, more complex relation to "the serious." One can be serious about the frivolous, frivolous about the serious.

42. One is drawn to Camp when one realizes that "sincerity" is not enough. Sincerity can be simple philistinism, intellectual narrowness.

43. The traditional means for going beyond straight seriousness—irony, satire—seem feeble today, inadequate to the culturally oversaturated medium in which contemporary sensibility is schooled. Camp introduces a new standard: artifice as an ideal, theatricality.

44. Camp proposes a comic vision of the world. But not a bitter or polemical comedy. If tragedy is an experience of hyperinvolvement, comedy is an experience of underinvolvement, of detachment.

"I adore simple pleasures, they are the last refuge of the complex."
—*A Woman of No Importance*

45. Detachment is the prerogative of an elite; and as the dandy is the 19th century's surrogate for the aristocrat in matters of culture, so Camp is the modern dandyism. Camp is the answer to the problem: how to be a dandy in the age of mass culture.

46. The dandy was overbred. His posture was disdain, or else *ennui*. He sought rare sensations, undefiled by mass appreciation. (Models: Des Esseintes in Huysmans' *À Rebours, Marius the Epicurean*, Valéry's *Monsieur Teste*.) He was dedicated to "good taste."

The connoisseur of Camp has found more ingenious pleasures. Not in Latin poetry and rare wines and velvet jackets, but in the coarsest, commonest pleasure, in the arts of the masses. Mere use does not defile the objects of his pleasure, since he learns to possess them in a rare way. Camp—Dandyism in the age of mass culture—makes no distinction between the unique object and the mass-produced object. Camp taste transcends the nausea of the replica.

47. Wilde himself is a transitional figure. The man who, when he first came to London, sported a velvet beret, lace shirts, velveteen knee-breeches and black silk stockings, could never depart too far in his life from the pleasures of the old-style dandy; this conservatism is reflected in *The Picture of Dorian Gray*. But many of his attitudes suggest something more modern. It was Wilde who formulated an important element of the Camp sensibility—the equivalence of all objects—when he announced his intention of "living up" to his blue-and-white china, or declared that a door-knob

could be as admirable as a painting. When he proclaimed the importance of the necktie, the boutonniere, the chair, Wilde was anticipating the democratic esprit of Camp.

48. The old-style dandy hated vulgarity. The new-style dandy, the lover of Camp, appreciates vulgarity. Where the dandy would be continually offended or bored, the connoisseur of Camp is continually amused, delighted. The dandy held a perfumed handkerchief to his nostrils and was liable to swoon; the connoisseur of Camp sniffs the stink and prides himself on his strong nerves.

49. It is a feat, of course. A feat goaded on, in the last analysis, by the threat of boredom. The relation between boredom and Camp taste cannot be overestimated. Camp taste is by its nature possible only in affluent societies, in societies or circles capable of experiencing the psychopathology of affluence.

> "What is abnormal in Life stands in normal relations to Art. It is the only thing in Life that stands in normal relations to Art."
> —*A Few Maxims for the Instruction of the Over-Educated*

50. Aristocracy is a position vis-à-vis culture (as well as vis-à-vis power), and the history of Camp taste is part of the history of snob taste. But since no authentic aristocrats in the old sense exist today to sponsor special tastes, who is the bearer of this taste? Answer: an improvised self-elected class, mainly homosexuals, who constitute themselves as aristocrats of taste.

51. The peculiar relation between Camp taste and homosexuality has to be explained. While it's not true that Camp taste *is* homosexual taste, there is no doubt a peculiar affinity and overlap. Not all liberals are Jews, but Jews have shown a peculiar affinity for liberal and reformist causes. So, not all homosexuals have Camp taste. But homosexuals, by and large, constitute the vanguard—and the most articulate audience—of Camp. (The analogy is not frivolously chosen. Jews and homosexuals are the outstanding creative minorities in contemporary urban culture. Creative, that is, in the truest sense: they are creators of sensibilities. The two pioneering forces of modern sensibility are Jewish moral seriousness and homosexual aestheticism and irony.)

52. The reason for the flourishing of the aristocratic posture among homosexuals also seems to parallel the Jewish case. For every sensibility is self-serving to the group that promotes it. Jewish liberalism is a gesture of self-legitimization. So is Camp taste, which definitely has something propagandistic about it. Needless to say, the propaganda operates in exactly the opposite direction. The Jews pinned their hopes for integrating into modern society on promoting the moral sense. Homosexuals have pinned their integration into society on promoting the aesthetic sense. Camp is a solvent of morality. It neutralizes moral indignation, sponsors playfulness.

53. Nevertheless, even though homosexuals have been its vanguard, Camp taste is much more than homosexual taste. Obviously, its metaphor of life as theatre is peculiarly suited as a justification and projection of a certain aspect of the situation of homosexuals. (The Camp insistence on not being "serious," on playing, also connects with the homosexual's desire to remain youthful.) Yet one feels that if homosexuals hadn't more or less invented Camp, someone else would. For the aristocratic posture with relation to culture cannot die, though it may persist only in increasingly

arbitrary and ingenious ways. Camp is (to repeat) the relation to style in a time in which the adoption of style—as such—has become altogether questionable. (In the modern era, each new style, unless frankly anachronistic, has come on the scene as an anti-style.)

"One must have a heart of stone to read the death of Little Nell without laughing."

—*In conversation*

54. The experiences of Camp are based on the great discovery that the sensibility of high culture has no monopoly upon refinement. Camp asserts that good taste is not simply good taste; that there exists, indeed, a good taste of bad taste. (Genet talks about this in *Our Lady of the Flowers*.) The discovery of the good taste of bad taste can be very liberating. The man who insists on high and serious pleasures is depriving himself of pleasure; he continually restricts what he can enjoy; in the constant exercise of his good taste he will eventually price himself out of the market, so to speak. Here Camp taste supervenes upon good taste as a daring and witty hedonism. It makes the man of good taste cheerful, where before he ran the risk of being chronically frustrated. It is good for the digestion.

55. Camp taste is, above all, a mode of enjoyment, of appreciation—not judgment. Camp is generous. It wants to enjoy. It only seems like malice, cynicism. (Or, if it is cynicism, it's not a ruthless but a sweet cynicism.) Camp taste doesn't propose that it is in bad taste to be serious; it doesn't sneer at someone who succeeds in being seriously dramatic. What it does is to find the success in certain passionate failures.

56. Camp taste is a kind of love, love for human nature. It relishes, rather than judges, the little triumphs and awkward intensities of "character." . . . Camp taste identifies with what it is enjoying. People who share this sensibility are not laughing at the thing they label as "a camp," they're enjoying it. Camp is a tender feeling.

(Here, one may compare Camp with much of Pop Art, which—when it is not just Camp—embodies an attitude that is related, but still very different. Pop Art is more flat and more dry, more serious, more detached, ultimately nihilistic.)

57. Camp taste nourishes itself on the love that has gone into certain objects and personal styles. The absence of this love is the reason why such kitsch items as *Peyton Place* (the book) and the Tishman Building aren't Camp.

58. The ultimate Camp statement: it's good *because* it's awful. . . . Of course, one can't always say that. Only under certain conditions, those which I've tried to sketch in these notes.

[*1964*]

1.4

Uses of camp
by Andrew Ross

One of America's most prolific proponents of Cultural Studies, sociologist Andrew Ross studies how capitalist production and reception of culture depends on the creation of value through labour, a view informed by theories of political economy and Marxism. In that view, culture is the result of surplus value created through the exploitation of labour. And what is popular in culture depends on systems of labour (like sweatshops, white/blue collar distinctions, recycling, . . .) and myths and beliefs of achievement and taste operating in a society (the American dream, professionalism, intellectualism, breadwinning, . . .). 'Uses of Camp' is part of Ross' investigation into the cultural roots of the connection between popular culture and intellectuals, one that is usually located within liberal politics. The essay takes Susan Sontag's observations on camp as a challenge to good taste as its starting point to explore the history of 1960s and 70s camp, kitsch, pop, and cult. At the core of Ross' argument is the belief that camp and cult are ways of generating surplus value (cultural capital and economic capital) out of previously neglected labour. Yet they also, through their eclecticism, allow for the mocking of the power structures responsible for forced distinctions between high and low culture, and they facilitate resistance against the mainstreaming of taste into 'midcults' (a term proposed by Dwight MacDonald denoting the acceptable-and-not-too-elitist taste culture of the American middle class). As such, camp and cult appear to side with the exploited labourer in the struggle to gain control over the meaning of cultural products, and their outrageousness becomes a conscious attitude of revolt. Among the films Ross uses are *Myra Breckinridge*, *Beyond the Valley of the Dolls*, *The Rocky Horror Picture Show*, *Pink Flamingos*, and *Eraserhead*. He also analyses the status of cult icons like Judy Garland and Bette Davis.

A note on extracting: this extract is pulled from Andrew Ross' monograph *No Respect; Intellectuals and Popular Culture* (New York: Routledge, 1989, pp. 145–170). For our selection, we have concentrated on the paragraphs of the chapter that highlight the theoretical and cultural aspects of 'camp', and the discussions of camp examples in film and rock culture. We would like to point readers to Ross' discussion of camp in the films of Andy Warhol, which closes the chapter and which we, for reasons of space, are unable to reproduce here.

"It's beige! *My* color!"

> (Elsie De Wolfe, on facing the Parthenon for the first time)

The best thing about subscribing to the *National Enquirer* is that it arrives in the mailbox the same day as the *New York Review of Books*.

(John Waters)

[. . .]

1969: The evening of the funeral of Judy Garland (a long time gay icon), members of the New York City Vice Squad come under fire, from beer cans, bottles, coins, and cobblestones, as they try to arrest some of the regulars at the Stonewall Inn in Christopher Street. The mood of the protesters, many of them street queens in full drag, had changed from that of reveling in the spectacle of the arrest, even posing for it, to one of anger and rage, as one of the detainees, a lesbian, struggled to resist her arrest. Within minutes, the police were besieged within the burning bar. Some of those present thought they heard the chant "Gay Power," while others only saw a more defiant than usual show of posing; it wasn't clear whether this confrontation was "the Hairpin Drop Heard Around the World" or the "Boston Tea Party" of a new social movement.

Later in 1969: A different scene of conflict at the Altamont free festival, the dark sequel to Woodstock, and the Stones again. Jagger is up front, berobed and mascara'd, swishing, mincing, pouting, and strutting before a huge audience barely in check, while on every side of the stage are posted Hell's Angels, confrontation dressers all— the sometime darlings of radical chic, which saw in them an aggressive critique of the counterculture's "male impotence." Here employed as soft police, they stare, bluntly and disdainfully, at the effeminate Jagger, some of them mocking his turns and gyres, while the off-stage violence escalates, to end soon in the death of Meredith Hunter, caught on film in *Gimme Shelter*, the Stones's blatant attempt at self-vindication, in which Jagger poses the rhetorical question: "Why does something always happen when we start to play that song?"—"Sympathy for the Devil."

There are many sixties themes that could serve to link each of these highly mediated moments together: the spectacle of narcissism, radical chic, carnivalesque conflict, and so on. The purpose which they will serve here is to introduce particular aspects of the history of camp, that category of cultural taste, which shaped, defined, and negotiated the way in which sixties intellectuals were able to "pass" as subscribers to the throwaway Pop aesthetic, and thus as patrons of the attractive world of immediacy and disposability created by the culture industries in the postwar boom years. On the importance to the sixties of this category of taste, George Melly, the English jazz musician and Pop intellectual, is adamant: camp was "central to almost every difficult transitional moment in the evolution of pop culture. . . . [it] helped pop make a forced march around good taste. It brought vulgarity back into popular culture . . ."

Beyond these few iconic moments, there is, of course, a much larger story to tell about the transitional function of camp as an *operation of taste*. It is a story of uneven development, because it demonstrates the different uses and meanings which camp generated for different groups, subcultures, and elites in the sixties. The exercise of camp taste raised different issues, for example, for gay people, *before* and *after* 1969; for gay males and for lesbians; for women, lesbian and straight, before and after the birth of the sexual liberation movements; for straight males, before and after androgyny had become legitimate; for traditional intellectuals, obliged now, in spite of their prejudices, to go "slumming," and for more organic intellectuals, whose loyalty to the Pop ethic of instant gratification, expendability, and pleasure often seemed to leave no room for discriminations of value; for disadvantaged working-class sub-cultures whose relation to Pop culture was a glamorous semiotic of their aspirations and dreams of social mobility and leisure, and for the middle-class counterculture, whose adherents could afford, literally, to redefine the life of consumerism and material affluence as a life of spiritual poverty.

While it would be wrong to see camp as the privileged expression of any of these groups, even the pre-Stonewall, gay male subculture for which the strongest claim can be made, there are certain common conditions which must be stressed. Just as the new presence of the popular classes in the social and cultural purview of the postwar State had required a shift in the balance of *containment*, so too, the reorganization of the culture industries, the new technologies and the new modes of distribution which accompanied that shift had yielded structural changes in the shape of aesthetic taste. New markets—the youth market and the swinging "Playboy" male in the fifties (to be followed by women in the sixties and gays in the seventies)—had generated massive changes in the patterns of consumption. Full employment, growing surplus value, and widely shared levels of material affluence provided a secure basis for the expressive leisure activities and the cultural risk-taking which characterized the sixties. In the writing of Tom Wolfe and others, the interlocking subcultures of the late fifties began to emerge as visible phenomena in the early years of the decade: "Practically nobody has bothered to see what these changes are all about. People have been looking at the new money since the war in economic terms only. Nobody will even take a look at our incredibly new national pastimes" among which Wolfe himself was to number stock car racing, demolition derbies, customized auto styling, surfing, the new teenage dance scenes, and many others.

[. . .]

Camp oblige

In her seminal essay, "Notes on Camp" (1964), Susan Sontag raises the question of survival in a quite specific way: "Camp is the answer to the problem: how to be a dandy in an age of mass culture." Her formula suggests that what is being threatened in an age of mass culture is precisely the power of tastemaking intellectuals to influence the canons of taste, and that the significance of the "new sensibility" of camp in the sixties is that it presents a means of salvaging that privilege. (The term "dandy," here, can be seen as standing for intellectuals who are either personally devoted to the sophistries of taste, or whose intellectual work it is to create, legitimize, and supervise canons of taste.)

The pseudo-aristocratic patrilineage of camp can hardly be understated. Consider the etymological provenance of the three most questionable categories of American cultural taste: schlock, kitsch, and camp. None are directly of Anglo origin, and it is clear, from their cultural derivation, where they belong on the scale of prestige: *Schlock*, from Yiddish (literally, "damaged goods" at a cheap price), *Kitsch*, from German, petty bourgeois for pseudo-art, and *Camp*, more obscurely from the French *se camper* (to posture or to flaunt), but with a history of English upper-class usage.

While schlock is truly unpretentious—nice, harmless things—and is designed primarily to fill a space in people's lives and environments, kitsch has serious pretensions to artistic taste, and, in fact, contains a range of references to high or legitimate culture which it apes in order to flatter its owner-consumer. Kitsch's seriousness about art, and its aesthetic chutzpah is usually associated with the class aspirations and upper mobility of a middlebrow audience, insufficient in cultural capital to guarantee access to legitimate culture.

Of course, kitsch is no more of a *fixed* category than either schlock or camp. These categories are constantly shifting ground, their contents are constantly changing; as is the case with "midcult," that which is promoted one year may be relegated down again the next. Neither can they be regarded as categories defined with equal objectivity but attributed different value, since schlock and kitsch are more often seen as qualities of objects, while camp tends to refer to a subjective process: camp, as Thomas Hess put it, "exists in the smirk of the beholder." If certain objects tend to be associated with camp more readily than others, they are often described as "campy," suggesting a self-consciousness about their status which would otherwise be attributed to the smirking beholder. Sontag downgrades this self-consciousness as too deliberate, reserving her praise for the category of *naïve* camp, perhaps because, with the latter, it is the critic and not the producer who takes full credit for discerning the camp value of an object or text. So too, the line between kitsch and camp partially reflects a division of audience labor between, in camp terminology, ignorati and cognoscenti. The producer or consumer of kitsch is likely to be unaware of the extent to which his or her intentions or pretensions are reified and alienated in the kitsch object itself. Camp, on the other hand, involves a celebration, on the part of cognoscenti, of the alienation, distance, and incongruity reflected in the very process by which hitherto unexpected value can be located in some obscure or exorbitant object.

But if camp, in this respect, has always been part of the history of pseudo-aristocratic taste, the "moment" of camp, in the sixties, was also seen as a democratic moment, and its influence continues to irradiate pop attitudes today. What were the conditions under which this democratizing influence came about?

To properly historicize that moment, we must first recognize that just as it is absurd to speak of a lasting canon or pantheon of camp texts, objects, and figures (though more or less definitive lists do exist for certain groups who use camp), universal definitions of camp are rarely useful. In Philip Core's encyclopedia of camp, for example, camp is loosely defined as "the lie that tells the truth" (after Jean Cocteau) or as "the heroism of people not called upon to be heroes," while Christopher Isherwood, in *The World in the Evening* (1954), finds that camp is a subjective matter of "expressing what's basically serious to you in terms of fun and artifice and elegance." This is why Sontag chose to write her essay about this "fugitive sensibility" in the more objective form of notes or jottings, for fear of writing a dry, definitive treatise that would itself be nothing but "a very inferior piece of camp." It appears, however, that she also wanted to avoid the argument that camp is a "logic of taste," with explicable, historical conditions; the determining grounds of taste, she prefers to say, are "almost, but not quite, ineffable."

More useful in this respect is Mark Booth's expanded and exhaustive account of Sontag's "pocket history of camp" (her note no. 14—embracing rococo, mannerism, *les précieux*, Yellow Book aestheticism, art nouveau, etc.), a history polemically guided by his thesis that "to be camp is to present oneself as being committed to the marginal with a commitment greater than the marginal merits." The advantage of Booth's formulation is that it helps to define camp in relation to the exercise of *cultural power* at any one time. Booth argues, for example, that, far from being a "fugitive" or "ineffable" sensibility, camp belongs to the history of the "self-presentation" of arriviste groups. Because of their marginality, and lack of inherited cultural capital, these groups parody their subordinate or uncertain social status in "a self-mocking abdication of any pretensions to power."

Unlike the traditional intellectual, whose function is to legitimize the cultural power of ruling interests, or the organic intellectual, who promotes the interests of a rising class, the marginal, camp intellectual expresses his impotence as the dominated fraction of a ruling bloc at the same time as he distances himself from the conventional morality and taste of the ascendant middle class. For example, the nineteenth-century camp intellectual can be seen as a parody or negation of dominant bourgeois forms: anti-industry, pro-idleness; anti-family, pro-bachelorhood; anti-respectability, pro-scandal; anti-masculine, pro-feminine; anti-sport, pro-frivolity; anti-decor, pro-exhibitionism; anti-progress, pro-decadence; anti-wealth, pro-fame. But his aristocratic affectations are increasingly a sign of his *disqualification*, or remoteness from power, because they comfortably symbolize, to the bourgeoisie, the declining power of the foppish aristocracy, while they are equally removed from the threatening, embryonic power of the popular classes.

Hitherto associated with the high culture milieu of the theater, the camp intellectual becomes an institution, in the twentieth century, within the popular entertainment industries, reviving his (and by now, her) role there as the representative or stand-in for a class that is no longer in a position to exercise its power to define official culture. As part of that role, he maintains his parodic critique of the properly educated and responsibly situated intellectual who speaks with the requisite tone of moral authority and seriousness as the conscience and consciousness of society as whole.

[. . .]

For the camp liberator, as with the high modernist, history's waste matter becomes all too available as a "ragbag," not drenched with tawdriness by the mock-heroism of Waste Land irony, but irradiated, this time around, with the glamor of resurrection. In liberating the objects and discourses of the past from disdain and neglect, camp generates its own kind of economy. Camp, in this respect, is the *re-creation of surplus value from forgotten forms of labor*.

By the late sixties, when the crossover appeal of camp was well established, this parasitical practice had become a survivalist way of life for the counterculture, whose patronage of flea markets was a parody, made possible by post-scarcity consciousness, of the hand-me-down working-class culture of the rummage sale. The flea market ethos, like many countercultural values, paid its respects to a modernist notion of prelapsarian authenticity. In an age of plastic, authentic material value could only be located in the "real" textures of the preindustrial past, along with traces of the "real" labor that once went into fashioning clothes and objects. By sporting a whole range of peasant-identified, romantic-proletarian, and exotic non-Western styles, students and other initiates of the counterculture were confronting the guardians (and the workaday prisoners) of commodity culture with the symbols of a spent historical mode of production, or else one that was "Asiatic" and thus "underdeveloped." By doing so, they signaled their complete disaffiliation from the semiotic codes of contemporary cultural power. In donning gypsy and denim, however, they were also taunting the current aspirations of those social groups for whom such clothes called up a long history of poverty, oppression, and social exclusion. And in their maverick Orientalism, they romanticized other cultures by plundering their stereotypes.

[. . .]

This process of camp rehabilitation is the basis of a vast and lucrative sector of the culture industry devoted to the production of "exploitation" fare. If the pleasure generated by bad taste presents a challenge to the mechanisms of control and containment that operate in the name of good taste, it is often to be enjoyed *only* at the expense of others, and this is largely because camp's excess of pleasure has very little, finally, to do with the (un)controlled hedonism of a consumer; it is the result of the (hard) *work* of a producer of taste, and "taste" is only possible through exclusion *and* depreciation.

The commercialization of camp/bad taste has run its course from the novels of Ronald Firbank to the nostalgia cable TV reruns of *The Donna Reed Show*; from the Beardsley period of the Yellow Book to exploitation publications like the *Weekly World News* and the *National Enquirer*. One important turning point was the television remake of *Batman* in the mid-sixties. Everyone "knew" about Batman and Robin, a fact that spoilt the jokes for the few. Pop camp reached its apotheosis in Roger Vadim's luxurious 1968 comic strip-based film *Barbarella* (with its gorgeous furlined spaceship, and the kinky naivete of its occupant, played by Jane Fonda), while the various parodies of James Bond movies exploited the hi-tech improbabilities of popular British spy culture.

1970 was the year that Hollywood fully caught up, with a trilogy of movies that featured what many cognoscenti came to see as the decadent, and not the vibrant, spirit of camp. Michael Sarne's much hyped *Myra Breckinridge*, based on Gore Vidal's entertaining novel, was a tired, laconic treatment of the gay camp fascination with Hollywoodiana, and it evoked a wave of scorn among critics for Rex Reed/ Raquel Welch's dual portrayal of transsexualism. *Beyond the Valley of the Dolls* overexposed the keen gluttony of Russ Meyer's earlier exploitation skin flicks like *The Immoral Mr. Teas, Faster Pussycat, Kill! Kill!*, and *Vixen*, while Roger Ebert's gildedtrash script for this most synthetic of movies demonstrated how camp deliberately aspires, as Mel Brooks put it, to "rise below vulgarity." Countercultural camp finally got a run for its money in Nicholas Roeg's *Performance* which brought together the working-class criminal subculture and the experimental rock avant-garde within the hallucinogenic milieu of an extended bad trip. In the artificial paradise of his house of pleasure and pretension, Mick Jagger's retired polysexual star, Turner (rock culture's Norma Desmond) acts out his liberated middle-class role—"Personally, I just perform"—to James Fox's confused Chas, his class opposite in masculinity, for whom "performance" is a category of work and not a way of life.

Each of these films was also a self-conscious attempt to produce a film with "cult movie" status, and thus to cash in on a ritual taste for the offbeat which had grown to considerable commercial dimensions by the end of the sixties. More successful was Jim Sharman's 1974 *The Rocky Horror Picture Show*, based on Richard O'Brien's play, an outrageous tongue-in-cheek tribute to the cult spectrum of late night picture shows—a trashy brew of B movie, schlock sci-fi, and junky horror productions. *Rocky Horror* became the queen of the midnight movie circuit, with its own ritualized audience subculture. Other cult favorites on the circuit include dozens culled from the gore factory of Roger Corman's New World Pictures, the full complement of George Romero horror films, from *Night of the Living Dead* (1968) onwards, and the low-budget charms of the rediscovered Ed D. Wood, Jr., whose prolific fifties output of films like the pro-transvestite *Glen or Glenda?* (1952) and the anti-militarist *Plan 9 from Outer Space* (1956) (featuring the all-time star camp cast of Tor Johnson, a 400 pound Swedish ex-wrestler; Criswell, the famous TV psychic; Vampira, as the mute, wasp-waisted ghoul woman; and a fading, stumbling Bela Lugosi in his last screen appearance) continues to posthumously earn him the top awards on the Golden Turkey circuit of best "bad films."

The most devoted interpreter of bad taste, however, has been the Baltimore film director John Waters, whose celebration of glamorized sleaze and trashola in films like *Mondo Trasho* (1969), *Multiple Maniacs* (1970), *Pink Flamingos* (1973), *Female Trouble* (1974), and *Polyester* (1981) is so tied to regional and "white trash" class specificity that its interest, if not its ever-ambiguous appeal, transcends the rote reshuffling of genre and stereotype that characterizes the more standard exploitation products. Only Waters would be capable of brilliantly confessing, in the most complete inversion of taste possible, to the guilty pleasure he experiences in watching art films:

> Being a Catholic, guilt comes naturally. Except mine is reversed. I blab on *ad nauseam* about how much I love films like *Dr. Butcher, M.D.* or *My Friends Need Killing*, but what really shames me is that I'm also secretly a fan of what is unfortunately known as the "art film." Before writing this sentence, I've tried to never utter the word "art" unless referring to Mr. Linkletter. But underneath all my posing as a trash film enthusiast, a little known fact is that I actually sneak off in disguise (and hope to God I'm not recognized) to arty films in the same way business men rush in to see *Pussy Talk* on their lunch hour. I'm really embarrassed.

In films like *Eraserhead* (1978) and *Blue Velvet* (1986), David Lynch has refurbished the more respectable side of the avant-garde cultivation of camp for crossover Hollywood consumption. On the other side of the taste divide, the popular market in hard-core porn, horror, gore, and splatter movies has entered a boom period in the last fifteen years as censorship laws have eased off. Today, the most advanced forms of bad taste vanguardism are located in a loosely defined nexus of cultish interests that have grafted the most anti-social features of "sick" humor on to an attenuated paranoia about the normality of the straight world. It covers particular obsessions with conspiracy theories (especially around the Kennedy assassination), bodily disorders and etiologies, religious cult tracts, mass murderer folklore, the psychopathology of atrocities, and exotic rituals, tribal practices, and bizarre customs as described in bogus ethnographic literature or in *Mondo Cane* (1963), the original Mondo film. There is a thin line between the sophisticated irony of this taste for the bizarre and the deeper, popular currents of involvement in the "cults" that have flourished within, alongside, and in the wake of the New Age movements—pseudo science (the paranormal, spontaneous human combustion, geocentrism, flying saucer contacteeism), pseudo religion (channeling, Space Jesii, breatharians, sub-Mormonism), weird politics (Is Hitler Alive? Is He Hiding the UFO Secret?), and other crankish excursions onto unorthodox cultural terrain.

From an institutional point of view, camp has become the resident conscience of a "bad film" subculture which has its own alternative circuit of festivals, promoters, heroes, stars, and prizes. Cognoscenti savor the work of directors like Ed D. Wood, Jr., Herschell Gordon Lewis, and Ray Dennis Steckler, while those with speciality tastes champion genres like biker films, nudist camp films, beach party films, industrial jeopardy films, women in prison films, and the like. Although it is specifically a low budget subculture, with considerable returns at stake nonetheless, it increasingly feeds off Hollywood's own recognition of the cost of its failures in the taste trade, and is thereby tied into the economic rhythms of the industry.

"Bad film" buffs are expected to know, moreover, that their taste is a product of the *labor of leisure*. In their preface to *The Golden Turkey Awards*, a semi-official organ of the bad film circuit, Harry and Michael Medved indirectly pay tribute to this work ethic when they compare their pursuit of bad films to the mystic:

> who climbed the walls of his town, day after day, staring off toward the horizon. He explained to his friends that he had to be there in order to await the arrival of the Messiah.
> "But don't you get tired of it?" they wanted to know.
> "Sure," he answered, "But it's steady work."

The camp value of these films is tied to a productivist ethic of labor, and to those for whom culture, even entertainment, has therefore to be "worked" at to produce meaning. Consequently, bad taste tends to be the preserve of urban intellectuals (professional and pre-professional) for whom the line between work and leisure time is occupationally indistinct, and is less regulated by the strict economic divide between production and consumption which governs the cultural tastes of lower middle-class and working-class groups. But while the taste for schlock has increasingly become a trademark of the postmodernist style of the yuppie class—the original "TV generation"—it has also spread, through the agency of late night television (*The David Letterman Show*), cable (*MTV* especially) and home video, well beyond its metropolitan force field into the heartlands, where young refugees from family morality have fashioned their sense of alienation out of the benign innocence of shopping mall culture (*Chopping Mall!*, 1986) just as their forebears made a cult out of "educational" films like *Reefer Madness* (1936), or the J.D. "problem" films of the fifties, like *Reform School Girls*.

If, however, we want to look at the effect on mainstream popular taste, then it is in the realm of performance rock that camp's penchant for the deviant has crossed over the threshold of restricted consumption into the mass milieux of homes, schools, colleges, clubs, and workplaces all over the country. For its teenage consumers, the outrageousness of performance rock has, among other things, always been something of a family affair—the object of what teenagers (and record company producers) imagine is every good parent's worst fantasy. It is almost impossible, then, to talk about the history of that ever shifting pageant of eroticized spectacle—from Elvis's gyrating hips to Annie Lennox's gender-blurred sangfroid, from the suggestive body language of Little Richard to the outrageous adult presence of Grace Jones, and the almost metaphysical, polysexual identities of Prince and Michael Jackson—without first discussing camp's influence on the changing social definitions of masculinity and femininity from the late fifties onwards.

Prisoners of sex?

Female and male impersonation, representations of androgyny, and other images of gender-blurring have all played an important historical role in cinema's creation of our stockpile of social memories. For the spectator, whose voyeuristic captivity (as captors *and* prisoners) of the cinema image can be read as an eroticized response to a psychic scenario on the screen, the suggestive incidence of cross-dressing among those memories is a provocative area of study. It has proved notoriously difficult, however, to provide a systematic account of how "masculine" and "feminine" positions of spectatorship are assumed as part of the process of reading and responding to these ambiguous images.

Molly Haskell has argued that the overwhelming disparity of images of female to male impersonation in films can be explained by the fact that, historically, male impersonation is seen as a source of power and aggrandizement for women, while the theatrical adoption of female characteristics by men is seen as a process of belittlement. Male impersonation is serious and erotic, while female impersonation is simply comical. In her book about cross-dressing in Hollywood cinema, Rebecca Bell-Metereau argues that Haskell's serious/comical distinction no longer applies to the whole range of female impersonations of "women of power" which have appeared over the last two and a half decades. So too, she argues that in the pre-1960 examples, "tragic" or "comic" readings of a film's treatment of cross-dressing are not simply the result of gender alignment. More important is whether or not the male or female imitation is "willingly performed and sympathetically accepted by the social group within the film."

Just as the reading of these images is inflected by the complex interplay between the film's spectacle of transgressive display and its narrative of social judgment, there is no guarantee that what is *encoded* in these film scenarios will be *decoded* in the same way by different social groups with different sexual orientations. This is nowhere more obvious than in the highly developed gay subculture that evolved around a fascination with classical Hollywood film and, in particular, with film stars like Judy Garland, Bette Davis, Mae West, Greta Garbo, Marlene Dietrich, Joan Crawford (and performers like Barbra Streisand, Bette Midler, Diana Ross, Donna Summer, Grace Jones, and many other disco divas). Denied the possibility of "masculine" and "feminine" positions of spectatorship, and excluded by conventional representations of male-as-hero or narrative agent, and female-as-image or object of the spectacle, the lived spectatorship of gay male and lesbian subcultures is expressed largely through imaginary or displaced relations to the straight meanings of these images and discourses of a parent culture.

[. . .]

Identification with the female film star's "power" is not, of course, without its contradictions, for representations of that power are not unconditionally granted within Hollywood film itself, where the exercise of such power in the service of some transgression of male-defined behavior would generally be met, within the narrative, by punishment and chastisement. As Michael Bronski argues, however, the mere idea that sexuality brings with it a degree of power, "albeit limited and precarious, can be exhilarating" for the gay male who "knows that his sexuality will get him in trouble." But what can the relation of this everyday triumph of the will to the commodified spectacle of a major star's "sexuality" tell us about the awesome power exercised through the institution of sexuality itself, a power that is more usually directed *against* women and sexual minorities? This is the question which gay politics came to ask of the pre-political culture organized around camp.

In answering that question, it is important always to bear in mind that the traditional gay camp sensibility was an *imaginary* expression of a relation to real conditions, both past and present—an ideology, if you like—while it functions today, in the "liberated" gay and straight world, as a kind of imaginary challenge to the new *symbolic* conditions of gay identity. Whether as a pre-Stonewall, survivalist fantasy, or as a post-Stonewall return of the repressed, camp works to destabilize, reshape, and transform the existing balance of accepted sexual roles and sexual identities. It seldom proposes a *direct* relation between the conditions it speaks to—everyday life in the present—and the discourse it speaks with—usually a bricolage of features pilfered from fantasies of the bygone.

This perception may help to answer, in part, the charge of misogyny that is often brought to bear, quite justifiably, upon camp representations of "feminine" characteristics. It could be argued, for example, that the camp idolization of female film stars contributes to a desexualization of the female body. In the context of classic Hollywood film, a social spectacle where women often have little visible existence outside of their being posed as the embodiment of the sexual, any reading which defetishizes the erotic scenario of woman-as-spectacle is a reading that is worth having. Indeed, in the classic camp pantheon, most film stars are celebrated for reasons other than their successful dramatization of erotic otherness. It is in this respect that gay camp looks forward to later feminist appraisals of the "independent" women of Hollywood, who fought for their own roles, either against the studios themselves, or in the highly mannered ways in which they acted out, acted around, or acted against the grain of the sexually circumscribed stereotypes which they were contracted to dramatize.

Bette Davis, whose looks excluded her from the stock image-repertoire of screen sexiness (one of her earlier directors complained "Who'd want to go to bed with her?"), was the most enduring example of the star whose screen identity could not be fixed by the studio machine, a woman who openly contested the terms of her contract with Warner Brothers, and whose wide variety of roles ensured that she escaped a life sentence of character typing. Aside from her superb acting skills, it was Davis's willed evasion of this fate that her fans saw reflected in the nervous and impetuous intensity with which she invests the celebrated "bitchiness" of her roles in such films as *Of Human Bondage* (1934), *Jezebel* (1938), *The Little Foxes* (1941), *All About Eve*, and *Whatever Happened to Baby Jane?* While the wide range of her mannered repertoire is often reduced in camp caricature to the famously over-used cigarette, or her wildly rolling eyes, it is clear that the sense of irony she conveyed through such gestures was more of a performance about the performance of her roles, rather than one which comfortably interpreted these roles. In contrast to Joan Crawford's earnest control over her roles, Davis could separate voice and body, image and discourse, and play off one against the other. But Mae West is the star who most professionally exploits the ironies of *artifice* when, like a female drag queen, she represents a woman who parodies a burlesque woman, and then seems to take on the role for real, as a way of successfully fielding every kind of masculine response known to woman. West pioneered a new bold, no-nonsense, no-romance relation with sex, while the sexual ambiguities of Garbo, Dietrich, and Hepburn all produced variations on the theme of androgyny-as-spectacle: prince of passivity, bird of paradise, and the go-getter.

Judy Garland, on the other hand, was a cult figure whose associated star persona had little to do with the ironic artifice of camp, since her roles insisted on her naturalness, innocence, and ordinariness, and, above all else, vulnerability. Richard Dyer has argued that she "is not a star turned into camp, but a star who expresses camp attitudes," as if she had been well versed in gay camp culture from the very beginning, and not just towards the end of her career when she ritually acknowledged the gay constituency of her most loyal audience. Her lack of glamor, and pronounced refusal of "feminine" grace meant that, like Davis, she fell outside of the conventional requirements of the Hollywood starlet, and this enabled her to enter into more unorthodox roles (the tramp-as-androgyne, tragi-comically beyond gender, is one which Dyer emphasizes). It was not until her personal hardships became public, and she embarked on a phase of repeated comebacks, that the conceit of survival in the face of all odds became an intrinsic part of her performing persona. It was in this period, right through the sixties, that her struggle between the role of self-destructive loser and resilient, irrepressible fighter took on a parable-like significance for a gay culture increasingly in search of overt rather than heavily coded forms of identification. The more recent commercial success of performers like Streisand, and Midler, while it reflects the genuine talents of these gutsy artistes, has been indissociable from the publicly visible support of a gay audience.

[. . .]

To non-essentialist feminism and to the gay camp tradition alike, the significance of particular film stars lies in their various challenges to the assumed naturalness of gender roles. Each of these stars presents a different way, at different historical times, of living with the "masquerade" of femininity. Each demonstrates how to *perform* a particular representation of womanliness, and the effect of these performances is to demonstrate, in turn, why there is no "authentic" femininity, why there are only representations of femininity, socially redefined from moment to moment. So too, the "masculine" woman, as opposed to the androgyne, represents to men what is unreal about masculinity, in a way similar to the effect of actors whose masculinity is overdone and quickly dated (Victor Mature is the best example, not least, I think, because of the symmetry of his names).

If camp has a politics, then it is one that proposes working with and through existing definitions and representations, and in this respect, it is opposed to the search for alternative, utopian, or essentialist identities which lay behind many of the counter-cultural and sexual liberation movements. In fact, it was precisely because of this commitment to the mimicry of existing cultural forms, and its refusal to advocate wholesale breaks with these same forms, that camp was seen as pre-political and out of step with the dominant ethos of the liberation movements. Nonetheless, its disreputable survival in gay culture, and its crossover presence in straight culture, has had a significant effect on the constantly shifting, hegemonic definition of masculinity in the last two decades.

Garland, Davis, and the other queens of Hollywood are one thing, Maria Montez, Tallulah Bankhead, Carmen Miranda, and Eartha Kitt are another. If the latter are also figures celebrated by gay camp, then it is not for their thespian talents or for their stylized parodies of femininity. On the contrary, the widespread cultivation of these exploited actresses (*Myron*'s cult of Montez is representative) is unarguably tinged with ridicule, derision, even misogyny. Their moments in the camp limelight cannot fail to conceal a "failed seriousness" that is more often pathetic and risible than it is witty or parodic. But to see how and where the contradictions of this cult homage are fully played out, we must look at the performance culture of female impersonation, the professional stage version of everyday gay camp.

[. . .]

As make-up and dressing-up became an everyday part of the flamboyant straight counterculture, "drag" took on the generalized meaning of everyday role-playing. Here, for example, is Myra Breckinridge's analysis of the male swinger:

> It is true that the swingers, as they are called, make up only a small minority of our society; yet they hold a great attraction for the young and bored who are the majority and who keep their sanity (those that do) by having a double sense of themselves. On the one hand, they must appear to accept without question our culture's myth that the male must be dominant, aggressive, woman-oriented. On the other hand, they are perfectly aware that few men are anything but slaves to an economic and social system that does not allow them to knock people down as proof of virility or in any way act out the traditional male role. As a result the young men compensate by *playing* at being men, wearing cowboy clothes, boots, black leather, attempting through clothes (what an age for the fetishist!) to impersonate the kind of man our society *claims* to admire but swiftly puts down should he attempt to be anything more than an illusionist, playing a part.

Myra concludes that it would be a healthy contribution to her mission of destroying "the last vestigial traces of traditional manhood" if this role-playing were to be encouraged. Her sentiments, at least, are defined by a clear political aim, and in this respect were hardly typical of the general tone set by the male swingers of the counterculture who pursued the golden fleece of sexual liberation in the late sixties. Countercultural liberation for straight men was one moment in the two decades of "permissiveness" (whose definition?) which began with the swinging *Playboy* ethic of mid-fifties and ended with the stirrings of the neo-conservative backlash in the mid-seventies. Barbara Ehrenreich has argued that the fifties "male revolt" against the suburban bondage of breadwinning, symbolized by the consumerist Playboy lifestyle, also delivered men from suspicions of homosexuality that had hitherto been attached to men who avoided marriage. So too, the "ethnicization" of homosexuality which gay liberation had fostered by advocating the policy of "coming out" meant that straight men could pursue their exploration of androgyny without the fear of their heterosexuality being questioned. The new macho man was gay. The radical "moment" of bisexuality was lost.

The privileges of androgyny, of course, were generally not available for women until well into the seventies, and only *after* male gender-bending had run its spectacular, public course through a succession of musical youth heroes: David Bowie (the first and the best, although Jagger and Lou Reed had been pioneers), Alice Cooper, the New York Dolls, Elton John, Iggy Pop, Marc Bolan, and other dandies of glam rock. It was not until punk ushered in a newer and more offensive kind of oppositional drag that women fully participated within rock culture in the confrontational strategies of posing and transgressing: Poly Styrene, Jordan, Wendy O. Williams, Patti Smith, and, above all, Souxsie Sue. When Annie Lennox appeared at the 1984 Grammy Awards ceremony in full Elvis drag, at least one sexual history of rock 'n' roll had come full circle. And as for Grace Jones, she is "acting the part of a *man*, not a boy," when she drags a male from her audience and simulates anal sex with him.

To look, today, for representations of the anti-social or threatening expressions of camp and drag, we must go to the outrageously spectacular heroes of the youth heavy metal scene. In popular rock culture today, the most "masculine" images are signified by miles of coiffured hair, layers of gaudy make-up, and a complete range of fetishistic body accessories, while it is the clean-cut, close-cropped, fifties-style Europop crooners who are seen as lacking masculine legitimacy.

Rock 'n' roll has long played the game of good boy/bad boy. If Bruce Springsteen embodies the stable, nostalgic image of traditional working-class masculinity, then it is the punks and the B-boys who represent the unruly, marginalized underside. In mainstream rock, however, it is the feminized cock rockers who are supposedly identified with the most retarded—aggressive, disrespectful, and homophobic—characteristics of working-class masculinity. It is ironic, then, to consider that when, in 1984, the affable Boy George received a Grammy Award on network television, he told his audience: "Thank you, America, you've got style and taste, and you know a good drag queen when you see one." Behind this ambiguous compliment, there was a long Wildean history of smug European attitudes towards American puritanism. But what did Boy George's comment mean in the age of Motley Crue, Twisted Sister, Aerosmith, Kiss, and Rapp, whose shared use of drag is directly tied to a certain construction of American masculinity? There is more than just class at stake here, although it is clear that heavy metal today is as much an assault on middle-class masculinity as it is an affirmation of sexist working-class bravado. What is also at stake, I think, is the international balance of patriarchal power. The brashness associated with heavy metal drag speaks, like Rambo's caricature of the he-man, to the legitimate power of American masculinity in the world today. By contrast, the jolly decorum of Boy George bespeaks the softer European contours of a masculinity in the twilight of its power. One is emboldened and threatening, the other is sentimental and peace loving.

[. . .]

1.5

Casablanca: Cult movies and intertextual collage
by Umberto Eco

Italian philosopher and semiologist Umberto Eco (1932-) takes a favourable position towards mass and popular culture. His writings on comic books, television,
cinema, and popular literature attempt to show how some popular culture texts
operate on the understanding that their audiences will pick up on, and appreciate,
their borrowing from and inferences of other texts. Such texts are cult texts. Eco
calls the hyperbolic chain of referents that these films call into being 'intertextuality' (one sign referring to another in another text to another in another text. . .).
Intertextuality poses a problem for any systematic, structuralist understanding of
how signs relate to reality, and can have precise, singular meanings. It invokes
ambiguity because signs can mean many things, and complicity because one has to
recognize the reference to other texts in order to enjoy the puns and plays. For Eco,
Casablanca is a perfect example showcasing the intertextuality of cult cinema,
because it is a 'paramount laboratory for semiotic research into textual strategies'.
The phrase shows how Eco's concern is mainly with the properties of the film, and
less with the playfulness of the audiences in placing the references. Nevertheless,
with Eco's essay, the theorization of cult acknowledges the importance of the
perceiver (audience, fan, public) for the first time. While Eco does not refer to
studies of cult audiences, and in fact ignores any real audiences, his emphasis on
how the semiotic signs and symbols in *Casablanca* are interpreted, and changed, by
viewers does stress the interaction between screen and spectator.

A note on extracting: the source for the version of this essay used in our reader is
the most quoted one, published in *Travels in Hyperreality* (London: Picador, 1986,
pp. 197–211), a collection of essays by Eco. Before that, it also appeared, in the
same format, in *Substance* (issue nr. 47, pp. 3–12), in 1985. In the source we used,
the essay is dated 1984, which is also the date we are using for it. As far as we were
able to establish, our reprint is the article in its most complete form.

Cult

"Was that artillery fire, or is it my heart pounding?" Whenever *Casablanca* is shown,
at this point the audience reacts with an enthusiasm usually reserved for football.
Sometimes a single word is enough: Fans cry every time Bogey says "kid." Frequently
the spectators quote the best lines before the actors say them.

According to traditional standards in aesthetics, *Casablanca* is not a work of art, if such an expression still has a meaning. In any case, if the films of Dreyer, Eisenstein, or Antonioni are works of art, *Casablanca* represents a very modest aesthetic achievement. It is a hodgepodge of sensational scenes strung together implausibly, its characters are psychologically incredible, its actors act in a mannered way. Nevertheless, it is a great example of cinematic discourse, a palimpsest for future students of twentieth-century religiosity, a paramount laboratory for semiotic research into textual strategies. Moreover, it has become a cult movie.

What are the requirements for transforming a book or a movie into a cult object? The work must be loved, obviously, but this is not enough. It must provide a completely furnished world so that its fans can quote characters and episodes as if they were aspects of the fan's private sectarian world, a world about which one can make up quizzes and play trivia games so that the adepts of the sect recognize through each other a shared expertise. Naturally all these elements (characters and episodes) must have some archetypical appeal, as we shall see. One can ask and answer questions about the various subway stations of New York or Paris only if these spots have become or have been assumed as mythical areas and such names as Canarsie Line or Vincennes-Neuilly stand not only for physical places but become the catalyzers of collective memories.

Curiously enough, a book can also inspire a cult even though it is a great work of art: Both *The Three Musketeers* and *The Divine Comedy* rank among the cult books; and there are more trivia games among the fans of Dante than among the fans of Dumas. I suspect that a cult movie, on the contrary, must display some organic imperfections: It seems that the boastful *Rio Bravo* is a cult movie and the great *Stagecoach* is not.

I think that in order to transform a work into a cult object one must be able to break, dislocate, unhinge it so that one can remember only parts of it, irrespective of their original relationship with the whole. In the case of a book one can unhinge it, so to speak, physically, reducing it to a series of excerpts. A movie, on the contrary, must be already ramshackle, rickety, unhinged in itself. A perfect movie, since it cannot be reread every time we want, from the point we choose, as happens with a book, remains in our memory as a whole, in the form of a central idea or emotion; only an unhinged movie survives as a disconnected series of images, of peaks, of visual icebergs. It should display not one central idea but many. It should not reveal a coherent philosophy of composition. It must live on, and because of, its glorious ricketiness.

However, it must have some quality. Let me say that it can be ramshackle from the production point of view (in that nobody knew exactly what was going to be done next)—as happened evidently with the *Rocky Horror Picture Show*—but it must display certain textual features, in the sense that, outside the conscious control of its creators, it becomes a sort of textual syllabus, a living example of living textuality. Its addressee must suspect it is not true that works are created by their authors. Works are created by works, texts are created by texts, all together they speak to each other independently of the intention of their authors. A cult movie is the proof that, as literature comes from literature, cinema comes from cinema.

Which elements, in a movie, can be separated from the whole and adored for themselves? In order to go on with this analysis of *Casablanca* I should use some important semiotic categories, such as the ones (provided by the Russian Formalists) of theme and motif. I confess I find it very difficult to ascertain what the various Russian Formalists meant by motif. If—as Veselovsky says—a motif is the simplest narrative unit, then one wonders why "fire from heaven" should belong to the same category as "the persecuted maid" (since the former can be represented by an image, while the latter requires a certain narrative development). It would be interesting to follow Tomashevsky and to look in *Casablanca* for free or tied and for dynamic or static motifs. We should distinguish between more or less universal narrative functions à la Propp, visual stereotypes like the Cynic Adventurer, and more complex archetypical situations like the Unhappy Love. I hope someone will do this job, but here I will assume, more prudently (and borrowing the concept from research into Artificial Intelligence) the more flexible notion of "frame."

In *The Role of the Reader* I distinguished between common and intertextual frames. I meant by "common frame" data-structures for representing stereotyped situations such as dining at a restaurant or going to the railway station; in other words, a sequence of actions more or less coded by our normal experience. And by "intertextual frames" I meant stereotyped situations derived from preceding textual tradition and recorded by our encyclopedia, such as, for example, the standard duel between the sheriff and the bad guy or the narrative situation in which the hero fights the villain and wins, or more macroscopic textual situations, such as the story of the *vierge souillée* or the classic recognition scene (Bakhtin considered it a motif, in the sense of a chronotope). We could distinguish between stereotyped intertextual frames (for instance, the Drunkard Redeemed by Love) and stereotyped iconographical units (for instance, the Evil Nazi). But since even these iconographical units, when they appear in a movie, if they do not directly elicit an action, at least suggest its possible development, we can use the notion of intertextual frame to cover both.

Moreover, we are interested in finding those frames that not only are recognizable by the audience as belonging to a sort of ancestral intertextual tradition but that also display a particular fascination. "A suspect who eludes a passport control and is shot by the police" is undoubtedly an intertextual frame but it does not have a "magic" flavor. Let me address intuitively the idea of "magic" frame. Let me define as "magic" those frames that, when they appear in a movie and can be separated from the whole, transform this movie into a cult object. In *Casablanca* we find more intertextual frames than "magic" intertextual frames. I will call the latter "intertextual archetypes."

The term "archetype" does not claim to have any particular psychoanalytic or mythic connotation, but serves only to indicate a preestablished and frequently reappearing narrative situation, cited or in some way recycled by innumerable other texts and provoking in the addressee a sort of intense emotion accompanied by the vague feeling of a déjà vu that everybody yearns to see again. I would not say that an intertextual archetype is necessarily "universal." It can belong to a rather recent textual tradition, as with certain topoi of slapstick comedy. It is sufficient to consider it as a topos or standard situation that manages to be particularly appealing to a given cultural area or a historical period.

The making of *Casablanca*

"Can I tell you a story?" Ilse asks. Then she adds: "I don't know the finish yet."

Rick says: "Well, go on, tell it. Maybe one will come to you as you go along."

Rick's line is a sort of epitome of *Casablanca* itself. According to Ingrid Bergman, the film was apparently being made up at the same time that it was being shot. Until the last moment not even Michael Curtiz knew whether Ilse would leave with Rick or with Victor, and Ingrid Bergman seems so fascinatingly mysterious because she did not know at which man she was to look with greater tenderness.

This explains why, in the story, she does not, in fact, choose her fate: She is chosen.

When you don't know how to deal with a story, you put stereotyped situations in it because you know that they, at least, have already worked elsewhere. Let us take a marginal but revealing example. Each time Laszlo orders something to drink (and it happens four times) he changes his choice: (1) Cointreau, (2) cocktail, (3) cognac, and (4) whisky (he once drinks champagne but he does not ask for it). Why such confusing and confused drinking habits for a man endowed with an ascetic temper? There is no psychological reason. My guess is that each time Curtiz was simply quoting, unconsciously, similar situations in other movies and trying to provide a reasonably complete repetition of them.

Thus one is tempted to read *Casablanca* as T. S. Eliot read *Hamlet*, attributing its fascination not to the fact that it was a successful work (actually he considered it one of Shakespeare's less fortunate efforts) but to the imperfection of its composition. He viewed *Hamlet* as the result of an unsuccessful fusion of several earlier versions of the story, and so the puzzling ambiguity of the main character was due to the author's difficulty in putting together different topoi. So both public and critics find *Hamlet* beautiful because it is interesting, but believe it is interesting because it is beautiful.

On a smaller scale the same thing happened to *Casablanca*. Forced to improvise a plot, the authors mixed a little of everything, and everything they chose came from a repertoire that had stood the test of time. When only a few of these formulas are used, the result is simply kitsch. But when the repertoire of stock formulas is used wholesale, then the result is an architecture like Gaudi's Sagrada Familia: the same vertigo, the same stroke of genius.

Stop by stop

Every story involves one or more archetypes. To make a good story a single archetype is usually enough. But *Casablanca* is not satisfied with that. It uses them all.

It would be nice to identify our archetypes scene by scene and shot by shot, stopping the tape at every relevant step. Every time I have scanned *Casablanca* with very cooperative research groups, the review has taken many hours. Furthermore, when a team starts this kind of game, the instances of stopping the videotape increase proportionally with the size of the audience. Each member of the team sees something that the others have missed, and many of them start to find in the movie even memories of movies made after *Casablanca*—evidently the normal situation for a cult movie, suggesting that perhaps the best deconstructive readings should be made of unhinged texts (or that deconstruction is simply a way of breaking up texts).

However, I think that the first twenty minutes of the film represent a sort of review of the principal archetypes. Once they have been assembled, without any synthetic concern, then the story starts to suggest a sort of savage syntax of the archetypical elements and organizes them in multileveled oppositions. *Casablanca* looks like a musical piece with an extraordinarily long overture, where every theme is exhibited according to a monodic line. Only later does the symphonic work take place. In a way the first twenty minutes could be analyzed by a Russian Formalist and the rest by a Greimasian.

Let me then try only a sample analysis of the first part. I think that a real text-analytical study of *Casablanca* is still to be made, and I offer only some hints to future teams of researchers, who will carry out, someday, a complete reconstruction of its deep textual structure.

1. First, African music, then the *Marseillaise*. Two different genres are evoked: adventure movie and patriotic movie.

2. Third genre. The globe: Newsreel. The voice even suggests the news report. Fourth genre: the odyssey of refugees. Fifth genre: Casablanca and Lisbon are, traditionally, *hauts lieux* for international intrigues. Thus in two minutes five genres are evoked.

3. Casablanca–Lisbon. Passage to the Promised Land (Lisbon–America). Casablanca is the Magic Door. We still do not know what the Magic Key is or by which Magic Horse one can reach the Promised Land.

4. "Wait, wait, wait." To make the passage one must submit to a Test. The Long Expectation. Purgatory situation.

5. "Deutschland über Alles." The German anthem introduces the theme of Barbarians.

6. The Casbah. Pépé le Moko. Confusion, robberies, violence, and repression.

7. Pétain (Vichy) vs. the Cross of Lorraine. See at the end the same opposition closing the story: Eau de Vichy vs. Choice of the Resistance. War Propaganda movie.

8. The Magic Key: the visa. It is around the winning of the Magic Key that passions are unleashed. Captain Renault mentioned: He is the Guardian of the Door, or the boatman of the Acheron to be conquered by a Magic Gift (money or sex).

9. The Magic Horse: the airplane. The airplane flies over Rick's Café Américain, thus recalling the Promised Land of which the Café is the reduced model.

10. Major Strasser shows up. Theme of the Barbarians, and their emasculated slaves. "Je suis l'empire à la fin de la décadence/Qui regarde passer les grands barbares blancs/En composant des acrostiques indolents. . . ."

11. "Everybody comes to Rick's." By quoting the original play, Renault introduces the audience to the Café. The interior: Foreign Legion (each character has a different nationality and a different story to tell, and also his own skeleton in the closet), Grand Hotel (people come and people go, and nothing ever happens), Mississippi River Boat, New Orleans Brothel (black piano player), the Gambling Inferno in Macao or Singapore (with Chinese women), the Smugglers' Paradise, the Last Outpost on the Edge of the Desert. Rick's place is a magic circle where everything can happen—love, death, pursuit, espionage, games of chance, seductions,

music, patriotism. Limited resources and the unity of place, due to the theatrical origin of the story, suggested an admirable condensation of events in a single setting. One can identify the usual paraphernalia of at least ten exotic genres.

12. Rick slowly shows up, first by synecdoche (his hand), then by metonymy (the check). The various aspects of the contradictory (plurifilmic) personality of Rick are introduced: the Fatal Adventurer, the Self-Made Businessman (money is money), the Tough Guy from a gangster movie, Our Man in Casablanca (international intrigue), the Cynic. Only later he will be characterized also as the Hemingwayan Hero (he helped the Ethiopians and the Spaniards against fascism). He does not drink. This undoubtedly represents a nice problem, for later Rick must play the role of the Redeemed Drunkard and he has to be made a drunkard (as a Disillusioned Lover) so that he can be redeemed. But Bogey's face sustains rather well this unbearable number of contradictory psychological features.

13. The Magic Key, in person: the transit letters. Rick receives them from Peter Lorre and from this moment everybody wants them: how to avoid thinking of Sam Spade and of *The Maltese Falcon*?

14. Music Hall. Mr. Ferrari. Change of genre: comedy with brilliant dialogue. Rick is now the Disenchanted Lover, or the Cynical Seducer.

15. Rick vs. Renault. The Charming Scoundrels.

16. The theme of the Magic Horse and the Promised Land returns.

17. Roulette as the Game of Life and Death (Russian Roulette that devours fortunes and can destroy the happiness of the Bulgarian Couple, the Epiphany of Innocence). The Dirty Trick: cheating at cards. At this point the Trick is an Evil one but later it will be a Good one, providing a way to the Magic Key for the Bulgarian bride.

18. Arrest and tentative escape of Ugarte. Action movie.

19. Laszlo and Ilse. The Uncontaminated Hero and La Femme Fatale. Both in white—always; clever opposition with Germans, usually in black. In the meeting at Laszlo's table, Strasser is in white, in order to reduce the opposition. However, Strasser and Ilse are Beauty and the Beast. The Norwegian agent: spy movie.

20. The Desperate Lover and Drink to Forget.

21. The Faithful Servant and his Beloved Master. Don Quixote and Sancho.

22. Play it (again, Sam). Anticipated quotation of Woody Allen.

23. The long flashback begins. Flashback as a content and flashback as a form. Quotation of the flashback as a topical stylistic device. The Power of Memory. Last Day in Paris. Two Weeks in Another Town. Brief Encounter. French movie of the 1930's (the station as *quai des brumes*).

24. At this point the review of the archetypes is more or less complete. There is still the moment when Rick plays the Diamond in the Rough (who allows the Bulgarian bride to win), and two typical situations: the scene of the *Marseillaise* and the two lovers discovering that Love Is Forever. The gift to the Bulgarian bride (along with the enthusiasm of the waiters), the *Marseillaise*, and the Love Scene are three instances of the rhetorical figure of Climax, as the quintessence of Drama (each climax coming obviously with its own anticlimax).

Now the story can elaborate upon its elements.

The first symphonic elaboration comes with the second scene around the roulette table. We discover for the first time that the Magic Key (that everybody believed to be only purchasable with money) can in reality be given only as a Gift, a reward for Purity. The Donor will be Rick. He gives (free) the visa to Laszlo. In reality there is also a third Gift, the Gift Rick makes of his own desire, sacrificing himself. Note that there is no gift for Ilse, who, in some way, even though innocent, has betrayed two men. The Receiver of the Gift is the Uncontaminated Laszlo. By becoming the Donor, Rick meets Redemption. No one impure can reach the Promised Land. But Rick and Renault redeem themselves and can reach the other Promised Land, not America (which is Paradise) but the Resistance, the Holy War (which is a glorious Purgatory). Laszlo flies directly to Paradise because he has already suffered the ordeal of the underground. Rick, moreover, is not the only one who accepts sacrifice: The idea of sacrifice pervades the whole story, Ilse's sacrifice in Paris when she abandons the man she loves to return to the wounded hero, the Bulgarian bride's sacrifice when she is prepared to give herself to help her husband, Victor's sacrifice when he is prepared to see Ilse with Rick to guarantee her safety.

The second symphonic elaboration is upon the theme of the Unhappy Love. Unhappy for Rick, who loves Ilse and cannot have her. Unhappy for Ilse, who loves Rick and cannot leave with him. Unhappy for Victor, who understands that he has not really kept Ilse. The interplay of unhappy loves produces numerous twists and turns. In the beginning Rick is unhappy because he does not understand why Ilse leaves him. Then Victor is unhappy because he does not understand why Ilse is attracted to Rick. Finally Ilse is unhappy because she does not understand why Rick makes her leave with her husband.

These unhappy loves are arranged in a triangle. But in the normal adulterous triangle there is a Betrayed Husband and a Victorious Lover, while in this case both men are betrayed and suffer a loss.

In this defeat, however, an additional element plays a part, so subtly that it almost escapes the level of consciousness. Quite subliminally a hint of Platonic Love is established. Rick admires Victor, Victor is ambiguously attracted by the personality of Rick, and it seems that at a certain point each of the two is playing out the duel of sacrifice to please the other. In any case, as in Rousseau's *Confessions*, the woman is here an intermediary between the two men. She herself does not bear any positive value (except, obviously, Beauty): The whole story is a virile affair, a dance of seduction between Male Heroes.

From now on the film carries out the definitive construction of its intertwined triangles, to end with the solution of the Supreme Sacrifice and of the Redeemed Bad Guys. Note that, while the redemption of Rick has long been prepared, the redemption of Renault is absolutely unjustified and comes only because this was the final requirement the movie had to meet in order to be a perfect Epos of Frames.

The archetypes hold a reunion

Casablanca is a cult movie precisely because all the archetypes are there, because each actor repeats a part played on other occasions, and because human beings live not "real" life but life as stereotypically portrayed in previous films. *Casablanca* carries the sense of déjà vu to such a degree that the addressee is ready to see in it what happened after it as well. It is not until *To Have and Have Not* that Bogey plays the role of the Hemingway hero, but here he appears "already" loaded with Hemingwayesque connotations simply because Rick fought in Spain. Peter Lorre trails reminiscences of Fritz Lang, Conrad Veidt's German officer emanates a faint whiff of *The Cabinet of Dr. Caligari*. He is not a ruthless, technological Nazi; he is a nocturnal and diabolical Caesar.

Casablanca became a cult movie because it is not *one* movie. It is "movies." And this is the reason it works, in defiance of any aesthetic theory.

For it stages the powers of Narrativity in its natural state, before art intervenes to tame it. This is why we accept the way that characters change mood, morality, and psychology from one moment to the next, that conspirators cough to interrupt the conversation when a spy is approaching, that bar girls cry at the sound of the *Marseillaise* . . .

When all the archetypes burst out shamelessly, we plumb Homeric profundity. Two clichés make us laugh but a hundred clichés move us because we sense dimly that the clichés are talking among themselves, celebrating a reunion.

Just as the extreme of pain meets sensual pleasure, and the extreme of perversion borders on mystical energy, so too the extreme of banality allows us to catch a glimpse of the Sublime.

Nobody would have been able to achieve such a cosmic result intentionally. Nature has spoken in place of men. This, alone, is a phenomenon worthy of veneration.

The charged cult

The structure of *Casablanca* helps us understand what happens in later movies *born in order to become cult objects*.

What *Casablanca* does unconsciously, other movies will do with extreme intertextual awareness, assuming also that the addressee is equally aware of their purposes. These are "postmodern" movies, where the quotation of the topos is recognized as the only way to cope with the burden of our filmic encyclopedic expertise.

Think for instance of *Bananas*, with its explicit quotation of the Odessa steps from Eisenstein's *Potemkin*. In *Casablanca* one enjoys quotation even though one does not recognize it, and those who recognize it feel as if they all belonged to the same little clique. In *Bananas* those who do not catch the topos cannot enjoy the scene and those who do simply feel smart.

Another (and different) case is the quotation of the topical duel between the black Arab giant with his scimitar and the unprotected hero, in *Raiders of the Lost Ark*. If you remember, the topos suddenly turns into another one, and the unprotected hero becomes in a second *The Fastest Gun in the West*. Here the ingenuous viewer can miss the quotation though his enjoyment will then be rather slight; and real enjoyment is reserved for the people accustomed to cult movies, who know the whole repertoire of "magic" archetypes. In a way, *Bananas* works for cultivated "cinephiles" while *Raiders* works for *Casablanca*-addicts.

The third case is that of *E.T.*, when the alien is brought outside in a Halloween disguise and meets the dwarf coming from *The Empire Strikes Back*. You remember that E.T. starts and runs to cheer him (or it). Here nobody can enjoy the scene if he does not share, at least, the following elements of intertextual competence:

(1) He must know where the second character comes from (Spielberg citing Lucas),

(2) He must know something about the links between the two directors, and

(3) He must know that both monsters have been designed by Rambaldi and that, consequently, they are linked by some form of brotherhood.

The required expertise is not only intercinematic, it is intermedia, in the sense that the addressee must know not only other movies but all the mass media gossip about movies. This third example presupposes a "*Casablanca* universe" in which cult has become the normal way of enjoying movies. Thus in this case we witness an instance of metacult, or of cult about cult – a Cult Culture.

It would be semiotically uninteresting to look for quotations of archetypes in *Raiders* or in *Indiana Jones*: They were conceived within a metasemiotic culture, and what the semiotician can find in them is exactly what the directors put there. Spielberg and Lucas are semiotically nourished authors working for a culture of instinctive semioticians.

With *Casablanca* the situation is different. So *Casablanca* explains *Raiders*, but *Raiders* does not explain *Casablanca*. At most it can explain the new ways in which *Casablanca* will be received in the next years.

It will be a sad day when a too smart audience will read *Casablanca* as conceived by Michael Curtiz after having read Calvino and Barthes. But that day will come. Perhaps we have been able to discover here, for the last time, the Truth.

Après nous, le déluge.

1984

1.6

Science fiction double feature: Ideology in the cult film
by Barry K. Grant

Barry Keith Grant's main interest as a scholar is in the construction of popular genre cinema, a topic that became part of university curricula in the 1980s. Grant's *Film Genre Reader* (1984) was one of the first academic collections on genre cinema, and it paved the way for an understanding of how the likes of the horror film, science-fiction, and the fantastic function within popular culture. In his essay *Science-Fiction Double Feature: Ideology in the Cult Film*, which appeared in the first ever academic collection solely devoted to cult cinema (*The Cult Film Experience*), Grant treats cult cinema as a genre in its own right, like the Western or the musical, albeit a more slippery one. According to Grant, all cult films share a doublebinded (the 'double feature' of his title) involvement with 'transgression': they transgress boundaries of competency, taste patterns, exhibition routines, aesthetic styles, . . . As such they defy the view that film is typified by a unified mode of practices. Taking Eco's acknowledgement of the viewer one step further, Grant suggests that a cult film's appeal, then, is the result more of its interaction between text and spectator than of its own structures. He analyses *Night of the Living Dead* (which he calls the first genuine midnight movie), *The Rocky Horror Picture Show*, *La cage aux folles*, and *The Gods Must be Crazy* as instances of cult cinema. Grant argues that their ideological traits too, transgress boundaries, encouraging audiences to take threats against the 'Other' (the other gender, the other ethnicity, the other political view) less seriously, but in taming the 'Other', they also encourage viewers to laugh at the 'normal', and nowhere can they find themselves.

A note on extracting: *Science-Fiction Double Feature: Ideology in the Cult Film* is taken from J.P. Telotte's edited collection *The Cult Film Experience: Beyond All Reason*, published in 1991 by the University of Texas Press in their Texas Film Studies Series (convened by Thomas Schatz), pages 122–137. The essay is reprinted in full here.

Before examining the cult film as a cinematic category, we must first ask, "What is a cult film?" Despite the phenomenon's popularity, critical work in this area has been sparse and tentative, so this question is somewhat more difficult to answer than it might at first appear. We all know, say, a western or musical when we see one. By definition, westerns are overdetermined by their physical and temporal settings. They must be set in the West, that is, between the Mississippi River and California, usually between 1865 and 1890. Less determined in this regard, musicals may be set in any time or place, from Ernst Lubitsch's mythical prewar Europe to the contemporary ghetto of *West Side Story*. Still, musicals remain relatively easy to identify generically, since if a movie contains several instances of song and dance *within* its diegetic world, it is by definition a musical.

In contrast, the cult film can come from any genre. It can modify classic generic forms, as Philippe de Broca's *King of Hearts* does to the war film, or it may defy generic category, like David Lynch's *Eraserhead*. While its disparate generic affinities make the cult film far more slippery to grasp than conventional genre works, we can find a number of underlying similarities shared by this otherwise varied group of movies. Indeed, although these movies might differ on the surface, in what Edward Buscombe terms their "outer forms," they are similar on a deeper, ideological level, what Buscombe calls a genre's "inner forms" (12).

In his *Theories of Film*, Andrew Tudor explains a major problem of all genre definition, which he terms "the empiricist dilemma":

> To take a genre such as a western, analyze it, and list its principal characteristics is to beg the question that we must first isolate the body of films that are westerns. But they can only be isolated on the basis of the 'principal characteristics,' which can only be discovered *from the films themselves* after they have been isolated.
>
> (135)

Tudor's pragmatic solution to this problem of definition is to rely on what he calls a "common cultural consensus," to analyze works that almost everyone would agree belong to a particular genre and generalize from that point. But the problem is more acute for the cult film for two reasons: first, its disparate generic affinities make the category even more unwieldy than conventional genres; and, second, the lack of a substantial body of cult criticism provides little help in establishing a cultural consensus. Thus critical confusion over identifying particular cult movies inevitably arises. J. Hoberman and Jonathan Rosenbaum in *Midnight Movies*, for example, call *The Cabinet of Dr. Caligari* "the cult film *par excellence*" (23), while Danny Peary in *Cult Movies* nowhere even mentions it.

In the cinema the term "cult" tends to be used rather loosely, to describe a variety of films, old and new, that are extremely popular or have a particularly devoted audience. Cult films, most of us would agree, tend to construct a microcosmic community of admirers. But what exactly makes this different from phenomenally successful popular movies like *Star Wars* or *E.T.*, which might more accurately be described as examples of "mass cult"? Such movies perfectly fit Harold Wilensky's definition of mass culture as "cultural products manufactured solely for a mass market" (175). Indeed, the cuddly Ewoks of the last *Star Wars* episode seem designed expressly for their merchandising potential. A similar problem is raised by those movies that seem consciously calculated from the time of their production (or even before) to become instant cult films. Examples might include *Repo Man*, *Liquid Sky*, and *Blue Velvet*, movies that represent the fast food of cult rather than the slowly simmered fare like *Blade Runner*, which became cult when released on video after its theatrical run.

Despite the critical difficulties arising from the equivocal nature of the cult corpus, however, one useful idea that has been suggested about all cult movies is that in some way they involve a form of "transgression" and that this quality is central to their appeal. This transgression can manifest itself in terms of subject matter, as with the "difference" evoked by Tod Browning's *Freaks* (1931); or in terms of attitude, as in the cheerful embrace of an aesthetic of the ugly—or perhaps simply the tacky— in John Waters' *Pink Flamingos* (1975). Transgression can manifest itself as well in a film's style, as in the Artaudian cinema of cruelty approach of Alexandro Jodorowsky's *El Topo* (1973), or in the kinetic visual pyrotechnics of George Miller's *Mad Max* movies.

Thus the films of Edward D. Wood, Jr., widely acknowledged as the worst filmmaker of all time, are cult because they transgress basic technical competency, even as they affront the consumer who shells out the considerable cost of a ticket at the box office. Wood's lurid 1952 transvestite movie, *Glen or Glenda?* (a.k.a. *I Changed My Sex*), is cult partly because of its subject but, more important, because it is so ludicrously inept as a documentary. Similarly, his 1956 effort, *Plan 9 from Outer Space*, is a cult favorite because it is so *obviously* awful in the context of the well-made classical narrative.

This embrace of "badness" also accounts for the cult status of such unhorrifying horror films as *Attack of the Killer Tomatoes* and antidrug propaganda movies like *Reefer Madness* (1936), a film which claims that smoking marijuana leads to addiction, rape, murder, and insanity. By the same reasoning, Frank Capra's *Why We Fight* series of World War II films, which are just as sensationalist in their bellicose jingoism, are not cult, since they are slickly made and have proven their ability to persuade an audience.

It has also been suggested that the element of transgressive difference central to cult films may be due largely to an alternative method of distribution or exhibition. This certainly applies to some of the midnight movies, which went against the logic of traditional "prime-time" exhibition. Thus, if John Waters' recent *Hairspray* (1988) does not achieve the cult status of his other films, it may be because it was released as a mainstream movie with a PG rating. But this idea seems more problematic when applied to many classical cult films, such as *Citizen Kane* (1941), *Forbidden Planet* (1956), or *Black Sunday* (1975), movies originally both produced and marketed through conventional studio channels.

While it is true that cult films seem commonly to offer some form of transgression, what these movies more precisely have in common, what essentially makes these movies *cultish*, is their ability to be at once transgressive *and* recuperative, in other words, to reclaim that which they seem to violate. Further, they tend to achieve this ideological manipulation through a particular inflection of the figure of the Other. Common enough in genre movies generally, in the cult film the Other becomes a caricature that makes what it represents less threatening to the viewer. As in classic genre films, then, the viewer ultimately gains the double satisfaction of both rejecting dominant cultural values and remaining safely inscribed within them.

Because of this structural doublethink of cult movies, it is not surprising that they have also been defined in terms of "sameness" rather than difference. Peary, for example, while hypothesizing the cult film's difference, oddly claims that sometimes films become cult by offering " 'definitive' performances by stars who have cult status" (xiii). Hence the cult appeal of almost any film with actors like Humphrey Bogart, Marlon Brando, James Dean, Mae West, Marilyn Monroe, and even Ronald Reagan. Presumably this is why Peary discusses in his book movies like *All About Eve*, *Top Hat*, and *A Hard Day's Night*—works that perfectly capture the appeal of Bette Davis, Astaire and Rogers, and the Beatles, respectively. Movies that fulfill this function of showcasing the iconographical significance of their stars are necessarily more conventional than different, since they must rely for their meaning on the culturally accepted values of the star. This is quite opposite the strategy of "casting against type," which is more a strategy of difference.

In yet another approach, Umberto Eco suggests that cult movies work by a kind of collage effect. "In order to transform a work of art into a cult object," he says, "one must be able to break, dislocate, unhinge it so that one can remember only parts of it, irrespective of their original relationship with the whole." This seems yet another aspect of the cult film's transgressive nature, since this collage structure is at odds with the usual appreciation of a work of art as an aesthetic unity (in Cleanth Brooks' famous phrase, the "well-wrought urn") and Hollywood's ideal of seamless ("classical") construction. For Eco, a cult movie survives by becoming "a disconnected series of images, of peaks, of visual icebergs. It should display not one central idea but many. It should not reveal a coherent philosophy of composition" (3–4). While Eco considers only *Casablanca* specifically, the idea seems to apply to many other cult films as well. *The Rocky Horror Picture Show*, perhaps the most obvious example, loosely joins elements of the horror, science fiction, and musical genres, with plenty of self-conscious allusions peppered throughout the text; *Mad Max*, to take another example, combines science fiction, road movies, and westerns. These films would seem to demonstrate Eco's assertion that "a cult movie is the proof that . . . cinema comes from cinema" (4).

Clearly, though, mainstream films have manifested this quality for decades. Neoformalist critics have recently argued for a view of Hollywood cinema as "a unified mode of film practice" with its origins dating as early as 1917 (Bordwell, Staiger, and Thompson). Eco's notion of a collagelike assembly of interchangeable parts is, in fact, an essential element of genre films, the mainstay of classical Hollywood cinema, whether among works of a particular genre or across different genres. *Casablanca*, Eco claims, "became a cult movie because it is not *one* movie . . . [but] the movies" (12); yet this same generalization can easily be made about hundreds of other undistinguished and now forgotten Hollywood films.

And so we define cult movies by the seemingly contradictory qualities of sameness and difference. The reason for this is that they are, in fact, at once different and the same, transgressive and recuperative. However, in the context of the cult film, it is not enough simply to talk about such properties in terms of the text alone. To understand why, let us consider the term "cult" itself. The first definition of the word offered by the OED is "worship; reverential homage rendered to a divine being or beings." In the case of cult movies, the "divinity" is the shimmering series of images cast on the silver screen which our devoted attention lifts above the realm of the merely representational and the secular. So the viewer's relation to the work is a crucial element of cult in film. With cult movies like *The Rocky Horror Picture Show*, where audience participation was first accepted and then ritualized until it became at least as much an attraction as the film itself, the term fits the OED's other, complementary definitions: "A particular form or system of religious worship; esp. in reference to its external rites and ceremonies," and "Devotion or homage to a particular person or thing, now esp. as paid by a body of professed adherents or admirers." In the first case, the emphasis is on the *object* of worship; in the second, on the *act* or *nature* of the worship; and in the third, on those who *engage* in the worship.

J. P. Telotte has observed that the close relation between the cult film as a text and as an experience allows us to conceive of both aspects together as what he calls the cult "supertext." He sees this feature of the cult film as distinguishing it from more traditional, conventionally defined genres (see the essay "Beyond All Reason" in this volume). The rapt attention of Woody Allen's Allan Felix in *Play It Again, Sam,* his face bathed in the beatific light of the movie screen as he reverently mouths Bogie's final speech to Ingrid Bergman on the airport runway in *Casablanca,* is the perfect cinematic expression of this cult "supertext." Now, since a movie's cult appeal becomes manifest in a particular way of experiencing it (in its most extreme form, as ritualized response), it seems logical to focus on this heightened relationship between spectator and text, a more intimate one than in the usual viewing experience.

Let us begin our examination of specific cult films with *Night of the Living Dead* (1968), probably the first genuine midnight movie. Along with the earlier *Psycho,* it helped establish what many critics have identified as a trend toward a progressive sensibility in the contemporary horror film because of its critique of dominant ideology through its treatment of the monster. According to Robin Wood, the horror film is structured by the simple formula of "normality, the Monster, and, crucially, the relationship between the two" ("Introduction" 14). This equation is fundamentally ideological. In the classic horror film, the normal characters successfully resist the threat of the monster which, in Wood's reading, represents the desires of the id that challenge dominant ideological values and thus must be denied or repressed. This denial takes the form of a distorted Other, a projection outward of unacceptable desires by way of denying them within ourselves. One of Freud's examples is witches, which he explains as psychic projections of repressed desire onto a scapegoat group (72). In the horror film, the threatening appearance of the monster signifies, as Wood appropriates Freud, an inevitable "return of the repressed." The 1956 horror and science fiction classic *Forbidden Planet,* with its expressly identified "monster from the id," only makes explicit this genre's underlying thematic concern.

The figure of the Other, as Roland Barthes explains, is a major strategy by which a dominant ideology maintains its hegemony (151–152). In some progressive horror films, like *Night of the Living Dead,* the classic relationship between the normal and the monstrous is subverted, or at least reversed, so that the normal characters appear as morally or psychologically "monstrous" as the monster is physically. Thus the progressive text questions the classic horror film's assumed values of "normalcy."

Night of the Living Dead consistently reverses generic conventions: the military is inept, the hero is black—and he dies, religion fails to ward off the monsters, and so on. The film also locates the monstrous *within* the normal—in the family patriarch Harry Cooper, as well as in the sibling relationship of Johnny and Barbara. Elliott Stein suggests that the zombies are metaphorical of Nixon's "silent majority" (105). While

I essentially agree with this reading, it does depend upon, first, an awareness of generic expectations and how they are thwarted and, second, the viewer's reflection upon these generic subversions and his or her reactions to them.

In fact, most viewers of *Night of the Living Dead* probably think little about its thematic implications, particularly when it comes to acknowledging their own moral culpability. Instead, they respond to its visual power and graphic violence. This is also the explanation for the popularity of Hitchcock's thrillers, despite the textually convincing case for their "therapeutic" value and their similar implication of the audience in their narratives.

Horror films that emphasize violence at the expense of character, plot, and theme are sometimes called "splatter" movies. As John McCarty describes them, such films "aim not to scare their audiences, necessarily, nor to drive them to the edges of their seats in suspense, but to *mortify* them with scenes of explicit gore. In splatter movies, mutilation is indeed the message—many times the only one" (1). McCarty identifies *Night of the Living Dead* as "the first official splatter movie to gain a real reputation" (3). Of course, such films are in one sense transgressive, since they treat violence in a way that challenges conventional notions of good taste. However, one's experience of such movies is most often an unconstructive, unfocused visceral response that is more accurately described as a gut reaction rather than as a truly transgressive experience. It is perhaps no more transgressive than applauding a good body check in a hockey game.

This point was emphatically demonstrated during Robin Wood's retrospective of horror films at the 1979 Toronto Film Festival. There, George Romero, director of *Night of the Living Dead*, was asked about the ideological implications of his work. The audience, however, was impatient with such talk, became rude, and shouted for him to leave the stage so they could enjoy the movie. The majority of the audience, even in this supposedly sophisticated context, clearly just wanted to have a good time and to see the "good parts." This film's reception thus brings into focus a critical problem shared by many horror films: the discrepancy between textual interpretation and actual viewer reception. The fact that the film can be read as a biting critique of the American middle class accounts for little of its cult appeal, although for those who can perceive it, this theme lends a degree of respectability to what Alex in *A Clockwork Orange* would call "a real horrorshow."

The Rocky Horror Picture Show, like *Night of the Living Dead*, is an ambiguous text that can accommodate opposing readings. Like Romero's film, it reverses some of the genre's classic conventions in a manner demonstrating a conscious awareness of generic traditions. It is a generic pastiche with many elements of horror, science fiction, and the musical. And it signals this "collage" quality from the opening credit sequence, as a pair of lips sing "Science Fiction Double Feature," a song that alludes to many classic science fiction films.

Despite the sameness implied by its dense intertextuality, the film also seems to diverge significantly from the horror and science fiction genres, in part by reversing the conventional appearance and sexual significance of the monster in relation to the normal. The eponymous creature is a good-looking hunk of a guy, while the "normal" couple, Brad Majors and Janet Weiss, are depicted as heavily repressed. Dr. Frank-N-Furter (Tim Curry in black garterbelt, hose, and heavy, sensuous makeup) is at once the standard, overreaching scientist figure and alternate monster who, as his name crudely suggests, threatens to overwhelm the normalcy of the bland bourgeois couple with his unrestrained sexual appetite and pursuit of physical pleasure.

When Brad and Janet, played as wimpishly as possible by Barry Bostwick and Susan Sarandon, arrive at the doctor's castle after having a flat tire, their repressed nature is challenged. "Don't judge a book by its cover," sings Furter, as he proceeds to seduce first Brad and then Janet. The seduction scenes are photographed in the same manner and the dialogue is identical in each, suggesting the common nature of desire, whether hetero- or homosexual. Such an attitude is in direct opposition to the dominant heterosexual, monogamous values of Western culture. "Be it, don't dream it," croons Furter as he urges them to be honest and unrepressed. The flat tire thus becomes emblematic of the breakdown of Brad and Janet's bourgeois values, an idea reinforced by both a visual reference to Grant Wood's famous "American Gothic" painting during the opening wedding scene and by Nixon's resignation speech, heard on the car radio just before their tire deflates.

In the climax, Riff-Raff and Magenta, Furter's two alien assistants, burst into the lab, stating that the doctor must be terminated because of his excessive pursuit of pleasure. His death occurs in a scene marked with castration imagery (the falling RKO tower, the reference to King Kong's death on the Empire State Building) and, significantly, results from a laser blast from Riff-Raff's weapon, which resembles the pitchfork in Wood's painting. Thus the middle American empire strikes back to restore dominant sexual values. (It is no coincidence that Richard O'Brien, the actor who plays Riff-Raff, appears earlier as the priest performing the marriage ceremony.) The film seems in the end to call the stability of the heterosexual couple's relationship into question, since Brad has come out of the closet and Janet has revealed her hidden lust ("Touch-a, touch-a, touch me/I wanna be dirty," she sings). But narrative closure results, and dominant sexual values are restored as the couple survives and Furter is eviscerated.

In this context, the film's use of the musical genre becomes especially significant. The musical traditionally develops two central themes: constructing a sense of community and defining the parameters of sexual desire. These themes are, of course, intimately related, since unchanneled desire poses a threat to the dominant ideology of heterosexuality and monogamy so insistently represented in classical Hollywood cinema. *Rocky Horror* shows just how close the musical and horror genres really are. And just as classical musicals inevitably end in the valorized union of the monogamous couple—*Seven Brides for Seven Brothers* is the ultimate example— so Brad and Janet, with the elimination of the Furter between them, can come together as promised at the beginning when Janet catches the bridal bouquet at the wedding.

Given this example, Hoberman and Rosenbaum seem right in identifying alternate sexuality as a pronounced motif in cult movies (263), but it is equally important to consider *how* the alternative is used or consumed by audiences. *Rocky Horror*, for example, develops a strong sense of community generated by individuals in the audience dressed similarly, in the manner of the characters. But the predetermined costumes, repetition of the characters' lines at specific times, and the ritualization of certain acts during the screening (throwing rice or toilet paper) ultimately reconstitutes *outside* the film a community not unlike the one lampooned *within* it. The rote quality of these rituals, which discouraged the spontaneous improvisation by newcomers, suggests that this community is in its own way every bit as conformist and repressive as the middle class satirized on the screen.

The costuming and play-acting aspects of the *Rocky Horror* experience also foreground style over meaning, making it, in effect, an expression of the camp sensibility that Susan Sontag has described. According to Sontag, camp attacks the serious in a way that irony and satire, because of contemporary media saturation, can no longer do (288). Thus she says, "Camp asserts that good taste is not simply good taste; that there exists, indeed, a good taste of bad taste" (290). Certainly this helps explain the appeal of cult films like Edward Wood's, of *Eraserhead*, of *Killer Tomatoes*, of splatter movies, and of Russ Meyer's *Beyond the Valley of the Dolls*. Waters' *Pink Flamingos* ends with Divine eating dogshit in perhaps the ultimate image of the cult film as bad taste! Camp, then, partially accounts for one significant aspect of the cult film's transgression, for to like these movies is to embrace aesthetic—and, by extension, social—values in apparent opposition to the accepted norm. To like them, or to claim to, clearly sets one apart from the "decency" of the mainstream.

The celebration of sexual alternatives also seems to be at the root of the cult appeal of Edouard Molinaro's popular gay sex farce *La Cage Aux Folles* (1979). In his essay on horror films, Wood offers "deviations from ideological sexual norms" as one version of the Other ("Introduction" 10), and indeed, the film appears to be structured somewhat like a horror film. The normals are the Charrier family, the heterosexual parents of Andrea, who are contrasted to the gay couple, Renato and Albin. The gay couple may at first seem monstrous to the average viewer, but ultimately they appear to be like any normal—that is, heterosexual—couple.

The Charriers are made laughable by their strict conservative moral code, exaggerated to the point that M. Charrier works as the secretary for the Union of Moral Order. That his values are both silly and unrealistic is made clear by his ludicrously excessive response to what he considers moral turpitude and by the fact that the president has been found dead in the arms of a prostitute—a black, underage one at that!

The gay couple are clearly the sympathetic characters in the film, the heterosexual ones rather unlikable in varying degree. While the Charriers, for instance, are interested only in marrying their daughter to help restore M. Charrier's failing career, Renato and Albin would sacrifice their personal integrity by denying their gayness so that Laurent's marriage will be approved by his conservative in-laws-to-be. Their parental sacrifice is so noble that they even allow their apartment to be redecorated—and in a nice visual metaphor for this sacrifice, the erect penis of an erotic statue is accidentally snapped off by Renato as he moves it. Laurent himself is so eager to hide the truth of what he euphemistically terms his father's "special" quality that he begins to transform the apartment even *before* consulting Albin.

Aside from its generally sympathetic treatment of the gays, the film occasionally challenges the viewer in another way by suggesting a discrepancy between appearance and truth in sexual terms, and so periodically thwarting our probable response. The initial meeting early in the film between Renato and Laurent, for example, seems at first to be a clandestine sexual rendezvous between the two—a likely response for a straight viewer because of the popular stereotype of gays as sexually profligate. Similarly, the dominant macho image of masculinity is undermined by being revealed *as* an image, particularly in the scene where Renato tries to teach Albin to butter his toast like a man and to walk "like John Wayne." The scene culminates with Renato assuming this macho pose himself and, to Ennio Morricone's music (the composer who provided the distinctive music for Sergio Leone's cult westerns with Clint Eastwood), walking through the contemporary equivalent of the saloon doors to confront a gay basher—only to be pummeled himself. The Wayne tough-guy image is thus undercut by the incongruity of the person adopting it, and so, as a result, revealed as fantasy.

But again, while *La Cage Aux Folles* would seem to attack dominant sexual ideology, its challenges are not sustained to any significant degree. For example, the characters remain too simplistic to make the conflict really work. The gay characters hardly rise above the level of stereotype to become fully rounded figures. They are depicted in clearly defined male and female roles, although Albin, as the neurotic drag queen, is, as we might expect, more broadly played. The film mocks the prissy self-preoccupation typical of the role with Albin's first appearance, hiding petulantly beneath a bedsheet because he feels he is aging. His self-pitying monologue stops only when the doctor, summoned because he knows what is "important" to Albin, makes him forget his own problems to consider the pros and cons of cooking with a particular kind of pan. Renato, by contrast, is not nearly as comical a figure, since he remains in part "a man," capable of heterosexual experience and reproduction. So he is depicted with the conventional signifiers of masculinity: he is hairy (Simone, Laurent's mother, specifically admires his chest hair), more rational than Albin, and the one in charge of the family business.

The narrative itself is also quite conventional, seeming in fact much like a television sitcom. As in the typical situation comedy, most of the action takes place in one domestic space, the gay pair's apartment; and this space is treated circumspectly: we see neither the bedroom nor the bathroom—according to Horace Newcomb, a convention of the TV sitcom (29). Physicality is, in fact, deemphasized throughout the film. There is virtually no sexual or even intimate scene between the two gay men, and the only scene of this kind we do see is between Renato and Simone. Like many newer sitcoms (e.g., "Cheers," "Three's Company," "Bosom Buddies"), *La Cage Aux Folles* spices its situation with a twist of sexual difference while directly avoiding that difference itself.

The narrative conflict is never really resolved, or even concluded; rather, it simply stops. In the climax, Albin takes off his wig to reveal that he is actually a gay male and not Laurent's mother, which immediately precedes a larger "unmasking" as the transvestites from the adjacent La Cage Aux Folles Club come through an adjoining door. The alternative sexuality the Charriers had wished to repress here seems joyously to return. But then the plot conveniently arranges for Charrier to have to dress in drag (even his wife "lets down her hair") in order to escape the club undetected by reporters. Albin finds them a way out, the problem is solved, life goes on, and the film is over. With such disguises, confusions, complications, and a pat conclusion, the film's narrative neatly fits the conventional TV sitcom plot structure (Newcomb chap. 2). Charrier in drag is finally much like Lucy Ricardo trapped in one of her situations—and he has no explaining to do. So the specifics of the disguise become less important than the plot mechanics that end the story. In the end the viewer feels "progressive" by laughing at the film's representative "normal" characters for their uptight attitude, while at the same time remaining safely distant from gayness through the comforts of stereotype and popular narrative formula, as well as through the comic deflation of the sexual issues seemingly addressed. Such a strategy would seem to explain the enormous popularity of this film in North America at a time when gay bashing was rumored to be increasing dramatically.

Yet another form of the Other noted by Wood is a specific ethnic group or, more generally, another culture ("Introduction" 10). A good example of the cult treatment of this type occurs in *The Gods Must Be Crazy*, an enormously popular South African comedy directed by Jamie Uys. The film begins by unambiguously contrasting modern, technological (white) society with the pastoral simplicity of the (black) Kalahari bushmen. Their Rousseauesque simplicity, completely in harmony with nature, seems to give them an edge over the "civilized" whites trapped in the urban ratrace.

But despite this initial explicit comparison, clearly favorable to the bushmen, the white viewer's sense of cultural superiority is then systematically restored by a voice-of-god narrator who presumes to tell us everything that the bushman !Ky thinks—although he makes no such presumption for any of the white characters. The narrator emphasizes !Ky's naivete as either exotically charming or laughably simple. He tells us, for example, that !Ky perceives land rovers as strange animals with round legs. One might justify this narration as a parody of the typical voice-of-god narrator in the tradition of travelogue documentary (e.g., Buñuel's *Land without Bread*) and thus in keeping with the film's humorous spirit. But such an argument falls apart because the narrator's knowledge and authority are in no way undercut in the film.

Following the contrast between the two cultures, the first of three interwoven plots is introduced. A thoughtless airplane pilot drops an empty Coke bottle into a family of bushpeople, who begin to covet it and fight over it; so to resolve these disputes !Ky must trek to the end of the earth and toss the bottle off, returning it to the gods. Then begins a plot concerning black revolutionaries in a neighboring country, followed by the romantic narrative involving Andrew Styne, a white biologist, and Kate Thompson, a schoolteacher. The three plots merge, as the rising action builds to a climax: Styne's rescue of Kate and the black schoolchildren who had been taken hostage by the revolutionaries.

But as these plots come together, the black characters are displaced by the white. The threat posed by the revolutionaries is defeated by the white man, with his ingenuity and technology—supported by the cheerful, obedient black servant, his version of a faithful Indian companion. It is Styne who devises the rescue plan and gives the orders, who uses his telescope and animal tranquilizer as tools, while !Ky comically drives the jeep backwards and is given no opportunity to employ the bushmen's own natural tranquilizer said earlier to be so useful in hunting.

The whites are presented as ecologically concerned (Styne's job) and sincerely interested in the welfare of blacks, while the blacks are depicted as childlike (as seen in the simplicity of !Ky and the literal "innocent children" kidnapped by the political radicals), gratefully subservient, or bumblingly dangerous (the inept revolutionaries manage to trip on banana peels while fleeing from government troops; later they hit the helicopter with a bazooka purely by accident). The conventional romance between the two white characters is increasingly foregrounded at the expense of !Ky's story. Their union at the end provides a narrative closure, capped by an abrupt coda informing us that! Ky has successfully completed his quest. Ultimately, then, the film claims to envision blacks as morally noble, even socially superior people, but in its narrative structure inscribes them as inferior to the whites, who are seen as necessary for maintaining social order (read apartheid).

In this way the film works like *La Cage Aux Folles:* while that film makes homosexuality safe for straight audiences, *The Gods Must Be Crazy* makes blacks safe for whites. In fact, its vision of blacks is not much of an advance over Hollywood's traditional stereotyping of them. As Roland Barthes says, "How *can* one assimilate the Negro . . .? There is here a figure for emergencies: exoticism. The Other becomes a pure object, a spectacle, a clown" (152).

Interestingly, all of the films discussed here share a strategy of presenting a conflict between the normal and the Other, and of making a clownish spectacle—of caricaturing—the normal while minimizing the threat of the Other. Even the least comic of these movies, *Night of the Living Dead*, lapses into this approach in its treatment of the sheriff, who, along with Harry Cooper, carries the metaphoric burden of equating the living dead with the normal. He gets the lines that always bring the laughs from the audience. When interviewed on TV, for example, he offers the opinion that the zombies are "dead; they're all messed up." In Romero's sequel, *Dawn of the Dead* (1978), the threat of the zombies is to a large extent reduced to a comic treatment. The film takes place almost entirely in a large suburban shopping mall, where the zombies tend to congregate. One of the living characters hypothesizes that they are drawn there by instinct, by a dim memory of their former existence; and indeed, except for their pallid skin, they look surprisingly like shoppers going about their business to the strains of the ubiquitous Muzak.

Because such characters emphasize the comic nature of normalcy or bourgeois life at the expense of any positive or redeeming features, they tend to flatten into caricature. This tendency toward caricature may be essential to the cult film, making an otherwise bitter pill somewhat easier to swallow. While cult movies gain some appeal through this textual strategy, they lose much potential power. As Sontag remarks of camp, it is "art that proposes itself seriously, but cannot be taken altogether seriously because it is 'too much' " (284). Thus Leslie Fiedler, while championing Russ Meyer as the great American filmmaker of the seventies, notes that, for all the depiction of blood and death in *Beyond the Valley of the Dolls,* "one leaves the theatre feeling exhilarated, amused—assured at the level of absolute childlike credence that nowhere is blood or death real" ("Beyond" 5).

Like classic genre films, cult movies work in terms of clearly defined oppositions. Their conflicts invariably can be reduced to some version of white hats versus black hats. And, too, they provide satisfactions similar to those of generic entertainment. The difference is that the genre movie tends to deemphasize its potential transgression. In gangster movies, for instance, we identify with the kinetic charisma of Edward G. Robinson or James Cagney for virtually the entire film, until the climax, of course, when the gangster meets his inevitable fate and social order is restored. We may have been vicariously antisocial for ninety minutes, but we are emphatically reformed in the last five. In musicals we identify with the sexual sophistication of Fred Astaire or bravado of Gene Kelly, but we are always satisfied when in the end their desire focuses on one partner only, and they dance in harmony to valorize the monogamous couple. But cult movies, like splatter films, boast of their transgressive qualities through excesses of style or content, treating normally taboo subjects or violating commonly accepted standards of taste. Yet they too end, like genre films, recuperating that which initially has posed a threat to dominant ideology.

This is not to claim, however, that no cult films are genuinely disturbing, for clearly some are—*Freaks, Flaming Creatures*, and Kenneth Anger's films, for example. But *Freaks* was banned for decades; *Flaming Creatures* was withdrawn from exhibition in New York during a lengthy litigation; and Anger's films showed only in a few art cinemas in major cities. These movies exist at a far remove from the mainstream narrative tradition that dominates the cult marketplace. For in those cult movies, ideological transgression is consistently recuperated by textual strategies and the very level of reception.

Cult films encourage viewers not to take very seriously the threat of the Other. At the same time, they prod us to laugh at representations of the normal, usually our own surrogates on the screen. Thus viewers cheer when in *The Texas Chain Saw Massacre* and other, less interesting splatter movies like *I Spit on Your Grave* and the various *Friday the 13th* films, their figures of identification are killed off serially in ever more prolonged and gruesome ways. People become, in these films, objectified bodies submitted to the inevitable fate of special effects and dismemberment. We hardly think of these characters as people, but rather as excuses, or pretexts, for splatter. In short, in cult movies viewers laugh at the normal, tame the Other, but nowhere see themselves. Perhaps this is why cult audiences tend to be composed of teenagers, disenfranchised youths who are caught between childhood and adulthood, who have little sense of belonging. There are, of course, other reasons for the cult appeal of specific movies, but it would seem that this "double feature" of transgression and recuperation accounts for much of the appeal of these otherwise diverse films we have come to describe with the unwieldy term "cult."

1.7

Semiotics by instinct: 'Cult film' as a signifying practice between film and audience

by Anne Jerslev

Danish media scholar Anne Jerslev was one of the first European academics to make the study of cult cinema her core interest. She published a book on cult cinema in 1993 (*Kultfilm & Filmkultur*, 1993), a study of David Lynch (1991), and researched violence in cinema and *The Lord of the Rings* as well. For Jerslev, cult cinema's significance lies in the interaction between film and audience. But unlike Eco or Grant she does not use the framework of intertextuality or genre to typify cult cinema's uniqueness. Rather, Jerslev departs from the 'event' aspect of a cult film screening to emphasize that instead of 'indicating a certain genre, [cult cinema] may be conveniently attached to a certain mode of reception'. In doing so, Jerslev brings the study of cult back to the 'experiential' level of engagement where Benjamin had located it (without referencing Benjamin however). Jerslev refuses to use the concept of identification with the screen, and stresses that cult cinema does not just mobilize audiences emotionally but also cognitively – it challenges audiences to play a game with the text's features, creating the possibility for ironic, sovereign, and distanced viewing (she calls it a 'position of playful mastery'). Jerslev uses *The Big Sleep* and *The Rocky Horror Picture Show* (which was already analysed by Grant, but also empirically studied by Bruce Austin – see section 4) as case studies. Jerslev claims that audiences do make sense of *The Rocky Horror Picture Show* using many of the intertextual cues Eco put forward. But they do so being fully aware of the ramifications and implications, using them as 'semiotics by instinct', enabling them to, should they so wish, read the text against its intentions and properties.

A note on extracting: this essay is reprinted from Michael Skovmand and Kim Schrøder (eds). *Media Cultures: Reappraising Transnational Media*. London: Routledge, pp. 181–198. The essay is reprinted here in full.

On 7 February 1979 Howard Hawks' film *The Big Sleep* reopened at a major art cinema in Copenhagen. An expectant mumble was heard in the crowded audience before the lights went out; I felt like a member of a theatre's audience just before the curtain rises: an experience one mostly gets secondhand nowadays, watching films about theatre. I felt like a connoisseur among other connoisseurs. It seemed that all of us had watched *The Big Sleep* at least once before. We knew when the highlights were coming and it seemed to us that they were performed in that very same moment just for us. Every now and then, from somewhere in the rows a few lines would be cited that Bogart and Bacall were to sneer politely at each other on the screen seconds later. And right after the famous café-scene where the two of them are testing each other verbally via horse metaphors, a great many people in the audience applauded loudly. When the film was over everybody applauded vehemently and whistled as if to get the actors back on stage.

Cult films as deconstruction

This bit of memory describes precisely a historically specific construction of a cult event in relation to cinema and a certain film. One might also say that it describes the putting into existence of a cult film. I am going to use this memory as a point of departure for a discussion of the very concept of *cult film. And* I am going to discuss the meaning resulting from the clash between an audience and a 'cult film' to come, a signifying practice that I shall call a *cult event* or *cult culture.*

I find this specific clash interesting for two reasons, both as a cultural practice and as a sort of textual staging. In the first place, it may be read as signifying postmodern culture in a wider sense. I use the concept postmodern here merely to indicate a mode of comprehension that transgresses modernity's hierarchised construction of mean-ing: the cult event speaks of a cultural practice that invalidates already fixed cultural codes, and constructs a certain relation between the filmic texts and their audiences on grounds of a perceptual cognition structured as an 'intertextual encyclopedia'; Umberto Eco (1984, 1985) uses this concept to describe the extensive visual con-sciousness of a modern audience that structures perception and cognition into a pattern of pleasurable repetition. Second, the cult event is interesting because its discursive practice can to a certain extent be regarded as a symbolisation of the structural codes of contemporary media reception, both in the cinema and in front of the TV set.

In the first of two articles on cult films in the Swedish film journal *Chaplin*, critic Olle Sjögren writes that

> The concept of cult film has turned into a public relations device in Sweden. But underneath the term hides an internationally widespread movement of heretics, constantly fighting against pompous orthodoxy, morally as well as aesthetically.
> (Sjögren 1988 – my translation)

Sjögren's statement represents a widespread understanding of the cult film genre as constituting a sub-cultural movement, circulating in another cultural and institutional environment than the cinema of popular culture. But I would suggest that it has now become necessary to revise or to expand the use of the concept, as we approach the end of the century. I shall argue below that 'cult film' has lost part of the specific sub-cultural meaning traditionally attached to it. The problem is not that film market-ing has usurped the concept, but rather that: when any film can be marketed com-mercially as a cult film – i.e. labelled a cult film before it has even been shown in a cinema – then the public relation business has labelled a tidal change in media culture. I'm not arguing that cult film is a concept deprived of any meaning, but rather than indicating a certain genre it may be conveniently attached to a certain mode of reception. In view of the amount of private video recorders that allow for screenings of the horror and splatterlike part of what Sjögren calls the aesthetics of heretics, and in the light of the continuing blurring over at least two decades of any certainty about art being the site of moral or aesthetic truth in contemporary culture, I find it difficult to understand cult films as merely subversive and consequently oppositional to popular media fiction.

Speaking of cult films and cult events I am primarily – and this is exactly my point – referring to a circulating and interdependent structure of meaning, involving an audience and a film. I am considering the cult event as an ancestral form of a more widespread culture of reception around 1990, thus representing a sort of cultural mentality to be found in the visual texts and then transformed and developed into a specific cult discourse by the cinema audience.

It is by focusing both on the aesthetic and the narrative similarities between contemporary fiction films and on the fact that, generally speaking, the audience around 1990 has changed in a crucial way in comparison with that of the 1970s, that the concept of cult film may be given a new significance. This is what interests me in this chapter. At the same time it is evident that films which deal with the lives and opinions of outsiders or in other ways address specific groups of spectators may still be part of sub-cultural activities.

In my previous description of the *Big Sleep* event, I focused on a specific circulation of meaning between cinema audience and film. The condition for this interaction is first of all a distance of time, in several ways: as 1970s spectators we were watching a film made in 1946, but at the same time (1979) we were spectators on an opening night, as if the film had been made that same year. We knew the film by heart, and yet we were in anticipation, as if we were going to watch a much-discussed film that had finally reached the country. The result of these clashes and contradictions of time was that we became highly aware of the viewing situation and of ourselves being constructed as spectators. Considering German theorist Gunther Salje's definition of the spectators' position vis-à-vis the film as 'das stumm-passive sich-fallen lassen' (Salje 1977: 273); or Christian Metz' reference to 'the spectator's solitude in the cinema' and his statement that the cinema audience does not, like the theatre audience, constitute 'a true "audience", a temporary collectivity' (Metz 1982: 64), the cult event calls for theoretical concepts that are able to account for and to emphasise the ambiguity of the setting and the circulation of meaning.

But the circulation between audience and film also signifies an emotional distance, because of the fact that we know the film, though some of us probably better than others. Consequently, we do not merely or necessarily participate by identifying with the narrative development or the history of Bacall or Bogart. Because we know the story, we immerse ourselves in it. Rather, because we know the story, the pleasure of watching is derived from a position of sovereignty where hypothesis-making becomes a play-act, and the question 'What happens next?' is asked from a position of playful mastery, because we already know the answer. While the 'stereotyped frames' unfold in front of our eyes and ears – this is what Eco terms the stereotyped pattern of situations and narrative segments in genre films – we hasten devotedly towards the next beloved sequence before it has actually been projected. It is thus segmented and separated from the previous as well as the following scene, and this is why the virtuous repetition of the same few sentences is followed by applause and whistling.

The historical distance between film and audience even prolongs the intertextual references prospectively: not only is the spectator familiar with *The Big Sleep*, but this film points towards other and more recent films: other Marlowe interpretations, film noir remakes, other and more recent secondary texts: extra-textual media gossip about the characters who were also lovers in real life, and so on.

I will now move on to a 'classic' example of a film cult event. But first let me summarise: what quite obviously happened in the Copenhagen cinema may be interpreted as a textual deconstruction, a dismantling of the text as a coherent signifying system. But this deconstructive effort is made possible only because the film itself offers it as a possible way of reading: because the film itself is not as discursively coherent as it seems; because even a dozen viewings does not prevent the spectator from a feeling of confusion, of never quite understanding what has really happened and who really killed whom; and also because the film changes its story and narrative mode halfway through, from film noir to a love story. Altogether, the pleasure of repetition, the historical distance as well as the incoherent narrative make up a signifying practice that can be labelled a cult event: the cult event transforms the film into a cult film and positions the spectators as a cult audience.

So the concept of repetition is central to this retheorising of the term cult film: one of the characteristics of the *Rocky Horror Picture Show* audience, as I am going to demonstrate, was that they had literally seen the film dozens of times. But repetition may also be theorised as a feeling of déjà vu, put into play by the aesthetically conscious intertextual circulation that is characteristic of contemporary media fiction. Both kinds of repetition make deconstruction a possible mode of reception. So in order to understand the specificity of the contemporary culture of media reception, it is crucial to conceptualise intertextual deconstruction.

What happened in the Copenhagen cinema happens, of course, more evidently when one is watching a 'real' cult film, for example an 'outlaw' film or a 'midnight movie': some of the best-covered events, theoretically as well as journalistically, are the notorious screenings of Jim Sharman's and Richard O'Brien's *The Rocky Horror Picture Show* (1975). What takes place ritualistically is, for example, that

> Throughout the showing of the film fans call for camera cuts and character action. They ask questions of the characters, respond to the characters' comments, and add lines to the film's dialogue. The fans also 'help' the characters – by providing flashlights to show the way to Brad and Janet as they trudge through the dark, rainy night, for example. In addition, the audience adds its own special effects, such as hurling toasts when a toast is proposed in the film, and squirting one another with water pistols in the rain sequence.
>
> (Austin 1981: 46)

The internationally distributed, ritual performances of *The Rocky Horror Picture Show* audience are well analysed – ever since the film gained its status as a cult film after it had been scheduled in a small Greenwich Village cinema, from April 1976 until four or five years later. Jonathan Rosenbaum states (Hoberman and Rosenbaum 1983) that in the beginning the audience formed a sub-cultural group of sexual minorities. But after the midnight shows had become famous they were not only squeezed into the cultural hegemony by the mass media, but were also attended eagerly by students, chasing the possibility of establishing themselves as a new *avant garde* of the cinema and thus filling the cultural gap after the sixties nouvelle vague audience. Here, however, I am not interested in discussing whether the cult event might be understood as a sub-cultural manifestation or not, but rather in examining the specific discourse of the cult event.

What seems to be the heart of the matter in the cult culture is the deconstruction (either obvious or less obvious, but always playful) of the film text's position of superiority; of the text unfolding itself in front of the reader, thus placing and constructing a position of reading for the spectator. This deconstructive discourse is called 'radical bricolage' by Corrigan (1986). The textual discourse is put into play by means of the spectators pretending to be directors of and actors in the film at the same time. The cult event may be understood at the same time as a construction of and as a travelling through a fictional universe.

The literature of cult films – the average understanding

The concept of cult film, as I have theorised it, is not to be understood as some fixed structure of meaning inherent in the film text. It is not a genre concept, unless one goes along with Andrew Tudor's very interesting and polemical theorising of genre as a reception concept: 'Genre is what we collectively believe it to be' (Tudor 1976: 127). Cult film is fundamentally an event. A cult film is only brought into existence in so far as one talks of a certain interaction between a text and an audience. On the other hand, this specific relationship is made possible by certain textual arrangements and historical circumstances.

The existing literature on cult films has, however, aimed at anchoring the understanding of the concept by focusing entirely on aesthetic and thematic structures inherent in the films. As a result of this a great deal of the literature consists of collections of film abstracts and film commentaries, although with different analytical points of view (Heinzlmeier, Menningen, and Schulz 1983, Hahn and Jansen 1985, Peary 1981, 1983, 1989).

Austin (1981) is the only author to have made a systematic, quantitative study of a cult audience's behaviour of repetition (*The Rocky Horror Picture Show* audience). Rosenbaum analyses the audience of the same film (Hoberman and Rosenbaum 1983) qualitatively, referring among other things to interviews with famous 'regulars', the ever-present fans.

There seems to be something very paradoxical in these collections of cult films, in the very fact that they are placed in a collection, because 'cult film' is basically a historical conceptualisation of a film. What may be regarded as and inscribed as a cult film at a certain period, in one country, may go completely unnoticed somewhere else or at another time. Only the passing of time makes repetition possible. And repetition places the film as not-new in relation to the spectator.

Critics who do not just collect titles seem to agree that what characterises cult films and the cult event are: firstly the screening hour: late at night, often at weekends;

second low budgets and poor distribution, which place the films outside mainstream circuits. (Paradoxically this excludes a lot of the titles in the collections.) So there seems to be a common agreement in understanding the cult audience as oppositional to mass culture. Third, cult films are regarded as representations of the life of outcasts. This is the reason why there are similarities between what Chute (1983) names Outlaw Cinema and Hoberman and Rosenbaum (1983) Midnight Movies, and cult films. Finally most of the literature mentions the importance of the repetitive and creative audience behaviour when talking about cult films.

Cult films eventually become commercially successful. On the other hand one will also find in the literature of cult movies the assertion that cult films are not part of the industry's middle-of-the-road production. So Hahn and Jansen (1985) stress that cult films are blockbusters, but that not all blockbusters are cult films. Thus the undercurrent of the literature's statements is the conception of cult films as a sort of film art's trash-aesthetics and of the audience as the cinema's *avant garde*, fascinated by other films than the masses and being spectators in quite another way.

My objections to the authors who make cult film collections are, first, that they relate the concept to counterproduction – thus making reference to intellectuals and researchers who will be able to study popular culture and yet conceptualising this culture as 'camp', as Susan Sontag puts it. Second, 'cult film' becomes some sort of reversed sign of quality, signifying difference: an anthology of cult films is an anthology of films that are noteworthy, not for being art-movies, from an aesthetic point of view, but because they have been able to rise above the common denominator's darkness of commercial mainstream, gaining an audience that for this very reason love to watch them over and over again. Thirdly, I take issue with the anthologies' lack of interest in audience reception and patterns of audience behaviour. Analysis of the contextual setting of the film as an event is of the utmost importance in defining a film as a cult film, and conversely, the concept has no significance without reception analysis. And of course, audience behaviour must be the only reason for collecting films like *Blow-Up*, *Casablanca*, and *2001:A Space Odyssey* (Hahn and Jansen 1985) in the same anthology of *Kultfilme*.

In short: as I see it, the anthologies lack a historical and relative conceptualisation of cult films, and they fail to provide essential reflection on culturally determined signifying practices and signifying production.

Cult films and intertextuality

Now, if the literature mentioned above collects cult texts (films and stars) on the grounds of some vague notion of similarities between them as outlaw films – because of themes, production conditions, distribution, and/or audience composition – and if it is a common notion that cult films as cultural events are raised above economic calculations; if, on the one hand, the main argument is that either an audience's attachment to certain thematic positions or a place in a specific textual circuit makes a film a cult film – then, Umberto Eco argues, on the other hand, by using Michael Curtiz's *Casablanca* from 1942 as an example, what makes a film into a cult object comes from certain aesthetic or structural devices and a certain definition of quality.

Consequently, he finds that there are films which are 'born in order to become cult objects' (Eco 1984: 209). Eco's article is interesting because he is taking a precise analytical point of view in relation to this spectator–text interaction, arguing what kind of textual structures invite a cult culture's spectator position. What makes a film into a cult object, he argues, an object so dearly beloved that repetitions constitute the act of viewing, is precisely its deconstructive address:

> In order to transform a work into a cult object one must be able to break, dislocate, unhinge it so that one can remember only parts of it, irrespective of their original relationship with the whole.
>
> (Eco 1984: 198)

Thus *Casablanca* is not fascinating because it invites its audience to identify with the narrative puzzle: will Victor be safe and will Ilse go with him?, nor with the story of love between Ilse and Rick: a story of two persons who were meant for each other, but on whom Fate or world history played another trick. Yet, in a sense these proto-typical schemata are the reason for the film's appeal. *Casablanca* is loved because the archetypical configurations

> indicate a preestablished and frequently reappearing narrative situation, cited or in some way recycled by innumerable other texts and provoking in the addressee a sort of intense emotion accompanied by the vague feeling of a déjà vu that everybody yearns to see again.
>
> (Eco 1984: 200)

In Eco's opinion, it is the large collections of archetypes, narrative traces, scattered into a, generically speaking, quite incoherent narrative that make up for the emotional appeal. And in that sense he endows the cult object with a certain quality mark: 'Two clichés make us laugh but a hundred clichés move us' (Eco 1984: 209). The cult object is structured intertextually, or rather reverberates into the realm of the unconscious, conceptualised as a visual encyclopedia, 'the treasure of the collective imagination', as Eco calls it elsewhere (Eco 1985). But the intertextual traces are not obvious in *Casablanca* as they are in contemporary films. The quotation marks are not underlined, and the loss of coherence is hidden underneath the story.

This visual or 'encyclopedic expertise' is an actual cultural and cognitive fact; and this is why all new cult films relate to this structure of culture and mind:

> What Casablanca does unconsciously, other movies will do with extreme textual awareness, assuming also that the addressee is equally aware of their purposes. These are 'postmodern' movies where the quotation of the topos is recognized as the only way to cope with the burden of our filmic encyclopedic expertise.
>
> (Eco 1984: 209)

A modern cult film is merely one huge collection of quotations, no matter whether, intertextually, it points forwards: *Casablanca* refers to 'Play it again, Sam', or back-wards: 'Play it again, Sam' refers to *Casablanca*. The pleasure of watching the film is activated from the joy of recognition and the knowing expectation of what is to come, made possible by the intertextual references, subtle and yet so directly spoken; and/or the countless feelings of déjà vu, because nothing is spoken that has not been represented in some disguise before. In other words: all texts may be understood as variations, referring intertextually to one another and reverberating inside the spectator.

Taking Eco's point of departure one can easily characterise, for example, David Lynch's *Blue Velvet* as a contemporary cult film. It can be theorised as a 'postmodern movie', in Eco's terminology, in so far as the intertextual and intermedial references are its only mode of representation (its intertextual references are primarily to the œuvre of Alfred Hitchcock; its intermedial references are both to the common knowledge that actress Isabella Rossellini is the beautiful face of the beauty firm Lancôme's advertisements and to media gossip about Dennis Hopper's desperate private life).

Nevertheless, if as a spectator one is not able to catch the more or less evident references to *Rear Window* or *Vertigo*, to the Batman series of the fifties, to Brian de Palma's *Dressed to Kill* and to *The Rocky Horror Picture Show*, one can at least address and be addressed by the archetypical characters of the film: the Good and the Bad, the Child and the Adult, the Law and the Outlaw, and so on. Or one can be addressed by the familiar genres: the suspense and the horror film, and their classical scenarios: the lift, the dark staircase, the multilated body.

Blue Velvet can be labelled postmodern by the fact that it exposes its own quotation marks so clearly. The blue, waving velvet curtain that opens and closes the film – a film quotation itself – underlines the very conscious and calculated construction of the film, stating its meta-textual presence. Finally there is an abundance of punchlines in the film ('That's for me to know and you to find out', 'Bud – King of Beers', 'Touch me! Hit me!', 'I close my eyes, then I drift away' – the Roy Orbison song that the awful Frank's perverted friend Ben mimes). These fragments of texts are framed by sketches, incoherently narrativised, to tell a story of a severed ear and a mysterious woman, Dorothy, the riddle of whom it is the project of the main male protagonist to solve. Perhaps! *Blue Velvet* thus fits very precisely into Eco's theorising about the concept of cult film, as he distils from a number of films their structural similarities: they are at once popular films and meta-films, referring to their own structuration.

But contemporary discussions of the dissolution of classic narrative discourses may imply that Eco's definition of a cult film is suitable for a wide range of films: that, by conceptualising cult film, Eco theorises fiction film in a wider sense as well as structures of a historically specific mode of reception. Here I am talking about a certain intertextual codification of and address to perception and experience. This is necessarily the case with contemporary screenings of *Casablanca*.

Eco himself seems to consider this historicisation by introducing the concept of Cult Culture. After having demonstrated intertextuality in Steven Spielberg's film *E.T.*, he remarks that

> The required expertise is not only intercinematic, it is intermedia, in the sense that the addressee must know not only other movies but all the mass media gossip about movies. This third example presupposes a *'Casablanca universe' in which*

cult has become the normal way of enjoying movies. Thus in this case we witness an instance of metacult, or cult about cult: a Cult Culture.

(Eco 1984: 210, my italics)

This cult cultural discourse, then, which addresses the fiction deconstructively, talkatively, more or less yellingly and more or less theatrically, is not something special. It is not to be understood as a sub-cultural discourse, but signifies a more widespread cultural setting, cutting the film text loose from its attachment to the screen in front of the spectator. For the film is always defined intertextually. And so are perception and reception.

The contemporary audience may thus be conceptualised as an audience of *semiotics by instinct*. And cult culture may be understood as a deconstructive and repetitive discourse, put into action by the possibility of activating intertextual codes, or in other words, references to the visual encyclopedia. In speaking about a meta-semiotic culture, one will necessarily have to address the unconscious in textual metaphors!

Seen through the magnifying glass of history, the low-budget film *The Rocky Horror Picture Show* is a classic example of this cult culture. The spectators' playing with the film – their deconstructive game – is made possible by repetition. The audience destroy the common opposition between temporal presence and temporal distance, and between actor (represcnter) and character (represented), that distinguishes theatre and cinema (see Metz 1982); and they replace the voyeuristic desire that constitutes cinema, so to speak, with a performance where voyeuristic and exhibitionistic pleasure are inseparable. And again, the cult culture is made possible by the fact that *The Rocky Horror Picture Show*, as a cult text, is structured as an intertextual collage. Its narrative oscillates consciously between different genres that are also constantly being interrupted by song and dance acts. It quotes innumerable other Hollywood films, for example *King Kong, Sunset Boulevard, Dr Strangelove,* and *Frankenstein's Bride* (see Rosenbaum, in Hoberman and Rosenbaum 1983). And the cult event itself, the performance in the cinema, consists of an endless chain of signifiers: a famous New York 'regular' plays the actor Tim Curry, who plays Frank-n-Furter. After a few years of screenings another 'regular' played the famous first 'regular', who plays Tim Curry, who plays Frank-n-Furter, and so on. And when Tim Curry announced his presence at a show in one New York cinema, he was, according to Rosenbaum, refused admission with the explanation that he was the third Tim Curry to arrive that day.

Finally, *The Rocky Horror Picture Show* performance appears in other films around 1980: in a sequence in Alan Parker's film *Fame,* two of the characters join a screening of *The Rocky Horror Picture Show* (Parker had Sal Piro, one of the famous 'regulars', as a consultant on the sequence). And thus the chain of signifiers continued as an audience watching *Fame* in a cinema in Florida rose to their feet and performed a *Rocky Horror* dance ('time-warped') that the cult audience in the represented film *Fame* dance in front of the screen together with the fictive characters of *The Rocky Horror Picture Show*!

Reception of media fiction is cult culture

If the concept of cult culture is to be understood more generally as a way of theorising the contemporary reception of media fiction, then cult cultures are constituted not only in the darkness of the cinema, but also in the twilight in front of the TV set, and around the video recorder.

Schrøder (1989) refers to an audience performance in a Los Angeles gay night club that seems very similar to that of an original sub-cultural cult audience. Only here the audience are watching *Dynasty* on a wall of several TV monitors – playfully, as Schrøder puts it, deconstructing the fictional text talkatively in exactly the same way as *The Rocky Horror Picture Show* audience.

Similarly, adolescent cultural practices around the video recorder may lend themselves to description in cult culture terms. Consider the following extract from an interview in 1987 with two adolescent boys (Peter and Michael) about their experiences with video films:

Interviewer: 'Now, could you tell me why it is fun to watch the movies together with your friends?'
Peter: 'Yeah, you know, it's like with Michael, I don't think that his parents would like us to sit and scan forwards and backwards all the time. We scan to see . . . to see the funny parts.'
Michael: 'When you're with your Dad and Mum, right, they laugh y'know. It's not like with your pals, it's like . . . I think it's a lot more fun!'
Peter: 'We were hysterical, weren't we? . . . it was so funny!'
Michael: 'The night before I was laughing for a while with my Mum and Dad. You just laughed at the scene and then it finished and then it wasn't fun anymore. But when I'm with Peter, it was a scream. I was laughing for five minutes. It's like, no matter what happens, we were just screaming away. When Peter starts laughing, I start as well. And when I start laughing, Peter does. And it just goes on and on. No matter what happens we start laughing . . . But then, there were no grown-ups at home!'

There seems to be a lot going on between the two boys and their film and, of course in a less direct way, between the boys and their parents. The interesting thing here is that what structures the two boys' scanning of the tape forwards and backwards with the remote control unit is an instinctive and deconstructive reading, a dissolution of the textual layers of meaning into a kind of bodily rejection of the film's address and positioning of the subject. And equally, part of the deconstructive reading is a rite of repetition as the boys rewind to the same pleasurable segment over and over again. Contrary to the previous examples of cult culture, this small boys' audience does not refer to the fictional text in a dialogic way. Part of their pleasurable reading comes from their very obvious creation of an interpretative community by means of their control over the remote control unit – and thus by means of their changing the script and creating a reading position of their own. Moreover, on a more general level, the difference between cinema and video is that the boys may watch the video film once, but their favourite spots several times. The cinema audience watch both the film and their favourite sequences the same number of times. The boys are decomposing narrative time, whereas the cinema audience – either because they have literally seen the film before or because of the intertextually created impression of déjà vu – decompose narrative space.

Much visual fiction today, films as well as TV serials, on account of their textual construction, carry the possibility of constituting and thus participating in a cult culture. And structurally the contemporary reception mode approaches the cult culture of *The Rocky Horror Picture Show.*

I have already mentioned David Lynch's *Blue Velvet* as an example of an inter-textual collage. His *Wild at Heart* is evidently structured meta-textually in the same way, carrying with it film history in an even more explicit way. The same goes for TV fiction, as Olson (1987) has demonstrated, talking about popular TV fiction as self-reflexive meta-television, 'putting readers in a powerful position and saluting them for their sophistication' (Olson 1987: 284). In other words, the encyclopedic expertise is activated through the meta-televisual address to a skilled TV viewer (Olson uses, among other examples, the highly self-reflexive TV serial *Moonlighting*). On the other hand, this TV viewer often uses these skills for channel switching, thus playing with the very act of television watching – something which is particularly characteristic of youth audiences, who deconstruct any text, not just those which invite a deconstructive reading.

The 1970s cult culture of *The Rocky Horror Picture Show*, which was quickly extended from sub-cultural or minority groups to a wider youth audience, can thus, as a historical phenomenon and discursive practice, be regarded as a culturally as well as a geographically specific and limited media event. It arises locally, outside mainstream culture, but not directly in opposition to it.

Nowadays, I would suggest, it may be meaningful to conceptualise cult film in another manner. In the wider sense outlined above, it broadens the understanding of historically specific structures of media reception in relation to popular films and TV fiction as a whole. Cult culture focuses on the general invalidation of unambiguous codes. Whether (part of) the fiction is watched once or several times; whether it addresses its spectator with immense intertextual awareness, as is the case with *Blue Velvet, Twin Peaks* or *Moonlighting*; or whether, as a genre variation, it inspires the feeling of déjà vu, as with *Casablanca* or *The Big Sleep*, the contemporary audience partake in a semiotic discourse, a 'dialogue' with a present fictional text, placed in a different way from being presently unpresent (Metz 1982). Similarly, the spectators inscribe the characters into this discourse as if they were 'real' persons. And vice versa: the spectators inscribe themselves as actors in a story and a script that they write themselves. The audience play 'reality' as if it were theatre and the film as a reality that they consciously know as being represented.

In a sense the cult event refers to a signifying practice that transgresses – or at least is not similar to – postmodernism's founding concept of the circulating signifiers. On the contrary this audience discourse may be conceptualised as a way of making sense of important basic experiences of our 'optical empire' (Chambers 1986) – i.e. the experience of being a spectator as an everyday experience. In the discourse of cult culture there is a constant testing of and repetition of being (part of an) audience. Regarded as a historically specific phenomenon, cult culture transforms the specta-tors into an audience. If the spectator is inscribed as a subject in relation to classic

Hollywood narratives, one may, by contrast, from the point of view of cult culture, speak of 'the subject' being inscribed as a member of an audience in and through the cult event. The contemporary cult audience are adults and without illusions. They are definitely aware of what they are going to get. The fictional spell and movement of innocent days is replaced by a more or less undisguised direction of repression of excess and boredom.

1.8

'Trashing' the academy: Taste, excess and an emerging politics of cinematic style
by Jeffrey Sconce

Trashing the Academy is the first grounded attempt at theorizing cult cinema, taking into account its sociology, aesthetics, reception, and its political ramifications. A Ph.D.-graduate from the influential film studies programs at the University of Wisconsin, Madison, American scholar Jeffrey Sconce builds on the work of Pierre Bourdieu on taste preferences and their relations to class and (sub)cultures (see section 4). Sconce describes how different kinds of 'anti-establishment' taste cultures are not just the effect of the class position of audiences (low taste for lower classes), but are also, and perhaps even more, directed by attitudes to consciously object to certain hierarchies in taste. It is because of this attitude towards film (one that champions excess and bad taste) that films of the most divergent plumage can be lumped together under one umbrella. Sconce calls that attitude 'paracinema'. It is an aesthetic attitude of the films (and their audience at the same time) that becomes, as a mode of resistance, a political one. As such, paracinema (exemplified by films such as Ed Wood's *Glen or Glenda*, Larry Buchanan's *Curse of the Swamp Creature*, and Dwain Esper's *Maniac*) is a result of alignments against canons, proper tastes, midcults, and any force that aims to channel taste – and in doing so it becomes a counter-taste. The politicization of the attitude lifts Sconce's consideration of cult cinema's receptions beyond that of fandom (which had become in the mid-1990s a dominant framework for considering cult receptions), and gives it a theoretical platform of its own. *Trashing the Academy* is also very timely. Its publication comes right after the first individual considerations of cult cinema from scholars. In addition, it takes the wave(s) of encyclopedic overviews of cult cinema as a point of reference, *and* it makes them subject to the study of cult itself, demonstration how cult cinema's appeal has moved, since the 1980s, well beyond the films only, to become a cult(ure) itself.

A note on extracting: because of its significance for the study of cult, we have decided to reprint *Trashing the Academy Taste, Excess, and an Emerging Politics of Cinematic Style* in its full length. The essay first appeared in 1995, in the British film studies *Screen*, volume 36 (issue 4), pages 371–393. It has since been reprinted a few times, often in extracted form.

Nobody likes movies like *Teenagers from Outer Space* or *Wrestling Women vs. the Aztec Mummy* save any loon sane enough to realize that the whole concept of Good Taste is concocted to keep people from having a good time, from reveling in a crassness that passeth all understanding. . . . But fuck those people who'd rather be watching *The Best Years of Our Lives* or *David and Lisa*. We got our own good tastes . . .

Written five years before Pierre Bourdieu published his monumental study on the social construction of taste, Lester Bangs's diatribe against a nebulously defined group of cultural custodians epitomizes Bourdieu's contention that 'tastes are perhaps first and foremost distastes, disgust provoked by horror or visceral intolerance of the tastes of others'. 'It is no accident', writes Bourdieu, 'that when they have to be justified, they are asserted negatively, by the refusal of other tastes'. Thus, in the spirit of Lester Bangs, the editors of *Zontar*, a Boston-based fanzine devoted primarily to the promotion of 'badfilm', note that their publication 'is *not* for the delicate tastebuds of the pseudo-genteel cultural illiterati who enjoy mind-rotting, soul-endangering pabulum like *Joseph Campbell and the Power of Myth* and the other white-boy 'new-age' puke-shit served up from the bowels of PBS during pledge-week'. Meanwhile, a 1990 issue of *Subhuman*, a fanzine featuring articles on cinematic manifestations of 'necrophilia, 3-D surrealism, animal copulation, pregnant strippers, horror nerdism, and bovine flatulence', labels itself a journal of 'eccentric film and video kulture'.

The stridently confrontational tastes espoused by Bangs, *Zontar* and *Subhuman* over this fifteen-year period describe the gradual emergence of a growing and increasingly articulate cinematic subculture, one organized around what are among the most critically disreputable films in cinematic history. Publications devoted to this 'trash' cinema include such magazines, fanzines and makeshift journals as *Psychotronic Video*, *Zontar*, *Subhuman*, *Trashola*, *Ungawa*, *Pandemonium*, and the RE/Search volume, *Incredibly Strange Films*. The most visible document of this film community is Michael Weldon's *Psychotronic Encyclopedia of Film*, a subterranean companion to Leonard Maltin's *Movies On TV*, which catalogues hundreds of bizarre titles culled from Weldon's late-night television viewing marathons in New York City. Taken together, the diverse body of films celebrated by these various fanzines and books might best be termed 'paracinema'. As a most elastic textual category, paracinema would include entries from such seemingly disparate subgenres as 'badfilm', splatter-punk, 'mondo' films, sword and sandal epics, Elvis flicks, government hygiene films, Japanese monster movies, beach-party musicals, and just about every other historical manifestation of exploitation cinema from juvenile delinquency documentaries to soft-core pornography. Paracinema is thus less a distinct group of films than a particular reading protocol, a counter-aesthetic turned subcultural sensibility devoted to all manner of cultural detritus. In short, the explicit manifesto of paracinematic culture is to valorize all forms of cinematic 'trash', whether such films have been either explicitly rejected or simply ignored by legitimate film culture. In doing so, paracinema represents the most developed and dedicated of cinephilic subcultures ever to worship at 'the temple of schlock'.

The caustic rhetoric of paracinema suggests a pitched battle between a guerrilla band of cult film viewers and an elite cadre of would-be cinematic tastemakers. Certainly, the paracinematic audience likes to see itself as a disruptive force in the cultural and intellectual marketplace. As a short subject, this audience would be more inclined to watch a bootlegged McDonald's training film than *Man with a Movie Camera*, although, significantly, many in the paracinematic community would no doubt be familiar with this more respectable member of the avant-garde canon. Such calculated negation and refusal of 'elite' culture suggests that the politics of social stratification and taste in paracinema is more complex than a simple high-brow/low-brow split, and that the cultural politics of 'trash culture' are becoming ever more ambiguous as this 'aesthetic' grows in influence. In recent years, the paracinematic community has seen both the institutionalization and commercialization of their once renegade, neo-camp aesthetic. Although paracinematic taste may have its roots in the world of 'low-brow' fan culture (fanzines, film conventions, memorabilia collections, and so on), the paracinematic sensibility has recently begun to infiltrate the avant garde, the academy, and even the mass culture on which paracinema's ironic reading strategies originally preyed. Art museums that once programmed only Italian Neo-Realism or German Neo-Expressionism now feature retrospectives of 1960s Biker films and career overviews of exploitation auteurs such as Herschell Gordon Lewis and Doris Wishman. No doubt to the dismay and befuddlement of cultural hygienists like Allan Bloom and James Twitchell, academic courses in film studies increasingly investigate 'sleazy' genres such as horror and pornography. Recently, the trash aesthetic has even made inroads into mainstream popular taste. The ironic reading strategies honed by the badfilm community through countless hours of derisive interaction with late-night science fiction are now prepackaged for cable in programmes such as *Mystery Science Theatre 3000*. Similarly, Turner Network Television now presents a weekly sampling of the paracinematic pantheon in Friday night, '100% Weird' triple features. Even Blockbuster video, America's corporate bastion of cinematic conservatism, features a 'le bad' section in many of their stores, where patrons can find the work of John Waters, William Castle and other 'disreputable' filmmakers. Perhaps most incredibly, *Batman's* director Tim Burton recently directed a multi-million dollar biopic of Ed Wood Jr, the director of such paracinematic classics as *Plan 9 From Outer Space* (1959) and *Glen or Glenda* (1953), an artist who himself never spent over a few thousand dollars on any one picture. Clearly, in cinematic circles of all kinds, there has been a significant realignment on the social terrain of taste, a powerful response to what has been termed 'the siren song of crap'.

At first glance, the paracinematic sensibility, in all its current manifestations, would seem to be identical to the 'camp' aesthetic outlined by Susan Sontag some thirty years ago. Without a doubt, both sensibilities are highly ironic, infatuated with the artifice and excess of obsolescent cinema. What makes paracinema unique, however, is its aspiration to the status of a 'counter-cinema'. Whereas 'camp' was primarily a reading strategy that allowed gay men to rework the Hollywood cinema through a new and more expressive subcultural code, paracinematic culture seeks to promote an alternative vision of cinematic 'art', aggressively attacking the established canon of 'quality' cinema and questioning the legitimacy of reigning aesthete discourses on movie art. Camp was an aesthetic of ironic colonization and cohabitation. Paracinema, on the other hand, is an aesthetic of vocal confrontation.

Who, exactly, is the paracinematic audience at war with, and what is at stake in such a battle? Consider the following diatribe from *Zontar*:

Where the philosophical pygmies search the snob-ridden art galleries, flock to the false comfort of PBS-produced pseudo-gentility, WE look elsewhere. We seek the explanations for the decline of Hu-Manity in the most debased and misunderstood manifestations of the IDIOT CULTURE. Monster movies, comic books, cheap porn videos, TV preachers, of course!!! But we search ever deeper into the abyss. The Home Shopping Network. Late-Night Cable TV-Product Worship-Testimonial Shows. Tiffany Videos. We leave purity to those other assholes. The search for BADTRUTH is only for the brave few, like you, whose all-consuming HATE is powerful enough to resist the temptations of REFINEMENT, TASTE, and ESCAPISM—the miserable crumbs tossed from the table by the growing mass of REPUBLICAN THIRTYSOMETHING COUNTRY-CLUB CHRISTIAN ZOMBIES who now rule this wretched planet.

The paracinematic audience promotes their tastes and textual proclivities in opposition to a loosely defined group of cultural and economic elites, those purveyors of the status quo who not only rule the world, but who are also responsible for making the contemporary cinema, in the paracinematic mind, so completely boring. Nor does the paracinematic community care much for the activities of film scholars and critics. For example, an editor of *Zontar's Ejecto-Pod*, a sister publication of *Zontar*, encourages readers to hone their knowledge of trash-culture classics ridiculed by the academy (in this case the sword and sandal epic, *The Silver Chalice* [Victor Saville, 1954]), thereby 'amazing your friends and embarrassing the jargon-slinging empty-headed official avatars of critical discourse'.

At times, factions of the paracinematic audience have little patience even for one another. This rift is perhaps most pointedly embodied by the competing agendas of *Film Threat* and *Psychotronic Video*, two fanzines turned magazines with international circulations that promote rival visions of the 'trash' aesthetic. While *Psychotronic* concentrates on the sizable segment of this community interested in uncovering and collecting long lost titles from the history of exploitation, *Film Threat* looks to transgressive aesthetics/genres of the past as avant-garde inspiration for contemporary independent filmmaking, championing such 'underground' auteurs as Nick Zedd and Richard Kern. In a particularly nasty swipe, a subscription form for *Film Threat* features a drawing of the 'typical' *Film Threat* reader, portrayed as a dynamic, rockabilly-quiffed hipster surrounded by admiring women. This is juxtaposed with a drawing of the 'typical' *Psychotronic* reader, depicted as passive, overweight and asexual, with a bad complexion.

Despite such efforts at generating counter-distinction within the shared cultural project of attacking 'high-brow' cinema, the discourses characteristically employed by paracinematic culture in its valorization of 'low-brow' artefacts indicate that this audience, like the film elite (academics, aesthetes, critics), is particularly rich with 'cultural capital' and thus possesses a level of textual/critical sophistication similar to the cineastes they construct as their nemesis. In terms of education and social position, in other words, the various factions of the paracinematic audience and the elite cineastes they commonly attack would appear to share what Bourdieu terms a 'cultural pedigree'. Employing the terminology of US sociologist Herbert Gans, these groups might be thought of as radically opposed 'taste publics' that are nevertheless involved in a common 'taste culture'. As Gans writes: 'Taste cultures are not cohesive value systems, and taste publics are not organized groups; the former are aggregates of similar values and usually but not always similar content, and the latter are aggregates of people with usually but not always similar values making similar choices from available offerings of culture'.

Whether thought of as a subculture, an aesthetic or a sensibility, the recent flourishing of paracinema represents not just a challenge to aesthete taste, but the larger fragmentation of a common taste culture, brought about by various disaffected segments of middle-class youth. Although it would be difficult to define the precise dimensions or identify the exact constituency of this particular taste public, I would argue that the paracinematic community, like the academy and the popular press, embodies primarily a male, white, middle-class, and 'educated' perspective on the cinema. Representations of this 'community' are rare, but can be glimpsed, among other places, at the fringes of Richard Linklater's ode to baby-buster anomie, *Slacker* (1991). Linklater documents the desultory activities of bored students, would-be bohemians and miscellaneous cranks, all of whom exist at the economic and cultural periphery of a typical college town. In a more reflexive turn, a fanzine from San Francisco describes the world of 'low-life scum', disheveled men in their twenties manifesting 'a fascination with all things sleazy, bizarre, and macabre'. Paracinematic interests also often intersect with the more familiar subcultures of science-fiction fandom. Regardless of their individual interests and ultimate allegiances, however, the paracinematic audience cultivates an overall aesthetic of calculated disaffection, marking a deviant taste public disengaged from the cultural hierarchies of their overarching taste culture.

Such acrimonious battles within a single taste culture are not uncommon. As Bourdieu writes: 'Explicit aesthetic choices are in fact often constituted in opposition to the choices of the groups closest in social space, with whom the competition is most direct and most immediate, and more precisely, no doubt, in relation to those choices most clearly marked by the intention (perceived as pretension) of marking distinction vis-a-vis lower groups'. As the alienated faction of a social group high in cultural capital, the paracinematic audience generates distinction within its own social space by celebrating the cultural objects deemed most noxious (low-brow) by their taste culture as a whole. Paracinema thus presents a direct challenge to the values of aesthete film culture and a general affront to the 'refined' sensibility of the parent taste culture. It is a calculated strategy of shock and confrontation against fellow cultural elites, not unlike Duchamp's notorious unveiling of a urinal in an art gallery. As Bourdieu states: 'The most intolerable thing for those who regard themselves as the possessors of legitimate culture is the sacrilegious reuniting of tastes which taste dictates shall be separated'. By championing films like *2000 Maniacs* (Herschell Gordon Lewis, 1964), *Bad Girls Go to Hell* (Doris Wishman, 1965), and *The Incredibly Strange Creatures Who Stopped Living and Became Mixed-Up Zombies* (Ray Dennis Steckler, 1963), and by associating themselves with home shopping networks, pornography and TV preachers, this community is, in effect, renouncing its 'cultural pedigree' and attempting to distance itself from what it perceives as elite (and elitist) taste.

Despite the paracinematic community's open hostility to the 'jargon-slinging avatars of critical discourse', many scholars see this trend towards the valorization of 'trash' at work in the academy itself, especially in the realm of media studies. In ' "High culture" revisited', for example, Jostein Gripsrud argues that a major segment of contemporary media scholars routinely attacks all forms of high culture while indiscriminately valorizing mass culture in its place. As Gripsrud states somewhat sarcastically, 'Presenting oneself as a soap-fan in scholarly circles could be considered daring or provocative some ten years ago. Nowadays it is more of a prerequisite for legitimate entry into the academic discourse on soaps in some Anglo-American fora.' Gripsrud speculates that this proclivity among many contemporary scholars to condemn high culture and valorize mass culture is a function of their unique trajectory in social space. 'Such upwardly mobile subjects are placed in a sort of cultural limbo, not properly integrated in the lower-class culture they left, nor in the upper-class high culture they have formally entered. Since they are newcomers, they are faced with a need to make choices concerning what to do in and with their acquired position.' Gripsrud believes that the valorization of mass culture serves as a form of 'symbolic homecoming' that allows such scholars to 'strive for or pretend re-integration into the classes they once left, preferably as "leaders" in some sense, "voices" for the people'.

Gripsrud's depiction of the intellectual in limbo is a particularly apt description of the contemporary graduate student, the figure within the institution of the academy who is perched the most precariously between the domains of cultural, educational and economic capital. Not surprisingly, paracinematic culture is a particularly active site of investment for many contemporary graduate students in film studies. Often, the connections between graduate film study and paracinematic culture are quite explicit, since many students now pursuing an advanced degree in film began as fans of exploitation genres such as horror and science fiction. Some students retain their interest in trash culture as a secret, guilty pleasure. Others, however, increasingly seek to focus their work on these previously marginalized and debased forms of cinema. Influenced by the importation of cultural studies to the USA during the 1980s, and writing in the wake of film scholars who were increasingly willing to address tradition-ally 'untouchable' cinematic genres such as horror and pornography, many students in media studies wish to continue pushing the limits of the traditional cinematic canon and the constraints of conventional academic enterprise. At stake is a sense of both institutional and cultural distinction. As John Fiske writes, 'Many young fans are successful at school and are steadily accumulating official cultural capital, but wish to differentiate themselves, along the axis of age at least, from the social values and cultural tastes (or habitus) of those who currently possess the cultural and economic capital they are still working to acquire'. As paracinematic texts and concerns increasingly infiltrate film studies, however, many graduate students find themselves caught between the institutional discourses (and agendas) of the film elite as repre-sented by the academy, and the 'fan' activities of the paracinematic community with which they feel a previous affinity. Raised in mass culture, such students are not always willing to give up the excesses of the drive-in for the discipline of Dreyer. The question is what to do with such textual experience and expertise.

Debate within the academy over the politics of the canon is not new. Nor is it unusual for 'fan' cultures to make themselves heard within the academy (most film scholars, one would assume, study the cinema because they were fans first). What is unusual in paracinematic culture's gradual infiltration of the academy is the manner in which this group so explicitly foregrounds the cultural politics of taste and aesthetics, not just in society at large, but within the academy itself. Graduate students with an interest in 'trash' cinema often find themselves in the ironic position of challenging the legitimacy of the very institution they are attending in order to obtain cultural validation and authority over issues of politics and taste. Such students are struggling to make the transition from a mere fan to an accredited scholar. Though both fan and scholar may be equally dedicated (and even knowledgeable) in their involvement with a particular cultural form, they differ tremendously in terms of their respective status within society as a whole. In a hierarchical social system marked by the differential circulation of cultural and economic capital, graduate students seeking to make this crucial transition of accreditation must submit themselves, quite literally, to the *discipline* of film studies in both its institutional and punitive forms. In doing so, the discipline works to shape both knowledge and taste, linking them in a process that is every bit as political in the academy as it is in the culture the academy seeks to study. As Bourdieu notes, 'At stake in every struggle over art there is also the imposition of an art of living, that is, the transmutation of an arbitrary way of living into the legitimate way of life which casts every other way of living into arbitrariness'. In this way, the legitimizing function of the academy in issues of knowledge, taste and aesthetics works to conceal relations of power and control, both within the institution itself and the society that sanctions that institution's cultural authority.

By challenging this disciplinary authority, the paracinematic audience, both academic and non-academic, epitomizes what Bourdieu terms the 'new style autodidact'. As described by Bourdieu, the autodidact is a figure alienated from the legitimate mode of educational and cultural acquisition. Estranged or excluded from legitimate modes of acquisition, autodidacts invest in alternative forms of cultural capital, those not fully recognized by the educational system and the cultural elite. Bourdieu describes two backgrounds typical of this new style autodidact:

> 'middle-ground' arts such as cinema, jazz, and, even more, strip cartoons, science-fiction or detective stories are predisposed to attract the investments either of those who have entirely succeeded in converting their cultural capital into educational capital or those who, not having acquired legitimate culture in the legitimate manner (i.e., through early familiarization), maintain an uneasy relationship with it, subjectively or objectively, or both. These arts, not yet fully legitimate, which are disdained or neglected by the big holders of educational capital, offer a refuge or a revenge to those who, by appropriating them, secure the best return on their cultural capital (especially if it is not fully recognized scholastically) while at the same time taking credit for contesting the established hierarchy of legitimacies and profits.

The autodidact is a person who invests in unsanctioned culture either because he or she can 'afford' to, having already made a successful conversion of legitimate cultural and educational capital into economic capital, or who feel, because of their tentative and at times alienated relationship with 'legitimate culture', that such disreputable investments are more durable and potentially more 'rewarding'.

It should not be surprising, then, that paracinematic fans, as exiles from the legitimizing functions of the academy, and many graduate students, as the most disempowered faction within the academy itself, both look to trash culture as a site of 'refuge and revenge'. Such autodidacticism constitutes, for Bourdieu, a form of 'counterculture', one working to free itself from 'the constraints of the scholastic market'. 'They strive to do so by producing another market with its own consecrating agencies', writes Bourdieu, 'capable of challenging the pretension of the educational system to impose the principles of evaluation of competencies and manners which reign in the scholastic market.' For its audience, paracinema represents a final textual frontier that exists beyond the colonizing powers of the academy, and thus serves as a staging ground for strategic raids on legitimate culture and its institutions by those (temporarily) lower in educational, cultural and/or economic capital. Such a struggle demonstrates that battles over the canon, in any discipline, are as much conflicts over the processes and politics by which an entire academic field validates its very existence and charts its own future, fought by groups within the academy as stratified in their institutional power as society at large is stratified in terms of cultural and economic power.

On one hand, it would be easy to explain the turn towards trash cinema as yet another example of the generational politics of the canon in the academy, a struggle that legitimated cinema in the face of literature, Hollywood in the face of art cinema and, most recently, television in the face of Hollywood. But there is more here than a struggle over the canon and the politics of object choice. The study of trash cinema suggests a struggle over the task of cinema scholarship as a whole, especially in terms of defining the relationship between aesthetics and cultural criticism. Whether attacking traditional cultural markets and intellectual institutions as a fan, or attempting to bridge the two worlds as a student, the paracinematic audience presents in its often explicit opposition to the agendas of the academy a dispute over *how* to approach the cinema as much as a conflict over *what* cinema to approach. At issue is not only which films get to be studied, but which questions are to be asked about the cinema in the first place. What I am interested in exploring in the remainder of this essay is the relationship between paracinematic culture and the aesthete culture this group associates with the academy, as well as the place of the contemporary graduate film student in bridging these two often antagonistic sensibilities. How are these groups similar, how do they differ and, perhaps most importantly, how might the trash aesthetic ultimately impact the academy? I am particularly interested in how the two communities approach issues of cinematic 'style' and 'excess'. I will argue that paracinema hinges on an aesthetic of excess, and that this paracinematic interest in excess represents an explicitly political challenge to reigning aesthete discourses in the academy. The cultural politics involved in this struggle, however, can be clarified by first examining similarities between aesthete and paracinematic discourses on cinema.

Counter-cinemas

Throughout the history of cinema studies as a discipline, the cultivation of various counter-cinemas, exclusive cinematic canons that do not easily admit the textual pleasures of more 'commonplace' audiences, has been a crucial strategy in maintaining a sense of cultural distinction for film scholars. Frequently, the promotion of such counter-cinemas has been organized around what has become a dominant theme in academic film culture: namely, the sense of loss over the medium's unrealized artistic and political potential. From this perspective, the cinema once held the promise of a revolutionary popular art form when, as Annette Michelson writes, 'a certain euphoria enveloped . . . early filmmaking and theory'. '[T]here was', she continues, 'a very real sense in which the revolutionary aspirations of the modernist movement in literature and arts, on the one hand, and of a Marxist or Utopian tradition, on the other hand, could converge in the hopes and promises, as yet undefined, of the new medium'. Instead, these hopes were dashed by the domination of the public taste and mind by Hollywood cinema. And while there has never been a shortage of critical interest in the classical Hollywood cinema, championing counter-cinemas that break with the conventions of Hollywood production and representation remains a central project of film aesthetes and academics. This critical programme proceeds both artistically, by valorizing a body of 'art' films over the mainstream, commercial cinema, and politically, by celebrating those filmmakers who seem to disrupt the conventional narrative machinery of Hollywood.

In cultivating a counter-cinema from the dregs of exploitation films, paracinematic fans, like the academy, explicitly situate themselves in opposition to Hollywood cinema and the mainstream US culture it represents. United with the film elite in their dislike of Hollywood banality and yet frequently excluded from the circles of academic film culture, the paracinematic community nonetheless often adopts the conventions of 'legitimate' cinematic discourse in discussing its own cinema. As Fiske notes, fan groups are often 'aware that their object of fandom [is] devalued by the criteria of official culture and [go] to great pains to argue against this misevaluation. They frequently [use] official cultural criteria such as "complexity" or "subtlety" to argue that their preferred texts [are] as "good" as the canonized ones and constantly [evoke] legitimate culture . . . as points of comparison.' Elite discourse often appears either earnestly or parodically in discussions of paracinematic films. A fanzine review of the obscure 1964 film, *The Dungeons of Harrow*, is typical. The fanzine describes the film as 'a twisted surreal marvel, a triumph of spirit and vision over technical incompetence and abysmal production values. The film can be seen as a form of art brut—crude, naive, pathetic—but lacking the poetry and humour often associated with this style. Perhaps art brutarian would better serve to describe this almost indescribable work.

As in the academic film community, the paracinematic audience recognizes Hollywood as an economic and artistic institution that represents not just a body of films, but a particular mode of film production and its accompanying signifying practices. Furthermore, the narrative form produced by this institution is seen as somehow 'manipulative' and 'repressive', and linked to dominant interests as a form of cultural coercion. In their introduction to *Incredibly Strange Films*, V. Vale and Andrea Juno, two of the most visible cultural brokers in the realm of paracinema, describe why low-budget films helmed by idiosyncratic visionaries are so often superior to mainstream, Hollywood cinema.

> The value of low-budget films is: they can be transcendent expressions of a single person's individual vision and quirky originality. When a corporation decides to invest $20 million in a film, a chain of command regulates each step, and no one person is allowed free rein. Meetings with lawyers, accountants, and corporate boards are what films in Hollywood are all about. . . . Often [low-budget] films are eccentric—even extreme—presentations by individuals freely expressing their imaginations, who throughout the filmmaking process improvise creative solutions to problems posed by either circumstance or budget—mostly the latter. Secondly, they often present unpopular—even radical—views addressing social, political, racial or sexual inequities, hypocrisy in religion or government; or, in other ways they assault taboos related to the presentation of sexuality, violence, and other mores.

Such rhetoric could just as easily be at home in an elite discussion of the French New Wave or the American New Cinema. Products of a shared taste culture, paracinematic cinephiles, like the scholars and critics of the academy, continue to search for unrecognized talent and long forgotten masterpieces, producing a pantheon that celebrates a certain stylistic unity and/or validates the diverse artistic visions of unheralded 'auteurs'.

Zontar, for example, devotes almost all of its attention to the work of Larry Buchanan, who is celebrated as 'the greatest director of all time' and as a maker of films that must be regarded as 'absolute and unquestionable holy writ'. Elsewhere, *Zontar* hails Buchanan as 'a prophet of transcendental banality . . . who eclipses Bergman in evoking a sense of alienation, despair and existential angst'. As this rather tongue-in-cheek hyperbole suggests, paracinematic culture, like that of the academy, continues to generate its own forms of internal distinction by continually redefining its vanguard, thereby thwarting unsophisticated dilettantes and moving its audience as a whole on to increasingly demanding and exclusive paracinematic films. In its contemporary and most sophisticated form, paracinema is an aggressive, esoteric and often painfully ascetic counter-aesthetic, one that produces, in its most extreme manifestations, an ironic form of reverse elitism. 'The fine art of great bad-film is not a laughing matter to everybody', says one fan. 'Its adherents are small in number, but fanatical in pickiness. Badness appreciation is the most acquired taste, the most refined.'[31]

Invoking Larry Buchanan, the mastermind of films like *Mars Needs Women* (1966) and *Zontar the Thing from Venus* (1966), as a greater director than Ingmar Bergman, however, reaffirms that the paracinematic community defines itself in opposition not only to mainstream Hollywood cinema, but to the (perceived) counter-cinema of aesthetes and the cinematic academy. Again, as with any taste public, this elite cadre of 'aesthetes' cannot be definitively located in a particular author, methodology, or school of academic/journalistic criticism. Paracinematic vitriol also often ignores the fact that low-budget exploitation films have increasingly become legitimized as a field of study within the academy. For purposes of distinction, however, all that is required is a nebulous body of those who do not actively advance a paracinematic aesthetic. As Vale and Juno state broadly in their introduction to *Incredibly Strange Films*:

> This is a functional guide to territory largely neglected by the film-criticism establishment. . . . Most of the films discussed test the limits of contemporary (middle-class) cultural acceptability, mainly because in varying ways they don't meet certain 'standards' utilized in evaluating direction, acting, dialogue, sets, continuity, technical cinematography, etc. Many of the films are overtly 'lower-class' or 'low-brow' in content and art direction.

Vale and Juno go on to celebrate this cinema for its vitality and then identify what is at stake in this battle over the status of these films within the critical community. In a passage reminiscent of Bangs and Bourdieu, they state, 'At issue is the notion of "good taste", which functions as a filter to block out entire areas of experience judged—and damned—as unworthy of investigation'.

Style and excess

Graduate students entering the academy with an interest in trash cinema often wish to question why these 'areas of experience' have been 'judged and damned' by earlier scholars. But though they may attempt to disguise or renounce their cultural pedigree by aggrandizing such scandalous cultural artefacts, their heritage in a 'higher' taste public necessarily informs their textual and critical engagement of even the most abject 'low culture' forms. Gripsrud argues that 'egalitarian' attempts on the part of the culturally privileged to collapse differences between 'high' and 'low' culture, as noble as they might be, often ignore issues of 'access' to these two cultural realms. As Gripsrud writes, 'Some people have access to both high and low culture, but the majority has only access to the low one'. Gripsrud describes high culture audiences that also consume popular cultural artefacts as having 'double access', and notes that this ability to participate in both cultural realms is not randomly distributed through society. As Gripsrud observes, 'The double access to the codes and practices of both high and low culture is a *class privilege*'.

The phenomenon of double access raises a number of interesting political issues concerning the trash aesthetic. For example, when Vale and Juno write that these films address 'unpopular—even radical—views' and 'assault taboos related to the presentation of sexuality [and] violence', this does not mean that paracinema is a uniformly 'progressive' body of cinema. In fact, in subgenres ranging from the often rabidly xenophobic travelogues of the 'mondo' documentaries to the library of 1950s sex-loop star Betty Page, many paracinematic texts would run foul of academic film culture's political orthodoxy. But, of course, this is precisely why such films are so vociferously championed by certain segments of the paracinematic audience, which then attempts to 'redeem' the often suspect pleasures of these films through appeals to ironic detachment. Double access, then, foregrounds one of the central riddles of postmodern textuality: is the 'ironic' reading of a 'reactionary' text necessarily a 'progressive' act?

As pivotal as double access is in considering conventional debates over representational politics, the influence of high cultural capital is equally foregrounded in how the academy, the paracinematic audience, and the students who claim membership in both realms attend to the question of cinematic style. Of course, the ability to attend critically to a concept such as style, whether it manifests itself in Eisenstein or a Godzilla movie, is a class privilege, requiring a certain textual sophistication in issues of technique, form and structure. Though paracinematic viewers may explicitly reject the pretensions of high-brow cinema, their often sophisticated rhetoric on the issue of style can transform low-brow cinema into an object every bit as obtuse and inaccessible to the mainstream viewer as some of the most demanding works of the conventional avant garde. Both within the academy and the paracinematic community, viewers address the complex relationship between cinematic 'form' and 'content', often addressing style for style's sake. This is not to say, however, that the paracinematic community simply approaches trash cinema in the same terms that aesthetes and academics engage art cinema. There is, I would argue, a major political distinction between aesthete and paracinemaic discourses on cinematic style, a distinction that is crucial to the paracinematic project of championing a counter-cinema of trash over that of the academy. In other words, though the paracinematic community may share with academic aesthetes an interest in counter-cinema as technical execution, their respective agendas and approaches in attending to questions of style and technique vary tremendously.

For example, film aesthetes, both in the academy and in the popular press, frequently discuss counter-cinematic style as a strategic intervention. In this scenario, the film artist self-consciously employs stylistic innovations to differentiate his or her (usually his) films from the cultural mainstream. James Monaco's discussion of the French New Wave is typical in this regard. 'It is this fascination with the forms and structures of the film medium . . . that sets their films apart from those that preceded them and marks a turning point in film history'. Similarly, according to David Bordwell's concept of parametric narration, a filmmaker may systematically manipulate a certain stylistic parameter independent of the demands of the plot. Such films are rare and are typically produced by figures associated with 'art cinema' (Bordwell identifies Ozu, Bresson and Godard as among those having produced parametric films). The emphasis here is on applied manipulation of style as a form of systematic artistic experimentation and technical virtuosity. 'In parametric narration, style is organized across the film according to distinct principles, just as a narrative poem exhibits prosodic patterning or an operatic scene fulfils a musical logic.

Paracinematic films such as *The Corpse Grinders* (Ted V. Mikels, 1972) and *She Devils on Wheels* (Herschell Gordon Lewis, 1968) rarely exhibit such pronounced stylistic virtuosity as the result of a 'conscious' artistic agenda. But this is not to say that issues of style and authorship are unimportant to the paracinematic community. However, rather than explore the systematic application of style as the elite techniques of a cinematic artist, paracinematic culture celebrates the systematic 'failure' or 'distortion' of conventional cinematic style by 'auteurs' who are valued more as 'eccentrics' than as artists, who work within the impoverished and clandestine production conditions typical of exploitation cinema. These films deviate from Hollywood classicism not necessarily by artistic intentionality, but by the effects of material poverty and technical ineptitude. As director Frank Henenlotter (of the *Basket Case* series) comments, 'Often, through bad direction, misdirection, inept direction, a film starts assuming surrealistic overtones, taking a dreadfully cliched story into new frontiers— you're sitting there shaking your head, totally excited, totally unable to guess where this is going to head next, or what the next loony line out of somebody's mouth is going to be. Just as long as it isn't stuff you regularly see.' Importantly, para-cinematic films are not ridiculed for this deviation but are instead celebrated as unique, courageous and ultimately subversive cinematic experiences. For this audi-ence, paracinema thus constitutes a true counter-cinema in as much as 'it isn't stuff you regularly see', both in terms of form and content. Henenlotter continues, 'I'll never be satisfied until I see every sleazy film ever made—as long as it's different, as long as it's breaking a taboo (whether deliberately or by misdirection). There's a thousand reasons to like these films.'

While the academy prizes conscious transgression of conventions by a filmmaker looking to critique the medium aesthetically and/or politically, paracinematic viewers value a stylistic and thematic deviance born, more often than not, from the systematic failure of a film aspiring to *obey* dominant codes of cinematic representation. For this audience, the 'bad' is as aesthetically defamiliarizing and politically invigorating as the 'brilliant'. A manifesto on acting from *Zontar* further illustrates the aesthetic appeal of such stylistic deviation among this audience:

> Transparent play-acting; mumbling incompetence; passionate scenery-chewing; frigid woodenness; barely disguised drunkenness or contempt for the script;— these are the secrets of Zontarian acting at its best. Rondo Hatton's exploited acromegalic condition; Acquanetta's immobile dialogue readings; the drunken John Agar frozen to his chair in *Curse of the Swamp Creature*;—these great performances loom massively as the ultimate classics of ZONTARISM. These are not so much performances as revelations of Human truth. We are not 'entertained,' we rather sympathize with our suffering soul-mates on screen. These performances are not escapist fantasy, but a heavy injection of BADTRUTH.

The Zontarian moment of the 'badtruth' is not unlike the Surrealist notion of the 'marvellous' (and indeed, the Surrealists were perhaps the first cinephiles with an interest in bad cinema). As with the marvellous, the badtruth, as a nodal point of paracinematic style, provides a defamiliarized view of the world by merging the tran-scendentally weird and the catastrophically awful. Thus, rather than witness the Surrealists' vision of the exquisite chance meetings of umbrellas and sewing machines on a dissecting table, the paracinematic viewer thrills instead to such equally fantastic fabrications as women forced to duel in a syringe fight in the basement of a schizo-phrenic vaudevillian who has only moments earlier eaten his cat's left eyeball (*Maniac!* [Dwain Esper, 1934]), Colonial era witches and warlocks crushed to death by men in Levis corduroys who hurl bouncing Styrofoam boulders (*Blood-Orgy of the She-Devils* [Ted V. Mikels, 1973]), a down and out Bela Lugosi training a mutant bat to attack people wearing a certain type of shaving lotion (*The Devil Bat* [Jean Yarborough, 1941]), and leaping, pulsating brains that use their prehensile spinal cords to strangle unwary soldiers and citizens on a Canadian rocket base (*Fiend Without a Face* [Arthur Crabtree, 1958]).

Paracinematic taste involves a reading strategy that renders the bad into the sublime, the deviant into the defamiliarized, and in so doing, calls attention to the aesthetic aberrance and stylistic variety evident but routinely dismissed in the many subgenres of trash cinema. By concentrating on a film's formal bizarreness and stylistic eccentricity, the paracinematic audience, much like the viewer attuned to the innovations of Godard or capable of attending to the patterns of parametric narration described by Bordwell, foregrounds structures of cinematic discourse and artifice so that the material identity of the film ceases to be a structure made invisible in service of the diegesis, but becomes instead the primary focus of textual attention. It is in this respect that the paracinematic aesthetic is closely linked to the concept of 'excess'.

Kristin Thompson describes excess as a value that exists beyond a cinematic signifier's 'motivated' use, or, as 'those aspects of the work which are not contained by its unifying forces.' 'At the point where motivation ends', Thompson writes, 'excess begins'. '[T]he minute the viewer begins to notice style for its own sake or watch works which do not provide such thorough motivation, excess comes forward and must affect narrative meaning. . . . Excess does not equal style, but the two are closely linked because they both involve the material aspects of the film.' Thompson writes of excess as an intermittent textual phenomenon, a brief moment of self-conscious materiality that interrupts an otherwise conventional, 'non-excessive' film: 'Probably no one ever watches only these non-diegetic aspects of the image through an entire film.' But, Thompson writes further, these non-diegetic aspects are nevertheless always present, 'a whole "film" existing in some sense alongside the narrative film we tend to think of ourselves as watching'.

I would argue that the paracinematic audience is perhaps the one group of viewers that *does* concentrate exclusively on these 'non-diegetic aspects of the image' during the entire film, or at least attempts to do so. Like their counterparts in the academy, trash cinema fans, as active cinephiles practising an aesthetic founded on the recognition and subsequent rejection of Hollywood style, are extremely conscious of the cinema's characteristic narrative forms and stylistic strategies. But, importantly, while cinematic aesthetes attend to style and excess as moments of artistic bravado in relation to the creation of an overall diegesis, paracinematic viewers instead use excess as a gateway to exploring profilmic and extratextual aspects of the filmic object itself. In other words, by concentrating so intently on 'non-diegetic' elements in these films, be they unconvincing special effects, blatant anachronisms, or histrionic acting, the paracinematic reading attempts to activate the 'whole "film" existing . . . alongside the narrative film we tend to think of ourselves as watching'. One could say that while academic attention to excess often foregrounds aesthetic strategies within the text as a closed formal system, paracinematic attention to excess, an excess that often manifests itself in a film's failure to conform to historically delimited codes of verisimilitude, calls attention to the text as a cultural and sociological document and thus dissolves the boundaries of the diegesis into profilmic and extratextual realms. It is here that the paracinematic audience most dramatically parts company with the aesthetes of academia. Whereas aesthete interest in style and excess always returns the viewer to the frame, paracinematic attention to excess seeks to push the viewer beyond the formal boundaries of the text.

Paracinematic excess: Ed Wood, Jr and Larry Buchanan

Ed Wood, Jr's status has long been high in the paracinematic community. Wood was an independent filmmaker in Hollywood during the 1950s, known primarily for his work with Bela Lugosi. His films are remarkably incompetent from a conventional perspective. Wood's dialogue was often awful, his actors alternately wooden and histrionic, and his sets pathetic and threadbare. Throughout his long career as a filmmaker, Wood was unable (or unwilling) to master the basics of continuity, screen direction or the construction of cinematic space. His *Plan 9 From Outer Space* is perhaps the most famous 'badfilm' of all, having become badfilm's equivalent of *Citizen Kane* as an inventory of characteristically paracinematic stylistic devices. Though Wood's films were initially read as camp, the critical discourse within paracinematic literature surrounding Wood has since shifted from bemused derision to active celebration. No longer regarded as a hack, Wood is now seen, like Godard, as a unique talent improvising outside the constrictive environment of traditional Hollywood production and representation. As one fanzine comments, 'Wood's films are now appreciated less as models of incompetence, and more as the products of a uniquely personal and obsessive sensibility that best expresses itself through madly deconstructed narratives enacted by a gallery of grotesque castoffs from the fringes of Hollywood bohemia'. This is certainly the perspective that dominates Tim Burton's cinematic treatment of Wood's career, *Ed Wood* (1994).

Wood's most notorious film and the movie that is central to his status as a paracinematic filmmaker is *Glen or Glenda*. As detailed extensively in Burton's biopic, Wood shot *Glen or Glenda* in 1953 to capitalize on the public hysteria surrounding the Christine Jorgenson sex-change operation. Also released under the titles *I Led Two Lives* and *I Changed My Sex*, the film purports to be an investigative examination of the sex-change issue. Instead, the film is an odd plea for public tolerance of transvestitism. The film's protagonist is a young man named Glen, a transvestite struggling with the decision of whether or not to tell his fiancee of his secret before their marriage. From this central conflict, Wood fashions a vertiginous film that in a bizarre and at times hallucinatory manner argues the virtues of transvestitism, giddily shifting from documentary to horror film, from police drama to sexploitation picture. In the midst of this generic turmoil, Bela Lugosi appears from time to time as a meta-narrational figure who punctuates the diegetic action with incomprehensible comments and bizarre non sequiturs.

A casebook example of stylistic deviation as the result of the unique conditions of production in exploitation cinema, *Glen or Glenda* is of particular interest for paracinematic viewers because of the extratextual identity of Ed Wood, Jr: Wood was himself a transvestite. He not only wrote and directed *Glen or Glenda*, but also starred as the troubled young transvestite, Glen. Fan legends (based on interviews with surviving crew members) have it that Wood directed most of the film while wearing his favourite chiffon housecoat and that he had an obsession with cashmere sweaters (a fetish dramatically enacted in the film's final scene). After his movie career ended in the 1960s, Wood went on to write a number of adult novels with transvestite storylines.

This extratextual information about Wood is key to the paracinematic positioning of his films as a form of counter-cinema. Knowing this information allows the paracinematic fan to more fully appreciate the complexity of the cultural codes at work in a film like *Glen or Glenda*. John Fiske argues that the cultural elite 'use information about the artist to enhance or enrich the appreciation of the work'. Within fan culture, on the other hand, 'such knowledge increases the power of the fan to "see through" to the production processes normally hidden by the text and thus inaccessible to the non-fan. In the case of Ed Wood, Jr, the paracinematic aesthetic combines an elite interest in 'enriched appreciation' with a popular interest in seeing through 'production processes'. Paracinematic fans use their knowledge of Wood's real life to 'enhance or enrich' their engagement in his films, much as elites use their knowledge of Godard's various positions in relation to Marxism to inform their viewings. Vital to paracinematic pleasure, however, is this process of 'seeing through' the diegesis. For a sophisticated paracinematic viewer, *Glen or Glenda* is compelling because it seemingly presents both the textual and extratextual struggles of a man set against the repressive constraints of 1950s sexuality, encoded in a style that also challenges the period's conventions of representation. Paracinematic fans appreciate films such as *Glen or Glenda* not only as bizarre works of art, but as intriguing cultural documents, as socially and historically specific instances of artifice and commentary. Set against the bland cultural miasma of the Eisenhower years, Wood and his film stand out as truly remarkable figures.

This interest in collapsing the textual and the extratextual, the filmic and the profilmic, is especially pronounced in Zontarian interest in Larry Buchanan, a Dallas filmmaker who made a number of AIP films for television in the mid sixties. Buchanan's films rank among the most low-budget productions ever attempted in commercial filmmaking. Often following scripts from old black and white features, these films were reshot in colour for the television market in two or three days for often less than a few thousand dollars. The finished products are a test of even the most dedicated paracinematic viewer's patience. With no money or time to reshoot, mistakes in dialogue, camera movement and sound recording remain in each film. The films are unwatchable for most mainstream viewers, and consequently have assumed an exalted status among the 'hardcore' badfilm faction of paracinematic culture.

As with the other visionary stylists in paracinema's shadow realm of autuerism, Buchanan is valorized for his unique artistic vision. *Zontar* positions Buchanan as a poor man's Carl Dreyer, celebrating his particularly bleak and sombre approach. Importantly, however, this bleak and sombre tone is as much a function of the conditions of production as the product of Buchanan's 'genius'. A common strategy when discussing Buchanan is to transform his films into profilmic parables of artistic tragedy. Differentiating Buchanan from the more accessible Ed Wood, Jr, for example, *Zontar*'s editors write, 'where Ed Wood's films ultimately reassure the comfortably "hip" viewer of the dynamic force of even the most downtrodden and despised corners of human experience, the films of Larry Buchanan can only induce a profound feeling of desperation, anxiety and terminal boredom. The texture is not that of a tatty side-show, but that of the endless despair and futility of human existence as reflected on the concrete pavement of a Dallas parking lot.' The Zontarian transformation of Buchanan's work thus shifts the diegetic frame so that the action on the screen becomes but the trace of an isolated moment of desperate human activity, a farcical attempt at 'art' taking place on a particular day many years ago in someone's garage, on a Dallas parking lot.

A contributor to *Zontar* describes this moment of profilmic nausea as personally experienced in the climatic revelation of the monster in the concluding scenes of Buchanan's *Curse of the Swamp Creature*:

> Seldom, if ever, has a more disappointing final monster revelation scene been filmed. . . . The monster is unbelievably, spectacularly cheap. . . . 'It' appears dressed in a white hospital smock, with rubber monster-gloves and a minimal mask-piece consisting of two painted PING-PONG BALL EYES set into a rubber bow. A skin-head wig and a couple of cruddy fangs complete the 'monster suit' . . . which is more embarrassing than scary . . . the CREATURE itself must be the least convincing creation in monster movie history. This is, of course, a subjective area, but I would rate it far worse than the ROBOT MONSTER and at least as bad as the CREEPING TERROR . . . though of a different order, naturally. THE MASTER DIRECTOR actually compounds the failure of his creature by withholding it for so long. By building to his epic anti-climax Buchanan makes the SWAMP CREATURE itself the essence of disappointment and failure . . . translated into cheap rubber and ping-pong ball eyes. The SWAMP CREATURE'S scaly rubber fright-mask is composed of the very substance of despair.

The swamp creature, intended to be a startling and menacing cinematic revelation, is, in the last analysis, simply an overweight actor standing in weeds with ping-pong balls attached to his eyes on a hot day in Dallas in 1966. For the paracinematic community, such moments of impoverished excess are a means toward collapsing cinema's fourth wall, allowing the profilmic and the extratextual to mesh with the diegetic drama. The 'surface' diegesis becomes precisely that, the thin and final veil that is the indexical mark of a more interesting drama, that of the film's construction and sociohistorical context.

The politics of excess

Thompson argues that the importance of excess is that it renews 'the perceptual freshness of the work' and 'suggests a different way of watching and listening to a film'.

> The viewer is no longer caught in the bind of mistaking the causal structure of the narrative for some sort of inevitable, true, or natural set of events which is beyond questioning or criticism. . . . Once narrative is recognized as arbitrary rather than logical, the viewer is free to ask why individual events within its structures are as they are. The viewer is no longer constrained by conventions of reading to find a meaning or theme within the work as the solution to a sort of puzzle which has a right answer.

Excess provides a freedom from constraint, an opportunity to approach a film with a fresh and slightly defamiliarized perspective. As Thompson argues, through excess 'the work becomes a perceptual field of structures which the viewer is free to study at length, going beyond the strictly functional aspects.' What the critical viewer does with this newfound freedom provided by the phenomenon of excess is, I would argue, a political question, and one that lies at the heart of the conflict between the counter-cinema of the academy and that promoted by paracinematic culture. The very concept of excess, after all, as a relativistic term that posits a self-evident 'norm', is an inherently political evaluation. Exploring these politics of excess presents a key area where students who possess a trash aesthetic may impact the academic institutions to which they belong by questioning the goals, strategies and techniques of academically enshrined versions of 'art' cinema and the 'avant garde'.

Specifically, the trash aesthetic offers a potential critique of two highly influential methodologies in film studies: neoformalist analysis and theories of 'radical' textuality. Paracinema suggests that the neoformalist emphasis on art as defamiliarization might be more complicated than the cataloguing of innovative, text-bound 'devices'. If the paracinematic community celebrates a film, either earnestly or parodically, as an invigorating artistic experience precisely because of its utter banality, does that constitute a form of defamiliarization? For whom and under what circumstances is any film defamiliarizing? Since any notion of aesthetics is inextricably linked to historical issues of representation and reception, what are the politics of a neoformalist analysis that ultimately constructs a hierarchy of 'skilled' and 'unskilled' audiences, artistic and non-artistic films? (Do we really want to claim that *Last Year at Marienbad* is somehow more 'artistic' than *Sweet Badass's Badass Song* or even *E.T.*? What exactly is the purpose of such aesthetic valuations other than to empower a certain critic or a certain cinema?) If nothing else, the trash aesthetic serves as a reminder that all forms of poetics and aesthetic criticism are ultimately linked to issues of taste; and taste, in turn, is a social construct with profoundly political implications.

Paracinema also offers a critique of the 'radical' aesthetic that seeks to liberate, or at least politically agitate, audiences through the application of disruptive textual devices, a project that coalesced in theoretical and critical writings in film studies during the 1970s and which continues to inform much work on avant-garde textuality. In many respects, paracinematic discourses on excess greatly resemble the symptomatic criticism so central to film studies during this formative period. As with the devotees of Sirk, Minnelli and Lewis, paracinematic viewers are interested in reading films 'against the grain', ever on the alert for the trash film equivalents of Comolli and Narboni's celebrated 'category e' films. And, as in the counter-cinemas explicitly designed by Godard or covertly implanted by Sirk, paracinema's retrospective reconstruction of an avant garde through the ironic engagement of exploitation cinema's history is a 'politicized' cinema to the extent that it demonstrates the limitations and interests of dominant cinematic style by providing a striking counter-example of deviation.

But while segments of academic film culture often appeal to a refined code of aesthetics to apprehend and explain the potentially disruptive forces of style and excess (an aesthetics most often intentionally applied by an 'artist' to be successfully decoded by an elite cinephile in a rarefied and exclusive circuit of textual exchange), paracinematic culture celebrates excess as a product of cultural as well as aesthetic deviance. Once excess cues the elite viewer to the arbitrary structure of a narrative, he or she can then study the 'perceptual field of structures' in the work itself in appreciation of artistic craftsmanship within a closed formal system. The paracinematic viewer's recognition of a narrative's artifice, however, is the first step in examining a field of structures within the culture as a whole, a passageway into engaging a larger field of contextual issues surrounding the film as a socially and historically specific document. As a consequence, paracinema might be said to succeed where earlier more 'radical' avant gardes have failed. It is doubtful that *Tout Va Bien* (Jean-Luc Godard/Jean-Pierre Gorin, 1973), or *Written on the Wind* (Douglas Sirk, 1956) for that matter, ever 'radicalized' anyone other than fellow academy aesthetes. Perhaps paracinema has the potential, at long last, to answer Brecht's famous call for an anti-illusionist aesthetic by presenting a cinema so histrionic, anachronistic and excessive that it compels even the most casual viewer to engage it ironically, producing a relatively detached textual space in which to consider, if only superficially, the cultural, historical and aesthetic politics that shape cinematic representation. In this respect, one might argue that while academy icons such as Godard and Sirk may have employed complex aesthetic strategies to problematize issues such as the construction of gender, Ed Wood Jr, by his own admission, actually fought in the Pacific during World War II with a pink bra and knickers worn underneath his combat fatigues. As to which form of political engagement and subsequent critical promotion by the academy will prove more provocative and productive, it is open for debate.

1995

1.9

Sleaze mania, Euro-trash and high art: The place of European art films in American low culture

by Joan Hawkins

American academic Joan Hawkins graduated with her Ph.D. from the University of California, Berkeley, where her ideas about cult cinema had been influenced by the work of Linda Williams and Carol Clover, on gender and the horror genre. While Hawkins' essay on cult cinema does not use feminism as an explicit approach towards cult cinema, it does address the issue of how 'the gendered body' is put on display in cult cinema – the body is sensationalized through its treatment as object of arousal or disgust. Significantly, her approach leads Hawkins to re-address a crucial balance in the high/low culture tension within cult cinema. Sconce had positioned paracinema almost exclusively within low culture (albeit with high culture pretences). For Hawkins, high-culture arthouse films are as susceptible to cult reception as low-end examples. She traces the American releases of European art-house cinema of the 1950s and 60s (*Rome Open City*, *Eyes Without a Face*, or *The War Game* for instance), and the distribution patterns of American avant-garde (*The Act of Seeing With One's Own Eyes* for instance, or the films of Kenneth Anger) to demonstrate how they received similar receptions as low-culture exploitation cinema, often sharing distributors and exhibition networks. For Hawkins, this similarity is not coincidental but is instead grounded in the (potentially) sensationalist characteristics these films share – it is what gives them a certain appeal, what makes them cult. Around the same time as Hawkins is laying her claim, similar observations are made by others, like Canadian scholar Mark Betz, and American academics Janet Staiger, Kevin Heffernan, Eric Schaefer [see section 2]. The combined work of these academics is important in that it rejoins the (prewar) interest in high-art cult with the study of post 1960s exploitation cults, thus providing for a coherent historical base of a reception theory of cult cinema.

A note on extracting: *Sleaze Mania, Euro-Trash and High Art: the Place of European Art Films in American Low Culture* originated as a chapter of Joan Hawkins' Ph.D. dissertation, and was published in *Film Quarterly*, volume 53 issue 2, pages 14–29. It is this version we reprint here. The essay has since been re-published, in an updated, elaborated version, in Joan Hawkins's book *Cutting Edge: Art-Horror and the Horrific Avant-garde*, published by The University of Minnesota Press, Minneapolis, pages 3–32, in 2000.

Open the pages of any U.S. horror fanzine—*Outré, Fangoria, Cinefantastique*—and you will find listings for mail order video companies which cater to afficionados of what Jeffrey Sconce has called "paracinema" and trash aesthetics. Not only do these mail order companies represent one of the fastest-growing segments of the video market, their catalogues challenge many of our continuing assumptions about the binary opposition of prestige cinema (European art and avant-garde/experimental films) and popular culture. Certainly, they highlight an aspect of art cinema which is generally overlooked or repressed in cultural analysis, namely, the degree to which high culture trades on the same images, tropes, and themes which characterize low culture.

In the world of horror and cult film fanzines and mail order catalogues, what Carol J. Clover calls "the high end" of the horror genre mingles indiscriminately with the "low end." Here, Murnau's *Nosferatu* (1921) and Dreyer's *Vampyr* (1931) appear alongside such drive-in favorites as *Tower of Screaming Virgins* (1971) and *Jail Bait* (1955). Even more interesting, European art films which have little to do with horror—Antonioni's *L'avventura* (1960), for example—are listed alongside movies which Video Vamp labels "Eurociné-trash." European art films are not easily located through separate catalogue subheadings or listings. Many catalogues simply list film titles alphabetically, making no attempt to differentiate among genres or subgenres, high or low art. In *Luminous Film and Video Wurks Catalogue 2.0*, for example, Jean-Luc Godard's edgy *Weekend* (1968) is sandwiched between *The Washing Machine* (1993) and *The Werewolf and the Yeti* (1975). Sinister Cinema's 1996–97 catalogue, which organizes titles chronologically, lists Godard's *Alphaville* (1965) between *Lightning Bolt* (1965) and *Zontar, the Thing from Venus* (1966).

Where separate genre and subgenre headings are given, the only labels which apply are the labels important to the fans who purchase tapes. European art and experimental film titles are woven throughout catalogue listings, and may be found under the headings "Science Fiction," "Horror," "Barbara Steele," "Christopher Lee," "Exploitation," "Weird Westerns," and "Juvenile Schlock." Where art films are bracketed off, they are often described in terms that most film historians would take pains to avoid. Instead of presenting Pier Paolo Pasolini's *Salò* (1975) as a work which explicitly links "fascism and sadism, sexual licence [sic] and oppression," as the *Encyclopedia of European Cinema* does, Mondo simply notes that the film "left audiences gagging."

The operative criteria here is affect; the ability of a film to thrill, frighten, gross out, arouse, or otherwise directly engage the spectator's body. And it is this emphasis on affect which characterizes paracinema as a low cinematic culture. Paracinema catalogues are dominated by what Clover terms "body genre" films, films which, Linda Williams notes, "privilege the sensational." Most of the titles are horror, porn, exploitation, horrific sci-fi, or thrillers; and other, non-body genre films—art films, Nixon's infamous Checkers speech, sword-and-sandal epics, etc.—tend to be collapsed into categories dictated by the body genres which are the main focus. Part of this strategy is economic. Consumers in search of a particular title or type of film have to literally read most of a catalogue in order to find everything that might be of interest. But the design of the catalogues also enforces a valorization of low genres and low generic categories.

Williams identifies three pertinent features shared by body genres (which she defines as porn, horror, and melodrama). "First," she writes, "there is the spectacle of a body caught in the grips of intense sensation or emotion" (142): the spectacle of orgasm in porn; of terror and violence in horror; of weeping in melodrama. Second, there is the related focus on ecstasy, "a direct or indirect sexual excitement and rapture," which borders on what the Greeks termed insanity or bewilderment (142–3). Visually this is signalled in films through what Williams calls the "involuntary convulsion or spasm—of the body 'beside itself' in the grips of sexual pleasure, fear and terror, and over-powering sadness" (143). Aurally, ecstasy is marked by the inarticulate cry—of pleasure in porn, of terror in horror, and of grief or anguish in melodrama (143).

Finally, body genres directly address the spectator's body. And it is this last feature which, Williams argues, most noticeably characterizes body genres as degraded cultural forms. "What seems to bracket these particular genres from others," she writes, "is an apparent lack of proper aesthetic distance, a sense of over-involvement in sensation and emotion . . . viewers feel too directly, too viscerally, manipulated by the text" (144). The body of the spectator involuntarily mimics "the emotion or sensation of the body onscreen" (143). The spectator cringes, becomes tense, screams, weeps, becomes aroused. This is such a pointed and calculated feature of body films that Mary Ann Doane, as Williams points out, "equates the violence of this emotion to a kind of 'textual rape' of the targeted . . . viewer" (144).

While Williams' assessment of the way body genres work—particularly the way they work in "specifically gendered ways" (144)—is excellent, the distinction between high and low, properly distanced and improperly involved audience response is not as neat as Williams suggests. Consider, for example, Amos Vogel's description of *The War Game* (Peter Watkins, 1965), a British art film which is frequently listed in para-cinema catalogues. "A terrifying, fabricated documentary records the horrors of a future atomic war in the most painstaking, sickening detail. Photographed in London, it shows the flash burns and firestorms, the impossibility of defence [sic], the destruction of all life. Produced by the BBC, the film was promptly banned and became world-famous and rarely seen." Similarly, Stan Brakhage's *The Act of Seeing with One's Own Eyes* (1972), which is hard to find outside experimental and avant-garde film venues, encourages an uncomfortably visceral reaction in the spectator. The chronicle of a real autopsy, the film is, Amos Vogel writes, "an appalling, haunting work of great purity and truth. It dispassionately records whatever transpires in front of the lens: bodies sliced length-wise, organs removed, skulls and scalp cut open with electric tools" (267). While such descriptive terms as "haunting work of great purity and truth" are seldom found in paracinema catalogues, *The War Game* and *The Act of Seeing with One's Own Eyes* do address the spectator in ways that paracinema fans would appreciate. Clearly designed to break the audience's aesthetic distance, the films encourage the kind of excessive physical response which we would generally attribute to horror. Furthermore, their excessive visual force and what paracinema catalogues like to term "powerful subject matter" mark them as subversive. Banned, marginalized through being screened exclusively in museums and classrooms, these are films which most mainstream film patrons never see.

Of course *The War Game* and *The Act of Seeing with One's Own Eyes* use sensational material differently than many body genre movies do. Seeking to instruct or challenge the spectator, not simply titillate her, films like Watkins' and Brakhage's are deemed to have a higher cultural purpose, and certainly a different artistic intent, from low-genre blood and gore fests. That is, high culture—even when it engages the body in the same way that low genres do—supposedly evokes a different kind of spectatorial pleasure/response than the one evoked by low genres.

Supposedly. But that doesn't mean that it always does. Consider the works of the Marquis de Sade, whose books are sold in mainstream bookstores and adult book-stores, and housed in university libraries. De Sade's works, which the intellectual elite views as masterful analyses of the mechanisms of power and economics, are also—at least if we are to take their presence in adult bookstores and magazines seriously—still regarded as sexually arousing, as masturbatory aids. Furthermore, as Jane Gallop's powerful admission that she masturbated while reading de Sade demonstrates, one set of cultural uses—one kind of audience pleasure—doesn't necessarily preclude the other. It is possible for someone to be simultaneously intellectually challenged *and* physically titillated; and it is possible for someone to simultaneously *enjoy* both the intellectual and the physical stimulation.

Finally, it is not so clear that low genres seek *only* to titillate. As Laura Kipnis remarks in her famous article on *Hustler* magazine, low genres, too, can be analyzed for serious content and purpose. Using a vocabulary similar to the one generally used to analyze the powerful cultural critique mounted by the high pornography of pre-Revolutionary France, Kipnis writes that "*Hustler* also offers a theory of sexuality—a 'low theory.' Like [Robin] Morgan's radical feminism, it too offers an explicitly polit-ical and counterhegemonic analysis of power and the body." The fact that it does so in a way that middle-class readers—Kipnis included—find disgusting is evidence that "it is explicit about its own class location."

In a similar fashion, low cinematic genres—as Clover, Williams, Robin Wood, and others have pointed out—often handle explosive social material which mainstream cinema is reluctant to touch. Carlos Clarens notes in *An Illustrated History of the Horror Film* that the B thrillers that Roger Corman's studios quickly cranked out depicted—for all their fabulous premises—a resolutely contemporary world, a world "usually ignored by Hollywood or blown up beyond recognition." And Eric Schaefer has demonstrated that, historically, art films which failed to get the Hays Office's coveted seal of approval were screened in bump-and-grind houses, marketed to patrons of body genre pictures as well as to European art film connoisseurs.

As these examples show, the categorical difference between low and high genres, body genres and elite art—both inside and outside the cinematic beltway—is a dif-ficult one to define. Even critics who make it their business to evaluate films on the basis of their artistic worth, intent, and merit sometimes find it hard to distinguish between low and high cinematic elements. Stephen Garrett's annotated article on the Production Code in *Hollywood Handbook*, for example, calls foreign films of the 1960s "erudite skin flicks," and Amos Vogel links horror, porn, avant-garde, and European art films under one heading: "subversive" cinema.

If the operative criterion in paracinema culture is affect, the most frequently expressed patron desire is to see something "different," something unlike contempor-ary Hollywood cinema. As A.S. Hamrah and Joshua Glenn put it, "Let's face it:

Hollywood films are cautious, uninventive, and bland, and young filmgoers are increasingly uninterested." Paracinema fans, like the cineaste elite, "explicitly situate themselves in opposition to Hollywood cinema" (Sconce, 381); and they do so in a way which academics would recognize as highly sophisticated. As Sconce notes, "the paracinematic audience recognizes Hollywood as an economic and artistic institution that represents not just a body of films, but a particular mode of film production and its accompanying signifying practices. Furthermore, the narrative form produced by this institution is seen as somehow 'manipulative' and 'repressive,' and linked to dominant interests as a form of cultural coercion" (381). Paracinema consumption can be understood, then, as American art cinema consumption has often been understood, as a reaction against the hegemonic and normatizing practices of mainstream, dominant, Hollywood production.

Providing for the demand for affective products and the demand for "something different"—something unlike contemporary Hollywood movies—often takes a company's list in what appears to be wildly different directions. Paracinema catalogues not only list classic films by Godard, Antonioni, and Bergman, they are often the only places where European cinema fans can find video titles which are otherwise not available for sale in the U.S. These include everything from the uncut horror films of Jess Franco to Peter Greenaway's *The Baby of Macon* (1993) to Jean-Luc Godard's historically important *Tout va bien* (1972). If "entertainment is one of the purest marketplaces in the world," as Robert Shaye Director of New Line Cinema, maintained during the 1993 GATT controversy, then the alternative mail-order video industry is one of the purest (i.e., uncontaminated by any prejudice) entertainment marketplaces around. Certainly, its mail order catalogues encourage a reading strategy much like the one which Fredric Jameson proposes in *Signatures of the Visible*. That is, they invite us to "read high and mass culture as objectively related and dialectically interdependent phenomena, as twin and inseparable forms of the fission of aesthetic production under capitalism."

Historically speaking, paracinema catalogues, with their levelling of cultural hierarchies and abolition of binary categories, are reminiscent of an earlier age—an age preceding what Lawrence W. Levine has called the "sacralization" of high art, when the mingling of high and low culture was commonplace. In his book *Highbrow Lowbrow*, Levine describes the historical emergence of a cultural hierarchy in the United States during the late nineteenth century. Prior to that time there was little cultural stratification—be it of cultural products or of audiences. This was a time when opera could exist *simultaneously* as a popular and an elite art form; a time when American audiences might hear a soliloquy from *Hamlet* and a popular song in the course of one evening's entertainment at a local venue. In the early nineteenth century, Levine tells us, no art form—opera, painting, theater—was "elevated above other forms of expressive culture . . .; they were part of the general culture and were experienced in the midst of a broad range of other cultural genres by a catholic audience that cut through class and social lines. This situation began to change after mid-century" (149).

The change, which Levine calls "the sacralization of culture," involved the establishment of a hierarchy of cultural products and spaces. Shakespeare's works were increasingly played "straight," without the accompaniment of farce (a form of entertainment usually scheduled between acts) or popular music; and gradually they acquired the patina of high art. They were seen as more culturally valuable or sophisticated than the travelling road shows which catered to "popular taste." The emergence of a growing differentiation of cultural products brought with it a nearly simultaneous differentiation of performance space and audience. Since tickets to the opera house, an edifice of high culture, commanded a much higher price than tickets to the music hall, audiences who attended performances at the opera house tended to be a much tonier crew than audiences who attended the newly devalued variety shows. More importantly, however, as certain cultural products picked up elite status, they also acquired a certain restrictive class inflection. Shakespeare not only moved into theaters, he moved off the boards. He was transformed, as Levine tells us, "from a playwright for the general public into one for a specific audience" (56). Shakespeare became high class and highbrow.

The reasons for the sacralization of high culture in the nineteenth century are, as Levine argues, complicated. Then as now, "culture"—as a concept—had politico-economic as well as aesthetic and social resonance, and "aesthetics by themselves cannot account for the nature of the mores and the institutions" that accompanied the historical development of high culture (228). As Levine writes, "these were shaped by the entire [historic] context—social, cultural, and economic—in which that development took place" (228). Certainly, the categorization and stratification of cultural products seems, at this remove at least, to be the logical aesthetic extension of the stratification, compartmentalization, and commodification that accompanied most cultural production during industrialization and the rise of capitalism. And as leisure activity—the freedom to not work or at least to have a wife who did not work for a salary—increasingly became both a signifier of social status and a reason for cultural consumption, it was only natural that the cultural products consumed during leisure time would themselves emerge as important signifiers of social prestige and class standing.

But while Levine stresses the need for a holistic paradigm to explain the cultural shift which occurred in the United States during industrialization, he also emphasizes the degree to which the sacralization of culture served particular partisan political goals. For Levine, cultural stratification was one logical outcome of a conservative political reformation. "It should not really surprise us," he writes,

> that the thrust of the Mugwumps—those independent Republicans whose devotion to the cause of orderly and efficient civil service reform led them to desert their own party in the election of 1884—was not confined to the political sphere. Once we understand that the drive for political order was paralleled by a drive for cultural order, that the push to organize the economic sphere was paralleled by a push to organize the cultural sphere, that the quest for social authority ("the control of action through the giving of commands") was paralleled by a quest for cultural authority ("the construction of reality through definitions of fact and value"), we can begin to place the cultural dynamics of the turn of the century in clearer perspective.
>
> (228)

Certainly, we can see the way that the impetus to sacralize specific cultural products, spaces, and historic artifacts as "culture" had the same sociopolitical and economic implications in the nineteenth century that it has today. The recent debates surrounding the educational curriculum (particularly regarding the canon and which books may or may not be considered "literature" by the public schools), the concern over the free circulation of both information and images on the Internet, the disputes over continued funding for the National Endowment for the Arts and the Public Broadcasting Service, and the public lambasting of violent and sexual content in rap music, popular Hollywood cinema, and commercial television by both politicians and intellectuals all demonstrate the degree to which culture, economics, and politics continue to be interrelated terms in a society very much concerned with issues of social control. Now, as in the late nineteenth century, "there is . . . the same sense that culture [in the sacralized sense of the word] is something created by the few for the few, threatened by the many, and imperiled by democracy; the conviction that culture cannot come from the young, the inexperienced, the untutored, the marginal" (252). And it is largely in opposition to this sense that "culture" is exclusionary and elitist that paracinema consumption must be understood. As Michael Weldon notes in the foreword to the *Psychotronic Video Guide*, "unlike other movie guides, nothing is omitted [here] because it's in bad taste. All of this stuff is out there. You should know about it" (vii).

Exploitation companies are not the only places which cater to European art film fans. Other—more upscale—video companies pick up most of the art film business, and while they don't carry some of the truly obscure titles that characterize Mondo or Cinemacabre's lists, they have a broader range of European art selections than the paracinema companies do (and their tapes are usually much better quality). Interestingly, like Mondo, they do attempt to cater to the horror tastes, as well as the art tastes, of their clients. Facets Multimedia, one of the most complete mail-order video services in the country, has listings for cult and horror films, as well as for hard-to-find avant-garde and European art titles. Even Home Film Festival, whose slogan, "the best films you never saw," specifically targets a middle-class art and independent film audience, has begun carrying some horror titles—*Night of the Living Dead* (1968), *Spanish Dracula* (1931), *Eyes Without a Face* (*Les Yeux sans visage*, 1959), *Nadja* (1995), and *Mute Witness* (1995), to name just a few. The fact that "art" companies as well as "sleaze" companies market both high art and low culture titles suggests that the sacralization of performance culture (its division into high and low art) never completely took root among art and horror/sleaze/exploitation film fans.

Of course, upscale mail-order video companies rely on a very different kind of product for the majority of their sales than do companies like Mondo or Video Vamp. In June, 1996, for example, the best-selling foreign title at Facets was *La Jetée* (1964), a title which was currently popular with film buffs because, as Facet's manager Milos Stehlik claimed, "it was adapted by Terry Gilliam for his 1995 hit *Twelve Monkeys*." Ranked number 2 was *Bread and Chocolate* (1974), an Italian comedy which had been previously unavailable on video. Jean-Luc Godard's *Numéro Deux* (1975), Luis Puenzo's *The Official Story* (1985), and Jean-Jacques Beineix's *Diva* (1981) followed as third, fourth, and fifth in popularity respectively (Nichols, H 29). The tendency here is for patrons to buy more contemporary titles or historical titles of current interest (Fox Lorber's video release of Jacques Démy's *The Umbrellas of Cherbourg*, 1964, for example, which followed the film's re-release in theaters, or *La Jetée*).

These are titles which the horror and exploitation catalogues, for the most part, do not even bother to carry. While the European *horror* film listings in exploitation publications include recent films as well as films of historical interest, the European art films which show up in these catalogues tend to date from the height of the art cinema movement, the period which Susan Sontag elegized in her *New York Times* article, "The Decay of Cinema." The post-1970 auteurs mentioned by Timothy Corrigan, Thomas Elsaesser, and Jill Forbes in their studies of postwar European and postmodern cinema are largely passed over in favor of the "classic" auteurs—Godard, Fellini, Antonioni, Buñuel. The most frequently represented American auteur is Orson Welles. Exploitation catalogues feature, then, art film titles which don't sell well in other venues: films of historical interest or titles which haven't been officially released. In that sense, it's not clear to what degree they actually compete with more upscale specialty video companies. What is clear is that the catalogue companies themselves comprise and address what Dick Hebdige might recognize as a true video subculture, a subculture identified less by a specific style than by a certain strategy of reading.

In addition to art, horror, and science fiction films, "paracinema" catalogues "include entries from such seemingly disparate genres" as badfilm, splatterpunk, mondo films, sword-and-sandal epics, Elvis flicks, government hygiene films, Japanese monster movies, beach party musicals, and "just about every other historical mani-festation of expoitation cinema from juvenile delinquency documentaries to . . . pornography" (Sconce, 372). As Sconce explains, this is an "extremely elastic textual category," and comprises "less a distinct group of films than a particular reading protocol, a counter-aesthetic turned subcultural sensibility devoted to all manner of cultural detritus. In short, the explicit manifesto of paracinematic culture is to valorize all forms of cinematic 'trash' whether such films have been either explicitly rejected or simply ignored by legitimate film culture" (372).

This valorization is achieved, he argues, largely through heavily ironized strat-egies of cinematic reading. Connoisseurs of trash cinema are always on the lookout for movies that are so awful they're good. But they also consume films which are recognized by "legitimate" film culture as masterpieces. And catalogue descriptions do attempt to alert the consumer that such films might require a different reading strategy—less heavily ironized—than other films listed in the catalogue. Sinister Cinema's description of *Vampyr* is a good example: "If you're looking for a fast-paced horror film with lots of action go to another movie in our listings. If you like mood and atmosphere this is probably the greatest horror movie ever made. The use of light, shadow, and camera angles is translated into a pureness of horror seldom equaled, in this chilling vampire-in-a-castle tale. One of the best."

Clearly, the description serves an important economic purpose. Customers are less likely to be disappointed, to return tapes, if they understand clearly what they're getting. But the delineation of important stylistic elements is instructional as well cautionary. It tells the collector what to look for, how to read a film which might seem lugubrious or boring. The fact that the catalogue lists two versions of the film—a longer, foreign-language version and a shorter version with English subtitles—marks the company's economic stake in serious collectors and completionists (people who collect many versions of the same title—the U.S. theatrical release, the director's cut or uncut European version, the rough cut, etc.). But it also gives the catalogue a curiously academic or scholarly air, which links Sinister Cinema to more upscale "serious" video companies like Facets.

While paracinema catalogues often tag art films as films which require a different reading strategy than *Reefer Madness* (1939) or *Glen and Glenda* (1953), they also tag certain B movies as films which can be openly appreciated on pure aesthetic grounds. In the same catalogue which characterizes *Vampyr* as "one of the best," for example, the reader can also find a listing for *Carnival of Souls* (1962), a B-grade American horror film which *The Encyclopedia of Horror Movies* calls "insufferably portentous." The script, the *Encyclopedia* tells us "harks back to those expressionistic dramas which solemnly debated this life and the next with heavy-breathing dialogue." For Sinister Cinema catalogue patrons, however, the film is described in terms not unlike the ones used to describe *Vampyr*: "A riveting pipe organ music score. Seldom have the elements of sight and sound come together in such a horrifying way. A haunting film that you'll never forget. Original uncut 80-minute version." Although this description does not praise *Carnival of Souls'* use of "light, shadow, and camera angles," its observation that "sight and sound come together in a . . . horrifying way" is a tribute to the film's formal style. And the use of the word "haunting" in the next-to-last line reminds the reader that schlock, too, can be beautiful. Like the Surrealist film critic Ado Kyrou, the writers for paracinema publications continually remind readers that low budget horror can sometimes be "sublime."

Negotiating paracinema catalogues often calls, then, for a more complicated set of textual reading strategies than is commonly assumed. Viewing/reading the films themselves—even the trashiest films—demands a set of sophisticated strategies which, Sconce argues, are remarkably similar to the strategies employed by the cultural elite.

> Paracinematic taste involves a reading strategy that renders the bad into the sublime, the deviant into the defamiliarized and in so doing, calls attention to the aesthetic aberrance and stylistic variety evident but routinely dismissed in the many subgenres of trash cinema. By concentrating on a film's formal bizarreness and stylish eccentricity, the paracinematic audience, *much like the viewer attuned to the innovations of Godard* . . . foregrounds structures of cinematic discourse and artifice so that the material identity of the film ceases to be a structure made invisible in service of the diegesis, but becomes instead the primary focus of textual attention.

> (388, emphasis mine)

Since Sconce is mainly interested in theorizing trash aesthetics, he doesn't take the "high" art aspects of the catalogues' video lists into account. So he does not thoroughly discuss the way in which the companies' listing practices erase the difference between what's considered trash and what's considered art through a deliberate leveling of hierarchies and recasting of categories. But his comments about "the viewer attuned to the innovations of Godard" help to explain the heavy representation of Godard's films in these catalogues. As Godard himself repeatedly demonstrated, there is a very fine line between the reading strategies demanded by trash and the reading strategies demanded by high culture.

Earlier I mentioned that the design of paracinema mail order catalogues—which list titles alphabetically or chronologically, and make no attempt to differentiate between high and low genres—encourages a kind of dialectical cultural reading. Certainly, it highlights an aspect of art cinema generally overlooked or repressed in cultural analysis, namely, the degree to which high culture trades on the same images, tropes, and themes that characterize low culture. "Film is a vivid medium," as Steven Shaviro notes. And there is something vividly scandalous and transgressive about the films of Peter Greenaway, Derek Jarman, Luis Buñuel, Jean-Luc Godard, and the other European filmmakers mentioned above. In fact, European art cinema has followed a trajectory in the United States not unlike that of pure exploitation cinema, in that historically it has been seen as delving "unashamedly into often disreputable content," often "promoting it in . . . [a] disreputable manner."

As Peter Lev notes, *Open City* (1945), "the first foreign-language film to earn more than a million dollars in the United States, is certainly not sexually explicit by contemporary standards. But some observers felt that *Open City*'s success in the United States was based on a salacious advertising campaign." Similarly, throughout the 1960s, the advertisements for Jean-Luc Godard's films tended to feature scantily clad women, images which were, American distributors felt, in keeping with the impression most Americans had of French cinema, as something sexy. And as late as 1972, Pauline Kael felt it necessary to distinguish *Last Tango in Paris*'s eroticism from that of exploitation films and to stress the movie's links to the world of high culture.

While Michael Mayer gives a long list of reasons for the rise in popularity of foreign films in the U.S. after the war—the Paramount decision, which had the effect of decreasing the number of films produced in the U.S., the increased American interest in all things foreign, the end of political isolationism, more travel opportunities, the increased sophistication of the viewing public ("the public no longer requires complete clarity on film")—most interesting for our purposes is the importance he places on the "violent" change in Americans' sexual mores. Certainly, this is the "lesson" which Hollywood learned from the rise of art cinema. As Kristin Thompson and David Bordwell note in *Film History*, "one way of competing with television, which had extremely strict censorship," as well as with European art films, "was to make films with more daring subject matter. As a result, producers and distributors pushed the code further and further."

For many Americans, however, throughout the late 50s and early 60s, European art cinema retained a scandalous reputation which marked its difference from Hollywood cinema (even a Hollywood cinema dedicated to "push[ing] the code further and further"). In 1960, the residents of Fort Lee, New Jersey, protested the opening of a "film art house" in their community. "It is a known fact that many of the foreign films are without doubt detrimental to the morals of the young and old," one pastor maintained. Apparently, the president of the Borough Council, agreed. "I would not hesitate to pass an ordinance barring all future theatres from Fort Lee," he claimed, "if that's the only way to keep this one out." And both Janet Staiger and

Douglas Gomery stress the degree to which the audience for art films in the U.S. has always been a "special interest group." Hollywood's need to compete for art film audiences, then, should be seen more as an indication of changing audience demographics (mainstream audiences were going less and less frequently to the movies; special interest groups were going more and more) than as an index of changing mainstream tastes. The moviegoing audience was not only becoming segmented, as Janet Staiger claims, it was becoming polarized (into mainstream and "alternative" or "fringe" audiences). Interestingly, the majority of historical titles on horror and exploitation video mail order lists are drawn from films made during the era when this polarization became pronounced. Agreeing with Richard Kadrey that "everything interesting is out at the edges," the catalogues celebrate the two extreme tastes of the postwar, youthful filmgoing public: low-budget horror, sci-fi, and exploitation films on the one hand; art-film "classics," on the other.

In addition to these, there is an interesting array of films which, put quite simply, are difficult to categorize. Films with high production values, European art-film cachet, and enough sex and violence to thrill all but the most jaded horror fan: Roger Vadim's *Blood and Roses* (1960), Stanley Kubrick's *Clockwork Orange* (1971), Harry Kuemel's *Daughters of Darkness* (1971), Georges Franju's *Eyes Without a Face* (1959), Roman Polanski's *Repulsion* (1965) and *The Tenant* (1976), to name just a few. There are films, like Tod Browning's *Freaks* (1932), which began their career as horror or exploitation films and were later revived as art films; films, like Paul Morrissey's *Andy Warhol's Frankenstein* (1973) and *Andy Warhol's Dracula* (1974), which belong to New York avant-garde culture as well as to horror; and experimental films, like the Surrealist classic *Un Chien andalou* (1929), which contain sequences as shocking as those in any contemporary splatter film. These are films which promise *both* affect and "something different"; films which defy the traditional genre labels by which we try to make sense of cinematic history and cultures, films which seem to have a stake in both high and low art.

Unlike *Nosferatu* or *Vampyr*—films which I earlier designated "the high end of horror"—these films still directly engage the viewer's body. Like the slasher films which Clover analyzes, many of them are "drenched in taboo" and encroach "vigorously on the pornographic."[54] All of them meet both Linda Williams' and William Paul's criteria for lower cinematic forms. In *Laughing Screaming*, Paul writes:

> From the high perch of an elitist view, the negative definition of the lower works would have it that they are less subtle than higher genres. More positively, it could be said they are more direct. Where lower forms are explicit, higher forms tend to operate more by indirection. Because of this indirection the higher forms are often regarded as being more metaphorical and consequently, more resonant, more open to the exegetical analyses of the academic industry.

This concurs with Williams' characterization of body genres as physically excessive, viscerally manipulative genres. For both Williams and Paul, so-called "low" genres lack "proper aesthetic distance" (Williams, 144). In fact, the title of Paul's book, *Laughing Screaming*, specifically foregrounds the kind of undistanced involuntary response—what Williams might call the ecstatic response—which direct, body-genre films evoke from the audience. As Williams notes, "aurally, excess is marked by recourse not to the coded articulations of language but to inarticulate cries" (143)—laughing, screaming—both onscreen and in the audience.

The films listed above are nothing if not direct. There may be a "metaphorical" significance to the slashing of a woman's eye in *Un Chien andalou*—in fact, feminist film theory would argue that there's a profound metaphorical significance to such an act—but that significance is very much bound up with the immediate physical jolt experienced by the spectator. Similarly, when Dracula vomits blood in *Andy Warhol's Dracula*, when Dr. Génessier peels the skin from a woman's face in *Eyes Without a Face*, and when Stephan, in *Daughters of Darkness*, whips his wife in an excess of sadistic sexual frenzy, the directness of the image, as Paul points out, "makes metaphoric significance seem secondary to the primary power" of the image itself (32).

Which is not to say these films don't simultaneously operate at the high end of the horror spectrum. They do. The pacing, the blatant disregard for the cause-effect logic of classical Hollywood cinema, the strategic use of discontinuous editing, the painterly composition of certain scenes all serve to mark these films as art cinema. The fact that the films seem to operate at both ends of the horror spectrum is at least partly responsible for the fact that the best of them were so poorly received at the time of their release. *Daughters of Darkness* was so unsuccessful in finding a generic niche, *The Encyclopedia of Horror Movies* notes, that it never received the attention it deserved. This "unsettlingly intelligent" and uncommonly beautiful film was not well received "by any of the established audiences for art cinema, horror or camp movies" (242).

A film which had an even more difficult time staking out its generic territory is Tod Browning's *Freaks* (1932). Initially made as a mainstream horror film at MGM, the film caused a scandal. Described in reviews as "loathsome" and "unwholesome," the film was pulled from mainstream distribution shortly after its initial release and leased to Dwain Esper (the prolific exploitation filmmaker), who showed it, under a variety of titles, on the exploitation circuit. Like *Daughters of Darkness*, however, the film had trouble finding an appropriate audience. Too sensational for mainstream filmgoers, the film simply wasn't sensational enough for many exploitation fans. As David Friedman notes, *Freaks* nearly caused a riot when Dwain Esper showed it to a North Carolina drive-in audience under the sensational title *Forbidden Love*. Led by the title and advertising to expect a softcore treatment of "love" between "a beautiful woman and a midget," the crowd had no patience with a movie which Raymond Durgnat later compared to the European art films of Buñuel. Esper managed to pacify the drive-in patrons by showing them a black-and-white nudist colony one-reeler that he had tucked in the trunk of his car, a film that apparently came much closer to satisfying their expectations than did Browning's creepy classic. Interestingly enough, *Freaks* was revived 30 years later as an "art film" and did very well, attracting favorable reviews by Raymond Durgnat and John Thomas, and captivating such notable patrons as Emile de Antonio and Diane Arbus. By 1967, David J. Skal notes, the film "had made it to the Museum of Modern Art" (21).

Finally, Michael Powell's art-horror masterpiece, *Peeping Tom* (1960), which *The Encyclopedia of Horror Movies* calls "one of the best and most disturbing films to be made in Britain," not only shocked audiences, it almost ruined the director's career (135). Known for making films like *The Life and Death of Colonel Blimp* (1943), *Black*

Narcissus (1947), and *The Red Shoes* (1948), Powell had previously flirted with the sensational in his work, but never so graphically and disturbingly as he did in *Peeping Tom*. The film disgusted reviewers. Derek Hill's now infamous review for the *Tribune* perhaps best sums up the critical response. "The only really satisfactory way to dispose of *Peeping Tom*," Hill writes, "would be to shovel it up and flush it swiftly down the nearest sewer. Even then the stench would remain." Interestingly, the film is now shown in art houses as well as in horror venues, and it is frequently taught—as an example of some of the best of British filmmaking—in university courses treating the history of British cinema.

In a way, hybrid genres like art-horror films simply point up the problems which have historically characterized all attempts at genre definition. As S.S. Prawer notes,

(i)   Every worthwhile work modifies the genre [horror] to some extent, brings something new to it, and therefore forces us to rethink definitions and delimitations.
(ii) There are borderline cases, works that belong to more than one genre—the overlap between the "fantastic terror" film and the "science fiction" film is particularly large.
(iii) Wide variations in quality are possible within a given genre.
(iv) There are works which as a whole clearly do not belong to the genre in question but which embody references to that genre, or contain sequences that derive from, allude to, or influence it. The first dream sequence in Bergman's *Wild Strawberries* . . . clearly . . . [belongs] in that category.

While Prawer is speaking here mainly of horror films, his remarks—as he himself points out—can be adapted to fit "genre studies in any medium" (37). Certainly, they can be adapted to fit other film genres. Film noir, the thriller, and melodrama have a great deal of overlap with other genres. Avant-garde cinema is just as divergent in scope and quality as horror cinema. The European art film is so diverse that it is generally not represented as a genre at all. And, as Jim Collins maintains in *Architectures of Excess*, the 80s and 90s have been marked by the increasing number of "eclectic, hybrid genre films": films such as *Road Warrior* (1981), *Blade Runner* (1982), *Blue Velvet* (1986), *Near Dark* (1988), and *Thelma and Louise* (1991), which "engage in specific transformations across genres." In fact, genre overlap and instability is so common, Robin Wood maintains, that the tendency to treat genres as discrete has been one of the major obstacles to developing what he calls a synthetic definition of the term.

Not only is there slippage between genres, there is slippage between evaluative classifications as well. As Eric Schaefer pointed out to me, if *Dementia* (*Daughter of Horror*, 1955) or *Carnival of Souls* (1962) had been made in Europe they would probably be considered art, or at least art-horror, films, instead of drive-in classics. Similarly, if *Eyes Without a Face* had been made in the United States, it would probably be considered a low-budget horror film. That is, in evaluative terms, the films would occupy not only a different generic niche, they would occupy a different artistic category or "class." The instability of film categorization (as high or low art) in all genres was illustrated when the July–August 1997 issue of *Film Comment* published a list of the top 30 unreleased foreign-language films of the 90s. Drawing upon a poll which queried such film scholars and critics as David Bordwell, Roger Ebert, Jonathan Rosenbaum, and Robert Sklar, Gavin Smith (writing for *Film Comment*) listed *Les Amants du Pont Neuf* (Léos Carax, 1991) as the second-best unreleased art house flick of the 90s. Thus the film was categorized as high art. In 1996, however, before the *Film Comment* poll results were published, the film was listed in a special paracinema company mailing, *Video Vamp Presents Celebrity Skin Videos*, as a "French sleaze classic." Clearly, as Jameson suggests, we need to rethink the emphasis we have placed on evaluation and essentialized categorization and replace it with a mode of assessment that's a little more dynamic.

As I've suggested, horror is not the only genre/category which is hard to pin down and it's not the only genre/category which continually flirts with the possibility of existing simultaneously as high and low art. To some degree, as William Paul asserts, all film still has something disreputable about it, all film still has to struggle to be seen as art at all. And yet, we do, as he also notes, consistently make distinctions between good cinema and bad, between artistic films and films that are "just entertainment." Even within as democratic a medium as film, we worry about "taste," a phenomenon which, social critics from Pierre Bourdieu to V. Vale and Andrea Juno maintain, is always already bound up with questions of class.

But while it is not the only popular genre which continually flirts with a kind of high-art double—in this case, the European art film or prestige import cinema— horror is perhaps the best vantage point from which to study the cracks that seem to exist everywhere in late twentieth-century "sacralized" film culture. Precisely because it plays so relentlessly on the body, horror's "low" elements are easy to see. As Joe Bob Briggs is fond of reminding us, fans of low horror are drawn by the body count ("We're talking two breasts, four quarts of blood, five dead bodies . . . Joe Bob says check it out"). And as catalogues from mail order video companies remind us, prestigious films, too, can play relentlessly on the public's desire—or at least its willingness—to be physically affronted. Like the lowest of low horror, European art films can "leave audiences gagging."

Joan Hawkins is an assistant professor in the Department of Communication and Culture at Indiana University, Bloomington. She is the author of *Cutting Edge: Art-Horror and the Horrific Avant-garde* (Minneapolis: University of Minnesota Press, 2000).

Note

A shorter version of this article was presented at the 1997 Society for Cinema Studies Conference. I would like to thank Chris Anderson, Carol J. Clover, Skip Hawkins, Eric Schaefer, Ann Martin, and the Editorial Board of *Film Quarterly*, all of whom read earlier versions of the essay and made helpful suggestions. Also, a special thanks to Eric Schaefer for his sensitive reading of the piece and the references he gave me.

1.10

Media fandom, neoreligiosity and cult(ural) studies
by Matt Hills

There is always the caveat that cult and fan audiences are not the same. British scholar Matt Hills managed to bridge fandom with cult cinema by approaching it from the perspective of the sociology of religion. Going back to Karl Marx, and French sociologist Emile Durkheim's work on religious cults, Hills argues that the 'worship'-like appeal of cult media needs to be understood both as a fetishism of commodity (like Benjamin does in relation to the work of art's 'aura'), but also, and importantly, as a 'project of the self' – a near spiritual attempt to develop one's cultural identity. This position is different from the one assumed by Bourdieu because it depends less on social positioning, and much more on self-reflexive attitudes towards culture. A fan of cult is a fan of specific films as part of an effort to achieve a personal significance, and objects of worship are chosen accordingly (like an 'attitude of coolness', or a location). Hills only occasionally uses film as an example for his theory on cult fandom. For the most part he refers to television series, like *The X-Files*, or *Dr. Who*. We need thus be careful to extend his ideas into the discipline of film studies. But in the twenty-first century cultural environment key characteristics that used to distinguish television from film, like 'home viewing', or 'serialization' (the succession of texts creating a continuous public presence) have become features of cinema as much as of television. Observe, for instance, the serializations of *Friday the 13th* (which are mostly straight to DVD – hence straight to home viewing), *The Lord of the Rings* (on which Hills has also written, see bibliography), or *Ginger Snaps* (which has combined public with home viewing instances, see section 4). As Hills puts it 'the common practices of cult film and television fans' stress the similarities more than the differences, at least at this theoretical level. In the end, Hills remains cautious: 'cult fandoms must be carefully distinguished from wider discussions of fandom within contemporary consumer culture'. But by stressing the individual's connection to cult (and not the system of culture, or social conditions) Hills has offered the theorization of cult cinema a nodal point.

A note on extracting: *Media Fandom, Neo-Religiosity and Cult(ural) Studies* was first published in the journal *The Velvet Light Trap*, in issue 46, pages 73–84. This is the version we reprint here. It has since, in a different version, also been published in Matt Hills' book *Fan Cultures*, published by Routledge in 2002.

Discourses of "the cult"

In his 1901–02 Edinburgh lecture series, William James referred to the "cult" surrounding Walt Whitman: "many persons to-day regard Walt Whitman as the restorer of the eternal natural religion. He has infected them with his own love of comrades, with his own gladness that he and they exist. Societies are actually formed for his cult; a periodical organ exists for its propagation, in which the lines of orthodoxy and heterodoxy are already beginning to be drawn" (98–99). It is striking that in a lecture dealing with "natural religion," James describes mediated celebrity as being "cult"-like and expressive of a nascent religiosity. Moving hurriedly from the beginning to the end of the twentieth century, we can observe a proliferation of contemporary media "cults" whose fandoms routinely cluster around and valorize film, television, and related popular cultural texts.

Certain films and television programs (and other media such as novels and popular music) can be defined as "cult media" through the fact that such media texts attract passionate, enduring, and socially organized fan audiences. Cult fandoms, however, must be carefully distinguished from wider discussions of fandom within contemporary consumer culture. As Brooker and Brooker note, "not all fans will be cult fans" (141). Fandom has been discussed as a matter of the intensity with which such audiences follow their chosen texts (Grossberg). Other criteria typically linked to media fandom have been interpretive—the construction of fandom as an interpretive community (Amesley; Jenkins)—or have involved the construction of cultural identities through fannish attachments to media texts (Tulloch and Jenkins). Abercrombie and Longhurst have sought to separate "fans" from "cultists" by emphasizing the manner in which cultists produce texts based on the object of their fandom and the extent to which cultists are organized into social networks. This definition is potentially unhelpful since, as its authors concede, "Cultists . . . are closer to what much of the recent literature has called a fan" (138).

While previous attempts at delimiting fandom and cult fandom have depended upon rewriting (or overwriting) the critical use of both terms, I want to attend to the discourses of the "cult" which are at play *within* media fandoms. Nevertheless, one useful distinction between "fandom" and "cult fandom" worth bearing in mind—apart from the necessary but tautological definition that cult fandoms relate to texts discussed as "cults" by their fans—concerns the place of cult fandom as an unfolding project of the self. John B. Thompson describes fandom as a *symbolic* project of the self, noting that "the deep personal and emotional involvement of individuals in the fan community is also a testimony to the fact that being a fan is an integral part of a project of self-formation" (224). By discussing cult fandom I want to extend this valuable insight. Cult fandom is thus defined here as a similar "project of the self" (occurring and enduring over time), one which is *not* primarily symbolic and secondarily emotional. Cult fandom is a project of the self which is primarily and significantly emotional; cult fans create cultural identities out of the *significance* which certain texts assume for them, rather than out of textual signification and hence out of rationalist or cognitive mechanisms of interpretation. Such fandom "has the power to *bring meaning*" (McLaren 242, my emphasis) to the fan's experience rather than being wholly or primarily about the interpretive construction *of meaning*. Hence, cult fandom exists "beyond reason," as J.P. Telotte has observed of the "cult film experience" and "its nearly worshipful audience" (5). This is not to allege irrationality, as certain pathologizing stereotypes do, but instead to consider cult fandom as a set of lived practices which may be more accurately considered within "practical logics" (Bourdieu 54) rather than contained within models of "interpretive community" which may be read as the projections of epistemocentric scholastic reason: "Projecting his theoretical thinking into the heads of acting agents, the researcher presents the world as he thinks it—as if it were the world as it presents itself to those who do not have the leisure (or the desire) to withdraw from it in order to think it" (Bourdieu 51). The "interpretive" approach to media fandom generalizes on the basis of the academic's social location and skills, presenting the fan audience as a set of hermeneutic readers such that these practices reflect the disposition of the academic as interpreter. To clarify this point, Bourdieu offers the example of Clifford Geertz's work on the Balinese cockfight as an instance of academic projection, noting that "in his 'thick description' of a cock-fight, Geertz 'generously' credits the Balinese with a hermeneutic and aesthetic gaze which is none other than his own" (52).

In the remainder of this essay, I will examine the extent to which the term "cult," used as a self-description within various subcultures of media fandom—as well as being used within journalistic (and, more rarely, academic) work on fandom—relates not to the interpretive models of scholastic reason but rather to modes of fan practice (practical reason) which can be described as "neoreligious."

But why *neo*religious? What is the distinction between religion and neoreligion? Derrida has recently discussed the matter of religion, wondering whether the term is not to be trusted: "We act as though we had some common sense of what 'religion' means . . . We believe in the minimal trustworthiness of this word . . . Well . . . nothing is less pre-assured . . . and the entire question of religion comes down, perhaps, to this lack of assurance" (3). Given this lack, I do not aim to install an ontological separation between an experience defined as "religious" and another defined as "neoreligious." Instead, I use the term "neoreligion" to indicate that we cannot assume a stable referent or thing called "religion." It is a gesture toward recognizing the fact that the proliferation of discourses of "cult" within media fandom cannot be read as the "return" of religion or the social relocation of "religion" (both of which assume religion's stability). In place of an ontology, then, I pursue a pragmatics of the term "cult" and its neoreligiosity (i.e., its appearance in unusual social locations such as the consumption of popular culture): "An analysis above all concerned with *pragmatic* and functional effects, more structural and also political, would not hesitate to investigate the usages or applications of the lexical resources [such as that of the "cult"], where, *in the face of new regularities, of unusual recurrences, of unprecedented contexts, discourse liberates words and meaning from all archaic memory and from all supposed origins*" (Derrida 35, my emphasis). I will examine the social logics underpinning the multivalent uses and contestations, the "new regularities," of the discourses of "cult" fandom. My focus falls on audience practices and experiences which have been semiotically placed within discourses of religion and which appear to share characteristics of what has been theorized as "privatized" and commodified religiosity (see Durkheim, Berger, and Luckmann for this debate) but whose discursively "religious" status is open to argument, particularly from those involved (see Doss; Cavicchi; and

Jindra, "*Star Trek* to Me" 220). By looking at such practices, we can map out both the particular social contexts and the specific experiences of fan audiences who take neither "religion" nor "the media" for granted but instead rework the meanings and the practices associated with both. The relationship between the media and "religion" must be considered as moving beyond mere film and television "representations" of a preexistent or somehow essentialized referent (a thing clearly identifiable as "religion"). *Religiosity is itself sociohistorically reconstructed and reconfigured (as neo-religiosity) through "cult media" and associated fan practices and experiences in such a way as to suggest that there is no essential thing which can be referred to as "religiosity."* I will pursue the broad theoretical outlines and repercussions of this hypothesis before presenting a brief case study of one cult text (*The X-Files*) and the discourses of religiosity which have circulated around it. By focusing on a single text in this manner, I will illustrate the shift in emphasis which such a theoretical perspective can provoke in the study of cult film and television.

Despite the term "cult media" occurring in a seemingly secularized and com-modified context, the prevalence of religious and quasi-religious discourses surround-ing the media "cult" is striking. Discussing the contested validity of the term "cult media" allows a consideration of the extent to which practices of media consumption can encapsulate affective processes (of embodied and practical reason rather than detached scholastic reason) within contemporary culture—processes which many exponents of cultural studies have tended to marginalize (with notable exceptions, such as the work of Grossberg). John Frow has recently made a timely statement relevant to these issues:

> Religion is an embarrassment to us . . . because we Western intellectuals are so deeply committed to the secularisation thesis which makes of religion an archaic remnant which ought by now to have withered away. This thesis . . . is wrong . . . both because organized religion is flourishing in many parts of the world, and because *religious sentiment has migrated into many strange and unexpected places, from New Age trinketry to manga movies and the cult of the famous dead . . . among the things we need to know about . . . is the history and sociology of religion . . . we need to take religion seriously in all of its dimensions because of its cultural centrality in the modern world.*
>
> (208–09, my emphasis)

This "embarrassment" has, I think, been on show in some recent studies of fandom (Erb; Jenkins; Lewis; Tulloch and Jenkins) which neglect the analysis of "cultishness" by defusing the religious connections and connotations of "cult" and polemically constructing the fan as a rational subject (although Lynne Joyrich's work on the "Cult of Elvis" and desiring "Elvisophilia" [Joyrich 83] forms a notable exception). Other studies (see Jensen) have considered the etymology of "cult" as a "cultural symptom" attached to fandom rather than as a substantive feature of fan activity and of the sense making of such activity. "Cult" is thus assumed to speak more to a series of theoretical and practical anxieties surrounding modernism (and its valorization of the rational, Enlightenment project; see Jensen, *Redeeming* 168–69) rather than to the figure of the fan. These argumentative positions cannot be sustained: the neoreligiosity of the fan experience and fan practices must be taken seriously within analysis without seeking refuge in evaluative terms which could link this sociohistorically reconstructed "religiosity" either with forms of obsessional neurosis (see Freud) or even psychosis (see Robins), thereby pathologizing or demonizing the cult fan.

Media scholarship must refrain from reproducing the "moral panics" of the mass media (Cohen), replete with their pathologized representations of the cultist proper (Barker) or the fan as a "cultist." However, by seeking to revalue positively the figure of the fan, cultural studies has tended to avoid discussions of fan "religiosity" for fear of merely replaying these journalistic "moral panics." This is a curious revaluation of fandom since (by default) it leaves the terms of antifan discourses intact rather than asking why many fans feel comfortable describing themselves as "cult" fans and thus attempting to engage with the lived fit of "cult" discourses and practices as they occur alongside the mass media's simultaneous use of "cult" discourses as a tool to belittle and demonize fandom. Just as new religious movements are deemed by the media to act as a threat to the rationalist "modern" self (as Eileen Barker illustrates in *The Making of a Moonie* [1984]), so too is cult fandom depicted as a threat to rational subjectivity, resulting in the "obsessed" fan being absorbed in a fantasy world (Elliott). The term "cult" is thus highly negatively charged within current constellations of meaning (Wright). In her introduction to Durkheim's *The Elementary Forms of Religious Life*, Karen Fields notes that " 'Cult' now connotes not just feasts and rites but excessive and perhaps obsessive ones, attached to beliefs assumed to be outlandish" (lvi). Fields adds that a strong case has been made for excising the term "cult" from serious scholarship because of the negative connotations it has acquired. If "cult" remains a useful term within both practical and theoretical systems, this must be *because* of the social conflicts, forms of experience, and sociological processes inscribed across its varied usages, not in spite of these complexities.

Cult fandom and the sociology of religion

Jindra and Frow represent voices in the wilderness insofar as each takes cult fandom's religiosity seriously and suggests that the sociology of religion can shed light on this phenomenon (see also Porter and McLaren). Although Jindra focuses specifically on *Star Trek* fandom as a religious phenomenon, he does not adequately address the significance of the term "cult" within *Star Trek* and related fandoms, discussing *Star Trek* fans as a unique phenomenon (Jindra, "*Star Trek* Fandom" 27) rather than as part of the wider discourses and experiences of *cult* fandoms. Of course, we might suppose that all religious sentiment has been cleansed from the word "cult" in its contemporary media-consumption-related contexts. This would tie in with a body of sociological theorizing about the processes of societal secularization, processes considered to be characteristic of modernity (Lyon; Beckford). However, many writers considering the sociology of religion focus on the distinctive possibilities for religion within the social structures of postmodernism (Berger; Luckmann). Organized (institutional) religion may have declined in the West, but a privatized and individualized space remains open to the voluntaristic adoption of sacred themes and ideas, and it is here that discourses of "cult" media and fandom find a specific social and historical context. As Doss observes,

What does it mean when adherents deny the religiosity of something that looks so much like religion? . . . Aware of their marginalization by the media, it isn't surprising that many fans hotly deny fidelity to any sort of Elvis cult or religion, suspicious of facile analyses that come close to equating them with the Branch Davidians or the Japanese followers of Aum Supreme Truth. . . . Americans continue to mix and match religious beliefs and practices, creating and claiming their own spiritual convictions out of that amalgamation. It may be that when Elvis fans protest that their devotion to Elvis is not "religious," they are really objecting to an institutional definition of the term. In fact, their privatizing veneration of Elvis is one strong historical form of American religiosity.

(74–75)

Examining particular ideas within the sociology of religion can help forge a route through the turmoil of the media "cult" in all its neoreligious and commodified forms. Emile Durkheim's work, which views religion and society as essentially linked, is a particularly valuable resource. The elementary form of religion is none other than society mistaking its own forces for those belonging to something external or other. Durkheim's intimate connection of society and religion implies that "there is something eternal in religion that is destined to outlive the succession of particular symbols in which religious thought has clothed itself. There can be no society which does not experience the need at regular intervals to maintain and strengthen the collective feeling and ideas that provide its coherence and its distinct individuality" (429). Of course, we must refrain from easily equating "religious-proper" definitions and issues with those of media cults. Such a move would generate the danger of a facile agreement with Durkheim's sociological functionalism, a factor which must be carefully tempered by considerations of the media cult's historical specificity. Rather than viewing the media cult as a "clothing" of particular symbols which cloaks an otherwise "eternal" religion ("eternal" because of its function within social relations), it is important to side-step this trap of transhistorical functionalism.

One approach which remains more alert to issues of historicization is offered by Thomas Luckmann. The media cult seems to fit into Luckmann's predictions regarding an historical shift from religion to religiosity. In 1967 Luckmann predicted a move from socially organized religion to "individual religiosity" revolving around loosely connected themes and deriving from the individual's familial and consumerist experiences in the private sphere. Luckmann thus considered *the emergence of an historically novel form of religion*:

lacking an over-arching coherence or structure . . . it will consist of an assortment of sacred themes chosen by the individual . . . the selections will express flexible and unstable arrangements of personal priorities which have little or no backing from public institutions . . . *They represent consumer preferences* and are therefore congruent with the individual's sovereign status and location in modern society.

(As summarized in Beckford 103, my emphasis)

For Luckmann the neo- and "invisible" religion of modern society exists in the selections of the individual within the private sphere as a matter of consumption. These selections, not the social groupings of Durkheimian rites, confer an attenuated "sacredness" upon a contingent grouping of "themes" and commodities.

Both Luckmann and his colleague in the sociology of religion, Peter Berger, agree that the production of the sacred (a socially bounded space within which religious ritual can occur, securely set apart from everyday life; see Porter) depends upon the everyday and proximate form of the "profane" world. The seeds of the sacred are contained *within* the most available, unremarkable, and habitual aspects of the profane world, and it is the shielding of the "sacred" from the "profane" (or everyday) which seeks to obscure this fact and elevate the "sacred." Consider how cult fans often consume their texts ritualistically by setting "bounded" spaces around such consumption (they view alone or in silence and without interruptions), a situation unlike most television consumption (see Ellis). What is "sacred" must be protected from collapsing back into the "profane"—hence the rituals enabling the transition between separated states. It is this very arbitrariness of the sacred which produces the force of social convention *and* allows for the possibility that new sacred forms may emerge from novel sociohistorical contexts (mass mediation) and objects ("cult" film and television texts). That is, new forms of the "sacred" may emerge from the historical contingencies produced by late capitalism. If the "sacred" is built out of material readily at hand, encountered regularly and in a bounded manner by any given individual, then media consumption suggests itself as an obvious candidate for any such process. Luckmann's work effectively detaches "religion" from organized and institutional forms, suggesting that religious impulses toward the formation of symbols carrying transcendental significance for the self may be rediscovered in a variety of unexpected and increasingly individualistic locations: "Friends, neighbours, members of cliques formed at work and around hobbies may come to serve as 'significant others' who share in the construction and stabilization of 'private' universes of 'ultimate' significance. If such universes coalesce to some degree, the groups supporting them may assume almost sectarian characteristics and develop what are called secondary institutions" (106). Although Luckmann's work appears alert to issues of historicization, it risks equating "religion" with sociality per se (one of the difficulties which may arise when applying Durkheim's sociology of religion; see Berger). And though Luckmann's theorization appears to tally with the situation of the cult fan, its emphasis on religiosity as a stable referent must be discounted via a consideration of cult fandom as neoreligiosity—that is, not as religion that returns but as a form of practical reason and discourse which reconstructs and contests the referent "religion."

Marx and the nonsecrets of "cult value"

Against this revised Durkheimian and discursive focus, Marxists might counter that the phenomenon of the media cult presents nothing more than an instance of the fetishism of the commodity. For Marx, religiosity is never alien to the commodity form but represents the closest analogous social product. Both religion and the commodity present the self-same "fetishism" through which material social relations are displaced. Thus, from a Marxist perspective, it is meaningless to argue that the "sacred" media cult distinguishes itself from other forms of consumption through a secularized religiosity. No such distinction exists within the Marxist lexicon, since religion and the commodity are deemed to act as two sides of the same coin of reification. By this token, to propose neoreligiosity as a sociohistorical valuation and aspect of media consumption would be considered misguided: the neoreligion of the media cult could only represent the manifestation of latent qualities of the commodity in general.

However, only by reducing "religiosity" (meaning the sociohistorically specific privatized construction of the sacred; see Doss; James; Luckmann) to religion-as-system (that is, to an objective and alienated social "fact") can a Marxist stance with regard to the media cult be retained. A key problem with adopting a Marxist framework in relation to the media cult lies in the commodity-religion analogy upon which Marx's argument hinges (Marx 165), which provokes the question, What, if any, are the logical consequences of the Marxist commodity-religion analogy being realized within fan discourses of "cult" media?

The fans' realization of Marxist analogy poses difficulties insofar as the "secret" of the commodity (Marx 163) cannot be assumed to represent much of a secret within cult practices; social relations are written *on* and *through* the cult media commodity in this instance, rather than being frozen as a set of relations between things, since these "things" refuse to remain "dead" within fan speculations, relationships, and social organizations. The cult as a commodity does not hide its "theological niceties" (Marx 163) from analysis: fans' valorization is on open display, and the "misty realms" of religion are often self-reflexively invoked rather than requiring critical exegesis. What is latent in Marx has become manifest in the culture of cult media. The practices and experiences of cult fans, set within a particular sociohistorical context of privatized religiosity achieved through media consumption, thus begin to unpack the antireligious presuppositions of Marxist thought (see Lowentrout). It is worth noting that Walter Benjamin's discussion of "cult value" replays Marx's emphasis on the "hidden," although for Benjamin this cult "hidden-ness" is not part of the mechanism of the commodity itself but part of an attempt to retreat from the exchange value of commodification: "Today the cult value would seem to demand that the work of art remain hidden . . . [just as] certain sculptures on medieval cathedrals are invisible to the spectator on ground level" (Benjamin 218). Hidden-ness is revalued by Benjamin, with the residues of the artwork's "aura" depending on a retreat from "exhibition value." The media cult deconstructs these oppositions between "visibility" (the commodity) and hidden-ness (the "auratic" artwork), being visible/exhibited and ritualistically auratic for its cult fans.

Yet the media "cult" is emphatically *not* a "religion" in the traditional sense of the word, despite seeming to possess some elements of "religiosity." If not absolutely an "invisible religion," given the unacceptable equation of "religion" with culture *tout court* which this implies—the media "cult" remains at least partially within Durkheim's model, particularly with reference to the arbitrary nature of the sacred and the protection of the sacred/profane boundary. By problematizing—but nevertheless taking seriously—the "religious" status of cult media, I am following Natalie Heinich's exemplary study of the "cult" of Van Gogh. Heinich marks out the operation of "neoreligiosity" within an "anthropology of admiration" (she pointedly does not refer to fandom in this context) which surrounds the reception of Van Gogh's art. In common with my approach here, Heinich does not assume that "religion" can be identified as a given but rather that it is (re)constructed within a sociohistorical context:

> References to religion are in no way metaphorical. I have not proceeded "as though" art were "a kind of" religion, fabricating a rhetorical trope, weaving a metaphorical thread, which could not be faulted any more than it could be taken seriously. . . . To understand the Van Gogh effect, we therefore had to extricate ourselves from the *a priori* categories of "religion" and "art," and to regard them not as given facts, but as mental constructs, which organize the perception of phenomena that, under various forms, are common to different universes.
>
> (150)

Reinstating neoreligiosity within cult(ural) studies

Cultural studies is marked by the absence of a critical discourse which takes seriously the dimensions of affect and neoreligiosity within contemporary media and (fan) audience experiences. It surrenders, by default, to journalistic and hegemonic antifan discourses which simplistically reduce fan culture to fan cult "as though" fandom were "a kind of" religion. In short, cultural studies participates in this equation by refusing to contest and complexify it.

The common devaluation of both cult activities and "cult" media consumption by fans (notably fused in U.K. press coverage of the Heaven's Gate cult; Krips 1–3) rests on a homology between cult members and cult fans whereby both challenge modernist ideals of cognitive and rationalist conduct by displaying affective and mimetic engagements with texts/icons. This modernist-Enlightenment rejection of religion and religiosity acts as a philosophical determinant of cultural attitudes here, both outside and inside the academy. Thus it is unsurprising to find neoreligiosity devalued within cultural studies. Frow argues that it is "the failure of cultural studies—with rare exceptions—to come to terms with, to theorise in any adequate way, what is perhaps the most important set of popular cultural systems in the contemporary world, religion in both its organised and disorganised forms" (207). He adds, "[W]e need to take religion seriously in all of its dimensions because of its cultural centrality in the modern world; and we need to do so without ourselves participating in those religious myths of origin and presence—the myth, for example, of the great star whose charisma is the cause rather than the effect of their fame—which are a constant theoretical temptation in the study of popular culture" (Frow 208).

Yet Frow is curiously devoted to a nondevotional reading of religion, one which is supposed to occur "without ourselves [i.e., cultural theorists] participating in those religious myths." This nonmimetic relationship between academic and fan is exceptionally difficult to sustain, not least because the academic who writes about (cult) fans, *whether or not he or she is self-identified as a "fan,"* takes up an affective relationship to the representation of fandom (even if only as a vehicle for propping up a rationalist academic self-identity) and becomes what Fredric Jameson describes as "something like a fan of fans" (282). Given its efforts to evade this second-order or metafandom, Frow's attempt to place religion on the cultural studies agenda partially replays the hegemonic position he seeks to oppose and remonstrate with, since he suggests that "we" (as academic rationalists) cannot surrender our intellectual distance and become corrupted by the myths of religiosity and fandom.

If neoreligiosity is to secure genuine consideration within cultural studies, with the media cult representing one form of neoreligious sentiment which can be analyzed simultaneously as a cultural practice, then the hegemonic position which Frow argues against while surreptitiously adopting must be thoroughly deconstructed, with the fluidity of (modernist-academic) "self" and (neoreligious-fan) "other" being recognized in its place.

Through such moves (see Gargani [126] for a discussion of how philosophical discourse must be opened to religious discourse), it is possible to reconstruct cultural studies as a form of cult(ural) studies. This would mean becoming more closely attentive to the kinds of lived (and intense) valorizations and privatized, neoreligious sentiments which are realized through the cultural practices of cult media fandoms. We must return to viewing discourses about the "cult" as symptoms of social struggle over the acceptability of the affective and the mimetic within contemporary culture, keeping in mind that such discourses attempt hegemonically to devalue both certain audiences (the fan portrayed as a "fanatic") and certain audience *experiences* (passion; attachment; immersion; involvement; devotion). Cult media and their fans must be approached not as if they *are* cults but rather as both willed managements of self-identity and "will-less" devotional practices of subjectivity (see Mestrovic 28). This movement from cult-as-thing to cult-as-process invites the twin dangers of religious essentialism and religious functionalism, but neither possibility should be allowed to close down prematurely our consideration of the practices of cult fandom, thereby returning us to the modernist's "embarrassment" over issues of religiosity within contemporary culture. As Daniel Cavicchi observes, "[W]hile religion and fandom are arguably different realms of meaning, they are both centred around acts of devotion, which may create similarities of experience. In fact, fans are aware of the parallels between religious devotion and their own devotion" (51).

Yet the difficulty with Cavicchi's fan-ethnography is that he is so keen to avoid accusations of religious essentialism and functionalism that he oscillates between defining religion and fandom as relating to common experiences and subsequently defining the relationship between the two terms as being primarily discursive: "the discourse of religious conversion may provide fans with a model for describing the experience of becoming a fan" (51). In the former statement, common concerns and experiences link fandom and religion; in the latter, the *languages* of religion (and not a sociohistorically reconstructed religiosity) are used consciously as a model for discursively constructing "becoming-a-fan" stories. The difficulty with pursuing the latter strategy is that the qualities of will-less self-transcendence (the temporary loss of the self experienced through fan devotion) expressed in "becoming-a-fan" stories (Barker and Brooks) are displaced by a pure emphasis on fan rationality and on self-consciously maintained self-continuity. This highlights the ultimately limiting paradox of ethnographic work which seeks to more adequately represent fan voices; by positing fans as self-present, it overwrites and reduces the very fan experience (of "conversion") it seeks to capture. While Cavicchi's oscillation between experience and discourse may be inevitable (and it could be said that I replay it here to an extent),

I have sought to keep open the duality of cult fandom both as an affective loss of self and as a rational claim to social identity.

I have suggested that we cannot retreat to a purely discursive level; taking seriously the discourses of "cult" media means considering that these proliferating discourses may indicate a lived fit between fan experiences of media consumption and practices of neoreligiosity. In the following case study of the discourses of religiosity which circulate around *The X-Files*, I will conclude by indicating, albeit briefly, how these concerns may enable an innovative view of popular culture within cultural studies.

The X-Files as a media cult: contested discourses of religiosity

The journalistic material surrounding *The X-Files* is evidently vast, and to examine this thoroughly would constitute a book-length study. However, I will select two instances here which are discursively *symptomatic* of the manner in which cult media such as *The X-Files* engage with hegemonic contemporary culture rather than being fully "representative" of the discourse. The first is from the *New Statesman* (Justice); the second is from the *Sunday Times—Culture* supplement (Rizzio).

It might be objected at this juncture that to take journalistic coverage of *The X-Files* as my object of study is irrelevant to a consideration of the limits of cultural studies. In order to avoid this misreading, I must clarify the purposes of the following case study. By examining journalistic coverage of *The X-Files* I aim to illustrate how rationality is privileged within what Joli Jensen has termed the "media/modernity story" (177) and how the practical reason of cult fandom (a form of embodied and affective reason which cannot always articulate itself within a discursive field) is devalued and denigrated. I argue that privileging rationality over emotion (or, in Bourdieu's terms, scholastic reason over practical reason) is replayed in both journalistic and cultural studies discourses. Clearly, there may be forms of plurality and fragmentation within each terrain (neither "cultural studies" nor "journalism" are monolithic), but these pluralisms appear to be subject to nonrelativistic lines of force which define the norm (rationally centered subjectivity) and its degraded exception (affectively decentered subjectivity). By discussing *The X-Files* in terms of its "(post)modern" status (Meehan; Nelson; Kellner) and its "aesthetics" (Kellner), cultural studies scholars turn away from popular discourses put in play around cult fandom. Rather than engaging with these discursive struggles over the acceptability of affect and devotion within contemporary culture, such work retreats into an insulated language-game. In this theoretical game the critic remains a centered (and knowing) subject, and "epistemic doxa" (the dogmatism of centered and "detached" know-ledge rather than the exploration of affect and uncertainty; Bourdieu 15) remains firmly in place, albeit the unspoken or unwritten assumption underpinning what is written and said.

It might be objected that my emphasis on cultural studies as a rationalist project (in two senses of the term "project," to refer back to Bourdieu's discussion of Geertz) seems to make two fundamental errors. First, it fails to adequately define "the rational," and second, it fails to adequately consider the postmodern deconstruction of fixed knowledge and grand narrative. "Rationality" is perhaps as difficult to pin down as "religion," but my use of rationality refers to a restricted form of knowing which seeks to control or master (Elliott, *Subject*), which is detached from practical logics that cannot always explain themselves, and which either projects itself into the other or devalues this other as "barbarous" (Bourdieu). This "rationality" is never pure (it is always inhabited by its other) but seeks continually to disavow any relationality (see Derrida 28; Jensen, *Redeeming*).

Taking the latter point: on what basis can we assume that postmodern theory dispenses with modernity's inherited emphasis on privileged rationality? Does "theory" (whether modern or postmodern) not by definition presuppose a theory/practice break or division which is inadequately brought back into the process of theorization, being instead bracketed off? And if postmodern theory is about the displacement of instrumental rationality by other forms of (embodied and affective) reason, why does the term "postmodernism" itself inevitably require such cognitive mastery and arcane discussion and dispute? As Keller notes,

> Any mention of postmodernism inevitably invites and incites anxiety about what precisely the "p" word means. There are two fundamental traditions vis-à-vis the term "postmodernism," one critical of it and one celebratory, albeit in a cautionary fashion. Where its critics (e.g. Fredric Jameson, Terry Eagleton, Jurgen Habermas, Hal Foster) see an epistemology marked by a breakdown of tastes and standards, its proponents (e.g. Craig Owens, Linda Hutcheon, Charles Russell, Robert Venturi) see an expansion of or deemphasis of, and a challenge to, those very same things.
>
> (135)

It is as if the term "postmodernism" replays in miniature the flight from affect: its very referential uncertainty "invites and incites" a state of unpleasant affect (anxiety) which is warded off by arriving at a series of (safely contained and nominated) argumentative coordinates. If this containment depends on a certain dissonance gathered around and through "postmodernism," then theorists might continue to argue whether postmodernism allows a greater space for affect and its consideration (Elliott, *Subject* 135) or whether it actually continues the rationalist project of modernity (Mestrovic 20, 28).

It should be clear by now that my position throughout has been (and continues to be) that postmodern theory is *predominantly* (though not without exceptions) every bit as "abstract and placeless and . . . legitimising of rationalising ways of thought" (Wark 15) as modernity has been claimed to be. Indeed, in *Subject to Ourselves*, Anthony Elliott broadly contrasts modernity as rational mastery to postmodernity as reflexive scanning and fantasy. Having said that much, the first journalistic example I will examine—headed "We All Love X. But Why?"—accompanies an essay by Pat Kane which is presented as dealing with "the war between science and mystery." *The X-Files* is thus immediately aligned within a set of binary oppositions dealing with rationality versus (New Age) religiosity. This construction—with *The X-Files* somehow promoting or fostering an antiscientific worldview—is cemented by the final critical appraisal offered in the piece, a quotation from Richard Dawkins (described as "professor of the public understanding of science at Oxford University"). Dawkins states, "I find *The X-Files* pernicious because week after week it promotes the idea that a supernatural explanation should be favoured over a rational one. This undermines the rational world view that is our only hope" (Justice 26).

This "secondary discourse" (Fiske 108) is unusual in coverage of cult media insofar as its allegations of anti-Enlightenment and antimodernist irrationality are centered crudely on the text rather than upon the figure of the fan, which typically allows similar discursive mechanisms to be wheeled into play. However, there is a discursive slippage here, for by invoking the notion that the text "promotes the idea that a supernatural explanation should be favoured over a rational one," Dawkins implicitly characterizes both the audience and the text as lacking the virtues of (scientific) rationality. Audience and text are discursively collapsed together through a form of unidentified but profoundly deplored mimesis.

The X-Files is a helpful example of cult television and film, since its textual (and extratextual) romantic representations of Science versus its Other—variously constructed as religion or as mysticism—place religious discourses and experiences (both within the diegesis and within the fan community) squarely center-stage. This particular fragment of discourse—Richard Dawkins's view—echoes soundbites from critic Charles Shaar Murray, *Fortean Times* editor Bob Rikard, and *GQ* science editor Michael White. There is some apparent attempt at "balancing" the proscience and promystical edges of the "science versus religion" debate. Yet it is patently absurd, unless one is following a lay or folk theory of media influence, to use *The X-Files* within any such discussion. The "balancing" of soundbite quotations conveys the impression of having offered an adequate "public sphere" debate, drawing on conventions of journalistic impartiality to construct a spurious sense of legitimacy for the piece as a whole. What is significant here is that a cult text acts as a discursive site for articulating "rationalist" outrage at "pernicious" antirationalism. If the rational worldview is "our only hope" (a curiously messianic phrase), then one might wonder how and why this injunction has been played out across *The X-Files*. Why should Dawkins feel so threatened? How has the entire Enlightenment project been reduced to rubble by the popularity of one television program? I argue that Dawkins's critique—misguided and simplistic though it is—accurately picks up on the fan experience of religiosity or "fervour" which has gathered around the program as a cult text. The *New Statesman*'s construction of pseudodebate therefore operates as a function of the cult text's challenge to modernist hegemonic culture. An Oxford professor (and what finer hegemonic figure of rationality could one hope for?) would hardly be expected to defend the cult fan's affective and mimetic practices. The emphasis I place on considering hegemonic depictions of "cult" as a threat to rational subjectivity (both in terms of the media cult and the cult proper) is exemplified by Dawkins's intervention. Cultural studies must assess critically the social power and force of the discursive positions (science versus mysticism, Enlightenment versus religion) set in play around the media cult rather than merely assuming the legitimacy of a detached and modernist-academic discourse (as Frow ultimately does).

The second symptomatic moment of journalistic coverage that I will address is interesting because it also enacts a devaluation of religiosity within cult fandom but does so by emphasizing the ironic status of fans' religious language:

we have . . . the Almighty Cult of David Duchovny . . . and The Church of Our Guy David Duchovny. . . . The latter, apparently the brainchild of a teenager in Norwich, describes itself as 'a site devoted to the principle that the adoration of David Duchovny can bring you closer to the Truth' . . . Despite the apparent emphasis on heavily ironic, quasi-religious devotion, Duchovny also attracts his fair share of straightforward passion.

(Rizzio 5)

Quasi-religious discourses are repeatedly undermined here via the emphasis upon their "heavily ironic" status—a phrase introduced in the article's opening lines which inform the reader that devotional Websites are "often heavy on irony."

Yet there is no serious consideration as to why quasi-religious discourses have been selected by these cult fans, nor is there any attempt to view irony as anything other than a "joke." The univocality of such an attribution effects a form of discursive closure in the article. Irony could be approached otherwise; rather than being constructed as univocal (something which the article works hard to achieve), it could be used to acknowledge discursive hybridity. Linda Hutcheon, for example, has discussed the politics of postmodern parody as a politics of double coding which "both legitimises and subverts that which it parodies . . . [and whose] ironic reprise also offers an internalised sign of a certain self-consciousness about our culture's means of legitimation. How do some representations get legitimized and authorised?" (101, my emphasis). In the previous symptomatic instance (Justice 26), *The X-Files* became a vehicle for social struggle over the proper cultural space for rationality and the hegemonic (modernist) legitimation of this space. In this case, discourses of cult fans are delegitimated (they are plainly joking about the "religiosity" of their devotion) without considering the possibility that cult fans' "heavy" irony displays an acute awareness of the illegitimacy of fandom as worship within contemporary culture. Irony thus may be less of a "joke" and more of a discursive struggle, or at least may function as both joke and social struggle. Bakhtin has described the process of discursive "objectification" through which hegemonic or "persuasive discourses" can be rehearsed and reproduced:

This process . . . becomes especially important in those cases where a struggle against such images has already begun, where someone is trying to liberate himself from the influence of such an image and its discourse by means of objectification, or is striving to expose the limitations of both image and discourse. . . . One's own discourse and one's own voice . . . will sooner or later begin to liberate themselves from the authority of the other's discourse . . . [Through this double-voiced struggle] stylizing discourse by attributing it to a person often becomes parodic, although not crudely parodic—since another's word . . . mounts a resistance to this process.

(348)

Irony, Bakhtin suggests, can appear as a result of struggle over representative discourses. To his list of discourses and images (ethical, philosophical, and sociopolitical; see Bakhtin 347) we might add the devotional discourse of fandom and the image of a cult fan. The "objectification" of this image, and the fan's reclaiming of it, occurs against a powerful backdrop of delegitimation and stereotyping. To speak the quasi-religious discourses of the cult fan is to invite modernist and hegemonic ridicule. To "liberate themselves from the authority of the other's discourse" and to self-consciously revalue languages of devotion—contesting the "proper" space of the rational—propels cult fandom into a situation of inevitable polyphony, irony, and discursive instability. Ironically, of course, it may be too easy for the finer nuances of this discursive struggle to be hegemonically reencapsulated either as mere (i.e., insignificant) jokes or as "sincere" statements of a "religion," which reopens the space for, and of, modernist ridicule.

I will conclude this pointer toward the application of my ideas by addressing academic "coverage" of *The X-Files*, which is often roundly embraced as playing along the faultlines between modernism and postmodernism; see Kellner, Meehan, and Nelson's hesitant use of "(post)modern" (151, 155). The program has also been welcomed for making "*the sort of demands seemingly designed for academics like ourselves, always on the lookout for television material difficult enough to present a true challenge to our encyclopedic vocabulary of allusions and to our arsenal of critical methodologies* (semiotic, psychoanalytical, narratological, reader/viewer-response, deconstructionist, etc.)" (Lavery, Hague, Cartwright 14, my emphasis). My question here remains: Is *The X-Files* a challenge to "critical methodologies," or does it constitute a popular cultural space into which such methodologies can be projected, without their dislocation or disruption and seemingly without remainder? It seems that cultural studies has latched onto *The X-Files* as a mirror for its own theoretical concerns, rather than approaching the text outside of disciplinary language-games. This is far from being a "challenge"; it is a performance of theoretical mastery in place of a respectful approach to the specificity of "the text" and its coconstituting secondary discourses.

Roger C. Aden has extended Kellner and Meehan's modernist/postmodernist debate to argue that *The X-Files* constitutes a triangulation of discursive positions with the modernist ("The truth is out there") and postmodernist ("Trust no one") existing alongside the romantic ("I want to believe") (153). Meanwhile, dissenting voices have rejected the postmodernist thesis, seeing *The X-Files* as "post-postmodern" (Reeves, Rodgers, and Epstein 35) via its insistence upon an ongoing quest for meaning. This quest has also been interpreted as a reaction to "the decay of meaning in our lives" by Adrienne McLean, a reaction which operates phenomenologically as a "strong drive towards religious experience with rich liturgical overtones" (9). Such positions begin to take a more complex and unsettled approach to the text, but they continue to do so within frameworks which assume that "postmodernism" occupies an orienting position which must be countered. Even in such disputes, "postmodernism" continues to function as a ghostly center and legitimation within cultural studies approaches.

Perhaps by surrendering their current emphases on the arcane and scholastic games of "postmodernism-spotting," "po-mo bashing," or (post)modern hesitation (which, best of both worlds, means never having to definitively say "modernism" or "postmodernism"), academic discourses on *The X-Files* (and other cult texts) could (and, I argue, *should*) engage more forcefully with the debates and social struggles which emerge from journalistic and cult fans' secondary and tertiary texts/discourses.

Discourses and experiences of cult fandom call for a form of cult(ural) studies which knows when to call time on its own language-games and which knows that entering the discursive terrain of the media cult means *directly entering a hegemonic struggle over what constitutes "rational" and "proper" behavior within contemporary media culture,* rather than merely assuming the privilege of an unspoken epistemic doxa.

1.11

Cult fictions: Cult movies, subcultural capital and the production of cultural distinctions
by Mark Jancovich

By 2000, the rise in academic interest in cult cinema enabled a first full-fledged international conference on the subject, at the University of Nottingham, bringing together most of the scholars working on the subject, and becoming representative of the state of a rapidly emerging field. And where there is an emerging field, there is discussion and divergence of opinion, and reflection upon its history. In an essay that reflects some of the major strands of thought (and the tensions between them), organizer of the conference British scholar Mark Jancovich, brings the theorization of cult cinema down to a polar opposition between formalist and sociological approaches. Formalist approaches are concerned with identifying 'cultness' in the text, as a generic trait, a style, an aesthetic sensibility; sociological approaches are concerned with the reception and audiences of cult cinema, identifying 'cultness' in the conditions created by social positioning (sometimes individual postures, but also hierarchies of taste), and networks of access (distribution, modes of fandom, privileges, . . .). Using Pierre Bourdieu's work as a touchstone, Jancovich takes issue with what he calls Sconce's formalist theorization of paracinema as an aesthetic of liberation. Jancovich points out that the 'counter tastes' fans and paracinema-lovers display are, in fact, employing the same exclusionist strategies of aesthetics as the ones used against them – they are as 'bourgeois aesthetics' as the 'bourgeois aesthetes' they criticize. The affection for Ed Wood's and Hershell Gordon Lewis' films, and the disdain for, say, slasher movies (and their champions, special effects gurus Tom Savini or Dick Smith), are eclectic because they can afford to be: 'the privileging of form over function asserts the superiority [of the bourgeois] over those who [. . .] cannot assert the same contempt'. From a sociological perspective, Jancovich reminds us, these attitudes arose in college towns like Madison, Wisconsin or centres of academic liberalism (like Berkeley, or Austin), where films like *Reefer Madness* or *Maniac* could be relished by privileged students free from functional constraints. Jancovich suggests research should map the origins of cultdom by concentrating on the function and uses of 'micro-media' and 'invisible colleges' in the positioning of viewers of cult cinema. It will allow for fine distinctions between niche-cultures and subcultures based on existing cultural differences, and by displaying the myriad appearances of cults it does exactly what it should: stress the divergence of aesthetics and attitudes which make cult cinema stand outside the mainstream.

A note on extracting: *Cult Fictions: Cult Movies, Subcultural Capital and the Production of Cultural Distinctions* appeared in *Cultural Studies*, volume 16 issue 2, pages 306–322, in 2002. It is reprinted here in full.

Introduction

In textual poachers, Henry Jenkins claims that 'it was my fannish enthusiasm and not my academic curiosity that lead me to consider an advanced degree in media studies and to spend all of the time required to gain competency in that discipline' (Jenkins, 1992: 5). My own history is slightly different to that of Jenkins but like him, it was my fannish enthusiasm for cinema and popular culture, and my consequent knowledge of it, which directed me through my studies and which I eventually converted into economic capital by making a living out of its analysis.

In contrast to earlier generations of scholars, this 'fannish enthusiasm' has meant that there are many scholars of our generation who (when not disappearing into the excesses of cultural popularism) have tried to find a way of conducting research that is not based on a position of distance and disdain with regard to the popular, but from one which is informed by our knowledge and investments within the field, and yet is not uncritical of the relations of power within which it (like any other area of culture) is implicated. Elsewhere, however, I have expressed my concern at the ease with which – or even the inevitability with which – writing *as* a horror fan has transformed itself into writing as a *real* horror fan, a move which implicitly cast anyone who might construct and value the field in different ways as not simply naive, foolhardy and ignorant but as an implicitly *phoney* horror fan who has no right speak (Jancovich, 2000).

Of course, this is partly the aim of the strategy. Writing as a fan is frequently about writing as someone who knows the field and who is therefore more authoritative than the academic who merely talks about films and their fans from a position of distance and authoritative ignorance. But by failing to acknowledge the extraordinarily vicious struggles for distinction within and between fan cultures, this strategy also tends to repeat the same errors as that which it is supposed to criticize, to validate certain readings over others by casting some fans as authentic and authoritative and others as inauthentic and without the authority to define the field.

Indeed the distinction between the authentic and the inauthentic fan raises a number of problems that, it now seems to me, are central to an understanding of fans and the phenomena of cult movies. First, it raises issues about the ways in which authenticity works within these fields, but secondly, it illustrates the ways in which the notion of authenticity is used to produce distinctions not only between fans and the broader culture, but also within fan 'communities' themselves. The problem is that while there is much writing on the way in which 'dominant' or 'mainstream' cultures have produced distinctions between themselves and fans cultures, this writing either operates to normalize the fan or else accepts the subcultural ideologies on which fan communities are based, ideologies through which fan cultures present themselves as alternative, oppositional and authentic (Lewis, 1992).

Indeed, subcultural ideologies are fundamental to fans cultures because without them fans cannot create the sense of distinction which separates themselves as 'fans' from what Fiske has rather tellingly referred to as 'more "normal" popular audiences' (Fiske, 1992). In other words, in fan cultures, to be a fan is to be interesting and different, not simply a 'normal' cultural consumer.

The following essay will therefore concentrate on the phenomena of cult movies to examine the political workings of its subcultural ideologies. Indeed, the frequently stated problem of defining cult movies is precisely based on the fact that they are specifically defined according to a subcultural ideology in which it is their supposed difference from the 'mainstream' which is significant, rather than any other unifying feature. Rather than accepting this distinction between the cult and the mainstream, however, the following essay will also highlight the ways in which both these categories are constructed within cult movie fandom, and also examine the ways in which these distinctions are central to the complex operation of the cultural competences and dispositions within this field.

Using Sara Thornton's work on 'club cultures', the essay will examine both the ways in which the cult movie scene depends on a sense of its own distance from 'the media' and the academy, but also how these institutions are 'instrumental in the congregation of [fans] and the formation of subcultures' (Thornton, 1995: 121). Not only are cult audiences produced through the differential distribution of economic and cultural capital in which these institutions operate and which they act to regulate, but these institutions also provide the very mechanisms, spaces and systems of communication through which a sense of community is produced and maintained.

Indeed, the similarities between fan discourses and academic discourses should be no surprise. Nor is this simply to do with the fact that despite the class affectations of most cult movie fans, they are predominantly middle class and well educated in academic competences and dispositions. Joe Bob Briggs may play the role of a dumb, right wing red neck, but this is a performance designed to shock. It is not even a genuine identification.

It is also the case that, in the USA, the cult movie emerged out of the same processes as academic film studies before being exported to Britain. Cult movie fandom and academic film studies may have historically diverged into relatively independent scenes, but they both emerged through the art cinemas, college film societies and repertory theatres of the post-war period, and hence employ similar discourses and reading strategies. It should after all be remembered that the auteur theory was not only central to the institutionalization of film studies within the academy but that one of its foundational texts was Sarris's *Confessions of a Cultist* (Sarris, 1970).

Finally, then, to return to the original problem, the essay will attempt to show how and why the subcultural ideology which underpins cult movies fandom not only celebrates the unwatchable and/or unobtainable – that which is by definition usually unpleasurable or inaccessible to most viewers – but how this emerges from a need to produce and protect a sense of rarity and exclusivity. As Thornton puts it, 'subcultural capital is defined against the supposed obscene accessibility of mass culture' (Thornton, 1995: 121).

Form, function and cultural capital

The sheer eclecticism of the cult movie as a category is summed up well by Jeff Sconce who calls this body of films 'paracinema' and argues that it 'would include entries from such seemingly disparate subgenres as "bad film", splatterpunk, "mondo" films, sword and sandal epics, Elvis flicks, governmental hygiene films,

Japanese monster movies, beach party musicals and just about every other historical manifestation of exploitation cinema from juvenile delinquency documentaries to soft core pornography' (Sconce, 1995: 372). Even this description only touches on the range of films identified as 'cult'.

However, despite his use of Bourdieu to begin to discuss this scene, Sconce ultimately accepts its subcultural ideology and the supposedly oppositional identity that this bestows upon its members. Indeed, Sconce not only accepts 'paracinema' as a form of 'counter cinema' which is defined in opposition to a conformist 'main-stream', his argument overtly seeks to present it as an incisive critique of, and viable alternative to, established academic criticism.

For Sconce, paracinema is the product of 'a pitch battle between a guerrilla band of cult film viewers and an elite cadre of would be tastemakers' (1995: 372), and in terms of the academy it is as much a battle over the *purposes* of analysis as it is over the appropriate *objects* of analysis. As Sconce puts it, 'the paracinematic audience presents in its often explicit opposition to the agendas of the academy a dispute over *how* to approach cinema as much as a conflict over *what* cinema to approach' (1995: 380).

None the less, he proceeds to illustrate the points of agreement, or at least com-patibility, between paracinema and the academy, the first and most central of which is their shared opposition to 'mainstream, commercial cinema'. However, rather than investigate the contradictory and problematic nature of this concept, he conflates it with an equally problematic term, 'Hollywood', which he defines as 'an economic and artistic institution that represents not just a body of films, but a particular mode of film production and its accompanying signifying practices' (389).

This shared opposition to the 'commercial mainstream' is necessary to both camps because it presents them as standing in clear distinction to a conformist mass of viewers, and allows them to present their own favoured films as defamiliarizations of the 'signifying practices' associated with the mainstream. Indeed, as Bourdieu has shown, the concept of defamiliarization in its various guises underpins bourgeois aesthetics. It both privileges and legitimates a concentration on form over function, a tactic that clearly asserts the superiority of distanced aesthetic contemplation of form over the supposedly naive acceptance of illusionist mass culture (Bourdieu, 1984). It is hardly surprising, therefore, that, along with auteurism, Sconce finds that paracin-ema and the academy share a common preoccupation with the concept of excess, the supposed 'effects' of which are described in a passage from Thompson which he quotes:

> The viewer is no longer caught in the bind of mistaking the casual structure of the narrative for some sort of inevitable, true, or natural set of events which is beyond questioning or criticism . . . Once narrative is recognised as arbitrary rather than logical, the viewer is free to ask why individual events within its structures are as they are. The viewer is no longer constrained by conventions of reading to find a meaning or theme within the work as the solution to a sort of puzzle which has a right answer.
>
> (Kristin Thompson, quoted in Sconce, 1995: 391)

Excess is therefore seen as a quality of the text which 'provides freedom' by requiring 'a fresh and slightly defamiliarized perspective'. Excess prevents illusionism and foregrounds the formal features of the text.

However, Sconce argues that 'the trash aesthetic offers a potential critique of two highly influential methodologies in film studies: neo-formalism and theories of radical textuality' (1995: 391). For Sconce, neo-formalist criticism fails to acknowledge that taste is socially constructed and that it has political implications, and as a result, it falls back on 'a hierarchy of "skilled" and "unskilled" audiences, artistic and non-artistic films' (1995: 392). It fails to account for the fact that differences in reception may not be simply based on failures due to lack of knowledge, but are rather a product of the differential distribution of cultural competences and dispositions within society; that differences are the product of social inequality and the struggles which it produces. By contrast, Sconce argues, 'the trash aesthetic serves as a reminder that all forms of poetics and aesthetic criticism are ultimately linked to issues of taste; and taste, in turn, is a social construct with profoundly political implications' (1995: 392).

If 'paracinema' is supposed to take issue with the neo-formalist concept of aesthetics, it is supposed to also imply a critique 'theories of radical textuality' and their failure to look beyond the textuality of cinematic texts to the broader culture. Thus, he illustrates the similarities between 'paracinema' and the 'counter cinema' associated with Godard and 'Screen Theory'. However, he argues that while the filmmakers and critics associated with this area saw film style and excess as disruptive of the illusionism of 'mainstream, commercial cinema', 'paracinema celebrates excess as a product of cultural as well as aesthetic deviance' (1995: 392). This seems a little unfair to traditional 'Screen theory', which, whatever its limitations, at least believed that it was concerned with more than an 'appreciation of artistic craftsmanship within a closed formal system' (1995: 392). However much one might argue that the stylistic strategies failed to produce the political effects claimed for them, 'theories of radical textuality' were as much concerned as 'paracinema' that defamiliarization and anti-illusionism should be 'the first step in examining a field of structures within the culture as a whole, a passage into engaging a larger field of contextual issues surrounding the film as a socially and historically specific document' (1995: 392–3).

Indeed, Sconce himself even contradicts himself by failing to acknowledge the historical nature of paracinematic aesthetic, and by presenting the film texts associated with it as *inevitably* producing specific 'effects' regardless of the cultural competences and dispositions of specific viewers:

> As a consequence, paracinema might be said to succeed where earlier more 'radical' avant gardes have failed. It is doubtful that *Tout Va Bien* (Jean-Luc Gordard/ Jean-Pierre Gorin, 1973), or *Written on the Wind* (Douglas Sirk, 1956) for that matter, ever 'radicalized' anyone other than fellow academic aesthetes. Perhaps paracinema has the potential, at long last, to answer Brecht's famous call for an anti-illusionist aesthetic by presenting a cinema so histrionic, anachronistic and excessive that it compels even the most casual viewer to engage with it ironically, producing a relatively detached textual space in which to consider, if only

superficially, the cultural, historical and aesthetic politics that shape cinematic representation.

(1995: 393)

This not only contradicts his critique of neo-formalism in so far as it fails to see that these responses are not the 'effects' of texts but the products of different cultural competence and dispositions, it also privileges a particular disposition which as he himself has argued is essentially class based. It may provide a limited challenge to existing academic practice, but it also shares much in common with it. Indeed, its very dependence on the anti-illusionist aesthetic is itself bound up with bourgeois taste and its concentration on form over function, a taste that is itself the product of social inequality. As Bourdieu shows, and indeed as Sconce himself seems to have already acknowledged, the privileging of form over function asserts the 'superiority [of the bourgeois] over those who, because they cannot assert the same contempt for . . . gratuitous luxury and conspicuous consumption, remain dominated by ordinary interests and urgencies' (Bourdieu, 1984: 56).

In this way, what Sconce calls 'paracinema' is a species of bourgeois aesthetics not a challenge to it. Indeed, far from serving as a reminder that 'taste . . . is a social construct with profoundly political implications', paracinema is at least as concerned to assert its superiority over those whom it conceives of as the degraded victims of mainstream commercial culture as it is concerned to provide a challenge to the academy and the art cinema.

Producing the subcultural/inventing the mainstream

The image of mass culture as the inauthentic Other, and of the consumer of mass culture as the simple conformist dupe, recurs again and again within this fan writing. This becomes clear, for example, in the title of Martin's book on the 'video nasties', *Seduction of the Gullible*. In this book, Martin attacks those who campaigned against the 'video nasties' and rejects their claim that the 'lower classes' were too unsophisti-cated to handle the video nasties and that they would, therefore, be seduced and corrupted by exposure to them. Unfortunately, while Martin maintains that this view is patronizing to 'the lower classes', he presents most people as too gullible and con-formist to prevent themselves being seduced and corrupted by the British press who led the campaign (Martin, 1993). A similar problem can be found in Juno *et al*.'s *Incredibly Strange Films*, which repeatedly evokes the ideology of mass culture as can be seen, for example, in the their claim that 'our sophisticated, democratic western civilization regulates the population's access to information, as well as their innermost attitudes, through media – particularly film and video' (Vale *et al.*, 1986b: 4). In this work, the majority of the population are little more than mass cultural zombies and while these writers do claim that 'Aesthetics are not an objective body of laws', they simply see it as part of the 'fundamental mechanisms of how to control the population and maintain the status quo' (1986b: 4). This critique of aesthetics not only sits quite happily with a presentation of the population as an ignorant conformist mass, it also privileges a taste formation which is unable to acknowledge its own conditions of possibility.

However, if Sconce is right that these fans often found themselves battling against traditional aesthetics because 'explicit aesthetic choices are in fact often constituted in opposition to the choices of the groups closest in social space, with whom competition is most direct and immediate' (Sconce, 1995: 375), these fans often reserve their most direct and vitriolic attacks at the both the cultures of their parents and the tastes of other fans – fans who are dismissed as inauthentic. For example, *Incredibly Strange Films* frequently distinguishes itself from fans of the 1980s slasher film, who are presented, by comparison, as inauthentic and indistinguishable from the conformist masses. At one point, for example, writing about *The Wizard of Gore*, Mark Spainhower claims:

> the average moviegoer will certainly be mortified by *The Wizard of Gore*'s extreme sadism, as well as the 'seedy' quality which pervades all of Lewis's films. Absent are the sophisticated latex prosthetics of Tom Savani or Dick Smith, which, while technically virtuosic, appear merely slick and facile next to the crude and vicious carnage of the animal innard school which Lewis himself pioneered to hideous extremes.
>
> (Spainhower, 1986: 176)

Tom Savani* and Dick Smith are themselves, amongst sections of horror fandom, the subject of great adoration, but are hardly figures who would be familiar to the majority of moviegoers. The term 'average movie goer' is therefore an extremely slippery one that operates to conflate a small fan culture with the conformist mass and so produce a clear sense of distinction between the authentic subcultural self and the inauthentic mass cultural other.

On the other hand, Sconce's own account of 'paracinema' also tends to conflate major differences between the fan cultures that it discusses and so constructs its own sense of the 'real' authentic nature of this fan culture. At one point, he does acknowledge that 'factions of the paracinematic audience have little patience even for one another', and refers to a subscription form for *Film Threat* which portrays 'the "typical" *Film Threat* reader, . . . as a dynamic rockabilly-quiffed hipster surrounded by adoring women' who is 'juxtaposed to a drawing of the "typical" *Psychotronic* reader, [who is] depicted as a passive overweight and asexual, with a bad complexion' (Sconce, 1995: 375). Elsewhere I have discussed how similar oppositions are used between SF and horror fans as both fan cultures seek to dissociate themselves from the problematic image of the conformist dupe of mass culture by deflecting this image onto the other fan culture (Jancovich, 2000). Sconce, however, seeks to evade such conflict and simply claims that 'these groups may be thought of as radically opposed "taste publics" which are never the less involved in a common "taste culture"' (Sconce, 1995: 375).

This not only acts to repress the conflicts between these fan cultures, but also the differences on which they are based. For example, while *Incredibly Strange Films* takes a stand in opposition to standards of 'good taste' and champions the films of Edward

---

* Tom Savani should of course be Tom Savini – EM/XM

D. Wood Junior because of his inability/unwillingness to conform to these standards, the Medved brothers who did so much to promote him to legendary status take anything but a confrontational stance to 'Hollywood', 'mainstream, commercial culture' or 'good taste'. Indeed their *Gold Turkey Awards* sets itself up as a pastiche – rather than a parody – of the Oscars in which they hand out awards for failure rather than success (Medved and Medved, 1980). None of this is designed to oppose 'Hollywood', 'mainstream, commercial cinema' or 'good taste', but rather to affirm it. Indeed the enjoyment to be gleaned from these 'turkeys' is precisely their ludicrous ineptness, and this is set up in such as way as to presuppose and endorse the legitimacy of a norm from which they are claimed to differ. In this way, the mass culture critique gets directed at the 'bad movie' rather than mainstream Hollywood, so that the audience declares itself as sophisticated and independently minded through their recognition of the unselfconscious, moronic and conventional nature of these 'bad' films and their filmmakers. Indeed far from celebrating 'bad taste' as a critique of Hollywood and American society, Medved has become known for his book, *Hollywood vs. America*, in which he attacks 'mainstream Hollywood' itself for its 'bad taste' and its supposed opposition to traditional American values (Medved, 1992).

As a result, cult movie audiences do not share a single, and certainly not a uniformly oppositional, attitude towards legitimate culture. At least as often as they challenge legitimate culture, these audiences also attempt to raise the value of their own tastes by demonstrating their comparability with it. *Incredibly Strange Films*, for example, not only name checks avant-garde filmmakers such as Stan Brakhage (Vale *et al.*, 1986b: 4) and draws positive comparisons between the 'grossness' of *Daughter of Horror* with that of *La Grande Bouffe* (Morton, 1985a: 179) but it also claims that Ed Wood's strangeness 'borders on Dada' (Morton, 1986b: 159). Indeed, the emphasis on the oddity and strangeness of these movies is often discussed in terms of 'Surrealism', and the *Research Series* in which *Incredibly Strange Films* is an edition clearly places this book within the context of a supposedly 'alternative', 'underground' and 'transgressive' subculture in which similar topics include The Cramps, Kathy Acker, Annie Sprinkles, bell hooks, Susie Bright, J. G. Ballard, William Burroughs, Throbbing Gristle, punk rock and Octavio Paz.

Even within a single publication, the sheer eclecticism of the films discussed means that they are not read in one coherent way, but through a number of different and contradictory strategies that are constantly slipping into one another. In *Incredibly Strange Films*, for example, the tone moves between virtual contempt for the films discussed, through a patronizing affection for their pathetic failings, to a virtual awe-filled admiration for true works of art. The book also establishes different relationships to its subjects through its interviews. Frank Henenlotter, for example, is addressed as another cult fan whose views affirm, and are affirmed by, those of the interviewer. Herschell Gordon Lewis and others are cast as hacks who had little sense of what they were doing, but whose lifestyles and adventures are almost heroically outrageous, if completely 'cuckoo'. Finally, Larry Cohen is addressed as neither a cult fan, nor as a wacky freak, but rather as a serious auteur with an independent intelligence and an overtly oppositional politics. Indeed, it is the supposed subversiveness of Cohen's politics that concerns the majority of the interview.

These different concerns are held together in the book by a preoccupation with the supposed 'independence' of the true auteur. Rather than working within the commercial mainstream where 'lawyers, accountants, and corporate boards are what films in Hollywood are all about', the independent filmmaker is seen as operating within a 'non-commercial' sector which provides the possibility of 'unfettered creativity' and the presentation of 'unpopular – even radical – views' (Vale *et al.*, 1986b: 5). Unfortunately, rather than true individualism, it was precisely the commercial conditions of many of the films discussed which encouraged their more outlandish features and it is often the very banality or incoherence of their political positions which marks them out: why else would these fans celebrate educational films or industrial jeopardy films. In fact, cult movie audiences are less an internally coherent 'taste culture' than a series of frequently opposed and contradictory reading strategies that are defined through a sense of their difference to an equally incoherently imagined 'normality', a loose conglomeration of corporate power, lower middle class conformity and prudishness, academic elitism and political conspiracy.

Exhibition, the academy and the emergence of the cult movie

As Thornton has shown in her own work on subcultural ideologies, while this sense of opposition to, or difference from, the 'mainstream' eventually proves entirely contradictory, it is necessary in order to provide a sense of subcultural authenticity, both in the fan writing and in academic accounts like that of Sconce, which 'uncritically replay these beliefs' (Thornton, 1995: 96). As she argues, 'inconsistent fantasies of the mainstream are rampant in "subcultural studies"' and this is 'probably the single most important reason why subsequent cultural studies find pockets of symbolic resistance wherever they look' (1995: 93), and by the same logic, why everything can also look as though it has already been incorporated.

Thus, she shows that both the subcultures themselves, and the academic studies of them, frequently portray these groupings as 'somehow outside the media and culture', as 'grassroots cultures (which) resist and struggle with a colonizing mass-mediated corporate world' (1995: 116). By contrast, she argues that despite their oppositional ideology, these subcultures are not the products of an authentic self-generation which is later threatened with incorporation by the media, but rather that the media is central to both their formation and maintenance. Much the same is also true of the academy in the case of cult movie fandom.

Rather than emerging out of some spontaneous sense of affinity, cult movie audiences developed out of the audiences for the art cinema and repertory theatres, and it was these institutions that provided the spaces for congregation and often acted as the gatekeepers who classified and reclassified films through their advertising and exhibition. However, as Gomery has shown, the arts cinema in the USA was itself produced not through a rejection of commerce rather by through its imperatives. In the late 1940s and early 1950s, as the cinema audience declined, many cinemas converted themselves into arts cinemas as a way of avoiding closure. The audience for these new cinemas was not only class based but also, in the process, geographically exclusive. Before the 1950s, 40% of all art cinemas were in New York City, and 60% of the national revenues for the typical art film came from Manhattan alone. Even outside New York City, the scene was largely confined to college towns such as Ann

Arbor, Michigan and Madison, Wisconsin. None the less, as a specialist market, the art cinema circuit was a profitable one and, by 1952, it was hailed as the biggest news in movie exhibition. At this point, it was foreign films which dominated the programmes, especially after the success of Roger Vadim's *And God Created Woman* in 1956, a film which established the practice of selling art cinema to highly educated Americans on the basis of themes and materials which were supposedly unavailable or even taboo within 'Hollywood' product.

These cinemas continued to flourish throughout the 1950s and 1960s, but they were also complemented by another development, the emergence of the repertory film theatre. If the arts cinema had managed to define film as an art form, college film societies were formed to show reruns of old classics. By 1960, there were 250 college film societies, many of which would be converted into repertory cinemas during the 1960s (Gomery, 1992).

These developments also correspond to changing academic attitudes to film within the period. While the art cinema stage corresponded closely to the tastes of mass culture theorists such as Dwight Macdonald who dismissed Hollywood and championed the largely European avant-garde (Macdonald, 1963), the film societies corresponded closely to the tastes of auteur theorists such as Andrew Sarris who sought to displace the European avant-garde through a re-examination of the Hollywood cinema. If the first critical trend established the ideology of mass culture on which cult movie audiences would found themselves, an ideology in which Hollywood was distinguished from the cinema of independence, auteurism bequeathed an aesthetics of the 'underground' in which it was not high culture itself which was to be celebrated but rather the apparently worthless low budget quickie. Like the cult movie fans after him, Sarris overtly used the apparently 'low brow' rather than the 'high brow' to beat the 'middle brow' or 'mainstream'. Thus, while he celebrated movies made within Hollywood, he celebrated them as a critique of the Hollywood mainstream and this led him to privilege 'relatively conventional genre films' over 'so-called "big" pictures' because, in a argument directly repeated in *Incredibly Strange Films*, the former were not subject to the same close scrutiny by the head office and hence provided greater freedom for the director to express himself (Sarris, 1976: 247).

However, if Sarris provided the means of finding the artistic within the low budget film, it was the influence of French structuralism that offered a way of celebrating the inept or even downright awful. In their famous introduction to *Cahier du Cinema*, Comolli and Narboni offer a way of redeeming specific forms of non-avant-garde cinema that extended certain aspects of auteurism and mass culture theory but did not require a univocal celebration of these films. Their infamous 'category e' film did not necessarily present a conscious or even unconscious critique of the prevailing ideology, and was thus fully implicated in the supposed conservatism and conformity of mass culture, but for some reason, these films failed to work as intended. These films 'start out from a non-progressive stand point, ranging from the frankly reactionary through the conciliatory to the mildly critical', but for some reason, 'there is a noticeable gap, a dislocation, between the starting point and the finished product' (Comolli and Narboni, 1976: 27). For one reason or another, a film of this type 'lets us see' the ideology. Instead of appearing natural, transparent and obvious, the ideology is made manifest and visible, either because it is presented too baldly or because the film fails to smooth over its contradictions. It is through this kind of critical framework that cult fans can appreciate the likes of *The Phenix City Story* or *Reefer Madness*. They are not praised for their inherent artistry, but rather for either their remarkable lack of artistry or their bald, contradictory or even hypocritical, ideological positions.

This, however, frequently bleeds into another strategy, that of camp, and it is important to note the significance of this concept, particularly in the New York City art worlds of the 1960s. While Sconce tries to distance his conception of paracinema from an association with camp by presenting the former as confrontational and the latter as a form of 'ironic colonization and cohabitation', this distinction seems like simply another attempt to distinguish the authentic from the inauthentic fan. The films of John Waters and *The Rocky Horror Picture Show* were amongst the most prominent examples of the cult movie within the 1970s, but both of these are positively imbued with the aesthetics of camp.

They also emerge at what Gomery calls 'the apex of the repertory cinema (which) came with the phenomenon of the midnight movie in the 1970s' (Gomery, 1992: 194). These film showings began in New York and brought together an eclectic series of movies from excessively gorey art movies such as *El Topo*, horror classics such as Romero's *Night of the Living Dead* and the 3D version of Jack Arnold's *Creature from the Black Lagoon*, to movies such as *The Rocky Horror Picture Show* or John Waters' *Pink Flamingos*, both of which were self consciously designed as cult movies.

Rarity, exclusivity and cultural knowledge: mass, niche and micro media in the construction of the cult audience

Cult movie fandom was, therefore, not developed in opposition to either the commercial or the academic but grew out of a series of economic and intellectual developments in the post-war period, a process which created selective film markets that were defined by a sense of distinction from 'mainstream, commercial cinema'. Indeed, it is the very ideology which insists that these markets are free from economic criteria which needs to be criticized. As Bourdieu, Garnham and others have shown, it is the very sense of art as something which exists as outside of economic relations that needs to be challenged because the values through which art is legitimated and mass culture is rejected, 'far from being universal, are closely linked to the structural inequality of access to societies resources' (Garnham, 1977: 347). Not only is it the case that, as Bourdieu has shown, the dispositions through which both the art cinema and cult movie audiences both celebrate these films and define their distinction from, and superiority to, the consumers of 'mass culture' are produced on the basis of social and economic privilege, it is also the case that these dispositions are not natural but are themselves the products of economic investments, investments in books, magazines, cinema-going, etc.

It is, therefore, not just the academy and the art cinemas that are responsible for the organization of cult movie audiences, but, as Thornton has shown in relation to musical subcultures, the media more widely. Indeed, as Thornton has shown, the fact that fans are so often openly hostile to the media is itself one of the complex and contradictory consequences of the circulation of information. Rather than simply spontaneous, self-organizing subcultures, cult movie audiences are themselves brought together, and a sense of 'imagined community' is produced and maintained, *through* the media. However, the value of membership within these subcultures is based on a sense of exclusivity and hence the media also threatens these subcultures by blurring the very sense of distinction which underpins the sense of community. As Thornton puts it, the very notion of ' "selling out" means *selling* to *out*siders' (1995: 124). She therefore distinguishes between three media layers – micro, niche and mass – each of which have markedly different connotations, at least in part because 'their diverse audience sizes and compositions and their distinct processes of circulation have different consequences' (1995: 122).

These distinctions are useful markers but they are merely stages in a continuum. For example, if the popular press are mass media and the fliers for horror movie fan conventions are micro media, can we simply link *Premiere* and *Fangoria* together as niche media? *Premiere* is directed at a niche readership – movie fans – but *Fangoria* is directed at a niche within that niche – horror movie fans, and even then a niche within that niche. Even then one is still left with the problem of the fanzines that exist somewhere between niche publications such as *Fangoria* and micro media such as advertising fliers. What is more, the status of these change as they 'sell out,' as for example when Michael Weldon's fanzine *Psychotronic* spawns a publications such as *The Psychotronic Encyclopaedia of Film* (Weldon, 1983) published for a 'mass market' by Ballatine Press or more recently *The Psychotronic Encyclopaedia of Video* (Weldon, 1996).

Thus, the media exist not as a clearly defined Other to the cult movie audience, but rather as a complex range of communications systems that act to both compose and maintain the sense of an 'imagined community', but also threaten to destroy this sense through the profligate dissemination of their exclusive knowledges. Indeed, in cult movie fandom, information and inaccessibility need to be carefully regulated and balanced. For example, many publications present themselves as guides to an inaccessible 'underground' where knowledge is not only essential to appreciation and the making of distinctions, but as such, operates as a precious emblem of *insider* status. As a result, publications such as *Video Watchdog* and *Uncut* provide detailed knowledge about cult materials available (although inaccessibly so) on video and other formats. Both are concerned to identify or define the authentic version of the films that they discuss in a context where there are multiple versions within different media at different times.

In the case of *Video Watchdog*, this is usually associated with issues of technological reproduction, as well as a 'historical' concern with the significance of the film itself and reasons for the different versions. For example, in the case of a Kino Video release of *The Cabinet of Dr Caligari*, they write 'thanks to another superb restoration job by David Shepherd and film preservation associates, Robert Wiene's silent classic – which launched the mesmerizing invaluable movement of German expressionism – can now be appreciated with a clarity unseen for generations' (Cole, 1997: 9). They then move on to discuss the pros and cons of the various techniques used in the transfer.

Uncut, on the other hand, is much more interested in the search for the authentic original and focuses less on the 'classics' than on those films identified as 'video nasties' in Britain, and which have been cut and/or banned in the process. The pictures also draw attention to its main focus of concern: the moments of sex and/or violence which have been made precious through their status as 'taboo', and whose presence or absence now comes to signify authenticity and inauthenticity.

This raises another of Thornton's points. Like the rave scene in music, the cult of the so-called 'video nasty' was produced through the media and to some extent by the commercial motivations of distributors. For example, rather than simply the target of a right wing campaign, the 'video nasties' were to some extent the production of organizations such as Palace Pictures who had brought the rights to *The Evil Dead* and tried to produce a 'moral panic' as a way of not only advertising the film, but making it a precious and desirable object. As with many subcultures, the media did not simply attack a pre-existent and authentic subculture, but an engineered moral panic (even if it did get out of control) created both a cult sub-genre and an audience for it.

However, while niche publications such as *Uncut* act to disseminate information in order to produce a sense of community, they are also concerned not to disseminate it too widely. They frequently announce their selective nature – that they are not for everyone – and their combative style is at least as much to warn off 'outsiders' and to reassure insiders by advertising the inaccessibility of the scene.

Indeed, inaccessibility is maintained throughout the scene not only through the selection of the materials – they are not for everybody – but also through their virtual unobtainability. The privileging of banned material is most obviously explained in its celebration of that which is not even legally available. One has to be in the know to even get to see them. The inaccessibility of these films is even something that the magazines actually promote as one of the pleasures of the scene. For example, the editor of *Uncut* writes:

> Readers have requested that we feature the addresses of the companies that have released the videos under review, but I won't be doing that for a couple of reasons: a) some of the tapes are old and deleted and, b) this takes away half the fun of finally tracking down an exclusive and rare cassette! If it exists, keep looking – seek and you shall find . . .
>
> (Brown: 2)

However, this is slightly deceptive because it is this very exclusivity and rarity that makes forms of fan's knowledge culturally valuable within these scenes and their collections economically valuable. Hence Frank Henenlotter's contradictory reactions to the effects of video on the cult movie scene:

> It's a strange concept: all those obscure films that I would have risked injury and death to see (literally, in some of those theatres) are now available at your local clean video store! It's a little unnerving. I'm wholeheartedly in support of this, but I'm still not used to the fact that those films that I spent my whole life trying to see are now consumer items.
>
> (Vale *et al.*, 1986a: 8)

In this way, these publications (like the cinemas where the films are shown) also act as gatekeepers that manage the difficult balance between inclusion and exclusion on which the scene depends. However, even the fanzines should not be seen as the authentic voice of the scene. As Thornton points out, the fanzines of the rave culture came out after it was converted into a scene, a process that was produced through the entrepreneurial activities of event organizers and listings magazines such as *Time Out*.

Similarly, in the realm of the cult movie, my own entrance into the scene was not through 'word of mouth' or through fanzines, but through the reviews of listings magazines such as *Time Out* and the schedules and micro media of cinemas such as *The Phoenix, The Scala* and the *ICA*. However, even these were not the producers of the scene, but were largely importing a cult movie canon which had been constructed to a large extent in the USA, and New York in particular.

In conclusion, then, the cult movie has much to tell us about the politics of cultural consumption and its relation to issues of economic and educational capital. Most particularly, it requires a re-examination of one of the most problematic concepts within film studies – 'the mainstream, commercial cinema' – and the ways in which its inconsistent and contradictory uses arise from its function as the Other, the construction of which allows for the production of distinctions and sense of cultural superiority.

SECTION 2
Cult case studies

Introduction

While the first section of the *Cult Film Reader* focused on the theories and concepts, this section concentrates on the actual cult films and filmmakers themselves. By their very nature, cult films and filmmakers find themselves outside the norms, boundaries, and categories of mainstream cinema. Because they stand out it is extremely difficult to group them into movements or types. Moreover, many cult films thank their status to their unwillingness to adhere to routines and practices that would allow such classifications – they make it their business to challenge such attempts. They go against canons, genres and generalizations, whether these are aesthetic or ideological. In a crucial sense then, this section is heretic in that it attempts what the films and filmmakers themselves reject.

All of this means that any attempts to write the history of cult cinema, the story of its stars, villains, styles and streams, also needs to address the ways in which these histories are written. Because cult films challenge methodic examination, we need to expose the underlying assumptions of those examinations. Therefore, this introduction will first contain a brief discussion of the historiography of cinema and its relation to cult films' practices and reputations. Second, we will offer a necessarily sketchy and fragmentary historical overview of trends and tendencies in cult film. This canon of cult film is selective, singling out a small number of films and people who are considered instrumental in the development of cult cinema, and who feature in any consideration of its highlights. In each case we will make references to the more detailed case studies excerpted in this section.

Film historiography and cult films

Traditionally, film historical overviews – regardless of their approach – provide a coherent narration of developments that link chains of cause and effect together into one (or more) stories. They use techniques of evidence, argumentation, reasoning, logic and rhetoric to string those arguments into a thesis.[1]

Overviews of cult film usually resist this practice. Instead, they offer encyclopaedic overviews of cult films, organized by family name, by date of release, or sometimes simply alphabetically by title. In none of the cases do they claim to be complete – in fact, all such overviews stress the haphazardness and fragmentary nature of their efforts, and are frank and unapologetic about their lapses and omissions. Moreover, as most introductions to cult film overviews testify, even claims of evidence and logic are not often taken seriously. Much like the films themselves, a sweet sort of anarchy or surrealism, combined with irony, chance, accidents and exclusivity are part of the historiography of the cult film.

Two elements of the historiography of cult cinema akin to traditional scholarly work on film are biography and attention to detail. Much of cult cinema history is highly personal – tales of individuals resisting institutions or industrial routines, for instance. Much of cult film history is also marginal, captured through oral accounts or second-hand sources (private witnesses, tabloid journalism, fanzines) rather than production documents or even the films themselves. While occasionally unreliable or suspect, examples such as the biography of James Whale, studies of Johnny Depp, or interview books with Terry Gilliam, Werner Herzog or David Cronenberg (to name a few examples not further explored in this section) demonstrate how this personal approach can become an advantage, supplying accurate insights.[2] The study of cult films can turn the tool of biography into a razor-sharp instrument of dissection. It is the main reason why we have included in our bibliography a list of sources on individual directors.

The obsession with detail is also central to the study of cult cinema's history. Since so much of that history is anecdotal, incomplete and fractured – obstructing the kind of overarching narrative so typical for history writing – cult film history research tends to concentrate on microscopic moments, individual films, small cycles and genres, less popular and acclaimed personnel, and isolated incidents. There is both an advantage and a danger here. The advantage is that because of its reliance on detail, cult film study has to be precise – one cannot afford to have a name or date wrong since it would drastically alter the argument – one has to locate the exact source. To give two examples: studies of midnight movies with international careers, like *Daughters of Darkness*, need to pay detailed attention to the release pattern of the film in order to understand its significance; and research into the phenomenon of the video nasties needs to be exact about which versions of the 'nasties list' were used by different participants in the debates surrounding it.[3] The danger, of course, is that the details can obscure a broad understanding of the wider cultural implications cult cinema has, and that it ends up being a collection of details without wider application – what is it for then?

The study of cult film addresses this issue head-on. After all, studying films that have cult followings means placing them squarely in their cultural surroundings. The history of cult film is always also a cultural history. But the problem is that the locus of that culture is not so easy to define. Cult films' cultural impact is often less tangible than that of mainstream cinema – it deals with 'sensibilities' (Susan Sontag's term – see Section one), 'subjective opinions' (in the case of biographies), and 'trivialities' (details), impressions and particularities that are difficult to grasp and pin down. It deals with what people – practitioners and audiences alike – *experience*, not just what they testify. Maybe that is why the study of cult cinema, especially in its efforts to connect films to cultural surroundings, uses speculation. Jean Vigo's essay on *Un chien andalou* is an impressionistic account of such an experience, and it seems different from how Joan Hawkins links the films of Jess Franco to Spanish culture, or from the way in which

Lawrence O'Toole sees horror cinema as a cult particularly fitting the end of the 1970s.[4] But they all attempt to move from detailed observations to cultural interpretations. The problem they face is that their move is one between the very particular and the very general. Because of the span, it requires painstakingly careful attention to every step on the way. The essays in this section all demonstrate how much effort this takes.

At its best, then, the historical study of cult films combines detail and biography into a wider account of how this kind of cinema functions and what that tells us about the world we live in. As such, it can have policy applications, and it can even lead to a challenge of accepted practices within academia itself. Much in the same vein, cult films are suspicious of mainstream cinema; the study of cult film can be paranoid about the pervasiveness of accepted methodologies and routines that give us the 'wholemeal, fully approved' story of film. Details can play an essential part in deconstructing that story, questioning it and, at its extreme end, paranoia itself can become a technique of investigation – countering cultural homogeneity by cracking the code of the accepted canon.[5]

Finally, personality matters too. Traditional overviews of film history tend to 'erase' the personality of the writer or researcher behind a shroud of objectivity and evidence. But writers, critics and scholars of cult film are ready to admit, proud to declare, or reluctantly confess, their allegiances. They tend to indulge in offering the reader personal information, often in the form of confessions of 'guilty pleasures', or of embarrassing preferences.[6] There is an unusual partisanship in this almost endearing commitment, similar to that of the cult devotees themselves – one that we would not dare exclude ourselves from. This is not meant as a criticism: to a large extent, the historiography of cult depends on scholars who had to live an almost double life in order to be able to unearth any kind of information. Let us not forget that until quite recently one was not (*most certainly not!*) supposed to research such films. Now, cult film scholars have come out of the closet, and they have found audiences that not only read academic work on cult films, but also – by and large – appreciate it.

The canon of cult cinema

Given how unsettled the historiography of cult film is, what does the history of cult cinema, in all its personalized detail, look like? It cannot be anything other than a study of cases and therefore the following overview is of necessity piecemeal.

Roughly speaking the issue of cult films first appeared when fans of Mary Pickford or Asta Nielsen started paying attention to the films they appeared in. This first happened with slapstick films, which garnered a cult following not so much for their stars (though Charlie Chaplin, for one, was a cult case in himself) as for their anarchistic attitude, hedonism and rebellious dynamic – often disjointed in their storytelling, but never less than spectacular and frequently challenging accepted norms.[7] Buster Keaton's *Cops* (1922) is a terrific example. As Harry Potamkin's essay from Section one demonstrates, the object of cultdom gradually shifted, away from comedy to European art cinema. The impact of films like *Das Cabinet des Dr. Caligari* (1919), *Haxan* (1922), or *Pandora's Box* (1927), accompanied by controversies and bans was such that it opened up a totally new avenue of film appreciation, one which displays all the characteristics of cult film.[8] At a time when Hollywood championed the studio system, these films provided alternatives: they were disruptive, immoral, scandalous and almost occult in their observations and celebrations of 'difference'. The culmination of this sensibility came right before sound entered film history, with the surrealists and *Un chien andalou* (1928). Buñuel abandoned the continuity system completely, in favour of an associational mode that violated the logic of time and space, and added explicit imagery of a sexual and violent nature, spiced with illogical insertions that puzzled audiences. Add a tumultuous premiere, and you have a recipe for a cult film. Buñuel quickly found successors in Jean Vigo and Jean Cocteau.

When fascism and economic depression halted European developments, Hollywood's B-row took over. Influenced by a legion of European filmmakers who fled the old continent, Hollywood's chain-produced genre films started exploring the odd and unusual, going further than the studio executives cared to know. This created the opportunity for Todd Browning and James Whale to experiment with the permissible, and release cult favourites like *Dracula* (1930), *Frankenstein* (1930), *Freaks* (1932) and *Bride of Frankenstein* (1935) – all from Universal. Their popularity gave way to a veritable stream of horror, nurturing the talents of Robert Florey or Karl Freund. Parallel to that, the exoticism and erotic undertones of Friedrich Murnau and Robert Flaherty's *Tabu* (1931), led to suggestive pseudo-documentaries like *Trader Horn* (1931), which in turn spawned a series of exotic adventure serials, of which *King Kong* (1933) and *Tarzan and His Mate* (1934) were the most cultish – though one should not minimalize the appeal of swashbuckler and pirate movies.

After the installation of the Hays Code, such cult aesthetics (exotic, campy, outrageous, sexy, horrific, violent) were relegated to a near amateur level, where freelancers and occasional entrepreneurs like Louis Gasnier (and his *Reefer Madness*, 1934) used the veil of 'education' to still present titillating imagery. The new codeword was 'exploitation', and while the aesthetics were the same the emphasis shifted away from the films to the tricks that sell them.[9]

In the 1940s, film noir became the cult of the time. Marrying many of the stylistic achievements of the 1930s horror film, 1920s European expressionism and 1930s French poetic realism, the cool, brutality and fatalism of film noir became key aesthetic characteristics, illustrated by harsh contrasts, intimidating low-placed wide-angle perspectives and bold cutting. While the early 1940s saw some official recognition of cult aesthetics in the form of the acclaim of *Casablanca* (1942), the most cultish films noir were those in the margins, like *Detour* (1945), or the low-budget atmospheric thrillers of Val Lewton and/or Jacques Tourneur (*I Walked with a Zombie*, 1943). Incomplete themselves, they lifted fractured despair onto a level quite in tune with the horror of World War II.[10] The career of Orson Welles became emblematic for this attitude, as evidenced in Parker Tyler's essay in this section.[11]

Still, much went on below the radar of most critics. Especially since the 1950s, and the official denunciation of the Hollywood vertical integration (studios dominating production, distribution and exhibition), a small, gradually growing market for independent cinema emerged within which cult cinema found a nesting ground. Local cinema thrived, in the form of burlesque exploitation cinema (and occasional 16-mm pornographic features). Hardly visible on the official cultural map, they nevertheless attracted a determined clientele, and they offered a distinct set of aesthetic techniques – as Eric Schaefer shows in his essay in this section.[12] Next to that, the late 1950s and early

1960s saw European art-house films (like Rossellini's *Rome, Open City*), European lowbrow, low-budget exploitation films (Italian and Spanish horror cinema; erotic camp), and US-grown exploitation movies (like those from Roger Corman) find a niche with audiences appreciative of the popular music (like jazz or rock). The selfish characters without moral motivation, the sexual openness and directness of violent imagery, and the rough 'n' ready unpolished style these films offered – often undercut by a nihilistic and/or existentialist attitude towards contemporary 'issues' (especially in films openly soliciting youthful audiences). Several essays in this section chronicle parts of this vibrant activity.[13]

Throughout the 1960s and into the 1970s, this vibrancy guaranteed visibility and continuity to a wide variety of exploitation and experimental cinema. It turned obscure underground fare like *Flaming Creatures* (1963), *Scorpio Rising* (1963), or Andy Warhol's films, into international cult phenomena and it was lenient and permissive towards films testing the boundaries of taste and decency (like *Plan 9 From Outer Space*, 1959; or *Sins of the Fleshapoids*, 1965).[14] It gave Corman the opportunity to offer chances to young talents like Francis Coppola, Martin Scorsese, Jonathan Demme and Stephanie Rothman (see the essay by Noel Carroll excerpted in this section).[15] Many genre-exploitation efforts became self-reflexive (another trend noted by Carroll), turning their appreciation into a game at once playful and political – for the first time cult cinema began to behave in a revolutionary way, conscious of its resistance against oppression. In the wake of the hugely influential *Easy Rider* (1969), it became an attitude acutely present in rebellious road movies and action-romps that operated on the wrong side of the law, like *Get Carter* (1971).[16]

Of all genres, the ones most commonly associated with this combination of reflexivity, playfulness and politics are pornography, horror and blaxploitation.[17] The first two openly celebrate activities seen as hugely problematic in contemporary society: sex and violence. But films like *Deep Throat* (1972), *Behind the Green Door* (1973) or *Emmanuelle* (1973) not only portrayed full-on sex and erotica, they also replaced much of the false prudence of earlier erotic cinema with a frankness and playfulness unseen before – the cult of hedonism at its height. The horror film became the most openly political of all genres, and its violence was turned into a force of social critique. Building on *Psycho* (1960), *Invasion of the Body Snatchers* (1956) and *Night of the Living Dead* (1968), films like *The Texas Chainsaw Massacre* (1974) or *Shivers* (1975) portrayed gruesome acts of violence – often misogynist – without cathartic relief, offering themselves as cultural critiques, as Janet Staiger argues in her essay in this section.[18] Blaxploitation combined open sexuality and violence with generic playfulness (referencing virtually every possible genre), but its focus on black ethnic characters in often urban settings gave it both a bold attitude and a social significance – like feminist cinema it showed how groups routinely disenfranchised could subvert the norms and practices of their cinematic representations.[19]

Of the many factors facilitating the momentum, the most significant were a vibrant exhibition circuit – comprising art houses, grindhouses, drive-ins and campus societies – and an equally vivid film press, encompassing liberal criticism as well as widely available fan magazines and underground publications. The most notorious of these exhibition circuits was the 'midnight movie' phenomenon. Instigated to facilitate late-night urban screenings of cinema unsuitable to be programmed at other times (too risky for regular evenings, too shocking for matinées), it became an eclectic network for audiences craving unusual, subversive films, and anything daylight shun. *El Topo* (1970) is usually credited with being the first midnight movie. Others include *Night of the Living Dead* (1968), *The Texas Chainsaw Massacre* (which was first tried as a matinée, with predictably upsetting results), the obscene *Pink Flamingos* (1972) and the ultimate cult film, *The Rocky Horror Picture Show* (1975) – ultimate because of the insistently outrageous active audience celebrations it received (and still receives).[20] The unsettling combination of film noir, surrealism and avant-garde *Eraserhead* (1977) is usually seen as the last of the original midnight movies; its characteristics are investigated in Steven Schneider's essay in this section.[21]

By the late 1970s much of the momentum was destroyed by a recovery of mainstream taste (fuelled by some of the Corman babes, quick in recuperating runaway genres), and the emergent technologies or repeat-home viewing. While other cults floundered, the horror genre retained its reputation – as Lawrence O'Toole describes, it even gained notoriety.[22] A determined network of horror and fantasy festivals was instrumental in this survival, as were innovative appropriations of video technology – giving way to a new way of experiencing horror: remote in hand, finger on the pause and rewind buttons to fully enjoy the spectacle of special effects (what Philip Brophy quickly termed 'horrality').[23] The trend was exemplified by splatter films like *Scanners* (1981), video nasties (especially *Evil Dead*, 1983), mondo-films like *Cannibal Holocaust* (1979), rape-revenge movies like *House on the Edge of the Park* (1980), *Italian giallo* (especially those films by Lucio Fulci and Dario Argento), and the incredible appeal of slasher serials, like *Friday the 13th* (1980 onwards) – topped off by Peter Jackson's inventive, and aptly named *Bad Taste* (1987 – see Section three). While all this horror also meant endless repetition, and a phase of mannerisms that extended for almost a decade, that did not seem to deter cultists – quite the opposite: in the era of repeat viewings, repetition became a virtue.

Tied into that element of repetition, the biggest change to cult aesthetics in the 1980s was that it substituted its preference for decadence and revolution (its relentless drive forward) for nostalgia and deconstruction of the concept of time. As pointed out above, the destruction of logical progression of time was already present in cult cinema since *Un chien andalou*, but in the 1980s it became its determining factor. Next to an endless stream of remakes and sequels, films like *Back to the Future* (1985), *Peggy Sue Got Married* (1986), science fiction utopias and dystopias (*Blade Runner*, 1982; but also the rock 'n' roll fable set in 'another time, *Streets of Fire*, 1984), or John Hughes' teen comedies, combined a yearning for traditional values with a ruthless breakdown of consumer society. Time-travel and nostalgic self-awareness of the past became the prevailing tools to disrupt continuity and realism. Visually, special effects and postmodern homage (borrowing styles from earlier decades) aided that disruption. Similar sentiments seemed to surface in metaphysical meditations like *Le grand bleu* (1988) and *Blue Velvet* (1986), or action-packed epics like *Raiders of the Lost Ark* (1981) or *Das Boot* (1981). As a consequence, cult cinema became timeless, and film history itself became a cult.[24] *Casablanca* and *It's a Wonderful Life* found renewed followings, and *Nuovo Cinema Paradiso* (1989) combined a pining for the 'good old days' with a lament of 'loss'. New and past cults together offered a counterpoint to the decade's desperate search for values outside its own framework of relentless capitalism. If nothing else, the

1980s' self-awareness established cinema's 'cult appeal' as a prime source of attraction for audiences. For the first time, 'cult' became an aesthetic denominator in its own right.

The 1990s continued to contain most of the aesthetic traits that cult film had acquired over the decades. Actually, during this decade everything seemed to qualify as cult, from the small independent films of Jim Jarmusch, Pedro Almodovar and Hal Hartley to the supersized mainstream of *Titanic* (1997) – a film that redefined the size of cult cinema (masscult now really meant mass-cult), its instantaneity, and the concept of repeat-viewing. In such a climate a canon becomes almost impossible to detect, and partly that was what 1990s cults were all about – all aesthetic pretensions could remain intact, fandom commitments became 'normal', and everyone's favourite was a candidate for best cult ever at some point (or one could see it as the typically 1990s' lack of commitment – the 'I didn't do it, it's not my problem' attitude). Amidst that, a key characteristic of 1990s' cult became its move from a single medium-carrier (cinema) to multimedia platforms (video, TV, CD and later also DVD and the internet). This dispersal is best exemplified by the overlap between cult film and cult television. As Matt Hills' essay from Section one indicated, *The X-Files* took on most of the aesthetic properties of cult cinema and quickly became a powerful cult (similar to *Star Trek*, which Henry Jenkins singles out in his essay in Section four).[25] It is also visible in the ease with which directors like Mel Damski or Rachel Talalay, previously active in cult genres like horror and spoofs, went on to direct postmodern television pastiches like *Ally McBeal*. J.P. Telotte's essay on the multi-platform existence of *The Blair Witch Project* (2000) is a clear indication of this characteristic.[26]

Simultaneously, and almost as a reaction, cult purism dictated a retreat into even more obscure niches, championing only the most tough and taste-challenging films. As we will see in Section three, a lot of this material was found outside the western hemisphere – in Asia, Latin America or the Middle East – or it became distinctly subcultural (in the case of anime, gothic horror, erotic thrillers, or queer and lesbian cinema). By the beginning of the twenty-first century this caused a virtual split in cult aesthetics and its canon, with immediate (and sometimes preprogrammed) blockbuster cults like *Star Wars* (1999–2005), *The Lord of the Rings* (2001–3), *Harry Potter* (2001–), or *Pirates of the Caribbean* (2003–7) on the one hand, and slow-brewing, tiny, hidden cults like *Cube* (1997–2004), *Baise-moi* (2000), *Ginger Snaps* (2000–4), *Donnie Darko* (2001), or the films of Jörg Buttgereit on the other hand. In between these two poles, remakes of cult oldies occupied what Dwight MacDonald calls a 'midcult', sizeable and with the necessary edges, but somehow missing the authenticity of genuine cults.[27] Now that 'cult' has become a recognized term, it also seems to want its internal aesthetic distinctions.

Notes

1   There has been discussion within film studies about the best possible approach to film history, largely between teleological and ontological schools of thought. For overviews, see Allen, Robert and Douglas Gomery (1985) *Film History: Theory and Practice*, New York: Knopf; and Bordwell, David and Kristin Thompson (1994) 'History, historiography, and film history, in *Film History, an Introduction* (1st edn), New York: McGraw-Hill, xxxi–xlii.

2   See, for instance: Curtis, James (2003) *James Whale: A New World of Gods and Monsters*, Minneapolis, MN: University of Minnesota Press; Cronin, Paul (ed.) (2003) *Herzog on Herzog*, London: Faber & Faber; Christie, Ian (ed.) (1999) *Gilliam On Gilliam*, London: Faber & Faber; Rodley, Chris (ed.) (1997) *Cronenberg on Cronenberg* (2nd edn), London: Faber & Faber; Pomerance, Murray (2005) *Johnny Depp Starts Here*, New Brunswick, NJ: Rutgers University Press.

3   Mathijs, Ernest (2005) 'Bad reputations: The reception of trash cinema', *Screen*, 46(4), 451–72; Egan, Kate (forthcoming) *Trash or Treasure? Censorship and the Changing Meanings of the Video Nasties*, Manchester: Manchester University Press.

4   Vigo, Jean (1932) '*Un chien andalou*', in Luis Bunuel and Salvador Dali, *Un chien andalou*, London: Faber & Faber, xxv–xvi; Hawkins, Joan (2000) *Cutting Edge: Art Horror and the Horrific Avant-Garde*, Minneapolis, MN: University of Minnesota Press; O'Toole, Lawrence (1979) 'The cult of horror', *Maclean's*, 16 July, 46–7, 49–50.

5   One example of this is the discussion of David Cronenberg's *Videodrome* in Jameson, Fredric (1992) *The Geopolitical Aesthetic: Cinema and Space in the World System*, London: British Film Institute. Another excellent example is Robert Ray's speculation on the course of the history of cinema through a detailed 'what-if' exercise. Concentrating on the 'mystery' of the disappearance of inventor Louis Le Prince, Ray asks what this single event might mean for how we write on cinema, not just in the case that the event turned out to be different (or indeed if we even had any further information on it), but in the case of how we *acknowledge* it differently (choosing to see it as more crucial than we do now). See, Ray, Robert B. (1993) 'Film studies/crisis/experimentation', *Film Criticism*, 17(2–3), 56–78.

6   A case in point is the confessional tone of some parts of Welch Everman's introduction to his *Cult Horror Films* – see Everman, Welch (1993) *Cult Horror Films*, New York: Citadel Press, 4, 8.

7   One only needs to check Kenneth Anger's account of the infamous Fatty Arbuckle trial to see how mainstream America thought of this. See, Anger, Kenneth ([1974] 1957) *Hollywood Babylon*, London: Arrow Books.

8   See, Budd, Mike (1984) 'Authorship as commodity: The art cinema and the *Cabinet of Dr. Caligari*', *Wide Angle*, 6(1), 12–19; Thompson, Kristin (1990) 'Dr. Caligari at the Folies-Bergere', in Mike Budd (ed.) *The Cabinet of Dr. Caligari: Texts, Contexts, Histories*, New Brunswick, NJ: Rutgers University Press, 121–69; Peary, Danny (1981) *Cult Movies*, New York: Delta Books, 247–49; Mathijs, Ernest (2007) 'Benjamin Christensen', in Steven Jay Schneider (ed.) *501 Movie Directors*, New York: Quintet Books.

9   Of indispensable value in the study of this era are: Doherty, Thomas (1999) *Pre-Code Hollywood: Sex, Immorality and Insurrection in American Cinema 1930–1934*, New York: Columbia University Press; and Schaefer, Eric (1999) *Bold! Daring! Shocking! True! A History of Exploitation Films, 1919–1959*, Durham: Duke University Press.

10 As if to demonstrate how cults always clash, the cult of the musical provided relief from the war – displaying a cunningly naïve romanticism (smart yet unassuming). At this point soundtracks started to become a core element of cult aesthetics, developing from the quasi-innocent tunes in *Meet me in St. Louis* (1944), through reflexive musicals about music (*Singing in the Rain*, 1952), to swinging vehicles for rock 'n' roll artists (*The Girl Can't Help It*, 1956; *King Creole*, 1958). It is worth remembering though that in spite of their popularity, musicals only really became cult objects once the genre itself went into decline.

11 Tyler, Parker (1970) 'Orson Welles, and the big experimental film cult, in P. Adams Sitney (ed.) *The Film Culture Reader*, Open Square Press, 376–86. If, at this point, anyone wonders how neatly this account of the canon of cult fits official histories of cinema, there

is a good reason. Until the 1970s, much film history overviews tended to prefer the eclectic over the normal, the exceptional and off-beat over the mainstream and popular, celebrating through outspoken critics careers that were at odds with mainstream taste – hence the occurrence of Hitchcock, Lang and Huston. As pointed out in Section one, cult was often accompanied by cultists – critics like Sarris or Parker Tyler or devoted, omnivorous collectors like Jacques Ledoux or Henri Langlois, who stood at the cradles of national film archives. To some extent, this parallel between cult and criticism represented a time when cult coincided with the canon because writing on the history of cinema was a cultist occupation. David Bordwell gives an excellent explanation for this collision in Bordwell, David (1997) *On the History of Film Style*, Cambridge, MA: Harvard University Press.

12 See, Schaefer, Eric (1997) 'The obscene seen: Spectacle and transgression in post-war burlesque film', *Cinema Journal*, 36(2), 41–66; Schaefer, Eric (2002) 'Gauging a revolution: 16mm film and the rise of the pornographic feature', *Cinema Journal*, 41(3), 3–26.

13 See, Staiger, Janet (1992) 'With the compliments of the auteur: Art cinema and the complexities of its reading strategies', in *Interpreting Films*, Princeton: Princeton University Press, 178–95; Hawkins, Joan (2000) *Cutting Edge: Art Horror and the Horrific Avant-Garde*, Minneapolis, MN: University of Minnesota Press; Everman, Welch (1993) *Cult Horror Films*, New York: Citadel Press/Virgin Books; Hentzi, Gary (1993) 'Little Cinema of Horrors', *Film Quarterly*, 46(3), 22–7.

14 Betz, Mark (2003) 'Art, exploitation, underground', in Mark Jancovich, Antonio Lazaro-Reboll, Julian Stringer and Andy Willis (eds) *Defining Cult Movies: The Cultural Politics of Oppositional Taste*, Manchester: Manchester University Press, 202–22; Staiger, Janet (2000) 'Finding community in the early 1960s: Underground cinema and sexual politics', in *Perverse Spectators: The Practices of Film Reception*, New York: New York University Press, 125–60.

15 Carroll, Noel (1998) 'The future of allusion: Hollywood in the seventies (and beyond)', in *Interpreting the Moving Image*. Cambridge: Cambridge University Press, 240–65.

16 Chibnall, Steve (2003) *Get Carter*, London: IB Tauris.

17 See, Mendik, Xavier (ed.) (2002) *Shocking Cinema of the Seventies*, Hereford: Noir Publishing.

18 Staiger, Janet (1996) 'Hitchcock in Texas: Intertextuality in the face of blood and gore', in Gunnar Iversen, Stig Kulset and Kathrine Skretting (eds) *As Time Goes By: Festskrift i anledning Bjorn Sorenssens. 50-ars day*. Trondheim: Tapir, 189–97.

19 Because of that political significance we have included in this section an excerpt on blaxploitation. See, Benshoff, Harry (2000) 'Blaxploitation horror films: Generic reappropriation or reinscription', *Cinema Journal*, 39(2), 31–50.

20 See the essay on *Rocky Horror's* audiences excerpted in Section four: Austin, Bruce (1981) 'Portrait of a cult film audience', *Journal of Communication*, 31 (spring), 43–54.

21 Schneider, Steven Jay (2004) 'The essential evil in/of *Eraserhead*', in Erica Sheen and Annette Davison (eds) *The Cinema of David Lynch: American Dreams, Nightmare Visions*, London: Wallflower Press, 5–18.

22 O'Toole, Lawrence (1979) 'The cult of horror', *Maclean's*, 16 July, 46–7, 49–50.

23 Brophy, Philip (1986) 'Horrality: The textuality of contemporary horror films', *Screen*, 27(1), 2–13.

24 As we have pointed out before, writing on cinema became a serious and profitable practice in the 1980s, and cult cinema received its fair share of attention, albeit – true to form – mostly eclectic overviews.

25 Hills, Matt (2000) 'Media fandom, neo-religiosity and cult(ural) studies', *The Velvet Light*

Trap, 46, 73–84; Jenkins, Henry (1992) *Textual Poachers*, London: Routledge; Jenkins, Henry (1989) '*Star Trek*: Rerun, reread, rewritten – fan writing as textual poaching', *Critical Studies in Mass Communication*, 5(2), 85–107.

26 Telotte, J.P. (2001) '*The Blair Witch Project Project*: Film and the internet', *Film Quarterly*, 54(3), 32–9.

27 Macdonald, Dwight (1960) 'Masscult and midcult', *Partisan Review*, (spring), reprinted in Dwight Macdonald (1962) *Against the American Grain*, New York: Random House, 3–75.

2.1

Un chien andalou
by Jean Vigo

Jean Vigo's (1905–34) preface to *Un chien andalou* is not so much a criticism as a feverish sketch, a pamphlet rather than a rhetorically crafted interpretation. As such, it stands at the beginning of a tradition of impressionistic and anarchistic criticism, to which some of the writings of Louis Delluc, Parker Tyler, Robin Wood and Robert B. Ray also belong (together with pop culture critics like Greil Marcus or Lester Bangs). At its core is the attempt to communicate the intensity and poetry of the text itself, not by dissecting it, but by trying to preserve some of its features – through inference rather than explication. While such attempts are always doomed to fail, they have nevertheless regularly been employed in relation to cult films, films which in themselves resist dissection and explanation. In this case, Vigo describes Buñuel's accomplishment in *Un chien andalou* as a 'stab in the back' and a 'kick in the pants', referring of course to the shock imagery of the film. Such shock value is a typical tool of cult films. Taking audiences unaware through shocking imagery yet suggesting that the shock, besides its exploitation intent, also has redeeming, cultural value (the 'weighty argument' Vigo refers to), pulls audiences out of normalized viewing positions, forcing them to adopt novel and uncharted reading protocols. In a fascinating preempt of 1930's socially inspired criticism Vigo also calls attention to the cultural context within which *Un chien andalou* was released, asking the reader to take into account Buñuel's Spanish origin, the film's social awareness and the impact of its cruel imagery – all aspects that are now frequently highlighted as key characteristics of a cult film.

A note on the extract: this preface first appeared in 'Vers un cinema social', and was published in 1930, at the advent of Vigo's own filmmaking career. It is reprinted here in the version that appeared in the Faber & Faber edition of the screenplay of *Un chien andalou* (London: Faber and Faber, 1994, pp. xxv–xxvi).

Foreword

Un Chien Andalou, though primarily a subjective drama fashioned into a poem, is none the less, in my opinion, a film of social consciousness.

Un Chien Andalou is a masterwork from every aspect: its certainty of direction, its brilliance of lighting, its perfect amalgam of visual and ideological associations, its sustained dreamlike logic, its admirable confrontation between the subconscious and the rational.

Considered in terms of social consciousness, *Un Chien Andalou* is both precise and courageous.

Incidentally I would like to make the point that it belongs to an extremely rare class of film.

I have met M. Luis Buñuel only once and then only for ten minutes, and our meeting in no way touched upon *Un Chien Andalou*. This enables me to discuss it with that much greater liberty. Obviously my comments are entirely personal. Possibly I will get near the truth, without doubt I will commit some howlers.

In order to understand the significance of the film's title it is essential to remember that M. Buñuel is Spanish.

An Andalusian dog howls – who then is dead?

Our cowardice, which leads us to accept so many of the horrors that we, as a species, commit, is dearly put to the test when we flinch from the screen image of a woman's eye sliced in half by a razor. Is it more dreadful than the spectacle of a cloud veiling a full moon?

Such is the prologue: it leaves us with no alternative but to admit that we will be committed, that in this film we will have to view with something more than the everyday eye.

Throughout the film we are held in the same grip.

From the first sequence we discern, beneath the image of an overgrown child riding up the street without touching the handlebars, hands on his thighs, covered with white frills like so many wings, we discern, I repeat, our truth which turns to cowardice in contact with the world which we accept, (one gets the world one deserves), this world of inflated prejudices, of betrayals of one's inner self, of pathetically romanticized regrets.

M. Buñuel is a fine marksman who disdains the stab in the back.

A kick in the pants to macabre ceremonies, to those last rites for a being no longer there, who has become no more than a dust-filled hollow down the centre of the bed.

A kick in the pants to those who have sullied love by resorting to rape.

A kick in the pants to sadism, of which buffoonery is its most disguised form.

And let us pluck a little at the reins of morality with which we harness ourselves.

Let's see a bit of what is at the end.

A cork, here is a weighty argument.

A melon – the disinherited middle classes.

Two priests – alas for Christ!

Two grand pianos, stuffed with corpses and excrement – our pathetic sentimentality.

Finally, the donkey in close-up. We were expecting it.

M. Buñuel is terrible.

Shame on those who kill in youth what they themselves would have become, who seek, in the forests and along the beaches, where the sea casts up our memories and regrets the dried-up projection of their first blossoming.
Cave canem . . .

All this written in an attempt to avoid too arid an analysis, image by image, in any case impossible in a good film whose savage poetry exacts respect – and with the sole aim of creating the desire to see or see again *Un Chien Andalou*. To cultivate a socially aware cinema is to ensure a cinema which deals with subjects which provoke interest, of subjects which cut ice . . .

2.2

The anxiety of influence: Georges Franju and the medical horrorshows of Jess Franco

by Joan Hawkins

From the sex, savagery and surgery scenarios of *The Awful Dr Orlof* (1962), to the nip and tuck excesses of *Faceless* (1988), Jésus (or Jess) Franco has consistently challenged boundaries of cult cinema by creating hyper-stylized scenes of sexuality and sadism. His work is the subject of Joan Hawkins' chapter, which is extracted from her volume *Cutting Edge: Art Horror and the Horrific Avant-garde*. Here, Hawkins takes Jeffrey Sconce's influential 'Trashing the academy' account of cult film as her starting point to explore the transgressive stylistic, representational and reception strategies of a number of European and American underground auteurs. In the case of Jess Franco, the author highlights a paracinematic film style (as identified by features such as interruptive zoom shots and discordant use of jazz scores) which belies his consistent critical placement as merely a European 'low' director. Hawkins then goes on to situate Franco's output as part of a wider (and more legitimate) Spanish cinematic tradition which uses violent and sexual imagery to provide an anti-fascist and anti-Francoist stance. In one of the many interesting developments in this chapter, the author also goes on to explore Franco's cross-cultural reception by American cult audiences who have received his output via the largely subcultural routes of the cult fanzine or bootleg video circuit. As she argues, for these fans the Franco canon is a source of fascination for its transgressive mixing of a frenzied film style with flesh-filled scenes of excess. Hawkins explores the paracinematic qualities of Franco's gender strategies with a closing analysis of *The Awful Dr Orlof*, which moves beyond a generic mad scientist as skin grafter narrative to reveal atypical avenues of female agency that remain taboo in more mainstream horror productions.

A note on the extract: this chapter has been extracted from a longer chapter on Jess Franco contained in Hawkins' volume *Cutting Edge: Art Horror and the Horrific Avant-garde*. The original chapter explored the prominence of Sadeian motifs and surgery as horror narratives across Franco's films and other examples of postwar European 'low' cinema. For Hawkins, these texts can be seen as intimately reflecting recent European traumas such as fascism and the horror of institutionalized methods of experimentation, while also pointing to issues of postwar reconstruction (such as the liberalization of Spanish cinema during the 1960s and 1970s). In the original version of this chapter Hawkins extends the anti-fascist reading of Franco by offering an excellent account of his 1988 film *Faceless* as both 'slick, sick' porn horror movie and a self-reflexive mediation on Nazi techniques of surgery.

You're amazing, Doctor. And so *different*.

—Nathalie to Dr. Moser, *Faceless*

For Europe's "low" horror directors, *Les yeux sans visage* was an influential film. Its combination of traditional Sadeian motifs with what might be called the horror of postwar anatomical economy—too few faces to go around—appealed to continental filmmakers who were trying to create a niche for themselves in a market heavily dominated by American and British horror. In addition, the film's invocation of death camp imagery seemed to lift a perhaps self-imposed political taboo. During the sixties and seventies, Italian horror directors made a string of low-budget SS sexploitation horror movies, frequently set in concentration camps. And the Nazi doctor—a figure of some anxiety in postwar Europe (just where exactly had all those sadistic physicians gone?)—showed up with increasing frequency in medico-horror tales.

In addition, the basic story of *Les yeux*—a father or other male relative kidnaps young women and surgically removes their faces to restore the face/beauty of his beloved daughter/sister/wife—became something of a stock tale in postwar European horror. Franju's movie was remade and reworked frequently, usually by directors who wanted to up the gore ratio. But at least one director—Spanish filmmaker Jess Franco—seemed to use *Les yeux*'s story to push Eurohorror into a new, more overtly sexual arena, and in so doing, he changed the face of European horror.

Jésus (Jess) Franco is known primarily as the maker of what Mikita Brottman has called "cinéma vomitif," and despite Franco's second-unit work on Orson Welles's *Chimes at Midnight* (1965) and his own later high-budget work, he generally receives attention only in publications devoted to body genres and low culture. Although the *BFI Companion to Horror* (1996) calls Franco (who has made more than 160 feature films) "a hyperactive presence" on the post-1959 European film scene and devotes a full page to his work, for example, another BFI publication, *The Encyclopedia of European Cinema* (1995), does not give him an entry at all.

To some extent, Franco's categorization as a "low" director is understandable. As Jim Morton points out, Franco often "makes his films quickly and seemingly with little regard to production values," and his graphic depictions of sex and violence link him to the category of "body genre" directors. Most of his films, as Jim Morton notes, are horror films, "and several concern the exploits of women in prison. . . . Because of their 'sexism' and 'bad taste,' his films are sometimes loathed by even staunch fans of weird films."

I've never seen Franco referred to as an "art" director, but he does have a following of fans who appreciate his films as much for their paracinema aesthetics as for their affective emphasis on sex and gore. As Morton points out, Franco's films have "a definite style and flavor," characterized by his "notorious" use of the zoom lens, his sometimes frantic dolly work, and what Tohill and Tombs call an underlying jazz rhythm or beat (79). At his best, Franco is an accomplished cinematographer. Orson Welles hired him to direct the second-unit photography on *Chimes at Midnight*, and although some critics speculate that Welles's decision was influenced as much by the American director's vanity as it was by Franco's talent, nobody underestimates the influence Welles had on the Spanish director. Some of Franco's shot compositions are simply stunning. And his deep-focus black-and-white work often screens like a low-budget version of Welles's and cinematographer Gregg Toland's own.

At his worst, Franco can be sloppy. He makes his films quickly to give them a "different and spontaneous look"; and as Tohill and Tombs point out, "sometimes it works, sometimes it doesn't" (88). The editing can be erratic. At times this leads to the syncopated jazz rhythm that critics praise in Franco's work. At others, it simply leads to confusion, as narrative continuity is totally jettisoned for the sake of affect or economy. And for the uninitiated, the slow pace of Franco's early films can be maddening. As Tim Lucas—writing for *Video Watchdog*—notes, Franco can be "clumsy" and "numbingly dull."

For many paracinephiles, though, any new Franco film is a big event. Franco himself is considered one of paracinema's important auteurs. And his work is frequently discussed in auteurist terms. "If I've learned anything from watching 90 Franco films," Tim Lucas writes in one *Video Watchdog* article about the Spanish director, "it's that these movies cannot be watched in the same way one might view any comparable English-language releases. With the films of Richard Donner or John Badham (to use examples of Franco's own favorite contemporary American filmmakers), if you've seen one of their films, you've seen them all. With Franco's films it's different: *You can't see one until you've seen them all.* A degree of immersion is essential." Franco, Lucas writes, is "the Henry Jaglom of Horror—casting himself and his actor friends in anguished, blood-and-semen-scarred scenarios that tell you more about his inner life than you really want to know." It isn't that these films are so exceptional in themselves, "indeed any one of them might seem just as disorienting or discouraging as any random selection to the Uninitiated—but rather that their maker's language at some indistinct moment begins to sink in, after one has seen a certain number of them, and this soft, persuasive language coalesces in some films more tangibly, more audibly, more obsessively, than in others."

[. . .]

Whereas Lucas compares Franco to Henry Jaglom, Tohill and Tombs situate him firmly in the Spanish tradition, likening him to compatriot auteurs such as Luis Buñuel and Pedro Almodóvar. "There's something rigid and fossilized about the Spanish film industry," Tohill and Tombs write.

> Filmmakers like Almodóvar, Buñuel and Franco aren't exactly the norm inside Spain. They're outsiders and wild men, guys who have an unholy fascination with sex, excess, and the dreamlike potential of film. To these men, predictability means stagnation and death. Like Buñuel, Franco is a born rule breaker, a man driven to make his own brand of sex soaked cinema, a maverick trailblazer who personifies the untapped potential of film. . . . Almodóvar, Buñuel and Franco are creative bedfellows. Each follows a different trajectory, but they all curve inexorably towards sex. Of the three, Franco has followed its steamy siren-call further and longer, he's taken his flesh-filled interest to the very limits of human imagination.
> (78–79)

The rhetoric here is inflated and lionizing, but the authors are right to link Franco to the other bad boys of Spanish cinema. Like Buñuel, Franco brings a certain surrealist sensibility to his work. And like Almodóvar, Franco grew up in fascist Spain. That is, he came of filmmaking age in a political and social climate in which explicit depictions of sex and violence really were transgressive, revolutionary, and often illegal.

Jess Franco began making horror films in the 1960s, sometimes called *los felices 60* (the happy sixties), a time of some liberalization in Spain. In 1962 Manuel Fraga was appointed as minister of information and tourism. He was, as Tohill and Tombs note, "a cautious liberal" (63). In cooperation with another government minister, Cinema Supremo José Garcia Escudero, Fraga allowed the rigid censorship laws to relax a little. New laws were enacted to help Spanish producers, quota systems designed to help the Spanish film industry were put in place, and in 1967, a system of *salas* (special theaters) modeled on the French cinéclubs allowed foreign films to be shown under "less rigid systems of control" (63).

This was "the Golden Age of Spanish cinema" under General Franco (63). Genre films were popular, and coproductions *(copros)* with other European countries gave Spanish directors a chance to work in the international arena, with American producers and directors as well as with European auteurs. *Los felices 60* were, however, short-lived. At the end of the decade, social controls were tightened. The government was concerned by the rising number of cheap coproductions and tried to limit them by imposing high minimum budgets. "This was combined with a general tightening up of the political situation, resulting in the removal of Fraga and an attempt to return to the 'good old days' of the 1950s. The immensely popular film clubs also came under close scrutiny" (Tohill and Tombs, 64).

But once a country's borders are opened, it's extremely difficult to close them again. In the 1970s, Spanish middle-class audiences started going across the border to see forbidden films in France. "Special trips were arranged to Biarritz and Perpignan to see films like *Last Tango in Paris* or *Decameron*" (64). French distributors were quick to seize on what seemed like a golden opportunity. Special "Spanish weeks"—in which films subtitled in Spanish would be shown to a largely Spanish audience—were arranged in the French border towns and advertised in Spanish newspapers.

[. . .]

Spanish horror was born out of financial necessity (66). When the government tightened restrictions on cheap coproductions, the Spanish film industry needed to find films they could make cheaply and export (in order to recoup the costs of their bigger-budget productions). Horror seemed the perfect choice. The films were popular, and they sold well. Drawing on the formulas already established by England, Italy, and the United States, the Spanish film industry churned out a large number of Hammer takeoffs, psycho killer flicks, and gothic supernatural thrillers. Most of the films were European and Euro-American coproductions; some of them were filmed outside Spain. The government budgetary restrictions were met by simply making two versions of each movie—one for export, and a tamer version for domestic and, in some cases, U.S. and British distribution.

[. . .]

Franco's status in the U.S. market

Franco's cultural significance and status in the United States is difficult to track. Until the 1986 publication of Phil Hardy's *Encyclopedia of Horror Movies,* nothing of significance had been written about Franco in English. Until the advent of home video, Franco's movies were largely unavailable to U.S. consumers. Never picked up for distribution by either exploitation entrepreneurs or late-night television, Franco's films remain largely unseen in the United States. Currently, he is best known to American horror fans as the director of *Count Dracula* (1971), a Spanish, German, and Italian coproduction starring Christopher Lee as a strangely lethargic count; *The Castle of Fu Manchu* (1968), another multinational production starring Christopher Lee; and *Deadly Sanctuary* (1970), an English-language French production based on the writings of the Marquis de Sade. Franco is also well known as the director of *Succubus* (1968), the first mainstream horror film to receive an X rating.

Although these film titles are available through companies such as Facets Multimedia, which cater to a wide range of video collectors and movie buffs, most of Franco's movies are available only through paracinema and psychotronic video catalogs. Because different versions of Franco's films were often released simultaneously, publications like *Video Watchdog* try to keep track of which video releases contain the most complete (uncensored) footage, and which versions come closest to Franco's own vision of the movies. These are not always the most explicit versions available. Franco is one of the few European directors who have publicized the distribution practice of adding hard-core inserts to body genre films. In an interview with Harvey Fenton and William Lustig, Franco describes seeing a "hard-core" version of a Christopher Lee movie in Paris.

> Christopher Lee . . . is one of the most proud men in the world, he would say things like "I don't want to kiss her on the mouth." And I saw a film of his, directed by Terence Fisher, with porno inserts . . . I saw that film and I laughed in my guts! I told Christopher immediately. I called him and said "I didn't know you had made a porno film!" And he went completely out of control, so I explained to him about the process and how the producers and distributors who had the rights for France and Germany and some other countries in Europe made these versions. And you know they are made with that awful quality also, because if you try to make a similar light or similar sets. . . . No, it's just *shit.*

[. . .]

It is perhaps in response to the distribution practice of adding hard-core inserts to already completed films that Franco himself began making "erotic" versions of his own horror movies. *La comtesse noire,* for example, was made three times—as a vampire film *(La comtesse noire),* as a horrific sex film (*La comtesse aux seins nus,* The Bare-Breasted Countess, 1973), and as what *Video Watchdog* calls a "non-supernatural hardcore picture" (*Les avaleuses,* The Swallowers, 1973). Even this practice, however, has not kept distributors from modifying Franco's horror titles to reach a wider "horrotica" audience.

What brings paracinephiles to Franco's work is a mixture of irritation at what

Video Watchdog calls "the insultingly mild horror product tailored to fit the MPAA straightjacket" and curiosity about a director who has a kinky sex-horror reputation. For many, as Tim Lucas writes, "Franco's defiantly uncommercial, acutely revealing taboo-breaking stance is like a breath of fresh scare, even when his movies are clumsy, which is (let's be honest) most of the time." The implied connections between sex and death, blood and semen, cruelty and sexuality, that haunt all horror are laid bare in Franco's work. In Franco's own version of *La comtesse noire*, for example, the countess sucks the semen of her male victims rather than their blood; in a parody of *Deep Throat* (1972), she fellates them to death. Similarly, it is an excess of sexual passion rather than the loss of essential bodily fluids that destroys her female partners. In *Gritos en la noche* (The Awful Dr. Orlof, 1962), Franco's first reworking of Franju's *Les yeux sans visage*, the doctor caresses his victims' breasts before beginning his horrific operation to remove their faces; after surgery, he chains his victims—in sadoerotic bondage fashion—in the tower. Tohill and Tombs call *The Awful Dr. Orlof* (Franco's first feature-length horror film) "a cinematic time bomb" and credit it with revolutionizing European horror (77). "Before *Orlof*," they write, "horror films had opted for the poetic approach, playing down the sexual element, only hinting at the dark recesses of the human psyche. With *Orlof* sex sizzled into the foreground, changing the face of Euro horror for the next twenty years (77).

[. . .]

The Awful Dr. Orlof

In many ways, *The Awful Dr. Orlof* is more like a *giallo*—a graphically violent Italian thriller—than like a horror flick. Oh, there are definite horror elements: the creepy Dr. Orlof stalking attractive women and kidnapping them, the laughably monstrous figure of Morpho, the amazing chateau with its winding candlelit passages, a beautifully shot opening abduction scene, and a restrained operating-room scene (the doctor makes an incision in a woman's chest). But the main driving force behind the narrative is the story of police inspector Edgar Tanner and his pretty fiancée, Wanda. Which is not to say the film adheres to all the genre conventions of a police story. In fact, one of the interesting things about the film is the way in which it continually raises genre expectations and then disappoints them: the police inspector doesn't solve the mystery, his girlfriend does; Orlof is not killed or arrested at the end, just momentarily halted in his nefarious operations; a woman in the tower who might still be alive is forgotten as the lovers walk away from the chateau. With the exception of Wanda and Tanner's survival, we never get quite the denouement we expect.

[. . .]

Although *The Awful Dr. Orlof* is in many ways a curiously unaffective and tedious film, it also has a distinctly edgy feel. This derives largely from its use of music and sound to create dissonance and build tension. In fact, in *Orlof* Franco uses music in a way that's reminiscent of the dialectical potential that Eisenstein ascribed to sound. That is, Franco uses music as a form of "temporal counterpoint" that creates a sense of "collision" and enhances the dramatic potential of the film. This is evident from the very first scene, in which the hard-driving (and very good) jazz score seems totally out of keeping with the 1912 "period piece" look of the film. And it continues throughout the movie as both the extradiegetic score and diegetic sound (echoes, reverberations) break in frequently as a marked juxtaposition to what is happening on-screen. Visually, canted framing, the occasional jump cut, and some inserted shots (shots of cats and an owl watching, for example) create a similar sense of conflict, but in terms of pure affect, this is a film that seems to be largely sound driven.

The score is not an easy-listening jazz score. This is bebop. The "background" music is characterized by unusual chord structures, accents on the upbeat, lengthened melodic line, and harmonic complexity and innovation. It's loud, and it demands attention. This is the kind of jazz that makes non-jazz lovers nervous, the kind of music that creates an aural distraction. And it's a heavy presence in the film. While some scenes include only diegetic sound, a surprising number are introduced with the clash of cymbals or a long, frantic drum riff that seems as though it should come at the end of a piece, not introduce it. The music gives the impression that we are always entering in medias res, joining a set that's already in progress.

The demanding nature of the jazz score in *The Awful Dr. Orlof* helps to situate the film within the same kind of liminal space occupied by Franju's *Les yeux sans visage*. Invoking both the cerebral work and reception associated with high culture and the physical affect and response associated with low sex-horror, the film seems permanently poised between high and low genres, belonging to both of them simultaneously.

Thematically, the film plays pointedly with parallel story lines, contrasting images, and twin motifs. Orlof's daughter Melissa, who spends all her time lying motionless in what appears to be a little chapel, has a Janus face. Half of her face, the half that remains hidden from the camera's and Orlof's view, is scarred; the half we see is lovely. Her visual twin in the film is Tanner's fiancée, Wanda (played by the same actress). Because Melissa seems to spend all her time in a supine, trancelike state, Wanda almost functions as her emissary out in the world. Certainly, Wanda provides the emotional center to a film that desperately needs one. She's the only character whose fate we even remotely care about. It is Wanda's resemblance to Melissa that first catches Orlof's eye, and it is Orlof's fascination with Wanda's good looks that, in part, links him to Tanner.

The connection between Orlof and Tanner is less physical (they don't look like twins, as Wanda and Melissa do), but it's more stylistically emphasized than the connection between the two women. The film moves frequently between Orlof's pursuits and Tanner's, and the cuts between scenes are masked often by a graphic Orlof-Tanner match. Orlof puts his head in his hands; cut to Tanner putting his head in his hands. Orlof strokes Melissa's hair; cut to Tanner stroking Wanda's hair. The men seem to mirror each other; they're paired or twinned in the way that criminals and crime fighters, monsters and exorcists, frequently are paired and twinned. And as in most crime and horror stories, the pairing here makes a certain amount of sense. Orlof started his career, the narrative tells us, as a prison doctor. It was in this capacity that he met and fell in love with a female convict named Armée and acquired the services of Morpho (incarcerated for raping and murdering his parents). Orlof helped Armée and Morpho to escape and then began the experiments that turned Morpho into the bug-eyed "sightless idiot" we see throughout the film.

If Orlof is a monster figure, then, his monstrosity predates his obsessive need to repair his daughter's damaged face. And it's interesting that his mad-science mania is linked in the film to the darker sides of law enforcement—incarceration, institutional medicine, experimentation on prisoners. The prison motif carries over into the chateau as well. If Dr. Génessier in Franju's *Eyes without a Face* embodies the modern clinical method (surgical mask, white coat, sterile environment), Orlof reminds one of a medieval torturer. He wears a day coat when he operates. Nothing in his operating room seems hygienic, and after surgery he chains his victims—in sadoerotic bondage fashion—in the tower.

[. . .]

Just as Franco emphasizes disturbing connections between the worlds of law enforcement and horrific crime (in this film, the monster-criminal seems to emerge from, and in some ways to represent, the dark side of the legal and penal system), so, too, he underscores the parallel links between high art and popular culture. Scenes at the opera segue into scenes at the cabaret. And here the points of similarity—men in darkened boxes watching women perform onstage—are markedly clear. Performance sequences at both the opera and the cabaret are framed and shot in identical fashion. Furthermore, the two worlds are linked through the figure of Wanda. A professional ballerina, Wanda performs at the opera, but determined to help Tanner solve his case, she also—unbeknownst to him—frequents the cabaret after hours. Dressed as a "shameless hussy" (English version) or "street girl" (French version)—another kind of gender performance—Wanda has absolutely no trouble passing as a club habitué. And the ease with which she migrates from the sacralized world of ballet opera to the eroticized popular milieu of the after-hours dance hall suggests that the difference between the two worlds is not so great as one might think.

There's a certain insistence on cultural transgressivity here, as high culture is emphatically paired with low culture. There's also a certain insistence on the way both high art and popular culture fetishize the female body, female performance. The dress Wanda is wearing the night that Orlof picks her up has the same heart-shaped bodice that her tutu has; and her pose, drinking cognac at the bar—upper body inclined slightly forward, head lifted, one leg stretched *en arrière*, slightly behind the other— resembles a dancer's attitude. Furthermore, she has come to the bar specifically to attract Orlof's gaze, and as she drinks her cognac she looks toward the balcony, searching for his face in the darkness—the same way that she had glanced earlier at the darkened opera balcony, looking for Tanner.

Wanda is, as I mentioned earlier, the most interesting and emotionally compelling character in the film. What I find particularly interesting, though, is the way she is given command of the gaze. Unlike the fetishized female Hollywood character described by Laura Mulvey, who is always the object—never the subject—of an active (male) gaze, Wanda becomes the chief investigator on the Orlof case. From the moment she first sees Orlof's eyes on her, she turns the tables and makes him the object of her active, inquiring, investigative gaze. She puts herself in danger, in the hope that he will invite her home. And when he does, she uses her time in the chateau to investigate Melissa's room and to search the tower. It is she who actually solves the case. And although she *almost* becomes Orlof's final victim, ultimately she is not punished for assuming the active male gaze and usurping police and patriarchal authority. She does not have to go through a protracted traumatizing battle at the end of the movie, the way final girls in slasher films do, and when Orlof is finally dispatched at the end, her role in solving the case is explicitly acknowledged by Tanner. "You're the best detective," he tells her. "My right hand from now on."

It's tempting to dismiss Tanner's final comments as another example of the patronizing "brave little woman" speech that screen detectives frequently make to their girl Fridays. But here Tanner's speech serves to codify, or formally acknowledge, a kind of validation that the film has already shown. Throughout *Orlof*, much of the camera movement and many of the camera angles are motivated by Wanda's gaze. Certainly, her point of view drives most of the narrative in the second half of the film. If classical Hollywood cinema can sometimes be seen, as Laura Mulvey argues, as being organized around the male gaze, here it is, at least occasionally, linked to an active female gaze. In a way, then, *Orlof* seems to foreshadow some of the remarkable Spanish art house films of the 1970s. Like Victor Erice's *El espíritu de la colmena* (1973) and Carlos Saura's *Cría cuervos* (1975), both of which use the gaze of a female child to destabilize the dominant militaristic male gaze, *The Awful Dr. Orlof* subtly challenges police hegemony and control through the measured use of a female's point of view.

[. . .]

Cultural capital

Within dominant cultural codes, both *The Awful Dr. Orlof* and *Faceless* qualify as "bad art," as works that often look sloppy, that privilege affect over meaning and story, and that resist cohesion. But both works also enact an aesthetic shared by fans of low Eurohorror—a tendency toward excess, syncopated rhythms, and surreal frame compositions. They draw on what Bourdieu would call a "cultural accumulation" that is shared by paracinephiles and Eurohorror afficionados, a "cultural accumulation" that accrues from both "high" and "low" culture. To really appreciate Franco's films, it helps to know something about—or at least like—jazz (which Bourdieu links to "aristocratic" culture, the cultural elite), the works of the Marquis de Sade, European art films, other horror movies, porn flicks (Brigitte LaHaie, one of the stars of *Faceless*, made her name as an actress in adult movies), Nazi/SS exploitation films, American action movies, cop shows, and fascist history and culture. In fact, without such cultural accumulation, it's difficult, as Tim Lucas points out, to "get" or even like the films. There's simply not enough *affect* to help the viewer over the slow parts.

The idea that viewers have to learn to like Franco's style, have to learn how to watch his movies, removes the director's work from the arena of what Adorno would call true "mass culture." Here, as in Bourdieu's descriptions of mainstream elite culture, the viewer has to be educated into the system. The more Eurohorror experience one has, the more one is likely to be willing to immerse oneself in Franco's work, to put in the time that's necessary for a complete understanding of the director's "soft persuasive language." And because the cultural codes that Franco draws on derive both from a classical European education and from the "low" culture world of body genre movies, his films occupy a liminal cultural site much like the one occupied by Franju's *Les yeux sans visage*. Despite the raw visual quality of most of the films, they can still be situated at the intersection of high and mass culture, the place where traditional distinctions between high and mass culture become unhelpful, if not completely meaningless.

That Franco's images are raw, too raw and grainy for most mainstream film buffs and too gory for many mainstream viewers, links them to a certain "classed" and politicized taste. Within Spain, it links them historically to an antifascist aesthetic, a subversive tradition of controlled resistance that has a certain cultural resonance inside contemporary American paracinema circles as well. American low-horror fans turn to European cinema when their irritation at the "MPAA straight-jacket" begins to outweight their impatience with a set of film codes they have to learn to decipher. As Lester Bangs puts it, "we got our own good tastes." And those "good tastes" often encompass works that are difficult, that require cultural experience to properly decode. That is, the "good tastes" of low culture are every bit as complex, nuanced, and acculturated as is the elite taste for classical music, European art movies, and modern art.

[. . .]

2.3

The obscene seen: Spectacle and transgression in postwar burlesque films
by Eric Schaefer

In his article, Eric Schaefer offers the first theoretical account of a primary postwar American cult cycle: burlesque cinema. These song, dance and strip narratives are analysed by the author across the timescale of 1945–60. Schaefer makes clear that the remit for his study is twofold: not only to cast light on a long-forgotten cult film cycle, but also to consider the extent to which the burlesque film format eschews the heterosexual constraints of mainstream erotic cinema to offer an interesting case study of gender transgressions in a postwar American context. In terms of his first objective, Schaefer provides an illuminating account of burlesque cinema in the light of wider US traditions of popular theatre as well as the more specifically defined concerns of cult film cycles. In particular, he situates the rise of burlesque as a cinematic format within the wider remit of exploitation traditions such as the sex hygiene movie. In so doing, the author offers a fascinating account of the ways in which the burlesque film functioned as a form of cult bricolage, where titles could be endlessly re-cut and re-titled in order to fit the requirements of both differing grindhouse audiences and regional censorship constraints. Noting that the centrality of striptease as a key feature of burlesque becomes more prominent after 1945, Schaefer goes on to consider the role of gender transgressions within this format. Although the coding and construction of the burlesque strip routine would appear to function as an unproblematic mode of male desire, the author notes its frequent use of transgendered male performance as a mechanism for undermining the supposedly heterosexual drive of such routines. Equally, as defined by such celebrated burlesque icons as Betty Page, the author argues that this cult cycle offers an appropriate underground antidote to the dominant presentation of the domesticated and desireless American woman in contemporary Hollywood.

A note on the extract: this article first appeared in *Cinema Journal*, 36(2), winter 1997. The original article contained an extended section on the roots of burlesque cinema and its links to popular forms of American theatre. As well as containing an extended consideration of the reception of such pulp formats, the original article also contained additional material considering the role of humour as male denigration in the postwar burlesque movie.

In their original historical context, burlesque films of the period 1945 to 1960 displayed excess, parody, polymorphous desire, and gender fluidity, qualities that challenged normative gender roles and restrictions on sexual expression.

Striptease . . . is based on a contradiction: Woman is desexualized at the very moment when she is stripped naked. We may therefore say that we are dealing in a sense with a spectacle based on fear.

—Roland Barthes

I was unknown. I was not being brought into the eye of the public by a major studio, or press agents or that sort of thing. I had to make my name known and appearing in these little movies was just one more chance for the public to get to know me and get interested in me.

—Lili St. Cyr

By 1954 Lili St. Cyr was known, and almost every inch of her body had been seen, by "the eye of the public." St. Cyr was perhaps the most renowned stripper of the 1950s, and the "little movies" that helped thrust her name and body into the public arena were burlesque films. These movies were not sanitized Hollywood representations of "burley" shows but were instead recordings of authentic performances complete with striptease dances captured on film for the exploitation movie market. The burlesque film thrived on the fringes of American cinema in the years following the end of World War II, conveying the unvarnished sexual spectacle forbidden in movies governed by the Production Code. But because of their "low" nature and marginal status vis-à-vis mainstream product, burlesque movies have been ignored by film historians as well as other scholars of the postwar period.

This article has two primary purposes. First, it serves as an introduction to a largely forgotten body of theatrical films made and exhibited in the United States from the period roughly bounded by 1945 and 1960. Burlesque movies were situated within the broader context of "classical" exploitation films, a form that paralleled the classical Hollywood studio era but dealt with those subjects forbidden by state and municipal censorship and the mainstream industry's self-regulatory mechanisms: sex hygiene, nudity, drug use, and so on. Although the term "exploitation film" has changed over time to include all manner of low-budget films, my use of it conforms to the original application in the early thirties, when it designated low-budget movies that lacked recognizable stars or conventional genres and required some sort of special exploitation to be put over. The vast majority of these films had a salacious edge, employed lurid advertising, were shown to audiences often segregated on the basis of sex, and featured the sale of sex hygiene books or other racy tracts during performances. It was understood in the trades that exploitation movies were exhibited in theaters as special "adults-only" programs for a few days at a time or played houses that specialized in "slightly lurid and indecorous roadshow attractions." Such motion pictures were distributed on a states' rights basis or were "roadshowed" by distributors who drove from town to town ferrying both prints and promotional material. Burlesque films were made by those who came out of this tradition and were not associated with the relatively more respectable "teenpic" brand of exploitation purveyed by Arkoff and Nicholson, Corman, and others in the fifties.

My second purpose is to ask what burlesque films were saying to their postwar audiences about gender and sexuality. When the burlesque genre appeared, the terms "male role" and "female role" as well as the overarching term "sex role" had been in circulation for some time. R. W. Connell has written that these concepts became enormously influential in establishing normative (i.e., expected or approved) "sex roles" and patterns of deviance. The display of women for erotic contemplation might seem, at first glance, to fit within certain normative gender patterns of the 1950s, when dominant social and cinematic practices worked to contain female sexuality and to naturalize gender roles based on an active/male passive/female construction while negating other forms of desire. However, I will show that in their original historical context burlesque films displayed considerable ambiguity rooted in the variability of gender distinction and the polymorphous quality of desire conveyed by the films. As such, the burlesque film contained the potential for social transgression, clearly revealing that we cannot immediately or always assume that "the gesture of stripping in relation to a female body is already the property of patriarchy."

[. . .]

The burlesque film rose from the ashes of burlesque theater in the late 1940s, a revival that marked yet another reincarnation in the history of the ever-changing entertainment form. Yet this revival should not have been totally unanticipated, for as Epes W. Sargent wrote in *Variety* in May 1937, as burlesque was being swept off the New York City stages, "Burlesque is elastic; more so, perhaps, than any other form in theatrical entertainment." In *Horrible Prettiness: Burlesque and American Culture*, Robert C. Allen traces the history of burlesque as it was transformed from a middle-class entertainment that relied upon parody and spectacle in the form of transgressive female sexuality to a working-class form that existed primarily as a vehicle for female nudity. According to Allen, burlesque was systematically marginalized beginning in the 1870s, "its performance structure and content separated from that of vaudeville and its venues removed from the realm of bourgeois theater and into urban houses catering almost exclusively to its male audiences." The incorporation of the "cooch" dance (belly dancing) into the burlesque repertoire around the turn of the century helped push parody, song, and an inversive/transgressive female sexuality to the background. Allen concludes that "the cooch dance linked the sexual display of the female performer and the scopic desire of the male patron in a more direct and intimate fashion than any previous feature of burlesque." But this point is open to debate, particularly in the 1950s and in burlesque's incarnation on film.

The striptease dance is generally considered the single most distinguishing feature of burlesque theater. Its origins are obscure and the subject of conflicting legends. But as Allen and others have noted, it did not become a standard element in burlesque until the mid-1920s. It is this period, from the mid-1920s to the mid-1930s, that is paradoxically considered as both burlesque's "golden age" and an era of "nudity, smut, and decline." Comics like Bud Abbott and Lou Costello, Phil Silvers, and Red Skelton purveyed the laughs before being lured to more respectable and higher-paying media like radio, movies, and television. Strippers such as Gypsy Rose Lee, Ann Corio, Georgia Sothern, and Rose La Rose paraded down the runways and into national prominence while providing burlesque with sexual spectacle that was franker than ever before.

[. . .]

By the late 1940s the move toward feature-length theatrical burlesque films was under way. At least one reason for the proliferation of burlesque features can be traced to the fact that many old-line exploitation producers, notably J. D. Kendis, Willis Kent, and the Sonney family, found their stake in the lucrative sex hygiene field diminishing. That genre had been an exploitation mainstay since World War I, but newcomer Kroger Babb's *Mom and Dad* (1944) succeeded in cornering the postwar market with its aggressive roadshow campaign and modern gloss. *Mom and Dad*'s story of a high school girl "in trouble" inspired three direct imitations, *Because of Eve, Street Corner*, and *The Story of Bob and Sally* (all 1948), made by other upstart companies. The four contemporary films were eventually linked in a consortium called Modern Film that dominated the sex hygiene field throughout the fifties. With a traditional income generator in new hands, the older concerns were forced to innovate to remain competitive—and burlesque films supplied the requisite titillation that made the exploitation engine churn. Moreover, ten years and the intervention of the war had established some distance between burlesque's controversial status of the thirties and the postwar market. This distance allowed the exploiteers to construct burlesque as a bygone form of entertainment, despite its resurgence on the nightclub and theater circuit. "Old-fashioned burlesque—as you like it" and "Entertainment that amused and thrilled our Dads and Grand Dads" were just some of the lines used to introduce or advertise films to convey an attitude of preservation or historical significance, thus allowing burlesque films to hew to exploitation's traditional claims of an educational mission.

[. . .]

The burlesque film was a tremendously malleable form. Movies could be short or feature-length, recut, repackaged, and retitled with almost no effort, making them particularly attractive to exploitation producers and distributors alike. Shooting a burlesque film may have been far removed from the Edison Company's early experiments at the Black Maria in years but not in technique. Thus they offered several economic advantages to producers, chief among them being that they were simple, cheap, and quick to shoot. In the most basic form of the burlesque movie, performers danced, stripped, or did their comedy sketches in front of a single, static camera in one long take, ranging from three to ten minutes. Billiken's 1953 *Peek-a-Boo* is an archetypal canned burlesque film. The existing print of the film is divided into nine segments: the opening production number/comedy routine, set at a carnival sideshow; three additional comic sketches: the "Street Corner Doctor," the "Palace of Passion," and "Passion Candy"; a specialty dance routine by the DuPonts; and strip acts, including Sherry Winters, Virginia Valentine, Jennie Lee, and the top-billed Venus. Most of the comedy bits are accomplished in one long take. In the specialty number the Peek-a-Boo Lovelies dance for two minutes and forty-five seconds before being joined by a dance team, the DuPonts, he in a sailor suit, she in a calf-length gown slit to the hip. They do a pas de deux before being replaced by the Lovelies. The DuPonts rejoin the Lovelies for the final minute. The entire segment is comprised of only three shots. The strip routines average a little over four and a half minutes. The featured number by Venus which concludes the film runs nine minutes and four seconds. Camera movement is restricted to simple pans to keep the dancers at the center of the screen. The entire film consists of only fifteen shots, making the average shot length over four minutes long. Despite the advertising promises of "Legs! Laughs! Thrills! *But* Never a Dull Moment!" *Peek-a-Boo* is remarkably static, exhibiting little discernible technical difference from films made at the turn of the century.

Other films used two cameras, one in medium long shot with the performer(s) visible from head to toe, and one in a medium shot, showing the player in plan-American. The routine would then be assembled in the editing room, alternating between these two camera positions. Shot length in most of the films with two-camera set-ups was ten to twelve seconds. At other times burlesque films could use a single camera with multiple set-ups, usually for comic skits or more elaborate dance numbers. No matter how the camera was employed or how many were used, the primary goal was a clear, uninterrupted display of the performers, especially the strippers. Extended views of the strippers constituted the spectacle, or attraction, of the burlesque film, serving to displace the genre from prevailing cinematic representations of women—a point I will elaborate on below.

[. . .]

Although some figures from the period indicate that burlesque features could cost as much as $50,000, Dan Sonney's recollection that most came in at about $15,000 probably reflects the norm. The films were shot quickly, sometimes in less than a day. Lili St. Cyr's *Love Moods* (1952), a twenty-minute short that often received top billing on exploitation programs, was shot between shows at the Follies Theater in Los Angeles. According to St. Cyr, shows at the Follies would start "at twelve noon and go until midnight—2 A.M. on Fridays and Saturdays. So we had to squeeze this in between the shows somehow." With such low budgets and short schedules, the production values of burlesque movies were almost nonexistent. Sets were extremely limited. Standing scenery could be used if a film was shot on location at a burlesque theater, or a bare-bones set could be constructed for studio shoots. *Variety*'s review of *Teaserama* (1955) assessed the production values of that film: "Virtually all routines . . . are done on some inlaid linoleum against a background of some yard goods hung on a wall. With the exception of an occasional sofa, there are no sets or props as such." In many instances striptease dances were shot silent to save on the cost of synchronous sound shooting. Music and canned applause were added to the soundtrack later.

If simple and inexpensive production techniques were the first economic advantage of burlesque movies, the second was their relative indistinguishability from one another. Except for highly recognizable performers, like Lili St. Cyr and Tempest Storm, and the occasional specialty number, most burlesque features looked alike. Even though the films were made by several companies, their similarity can be attributed to the fact that there was a rather small corps of individuals who worked in technical capacities on the movies. Lillian Hunt, who operated the Follies Theater in Los Angeles, directed at least ten features, and a number of shorts and features were directed by W. Merle Connell. Connell and veteran exploitation cinematographer William C. Thompson often handled the camera chores, and Stanford H. Dickenson and Wilfred N. Rose received music credits on many of the films.

The indistinguishability between films relates to their structure and provided a third economic advantage. Burlesque features consisted of roughly eight to twelve discrete segments. Each act, whether a stripper, specialty number, or comic skit, stood alone with no relation to those that came before or after. Segments could easily be reordered without damaging the overall integrity of the film. Lili St. Cyr recalled that Irving Klaw's productions were shot in such a way to facilitate this recutting:

> Irving Klaw had this loft and he was acquainted with an awful lot of strippers. And he'd take them one at a time and shoot their various acts. . . . His mode of operation was that he would take these separate segments—one with me, and one with Betty Page, and all these other girls—then he would splice these together until he had enough time, fifty minutes or whatever, and make what he would call a full picture. But actually it was nothing but a bunch of segments of ten or twelve different girls doing their various acts. . . . He'd piece them together in several different movies. The one I did he put into several other movies that I heard about later.

The similarity of burlesque films and their segmented construction meant that acts could be added or cut from burlesque features without damage to continuity. They could then be retitled and reissued without much risk of engendering a negative reaction from their audience.

In addition to the feature-length form, burlesque films continued to be made as short subjects, reflecting their origins in peepshows. These were often paired with other types of exploitation features to lend additional spice to a bill. But distributors were also able to combine a number of shorts to create a feature-length program. Sonney Amusement Enterprises produced some comedy/specialty shorts, such as *In Your Hat* (1953), which could be coupled with strip shorts to give a patchwork show the feel of a full burlesque performance. *Vegas Nights*, a 1953 J. D. Kendis film, was largely made up of shorts produced by Klaytan W. Kirby in the late 1940s. While shorts could be built up to create ersatz or "new" features, individual routines could also be removed from features to be released as shorts. The "Cinderella's Love Lesson" number with Lili St. Cyr from Venus Productions' *Striporama* (1953) was just one such number to be distributed as a stand-alone short subject.

[. . .]

The incessant cutting and recutting resulted in multiple permutations of bur-lesque films, so we will probably never know exactly how many actual features and shorts were produced during this period. Between 1949 and 1959 at least fifty distinct burlesque features were on the market; others probably remain unidentified. Dozens of theatrical shorts were made during the same period, and many of the 16mm films made for peeps or home projectors apparently wound up as part of theatrical pack-ages and were also used between live sets in burlesque houses. But these numbers are deceptive since many features (and possibly some shorts) circulated under two or more titles. For instance, *B Girl Rhapsody* (1952) was also known, at different times and in different territories, as *B Girl Burlesque, Gay Burlesk, Girls of Pleasure, Hollywood Peep Show*, and *Peep Show. Midnite Frolics* had alternate titles as diverse as *Burlesk Follies, French Burlesque, Hot Cha Burlesk*, and *Stags and Strips*. Some of these reissues included cuts or the replacement of numbers. Since the practice of retitling and recutting burlesque films was so pervasive, since numbers could be shuffled or removed from features to be used as shorts, and since shorts could be cobbled together to create "new" feature-length presentations, it is more instructive to think of these films not as fixed individual texts but as potential permutations of a burlesque metatext. The conclusions I have reached in this essay are based on viewing over thirty-five features (some of which contain overlapping material) and more than five dozen short subjects.

As indicated above, the mode of production and style of burlesque films were mobilized to turn the representation of women—strippers—into spectacle. Unraveling the nature of that spectacle becomes the key to understanding how burlesque films addressed their audiences. Writing about stage burlesque, Allen indicates that "cooch" dancing, and later stripping, "linked the sexual display of the female performer and the scopic desire of the male patron" in an undiffused, unmediated fashion. "Her movements served no function other than to arouse and please him." In discussing the "silencing of the sexually expressive woman in burlesque in the 1890s," he observes, "she still had her body with its power to enthrall, captivate, and, to some extent, dominate her male partner in burlesque's scopic pax de deux [*sic*]. But without a voice it was all the more difficult for that body to reclaim its subjectivity." Allen suggests that in the twentieth century the burlesque performer's transgressive power was circumscribed by her construction as an "exotic other," removed from the world of ordinary women. Her power to reordinate the world was similarly limited by largely depriving her of speech.

Given the source of the spectacle in twentieth-century stage burlesque it is not surprising to find Allen aligning it with the scopic regime of sexist objectification/ fetishization of women most often associated with Laura Mulvey's essay "Visual Pleasure and Narrative Cinema." Indeed, it is difficult to resist the impulse to consider burlesque films from the same paradigm. Obviously, the strippers on screen were the "objects" of a gaze, but as Margaret Dragu and A. S. A. Harrison have noted, "The concept of the sex object is loaded with notions of oppression, but it is important to realize that unless there is something wrong with sex itself, there can be no evil in the creation of objects of sexual desire. The abusive attitudes that sometimes accompany desire are not inherent in desire itself and should not be allowed to taint our view of human lust." Without denying the importance that Mulvey's construct had as a political intervention when it first appeared, I maintain that the application of it, or any other closed explanatory system, in an unqualified fashion to burlesque films would be reductive. Not only does this system rest on a polarizing essentialism of the masculine and feminine, its explanations tend to evade history, the social, and the "messy" aspects of culture. As Liz Kotz has written about power and the striptease, the relationship between the viewer and the viewed is not only profoundly transactional but also profoundly contextual. By considering the social and historical context in which postwar burlesque films were made and viewed here I hope to broadly plot the ideological climate of the period in order to suggest that the genre was open to a broader range of readings than was possible under the essentialist foundations of the visual pleasure construct. Indeed, burlesque films of the 1950s had the potential to be socially transgressive in much the same way that Allen describes the first nineteenth-century burlesque shows as inversive/transgressive.

In 1963 Betty Friedan identified "the problem that has no name." Friedan pointed to "the feminine mystique" as the postwar ideology which told women that fulfillment could only be found in "sexual passivity, male domination, and nurturing maternal love." More recently Elaine Tyler May has described this as a social and philosophical process of "containment" and domestication of female sexuality which broadly paralleled postwar foreign policy objectives. According to May, "the sexual containment ideology was rooted in widely accepted gender roles that defined men as breadwinners and women as mothers. Many believed that a violation of these roles would cause sexual and familial chaos and weaken the country's moral fiber." May states that "knockouts and bombshells" could be tamed into chicks, kittens, and what became the symbol for commodified female sexuality—the Playboy bunny. Once tamed and taken behind the walls of the home "sexuality could be safely unleashed by both men and women, where it would provide a positive force to enhance family life." Women were encouraged to "catch a husband" or instructed "how to snare a male," but as May points out, "this catching was to be accomplished passively, with bait rather than a net." Hollywood movies had often focused on transgressive women, such as Mae West and a long roster of femmes fatales in the film noir, but they were inevitably contained through ideological/institutional apparatuses like the Production Code, narrative means, or both. The containment of female sexuality seems to have escalated in the 1950s in films like *The Tender Trap, The Seven Year Itch*, and *Pillow Talk*, with stars such as Debbie Reynolds, Marilyn Monroe, and Doris Day displayed as passive, available, and controllable mates or potential mates. Within this social and industrial context burlesque films—which were based on the spectacle of the uncontained, undomesticated female body—offered a sharp contradiction. The transgressive potential of the burlesque film was located in its nonnormative representation of sex/gender roles in the performances of the strippers as well as the comics in their routines.

   [. . .]

While narrative cinema at this time operated to contain female sexuality, the burlesque film was directly confronting viewers with the sight of women who were uninhibited in their sexual expression. In burlesque films women strutted, pranced, swung their arms, bumped their hips, poured out of, and then stripped off their costumes in what appeared to be a flood of uncontained sexual display. The women on screen met the gaze of the spectator, acknowledged that gaze, and defiantly invited him to look further. During the postwar years burlesque films were a "shock," and their star system offered a counterpoint to Hollywood's dominant image of passive female sexuality. Billing dancers like Mickey Ginger Jones as the "Wham-Wham Girl," Zabouda as the "Terrific Turkish Torso Twister," or Gilda as the "Sexiest Blonde in Show Business" played on their use of their bodies as a sexually, and potentially socially, disruptive force.

   The burlesque film undermined prevailing representations of female sexuality within American cinema during the 1950s as well as its very system of presentation. Writing about female comic performance, Henry Jenkins has responded to the formulation of "visual pleasure," noting that the idea of women-as-spectacle which freezes the flow of action for "erotic contemplation" results in a "conception of feminine sexuality [that] denies women any active role within the story, any chance of articulating their own pleasures and desires." Adopting Mary Russo's notion of unruly or grotesque women who "make spectacles out of themselves," Jenkins ascribes power to the female comic performer who is able to disrupt the flow of narrative, "to step out of character and adopt the role of pure performer": "If Mulvey's notion of spectacle asserts a socially learned desire to be looked at, Russo's notion of spectacle dares men to look while gleefully anticipating male displeasure with what they see. Russo stresses the 'liberatory and transgressive effects' of the disorderly woman and her unfit conduct, yet also recognizes the degree to which this unstable figure can be reread in misogynistic terms." Just as the female comic who becomes a "pure performer" by making a spectacle of herself holds transgressive potential in Jenkins's account of early sound comedy, the performative aspects of the stripper do much the same in the burlesque film. More to the point, the spectator's attention is held solely by the performance without the distraction or restrictions imposed by narrative.

What was the nature of the performance of striptease in postwar burlesque films? By removing articles of clothing in a highly ritualized and stylized fashion, the stripper not only became a potential object of erotic desire but in making a spectacle of herself she simultaneously made a spectacle of gender identity. As performers, strippers were not merely the bearers of meaning in films but active makers of meaning, calling attention to the performative aspect of gender. Judith Butler writes that "acts, gestures, and desires" are "performative in the sense that the essence or identity that they otherwise purport to express are fabrications manufactured and sustained through corporeal signs and other discursive means. . . . In other words, acts and gestures, articulated and enacted desires create the illusion of an interior and organizing gender core, an illusion discursively maintained for the purposes of the regulation of sexuality within the obligatory frame of reproductive heterosexuality." Striptease as performance was based on a complex relationship between dance, gesture, and costuming.

The aggressively erotic aspects of the dances further called into question the passive "nature" of female sexuality as it was constructed by the dominant culture during the postwar years. This broadened the transgressive potential of the striptease dance during the period. Butler continues,

> If gender attributes and acts, the various ways in which a body shows or produces its cultural signification, are performative, then there is no preexisting identity by which the act or attribute might be measured; there would be no true or false, real or distorted acts of gender, and the postulation of a true gender identity would be revealed as a regulatory fiction. That gender is created through sustained social performances means that the very notions of an essential sex and a true or abiding masculinity or femininity are also constituted as part of the strategy that conceals gender's performative character and the performative possibilities for proliferating gender configurations outside the restricting frames of masculinist domination and compulsory heterosexuality.

The burlesque film was a constant target of MPAA disapprobation and state and municipal censorship action—attempts that can be seen as efforts to maintain the "regulatory fiction" of fixed gender identity of which Butler speaks.

In her study of the female nude, Lynda Nead discusses the transformation of the female body into the female nude as a process of regulation: "It stands as a paradigm of the aesthetic of the beautiful, a testimony to wholeness and integrity of form. The female nude is precisely matter contained, the female body given form and framed by the conventions of art." Nead adds that "art is being defined in terms of the containing of form within limits; obscenity, on the other hand, is defined in terms of excess, as form beyond limit, beyond the frame of representation." Burlesque films were defined by the dominant ideology as obscene—excess and form without limit. For instance, a toned-down version of *Midnite Frolics* was presented to the Production Code Administration for a seal, only to be rejected. A file memo noted, "Although complete strip routines were not included, the picture contained a great amount of material which could not possibly be approved under the Code." The same excesses that caused the MPAA to deny the film a seal caused Maryland censors to require the deletion of dance scenes that would "tend to excite emotional reaction of an audience." The censors expressed particular concern over the movement of Mickey Ginger Jones's "unbrassiered breasts." It is significant that the concern of the censors was not with Jones's breasts per se but with the fact that they were "unbrassiered." By removing an article of clothing that marks difference, the stripper had thrown one of the marks of gender distinction out the proverbial window, and with it the notion of fixed gender identity.

Here then is the paradoxical nature of the striptease: the actions which mark it as erotic—the progressive removal of clothing—culminate in the "degendering" of the woman doing the dance when she is stripped naked. The degradation of the stripper often alluded to by critics does not occur on a personal level but is instead the degradation of a construction, the feminine, which is valued by the dominant society. We are left with flesh that is mere flesh, without social connotation. The stripped body exposes the "regulatory fiction" of fixed gender identity and is "obscene" because it has moved beyond acceptable representation of existing social norms. As such the stripper was at once an attractive and a repellent figure, both enticing and frightening. Jenkins notes that the "unstable" figure of the pure female performer did not only embody liberatory potential but could also be read in misogynistic terms. In making a spectacle of herself and exposing the performative nature of gender she was open to potential charges of "unladylike" behavior and antagonism. Thus the stripper oscillated between being a figure of desire and one of fear because of her instability within the social order. And this instability was directly linked to burlesque's obscenity.

If the obscenity of burlesque was located in its foregrounding of the performative aspects of gender by the stripper, then it reached its logical extreme in two popular Irving Klaw movies, *Varietease* (1954) and *Teaserama* (1955). These Eastman Color films featured top ecdysiasts, Lili St. Cyr in *Varietease* and Tempest Storm in *Teaserama*, and both films spotlighted the premiere pin-up queen of the era, Betty Page. Wedged between the striptease dances, the comics, and the specialty numbers in these films are two performances which crystallized the transgressive potential of the burlesque film. In *Varietease* a segment opens in an ersatz nightclub setting. A dancer, sitting at a table with a young man in a suit, rises and performs what can best be described as a sensual dance, though not a strip. When she returns to her seat she asks her male companion, "How did you like my dance?" He replies, "I liked it very much. But you know, if I was a woman I could do a dance that would hold any man." The dancer requests a demonstration. The film cuts away to a song number and then returns to the club setting, where the man, billed as Vicki Lynn, now wearing a red wig and dress, performs his own provocative dance. Upon completing the three-and-a-half-minute number he rejoins the woman at the table and—in case anyone has forgotten—whips off his wig and earrings and lights a cigar. Lynn also appears in *Teaserama*, this time emerging from the curtains in full drag, performing a strip, and finally pulling off his wig and the top of his costume to reveal his lack of breasts.

The sight of a man in a dress in the burlesque films is not, as one might expect given the period, demeaning, nor is it comic in the same way Milton Berle's cross-dressing was on the *Texaco Star Theater* television program. Butler indicates that

> drag fully subverts the distinction between inner and outer psychic space and effectively mocks both the expressive model of gender and the notion of a true gender identity. . . . *In imitating gender, drag implicitly reveals the imitative structure of gender itself—as well as its contingency.* Indeed, part of the pleasure, the giddiness of the performance is in the recognition of a radical contingency in the relation between sex and gender in the face of cultural configurations of causal unities that are regularly assumed to be natural and necessary. In place of the law of hetero-sexual coherence, we see sex and gender denaturalized by means of a perform-ance which avows their directness and dramatizes the cultural mechanism of their fabricated unity.

Lynn's drag numbers in *Varietease* and *Teaserama* are presented with the same degree of sensuality and tease as the strips by women. A man is shown to convincingly "perform" the role of a woman for men. That Lynn could perform for and be per-ceived as erotic to heterosexual men, particularly in *Teaserama*, prompts questions about the eroticization of bodies without regard to, or confounding, conventional notions of gender. At the same time such a performance begged questions about the fixity of desire and whether it was based on innate physiological traits or on constructions resulting from cultural mechanisms.

Vicki Lynn's two performances, albeit in popular examples of the genre, were by no means isolated instances of gender sabotage in the burlesque film metatext. Many comedy routines served to further undermine the notion of fixed gender identity. Most of the sketches employed in the movies had been used on the stage for years, and several are reinterpreted by different comedians in different films. Comedy in burlesque films can be broken down into two major categories: standard comedy and body comedy. Standard comedy routines tend to revolve around drunks or simple-tons, a wager, a misunderstanding between two parties, and related gags based on counting and multiplication. Body comedy is based on double entendre or "blue" material which centers on sexual desire, prowess, or bodily functions.

The comedy routines in burlesque films could be just as "obscene" as the dances as they parodied gender norms and expectations based on sexuality. Many routines poked fun at ideas of male sexual prowess, such as the travel agent skit with Harry Rose and straight man Bob Carney in *Naughty New Orleans* (1953). Bob says he has arranged for the toothless, pot-bellied Harry to fight a bull on his trip to Spain. He describes the scene in the arena to Harry, telling him that he must pull out his *mach-acha* and wave it at the crowd to acknowledge their applause. Incredulous, Harry asks,

"In front of all those people?" "Well naturally," Bob responds, "they expect it." Harry replies sheepishly with the punch line–cum–double entendre: "They're in for an awful disappointment." A similar picture of masculinity is provided in the "rendezvous" sketch, performed at least three different times in burlesque features. In this bit the comic expresses to the straight man his desire to do away with his wife. The straight man outlines an elaborate plan which involves wining and dining the wife and having a "rendezvous" (sexual intercourse) many times a day. He guarantees the comic that after a specified amount of time the wife will die. The day before the specified period ends the wife—invariably young and beautiful—turns up. She is radiant and tells the straight man how wonderful her life has been since she has been enjoying so many "rendezvous" with her husband. The comic then appears. He is a wreck, looking sapped and able to move only with the help of crutches. As the wife exits the comic tells the straight man that he is totally drained. But the joke, he says, is on his wife because—little does she know—tomorrow she'll be dead. In these sketches and many others like them, ideals of masculinity (strength, physical stature, musculature, and, of course, penis size) were subverted. Much like the striptease dance, the comedy routines questioned postwar gender norms. While women were presented as vital and powerful in burlesque films, men, as embodied in the comics, were depleted, flaccid, and weak, the antithesis of the contemporary masculine ideal of the strong, active provider.

[. . .]

To conclude, Allen writes that "within the liminoid setting of commercial popular entertainment sexual transgressions can become the basis for a reordination of power relations," yet he denies the reordinative potential of the striptease. Contra Allen, I would argue that within specific exhibition situations during the historical conjuncture in which they emerged, burlesque films—wherein the striptease was a defining feature—had transgressive potential. Burlesque films' existence on the fringes of that culture call into question the degree to which the movies were inscribed with dominant ideology. The striptease and comedy of the burlesque film transformed the theater in which it played into an especially liminoid space. Whether a grindhouse, which showed films that existed on the border between Hollywood product and the underground world of the pornographic stag reel, or the average movie theater, which interrupted its usual string of mainstream features to bring in a burley film for a few days or a midnight show, it was a place *in between*. This liminoid space was in between the legitimate and illegitimate, between the ordered and disordered, between fixed notions of gender and the polymorphous. In this space the audience could, for a time, question gender's supposed "essence" or basis in nature and imagine a world where gender hegemony was not as rigid or confining and where sexual desire was something mutual as well as diverse.

The nature of exploitation production in general, and burlesque film production in particular, served to create a form of visual spectacle that was not tied to or contained by the constraints that attended conventional narrative entertainment. Insofar as she was unrestricted by narrative, the stripper-as-spectacle's significance was as a signifier that moved beyond the limitations of story and directly into the broader social context. Much of Allen's critique of striptease rests on the stripper's "voicelessness." Yet in the century that had elapsed from the introduction of burlesque to the rise of the burlesque film, popular culture had shifted from a largely verbal system to one heavily based on images. Reordinative power no longer rested on the carefully organized, linear verbal patterns of the symbolic order of language as much as on the apparently chaotic, random, and, at times, contradictory signifiers of images. Indeed, it would seem that the visual display of the woman, stripped of gender and rendered unstable, often left the male audience itself inarticulate, if not "voiceless." The creation of a female figure who was at once sexually desirable and fully capable of sexual desire was stupefying. Writing about the striptease in 1926, Edmund Wilson observed of the audience, "They have come for the gratification that they hope to derive from these dances; but this vision of erotic ecstasy, when they see it unveiled before them—though they watch it with fascination—frightens them and renders them mute." Similarly, in the epigram which opens this essay, Roland Barthes describes the spectacle of striptease as one based on fear. By refining his observation that "woman is desexualized at the very moment when she is stripped naked" to "the woman is degendered" we can come to an understanding of this fear. The confounding amalgamation of pleasure and discomfort produced by burlesque movies and the striptease was not so much the result of castration anxiety or other psychological constructs as it was the disturbing awareness that gender identity is not immutable but socially constructed.

I do not want to give the impression that the burlesque film was a radical form in which women burst out of oppressive sociocultural restraints and where the largely male audience entered into deep reflection about sexual inequalities and sprang from the theater, resolved to initiate change. But I do want to suggest that within the boundaries of the burlesque film the sexually expressive woman was not merely an "exotic other" but an entirely new norm. By exposing the performative nature of gender, burlesque films could reveal that, as Butler states, "there is no pre-existing identity by which an act or attribute might be measured," and as such "there would be no true or false, real or distorted acts of gender, and the postulation of a true gender identity [was] revealed as a regulatory fiction." This revelation could strip away "the very notions of an essential sex and a true and abiding masculinity and femininity," thus allowing the possibility for "proliferating gender configurations outside the restricting frames of masculinist domination and compulsory heterosexuality." While on the one hand burlesque films might have reinforced misogynistic or homophobic notions for some viewers, for others they may have had a more positive influence. Lynne Segal suggests that "recognizing the fluidity and variability of sexual and gender attributes within oneself and others can have other outcomes: positive identifications, conscious desires, intimacies, solidarities and support with and for subordinated 'others.' " The awareness of the possibility of new norms held the key to the burlesque film's reordinative potential.

The introduction of the "nudie-cutie" at the end of the 1950s, of which Russ Meyer's *The Immoral Mr. Teas* (1959) is generally considered the first and most famous, pushed the burlesque film off the exploitation circuit. Nudie-cuties, which also effectively ended classical exploitation and inaugurated "sexploitation" as a form, featured women lounging around in the nude in a variety of locations and situations. The spectacle of the female body in burlesque films was thus displaced by more conventional representations of passive female sexuality—at least at the beginning of the sexploitation cycle. But for a time burlesque films challenged gender norms through excess, parody, and the creation of new norms. Segal writes,

> The first point for sex and gender saboteurs is to acknowledge the real constraints of women's limited social power and submissive or compliant cultural legacies, the second point, in contrast, is to acknowledge that the codes linking sexuality to hierarchical polarities of gender, though always present, are never fixed or immutable. On the contrary, they are chronically unstable and actually very easy to subvert and parody—however repeatedly we see them recuperated.

Even if gender norms were continually recuperated, burlesque films, with their unique history and mode of production, had the capacity to expose the instability of those norms and deny their hegemony. For the men—and those women—who saw them, burlesque films offered alternative models that challenged restrictions on sexual expression and forms of desire which were channeled along rigidly defined lines. Such films may not have only gotten viewers "interested" in the likes of Lili St. Cyr, they may have made them more accepting of the nonnormative sex and gender roles that she represented and in turn helped pave the way for the sexual revolution and second-wave feminism during the 1960s.

2.4

Orson Welles and the big experimental film cult

By Parker Tyler

Of all vanguard American film critics trying to build an aesthetics of film, and there were several, Parker Tyler is the most surreal; his sense of what art should be and do was informed more by what he thought to be its subconscious, hidden motives, than by its overt concerns. For Tyler, themes are only interesting in as much as they cover the real intent of a movie (unbeknownst to itself). Tyler first attempted to construct an aesthetics that would incorporate popular cinema (Hollywood included), European art-house cinema and experimental film, all bound together by their explorations of desire and trauma. But when that proved impossible Tyler diverted his attention to cult and camp – to movies which revelled in style and excess, and which relied upon 'film buffs' to appreciate their eccentricities. These are the movies Tyler explores in his *Underground Film* book. One of the directors Tyler singled out for his cultist appeal was Orson Welles. The main reason why Welles represents a cult is because his films are failures – 'grandiose failures', Tyler calls them. Welles belongs, with Erich Von Stroheim, Robert Florey or Preston Sturges (or Jean Vigo and Jean Cocteau in Europe) to the canon of filmmakers who, by sheer dint of talent and vision, are among the best ever but who, judged by their actual accomplishments never really made a consistent impact. They are cult because of their unevenness – and it shows the importance of unevenness, incompleteness in a cult. And anything unfinished, unpolished, anything with its guts still hanging out, is cult. Tyler uses examples from the butchered *The Magnificent Ambersons, Mr. Arkadin*, the stealthily shot *Touch of Evil*, and Welles' less than perfect Shakespeare adaptation *Othello* as examples (he could also have used the then still unknown Kafka adaptation, *The Trial*). They demonstrate how Welles is a figurehead for a certain kind of filmmaker whose films will bode well with movie buffs, and will lead to cults, because he reminds viewers of the gorge that lies in between vision and reality.

A note on the extract: the original article first appeared in *Film Culture*, 26, in the summer of 1963. It is reprinted in P. Adams Sitney's edited collection of material from the journal, *The Film Culture Reader*, published by Praeger Press in 1970, and republished by Copper Square Press in 2000, pages 376–386. We have deleted some passages that go into detail about Welles' films, and have maintained material from pages 376–383, 384, 385 and 386.

A dialect is a special form of communication, a language set apart for special uses. In the case of film, which, in the main, uses direct images, a "film language" may be said to exist. There are many reasons why this dialect, today, governs both big and little film cults. Devoted filmists are still jealous of the medium they admire, especially jealous because, even after films assumed a secure place as a medium of human expression, the arrival of the soundtrack made words into a major element of film, and thus offers, nowadays, literature as a complement to spectacle. In the eyes of enthusiasts, filmic interests must be guarded *against* words even when the film uses, collaborates with, words—that is, when the sound track has speech, music, and other sounds. In this situation, many ironies adhere to the "pure dialect" of the film language. The figure of Orson Welles suggests to me the chief irony for he is curiously distinctive and interesting in the light of film history.

If we can consider the big and the little Experimental Film cults as two separate camps, Orson Welles, somewhat like a colossus, has a foot in each. Lately there have been many signs of the stepped-up growth of the *big* cult. It is not only that the commercial film itself, mostly in France and Italy, has recently adopted so-called art devices (conspicuously in *Last Year at Marienbad*), but also that, on the other side, the little Experimental, or avant-garde, Film has manifested a progress of its own toward greater physical stature, and in this respect challenges the commercial film. *No More Fleeing* (1957) from abroad and *Narcissus* (1957) in this country were of short "feature length" in contrast with the brief avant-garde tradition of 20 minutes or under: the length of the standard "short subject." Cocteau's *Blood of a Poet* (1930) was, so to speak, an ambitiously long short film, as were *Lot in Sodom* and, later on, *Dreams That Money Can Buy*.

Feature films in the commercial field have themselves become longer and longer in recent decades. Thus the newer Experimental Films should not surprise us by their ambitious lengths. One may point not only to Stan Brakhage's work, lately geared to feature length in perpetual motion, but also to essays in the "major statement" length instanced by *Guns of the Trees*. Of course, there are reasons both economic and cultural for the upsurge of sheer production in the Experimental field—a longer individual possession of the screen being as inevitable as the rise in the number of films. In effect, their makers have procured more and more generous backing. What seems most interesting in this intensification of filmic activity, on the art level, is the way in which the commercial and noncommercial films seem literally to have joined forces. This could not be "purely coincidental" (nothing of importance is purely coincidental), and if one looks for the reasons, one may be reminded that, as I have mentioned, the two Experimental cults have really *always* existed. The little one, by now, has had considerable recognition and documentation, while the big one has been rather ambiguous all along. Mainly, the latter has been the preoccupation of the audience we call "movie buffs": those who cherish the stylistic bents of certain well-remembered commercial directors; those who do their best to pretend that such directors do not fall victim to the demands of the commercial studios; those who believe that the "big" contributions to the art of the film may be regarded as intact.

That such admired directors—Griffith, von Stroheim, Vidor, Lubitsch, Dreyer, Lang, Pabst, von Sternberg, Murnau, Renoir, Feyder, Cocteau, Korda, Ford, Hitchcock, Huston, Bergman—have made special contributions to film style and some worthy, memorable films, I readily admit. But that their contributions make an intact art, free of serious blemishes, is most debatable and (I believe) a fallacy. Furthermore, the cult of the Experimentalists—from Dali-Buñuel to the present—is in precisely the same position as its "big brother." Though motivated by purer aesthetic promptings, the little Experimentalists have lacked, usually, the imagination as well as the material means to make independent and intact works of art, whether long or short. Paramount, as the Experimentalist or avant-garde virtue, doubtless, is the drive toward poetic statement, and this, by all means, has been the special property of the *little* cult.

Inevitably, the question must arise as to what degree the Big Cult—let us capitalize the term—shares in this same virtue, and furthermore what, if anything, the Big Cult has had with which to *replace* the virtue of "poetic statement." *Last Year at Marienbad*, while I think it not nearly so important as ostensibly serious people think it, is a very recent proof that a big commercial film can behave just like a little avant-garde film; that is, it can take a quite elementary situation of human psychology and emotion and treat it in a radically *filmic* way. *Marienbad* does not fear to make the imagination into a filmic instrument, to deliver us into a world of feeling composed from pieces of visible reality, objective nature; in brief, it does what, as to filmic method, was done by the makers of *The Cabinet of Dr. Caligari*, by Cocteau in *The Blood of a Poet*, and by Maya Deren in her films. I do not mean that each Big and Little film-maker has not had his own distinctive style and purpose; I mean that a good percentage of both types meet on generic avant-garde ground. On the other hand, one realizes that, for certain movie buffs, *Marienbad* is to be regarded, for that very reason, as arty and too special; as neither pure, broad, nor deep enough. For the same reason, too, Cocteau is still shunned by certain film purists for being too literary, too much a scion of "Classic" ideas about life.

Now who would fit the bill, so to speak, as the hero of the Big Experimental Film Cult: a type director of films that maintain touch with real contemporary life and yet are cinematic and inventive and the vehicles of a true film style? I have named my candidate for the honor: Orson Welles. Welles is a darling of the movie buffs young and old, and after more than two decades, he is still operating in high gear. I would agree that he has an indisputable flair for film-making; possibly he outranks, on the international level of esteem, all his competitors in terms of the universal affection aroused in serious admirers of the film art. Yet consider: Welles has consistently been as unfortunate as was another much esteemed, Big Cult man, von Stroheim, at least in the latter part of that departed director's career.

Erich von Stroheim's directorial creativeness ended with a film molded so contrarily to the way he wanted to do it that he disowned it. This was his version of Strindberg's *Dance of Death*, never seen publicly in the United States and a maimed, highly unmemorable, film. Von Stroheim's *Greed* (even as preserved to us in its defective state) ranks today as a world classic, close in universal evaluation to Welles's *Citizen Kane*—the only film which, for his part, Welles is willing to recognize as even nearly his own (I except, tentatively, the still unreleased *The Trial*). The plain moral is that esteem, in the Big Experimental Cult as in the Little, is based typically—insofar as separate and "intact" works of art are concerned—on promise, approximation or intention rather than on achievement.

It seems an illuminating point that Welles and von Stroheim, two of the most valued film directors in history, have produced in the main only "token" works of art. Thus, I think that any responsible estimate of their total output must emphasize, first, its fluid filmic idiom and, second, beware of treating it as a set of distinct and individual films. It becomes preferable to say that these two men are masters of a film style never ideally visible in *one* given work but in arbitrary, uneven pieces that hang together (in each man's case) as a certain trend or emphasis; a certain type, or series, of devices. As we know since the publication of Kracauer's *Theory of Film*, there exists a tendency to think of film not as a group of separable works of art but as a continuous "reel" of imagery, revealing what Kracauer calls "flow of life" rather than "work of art." If some are disinclined to accept that theorist's reasoning and strict terminology, it is probably because his viewpoint puts just such heroes as Welles in an overtly compromised artistic position. The movie buffs, that is to say, desire to think the film language an "art" of its own, regardless of how continuously or discontinuously it "flows." Yet, to me, there is pertinence in the flow theory because it absolves the director from responsibility to the specific and individual work, making him master of a potential art: an art visible, precisely, through persistently "flowing" signs, however well- or ill-connected.

Does my argument raise doubt in the reader? Well, take two virtually "intact" works of the revered master, D. W. Griffith: *The Birth of a Nation* and *Intolerance*. The former was badly cut up, so much so in some sequences as to look absurd—how can we tell, even in "restored" versions, what it was meant to be or should have been? Then, assuming we have the bulk of *Intolerance* and may consider it intact, it is still superficial and, in ways trivial, by any informed standard of history or fiction. Yet among the buffs, the legend persists that Griffith's film style, or film sense if you will, entitles him to be called a "master." True, speaking hypothetically, a mauled text or staging of a Shakespeare play still shows "the hand of a master." In fact, plays suspected of being *re*written by Shakespeare from pre-existing texts may be said to show just that: the hand of a master. But, in many plays accredited as intact Shakespeare, we have the proof of Shakespeare as creator of deep, true, and full works of art, all indisputably one master's. A thumbprint may guarantee an individual but not a work of art; so with film style in the loose sense it is predominantly held. Eisenstein and Cocteau come closest, along with a few isolated works by others. What I take leave to call the Big Experimental film-maker is another matter. His image, as represented best by Welles and von Stroheim, suggests the peculiar and challenging ambiguity of the film itself as a creative art. To me, at least, it suggests that the film director, as incarnated in the Big Experimental Cult, stands midway between the creative artist and the stage director in the theater, between the composer and the musician in the concert hall, between the creator and the adapter-interpreter.

In film, editing and style-accents no more comprise a whole and creative art than do rhythm and touch in a pianist playing another man's composition. In many commercial studios, even where distinguished directors are concerned, the final editing is usually taken out of the director's hands (with or without his wish or consent) and practiced by a specialist. Poor editing, as everyone knows, can cripple a film's style and its basic message. The same happens, for good or ill, in novels as in films, as well as in such methodical collaborations in the theater as have taken place between Elia

Kazan and Tennessee Williams. No inevitable argument exists against the idea of such collaborations, especially if between talents in two distinctive media: think of Mozart's magnificent *Don Giovanni* with its book by Lorenzo da Ponte. A superb collaboration in avant-garde art was that between Virgil Thomson and Gertrude Stein in two modern operas, *Four Saints in Three Acts* and *The Mother of Us All*; participating in the former with writer and composer, it should be noted, were also the scenarist, Maurice Grosser, who supplied a scenic conception for Miss Stein's bare verbal text, and Florine Stettheimer, who gave physical form to the conception with sets and costumes of her own imagining.

Such complex collaborations as those just mentioned are often the case in films, whatever the creative value of the result. But, especially important, in films, is that the director be his own scenarist, and preferably also his story's inventor, *or* that he collaborate as closely as possible with a sympathetic script-writer—as did Fellini with Antonioni, Eisenstein with Alexandrov. That such collaboration pay off in artistic gain is put beyond doubt in Antonioni's case because this film artist eventually became a director of his own scripts. Prime and happy examples of collaboration in the commercial film would number those between script-writer Zavattini and two directors: De Sica and Fellini. These observations are made purposely to distinguish between such generic cases and what I mean by the Big Experimental Cult. Whatever Welles's collaborations, whether with Shakespeare or a twentieth-century novelist, or with himself, he remains a Cult hero, a film artist of ambiguous successes; a lone wolf, as it were, whose egoistic failures have stacked up to make him both notorious and famous.

Exactly the same is true of virtually all the better known little Experimentalists. Faults, misfires, technical makeshifts, incomprehensible negligence, can easily be spotted in their works—yet nominally they remain "little masters." One is tempted to say that the representative of a film cult establishes the fact that filmic *activity* is being preferred over filmic *achievement*, a filmic *direction* over a filmic *goal*. This does not happen through any basic identification of aim, or even sensibility, between big cult and little cult, or among members of either. Think how hard it would be to equate Welles with von Stroheim (despite "resemblances") by way of such a measure! Rather, the Cult hero of film necessarily represents the extravagance, the very vice, of being willy-nilly "filmic." In short, this hero is one ready to pay any price to be his own "filmic self."

On occasion, the emergence of a commercially nourished director as the incarnation of the Film Cult that his admirers dream him, may be attended with anticlimax and embarrassment. Such was Josef von Sternberg's strange "debut" in the film he made in Japan, *Anatahan*, supposedly beyond the curse of the commercial studio; it was a sort of "film-maker's film." Yet *Anatahan* is remarkably weak and undistinguished. The truth is that von Sternberg revealed himself quite uninspired and impotent when lacking luxurious physical means and really dynamic actors. This case of von Sternberg's suggests that the most original and creatively active of important film-makers who have gone in for the "big money," have operated on the basis of bankrupting their backers. This is notoriously true of both von Stroheim and Welles, who, at their peak, ran deeper into the red, the more they took over the reins, the more they became wayward "stylists."

We might well pause, I think, to entertain a thought from the opposite direction. Suppose we take two more recently developed directors who are also "stylists" and yet who combine financially successful film-making with being "themselves," I mean Ingmar Bergman and Michelangelo Antonioni. At the moment, both Swede and Italian have arrived at international renown among the cultists, the buffs themselves. Bergman has actually replaced his much less active Scandinavian predecessor, Dreyer, as a cult ornament and big "Experimentalist" hero. It is doubtful, surely, if Dreyer's *oeuvre* of the last thirty-five years has provoked as much intense admiration as some half-dozen Bergman films have received in the last decade. I think the reason for this successful breakthrough of the avant-garde movement into the commercial film domain is because men such as Bergman and Antonioni have imitated, in substance, the best examples of little Experimental film-making, as begun in *L'Age d'Or* and *The Blood of a Poet*; they take personal charge of the story invention and the scenario and, to some extent, the camera itself.

Every striking success in collaboration, visible in recent years among commercial films, has the marks of Cocteau's personalism or of organized teams such as Zavattini-De Sica, Zavattini-Fellini, Antonioni-Fellini, Bergman as Sjöberg's scriptwriter in *Torment*, Duras-Resnais, and Robbe-Grillet playing composer to Resnais's musicianly *Marienbad*. We had Buñuel becoming his own Dali, Bergman his own Sjöberg. A very tempting speculation is that the Big Experimental Cult is the paradoxical result of the failure by brilliant film directors to find stories or story-ideas by talented collaborators sympathetic enough to work with them hand-in-glove, powerful enough to send them to school to invent their own stories. For example, I believe that Eisenstein (whom I regard as the most artistically successful director in film history) learned much, as he lived through the years, from both his scriptist, Alexandrov, and his camera man, Tisse. He learned better how to invent in terms of story, dialogue, and photographic vision. By the time of his last work, *Ivan the Terrible*, he knew by practice every "in" and "out" of the complex filmic process. Today, Antonioni and Resnais (not to mention Truffaut and other lesser lights) have earned more, and more insistent, *bravos* than a Cocteau or a Dreyer did while working through three decades instead of one—and so has Kurosawa, who has been known to the West for only ten years or so. Then why is Welles, today, the same toddler among tremendous effects as he was when his startling gift for the stage—revealed by the old Federal Theater Project—took him posthaste to Hollywood? Partly the answer is that he "collaborated" with the most culturally backward of the national industries. But it is also because of personal psychological reasons.

Simply what he *is* and *has been* makes Welles the quintessential type of Big Experimental Cult hero—always achieving failure yet bringing it off brilliantly, decking it with eloquence and a certain magnificence; fusing, in each film, the vices and the virtues appropriate to them. Welles is the eternal Infant Prodigy and, as such, wins the indulgences of adult critics and the fervid sympathy of the younger generation, which sees in him a mirror of his own budding aspirations and adventurous near-successes. Beside him, Stanley Kubrick and John Cassavetes look middle-aged, however one adds up the latter two's merits. Welles does "big things" with fabulous ease and against manifest odds. Careful assessment of the actual results displays, along with the marred success, needless audacity and impertinent novelties. He puts on an intellectual circus even when engaged cinematically with Shakespeare.

[. . .]

All Welles's heroes are "big doers" who crumble; *magnificos* who are crushed by secret starvation of personal desires or a cancerous guilt. Fair, hale, noble, with a beard (as in *Othello*) or middle-aged, ignoble, and ugly (as in the police chief in *Touch of Evil*), Welles as actor-director shows high human ambition in the grip of an obscure corrosion. The inquisitive reporter bent on searching out the magnate Kane's secret, the adventurer hired by Arkadin (another kingpin of wealth) to discover his own past, bear the same relation to the Wellesian type as Iago does to Othello: He is the chosen nemesis. The hero of *Citizen Kane*, despite all appearances, had been doomed to unhappiness; the reporter's quest simply reveals the technical origin of this unhappiness: a mechanism that has done its work. Welles's hireling hero is the *other self*, enlisted precisely to be the means of revelation to himself and the audience.

[. . .]

I have long maintained that film presents an unusually glib medium for parody and charade of many kinds. As Hollywood parodies itself and its material (as in *Sunset Boulevard* and just lately in the unspeakable *What Ever Happened to Baby Jane?*), Welles does the same in his own line. As a personality, Mr. Arkadin is the summit of the Kanes and the Ambersons: their melodramatic muse with an infusion of tragic grandeur. Note that Arkadin wears the most artificial makeup ever affected by Welles as an actor: he has Rochester's nose (in *Jane Eyre*), a palpably false hairline and the beard of a tragedian. During *Mr. Arkadin* someone compares him to Neptune; my guess is that he is familiar with the famous Greek bronze, so marvelously preserved, of Poseidon and deliberately tried to reproduce its head.

If we look closely enough at Welles's theatrical disguises, bearing in mind the abovementioned parable, we have, I believe, a perfect image of film as the great adventure of true Experimentalism: a sort of "confidence game" with laudable motives. Its hero is the substance of film cults at their "cultiest." Welles provides the complete Baedeker to failure as to success: An adolescent make-believer is posturing as an adult artist, and doing it so well, at times, that the imitation takes on a fabulous reality. The resultant charlatanry is not deliberate but the product of Welles's supreme confidence that he can overcome all defects of acting and story with his personal gifts.

[. . .]

This actor-director's main contribution to acting (as his boyish Othello showed) is a beautiful voice and a prodigal physical presence, the latter of which he invariably overdramatizes, on the screen, with foreshortening from below. In the little Experimental field, the same adventurism—let us call it Wellesian adventurism—is repeated again and again with varying, lesser means: the same, virtually automatic, egoism; the "necessary" self-reliance; the relentless exploitation of the "filmic," no matter what the material. One could easily list and identify all the parallels . . . Even were Orson Welles to repudiate these parallels, he is their cultural progenitor as much as is Cocteau, perhaps more than Cocteau. Welles, more than any one person in the world at this moment, is a cult incarnate—whether we approach his example from the side of the Little or the Big Experimentalists. He may never do a complete and untarnished work of film art, at once deep in theme and adequate in execution. Yet as a tireless infant Hercules, he has shaken the film firmament, and may (bearded or unbearded) do so again.

2.5

Little cinema of horrors
by Gary Hentzi

While many critics in the volume use interchangeable terms such as 'alternative', 'extreme' or 'underground' to describe the excessive pleasures of cult, film studies author Garry Hentzi uses the term 'psychotronics' to describe a specifically American form of exploitation film experience outlined in his article. The term (derived from the much quoted American pulp film journal *Psychotronic Encyclopedia of Film*) refers to a so-bad-it-is-good format of filmmaking pioneered between the 1950s and 1970s for American drive-in and grind-house audiences. For Hentzi, these bad film aesthetics can be exemplified by cult auteurs such as Russ Meyer, Jack Hill, Ed Wood and Ted V. Mikels, whose work he outlines in his piece. Rather than dismissing these texts as deficient, dysfunctional or even deviant (in their warped sexual politics) Hentzi identifies a camp, excessive film aesthetic in the psychotronic text that bonds maverick moviemaker and moviegoer alike. Moreover, these works often contain complex, self-reflexive qualities that not only draw attention to the poverty-row conditions under which they have been constructed, but also the more classy, complex and ultimately ideologically laden cinematic texts produced by the mainstream cinematic machine. Hentzi demonstrates the features of stylistic and theatrical excess that the psychotronic text contains with readings of a number of American cult classics including *The Corpse Grinders* (1972), *The Killer Shrews* (1959), *Plan Nine From Outer Space* (1959) and *Spider Baby* (1968).

A note on the extract: this article was first published in *Film Quarterly*, 46(3), and is reproduced here in its entirety.

Against a black screen divided by vertical white lines quivering in sympathy like a decibal meter, a portentously accented speaker, Hollywood-British, delivers the following remarks in a tone of mounting dread:

Ladies and gentlemen, welcome to violence—the word and the act. While violence cloaks itself in a plethora of disguises, its favorite mantle still remains sex. Violence devours all it touches, its voracious appetite rarely fulfilled. Yet violence doesn't only destroy; it creates and molds as well. Let's examine closely, then, this dangerously evil creation, this new breed encased and contained within the supple skin of Woman. The softness is there, the unmistakable smell of female—the surface shiny and silken, the body yielding yet wanton. But a word of caution: handle with care and don't drop your guard. . . .

Better than any description, this opening voice-over from Russ Meyer's 1966 tour de force of sexploitation, *Faster, Pussycat! Kill! Kill!*, conveys the ineffable quality, the mixture of engaging enthusiasm and shameless cliché that defines the cult of psychotronics. A meaningless word suggesting a teenager's idea of the far-out, psychotronics is the name of both a fan magazine and a catch-all genre of films which includes everything from aging horror movies to juvenile delinquent and biker films, drug films, women-in-prison films, mondo movies, and pornography that predates the hard-core era, as well as certain especially naïve or grisly educational shorts (for example, the ubiquitous *Signal 30*, shown in practically every driver's ed class in the country for over two decades). A list of typical titles has some of the same garish poetry as tabloid headlines: *Attack of the Giant Leeches; Color Me Blood Red; Zontar, The Thing from Venus; The Thrill Killers; Marihuana, Weed With Roots in Hell; The Astro-Zombies; They Saved Hitler's Brain; Cat Women of the Moon; The Nasty Rabbit.* Inseparably associated with these movies are the names of a small coterie of directors especially esteemed for their uncompromising trashiness—Ted V. Mikels, Herschell Gordon Lewis, Ray Dennis Steckler—some of whom are already well known, like the late Edward D. Wood, Jr., of *Plan Nine from Outer Space* fame, whose jaw-dropping dialogue ("All you of earth are idiots") is familiar from innumerable campus screenings.

What could be motivating this passionate turkey gourmandise? First of all, it must be said that the psychotronic sensibility is heterogeneous and often plainly suspect. At its worst, the writing in such organs of taste as *Cinemaphobia*, the *Trashola Newsletter*, or the compendium volume *Incredibly Strange Films* merely reflects the kind of delight in noxious extremity associated with heavy metal music and other adolescent male enthusiasms, e.g., "*Blood-sucking Freaks* is a mean, sleazy, misogynistic movie with no socially redeeming values. It should not be missed by any fan of deviant cinema." Yet there is also a substantial overlap with camp taste, and many of these films display all the characteristics of a successful piece of camp: visible artifice, outrageous exaggeration, and a healthy dose of self-love.

In fact, the studied goofiness of titles like *Three on a Meathook* or Steckler's *The Incredibly Strange Creatures Who Stopped Living and Became Mixed-Up Zombies* evinces a certain level of awareness on the part of the directors, who have accepted the unlikelihood of their making a good film and so are aiming for a campy one instead. Occasionally these howlers are even planted right in the films themselves, as at the end of *The Killer Shrews*, which sends up the Hollywood convention of the parting witticism. "In twenty-four hours, there'll be one shrew left on the island, and he'll be dead of starvation," muses the pedantic scientist, still intrigued by the prodigious appetite of the monsters. "An excellent example of overpopulation." "You know something, doctor," Our Hero replies, cozying up to his love interest (played by Ingrid Goude, Miss Universe of 1957), "I'm not gonna worry about overpopulation just yet."

Nevertheless, if these films sometimes grin and shrug their shoulders at their own badness, they also ask to be judged according to the specialized criteria applied to movies made expressly for the drive-in and grind-house circuit during the golden age of the fifties, sixties, and early seventies. Discussing his exclusion from the centers of power in the film industry, Ray Dennis Steckler goes right to the heart of the matter: "Hollywood is a situation where it really is *all money*." Instead of the latest Cadillac or some other movie business status symbol, "it's important to have film in the refrigerator . . . and to be ready to *go* when I have an idea." Or consider this vein of braggadocio from Ted V. Mikels: "We built a corpse-grinding machine for about $38 [this in reference to one of his most celebrated efforts, *The Corpse Grinders*]. If a studio were building something like that, $38 wouldn't even buy the *coffee* they'd drink. . . ." Freedom, individualism, and inventiveness in the face of fiscal limitations—these time-honored Yankee values are part and parcel of the schlock moviemaker's creed, and the psychotronics pantheon offers numerous examples of American ingenuity in action. Steckler's own "incredibly strange creatures" are fellow beatniks in papier-mâché masks. And in Ray Kellogg's *The Killer Shrews*, inspired cinematic *bricolage* puts on the emperor's new clothes when the monsters turn out to be dogs, wearing what look like tattered throw rugs over their backs and trailing stiff, Cowardly Lion-type tails, their unrodentlike mannerisms explained as the effect of "mutation." This kind of resourcefulness promised great things, and Kellogg did not disappoint: his all-American talents found their natural vehicle a few years later when he was chosen to direct John Wayne's yahoo-epic *The Green Berets*.

While the career of someone like Kellogg reminds us of how easily the qualities that sustain American individualism can be co-opted when profit remains the ultimate goal, his ability to make movies for next to nothing points to a major source of the psychotronic appeal. For these are above all low-budget movies, turned out by a kind of film industry underclass, who pride themselves on their ability to do without, and look on the privileges of their rich relatives with a mixture of envy and disdain. As a result, in their films we can *see* money—or rather the lack of it—and this fascinates us because of the way it exposes the conditions under which more successful Hollywood illusions are created. At this point, certain historical facts become inescapable. Most of the films admired by psychotronics enthusiasts are at least ten or fifteen years old, or more, and the beginnings of the cult itself date from around the same period. The reasons for this coincidence go beyond the death of the drive-in and the rise of home video, for the last decade and a half has seen an unprecedented increase in the production of big-budget spectacles, whose astonishingly convincing special effects are matched only by the unsurpassed shallowness of their conception.

In the presence of such a mindless display of wealth, ironic distance is invaluable, and a preference for cheap bad movies over expensive ones even comes to possess a certain subversive air. This at least is the implication of one petulant enthusiast, who observes that "people point out the flubs and continuity errors in [Ed Wood's] films, yet these same people are likely to become angry when you point out the numerous flubs in such favorites as *E.T.* or *Star Wars*." Spielberg and Ed Wood are both responsible for trash; however, the latter's childishness was genuine and didn't require a fortune to make its presence felt.

Psychotronic movies set out to give us convincing monsters, but their inevitable failure reminds us of the link between money and magic in our lives. This would be no strong recommendation, however, were it not for the films' unwillingness to take themselves too seriously. For an exemplary specimen of this lightheartedness, consider one of the authentic discoveries of recent years, Jack Hill's *Spider Baby*, which was shot in 12 days in the summer of 1964, though not released until 1968. The plot of the film is standard: a reclusive blue-blood clan afflicted with a bizarre heredi- tary illness dispatches some profit-minded interlopers with the help of the faithful family chauffeur (Lon Chaney, Jr.). While this moral scheme has a certain thematic relevance in view of the director's contempt for budgetary constraints, much of the film's appeal is traceable to the performance of a young actress named Jill Banner, whose Lolita-like qualities in the role of the problem child have the feeling of a found object.

And as is so often the case with psychotronic films at their best, the thin artifice of character, setting, and incident becomes vitalized by our awareness of the real people behind it—in this case, an inspired teenager playing at acting weird. *Spider Baby* is, moreover, a fairly self-conscious piece of camp (as opposed to the innocent, Ed Wood variety) and includes an assortment of inside jokes designed to call attention to the familiarity of the genre and its stars. One of the more sympathetic characters turns out to be a horror movie fan and offers an imitation of the mummy's walk over dinner ("step-scraaape, step-scraaape"); then, with Chaney himself sitting a few places away, she curls her lips and snarls like the wolfman. On its limited budget, *Spider Baby* can't hope to deliver the thrills of those pioneering efforts, but it does manage a modest eccentricity and charm that are outside the repertoire of all but a very few horror movies.

This is perhaps the most important irony of the psychotronics phenomenon: that however extravagant the intentions of these film-makers may have been, they ended up showcasing what was closest to home. At the same time, if their films are a celebra- tion of ordinariness, they also remind us of just how strange the ordinary can be in America and of how carefully polished an image of ourselves we are given by main- stream cinema. As with all social developments that are subject to the rhythms of popular culture, this one will probably have a limited life span and is unlikely to benefit from too much self-analysis. At the moment, however, it remains a typically idiosyncratic example of the alternative sensibilities that flourish in the vacant lots and junkyards of the global village.

The word psychotronic *was first used by Michael Weldon, whose* The Psychotronic Encyclopedia of Film *(New York: Ballantine Books, 1983) provides the most complete filmography. Weldon apparently thought he had coined the word himself until he was reminded of a film entitled* The Psychotronic Man *(dir. Jack M. Sell, 1980), about a crazed barber who acquires the power to kill people by blinking at them. Weldon is also the editor of* Psychotronic *(151 1st Ave. Dept. PV, NY, NY 10003) and has a store of the same name in New York's East Village (305 E. 9th St.). Another essential reference is* Incredibly Strange Films, *ed. Jim Morton (San Francisco: Re/Search Publications, 1986), which is the source of a number of the quotes in this article.*

2.6

What is a cult horror film?
by Welch Everman

American academic Welch Everman used his years of teaching at the University of
Maine to compose a collection of cult cinema that has as its only common feature
the fact that it is in some way or another related to the horror genre. Everman
organized his collection alphabetically. The films come from all around the world
(with notable presences for the USA, the UK and Italy), and date mainly from the
late 1950s to the early 1980s, with a heavy emphasis on the 1970s. The most recent
film is from 1985, *The Bride*, and the oldest is *Freaks*, from 1932. In the introduction Everman lists a few key characteristics of cult horror films. The first he highlights is the 'badness' of the films, a production problem (wrong casting, low
budget), but also as an aesthetic quality: the badness makes them 'kind of offbeat,
kind of weird, kind of strange'. Next, cult horror films share a loyal fandom, a niche
audience 'that will literally watch anything as long as it is a horror flick'. Third, cult
horror films are almost always made outside Hollywood, as independent efforts.
Fourth, Everman singles out the 'aura' of cult horror films, which is in his view a
'something' that makes them special, like the early appearance of an actor who
would later become a big star (Jack Nicholson in *The Terror*, or Nancy Reagan in
Donovan's Brain), or the late appearance of a star in decline (Yvonne De Carlo in
Cheerleaders, or Bela Lugosi in *Plan 9 from Outer Space*), or the use of a certain
effects, props, or styles (3D, killer babies, Dracula's dog etc.). Finally, Everman
observes that cult horror movies are both conservative in their ideology (a desire
for a return to order is prevalent), yet they tend to reject authority (anything
uniformed is evil or inadequate). Above all, cult horror films are horrific, offering a
wide range of threats to the integrity of society and the human body and as such
they act as a warning for all that can go wrong, and that is part of their appeal.

A note on the extract: this essay is the introduction to Welch Everman's encyclopaedic overview *Cult Horror Films: From Attack of the 50ft Woman to Zombies of
Mora Tau*, published by Citadel Press in 1993. We have deleted from this essay the
notes on how the book is organized, and have retained the part that attempts to
define cult horror – pages 1–4.

The phrase *cult horror film* has come to mean "bad horror film," and that's a bit
unfair—but only a bit. The truth is that, yes, most movies that are called cult horror
films *are* bad, and that's certainly true for most of the movies discussed in this book.

They have minimal budgets, they are poorly written and directed, the production values are near zero, and the acting is appalling. A lot of these films, though, are so bad they're good—or at least they're funny. Take a look at *Werewolf of Washington, Dracula's Dog*, or *Blood Orgy of the She Devils* and you'll see what I mean. On the other hand, some of these movies—like *Hillbillys in a Haunted House* and *Tentacles*—are so bad they really *are* bad, and others—such as *The Mind Snatchers, The Asphyx*, and *Donovan's Brain*—are very good, low budgets and all.

In other words, cult horror films are not necessarily bad, and even when they are, they aren't necessarily a total loss. What these films seem to have in common is that they're all kind of offbeat, kind of weird, kind of strange. Brains float in fish tanks, giant creatures level major metropolitan areas, presidential advisers turn into werewolves, and vampire dogs roam the countryside in search of victims. Some cult horror films are mindless copies or very conscious rip-offs of bigger-budget movies, while others are so original and so idiosyncratic that they hardly make any sense at all.

Maybe it's easier to say what cult horror films are not.

Cult horror films, first of all, are not for everybody. Horror movies are always popular—it is very likely that nobody has ever lost money making one of these films. But the word *cult* suggests a small group of loyal fans, so a cult horror film would seem to be one made strictly for the horror audience, the audience that will literally watch anything as long as it's a horror flick. By this definition, blockbuster hits such as *The Exorcist*, the *Alien* series, and *Bram Stoker's Dracula* would not be cult horror films because they are made to appeal to a more general audience. On the other hand, only a true horror film fanatic would sit through *Satan's Cheerleaders* or *The Corpse Grinders*.

Cult horror films, then, are not classics and never will be. Classic horror films are those that have influenced the entire history of horror movies—James Whale's *Frankenstein*, Tod Browning's *Dracula*, George Waggner's *The Wolf Man*, and so on. It isn't very likely, however, that movies like *Dracula vs. Frankenstein, Mansion of the Doomed*, or *The Vampire Lovers* will have any lasting effects on the genre.

And, for the most part, cult horror films are not products of the big Hollywood studios. The vast majority are independent productions, and a lot of them were not made in the Untied States. When connoisseurs of cinema talk about foreign films, they usually mean movies like *Kagemusha, Juliet of the Spirits, Christiane F.*, or *Jules and Jim*. When cult horror film fans talk foreign films, they mean *Godzilla on Monster Island* (Japan), *Curse of the Devil* (Spain), *Torso* (Italy), *Mary, Mary, Bloody Mary* (Mexico), or *Brides of Blood* (the Philippines).

In his essay "The Work of Art in the Age of Mechanical Reproduction," German philosopher Walter Benjamin wrote that the object of cult worship is invested with an aura, an indefinable something that sets it apart from ordinary objects, making it special, unique, one of a kind (in *Illuminations*, Hannah Arendt, ed., Harry Zahn, trans., New York: Schocken Books, 1969, p. 226). The aura defines a religious object—the relic of a saint or the place where a miracle has occurred. In our own time, objects of art are also invested with the same kind of aura—it's the aura that makes a Picasso painting different from a cheese knife, a coffee cup, or any other mass-produced object. Cult horror films seem to have auras, too, something that makes them special—though, in many cases, the aura is more like an aroma and not a particularly good one.

For example, a horror film might become special because it marks one of the first efforts by an actor or a director who would later go on to bigger, better, or at least different things. Roger Corman's movie *The Terror* is a cult film partly because of Jack Nicholson's early appearance in a starring role. A brief appearance by Tom Hanks in *He Knows You're Alone* adds a lot to an otherwise pedestrian slasher flick, and *Donovan's Brain*—already a fine film—gets an aura boost from the presence of Nancy Davis, who would become First Lady Nancy Reagan. *Dementia 13* is an early and impressive effort by director Francis Ford Coppola, and *Land of the Minotaur*—a loser on almost every count—can boast of a musical score by Brian Eno. Well, everybody has to start somewhere.

A horror film might also gain special cult status because it features a late appearance by a fading star—Richard Basehart and Gloria Grahame in *Mansion of the Doomed* or Yvonne DeCarlo and John Ireland in *Satan's Cheerleaders*. And the presence of a name horror star—Boris Karloff, Bela Lugosi, or Lon Chaney Jr.—might add a bit of an aura even to low-budget quickies such as *The Terror, Plan 9 From Outer Space*, or *Hillbillys in a Haunted House*.

A cult horror film might have something else going for it, something to set it apart. It might be the first of its kind, as *Blood Feast* is the first film to offer not only gallons of blood but also exposed entrails for our entertainment. Or it might be in 3-D or involve audience participation or simply present a new idea for a monster, such as the killer babies in the *It's Alive* series or the living dead Knights Templar in *Tombs of the Blind Dead* and its sequels. Or, for a variety of reasons, it might be weird enough or good enough or perverse enough or awful enough to stand out from the crowd.

The cult horror film, then, is unique and yet marginal at the same time. In general, most of what happens in popular culture happens in the margins. For every Madonna, there are hundreds of sleazy-nightclub singers working in out-of-the-way joints all over America, and for every blockbuster horror hit like *The Exorcist*, there are hundreds of marginal copies such as *Beyond the Door* and *House of Exorcism*.

But these marginal horror movies are interesting and popular, too—not with a mass audience but with the core of horror fans. And what is popular must say what we want it to say. Otherwise, we wouldn't like it.

So cult horror films must say what we want them to say, though we may not be readily aware of what these films are really saying to us. Still, every now and then, it might do us some good to take seriously what we would not normally take seriously and ask these cult horror movies what they are all about.

Most horror filmmakers don't have a particular message in mind—they just want to make a buck. The best way to do that is to copy films that have already made a buck. That's why John Carpenter's *Halloween* led to an enormous wave of mad-slasher clones that are still being cranked out today. But even the most mindless copy of a successful horror film—even the copy of a copy and the copy of a copy of a copy—says something, whether the makers of the movie know it or not.

For instance, virtually all horror films are basically conservative. Think for a moment of how the horror film works. In the beginning, things are okay. Then something unusual turns up—a vampire, a werewolf, an alien, a monster of some sort, a guy in a hockey mask—and everything is a mess. But someone figures out how to solve the problem, and in the end, things are pretty much as they were in the beginning.

This basic horror-film formula assumes that the way things are is the way things ought to be, and so the goal of the movie is to get everything back to the way it was, back to normal. This is a fundamentally conservative view of the world. Horror films are often conservative in more specific ways: for example, in their treatment of women as helpless, powerless victims or in their view of anyone who is different as dangerous and deserving of death.

On the other hand, these same movies often raise important questions about the way things are. Many horror films question authority or reject it outright. It isn't at all unusual to see the government, the military, the police, and scientists depicted as ineffectual or evil. Beginning in the 1970s, the ecological horror film started questioning the way we were treating Earth. During that same decade, the true horror-film heroine began to emerge—the woman who could deal with the problems that had once been the province solely of men.

Any particular horror movie can be offering a number of mixed and contradictory messages—for example, that women ought to be helpless, but if they are, they deserve whatever happens to them, or that nuclear weapons are really bad and can create monsters, but when we use them against the monsters they have created, then these weapons are really good. As Stephen King points out in his book on the horror genre, *Danse Macabre* (New York: Berkley Books, 1983, p. 177), it isn't unusual for a particular horror movie to be conservative, even reactionary, and liberal, even revolutionary, at the same time.

[. . .]

WELCH EVERMAN
March 1993

2.7

Blaxploitation horror films: Generic reappropriation or reinscription?
by Harry Benshoff

While African-American representations in urban crime or blaxploitation cinema have become a source of critical interest for film critics and race theorists alike, Harry M. Benshoff's article offers a cult case study of the largely untheorized areas of blaxploitation horror (1969–76). As defined by titles such as *Blacula* (1972), *Ganja and Hess* (1973), *Sugar Hill* (1974) and *Abby* (1974), this cycle subverted established genre imagery of the racial Other as monster to filter wider issues of black nationalism, pride and machismo that were sweeping the USA at the time. For Benshoff, the blaxploitation horror cycle remains a fascinating cult format, which was largely rejected as regressive by African-American critics during the period, yet seemingly able to draw out a number of ethnic issues (such as references to the Black Panthers and the threat of white racism) to make some very potent, political pulp points. Indeed, as Benshoff remarks via detailed study of texts such as *Blacula* and *Sugar Hill*, the ethnic monsters that these texts represent clearly stand as allegories of the wider African-American experience. Thus, the fatal hero of *Blacula* becomes enslaved to his condition after infection by a racist undead oppressor, while the zombies of *Sugar Hill* are former slaves who rise up with their ancestral chains and shackles intact. While Benshoff convincingly outlines a political dimension to the blaxploitation craze, he finds a more problematic source of contradiction in the cycle's depiction of gender and sexuality. In particular, he notes that it is not uncommon for these texts to redefine the Other as female or non-heterosexual (as the treatment of the comic interracial couple in *Blacula* indicates) or else use the theme of female black monsters to create a new trope of pseudo-racist imagery (as the author indicates in his analysis of the heroine's dual white/black constructions in *Sugar Hill*). Rather than reject this cult cycle for the sexual contradictions it contains, Benshoff argues that blaxploitation horror remains an interesting footnote to black American cinema for its innovative ability to highlight issues of racial inequality within well-worn genre patterns.

A note on the extract: this article was first published in *Cinema Journal*, 39(2), winter 2000. The original version of the article contains a longer introductory section which outlines the concept of the monster as Other in more detail, as well as elaborating on the theme of racial threats within American horror cinema. The original article also contains a fascinating section on art-house blaxploitation horror, which analyses *Ganga and Hess* as an example of a experimental black film aesthetic.

This essay explores how the concept of African American agency historically nego-tiated the generic structure of the horror film during the years of the blaxploitation film craze (roughly 1969–76). This is an important topic, since the American hor-ror film often hinges on filmically constructed fears of the Other—an Otherness both drawn from and constitutive of any given era's cultural history. As many theorists have pointed out, the generic pattern of the classical American horror film oscillates between the "normal," mostly represented by the white, middle-class hetero-sexuality of the films' heroes and heroines, and the "monstrous," frequently colored by racial, sexual, class, or other ideological markers. Since most of the horror films produced in America have been created by white filmmakers, it should not be surprising that the vast majority of those films use race as a marker of monstrosity in ways generically consistent with the larger social body's assumptions about white superiority.

By way of contrast, I explore how the discourse of race plays out in blaxploitation horror films. How are the generic tenets of "normality" and "difference" refigured (if they are) when viewed through the lens of a marginalized racial collective? In what ways might these films have addressed the specific fantasy needs of the black social imaginary? Ultimately, for some viewers, blaxploitation horror films mounted a chal-lenge to the Other-phobic assumptions of the genre's more common reception. However, while appearing to critique white racism in America, most of these films were unable to withstand the genre's more regular demonization of gender and sexu-ality, which are arguably more deeply embedded as monstrous within both the horror film and the culture at large.

The issue of African American agency is complicated by the fact that many of the films discussed below had white directors, editors, producers, and crews. Given the "leaky" or incomplete nature of traditional auteur (and genre) theory in light of poststructuralist reformulations and cultural studies, a provisional definition of the blaxploitation horror film should be proffered: a horror film made in the early 1970s that had *some* degree of African American input, not necessarily through the director but perhaps through a screenwriter, producer, and/or even an actor. The label "blax-ploitation horror films" thus signifies a historically specific subgenre that potentially explores (rather than simply exploits) race and race consciousness as core structuring principles. However, as the meaning of any text is also shaped by its readers, I also include in my definition the historical African American audiences to whom these films were marketed.

This project thus underscores not only the changing social understanding of the American horror film but also the changing social meanings of "African American-ness." As Ed Guerrero notes:

The social and political meanings of "race," of course, are not fixed but are matters of ongoing construction and contestation; whether in volatile debate or subtle transactions, the negotiation of racial images, boundaries, and hierarchies has been part of our national life from its very beginnings. The turbulent power of race is evinced by the varieties of ways in which the images and historical experi-ences of African Americans and other people of color are symbolically figured in commercial cinema.

Those symbolic figurations in turn contribute to the ongoing construction of racial meaning and identity within specific social and historical contexts. I mean to situate my comments about race and genre away from the essentialist position that conceives "of ethnicity and cultural identity as a predetermined, immutable condition beyond circumstances and rational control" and toward the position that views ethnicity and race as culturally and socially constructed, what Werner Sollors has called a model of identity by "consent" rather than "descent." Identity "is a process located in the core of the individual and yet also in the core of his [or her] communal culture," a process that depends on the subject's interaction with cultural artifacts both high and low, sacred and profane, from the "high" art of literary masterpieces to the "low" art of horror films.

[. . .]

The blaxploitation context

Blaxploitation filmmaking contributed to the ongoing social construction of race during an especially labile era of the nation's civil rights struggles. During these years, the ideologies of black nationalism, black pride, and black macho became dominant social expressions of racial identity for many African American men and women. In general, blaxploitation films depicted a stronger, more militant image of African Americans who triumphed over (frequently racist) white antagonists. As one black critic succinctly put it, "Black heroes were winning and community identification was intense." The effect of this change on the construction of cinematic narrative was to flip the terms of the hierarchical white-black opposition rather than necessarily oppose it. The reaction was a profoundly cathartic one for many black filmgoers at the time, but this reformulation is also necessarily more nuanced depending on the generic structures being reworked. For example, most black film critics of the era saw this racial rearticulation as a positive development in genres such as the western or the police thriller. In the case of gangster films and horror films, however, in which the protagonists were more complicated antiheroes, the middle-class black press often became quite hostile, arguing that the films were potentially damaging to the black psyche and/or to the struggle for equal rights.

Most blaxploitation films tended to be easily identifiable as genre films, and, as such, most filmgoers and critics alike usually understood them to be "escapist entertainment" rather than serious sociopolitical tracts about race in America. [. . .] however, some black filmmakers were in positions of industrial power and/or authorial sophistication that enabled them to address those tensions between Hollywood form and black audiences. Both African American and white filmmakers began to reappropriate generic forms for more overtly political goals, specifically, to critique the white power structure. Many blaxploitation films contain much harsher critiques of American racism than do the correspondingly "serious" black films of the era, such as *Sounder* (1972) or *Lady Sings the Blues* (1972). In fact, some in the white media establishment acknowledged blaxploitation film's political charge, as evidenced by a 1974 *Variety* article that asserted that blaxploitation films were not performing well at European box offices because "Europeans are simply more prejudiced than American audiences and are less willing to accept the black-dominated features, many of which are both anti-capitalistic and anti-white in implication."

The black press of the era also began to see important political meanings in allegedly meaningless genre films. For instance, the black western *Buck and the Preacher* (Sidney Poitier, 1972) was noted for making "a social statement, having to do with Blacks' relationship with Indians in the old West." Within the horror genre, lingering racist tropes, such as the black ape-man myth, were now readily identified and exposed. In 1976, for example, the following short piece ran in *Jet* magazine, attesting both to Hollywood's institutionalized racism and the black press's commitment to exposing it: "Black actors in Hollywood are upset because the producers of the forthcoming movie *King Kong* are looking for an 'ape-like' black person to play the title role. According to black actors who tried out for the role offered by [Dino] De Laurentiis Studios, they were asked to jump around and hop, bent over like a gorilla. In the wake of the odd audition, gossip among black actors resulted in strongly negative reactions." Paradoxically, only a few years earlier, black actors and stuntmen had chastised Hollywood for *not* casting them as ape-men in *Planet of the Apes* (1968). These two incidents underscore the difficulty of constructing and casting monsters in a politically sensitive era, as well as the wide variety of responses in black communities to the question of what constitutes a "positive" media image, an aspect of blaxploitation film reception that was widely and passionately debated.

Blaxploitation horror films were rarely referenced within those debates, possibly because black youth were thought to be less likely to emulate a supernatural creature than to emulate a drug dealer (as was argued about the potential social effects of *Superfly* [1972]). Nonetheless, *Blacula* (1972), the first and most commercially successful of these films, was singled out for condemnation by the media watchdog group, the Committee against Blaxploitation (CAB). Junius Griffin, of the Hollywood office of the NAACP, became embroiled in a battle of words when he suggested that "if black actors can play demeaning roles in *Blacula*," then he could see no reason why (white actor) Anthony Quinn should not play the proposed role of Haitian revolutionary Henry Christophe instead of *Blacula* star William Marshall. Other black critics grew tired of blaxploitation-bashing and cited *Blacula* as being less exploitative than the usual fare. Still other black reviewers picked up on the film's more overtly political significance: "I have . . . chosen to look upon the entire film as an effort by those responsible to show satirically the black man's plight as a victim of white vampirism. . . . Those who enjoy seeing the establishment take a whipping will be interested in the number of L.A. Police done in by this midnite creeper."

White media critics were also confused over the meaning of the film. Some opined that *Blacula* was "remarkably free of the effects of the 'frought-with-significance' syndrome." Still others noted that the film was "something more than just an exploitation of the black and the horror box-office market. . . . The film is both a tender love story and a statement about society's outcasts." White-dominated fan organizations lauded the film. The Count Dracula Society called it "the most horrifying film of the decade," and the Academy of Horror Films and Science Fiction Films named it the "Best Horror Film of 1972."

Nonetheless, even as middle-class black audiences and the champions of "respectable" cinema might have been made uneasy by the exploitative and/or generic nature of *Blacula*, extratextual uses of the film became important to the struggle for racial advancement. For example, in both Los Angeles and San Francisco, gala premieres of *Blacula* were held in the black community. The *Los Angeles Sentinel*, a weekly independent black newspaper, ran a two-page photo spread on the film's premiere, which was hosted by the Regalettes Social and Charity Club. The article noted that it was the "first ever Hollywood premiere hosted by a black organization"; however, the paper's entertainment critics, Bill Lane and Gertrude Gipson, remained silent on the quality of the film itself, possibly because of the confusion over whether or not *Blacula* represented a "positive" depiction of African Americans and their concerns. *Ebony* noted that "although well attended, horror flick [*Blacula*] met with mixed reaction because of [its] bizarre nature."

Blacula was so successful at the box office that American International Pictures (AIP) announced its intentions to remake all the classical Hollywood horror films with black casts. AIP ended up producing and/or releasing *The Thing with Two Heads* (1972), a sequel to *Blacula* entitled *Scream Blacula Scream* (1973), *(The Zombies of) Sugar Hill* (1974), *Abby* (1974), and *J.D.'s Revenge* (1976). Smaller independent companies released *Blackenstein* (Exclusive International, 1973) and *Dr. Black, Mr. Hyde*, aka *The Watts Monster* (Dimension Films, 1975/1979), while Twentieth Century-Fox distributed *House on Skull Mountain* (1974). Universal announced plans for a film entitled *The Werewolf of Watts*, which was never made. Also announced but never made were *The Devil's Door* (with William Marshall), *Blackenstein II*, and *Fall of the House of Blackenstein*. While the degree of black involvement varied from film to film (*House on Skull Mountain* was produced by blacks), only *Blacula* and *Dr. Black, Mr. Hyde* were directed by an African American, William Crain, who since that time has worked more extensively in television (*The Rookies, Mod Squad, Starsky and Hutch*) than in film.

Like most blaxploitation films, these horror films were notable for their popularization of urban black culture and the showcasing of African American talent. Most have at least one nightclub scene wherein black musical artists perform, and Motown Records released soundtrack albums for several of the more popular AIP films. *Sugar Hill* opens with a cabaret act scored with The Originals's "Supernatural Voodoo Woman," crystallizing the film's revenge narrative ("Do her wrong and you won't see the light"). Michael Jackson recorded a tender ballad as the theme song to *Ben* (1972), the horror-thriller sequel to *Willard* (1971), about a boy and his people-eating rat, and the artist soon to be known as Prince wrote the music for *J. D.'s Revenge*.

The films are also steeped in African American culture of the early 1970s; references to the Black Panthers, Afrocentric style, soul food, white racism (both institutionalized and personal), and urban ghetto life abound and in many cases are critically commented upon. (From *Blacula*: "Funny how so many sloppy police jobs involve black victims.") *Blackenstein* makes it explicit that its black Vietnam veteran lost his limbs in a white war; he is still preyed upon by white mad science when he is turned into a monster. And many of the films draw heavily on voodoo as a "more authentic" expression of the African American supernatural, especially after *Jet* magazine wondered in print "why there should be a film based on the Dracula legend when there is voodoo in the black experience." Indeed, voodoo subsequently figured in the *Blacula* sequel and in the "old dark house" thriller *The House on Skull Mountain*, as well as in *Sugar Hill*, much as it did in the blaxploitation-influenced James Bond film *Live and Let Die* (1972). Although these developments might seem racist in films made solely by whites (i.e., using African or African American culture as the signifier of exoticized horror), within these films they usually represent a form of black cultural empowerment over a rational white discourse.

Monstrous metaphors

Tying into the Afrocentric culture of late 1960s/early 1970s, many blaxploitation horror films reappropriated the mainstream cinema's monstrous figures for black goals, turning vampires, Frankenstein monsters, and transformation monsters into agents of black pride and black power. "Normality," represented by black hetero-sexual couples and black (and white) authority figures, also appears in these films, but unlike most Hollywood horror films of previous eras, audience sympathy is often redirected away from those figures and toward the figure of the monster, a specifically black *avenger* who justifiably fights against the dominant order—which is often explicitly coded as racist. Ad campaigns for the films assured patrons they would see Blacula set a "death trap for *revenge*" and partake of an "orgy of *vengeance*." Some of the films, such as *Sugar Hill*, are predicated solely upon this formula. After a racist white Mafia gang murders her lover, Sugar Hill raises zombies from the dead to avenge herself. She does so triumphantly, and the film ends with the white gangsters dead and Sugar's zombies returning to the underworld. Unlike the classical Holly-wood horror film narrative, there is no need to punish or destroy the monsters. In fact, the reverse is true: the monsters kill the racist agents of "normality," and the audience is expected to cheer these developments. As *BoxOffice* noted at the time, director "Maslansky realizes that urban audiences will be rooting for Sugar."

Central to these films' reappropriation of the monster as an empowering black figure is the softening, romanticizing, and even valorizing of the monster. In *Dr. Black, Mr. Hyde*, Bernie Casey plays Dr. Henry *Pride*, a prize-winning medical researcher assisted by Dr. Billie *Worth* (Rosalind Cash); both doctors serve the black community by working at the free clinic and the local arts center. Blacula is actually an African prince named Mamuwalde, much more of a lover than a fighter, who tenderly tries to find his reincarnated princess. In the sequel, *Scream Blacula Scream*, Prince Mamu-walde even tries to cure his vampiric ways. The cure fails, and the film ends with an extremely high-angle freeze frame of the tortured creature, while the theme song *Torment* is heard over the credits—"I lived in endless empty space, so alone, so empty . . . Hoping that in you there was a power . . . to end this search for my soul/A power that would give me freedom, freedom, freedom." Frozen in time by the freeze frame and disempowered by the high-angle shot, the vampiric Mamuwalde is finally trapped as more tragic than evil, more a doomed freedom fighter than a monster.

In another possible attempt to dampen the monster's evilness, Blacula's first attack in the first film is directed at an interracial gay couple who have inadvertently brought his coffin to America to sell in their antique store. Although the film was ahead of its time in representing an interracial gay relationship (and tying it to black revolutionary power), it possibly situates the couple as Blacula's first victims to make Blacula seem *less* of a monster, because the gay couple's deaths are somehow deserved (or at least comedic). One recent account of the film reads it that way, claiming that

Blacula is "appalled by contemporary customs and morals, putting the bite on drug dealers and homosexual antique dealers to help clean things up." (The reviewer's homophobia aside, there are no drug dealers in the film or any indications that Blacula is appalled by today's "morals.")

In blaxploitation horror films, the monster often becomes an allegory for the historical experience of African Americans. *Blacula*'s vampirism is an explicit metaphor for slavery: bitten by the racist Count Dracula centuries ago ("I shall place a curse of suffering on you that will doom you to a living hell"), the curse of vampirism becomes the lingering legacy of racism. Indeed, Blacula explicitly states that he was "enslaved" by the curse of vampirism. What he finds so distasteful about his state is that he must now enslave others, biting them and turning them into his minions. Even more forthrightly drawing on that history, in *Scream Blacula Scream*, the count is harassed by two pimps; before breaking their skulls he tells them, "You've made a slave out of your sister and you're still slaves imitating your slave masters!" And in *Sugar Hill*, the heroine's "zombie hit men" are explicitly marked as former slaves through both dialogue and the prominent placement of their rusting shackles within the mise-en-scène. At least one critic argued that the film's "vengeance is given a certain historical-political dimension. [Gangster] Morgan's gang, represented throughout as the arm of white exploitation and racism, is obliterated by the corpses of black slaves in a dream of apocalypse out of Nat Turner."

[. . .]

Gender and sexuality

J. D.'s Revenge is a rare blaxploitation film in that it calls into question the black macho ethic. Most of the other blaxploitation horror films, like blaxploitation films in general, tend to uphold male-dominated (hetero)sexuality and participation in the genre's usual demonization of women and nonpatriarchal sexualities. For example, *Abby* (1974), an obvious gloss on *The Exorcist* (1973), makes a sexualized woman into a monster. Abby starts out as a sweet-natured preacher's wife who sings in the choir, runs the youth program, and is a marriage counselor, but she becomes possessed by the spirit of Eshu, the African trickster god of sexuality. Soon Abby is masturbating in the shower, coming on to her clients, and tricking at local nightclubs. Following the reactionary narrative logic of this type of film, Abby's father-in-law, a theologian, calls upon both African and Western gods and drives the demon from her body, restoring her to her proper role as wife and daughter. Somewhat ironically, this film allowed its script to undergo revisions suggested by African American input (a move AIP made to appease critics of its earlier blaxploitation films). *BoxOffice* noted before the film was released that it "will be avoiding some of the clichés about black people and will be more in line with the present thinking of CORE and other groups about how they should be portrayed on screen." Perhaps these revisions were responsible for the positive depiction of black Christian religiosity, but they were at the expense of demonizing women, sexuality, and the Yoruba god Eshu, who herein becomes steeped in a Western, sex-negative Christian ideology. Although this development may have pleased some middle-class black Christians, the reviewer at the adult-entertainment magazine *Players* opined that *Abby* "represents black exploitation at its worst."

Nonetheless, *Abby* has a black woman protagonist, a trope of later blaxploitation films such as *Coffy* (1973), *Cleopatra Jones* (1973), and *Friday Foster* (1975). Both black and white critics had decried the overwhelming sexism in earlier blaxploitation films, and filmmakers had responded by inserting female protagonists into the formerly male "avenger" role, another flipping of binary concepts that had the potential to reveal an inherent hierarchy. For example, the press judged Blacula's monstrous appetites to be "noble, even tragic," whereas *Abby*'s appetites were figured as grotesque and in need of eradication. *Sugar Hill* comes closer to some kind of gender equality, since Sugar is smart, strong, and independent and has her own career. Yet her mission for revenge is predicated solely on the loss of her man, and, as is typical of these films, Sugar is sexually objectified throughout. Even her career as a fashion photographer conveniently allows the filmmakers to include a bikini photo shoot.

The black women's fashion magazine *Essence*, in which one might expect to find more information about woman-centered black films (especially since some of their lead actresses were ex-fashion models), employed a male film critic during these years. He occasionally cited the sexism of the more popular blaxploitation films but rarely mentioned the developing "blaxploitation superwoman." This is not surprising given the scapegoating of strong women within the era's black macho culture and *Essence*'s editorial goal of helping black women assimilate into traditional (i.e., passive and cosmeticized) models of Western femininity. The magazine's first film article by a woman critiqued the sexism of blaxploitation films, but it was the readers who more regularly proffered negative critiques: "We pay to see our morals degraded, our culture laughed at and the perpetuation of the myth that some of us would rather lie on our backs than use our minds. The majority of the money-making 'black' movies depict the black woman as superwoman, a hustler's ole lady or a prostitute."

As Michele Wallace has demonstrated in her essays on black macho, there was little chance that the black superwoman would empower most black women of the early 1970s. Indeed, both conservative Christian pundits *and* radical black militants often cited strong black women (and effeminate or gay black men) as something that was "wrong" with black culture. An attack on black men's fashions from this era ("an appearance often inspired by homosexual designers") decried "the drugging and faggotizing of black men in recent years [which was] robbing black people of the spirit and man-force essential to the reversal of the European destruction machine." Like the black macho ethic in general, most blaxploitation horror films attempted to advance the race by promoting the strong black male avenger; even if monstrous, he was romanticized and celebrated. Female monsters were more regularly deemed truly monstrous because of their wanton sexuality (*Abby*) or were contained within patriarchal parameters through both plot and cinematographic objectification (*Sugar Hill*).

Many critics of these films may have condemned the blaxploitation horror film simply because of its generic imperatives—African American monsters, no matter how likable, justified, heroic, or interesting, were still monsters, and, in most cases, the films used signs of African and African American culture to signify horror. One encounters the same problem in attempting to reappropriate the genre as "progressive" for any specific cultural group because the very formula of the genre demonizes difference, be it based on gender, sexuality, or race. In *Sugar Hill*, for example, Sugar wears a full black Afro hairdo when murdering her enemies but lightened and straightened hair in her "normal" life. Sugar's Afrocentrism, like her use of voodoo, is a sign of her power but also of her monstrosity and violence. In the same film, pop-eyed black zombies, shot with a subjective camera, suture the spectator into the victim's position and ask him/her to be afraid of blackness à la classical Hollywood horror films. Finally, stock Hollywood musical tropes, such as "primitive jungle drums," are used to invoke fear—a practice that has not changed very much over the years.

The lingering racist discourse of Negro bestiality is also evident in these films' makeup codes. Black monsters tend to be more animalistic than white monsters: when Blacula gets his blood lust up, for example, he becomes almost lupine, with a hairy face and brow, a trope usually not used for more debonair white vampires. The possessed woman in *Abby* also has facial hair and a deep voice (drawing on gender-blending queer fears as well as bestial/racial ones), and in *Blackenstein* the monster has hairy hands, while his Afro-natural hair is molded into a square, box-like head reminiscent of Boris Karloff's Frankenstein monster. Blaxploitation horror films may have attempted to reappropriate the genre for racial advancement, but the genre's deeply embedded structure still worked to reinscribe racist tropes.

[. . .]

Conclusion

Blaxploitation horror films had a significant impact on the genre's evolution. As pop-culture signifiers of the growing public awareness about race and racial inequity, these films exposed and opposed the genre's historically racist structuring principles, even though female gender and sexuality were still often figured as central conceits of monstrous Otherness. By embracing the racialized monster and turning him or her into an agent of black pride and power, blaxploitation horror films created sympathetic monsters who helped shift audience identification away from the status quo "normality" of bourgeois white society. In some cases, they exposed white "normality," and especially white patriarchy, as productive of monsters. And, as is frequently the case with subcultural aesthetic innovations, those practices predated the mainstream media's eventual co-optation of them. For example, the softer and romanticized *Blacula* character became a staple of Hollywood's big-budgeted *Dracula* remakes, both in 1979 and 1992. The philosophical musings of *Ganja and Hess*'s vampires became the cornerstone of Anne Rice's highly successful *Vampire Chronicles*, another recent genre reworking that attempts to mine the genre for more politically correct ideas.

While many media critics did (and still do) decry blaxploitation filmmaking, it nonetheless enabled many black film artists to gain a foothold in the industry, even as white Hollywood profited from the films' success. Many black leaders called for Hollywood to be more sensitive to black concerns and to divert some of the films' earnings back into black communities, while still others called for the formation of radical independent black filmmaking co-ops organized from preexisting black theater groups. Others, like Bill Lane, the pragmatic film commentator for the *Los Angeles Sentinel*, found himself defending blaxploitation movies even though he understood their potentially problematic implications. Lane also understood the films' marketplace and the need for commercially viable (i.e., Hollywood-style) product when he wrote: "Just say black producers suddenly got hold of unlimited film-making funds, and they decided to turn out only 'meaningful' black movies. They'd be broke in a year." Such was the case with *Ganja and Hess*'s production team of Quentin Kelly and Jack Jordan. They wanted to make "quality" films, not "headbusting films [in which] blacks beat up on whites," but their films did not find an audience.

[. . .]

Even today, despite the postmodernist pressure encouraging the collapsing of boundaries, many specific filmic and cultural categories remain firmly in place. Serious art films are worthy of consideration by high-minded adults, while genre films remain exploitative nonsense for younger viewers. The recent box-office failure of *Beloved* (1998) would seem to attest to the earlier audience's inability to accept serious message filmmaking and horror movie iconography both in one text. On the opposite pole, many critics and fans of the horror genre feel that the film fails "as a horror film" if it draws attention to sociopolitical ideas, that by making people think they will stop being scared. But that is precisely the point, for surely what is most political about a horror film is what scares the audience in the first place. Acknowledging and understanding how the deep structures of popular generic media figure race, gender, sexuality, or any discourse of Otherness is an important aspect of media studies; these forms and artifacts help define the current and future landscape of media culture and, by extension, our own social and historical realities.

2.8

Carter in context
by Steve Chibnall

Adapted from his book-length study of the gritty British urban thriller *Get Carter*, Steve Chibnall's chapter '*Carter* in context' provides a powerful analysis of the film's transition from cult to crime classic, as well as analysing the social factors which underpinned this urban thriller. Chibnall begins his analysis by drawing on notions of the active cult consumer to explain how Mike Hodges' film was initially reclaimed by fan communities rather than critics, following the mixed reception of the film's 1971 release. For the author, these modes of active appreciation are still evidenced via websites and Carter 'communities' dedicated to amassing memorabilia and off-screen anecdotes around the film's production, as well as reenacting key scenes and snatches of dialogue from the text. However, as Chibnall is keen to point out, in the case of *Get Carter*, cult status is assured by not only its active fan following but also key textual features which appear confrontational or non-conformist to more mainstream productions. In the case of *Carter*, the theme of an amoral gangster driven by a very moral quest of family vengeance, while familiar to longstanding fictional forms such as Jacobean tragedy, remained relatively rare within the realms of British crime cinema during the decade. While plotting *Get Carter*'s influence on the contemporary cinematic scene, Chibnall also equates its cult condition to an ability to mirror wider tensions occurring in 1970s Britain. These included contemporary moral panics over cross-regional criminal networks, local government and police corruption and the widespread proliferation of new forms of pornographic short films or 'rollers', as Chibnall defines them. The chapter also offers a fascinating insight into the creative team behind this cult crime caper and outlines the influence that the pioneering exploitation producer Michael Klinger exerted over the *Carter* phenomenon.

A note on the extract: this chapter has been extracted from the longer opening section of Chibnall's book *Get Carter*. The original chapter offers an in-depth account of the film's production, casting and social context, while situating *Get Carter* alongside a range of cinematic influences from American Westerns and film noir, to British social realism and the swinging London films of the 1960s. The chapter also offers an insight into contemporary social and political events occurring in the North of England at the time of the film's production.

[. . .] It took almost twenty-five years for the critical orthodoxy to accept that the cult followers of Mike Hodges' dark and downbeat tale of fear and loathing in Newcastle had some justification for their reverence. Clearly, the film had not changed, but something in the culture of its reception most certainly had. When Hodges spoke about his film at a screening at the National Film Theatre on 23 September 1997, he indicated that he had come to regard making a film as 'putting a message in a bottle', packing it with meaning and waiting for it to be washed up on some receptive shore. By the turn of the millennium, *Get Carter* was basking on the beach. [. . .]

In her 1985 essay on the politics of film canons, Janet Staiger pointed to a developing strand of film studies that questioned the idea of a single 'correct' interpretation of any text, and 'concentrated instead on how institutions and ideologies have established appropriate methods of understanding a work'. This involved, she suggested, an analysis of 'a politics that marginalises and devalues non-elite reading strategies'. Staiger's concerns with reading communities, interpretive strategies and the politics of admission to institutional canons were never more relevant than in the case of *Get Carter*, a film that has undergone a transformation from underground cult to overground classic. Staiger likened institutional anxieties about the dissolution or dilution of the film canon to the fears expressed in Umberto Eco's *The Name of the Rose* about 'dwarfs with huge bellies and immense heads' taking charge of the monastic library. Well, if the critical rehabilitation of *Get Carter* is anything to go by, the British Film Institute has recently become populated by rotund people of small stature. Its millennial poll of the great and the good of British cinema placed *Carter* among the top twenty treasures of the nation's cinematic heritage.

If *Get Carter*'s place among the pantheon of British cinema classics has only recently been established, its status as a cult movie has long been unquestionable. Anyone in doubt should visit the sumptuous Web site (www.btinternet.com/~ms. dear) that devotee Mark Dear operates as a shrine for the film's fans. Replete with poster reproductions from all over the world, rare stills, accounts of the film's shooting and critical reception, chat room, and prize awards for the winners of its trivia quiz, the site speaks eloquently of the enthusiasm of generations of *Get Carter* adherents. This enthusiasm is not confined to the manipulation of a computer mouse. The *Get Carter* Appreciation Society marked the thirtieth anniversary of the film's location shooting by re-enacting various scenes in Newcastle and Gateshead on 28 July 2000. Organised by Chris Riley, a Tyneside solicitor, the event centred on the decaying Owen Luder-designed car park on the corner of West and Ellison Streets in Gateshead, the scene of Carter's murder of the 'big man' in 'bad shape', Cliff Brumby (Bryan Mosley). The car park had become 'a monument to the film', said Riley, but was targeted for demolition to make way for new developments in the town. Now fully conversant with its cultural responsibilities, Gateshead Town Centre Regeneration announced plans to present the man who played Carter, Michael Caine, with a piece of concrete from the site once the bulldozers have done their work. A spokesman for the organisation acknowledged the solemnity of the occasion when he told the press on 3 August, '*Get Carter* was a great movie and there is a lot of affection for that car park.' The growing significance of the film to a sense of local identity was acknowledged in January 2002 when Newcastle radio station Century FM dedicated a day to *Get Carter*, asking listeners to phone in with their memories of the making of the movie.

Ultimately, cult movies are defined by their appropriation by active audiences, but films do not have an equal chance of being appropriated. Commentators have frequently noted that certain textual characteristics offer greater possibilities for cultish adoption than others. Movies that acquire a cult following are often challenging and confrontational in their style, imagery and themes. They will usually transgress genre boundaries, exhibiting an 'unhinged' quality, which revels in excess. Their narratives are likely to offer scope for metaphorical or allegorical interpretation, and may resonate with deep-seated cultural myths. More often than not, they will be highly self-aware, containing coded references and intertextual allusions that allow opportunities for detective work. Frequently, too, the cult film will feature a charismatic protagonist or antagonist who becomes an unconventional object of identification for viewers, provoking ambivalent feelings in the process. None of these characteristics is sufficient in itself to guarantee cult status, but the accumulation of these textual aspects will increase a film's chances of adoption. *Get Carter* is a perfect example.

Carter as tragedy

> 'Tragedy is born in the west each time that the pendulum of civilization is halfway between a sacred society and a society built around man.'
>
> Albert Camus, *Selected Essays and Notebooks*, Harmondsworth:
> Penguin, 1970, p. 199

Get Carter is a film about crooks and, therefore, easily classified as a gangster or crime film. Its narrative of a murder solved by a lone investigator in a city rife with corrupt practices links it to the hardboiled private eye fiction of Chandler and Hammett, and its nihilistic tone, amoral atmosphere and *mise-en-scène* of urban decay recall American film noir. [. . .]

To think of the terraces and back alleys of Tyneside as merely substitutes for the mean streets of Los Angeles [. . .] however, is to ignore the fact that the generic roots of *Get Carter* run deep into European soil. Its theme of family revenge goes back to Greek classical drama and the tragedies of Seneca (*Thyestes, Medea* and *Agamemnon*), but its most salient ancestry is the dark and violent theatrical tradition of revenge tragedies that begins with Jacobean plays like John Webster's *The White Devil* (c. 1610) and *The Duchess of Malfi* (1612) and continues to be revived in films like *The Cook, the Thief, His Wife and Her Lover* (Peter Greenaway, 1988) and *Gangster No. 1* (Paul McGuigan, 2000). In Jacobean tragedy, the centre of violence and corruption is generally the court of the city state. *Get Carter* updates this trope by depicting Tyneside as a local state in which venality and the rule of force go largely unchallenged and, in Albany's words in *King Lear*, 'humanity must perforce prey upon itself'.

The nihilistic mood of Jacobean tragedy, and its pessimistic depiction of an anomic society being eaten away from within, transfers easily to the dawn of the 1970s. Camus' description of the conditions in which tragedy thrives as a dramatic genre – an era in which 'man frees himself from an older form of civilization and finds that he has broken away from it without having found a new form which satisfies him' – is as relevant to the end of the 1960s as to the end of the sixteenth century. Both were periods of transition in which dominant cultures and moralities were forced to give ground to emergent forces. *Get Carter*'s lawlessness recalls an earlier Elizabethan age in which medieval conceptions of personal honour and private justice were being challenged by the extension of state power and a public administration of justice. Carter's is a 'blood revenge', the survival of a culturally sanctioned response to the murder of family members in the era before the codification of law and the universal authority of the state. And, like the Elizabethan dramatists before him, Hodges is careful to link the theme of revenge with an attack on the corruption endemic in the local state and the sense of a society disintegrating and out of control. As he once remarked, 'The film is not just about the villain. It's about observing the social structures and the deprivation of the country from which this character comes.'

A similar vision of social dissolution and anomie had already been explored in Hollywood. Don Siegel had persuaded Clint Eastwood to discard his poncho to play a tough, unorthodox cop, a figure alienated from the city he visits in *Coogan's Bluff* (1968). Eastwood would play much the same role for Siegel in *Dirty Harry* (1971), a film made at roughly the same time as *Get Carter*. The closest affinities with Mike Hodges' film, however, are to be found in an American movie made by the British director John Boorman. In *Point Blank* (1967), a coldly violent thriller adapted from a Donald Westlake novel, Lee Marvin plays Walker, a professional criminal dedicated to avenging the wrongs done to him by his wife and her gangster lover. The film resembles *Get Carter* not only generally in its narrative structure, amoral atmosphere and sudden explosions of violence, but specifically in some of its textual details. Both films, for example, have a sequence in which a man is thrown from a tall building and either lands on, or narrowly misses, a car below, and both feature the shooting of a man named Carter by a sniper. In the case of *Point Blank*, Carter is a crime boss who proclaims that 'profit is the only principle', a doctrine to which Walker might also subscribe if he was not so obsessed with revenge.

[. . .]

As in the bleakest of film noir, the world evoked by *Get Carter* is a predatory sea in which sharks prey on their own kind as well as the little fish. It is a cycle of death in which killers eventually become victims themselves. Michael Caine was himself conscious of how the class system under which he was brought up made it very difficult for the children of the terraces and tenements to break the cycle of replication: 'If you are born into that working-class milieu as I was and as virtually every violent criminal is, then you're sure to want something different. And if the world hits you violently enough, then you will act in a violent way to alter your circumstances.'

[. . .]

The character of *Carter*

> 'Injuries are not revenged except where they are exceeded.'
>
> Seneca, *Thyestes*, II.195

Like Travis's crusade in *Taxi Driver* (Martin Scorsese, 1976), Carter's merciless assault on the rats of his urban sewer tackles the symptoms rather than the causes of moral decay and is inflected with the same hypocrisy. Carter apparently stands for the old world, the world of his childhood when family and community provided the city with a soul. His crusade is the reassertion, not of family values, but the value of family. The gangsters of Newcastle express their contempt for family relationships by murdering his brother and luring his niece/daughter into pornography. Carter sets out to make them regret this affront to his family name. But ironically, he, too, is infected with the malaise of his age. His value system is really little different from that of the men he pursues. He shows neither compassion for his victims nor much remorse for his crimes, and his hypocrisy about the value of the family is evidenced in his affair with his brother's wife. In truth, he is less family-centred than self-centred. The abuse of his family is a personal affront, a challenge to his own reputation as a hard man. Significantly, Hodges makes no attempt to show the event (the murder of Frank Carter) that triggers his protagonist's drive for vengeance. In this way, the director loosens the empathic bond that ties the viewer to the revenger in most dramas of this type. Carter's cold rage is never given the emotional support the depiction of the crime committed against his brother might draw from audiences. Moreover, Carter's fraternal relationship to the victim suggests that his wrath indexes loyalty due to another member of a homosocial order rather than the wider heterosocial order of the family.

Michael Caine saw his performance as an ethnographic exploration of the moral beliefs and social mores that underlie the gangster's presentation of self:

> The problem with a lot of British gangster films is that the gangsters are portrayed either as funny or stupid. But real gangsters are neither. I should know, 'cos I grew up with them. The razor gangs down the Elephant and Castle. They're serious blokes. Serious and bright. And very scary. That's how I played Carter. Of course he's a villain. But he doesn't regard himself that way. He doesn't see himself as a bad man. He might do bad things. But he feels completely justified.

Carter rails against the corrupt world but, ultimately, can transform neither the world nor himself. In this he strongly resembles the malcontent of Jacobean revenge tragedies, the figure Jonathan Dollimore labels the 'contradictory Jacobean anti-hero' and describes as:

> malcontented – often because bereaved or dispossessed – satirical and vengeful; at once agent and victim of social corruption, condemning yet simultaneously contaminated by it; made up of inconsistencies and contradictions which, because they cannot be understood in terms of individuality alone, constantly pressure attention outwards to the social contradictions of existence.

Dollimore notes that the malcontent he is describing not only serves as a means of exposing a malaise at the heart of the social order, but constitutes 'a prototype of the modern discontented subject'. Carter embodies Dollimore's contradictory revenger striding blindly out of the 1960s: a social sanitiser infected with the germs he seeks to sterilise, his righteousness compromised by his own corrupt morality. But this is no world for the righteous. Newcastle's mean streets are not for knights to go. Carter, unlike Raymond Chandler's Marlowe, is himself mean without the slightest trace of chivalry. He is more Mike Hammer than Philip Marlowe – frequently described by those he encounters (and sleeps with) as a 'bastard' – but Hodges likes to believe that the character retains the vestiges of a moral conscience: 'Carter had to be callous, but he knows he is sick, that he's not like normal people. When he sees the car [with a woman in the boot] tipped into the dock, I see regret in his face.' The regret may not be obvious to all viewers, but the film's triumph is to raise this cold sociopath, against our better judgement, to the level of tragic hero. We might not go as far as Michael Caine did in a television interview and describe Carter as 'an upstanding citizen with the right moral values', but we find it difficult not to side with this character who, after all, is the only candidate for sustained audience identification in the film. We find it hard not to respect Carter, although he does nothing to deserve it. We are tempted to admire Carter, although there is nothing admirable in his behaviour. Our identification with the character is made guilty by the acknowledgement that we are colluding in murder. The revelation of *Get Carter* is the realisation of just how vulnerable our own moral codes have become. It was a revelation experienced by Hodges, himself, when he first viewed his creation with its intended audience: 'I had assumed that, like me, the audience would hate Carter and would also be shocked by the film. But what surprised and frightened me in many ways was that they actually liked him.'

This identification with a protagonist in a way that entails the suspension of conventional morality is a typical mechanism of cult movie appreciation. For the most part, Hodges scrupulously avoids standard mechanisms of identification like the point-of-view shot, and frequently adopts a mediated view of his protagonist, but identification is ultimately facilitated by the inevitability of the character's fate (subtly suggested by Hodges and evident after the initial viewing), and the feelings of social estrangement he embodies. Dollimore points to the importance of this sense of estrangement in his social-psychological profile of Vindice, the doomed protagonist of *The Revenger's Tragedy*. Estrangement from society, Dollimore argues, provokes 'an aggressive reaction; heroic or criminal it adds up to the same thing: a desperate bid for integration'. This bid is futile, however, because characters like Vindice – or Carter – are bent on destroying 'that which they are within and which they cannot survive without'. The underworld is the air Carter breathes, and if he destroys or abandons it, he suffocates. This is why Dollimore argues that for the revenger to seek reintegration is to 'embrace destruction'. This is the 'vital irony' that supplies *Get Carter* with much of its fascination and underlies the 'subversive black camp' with which revengers' tragedies so often relieve their 'deep pessimism'.

It might be argued that the futility of Carter's crusade positions him as a classic film noir victim-hero. But if, in its moral bleakness and pessimism, the film resembles much of the noir canon, Carter's character breaks genre conventions. He is not the vulnerable man ensnared by a lethal spider woman, but a brick-hard killer who uses and abuses women as it suits him. Rather than a victim, he is a vortex that sucks all the characters he encounters into its downward spiral. His destruction conforms to the conventions of classical tragedy rather than to those of film noir. Carter is a victim of his 'fatal flaws', a manipulative and compassionless attitude to others, and an overbearing pride and arrogance that fuels his need to respond to any perceived affront and convinces him of his invulnerability. The faults in his character are a cipher for wider cultural ills, just as they are in Greek and Jacobean drama. As J. W. Lever wrote of the protagonists of tragedy in a book published in the same year *Get Carter* was released, 'the fundamental flaw is not in them but in the world they inhabit, in the political state, the social order it upholds'. If Carter is redeemed it is not by his willingness to give love, or even by the sentimentality he shows towards his kith and kin, but by his status as martyr for the social order he represents.

Fatal though his flaws may be, they continue to exert a powerful attraction for audiences, not least because in other circumstances they could so easily be construed as virtues. Carter is brave and tenacious, unshakably committed to his chosen course of action and confident in its execution, but above all he exhibits 'a cool, flip, tough arrogance' that links him to contemporary protagonists like Harry Callahan (*Dirty Harry*), Walker (*Point Blank*), and Coogan (*Coogan's Bluff*) and continues to recommend him to new generations of viewers. 'I modelled him on an actual hard case I once knew,' Caine once revealed. 'I watched everything the man did. I even saw him once put someone in hospital for eighteen months. Those guys are very polite, but they act right out of the blue. They're not conversationalists about violence, they're professionals.'

The creation of *Carter*

'You have to be ruthless. When you write you are drawing on your own emotions and relationships, your family and friends – and if this means you are exploiting people, well – it has to be done. My wife has come to terms with this now, I think – but my parents, for example, still find it painful to be "used".'

Ted Lewis, interviewed in 1969

Jack Carter was the creation of Ted Lewis, a heavy-drinking commercial artist in his late twenties. Born in Manchester soon after the outbreak of World War II, he was brought up in Barton-on-Humber, where his father was a quarry manager. After attending Hull School of Art, he worked as a book illustrator, an animator and an art director at an advertising agency in London. In his spare time, he wrote stories with strongly autobiographical content. Hutchinson's publication of his first book, *All the Way Home and All the Night Through*, in 1965, encouraged his literary ambitions, and he began to devote an increasing proportion of his time to his second novel.

Jack's Return Home was written in 1968, a year of political turmoil in which the established order was subjected to a sustained attack by a young intelligentsia. But, although Lewis's book may share some of the pent-up rage of the revolutionary left, it has none of its optimism or idealism. In spirit, it harks back two, three or even four decades to the hardboiled literary tradition of *Black Mask* magazine, and the radical cynicism of Dashiel Hammett and the sardonic detachment of Raymond Chandler. Lewis's prose has something of the simplicity and directness of Hammett and the world-weariness of Chandler, but his story also resembles the criminal-centred narratives of second-generation hardboiled writers like Jim Thompson and David Goodis. The book is written in the first person in the vernacular of Humberside, and manages to remain convincingly in character through to the end and the (probable) death of its narrator. In doing so, it conveys what Robert Murphy has called a 'provincial authenticity' that marries its American sensibilities to a line of British low-life thrillers by authors like James Curtis, Gerald Kersh and Arthur La Bern.

[. . .]

The man who would bring *Jack's Return Home* to the screen, independent producer Michael Klinger, was a unique figure in the British film industry. He was a showman able to bridge the sizeable gap between commercial sexploitation and a cinema of genuine artistic experimentation. The son of a Polish tailor, Klinger was born in Soho in 1920 and thoroughly imbibed its ethos of rule-breaking and shrewd deal-making. He started out as a disc jockey, but by the late 1950s, he was cashing in on the Soho striptease boom by managing the Nell Gwynne club. The club's performers supplied much of the subject matter for the epidemic of 8mm 'glamour' films that began to be produced for the home-viewing market at the time, and would later feature in the plot of *Get Carter*. It was at the Nell Gwynne that Klinger met Tony Tenser, then head of publicity for Miracle Films, a UK distributor for racy continental pictures. In 1960 they went into partnership and opened the Compton Cinema Club to show uncertificated movies to a 'sophisticated' membership. As Compton-Cameo Films, they quickly branched out into film distribution and production, beginning with naturist epics like Harrison Marks' *Naked as Nature Intended* (1961), and taking the fading British social problem cycle in a more consciously exploitative direction with cautionary tales such as *That Kind of Girl* (Robert Hartford-Davis, 1963) and *The Yellow Teddybears* (Hartford-Davis, 1963). The following year, Compton-Cameo extended its portfolio by backing the mondo documentaries being made by Stanley Long and Arnold Louis Miller: *London in the Raw* (1964), *Primitive London* (1965) and the docu-drama *Secrets of a Windmill Girl* (1965).

Its ability to supply a niche market with titillating fare was fast making Compton-Cameo one of the most financially successful independent companies in British film-making, but Klinger was to demonstrate that his interest in cinema went deeper than catch-penny sensationalism by backing the talent of a promising director from his father's homeland. The production of Roman Polanski's *Repulsion* (1965) and *Cul-de-sac* (1966), followed by Peter Collinson's obtuse and Pinteresque *The Penthouse* (1968), established Klinger as a cineaste and risk-taker to complement his reputation as a showman and deal-maker. *The Penthouse* was Klinger's first solo production after his split with Tenser, and was quickly followed by *Baby Love* (Alastair Reid, 1968), the controversial story of a suburban Lolita. In 1969, with the conviction of the Kray brothers making headlines, Klinger decided that it was time to produce a tough gangster picture. His friend the producer/director Peter Walker had been quicker off the mark with his own low-budget crime film *Man of Violence* (1970), filmed in the summer of 1969. Klinger was invited to view the first print of the film with Walker later in the year and, after informing its director that it was 'a load of old crap, son', he announced, 'I'm going to make a gangster film, but it's going to cost a lot more than this and it's going to be better.' A trawl of publishers for suitable properties turned up *Jack's Return Home*, and Klinger recognised its potential immediately. His creative imagination quickly linked the book to the promise shown by a new writer-director whose work Klinger had seen on Thames Television a few nights earlier, on

17 November 1969. The programme was an eighty-minute filmed teleplay entitled *Suspect*, and its creator was Mike Hodges. The jigsaw that was to be *Get Carter* was beginning to fall into place.

[. . .]

Mike Hodges came from a very different background from both Michael Klinger and Ted Lewis. He was brought up in comfortable circumstances in the west of England, qualifying as a chartered accountant at the age of twenty-two in 1955. But after his National Service, he decided to turn his back on accountancy and try his luck in the television industry as a teleprompter operator. By the early 1960s, Hodges had written his first television play and, ironically for an atheist socialist, had been appointed as the editor of an ABC Television religious programme for young people. After an abortive attempt to make a documentary on Stephen Ward and the Profumo affair, Hodges successfully pitched an idea for a film on undertakers to Granada's *World in Action*, and began a two-year association with the programme. Between 1963 and 1965, he travelled widely, making programmes in Canada, the USA and Vietnam, before transferring to the ITV arts programme *Tempo*, where he made profiles of designers, writers and film directors including Orson Welles and Jean-Luc Godard. The profiles were made in the style of their subject, and Hodges further experimented with form in his contributions to a series of films on media culture. By the time Ted Lewis was working on *Jack's Return Home*, however, Hodges was also ready to work on a thriller because, as he told Mark Adams, 'Done well they can be like an autopsy of society. Crime is a wonderful way of really looking at what is going on.' The result was *Suspect*, the film that brought him to Klinger's attention.

Mike Hodges received the proofs of Lewis's novel on 28 January 1970 and knew very soon after starting to read that this was a project that he wanted to take on. As Hodges set to work on his script, Klinger's mind turned to the question of a star for the film. With the confidence afforded by the involvement of a Hollywood major, he approached Michael Caine's agent Dennis Selinger. His timing was impeccable. Hodges' second Thames Television play *Rumour* had been broadcast (2 March 1970) while the proposal was being considered and had been greeted with enthusiasm by both Caine and Selinger.

[. . .]

Hodges saw his film as a tragedy in the tradition of Elizabethan drama and grand opera, rather than as an action thriller. It would, however, be a tragedy anchored to real contemporary social conditions, and would tap into the rage of the times. The screenplay was written in a climate of disintegrating social order. Persistent rioting in Ulster had brought British Army intervention and the formation of the Provisional IRA, and in England there was widespread student unrest, including bombings and violent demonstrations. The press was gripped by a moral panic about the activities of 'skinheads', and 'queer-bashing' and 'Paki-bashing' entered the language. As 1970 began, Britain was experiencing a spate of bank robberies, and its first case of abduction for gain. In the aftermath of the Kray twins' imprisonment, it was an active time for gangland, with the killing of Eddie Coleman in March. It was this apparently accelerating descent into disorder that helped sweep the Conservative Party to power in the summer's general election, and informed a number of contemporary film-makers' explorations of the morality of violence. While Hodges planned *Get Carter*,

Kubrick was making *A Clockwork Orange* (1972), Ken Russell was working on *The Devils* (1971), and Sam Peckinpah was developing *Straw Dogs* (1971).

[. . .]

High rollers and heavy rollers

'Princes give rewards with their own hands
But death and punishment by the hands of others.'

Gasparo, in John Webster, *The White Devil*, V.vi.191–2

The well-publicised trials and convictions of the London gangs run by the Kray and Richardson brothers had, by the end of the 1960s, rekindled the commercial potential of the gangster film in Britain. Although the Great Train Robbery of 1963 had inspired one notable film – *Robbery* (Peter Yates, 1967) – the genre had become unfashionable as the upbeat mood accompanying 'Swinging London' switched the attention of film-makers towards lighter subjects with greater international appeal. The major backers of British film-making at the time were the Hollywood studios and, as far as they were concerned, crime subjects were best treated in a spectacular (James Bond) or comedic (Ealing) fashion. Their preferred solution was the caper film, a sub-genre that seemed to capture the frivolousness and irreverence of the era. Michael Caine had already starred in a number of capers, including *Gambit* (Ronald Neame, 1966) and *The Italian Job*. But with the arrest of the Krays, the spotlight was suddenly illuminating the darker recesses of the criminal underworld. There was a realisation that British criminals might now be convincingly depicted as being as tough and ruthless as their American counterparts. A sensitive observer like Mike Hodges quickly appreciated the need to revise the customary representation of the British gangster:

> British criminals never did anything we saw people do in American film noir; nothing really unpleasant or sadistic. Then it all changed with the Krays and the Richardsons trials. Suddenly one realized there was a whole other game going on. And it wasn't just in London. There was a killing in Newcastle in a nightclub called La Dolce Vita, for example.

Although the murder took place after a visit to La Dolce Vita rather than on its premises, the name of the club with its connotations of style and hedonism perfectly captured the transformation that took place in Tyneside's nightlife after the Betting and Gaming Act of 1960. Previously, 'clubland' in the north-east context had meant the 1,500 working men's clubs where the toilers in the area's heavy industries could refresh themselves with local brown ale and watch a modest cabaret. But as improving wage levels and permissive legislation came together in the early 1960s, a new gloss was given to the entertainment business. The working men's clubs were stocked with newly legal 'one-armed bandit' slot machines, and the underground gambling dens surfaced as exotic casinos on the American and continental models. With its work hard/play hard tradition, Newcastle became the Las Vegas of the north. A new breed of entertainment entrepreneurs, often with criminal links, emerged. Together with those reaping fat profits from the architectural transformation of northern cities, they lived an ostentatious lifestyle, stirring contradictory emotions of envy and disgust among ordinary Geordies. Some of these clubland cavaliers moved north from London, where the voracious demands of protection racketeers were inhibiting business expansion. The north-east gold rush would quickly be slowed by the erosion of the area's economic infrastructure, but for a decade it roared ahead, drawing in claim jumpers as well as prospectors, and redrawing the map of Tyneside's underworld.

In *Get Carter*, the profiteers of the new leisure culture are represented by fruit machine distributor Cliff Brumby and the 'governor' of Tyneside, Cyril Kinnear, who has a business arrangement with the powerful London mobsters, the Fletcher brothers. Kinnear supplies pornography for the Fletchers to distribute. In return, they supply Kinnear with back-up enforcement services and the insurance supplied by their reputation in the criminal community. This symbiotic relationship has been forged by the hospitality offered by Kinnear during a visit from the Fletchers. There are striking parallels with the *modus operandi* of the Kray brothers.

By 1963, having established their power base in the East End of London, the Krays were looking to extend their business nationally and internationally. They took over two clubs in Birmingham and one in Leicester, and they negotiated a reciprocal agreement with a leading Glasgow mobster who supplied a gunman for one of the Krays' 'hits' in London. The twins were also courting American Mafia contacts, and were impressed with their practice of importing hitmen from other cities to carry out murders. They first developed an interest in Newcastle when their showbiz friend, the American singer Billy Daniels, was booked to appear at the city's La Dolce Vita Club in 1964. Fellow villain Eric Mason arranged hospitality from the club's owners, David Marcus and Norman Levy. The Levys sent two Rolls-Royces to meet the seven-strong Kray party at Newcastle station. 'As the evening progressed,' recalled Mason, 'we met the guys who ran things in Newcastle.' Among those introduced to the twins was the playboy Angus Sibbet, an operative of the slot machine and nightclub magnate Vincent Landa. Another of Landa's employees, the flamboyant East Ender Dennis Stafford, was already known to the Krays as someone who had crossed them as a juvenile. In 1967, Stafford, together with Landa's brother Michael Lavaglio, would be convicted of Sibbet's murder. The conviction, however, was one of the most unsafe in recent memory.

After meeting the men who ran Newcastle, it seems that the Kray twins, who already profited from slot machines in London's West End, decided that they would like a 'slice of the action' in the north. In the summer of 1966, they returned to La Dolce Vita with the legendary boxer, Joe Louis, for whom they had fixed up a series of personal appearances in northern clubs. Their relationship with the Levys was firmly cemented. Acknowledging the £5,000 donated by the Levys towards the twins' defence fund after their arrest, Ronnie Kray later described them as 'good friends at a time when good friends were hard to find'. The Krays also paid a visit to Landa's flagship gambling club, the Piccadilly, which was managed by Stafford. They were shown round by Sibbet's minder. Soon afterwards, Landa's business empire came under sustained attack. When offers of 'protection' were declined, three premises were burned down, including the Piccadilly Club. Whether or not the Krays played any part in Sibbet's murder remains a matter of conjecture. Sibbet was known to be embezzling substantial sums from the takings of his employer's machines, and paying sweeteners to club stewards, and this may have supplied a motive for his killing. Certainly, the case raised considerable doubts about the probity and impartiality of a Durham Constabulary which rushed to judgement on Dennis Stafford, a petty criminal whose *chutzpah* had frequently left the police and prison services with egg on their faces. The mysterious death of Vince Landa's bad lieutenant shed a dark light on the murky world of the north east's gangland, suggesting much more about its internal and external connections than it confirmed. Hodges researched the case carefully in his preparations for his film, and emphasised its relevance by using Landa's hastily vacated country house as the location for Kinnear's home. The house was within the jurisdiction of the County Durham Police Authority which, under the chairmanship of Cunningham was, one might say, rotten from the top down.

Rollers

'A black and white roller used to cost us two and a half quid. It sold for anything from £10 to £15. Colour rollers: the 200 foot was a fiver, that started at £25, and the 400 foot, which was two films in one, the sky was the limit.'

Derek Cox, porn shop manager in 1960s Soho

At the beginning of 1971, shortly before *Get Carter*'s release, police at Grimsby docks discovered 1,300 reels of pornographic film (known in the trade as 'rollers') and ninety-six sets of obscene colour slides in a cargo of animal offal. Grimsby is a stone's throw from Lewis's original setting for his story. The late 1960s and early 1970s were growth years for the porn trade. What had been a small underground cottage industry was transformed by changes in public attitudes, substantial increases in supply and, in London, the corrupt practices of that squad of police officers charged with the control of obscene publications. Soho had long been the centre of the trade in Britain, and from the mid-1950s it was dominated by a syndicate controlled by the vice barons Bernie Silver and Frank Mifsud. By the time Lewis was writing his book about the supply of films to the trade, they had been joined by two other major players: John Mason and Jimmy Humphries. Their businesses were effectively licensed and protected by an elaborate system of illicit payments to the Metropolitan Police's Obscene Publications Squad (OPS) and their senior controllers at West End Central and Scotland Yard. By 1970 the number of shops in Soho selling erotic materials had grown to over forty, most of them dealing (via their back rooms) in hard-core magazines and films imported from Scandinavia and the USA.

The presentation of the erotic on screen is as old as cinema itself, but before the late 1950s, the exhibition of 'blue' films was a strictly clandestine affair in Britain. It was a question of knowing someone who might know a man who could arrange a private screening at a stag party or similar single-sex gathering. The films were invariably foreign, usually French or American in origin. What changed this situation was as much an advancement in technology as a loosening of moral prohibitions. The availability of affordable 8mm cameras and film projectors for domestic use opened up new opportunities for producers of 'glamour' magazines like the photographer George Harrison Marks. In 1958, he began to produce and distribute three-minute soft-core reels featuring his models in states of undress. His challenge was quickly taken up by competitors such as Stanley Long and Peter Walker, and the films began to get longer and more elaborate as business boomed in the early 1960s. One of these films, *Soho Striptease* (Roger Proudlock, 1960) featured the performers from Michael Klinger's Gargoyle Club, and first introduced the future producer of *Get Carter* to the possibilities of film-making.

As competition in the 8mm glamour film business intensified, one or two producers decided to chance their arms with stronger fare. Unlike the products of Marks, Long and Walker, which were on discreet but open sale at legitimate retailers and via mail order, the work of underground hard-core film-makers Mike Freeman and Ivor Cooke was confined to the back rooms of Soho sex shops. The films began as silent reels in monochrome, but by the end of the 1960s, they had been upgraded to colour and sound. Freeman, however, had little opportunity to take advantage of technological improvements. He was sentenced to eighteen months' imprisonment on obscenity charges in 1966, and not too long after his release was back inside on a life sentence, having killed a man he claimed was a hitman sent to carry out an underworld contract on him. The vacuum left by Freeman was quickly filled by the shameless John Lindsay, a Scottish photographer who began to shoot blue films around 1969, at the start of the extension of the pornography business to new markets. Happy to publicise his activities, Lindsay allowed one of his filming sessions to be recorded by Stanley Long for his documentary *Naughty* (1971). His brazenness may have had something to do with the protection afforded by the systematic bribes he was paying to the OPS. The session was filmed at about the time of *Get Carter*'s release, and the title of the resulting blue movie, *Sex After School*, echoed the name given to the faux stag film that Carter sees in Newcastle, *Teacher's Pet*. Although Lindsay used adult performers, he liked to give the impression that they were younger, even at one time filming in a genuine school (with the connivance of the caretaker and head boy). Although there is no contemporary evidence of the production of hard-core films in the north of England, the nearest real-life equivalent to *Get Carter*'s Cyril Kinnear was a home counties pornographer called 'Big Jeff' Phillips. His main business in the early 1970s was the importation of Danish porn films for the Soho market, but he also made some of his own. Shortly before committing suicide in 1975 he described his entry into film-making to the *Sunday Mirror*.

> I started from nothing ten years ago and soon made a fortune. It was easy – I got a good movie camera, hired men and girls from the coffee bars and pubs around Soho for a fiver or a tenner a time and made the films in flats or houses borrowed from friends. They were filthy of course but technically very good. I sold them myself at first for £100 or £200 a copy. Then I was 'sent for' by a big dealer in porn [. . .] who persuaded me to deal only through him. [. . .] I could get £1,000 a copy for my movies through him. He also arranged introductions to detectives who named their price for leaving my business alone.

Phillips was able to buy himself a white Rolls-Royce, two blocks of flats, houses in Esher and Kingston, and a mansion in the Berkshire countryside. The mansion, which the *Sunday People* exposed as 'the stately home paid for with filth', was called 'High Crockett'. Kinnear's country seat was named 'The Heights'.

But although *Get Carter* is ostensibly about the blue film racket, the corruption of Doreen by pornographers is also a metaphor for a much more general malaise affecting urban Britain at the end of the 1960s. Hodges remains in no doubt that the scandals of the era were interconnected. He knew, for example, from the scandals that had rocked first the Sheffield and then the Leeds Constabulary shortly before *Get Carter* that police impropriety was not confined to London: 'I had worked on *World in Action*, so I knew there were whole strata of the police force which were corrupt. You sensed that. *Carter* wasn't just about pornographic films – it extended to local councils and building controls, undercurrents which eventually proved true with T. Dan Smith and Poulson.' Hodges never makes these connections as explicit as Lewis does in his novel, but they none the less ground the narrative implicitly in the secret sub-world of the local state. Beneath the dramatic surface of *Get Carter* lies a network that links un-civil servants, jerry builders and the cash to be made from bent coppers, squandered sixpences and pounds of porn.

2.9

The future of allusion: Hollywood in the seventies (and beyond)
by Noel Carroll

American philosopher Noel Carroll was introduced to alternative cinema in all its myriad forms while doing his graduate studies in cinema at New York University. As a film critic, Carroll's work is characterized by an emphasis on art cinema, which he approached through what he himself calls 'explicatory criticism' (a combination of new criticism, formalism and close analysis). Carroll published his criticisms in a wide range of journals, including *Millennium Film Journal*, *Artforum* and *October*. Occasionally, Carroll would write on popular cinema, and this is one such essay. It isolates what Carroll believes to be a new trait of 1970s popular cinema, namely its playful acknowledgment of cinema history itself within new narratives and styles; it leads to homage, imitation, inferences, references, intertextuality, plagiarism and reflexivity – in short, movies quoting movies. Carroll calls it 'allusion'. He sees it as the result of 'informed, college-educated' moviegoers' and fans' increased awareness of cinema history and, subsequently, a new generation of moviemakers' desire to acknowledge this, demonstrating how their films latch onto the legacy of cinema. Since the 1970s it is seen as a core feature of cult cinema – offering avid audiences a privileged sensation of appreciation (and a step up from other audiences). For Carroll, exploitation film producer Roger Corman is instrumental in the creation of this sensibility. He offered young directors (at the margins of Hollywood) the chance to make quick, dirty films – encouraging them to rip off successful styles and tropes from films of the 1950s, and providing them with no-nonsense funds to shoot fast, include the necessary exploitation elements (sex and violence), and make it look slick, hip and topical. Corman made making movies look easy and fun. As Carroll writes, 'it was the not-so-secret daydream of many a cinephile to run away from school and join Corman – to make the old genres dance to a new theme, topical and metaphysical'. As such, Corman was responsible not just for introducing a new generation of filmmakers (Martin Scorsese, Francis Coppola, Jonathan Demme), but also for igniting genres with new élan, offering the 1970s a cultist sensitivity.

A note on the extract: this article was first published in *October*, 2, spring 1982, pages 51–81. It is reprinted in a collection of Carroll's criticisms, published by Cambridge University Press as *Interpreting the Moving Image*, pages 240–264. Our excerpts are taken from this reprint. We have chosen to focus on the excerpts that a) introduce the concept (p. 241), and b) single out the role of Corman in servicing the conditions under which allusion could become a cultist property (pp. 258–260).

[. . .]

Allusion, specifically allusion to film history, has become a major expressive device, that is, a means that directors use to make comments on the fictional worlds of their films. *Allusion,* as I am using it, is an umbrella term covering a mixed lot of practices including quotations, the memorialization of past genres, the reworking of past genres, *homages,* and the recreation of "classic" scenes, shots, plot motifs, lines of dialogue, themes, gestures, and so forth from film history, especially as that history was crystallized and codified in the sixties and early seventies.

During that period, a canon of films and filmmakers was forged. An aggressive polemic of film criticism, often called auteurism, correlated attitudes, moods, viewpoints, and expressive qualities with items in the putative canon. These associations became available to contemporary filmmakers, who were able to lay claim to them by alluding to the original films, filmmakers, styles, and genres to which certain associations or assignments were affixed in the emerging discourse about film history. Hence *Body Heat,* a film based on references to film history, a film that tells us that for this very reason it is to be regarded as intelligent and knowing, a film that demands that the associations which accrued to its referents be attributed to it and that it be treated with the same degree of seriousness as they were.

The strategies for making allusions are various. They include the outright imitation of film-historical referents; the insertion of classic clips into new films; the mention of illustrious and coyly nonillustrious films and filmmakers in dialogue; the arch play of titles on marquees, television screens, posters, and bookshelves in the background of shots; the retreading of archaic styles; and the mobilization of conventional, transparently remodeled characters, stereotypes, moods, and plots. I am grouping all these practices and strategies under the rubric of "allusion to film history" because the new films in question are structured by pertinent strategies and practices in such a way that (1) informed viewers are meant to recall past films (filmmakers, genres, shots, and so on) while watching the new films, and that (2) informed viewers are not supposed to take this as evidence of plagiarism or uninspired derivativeness in the new film – as they might have in the works of another decade – but as part of the expressive design of the new films. The force of *supposed to* in this formulation is conventional; it is a rule of seventies film viewing, for example, that a similarity between a new film and an old film generally can count as a reference to the old film.

[. . .]

Just outside the gates of the old Hollywood in the sixties were a number of those who would become lords and ladies of the new Hollywood. They were encamped and waiting at a small studio called American International Pictures. Among those who passed through AIP were Bogdanovich, Coppola, Scorsese, Milius, Hellman, Hopper, Jonathan Demme, Robert Towne, Jack Nicholson, Robert DeNiro, Bruce Dern, John Alonzo, Laszlo Kovacs, and Verna Fields. For financial reasons, AIP gave many young cinéphiles an opportunity to work – they were dirt cheap and they labored unstintingly for love of cinema. When the industry proper became interested in special-audience and youth films it was natural that AIP would be a source of talent, since for years it had, almost alone, farmed the fields of special-interest genres (such as motorcycle movies) and youth (and even younger) films. But AIP was important for the creation of the new Hollywood not only because it was a stepping-stone for future luminaries but because it provided an atmosphere which was not just congenial but also conductive to the aesthetic proclivities of the cinéphile.

The major artistic force at AIP was Roger Corman, a figure of great symbolic and inspirational, as well as instrumental, value for cinéphiles of the sixties. His was a life of film, the closest approximation around to the life of the American studio contract directors the American auteurists idolized. The very existence of Corman answered the cinéphiles' wish to believe that it was still possible to live and work like a Ford or a Walsh. Corman plied the *old genres*, moving from one to another, doing his job at a constant rate of productivity. Corman's individual films were less important than the fact that he was always immersed in the process of *film*. Corman appeared to be able to toss off films as quickly and as confidently as Mozart could symphonies. The number of camera setups Corman could run through from dawn to dusk was legendary; he could churn out a feature in three days, though he usually gave himself two to three weeks for a project. He worked quickly, improvising with surety, evoking the same kind of admiration for craftsmanship that Balanchine and Cunningham do in outsiders witnessing them in the thick of choreographing. Corman's creative speed and enormous output made him seem like a visitor from a bygone era.

His working procedures also recalled the hurly-burly days of early films – jumping into a car to drive over to a friend's house for some location shooting or cooking up a second film on the days remaining on the contract for the first. The working schedule was grueling, but it seemed tinged with adventuresomeness, freedom, and the fun of filmmaking. Corman's low budgets were often the mother of formal inventiveness; in the middle of an unadorned, almost TV-documentary-looking run of shots, his film might burst into an assertively edited sequence, a strikingly self-demonstrative camera movement, or a cheap, glaringly garish special effect that felt bold and experimental in contrast to the staid prevailing dicta of sixties Hollywood realism. Though overstated, his Poe films were refreshingly stylized in their use of color in a period of gray flannel films. Corman's indulgence in layers of albeit often strained religious and ritual allegory and literary conceits, as well as his willingness to shift from flat, homely, mundane images to self-declaiming stylization, gave his work a personal signature, a sense of irony; Corman was a literate director who stood apart, somewhat amused but also genuinely involved and entertained by his generally silly but at the same time oddly compelling little films. The films looked thrown together, a bit amateurish; they were often wooden, but would suddenly evince a feat of cinema that would appear to hail from nowhere. They could leap from cheap economical realism to montage to broad shtick. This gave his work a quality of freedom or free play that could be mistaken for Godard's, especially as the latter was misperceived in America.

Corman made parodies like *Bucket of Blood* ('59), *Little Shop of Horrors* ('60), *Creature from the Haunted Sea* ('61), and the funny, belligerently avant-garde *Gas*, ('70) that were directed at a special hip audience that accepted the *Mad Magazine, Comix* premise that being sophomoric can be sophisticated – an article of faith not unrelated to the mind set required to become a committed film fiend. In works like *St. Valentine's Day Massacre* ('67) Corman includes self-conscious bows to the historical gangster film, while in *Bloody Mama* ('70) he madly careens from dramatic to comic tones, from brutal to lyrical ones, while also taking potshots at media-made

America. Increasingly Corman's cinema came to be built with the notion of two audiences in mind – special grace notes for insiders, appoggiatura for the cognoscenti, and a soaring, action-charged melody for the rest. In this, he pioneered the two-tiered system.

It was the not-so-secret daydream of many a cinéphile to run away from school and join Corman – to make the old genres dance to new themes, topical and meta-physical, and to lard them with personal touches like the ones people were always finding in Ford, Hawks, Lang, and company. Everyone wanted to make a film rather than to write the Great American Novel; those with auteurist leanings wanted to be directors, directors of American genre films, ones with highly personal preoccupa-tions showing. Some actually carried through on their dream. And Corman was demanding, hard-driving, yet permissive taskmaster. The cinéphiles could have all the personal touches and artistic flourishes they wanted so long as they stayed on sched-ule, stayed within their budgets, and kept the sex and violence moving along briskly enough so that the drive-in audiences didn't start honking their horns. Corman asked no more of his epigones than he asked of himself.

[. . .]

2.10

Hitchcock in Texas: Intertextuality in the face of blood and gore

by Janet Staiger

Adapted from her volume *Perverse Spectators*, Janet Staiger's account of *The Texas Chain Saw Massacre* considers issues of humour and intertextuality as they impact on readings and receptions of this seventies cult classic. Staiger begins her article by considering the reasons *not* to invest critical attention on Tobe Hooper's 1974 shocker, noting that an initial viewing of the text offended her sensibilities on a number of levels. However, the author notes a gradual transition of her affiliations towards the film after noting its connections to the more critically celebrated *Psycho* (1960). For Staiger, Hitchcock's link to Texas (chainsaws) includes features such as the shared emphasis on a journey from civilized to uncivilized places, an uncanny fetishization of dead females as mummified remains, an unsettling emphasis on ocular imagery in pivotal scenes and the marked use of overhead camera movement in key sequences of assault. Having identified these connections between the reputable and disreputable cult text, Staiger notes how this not only frames her later interpretive strategies for reading *The Texas Chain Saw Massacre*, but also results in an increasing emphasis on the film's morbid humour as a central focus for the author's interest. For Staiger, the important aspect of her (re)-reading of this minor cult classic comes from her search for 'interpretive communities' or like-minded scholars able to read Hitchcockian/humerous references into the text as well as the range of parallels she identifies in both works. Staiger accurately identifies the degree to which a range of key readings of the film have identified similar themes and tropes in an article which focuses cult activity on the intertextual emphasis of the reader rather than the text.

A note on the extract: this chapter was first published in Staiger's volume *Perverse Spectators* and is reproduced here in its entirety.

At the university of Texas at Austin, I teach a course in Cult Movies which is really devoted to introducing my students to various theories of how readers use texts cognitively, sociologically, and psychologically. Since I live in Austin, Texas, I could scarcely avoid teaching *The Texas Chain Saw Massacre* (Tobe Hooper, USA, 1974), although written descriptions and word of mouth had made the prospect of actually watching the film more dreaded than anticipated. Watching a family of men attack four youngsters who happen to stumble into their home, presumably then using their bodies for Texas barbecue, did not excite me.

Indeed, the first viewing of the text affronted my feminist sensibilities. I was outraged by the images of abuse of both men and women, and at that point in my viewing career—raised on art cinema and Hollywood films, with only a few aggressive avant-garde texts as comparable in their onslaughts on the human body—I was, well, shocked! The class discussion was lively, however, and the movie seemed to serve a useful pedagogical purpose of questioning the social effects of cult movie behavior. Moreover, Robin Wood's excellent discussions of it as a comedy about the family worked well with my theoretical concerns. Thus, I kept the film in for the second time I taught the course.

Something strange happened to me that time, however. It has been common for my students to laugh at "inappropriate" places in films, and we often discuss laughter as a cathartic response for viewers. The second time through *The Texas Chain Saw Massacre*, though, I began to see all sorts of intertextual references to Hitchcock's *Psycho*, primed in part no doubt by Wood's essay, which discusses *Psycho* as a predecessor of *The Texas Chain Saw Massacre* in criticisms of the family. These intertextual references included:

1. Both films represent the protagonists keeping their dead and "living dead" ancestors mummified in the house.

2. Both films are structured around a car drive into an isolated area where a house seems to offer protagonists a chance for reestablishing social contact, but eventually the house provides precisely the opposite: a very antisocial contact.

3. Both films imply that the oddness of the children is a result of family relations.

4. Both films suggest serial killing is random and a matter of chance intrusion by unwitting victims.

5. Both films employ the same architecture for the house, in the case of *The Texas Chain Saw Massacre* even playing with the viewers' expectations about the spatial locations from which the murderers will come.

6. Both films use birds as motifs to accompany the serial killers (*Psycho*'s Norman Bates enjoys taxidermy; *Texas Chain Saw*'s family members have a pet chicken they keep in a birdcage).

7. Both films use excessive close-ups of eyes matched to other round objects as stylistic transition points and, upon further analysis, in a symbolic chain of meaning. In the case of *Psycho*, Marion's eye is graphically matched to the shower drain; for *Texas Chain Saw Massacre*, Sally's eye is matched to a perfectly full moon.

These references are probably sufficient to establish my argument that *Psycho* is a *complex* intertextual source for *The Texas Chain Saw Massacre*. However, my reading of the allusions began to go even further. Here are another two comparisons:

8. Both films have the threatening protagonists clean up the women's bodies using a broom, stuff the bodies and brooms in vehicles, nearly drive off, but return to turn out the lights. This occurs in *Psycho* as part of the cleanup of Marion's murder; in *Texas Chain Saw Massacre*, the victim Sally tries to escape one of the sons but unwittingly runs into the Father's barbeque shop, whereupon the Father stuffs her live into a gunnysack to bring back to the house.

9. Both films shoot one of the key attacks from an overhead camera position. In the case of *Psycho* this is during the death of the detective; in *Texas Chain Saw*

Massacre, the feeble attempt by Grandpa to whack Sally with the hammer has several overhead shots.

By the time I was seeing these allusions in my second viewing, I was laughing at scenes that had outraged me during my first viewing. Moreover, I was laughing in places that were not even in the loosest sense likely to have been placed there for comic relief and catharsis. As Michael Goodwin in an early review of *The Texas Chain Saw Massacre* pointed out, this is a film without relief of its horror: "Most horror films work on a cyclical structure in which the 'scare scenes' are separated by neutral sections of exposition. This was a nonstop nightmare in which the moment-to-moment texture is just as loathsome as the big horror scenes. . . . Even the comic relief is dire." Goodwin recounted that when the film was screened in a neighborhood theater in San Francisco in its early months, "people began to emerge from the theatre in a state of shock. Some of them made it to the bathroom before they threw up. Some didn't. The crowd was furious, the manager wasn't there to authorize refunds, and before things got straightened out a few punches were thrown" (p. 115).

This response to the film seems moral and appropriate. But what about mine? Especially since my class had now begun to worry about me. One way to reassure oneself that one is not perverted is to find a community of others—a subculture of like-minded individuals who mirror one's own nature. In my case I needed an interpretative community of fellow scholars who would also have the cultural capital to see the massive intertextual allusions to *Psycho* in *The Texas Chain Saw Massacre*.

I assumed I might find such a community in the reviewers of *The Texas Chain Saw Massacre* or, failing them, the scholarly commentators on the film. I checked the initial reviews of the film, starting in chronological order. The first one was from the *Hollywood Reporter*. Sure enough, John H. Dorr made a connection between the two films. He wrote,

> Made in Austin, Texas, largely by some very talented graduate students of the University of Texas, this Vortex/Henkel/Hooper Production is thoroughly professional, compelling, and gruesome. Squarely within the traditions of the "Psycho" genre, it is a fresh and extreme interpretation that should do for meat-eating what Hitchcock did for shower-taking. . . . "Everything means something I guess" is a throwaway line that nonetheless underscores the raw libidinal anarchy of this story and touches on the sense of humor lurking behind the mayhem.

Good for a start: Dorr connected the film to Hitchcock, *Psycho*, and a humorous subtext, but nothing he wrote indicated that he really saw the array of parallels that I did. Nor did the writer for the next review, which came from the *Los Angeles Times* and whose author, Linda Gross (honestly), saw no humor at all and called the film "despicable." *Variety*'s reviewer, "Mack," always a well-informed critic, made the Hitchcock/*Psycho* connection through *Psycho*'s own original intertext: Robert Bloch's novel about the incident in 1957 in which "Plainfield, Wis. authorities arrested handyman Ed Gein after finding dismembered bodies and disinterred corpses strewn all over his farmhouse."

If my interpretative community was not among the reviewers, perhaps it would be with academics who should be particularly used to looking for such allusions as part of their critical behavior. Within a year, Julian Smith began the serious recital of parallels in an essay for the *Journal of Popular Film*. Remarking on the film's humor, Smith recognized its already canonical place within the midnight movie scene then at its high point in America. Smith also put *The Texas Chain Saw Massacre* into the formula underlying the second parallel I noted: "the introduction of normal individuals into a strange and terrifying environment via an interrupted auto journey. Such films rely on lonely, sinister houses approached by car. The classic example— and a film that may well have inspired *The Texas Chain Saw Massacre*—is Hitchcock's *Psycho*" (pp. 105–6). Although Smith remarked on several of the parallels that I saw, he isolated them from any specific thread of intertextual analysis. Yet, he, like me, could not resist a grudging response of humor. He concluded his essay:

> Before I describe the last image, I should explain that this is a film that tries to be fair and open-handed . . . to both sides—to the travelers and to those who bestill them. Sally escapes, which pleases us, but is there a way to toss a bone, so to speak, to the family we have visited? They are, after all, worthy of our respect. They have responded ingeniously to their culture and environment. They speak for the value of traditional crafts and the sanctity of private property. They have not gone on welfare. They have decorated their home in a way that reflects their personality (grandmother and the family dog have been dried and put on display, their armchairs are armchairs). Besides, anyone who expresses himself with a chainsaw can't be all bad.
>
> (P. 108)

In the same year as Smith's critical essay, *The Texas Chain Saw Massacre* appeared in the London Film Festival, elevating it to the status of art object—which might have promoted more readings of intertextual influence. Even before then, it had been put into the Museum of Modern Art's permanent collection, screened at the 1975 Cannes Film Festival with films by Schroeter and Fassbinder, and reviewed favorably by Rex Reed. Guy Phelps in a 1976 essay, "Family Life," in *Sight and Sound* noted *Psycho*'s and *Texas Chain Saw Massacre*'s mutual intertextual debt to Ed Gein's story, but he went no further in detailing intertextual allusions.

Stephen Koch's 1976 diatribe against the film in "Fashions in Pornography" for *Harper's Magazine* described *The Texas Chain Saw Massacre* as "unrelenting sadistic violence as extreme and hideous as a complete lack of imagination can possibly make it." But his greater wrath was directed against any film buff who praised the film for its style and unrelenting form. Although Koch described the classic film buff's strategy of creating intertextual references as justifications for elevating a text to "art" from "trash," since the buffs praising the film were often arguing the film was just that— great trash—Koch was not moved to read it through a *Psycho* filter. Roger Greenspun rebuffed Koch in *Film Comment* in early 1977, but Greenspun spent most of the space of his article on cinematic homages to Hitchcock in Brian De Palma's *Carrie*, not on finding a similar potential in *Texas Chain Saw Massacre*.

However, Wood in his famous and valuable essay "Return of the Repressed" picked out the third parallel in December 1976: blaming the mother (or family) for the psychopathology of the killer. Wood's essay does much to trace a range of motifs in the formulas in which both *Psycho* and *The Texas Chain Saw Massacre* operate. Wood would have it that *Texas Chain Saw Massacre* is a "hideous parody of domesticity" (p. 12). Thus, Wood's primary intertext is to the family and not specifically to *Psycho*.

By 1977, *Texas Chain Saw Massacre* had been connected to other intertexts besides the representation of the family: Mary Mackey in the leftist journal *Jump Cut* read it as having "origins in class difference" and saw the chicken in the birdcage as "symbolizing, perhaps, the female principle trapped and fed on by the family." Sally's leap out the window recalled for Mackey the suicide in *The Birth of a Nation*. Tony Williams for *Movie* read *Texas Chain Saw Massacre* and other family horror films as part of the American myth of the degeneration of the hunter.

By now, I have come to the end of the 1970s, some five years after the film's release and elevation to the status of an object of intellectual scholarship, and certainly to a time of a devoted interpretative community of scholars of Hitchcock ready to read Hitchcockian influences into films. Somewhere further on in the 1980s, I am sure, all of the intertextual parallels I have seen (and possibly many more) were seen by someone. But I have not found an interpretative community to mirror me and authorize my laughter.

What can I conclude? That I remain a perverted reader? I hope not. I could justify the interpretations I have created by appealing to standing scholarly protocols for making interpretative arguments. These include:

1. *The Authorial Influence Warrant.* After all, Tobe Hooper acknowledges watching *Psycho* when working on *Texas Chain Saw*.

2. *The New Criticism Warrant.* The textual evidence "speaks" for itself.

3. *The Cultural Discursive Structure Warrant. Texas Chain Saw Massacre* is an interesting permutation of a series of discourses operating and transforming around the family and serial killing between 1960 and 1975.

All of those arguments are valuable and would make significant essays. Yet this essay has focused on me, as a perverted reader. Here I am more interested in why I (or any other reader) might make this interpretative move rather than in arguing for some historical or critical validity for the comparison. The issues of real influence—authorial or discursive—are not the point of this essay. The issues of textual and contextual evidence and proof are not the point of this essay.

The surface justification, of course, for my reading is that I have been primed to make this interpretation by the intertexts of the Bloch novel and the direct influence of *Psycho*. But that does not explain why I should find these intertextual references funny. According to Robert Stam, Robert Burgoyne, and Sandy Flitterman-Lewis' reading of Julia Kristeva's interpretation of Mikhail Bakhtin's notion of intertextuality, intertextuality is the "transposition of one or more systems of signs into another, accompanied by a new articulation of the enunciative and denotative position." That rearticulation, however, does not assume functions of cognition or affect for the reading subject who experiences or creates the transposition.

Research on intertextuality has focused on types of intertextuality, but little work has been accomplished on the functions of intertextuality for the reader or why a reader might be primed or cued to take up a particular function. In the case of *The Texas Chain Saw Massacre*, I would assert that I have been cognitively primed to make this humorous interpretation by several other contextual/intertextual situations:

1. Humor has long been associated with *The Texas Chain Saw Massacre*, from Wood's remarks about it as a family comedy to numerous cartoons, jokes, and comic skits. The images of the main characters, especially the brother who wields the chain saw, are part of American iconography and are routinely used for satire. *The Texas Chain Saw Massacre* is as ubiquitous in the American landscape as McDonald's.

2. Humor has also been long associated with Hitchcock. Since the 1950s and 1960s television programs, the text "Hitchcock-as-auteur" has had a connotation of having a morbid sense of humor. As Robert Kapsis points out, Andrew Sarris' 1960 review of *Psycho* counsels watching it a second time for "the macabre comedy inherent in the conception of the film." Allusions to Hitchcock texts are now available to be associated with the prospects of irony, parody, and the comic. Thus, despite Wood's appeal in the opening sentence of his book *Hitchcock's Films* that we take Hitchcock seriously, we can't take Hitchcock "seriously"—or at least only seriously.

Of course, cognitive priming is only part of the matter. As Freud notes about jokes, the economies of expenditure of energy are related to inhibition—either preventing an inhibition from being constructed or circumventing an inhibition already present. I do not have space in this essay to draw out the psychoanalytical mechanisms at stake, but obviously my personal invoking of the intertext of *Psycho* has been a means to defend myself from the sadomasochistic fantasies I am also constructing in viewing the text. By using the intertextual frame "Tobe Hooper has used Hitchcock's *Psycho* as an intertext for *Texas Chain Saw Massacre* and I am smart enough to see this," I am constructing for myself the role of a listener to a joke I am attributing to Hooper. Thus, I become complicit with Hooper in the mechanisms of a tendentious joke, rather than the joke's victim—the "average" viewer of the movie. I can laugh at the intertextual jokes rather than end up assaulted by the non-stop intensity of the plot.

I do not suppose that everyone laughing during *The Texas Chain Saw Massacre* is laughing for the reason that I have just suggested. The operations of the economies of the comic and the joke, particularly in the face of blood and gore, are quite complex. However, I would conclude by noting that scholars have produced substantial work on the types of intertextuality. Yet we have done very little work on the functions of intertextuality for the viewing subject. This is a worthy challenge as we try to sort out the political effects of texts on social subjects. The process of intertextuality clearly serves cognitive functions: we comprehend texts based on the series of other texts in which we insert the one we are viewing. Intertextuality also serves sociological functions such as the one implied by Koch's remarks: intertextuality permits scholars to align texts with other texts for the purposes of praising them as art or denigrating them as trash. Finally, intertextuality obviously serves affective functions, here to give me cultural capital and to let me laugh when I see the horror and humor of Hitchcock in Texas.

2.11

The essential evil in/of *Eraserhead* (or, Lynch to the contrary)
by Steven Jay Schneider

With his penchant for surreal narrative experimentation, oddball characterization and (un)healthy doses of the grotesque, David Lynch is a cinematic creator frequently categorized as 'cult'. However, in his chapter 'The essential evil in/of *Eraserhead* (or, Lynch to the contrary)' film producer and critic Steven Jay Schneider examines the paradoxes that surround the reception of Lynch's 1977 debut feature-length production. Despite its emphasis on the psychologically muted anti-characters, macabre erotic encounters, fantastical beheadings and monstrous foetuses that are anything but 'regular chickens', Schneider notes that critics have often denied the cult horror roots of Lynch's film. While much of the critical reception of *Eraserhead* has revolved around attempts to 'narrativize' and comprehend the text's discordant scenes, Schneider finds the film's fantastical roots in the horror genre as identified by Lynch's use of surreal set pieces, bizarre unmotivated character interaction and an emphasis on gross-out imagery. While it is the latter point which occupies much of the author's analysis (particularly in those scenes centring on the lead character's relations with his mutant offspring), he identifies five key scenes in which implied threat or monstrous representation indicate an off-centre, cult horror angle to *Eraserhead*'s appeal. As with other 'horror' classics such as *Black Sunday* (1960), *The Texas Chain Saw Massacre* and *Suspiria* (1977), Schneider sees the perverse fascination of Lynch's film in the uncanny way in which it violates existing physiological, cultural and conceptual categorizations identified by theorists such as Noël Carroll. From blurring of the boundaries between animate/inanimate characters to traversing the categories on inside and outside (with its celebrated internal-organ-explosion finale), this is a film that finds common currency in longer-standing splatter traditions, which Schneider explores in a concise and detailed manner via observation of key segments of the film.

A note on the extract: this chapter was first published in the Erica Sheen and Annette Davidson volume *The Cinema of David Lynch: American Dreams and Nightmare Visions*, which contains a number of interesting chapters dealing with the filmmaker's cult catalogue. The original version of this chapter contained additional sections on the narrative structure of *Eraserhead* as well as some further references to horror influences (such as Poe) as they impact on Lynch's work.

For various reasons, and in various ways, commentators on *Eraserhead* – David Lynch's first feature-length production, released in 1977 – have attempted to mitigate the film's cynicism and nightmarish qualities. It is as if they feel (but refuse to admit) that the picture cannot be celebrated as a work of brilliance unless its manifest horror is somehow redeemed. [. . .] In what follows, I will attempt to show how *Eraserhead* relies upon formal and thematic techniques familiar within the horror genre in order to engender its uncanny effects. To the extent that this analysis contradicts statements made by others, including Lynch himself, concerning the film's romantic, cathartic, even comedic dimensions, it will stand as a useful corrective to the naïve version of auteurism which so often accompanies the director's work. By contextualising *Eraserhead*, highlighting its debt to generic horror conventions both traditional and modern, the conception (including the *self*-conception) of Lynch as an eccentric *artiste* working in a cinematic vacuum may be somewhat damaged, though not his status as an innovative, immensely talented film-maker.

[. . .]

Eraserhead's horror effects

The following are brief descriptions of five of *Eraserhead*'s most unnerving scenes, in order of their appearance within the film. Although there is a degree of arbitrariness in the selections – there are, without a doubt, *other* unnerving moments, and perhaps not *everyone* will find those listed here especially effective or interesting – most of the scenes in question have been deemed worthy of attention in the critical literature on *Eraserhead*. After describing these scenes, I shall proceed to compare, contrast and analyse them in greater detail, and in the process situate them within various already-existent horror traditions:

(a) Early in the film, and after an innocent-enough walk home, Henry enters his apartment building and presses the elevator button. What follows after the doors open is an extremely disconcerting period of waiting (approximately 13 seconds) for them to close again, and then an equally disconcerting ride up to Henry's floor. It is not so much that anything 'happens' during this sequence – though the lights in the elevator flicker, and briefly go out a couple of times – but our sense of foreboding is primed nevertheless, and carries over to subsequent scenes.

(b) While alone at the table with Mary's father Bill (Allen Joseph) during his dinner at the Xs', Henry sits uncomfortably for what seems like an eternity while Bill just stares at him, his body completely still, his face frozen in the mask of a goofy smile. At the same time, in an effectively eerie juxtaposition of contrasting moods, Mary can be seen crying in the background.

(c) Henry and the audience suddenly discover (in the scene discussed briefly above) that the baby – already malformed and not entirely human – is sick, and not just sick, but suffering terribly.

(d) In the midst of a fantasy sequence that we eventually discover is a dream (or rather, a nightmare), Henry climbs up onto the stage inside his radiator and attempts to make physical contact with the blonde, ovarian-cheeked 'Lady in the Radiator' (Laurel Near) who occasionally performs a song-and-dance routine there for him. His attempt at touching her fails, however, and The Lady disappears in a flash of blinding white light. Henry backs up slowly as a small tree on a dolly rolls to centre stage. Then, just before the tree begins oozing blood down its sides, our hero's head literally pops off, only to be replaced by that of his mutant child's.

(e) Just prior to the film's epilogue, Henry takes a pair of scissors and cautiously yet determinedly cuts open the bandages in which his paraplegic infant has been mummified for what we can only assume has been its entire life. What gets revealed to Henry and the audience is far more disgusting than anyone could have guessed, far more than anyone could have imagined. After an extreme close-up of the baby's now exposed internal organs, out from every orifice mushrooms a foamy waste material that threatens to remain in a state of perpetual and ever-increasing discharge. (Kaleta's remark, quoted above, concerning the 'quantitative imagery' of *Eraserhead* is most appropriate here.)

One obvious difference between the first two scenes on this list is that the former involves just Henry and an inanimate object (the elevator), while the latter centres on a bizarre interaction taking place between two people, neither of whom we would be inclined to call 'normal', but one of whom – Henry – serves as our surrogate for much of the picture. Nevertheless, it could plausibly be argued that these scenes engender their disturbing effects primarily the same way: not through special effects, manipulative camerawork or hyperbolic gross-out shots, but through images which instil in viewers a palpable feeling of uncanniness. Before I defend it, this claim requires both qualification and clarification: the Lynchian uncanny is not – at least not primarily – explicable in Freudian/psychoanalytic terms (that is, via a return to consciousness of some previously repressed ideational content, or else via a reconfirmation in depicted reality of some previously 'surmounted' belief or beliefs), so much as in the terms proffered by Noël Carroll, a contemporary philosopher of film who attributes feelings of horror and uncanniness to apparent transgressions or violations of existing cultural (in some cases, conceptual) categories. Examples of such categories, according to Carroll, are the mutually exclusive dyads 'me/not me, inside/outside . . . living/dead' and human/machine (Carroll 1990: 32).

In both (a) and (b), Henry waits and waits . . . and waits . . . for something to happen (the elevator door to close; Bill X to stop grinning), without actively seeking to change his situation. In part, this is a symptom of his passivity, a character defect which is at least partially responsible for the problems he faces at home, and one which is dramatically overcome – with tragic consequences – when he finally decides to undress/murder his own child. But it is also no real surprise, since Henry has every reason (every *right*) to expect the 'somethings' in question to change of their own accord, and in a timely manner. It is precisely because Lynch intentionally primes, only to violate, Henry's – as well as our own – expectations concerning what is and is not 'appropriate' (standard operating procedure for a familiar piece of machinery; normal human social behaviour) that most viewers experience a feeling of uncanniness upon watching these scenes. At the imagistic level, both (a) and (b) also exhibit a *second* level of uncanniness: for there is a sense in which, arguably, the elevator displays a primitive consciousness of sorts, intentionally and perhaps spitefully 'teasing' Henry; and Bill X, by sitting utterly motionless for so long, in addition manages to violate the cultural/conceptual schema distinguishing animate from inanimate bodies. (Apparently this is a trait that runs in the X family, as Mary's grandmother displays some extreme corpse-like symptoms of her own.)

Without for a moment wishing to deny the effectiveness and creativity of the scenes in question, it should be pointed out that, at the level of *types* rather than *tokens*, the uncanny images just described do not originate with *Eraserhead*. On the contrary, the transgressive trope of non-living objects exhibiting some degree of proto-consciousness is a central feature of most – if not all – haunted-house movies (consider, for example, *The Haunting* (Robert Wise, 1964), *The Legend of Hell House* (John Hough, 1973) and *The Changeling* (Peter Medak, 1980)). Michel Chion writes that the shots of Henry waiting for the elevator and confronting evil in the form of electrical failures once inside it, 'betray the successfully assimilated influence of Kubrick, Fellini . . . and, of course, Tati' (Chion 1995: 31). With respect to Kubrick, it is true that his *own* unforgettable elevator sequence, in *The Shining*, appeared three years *after* Lynch's. Similarly, confusion over the ontological status of a particular individual – *Is s/he awake or asleep, conscious or unconscious, alive or dead?* – can be found in such a diverse collection of horror film narratives as *Mystery of the Wax Museum* (Michael Curtiz, 1933), *I Walked With a Zombie* (Jacques Tourneur, 1943), *House of Wax* (André De Toth, 1953), *A Bucket of Blood* (Roger Corman, 1959) and the post-*Eraserhead* pictures *The Texas Chainsaw Massacre 2* (Tobe Hooper, 1986), *The Serpent and the Rainbow* (Wes Craven, 1988) and *Se7en* (David Fincher, 1995). In the last example, a motionless, emaciated male figure is discovered tied to his bed in a dilapidated apartment by Detectives Somerset (Morgan Freeman) and Mills (Brad Pitt). Considering the wretched state of the body, and the largely 'realistic' world in which *Se7en* takes place, there seems no way this person could be alive. Curiosity and comfort lead the partners to bend over and examine the man, who suddenly jolts into consciousness with a vitality that fills most audience members with equal parts terror and disgust. Here we are approaching that most prolific of horror sub-genres, the zombie film, where the non-existent boundary separating animate from inanimate matter is frequently expressed by the term 'undead'. In Bill X's case, and especially that of Grandma X, however, a more fitting expression would be 'unliving'.

[. . .]

In order to further support these assertions, I propose to look more closely at another pair of scenes from the list above: (c) and (e). Because both scenes centre on Henry's freakish, physically- (not to mention psychologically-) indeterminate infant, it is no surprise that the predominant emotional response generated in each of them is disgust. Nor is the stylistic means by which Lynch seeks to achieve this response surprising, namely through the use of what I have been referring to as 'hyperbolic gross-out shots' (of the baby's face in the first instance; of its body in the second). A staple of modern horror fare, the technique of quick cutting to extreme close-ups of disturbing content became the defining feature of low-budget 'splatter' films, as pioneered by underground auteur Herschell Gordon Lewis (*Blood Feast*, 1963; *Color Me Blood Red*, 1965) and popularised in such immediate *Eraserhead* predecessors as Wes Craven's *Last House on the Left* (1972) – in which an innocent young girl is stabbed to death and disembowelled by her sadistic tormentors – and Tobe Hooper's *Texas Chain Saw Massacre* (1974). But considering that, in Lynch's film, the focus is primarily on the 'guts' component of the splatter sub-genre's 'blood-and-guts' formula, it would be remiss not to mention *Eraserhead*'s similarity in this respect to a pair of modern Italian horror classics: *Black Sunday* (Mario Bava, 1960) and *Suspiria* (Dario Argento, 1977).

In *Black Sunday*, there is an unprecedented and thus truly shocking moment near the end of the film in which the viewer is presented with a close-up of the reincarnated vampire-witch Aja's (Barbara Steele) rotting innards, which had previously been kept hidden by a mere article of clothing – just as the makeshift bandages encasing the Spencer baby's limbless body are the only things keeping its viscera 'under wraps'. Where are the layers of epidermis to protect this otherwise helpless being, to ensure that its insides *remain* inside? Although, as Freeland notes, nowhere in the published interviews does Lynch make actual direct reference to *Repulsion* (Roman Polanski, 1965), J. Hoberman and Jonathan Rosenbaum must be onto something when they describe the baby as 'an illegitimate monster – a mewling, eye-rolling first cousin to the skinned-rabbit centrepiece of Roman Polanski's [film]' (Hoberman and Rosenbaum 1983: 214). Whatever sympathy some viewers may feel for this creature – and let me emphasise the word *may* here, not wishing to assume any uniformity of audience response on this point – the 'monster' appellation is fitting. By fashioning Henry's baby skinless, boneless and poised to spill its guts out all over the place, Lynch forces Daddy and audience alike to contemplate a living, breathing (temporarily, at least) transgression of the deeply-entrenched cultural opposition, inside vs. outside.

[. . .]

With respect to (c), the sudden close-up of the baby in the throes of its mysterious, ulcerous illness finds an analogue in *Suspiria*, Argento's masterpiece of supernatural horror, released in the same year as *Eraserhead*. In this film, the discovery of infestation in the ceiling of a famous dance academy leads to a quick zoom-in to a nest of maggots, followed immediately by a close-up of a young girl's face covered with the vile insects – the resultant image is surprisingly similar to what we see of Henry's infant. Also crucial here is the sudden introduction of a high-pitched, monotonic, non-diegetic sound, an effect which serves as an aural correlate to the unsettling visuals. Lynch employs precisely the same technique in (c) – as well as in the scene when Henry discovers a multitude of stringy, sperm-like creatures (foetuses?) under the covers of his bed – resulting in nearly exactly the same bi-sensory shock effect.

Finally, we come to (d), a scene that stands alone in this brief survey not least because of its fantastic/surrealistic atmosphere and images. As is so often the case with highly effective horror scenes, even *knowing* what to expect here fails to provide a shield against its disturbing impact. In order to examine the reasons for (the 'causes of') this impact, I shall divide (d) into the following three segments: Henry's brief encounter with The Lady in the Radiator; his behaviour as the tree rolls out onto the radiator stage; and the loss and subsequent replacement of his head. What emerges from this division is that each sequence possesses its *own* horror effects, effects which nevertheless work together to add to the overall power of the scene, and which, after they are identified, serve to render the scene as a whole somewhat less mysterious (though certainly no less frightening).

In the first of the above segments, Henry approaches The Lady in the Radiator, whose chipmunk cheeks, adorable smile and saccharine voice still betray something distinctly ominous (I shall return to this point below). With a look of desperation mixed with apprehension on his face, he reaches out to touch her, but at the moment of contact the screen goes blindingly white and the omnipresent 'white noise' of mechanistic energy suddenly rises to a near-deafening crescendo (once again we are provided the auditory correlate to a striking visual display). Henry pulls back in surprise and, perhaps wanting to verify the strange cause-and-effect process he has seemingly initiated, tries touching her again – with the same result. Except that this time, after turning away momentarily, what he (and we) see in place of The Lady is the hideous visage of The Man in the Planet. This unexpected switch functions as a very effective scare tactic, as an associative link is established between apparent opposites (good and evil, appealing and repulsive, etc.) and what was originally thought to be safe is now revealed as a threat. Lynch would repeat himself 15 years later in the underrated *Twin Peaks: Fire Walk with Me* (1992) when the face of Laura Palmer's (Sheryl Lee) demonic attacker is momentarily replaced by that of her own father. But this tactic has a long history and can be found in numerous vampire, shape-shifter and *doppelgänger* films, as well as in such otherwise non-generic horror fare as *Don't Look Now* (Nicholas Roeg, 1973) and, more recently, *Jacob's Ladder* (Adrian Lyne, 1990).

In the second sequence from (d), Henry, even more unnerved after the shock of what just happened, slowly backs away from the centre of the stage, finally standing behind a railing as the tree makes its special guest appearance. Crucial to notice here (but next to invisible if one is not looking for it) is the compulsive manner in which Henry twists his hands around the rail, reminiscent of the fits experienced by Mary and her mother at the X family home, like a needle stuck in the groove of a phonograph record. Whether consciously registered by the viewer or not, Henry's repetitive, masturbatory hand motion only increases the overall feeling of dread and fearsome anticipation.

And we are not disappointed. For in the scene's final segment, Henry's head suddenly pops off, or, to be more precise, is forced off its moorings by an erect phallus erupting from somewhere inside his body. This shocking sight is accompanied by a loud noise reminiscent of a cartoon spring being released from a broken jack-in-the-box. His hands continue their circular movements around the railing, even though Henry is, at least for the time being, dead; think of a chicken with its head cut off, still running frantically around the pen until its body finally gets the message. Henry's decapitation is so horrific in part because of the way it happens. We have no time to prepare ourselves as the executioner readies his sword, the killer wields his knife, etc.; rather, it happens pretty much all on its own, via some kind of internal mechanism, and if Henry can lose his head so easily, what does that say about the rest of him . . . and us? I have made it this far without resorting to hackneyed Freudianisms, but the castration anxiety manifested in this sequence is just too transparent – and too effective – not to mention. The slow, steady rise of the baby's (penis) head in place of Henry's own signals Oedipal wish-fulfilment and in fact serves to over-determine psychoanalytic interpretation: are we witnessing Henry's nightmare, the baby's fantasy, both at once? Ultimately, the horror of this sequence is the horror of *attack from within*, whether psychically, socially ('As the internalisation of social labels, this interior "baby" is an impediment to the fulfillment Henry seeks' (Nochimson 1997: 160)), or at a more primitive, bodily level. In this respect, it bears comparison with such *Eraserhead* contemporaries as *Shivers* (aka *They Came From Within*) (David Cronenberg, 1975), *The Manitou* (William Girdler, 1978), *The Beast Within*

(Philippe Mora, 1982) and, of course, *Alien* (Ridley Scott, 1979), with its infamous male birthing scene of an extraterrestrial infant, a close cousin to Henry's own.

The essential evil in/of *Eraserhead*

The two-part thesis of this essay has been, first, that rather than treating *Eraserhead* as an isolated masterpiece, one whose 'genuine strangeness [of] cinematography . . . is not easy to define and cannot be reduced to the use of particular techniques' (Chion 1995: 42), the film's pervasive uncanniness is most fruitfully explained, though never explained away, when situated within the context of the horror genre and its established traditions; and second, that if such a reading of *Eraserhead* is at odds with Lynch's own denials of influence, so much the worse for the director (but not at all for the film itself). In support of these claims, I have analysed a number of *Eraserhead*'s most disturbing scenes, seeking to reveal and partially expose their dependence on and interaction with particular currents in horror film-making past and present.

As alluded to above, even the film's purported oases of contentment have a dark and ominous feel to them. Consider The Lady in the Radiator – whom Nochimson claims 'represents a feminine energy that prohibits castration' (Nochimson 1997: 164) and of whom Lynch disingenuously states that 'inside is where the happiness in her comes from. Her outside appearance is not the thing' (Lynch in Rodley 1997: 67) – what with her seductive song promoting suicide ('In heaven, everything is fine . . .'), her ritualised acts of violence (stomping to death the falling foetuses as part of a formal dance routine) and her funhouse-mirror Marilyn Monroe looks (those chubby cheeks are less cute than regressive, even grotesque). Similarly, Henry's night of passion with the Beautiful Girl Across the Hall possesses its share of distressing elements: for he must forcibly prevent the woman from focusing on the hysterical baby, who is indeed stuck witnessing a variant of the primal scene; and the couple's potentially 'romantic' dissolution into a pool of milky water closes with a disconcerting image of the woman's hair floating on the surface (what happened to *Henry's* famous coiffure? and is there any doubt that the woman's hair has become unattached from her scalp?). Although Freeland views Henry's infanticide as 'a matter less of revenge than of consuming curiosity or even mercy' (Freeland 2000: 230), we have already seen (with reference to Poe) that it is Henry's very obsession with 'ridding himself' of that which he is responsible for but cannot comprehend that renders his act of murder less merciful than (mono)maniacal.

There can be no denying the fact that *Eraserhead* is a complex and challenging film. The extent to which Lynch here renders plot and narrative subservient to what we have called 'the primacy of the audio-visual image' has been amply demonstrated. But it is an overstatement to claim that 'the uncanny in *Eraserhead* is what literally exceeds the limits of representation' (Freeland 2000: 234), or that 'all structures of representation . . . in *Eraserhead* . . . always feign totality in their absurd incompleteness' (Nochimson 1997: 158). The brilliance of this film lies in the director's extraordinary command of proven horror techniques: in *Eraserhead*, it is precisely what *can* be represented (despite its impossibility) that generates such powerful feelings of uncanniness, anxiety and disgust.

2.12

The cult of horror
by Lawrence O'Toole

Canadian film critic Lawrence O'Toole did not have to look far for inspiration for his article on the outrageous popularity of horror in the late 1970s: in his home-town Toronto David Cronenberg had just released *The Brood*, entrepreneurs like Garth Drabinsky were producing films like *The Changeling*, and even the Toronto Festival was preparing its special nights on horror (with critic Robin Wood inviting George Romero, Larry Cohen, Brian De Palma, Wes Craven, John Carpenter and David Cronenberg – all exponents of the brave new wave of horror). But O'Toole's observation goes beyond Toronto. He argues that North America was 'hell-bent for horror', and that the popularity of the scary movie genre reached gigantic proportions: everything from *Halloween*, through *Dawn of the Dead*, to *Alien* seemed not only a big success but also appeared to touch a cultural nerve, especially with younger generations of avid moviegoers. And it's not just movies: comic books, heavy metal music, punk rock, Stephen King, Ann Rice, even Meat Loaf all relied on horror imagery – and they all attracted wide fandom. O'Toole connects the cultist adoration for horror with contemporary religious cults (like the Jonestown cult), and threats of real horror (Skylab falling from the sky, nuclear melt-down, cancer), inferring that they are signs of a society looking for certainties where there are none. For O'Toole, that fear explains much of the appeal of horror. O'Toole uses *Alien, The Brood*, and *Love at First Bite* as examples to track the themes and metaphors of this new wave. Its main components are the emphasis on body horror (the monster comes from inside, or near you), the refusal to provide a comforting ending (either everyone dies or there is a 'big question mark'), and the exposition of fanaticism (not just in the portrayal of characters, but also in the relentless drive of horrific events happening on screen – there seem to be no more rest points). For O'Toole, the origin of the cult reception of these films lies in the college crowd midnight screenings of the mid-1970s, which brought films like *Night of the Living Dead, The Rocky Horror Picture Show* and *The Texas Chain Saw Massacre* to notoriety. The momentum of 'feeling for the genre' these films generated is now carried over into a wide cultural phenomenon, one to which Colonel Kurtz's 'the horror . . . the horror' seems an appropriate accompaniment.

A note on the extract: this article first appeared in the Canadian magazine *Maclean's*, on 16 July 1979, pages 46–50. We reprint it in full here. In its original publication format, the article was accompanied by two box inserts listing horror films and books and giving an overview of the ancillary industry of horror, sampling horror-related items from the toy and gadget industry.

Bloor Street, Toronto. A balmy summer evening. A long line snakes its way around a theatre where Alien, *the monster horror hit, is playing. Tittery, nervous laughter. Dissociated small talk to pass the time. Shuffling impatience and jittery little dances of anticipation. People have been known during showings of* Alien *occasionally to vacate their seats and vomit. "I hope you didn't snack up," one man says to a woman. The woman, who has the gaunt grace of a model, rubs the silky dress clinging to her midriff and says, "Oooh, I can't wait." The line begins to move. A serpentine, scared procession.*

North America is hell-bent for horror. The hottest ticket in every town is terror. In a society splintered by cults and stunned by crises, remembering Jonestown and awaiting Skylab's shower of metal, the cult of horror has metamorphosed into the biggest cult of all. The terror trade has made a killing everywhere—books, movies, Broadway, kids' toys and cereals, pop music and television. The malignancy of each medium is now the message, mirroring a malaise that can't be shrugged off by the pleasures of self-cleaning ovens in spotless suburban homes or the assurances of good and steady careers in bustling urban centres.

The times are palpably paranoid. The old memento mori—reminder of death —hangs in the air. There are global energy crises, threats of nuclear meltdowns, rising rates of teen-age suicide, bubonic plague in California. A few months ago snow fell in the Sahara—for the first time in recorded history. Nice people are rioting over gas for their cars. Cancer is still generally uncontrollable; all kinds of additives may be dangerous to your health. It takes no gift to be a 20th-century Cassandra.

Instead of avoiding the fearful—whether it be a description of the flutter of curtains in an insomniac's dark room or a visualization of a deformed birth—people are embracing it, finding romance (*Dracula*), orgies of death and dismemberment (*Dawn of the Dead*, Broadway's *Sweeney Todd*), cheap graveyard thrills (*Phantasm*), old-fashioned chills (*Ghost Story*) and even laughs (the vampire parody, *Love at First Bite*). What's happening may be a loose definition of decadence.

This summer the movie industry isn't releasing horror movies—it's *unleashing* them. All, even cheapies like *Halloween* and *Phantasm*, are hits. And the best, or worst, is yet to come. Booming in books as well, the terror trade finds a big audience in the extremely accessible paperback market. Horror is the grassroots genre: getting scared is the great equalizer.

George Romero, 39, who directed *Dawn of the Dead* and *Martin*, planted the seed of the current craze with the 1968 zombie cult movie *Night of the Living Dead*. He says that since *The Exorcist* made the horror movie venerable, not to mention lucrative, "you can get any script past the studio executives if it's in the genre." From the shower in *Psycho* to the beach in *Jaws*, horror has undergone a radical transformation. It has come out of the closet of the old dark house and moved into the wide-open spaces—even space itself. It has taken the old genre and, in Romero's words, "bared all the nerves," showing a world out of control. And if the world *is* out of control, psychologically it may be easier to revel rather than worry.

The state of the art in Hollywood is such that audiences can escape into horror— be totally drawn into it, be *alone* with it, yet know they have control over it. "Horror movies reduce you as a member of the audience to nothing," says Romero. "The rationale is, 'Since this is the way we're going why not celebrate it?' Audiences want the film to come to *them*, to expend as little thought and effort as possible." Technology has made that possible—manufacturing an incredible split-second reality in movies: you believe for the moment that a serpent-like infant is bursting through a man's stomach in *Alien* or that a zombie is tearing away a chunk of someone's flesh in *Dawn of the Dead*. Nobody *has* to suspend his disbelief—the movies suspend it for him. "And in the darkened theatre," says Romero, "it's every man for himself."

Alone—that's the operative word in horror right now.

"We live, as we dream—alone," wrote Joseph Conrad in *Heart of Darkness* in 1902. Not surprisingly, Conrad is enjoying a popular, as well as intellectual, revival (the heart of darkness theme in *The Deer Hunter*, the upcoming *Apocalypse Now* based on Conrad's novella itself, naming the spaceship Nostromo in *Alien*). With innocence apparently truncated at a very early age and the family fizzling as an institution, Conrad's notion of man as an island has never held such sway. And, in the four o'clock of the morning of the mind, prey to all kinds of disturbing persuasion, people look out for themselves first and foremost.

Alone. Birth, the first and most painful process in life, plays a large part in modern horror, eliciting fears that are primal and ineluctable. The monstrous infant ripping through the man's stomach in *Alien* looks around at the crew members of the spaceship as though to mark them for vengeance (and by the end has taken on more and more a human shape). An audience can't help but react on a deeply subconscious, disturbingly primal level. In *Prophecy*, the fetuses created by environmental tampering are unbearably malformed. They are our product. The reproductive system has become the repository of foulness, as in *The Brood*.

"The body is the wellspring of horror," says *Brood* Director David Cronenberg (see *Maclean's*, July 9) whose earlier, similar movies, *Shivers* and *Rabid*, have found ready audiences. "When you look in the mirror and your body is aging or rotting away with disease—that's real horror." Seldom has a culture had such an intense, microscopic look at how the body can be mangled: teeth sinking into necks, zombies tearing flesh, heinous births, genetic mutation, telekinetic bloodbaths. And instead of revulsion, the trend has induced the fascination that is born of fear.

Onward from the insidious impregnation of Rosemary by the Devil in Roman Polanski's *Rosemary's Baby* (to *Beyond the Door*, *It's Alive*, *The Exorcist*, *The Omen*), horror has chronicled—the breakdown of society right at the core of its atom—the nuclear family. "Probably the family is where we all learn about horror," muses the author of *Ghost Story*, Peter Straub. "Most of what I've been writing seems to hinge on the mechanism of buried guilt." Robin Wood, the organizer of more than 40 films for a horror festival scheduled for Toronto's Festival of Festivals in September, considers the horror film the most subversive genre of all: "In the XXX virtually every horror film of distinction has been centred on the nuclear family, with the monster identified as its product."

Fifth Avenue, New York. A blindingly bright, perfect spring day. People with money to spend and time to kill are swept along by the purling momentum. The mood is magnanimous. A thousand faces are on the verge of a giant smile. But detouring the friendly traffic, a crowd is milling in front of a bookstore's window display. Inside, impaled against a charcoal grey backdrop a woman wearing a crimson necklace is draped, lifeless, over a gravestone. The sun splashes against the window, reflecting the staring faces, frozen, caught in a spell. The book being advertised is Peter Straub's best seller, Ghost Story.

Horror writing had its beginnings in the Gothic novel of the late 18th century, with Horace Walpole (*The Castle of Otranto*) and Mrs. Radcliffe (*The Mysteries of Udolpho*), moving into the 19th century with Mary Shelley's *Frankenstein* and the writings of Edgar Allan Poe. It was a reaction against rationalism, but the romance has become nightmarish. The new delight in the drama of dread feeds off a blind faith: readers and audiences believe in the monstrous, or are willing to believe. The world of reason shut out, the experience becomes pristine, total, religious.

"Fear is a religious feeling," Philip Kaufman, director of the recent remake of *Invasion of the Body Snatchers*, has suggested. "Religion isn't as strong as it once was, so there's a demand for scary films by people who miss the old fears." That old thrill of accepting the inexplicable—Dante's "fear in the blood"—has been shrill throughout the '70s. Devilish spectaculars paraded religious symbolism: *The Exorcist*, *The Omen* and their sequels. The killer in Alfred Sole's *Alice, Sweet Alice* is a repressed religious fanatic. Carrie's mother, a fanatic as well, drives the teen-aged girl to wreak her telekinetic havoc.

"Horror," wrote Edgar Allan Poe, is "the soul of plot"—escapism in the extreme. With the world going out of kilter, some adhere to the afterlife, somnambulant before Billy Graham, Ernest Angley, David Mainse or Garner Ted Armstrong. For others, chaos inspires going to horror movies or reading horror stories. "We're in a period of outrageous uncertainty," explains Bob Kaufman, who wrote *Love at First Bite*, "and definition works. People don't want to think anymore. It's nice to go away for a few hours into a genre . . . the unreal is becoming real because there's a predictability about it. There is a beginning and an end, as opposed to our lives which go on and on." The less people can handle day to day, the more they look for escapism. "I think everybody has a lot of free-floating anxieties," says Stephen King, the 31-year-old writer whose last name perfectly describes his preeminence in the horror-writing field. "One way to get rid of them is to externalize them. Horror stories almost always put their finger directly on what's bothering people in the real world."

With society a circus of sensations, anything truly terrifying (by definition, truly surprising) is saliva for a jaded palate. Audiences are becoming desensitized to scares, perhaps because they live with so many, and because, visually, technology makes earlier ones quickly archaic. That's why motivation and logic don't often enter the movies anymore: people apparently want pure terror. Consider *Alien*'s success: "This monster kills to survive and it survives to kill," says H.R. Giger, the Swiss designer who created it; Director Ridley Scott describes his movie as "pure, linear horror." (People aren't totally desensitized yet, however: when Scott first screened the movie for a group of about 70, mostly families from an air base in England, *Alien* ran 11 minutes longer. Some of them fled vomiting. "It was just too intense," he admits.) Pure, linear horror: the crew of a spaceship alone with the ultimate carnivore.

Down to earth, another lonely crowd, teen-agers, their lives often a stretch of tedium battling for sovereignty over frustration, have been forefront in modern horror, victims of unnatural forces: *Carrie*, the boy and girl in *The Fury*, the blood-sucking title character of Romero's *Martin*, the malcontent pubescent girl in *Alice, Sweet Alice*. In a song by Toronto punk band The Poles, called *Cannibal Kids*, a young suburban girl named Lisa borrows dad's car and winds up queen of the cannibal kids at the local shopping mall. With teenagers, the nuclear family suffers its final split. Stephen King proposes an odd but reasonable theory of *The Exorcist*'s success: the book and the movie came out during the widest perceived chasm between gener-ations, when the younger one seemed out of control; subconsciously, there was an explanation for the behaviour of dirty, stringy-haired kids—they were possessed by the Devil.

Seventies' pop music for the teen-age lonely crowd, particularly punk and New Wave, is also full of the stylized violence of the horror phenomenon. Performers such as DEVO, Patti Smith, Warren Zevon, Blondie, Elvis Costello, the now defunct Sex Pistols—even Meat Loaf—have used images of old monsters and new technological ones to advance their message. Punk hasn't been a protest, but a party aboard a sinking ship, parasitically feeding off common fears and using the iconography of horror as statement of style. From The Rolling Stones' *Sympathy for the Devil* through David Bowie through Kiss, pop music has always had a soft spot for celebrating the ghoulish. "You listen to punk and it's a little bit like walking into a rock 'n' roll elevator with the doors opening in hell," remarks Stephen King. Now, discos' move into the mainstream has fostered a night-life culture in North America. "I love the night life," sings disco-discer Alicia Bridges in a paean to the decadence of dancing in the dark. The cosmetic fashion fuelled by it has been vampiric: pallor in the faces, highlighted bones, blood-red lips. Avant-garde fashion opts for your basic Dracula black.

The current cult of horror began with teens and the college crowd—midnight showings on the werewolf circuit nurtured the necrophiliac fantasies of a young, restless audience, one that had grown disillusioned and angry, or just bored, with the broken promises of the '60s. They went to see Romero's *Night of the Living Dead, The Texas Chain Saw Massacre* and, the daddy of them all, *The Rocky Horror Picture Show*. Now in its fourth year in Toronto, the story of a deadly dull middle-class couple coming upon a castle populated with transvestites and lovers of old horror lore sends its audience into paroxysms of joy, allowing them to disport their own personal fan-tasies in the theatre.

Having gathered momentum throughout the decade, the lore and feeling for the genre has planted itself firmly in common consciousness. Witness *Love at First Bite*—the top comedy hit of the year—or the Count on *Sesame Street*, who does numbers instead of blood counts. With the *Alien* around, the vampire has grown slightly benign, but is still a drawing card. The long-awaited movie version of *Dracula* is, intriguingly, R-rated and advertised as a "love story." Sex still sells, and the vampire offers a new twist to it. Asked what he thought love was like when he was human, the vampire in Anne Rice's brilliant novel, *Interview With the Vampire*, answers: "It was something hurried . . . seldom savored . . . something acute that was quickly lost. I think it was the pale shadow of killing." With the missionary position considered about as exciting as taking tea these days, new sexual frontiers are not scoffed at.

"Vampires have always had charisma and a kind of sexual dominance," boasts Stephen Kaplan, 39-year-old head of The Vampire Research Center in New York. "We recognize the times are super-hot." He claims to have interviewed more than 200 would-be and actual vampires (always with an assistant) and claims further to have documented 12 cases. "You know most of this fang stuff is passé. [Romero's *Martin* slits his victims' wrists.] People can operate with syringes, needles, that kind of thing."

To where does the terror trade point? *Apocalypse*, soon, it would seem to say. There's too much cynicism around to allow good to triumph over evil; now it's often the reverse, and if good triumphs it is increasingly marginal, increasingly temporary. Will Sigourney Weaver of *Alien* make it back to earth? Will the woman in *Prophecy* give birth to a mangled fetus? Will the surviving couple at the end of *Dawn of the Dead* make it to Canada in their helicopter? When horror shows don't end in destruction, they whimper away into a big question mark of a sunset. Someone's always left alone, in the dark.

"Lady," said the bum in Hitchcock's *The Birds*, "it's the end of the world."

Lady, it just might be the beginning of the end.

With files from Rita Christopher and Ann Johnston

2.13

The Blair Witch Project: Film and the internet
by J.P. Telotte

While other authors in the cult case studies section of this volume take specific films, or cult cinematic cycles as the objects of their study, it is the internet website for the 'Indie' horror hit *The Blair Witch Project* which forms the basis of J.P. Telotte's account. In this article, the author goes beyond the standard mythology of the film's production as ultra-low budget feature by two University of Central Florida graduates who sought to establish an alternative, ad hoc fan base for the film in the absence of big budget promotion. Rather, Telotte highlights the extensive marketing campaign which was mounted via *Blair Witch* distributor Artisan Entertainment through outlets such as MTV, ads in college newspapers and 'alternative' dailies. While the author concludes this systematic campaign is symptomatic of 'conventional' studio advertising of a small or niche genre product, where the *Blair Witch Project*'s cult status does come to the fore is in its website construction. Here, Telotte draws on digital gaming theorists such as Janet Murray to show how the film's internet promotion drew out a much more active audience than other comparable releases using such virtual technology. Indeed, Telotte employs concepts of 'immersion', 'agency' and 'transformation' to indicate the extent to which the film's website allowed its active audiences to submerge themselves within the fictional world of the text, participate in various tasks and enigmas that similarly faced characters within the text as well as transform their identities into differing roles pertinent to the production. Although Telotte does concede that some elements of audience activity (such as the trope of transformation) are curtailed in this cult website, his analysis does highlight the extent to which *The Blair Witch Project* perfectly tailored its marketing for a new generation of horror fans that like their darkest fears to be downloaded.

A note on the extract: this article was first published in *Film Quarterly*, 53(3), and is reproduced here in its entirety.

In discussing the structure and workings of the New Hollywood, Janet Wasko cautions against attending too much to the sort of stories it is producing or the myths it so readily fosters about how those movies are being made. As she notes, "By accepting the myths or concentrating primarily on aesthetic aspects of film technology, corporate influences on film activities, as well as the actual power structure of the industry, can be obscured." It is a caution that can serve us well when thinking about one of the most popular movie phenomena of recent times, *The Blair Witch Project*. A cheaply produced, independent horror film made by a couple of film school graduates from the low-profile University of Central Florida, it grossed nearly $150 million in 1999, garnered favorable critical commentary, turned its female protagonist into an over-night star, and earned both sequel and television deals for its co-writers/directors. And some measure of that public embrace of the film has to do with its apparently humble independent origins: its approximately $35,000 production cost, unsophisticated look, and unknown actors. It is, after all, manifestly unlike the high-budget Hollywood gloss with which we are so familiar and which has tended to dominate the recent box office. Yet, as the comment by Wasko might suggest, the story of *The Blair Witch Project* and its seemingly overnight success is far more complex, and that success a far larger lesson about what is happening in the U.S. film industry, particularly in its marketing efforts, than would initially seem to be the case.

In an era that has become practically defined not only by the effects of "mass media" but by the interweaving of many media, films today seldom really stand alone. Each new release operates—if it is to be at all successful—within a complex web of information sites: radio spots, theatrical trailers, various sorts of television promotions, billboards, product tie-ins, and, increasingly, the Internet. Certainly, the last of these is the newest marketing ploy, yet it is one that combines the lures of many more tradi-tional advertising techniques: the graphic pull of posters, the hyped language of the old-fashioned press release, interviews with stars via live-time chat rooms, publicity stills, sneak previews via downloadable video clips, offers of movie-related giveaways, and selections from film soundtracks. Today, in fact, almost no major film is released unaccompanied by its own carefully fashioned "official" Web site—one that can provide an extremely cost-efficient yet information-intensive medium for promoting the movie—and often by a variety of fan-created and fan-driven unofficial sites as well. The official Web site especially not only offers potential viewers the sort of information or lures that would, after the fashion of traditional film advertising, make them want to rush out and see the film. It can also effectively tell the "story" of the film, that is, as the film's makers and/or distributors see it and want it to be under-stood. For it can frame the film narrative within a context designed to condition our viewing or "reading" of it, even to determine the sort of pleasures we might derive from it. This establishing of context, this seemingly secondary "project," has been one readily acknowledged factor in the larger success of *The Blair Witch Project*, and one that merits further consideration for its comments on marketing in the con-temporary film industry.

Before we examine this secondary project, however, we need to note other factors that came into play in the case of *Blair Witch*. When Artisan Entertainment picked up *The Blair Witch Project* for distribution after its screening at the 1999 Sundance Film Festival for approximately $1.1 million, it continued a pattern for that minor-major studio of cheaply acquiring projects with an easily identifiable audience and then extensively promoting them to achieve a predictable if modest profit. This pattern is illustrated by such films as *The Limey* and *Pi*, the latter of which also benefited from an elaborate Web site. In the instance of *Blair Witch*, that promotional project certainly relied heavily on an extensive elaboration of a Web site already developed by the film's producers—hardly an uncommon add-on to the publicity push by this time, but one that has been given most of the credit for the film's success. Yet most accounts of the film's promotion overlook the extent of its *conventional* marketing project, one which included television advertising, especially on MTV; a series of ads in major college newspapers, alternative weeklies, and magazines with a young readership like *Rolling Stone*; and widely distributed posters for the "missing" principals of the film. As Dwight Cairns, Vice-President of Sony's new Internet Marketing Strategy Group, notes, "People tend to forget that the offline campaign . . . was so well integrated into what they did on the Web—the missing posters of the unknown cast, the TV spots perpetuating the myth that missing footage was found and that they should go to the site to see more. The Web was just another channel to deliver the message." Indeed, Amorette Jones, head of the Artisan marketing campaign for *The Blair Witch Project* and a veteran of marketing at such major studios as Universal, Columbia/Tri-Star, and MGM/UA, acknowledges a hardly modest $20 million marketing campaign for the film that included a series of ever-more-elaborate trailers, some of which were pointedly tied to playdates for *Star Wars: Episode One* in hopes of drawing in that same audience. As Jones admits, Artisan "did commercial things; we just did them in a non-commercial way."

This admission of the extent of the film's conventional publicity campaign per-haps helps to explain why other films have had trouble emulating the success of *Blair Witch*. Creating a "fun" Web site to lure young viewers, after all, is a relatively inexpensive and easy path for advertising, one which even allows the studio to begin to gauge—through a "hit" counter—the extent of potential viewer interest. And given Artisan's success, it is little wonder that other studios would try to follow suit, although as yet without similarly spectacular results. Marc Graser and Dade Hayes offer a partial explanation, noting that "calmer heads are realizing that the '*Blair Witch*' site was not an added-on marketing tool, but was designed as part of the film experience—one that tapped into fans of the horror genre." I would go a bit further and suggest that the selling of *The Blair Witch Project* and the *telling* of that film, its narrative construction, were from the start a careful match or "project," one that better explains both the film's success and why that success was so quickly and easily laid at the door of the now almost equally famous Web site.

Before pursuing this other project, the match between the filmic narrative and its electronic marketing, we first need to consider how such Web sites typically work, and thus why this Web site in particular might have played such a significant role in the film's success, quickly inspiring other film companies to follow suit in an effort to reach a key audience demographic online. As I have already noted, almost every major release today is preceded by a site designed to build audience anticipation for the film and, even after it has been released, to support that interest by feeding viewers additional information (behind-the-scenes facts, technical data, playdates for various markets, even the opportunity to purchase film-related souvenirs), and later to open up yet another avenue for profits by marketing tape and DVD copies of the film.

A selection of Web sites for similarly-themed films released in the same general period shows several typical levels of presentation. Those for *The Haunting* and *Stigmata* (both 1999), like the majority of official Web pages, are largely advertise-ments with little animation, offering basic data about the story, opening dates, and advance ticket-ordering information. Replicating the films' key advertising graphics against red or black backgrounds—colors obviously keyed to the films' horror genre—they seem like little more than electronic posters. The official *Urban Legend* (1998) and *Deep Blue Sea* (1999) sites provide a slightly higher level of information. The former, against a black-and-gold background, lists showtimes, offers credits and "behind the scenes" images, provides a library of contemporary urban legends, and invites visitors to participate in a sweepstakes contest. The latter, against a black-and-green background, offers images, text, and interviews with many of those involved in the production. Both are essentially press kits for the digital age, providing the sort of deep background typically found in their conventional counterparts. However, the Web sites for such films as *Lake Placid, House on Haunted Hill,* and *The Mummy* (all 1999) are far more complex affairs, not only providing the same sort of fundamental information—and measurably more—found in the previously noted sites, but also inviting a level of viewer interaction. These more elaborate sites all offer a storyline, cast list, background on the filmmakers, clips from the films, various electronic give-aways (such as downloadable screensavers and electronic postcards), chat rooms, and games keyed to the films' plotlines, set against the generically familiar black or dark red screens that immediately establish the horror-film tone. Such sites invite their visitors to linger, to explore, and, often with a few simple mouse clicks, to call the sites—and thus the films—to the attention of friends; they try to be fun and to encourage visitors to share the fun by viewing the sites and then, naturally, seeing the films.

Of course, such linkage is precisely the purpose. Thus, even as sites like those for *Lake Placid, The House on Haunted Hill,* and *The Mummy* provide their own level of entertainment to visitors, they also ultimately point to the film experience and suggest that we see their narratives within a tradition of cinematic horror. *The House on Haunted Hill* Web page quickly announces that the film is "a spine-tingling remake of William Castle's 1958 classic horror tale"; *The Mummy*'s site describes it as "a full-scale re-imagining of Universal Pictures' seminal 1932 film"; and *Deep Blue Sea*'s producer, Akiva Goldsman, explains that the movie is a "classic old-style horror film." While their games and on-line trailers afford net surfers a hint of the movies' atmosphere and some brief entertainment, these sites, in keeping with the long tradition of movie advertising, are basically "teasers," lures suggesting that the real thrills are to be found in the movies themselves—and in a *tradition* of similar movies. They *guide* our experience by situating their films in the context of the film industry and pointing to the entertainment power of the movies, particularly their special ability—one implicitly unmatched by the Internet—to transport us into another realm.

Artisan's own ambitious marketing campaign, and especially its Internet strategy, seems to have been designed to employ an element of this contextualizing, while also moving visitors in a direction different from the advertising sites just described. In fact, it seems to have been fashioned precisely to avoid the sort of situating at which these similar sites aim (including the hierarchical entertainment value of the movie itself that the established film industry would prefer to affirm), seeking instead to capitalize on the particular characteristics of this film. That campaign, which ended up as a television project as well, pitches the fictional movie as a documentary about three real student filmmakers who vanished while working on a documentary about a legendary witch near the town of Burkittsville, Maryland. The story unfolds through their own footage, accidentally discovered by student anthropologists a year after their disappearance and then pieced together by Artisan. The Web site that became the hub, although hardly the sole focus, of the campaign offered much additional material about the case of the missing filmmakers: information on the "Mythology" surrounding the *Blair Witch* legend, background on "The Filmmakers" who disappeared, a summary of "The Aftermath" of the disappearance, and a tour of "The Legacy" of these mysterious events—that is, of the various materials recovered in the search for the student filmmakers. All of these elements, the film's *back-story*, if you will, elaborately propagate the notion of authenticity, attesting to the film as, quite literally, a "found-footage" type of documentary rather than a fictional work, and more particularly, as a different sort of attraction than the movies usually offer, a reality far stranger than that found in any "classic old-style horror film." Rather, they suggest we see the film *not as film*, but as one more artifact, along with the materials gathered together at the Web site, which we might view in order to better understand a kind of repressed or hidden reality.

Thus *The Blair Witch* site, in contrast to those noted above, points in various ways away from the film's privileged status as a product of the entertainment industry. Or more precisely, its "project" is to blur such common discrimination, to suggest, in effect, that this particular film is as much a part of everyday life as the Internet, that it extends the sort of unfettered knowledge access that the Internet seems to offer, and that its pleasures, in fact, closely resemble those of the electronic medium with which its core audience is so familiar. *Blair Witch* co-creator Eduardo Sanchez has hinted as much when discussing the importance of his film's Web site. He offers, "It gave us a lot of hype for a little movie," while he also points to the fact that the site was effective primarily because it was so very different from other publicity pages with which Web surfers were familiar. Rather than "just a behind-the-scenes thing with bios," they aimed to create "a completely autonomous experience from the film. You don't have to see the film to actually have fun on the Web site, and investigate it and get creeped out. And that's kind of what you have to do" with such independent films. While operating within what has quickly become an established, if still evolving, electronic genre—that of the official film Web site—the *Blair Witch* page does rather more. It seems pointedly designed to suggest a level of difference from other sites, and to imply as well that the film, precisely insofar as it is *like* the Web site, *differs* from other films, even those within the horror genre. While it does provide what might be thought of as a kind of gaming experience, it does so in a far more complicated way than other sites; moreover, its key emphasis is on the complicated and mysterious nature of a world that would inspire such an experience. Thus, the *Blair Witch* site offered to those who had not yet seen the film but who might have heard some of the hype, as well as to those who had already seen it, a path of further investigation and a source of other, similarly creepy sensations—in effect, a *different context* for viewing the film.

And even as the site suggests that we see this film differently from other, more conventional works, it also points to the key terms of that difference, the central strategies shared by both Web site and film. To isolate these effects and better consider their implications for the film, I want to draw on Janet Murray's study of electronic narrative forms, wherein she describes how such texts, generally much more sophisticated than a typical advertising site, usually rely upon three "aesthetic principles" or characteristic "pleasures" for their lure—what she terms "immersion, agency, and transformation." The term "immersion" refers to the "experience of being sub-merged" in the world of the text, and thus to a certain delight in "the movement out of our familiar world" and into another realm, such as the complexly detailed medieval world of a game like *The Legend of Zelda.* By "agency," she means our ability to participate in the text, something we "do not usually expect to experience . . . within a narrative environment," but which is fundamental to the participatory investigation of a mysterious environment in a game like *Myst.* And "transformation" indicates the ability electronic texts give us to "switch positions," to change identities, role play, or become a shape-shifter—as freely happens in games like *Donkey Kong* and *Mortal Kombat*—within a world that is itself marked by a constant transformative potential. While not quite a game in the sense of those noted above, the *Blair Witch* site, largely because it does function as part of a larger narrative context, draws to varying degrees on each of these pleasures, which, it forecasts to those who have grown up with the computer and the Internet, extend into the world of the film as well.

While employing the same sort of dark and suggestive color scheme as other sites, the *Blair Witch* page especially distinguishes itself by its power of immersion. Rather than pointing to the entertainment industry, it lures visitors into a world that is, on the surface, deceptively like our own, and even anchors us in that realm of normalcy with maps, police reports, found objects, and characters who evoke the film's target audi-ence of teenagers or young adults (the missing student filmmakers and the University of Maryland anthropology class that, we learn, later discovered their film and various other artifacts). After establishing this real-world context and giving it authority, the site shifts from that anchorage into a completely "other" world, one of witchcraft, one connected to the repressed history of the mysteriously abandoned town of Blair, and one with a mythology all its own, attested to by a collection of woodcuts depicting witchcraft in the region and selections from the supposed book *The Blair Witch Cult,* which we are told "is on display at the Maryland Historical Society Museum." As site visitors move within that realm, they increasingly exercise an element of agency, exploring, like the missing filmmakers themselves, different dimensions of the mys-tery: gathering background on the region; pursuing the public debate about the miss-ing students through interviews with Burkittsville locals, parents of the students, and college professors of anthropology and folklore; reading pages of Heather's diary; looking over evidence accumulated by the local sheriff, the anthropology students, and the private investigator hired by Heather's mother. Through this agency effect, wherein we sort through a wealth of clues in any order we wish and try to put the pieces of a puzzle together, much in the fashion of *Myst,* we determine precisely how much we want to be "creeped out" by the materials made available to us. And in that "creeped-out" effect, we glimpse both the site's limited version of "transformation," as well as its key difference from the film itself.

Despite the densely structured nature of this world and its invitation to navigate its cyberspace, the site never quite gives us a full range of that other "characteristic pleasure of digital environments," of transformation. Here we cannot morph into another figure or become one of the three central characters; the best we can do is become the anonymous surfer of cyberspace or settle into the role of an investigator and adopt that posture as a satisfactory shift out of the self. The various interviews offered here—with, for example, Bill Barnes, Executive Director of the Burkittsville

Historical Society; Charles Moorehouse, a professor of folklore; or private investigator Buck Buchanon, among others—all place us in the typical position of the documentary audience, as recipients of the direct address of these speakers. To do otherwise, to allow us, even as a kind of investigative experiment, to temporarily "become" one of the lost students, would, of course, rub against the very texture of the film toward which this site does ultimately and so successfully point. For making the experience immediate rather than mediated could reassert a kind of cinematic context, reminding us of the extent to which subject position is always constructed by point of view in film, and would thus show the film not as another artifact, coterminous with the site, but as a kind of game played with—or on—us by the film industry. Simply put, it would work against the film's reality context. More to the point, the site mainly hints at the power of transformation because that closely allied pleasure is the payoff at the core of the film itself.

The Web site's ultimate aim, of course, is to encourage viewing the film, to help build its audience, which it does so effectively not only by allowing us these electronic pleasures, but by suggesting we might also find them, and perhaps something *more*, a content for this creepy context, in the film itself. Indeed, what *The Blair Witch Project* offers is some variation on the thrills of its Web site, along with a surprising level of transformation. In fact, after a number of studios tried to emulate the Internet-heavy approach of *The Blair Witch Project*, usually without reaping the same benefits, many in the industry recognized that its success derived from the way the Web site and film function together, *share* certain key attractions. As Marc Graser and Dade Hayes explain, an initial industry frenzy to mimic the *Blair Witch* Internet campaign has given way to a recognition "that the '*Blair Witch*' site was not an added-on marketing tool but was designed as part of the film experience—one that tapped into fans of the horror genre" in a special way.

In his review of *The Blair Witch Project*, Richard Corliss notes two "rigorous rules" that, he believes, account for its effectiveness as a horror film: "It will show only what the team could plausibly have filmed, and it will not reveal any sources of outside terror—no monsters or maniacs." That same sense of a restricted and thus logical agency and of a real rather than fantastic situation into which we can move are also crucial to the Web site. In effect, they point toward some of the ways in which those issues of immersion, agency, and transformation, all central to the context the Web site establishes, are key components of the film, contributing to its real-world context and conveying its specific pleasures.

The film offers us "no monsters or maniacs," no horror-movie fare of mad slashers, incarnate devils, or outsized monsters, because it is trying to immerse us in a world that, to all appearances, is coextensive with our own. In fact, the young filmmaker Heather worries specifically about making her film look too much like traditional horror movies. "I don't want to go too cheesy," she says, in a way that echoes the site's constant insistence on the real; "I want to present this in as straightforward a way as possible . . . the legend is unsettling enough." In keeping with this attitude, the film begins with domestic scenes: at Heather's house with Josh ("This is my home, which I am leaving the comforts of," she says as the film opens); at Mike's home as they pick him up and ask if they can meet his mother; at the grocery as they stock up on food for their excursion, the emphasis on buying marshmallows suggesting a typical scout camping trip. It then carefully moves us into another realm with the "ceremonial first slate" of the movie, used to introduce Burkittsville (which is, as Heather intones, "much like a small quiet town anywhere") with interviews of locals in the town and with the scene in the motel room before the filmmakers head into the woods. This location is pointedly different—the cemetery against which Heather films her introductory remarks in 16mm black-and-white quickly establishes that—but it remains a fairly known, sufficiently commonplace world, one of shopkeepers, waitresses, local fishermen. But the narrative quickly shifts into a realm in which neither the students nor the viewers can ever quite get their bearings as the filmmakers "start out off the map," repeatedly get lost, find they are going in circles, lose their map, and can make no sense out of their surroundings. And the shifting between black-and-white film and color video images only reinforces that disorientation. Finally, the climactic scene, in which Mike and Heather enter the ruined old house in the woods, recalls and mocks those initial domestic images of Heather's and Mike's homes with their implications of safety and security. We are simply left immersed in a world that has been completely transformed, one Josh had earlier, and quite accurately, summed up as "fucking crazy shit."

If the Web page is driven in large part by agency, the film links that thrust precisely to the powers of transformation. As Murray reminds us, "the more realized the immersive environment, the more active we want to be within it." Yet here, after a fashion long familiar from other horror films and their limited use of subjective camera, agency is evoked only to be frustrated, creating a sense of helplessness that is fertile psychic ground for horror. Although we find ourselves moving about in this world through our subjective incarnation as the filmmakers, we exercise no real control; as in so many slasher films, and as the *Scream* films repeatedly note and parody, we cannot stop these teenagers from running out into the dangerous dark where their fates are cinematically sealed. In its use of this effect the film recalls an earlier, landmark assay in this sort of cinematic narration, Robert Montgomery's subjective private-eye film *The Lady in the Lake* (1947). That film's experiment with agency, we might recall, fell flat with audiences, as one reviewer's frustrated feeling explains: "*You* do get into the story and see things pretty much the way its protagonist, Philip Marlowe, does, but *you* don't . . . get a chance to put your arms around Audrey Totter. . . . After all, the movie makers, for all their ingenuity, can go just so far." Here, though, the "pleasure"—along with the frustration—of agency dissolves into transformation, as we do indeed "become," by turns, Josh, Heather, and Mike, sharing their points of view and often even exchanging identities and point of view within the same scene, as one character's vantage through the color video camera shifts to that of another, filming in 16mm black-and-white, almost as if we were "team-playing" a video game.

That instability allows us to shift and share sympathies, as when Josh, filming Heather, upbraids her for getting them lost, while it also allows us another register of feeling when, from her subjective vantage, we see the familiar scenery that indicates they have gone in a circle, and the faces of Josh and Mike accusingly look to Heather. That same systemic instability allows as well for our acceptance of the shifty environment in which these events transpire, for our sense of a world that seems to operate from different principles and to speak in an indecipherable language of rock piles, stick figures, scrawled symbols, and strange voices. Transformation, especially via the extended subjective shot, then, becomes a key impulse that drives *The Blair Witch Project*, and a link as much to the realm of contemporary electronic narrative as to traditional horror films.

What may be just as significant as these simple alterations of extended subjective shots, though, is the film's self-consciousness, which constantly pulls us back from the typical film experience as if it were trying to reach for a more realistic context, one beyond the camera and its limited field of vision, one perhaps more in keeping with the Internet and its seemingly transparent access to the world. For while the camera is a device that appears to let us capture the real, to chronicle in "as straightforward a way as possible," it also constrains our experience by restricting what we can see, as is literally the case when Josh, Heather, and Mike run out into the night and we can see only as far as the limited light on their camera. Thus Josh tells Heather that he knows why she likes the video camera: "It's like a totally filtered reality."

In fact, the film ultimately challenges, even attacks our relationship to the cinema, the technological in general, and their usual filtering effect. For its three filmmaker-protagonists eventually prove ill-equipped for dealing with a natural and transformative world: their car can only take them so far; their map and compass prove useless; their cameras and sound equipment, designed to record the real, offer no insulation against a mysterious, perhaps even supernatural realm. And by funneling our relation to the natural world, even to one another, through the technological, the narrative evokes our own sense of being lost in the mediated contemporary world. Attacked for her attachment to the camera—an attachment that makes possible the film itself, we cannot forget—Heather is told to turn it off, put it down, help figure out their position and determine how to get out of it. Her reply, "No, I'm not turning the camera off. I want to mark this occasion," seems the response of someone who is already fully lost to and within the cinematic. From behind the camera, just as back in her home, she feels temporarily secure, pointed in a safe direction, able to document the "creeped-out" experience of her companions while remaining immune from its menace. And yet she is in the midst of that experience herself and unable, or unwilling, to face her own contingent situation, to see herself as lost and endangered here. Consequently, the extreme close-up of her face—cold, shaking, nose running—at the film's climax when she turns the camera on herself, works another and most effective "transformation" here. It shows her, and perhaps by extension us as well, as a frail contemporary human, immersed beyond all insulation by her technology, involved to such an extent that she can no longer find a safe distance, transformed from sceptical reporter to helpless victim of this quaint bit of local folklore.

In describing the success of *The Blair Witch Project*, Libby Gelman-Waxner has also linked the film's technological bent and its successful computer-based promotion. As she comments, its success must be "partially attributed to the heavy promotion of the movie on the Internet, and that makes sense: It's a movie for men and women . . . who prefer to see the world entirely through technology—it's nature downloaded." That is, it seems to present us with a kind of raw human experience framed by technology, a technology that allows us a safe, almost aesthetic distance on events—much as we might find on the Internet. That distance, with its built-in controls and a carefully established context, does seem a key to the film, albeit one whose import she does not quite fully gauge. For while that sense of distance suggests the film's packaging for Internet consumption, it also opens onto the film's own critique of a mediated environment, particularly of the cinema, essential to its context of difference. Perhaps it goes without saying that today's moviegoers, situated within a pervasive multimedia environment, experience the cinematic text differently, even much more sceptically than other generations of moviegoers. Certainly, the success of the *Scream* films suggests as much. But the link I have explored here points not simply to the measurably different ways in which we are now viewing and decoding those texts, but also to how our viewing experience and capacity for such decoding depend on a whole different register of experience, how various voices assist in constructing our experience, even constructing our critique of that experience. With *The Blair Witch Project*'s project, we can begin to gauge the dimensions of that construction, begin to make out what is so often obscured by mechanisms that are changing both the movies and our experience of them.

Paul Virilio has recently described the postmodern experience as like living in "the shadow of the Tower of Babel," not simply as a result of the many and different voices with which the multimedia environment bombards us but because of a certain dislocation that accompanies those various voices. For the electronic experience, he believes, with its tendency to bring together many and different places, to bind us within what he terms "glocalization," also leaves us without a real place—decentered and lost. *The Blair Witch Project*, along with its Internet shadow, seems to have effectively captured, and capitalized on, this sensibility. For it recalls the nature of the typical electronic document, the hypertext, which consists of a series of documents connected to one another by links; that is, it is a text of many fragments but no whole, no master text. And by virtue of its very lack of center, its absence of what Murray terms "the clear-cut trail," the hypertext invites us to find our own way, even to find some pleasure or profit in its very decenteredness. That absence of a center—or the lostness which the hypertext user shares in part with the three protagonists of *Blair Witch*—is simply part of the great capital of the Internet experience, something it typically barters with, plays upon by alternately denying and opening onto it. Here it is the stuff that can effectively "creep out" an audience. It is also something that the movie industry is quickly taking the measure of in its larger project of providing the postmodern audience with its peculiarly postmodern pleasures.

With this essay, more than simply describing the relationship between film and Web site, the product and its marketing, I hope to shed some light on the contemporary film industry. In today's wide-open media marketplace, the small, virtually unknown filmmaker often seems to function as successfully as the big studio in finding a venue for his or her work. Certainly, the proliferation of independent film festivals, the opening-up of direct-to-video distribution possibilities, the appearance of media outlets like the Independent Film Channel on cable television, and even the industry-feared Internet distribution of digitized films all support this notion and, in truth, lend it some substance. The well-made, small-budget, independently produced, and star-less movie does have a chance to be seen, picked up by a national distributor or cable outlet, and then offered to a wide audience. Yet reaching that wide audience remains a troublesome project, one with which the power structure of the industry is growing familiar, and for which it is constantly developing new strategies. These strategies then must take into account the changing nature of the entertainment form itself, particularly the increasingly substantial role of the computer and its offspring, the Internet—a medium that also threatens, much as television did, to supplant the film industry, in part by offering its own pleasures to a young audience that has grown up with electronic narratives. As Murray reminds us, "The computer is chameleonic. It can be seen as a theater, a town hall, an unraveling book, an animated wonderland, a sports arena, and even a potential life form. But it is first and foremost a representational medium, a means for modeling the world that added its own potent properties to the traditional media it has assimilated so quickly." And, I would add, it is a medium that, through the Internet and much as film has traditionally done, has begun to assert its own model for the world. It powerfully affirms its own authority, its own truth, its own priority at affording access to the world.

> **J. P. Telotte** teaches in the Literature, Communication and
> Culture Program at Georgia Tech.

SECTION 3
National and international cults

Introduction

This section covers the geographical range and cultural belonging of cult film – at the same time wildly global and firmly local. Because its appreciation relies on constantly moving, dynamic flows of reception, often in the margins of legitimate circuits of culture, it can literally pop up anywhere. Fans of horror, for instance, are avid in their scavenging to unearth and import obscure materials – they will carry the reels through customs themselves if they have to. At the same time, the devotion to films typical for cult requires a deep penetration of the local psyche – it has to *mean* something to the moviegoer in his or her daily life. In this introduction we will put national and international cult in perspective.

Still, unexplored areas continue to attract cultish fascination: 1920s audiences gazed at remarkable images of Ernest Shackleton's Antarctic expedition in *South* (1919–23), or marvelled at the underwater explorations of sea animals through the films of Jean Painlevé, whose surrealist affiliations added a remarkable poetry to the subject matter. Even after new technologies had explored all corners of the earth, filmmakers like Stan Brakhage or Godfrey Reggio could astonish audiences with unique explorations captivated in *Creation* (1979), *Mammals of Victoria* (1994), and *Koyaanisqatsi* (1983) and *Powaqqatsi* (1987) respectively. Or viewers could witness the intimate details of insect life in *Microcosmos* (1997), a cult favourite among biology teachers.

Rituals, cult and cultural belonging

In the case of cult film, cultural belonging is a peculiar concept: because cult films are already standing 'apart' in their own environments, they are not representative of their culture – at least not its mainstream. But at the same time they can (and do) carry some of the more edgy cultural sensitivities of a region or community. While this may not make them more comprehensible for foreign audiences, it may equip them with a sort of visceral impact that goes directly to the senses. *The Wisconsin Death Trip* (2000) and *Searching for the Wrong-Eyed Jesus* (2003) may seem elusive in their styles, and abrupt in their narrative (which often just seems to stagger along), but they do give the impression that they create a better understanding of a region (the Midwest or the Deep South), or a people (immigrants, settlers, locals). Similarly, the films of Álex de La Iglesia

(*Día de la Bestia*, 1995), Bigas Luna (*Jamón Jamón*, 1992) and Julio Medem (*Lúcia y el Sexo*, 2001) seem to provoke an insight into Spanish culture, though it is difficult to say exactly what that is. The films of Alejandro Jodorowsky are among the most complex and convoluted examples of this because their cultural origin is not limited to one region. *El Topo* (1970), the original midnight movie, combines Latin American, western, and European influences, and its narrative is near incomprehensible, but it still generates understanding. Its weirdness gives the impression that it communicates a certain cultural feel – maybe because by making us understand and appreciate what is *different* it also tells us what we perceive as normal, so we can resist it. As Hoberman and Rosenbaum show in their essay, that is exactly what attracted American audiences to the film.[1]

What cult films from outside an audience's own cultural surroundings make clear is that concepts of 'nation', 'state', and 'country' are useless – cult films are seldom nationalist in their inspirations, narratives or even their funding. Instead, they propagate rituals. Rituals are embodied, robust routines that provide cultures with a sense of belonging by reminding them of where and how their culture originated. And the closer to taboos and danger these rituals come, the more direct their communication of being and belonging is.[2] As we have seen already, cult films are filled with such moments – bodies threatened by, or in demand of, violence, sex, pollution, yukkie stuff, mutation and moral ambiguity are at the centre of their narratives.

Such moments may not be self-explanatory, but they signal where the cultural sensitivities of a region or community lie. Western audiences may not fully grasp the martial arts rituals from *A Touch Of Zen* (1969) or Bruce Lee's films, or the gendered sexual routines in Japanese Manga, or the rites of masculine bonding in heroic bloodshed gangster films from Hong-Kong, or the dance rituals in Bollywood – each of which are explored more in detail in the essays in this section – but they do recognize where the boundaries lie, where the taboos and dangers are, because cult films actively seek them out and exploit them.[3] This recognition has made films such as *Fists of Fury* (1971), *Enter the Dragon* (1973), *Surakksha* (1979), *Bandit Queen* (1994), *A Chinese Ghost Story* (1987), *The Killer* (1988) or *Akira* (1988) cult classics. It helps us to understand the cult appeal of Akira Kurosawa's samurai films, like *The Seven Samurai* (1954), *Yojimbo* (1961) and *Sanjuro* (1962), and their influence across continents on completely different cultural traditions.[4]

The danger in observing the rituals and taboos exposed in these movies is that they can lead to stereotypical ideas. Cult movies run the same risk of any other film – they simplify reality. Ultimately it depends on the audiences to look beyond that simplification. And in that respect, a somewhat strange shop clerk recommending a title you 'just have to see' is at least as good a guide as any handbook or *Rough Guide*.

Local traditions, global receptions and vice versa

Given the scale of many cult films it is amazing to see how well they do in foreign markets – it is often half a miracle they even receive distribution abroad (and of course sometimes they do not really officially get released at all), and when they do it is astonishing to see their impact, not so much in terms of immediate box office revenue but in long-term sedimentation within a foreign culture. We do not intend to elaborate here on the history of the international reception of the world's cult cinemas, but some territories are worth singling out, if only to demonstrate how the local and global plait unique cult traditions.[5]

We have already mentioned the international cult appeal of Akira Kurosawa, but it is worth noting how much he exemplifies a general pattern. Kurosawa's films have influenced western cinema (the spaghetti Western and George Lucas' science-fiction epics, to name two) as much as it has influenced him. Often called the 'most western of classic Japanese filmmakers' he has drawn from a wide variety of popular culture sources from Europe. As such his films are representative of the global exchange of influences that typifies cult cinema. Next to Kurosawa, the Godzilla films (especially the original *Gojira*, 1954) were borrowed from 1930s monster movies but given a local twist by linking the monster to the atomic bomb; and the yakuza films of Takeshi Kitano (starting with *Sonatine*, 1993) were influenced by spaghetti Westerns, the gangster films of Jean-Pierre Melville, and Scorsese's and Ferrara's mob films, and have in turn had a profound influence on contemporary crime cinema. Finally, Hayao Miyazaki's anime films (especially *Spirited Away*, 2001) drew on local Manga and international cartoon traditions (including *The Smurfs*) and in turn influenced Pixar and Dreamworks' animations. Monster movies, yakuza films, and anime are among Japan's most cultish exports products, and together their explorations of taboos and rituals around nuclear war, crime and/as business, and redefined gender roles, have helped audiences abroad see modern Japan.[6]

Italian cult cinema has a reputation that matches the acclaim of its most renowned auteurs. Italian horror is widely seen as one of the longest-lasting international cult traditions – starting with the films of Riccardo Freda (*I Vampiri*, 1956), Mario Bava (*Black Sunday*, 1960) and Antonio Margheriti (*Danza Macabra*, 1963). Its highpoint is usually situated in the mid-1970s to early 1980s, when Margheriti's Warhol-productions, Dario Argento, Lucio Fulci, Ruggero Deodato and Umberto Lenzi caused international furore – audacious, gory, visually stunning, and often banned from release. More recently, the films of Sergio Stivaletti or *Last House in the Woods* (2006) show the genre's appeal has not diminished among cult fans. But horror was only one aspect of Italian cult. To indicate the importance of Italian cult cinema we have included an essay discussing its prime representative, the *giallo* – often overlapping with horror, as Bava's *Blood and Black Lace* (1964), or Argento's *Deep Red* (1974) indicate. Next to that, Sergio Leone's and Sergio Corbucci's spaghetti Westerns unmasked the American Western myth in all its brutality. The Argento and Bertolucci co-scripted *Once Upon a Time in the West* (1968), with Peter Fonda in a memorable bad-guy role became a cult legend – partly because it was hardly ever shown in its intended uncut widescreen format.[7] Throughout the 1970s Italian cinema was notorious for the politically radical cinema of Pier Paolo Pasolini (*Il Decamerone*, 1971; *Salo, or the 120 Days of Sodom*, 1975), as well as churning out nunsploitation (*Killer Nun*, 1978), sleaze cinema (especially the films of Tinto Brass), poliziotteschi ('rogue cop' films like *Violent Professionals*, 1973), and the really nasty nazisploitation and mondo films. All of these expose rituals hidden in Italian culture, and all of them have found audiences across the globe. Italian cult cinema continues to have a large presence on the international scene.[8]

The films of Medem, Luna, and De La Iglesia mentioned above did not appear out of nowhere. They are part of a legacy of cult that originated in Mexico, expanded to Spain, and has, as Walter Salles testifies,[9] fared well on international markets. Luis Buñuel is *the* key figure in facilitating the international status of Latino cult, first in Mexico, then in Spain. His Mexican films helped an already active horror film culture, evidenced in *El Fantasma del Convento* (1934) or *El signo de la muerte* (1939),[10] slowly gain international cult appeal – viewers wanted to see more of this harsh magic realism (cruel *and* melodramatic) undercut with religious iconography that was simultaneously devout and ironic, and certainly morally ambiguous. After Buñuel's arrival it was exemplified in films such as *Susana* (1951), and from the 1960s onwards (and strongly influenced by the Cuban revolution *and* its cinema), in the caprioles of the masked wrestler El Santo (see, *El Santo and Blue Demon versus Dracula and The Wolfman* (1973).[11] In the 1960s, Buñuel introduced a similar trend in Spain, with his blasphemous and debauched *Viridiana* (1961), which was instantly banned but (of course) became a cult success worldwide. In its wake, Spain, like Mexico, developed a tradition that put rituals of revolution, violence and disfiguration in a political and religious frame, often spiced by the supernatural (see *Pyro*, 1963; or *Mark of the Werewolf*, 1967).[12] That cultural sensibility has since been carried further by numerous others, most notably Paul Naschy, Spain's most productive cult icon Jesus Franco (*Vampiros Lesbos*, 1971; *Female Vampire*, 1973), and most recently by Nacho Cerdà (his short *Aftermath*, 1994, was a cult in itself). But Latino cult films are not uniquely horror. The early outrageous comedies of Pedro Almodóvar, like *Labyrinth of Passions* (1982) are cult by any standard, as are most of Luna's and several of De La Iglesia's films.[13] Even here, cruelty and disfiguration remain powerful themes – Almodóvar explicitly acknowledges the link in the opening of *Matador* (1986), when he shows a (banned) scene of Franco's video nasty *Bloody Moon* (1980).[14] And in Mexico the sensual comedies of Alfonso Cuarón (*Love in Times of Hysteria*, 1991; *Y tu Mama tambien*, 2001), the gang-Western *El Mariachi* (1992), and the complex situation sketch *Amores Perros* (2000) have drawn large international cult followings. Spain and Mexico have also served as a location for producers trying to capitalize on the local sensibilities and their international cult appeal. Old Hollywood's attempts at Spanish language versions of its own hits are mostly just hilarious (and cult because of that), but Spanish and Mexican locations have played a significant role in the cult reputations of American and Italian Westerns alike.[15] The connection between Mexico and Spain was also physically consumed, when directors like Guillermo Del Toro (*Cronos*, 1993) combined the regions' cult potential to produce the unique *The Devil's Backbone* (2001) and *Pan's Labyrinth* (2006).

There are many other territories that have seen their local cult cinema receive international reputations. Western cultures like Australia (the *Mad Max* series), New Zealand (partly through Peter Jackson – to whom we devote an essay in this section),[16] and Canada (which in the wake of their notorious tax-break system produced a true avalanche of cult films like *The Changeling, Prom Night, Porky's* or *Christmas Story*),[17] have often explored the schizophrenic cultural situation of their histories (native versus settler) more directly in their cult films than in their 'official' mainstream cinema – or should we say, the films that have explored those issues have more often had a cult reputation, especially abroad, where audiences appreciated the taboos and ambiguity these issues brought with them. Surely, a lot of the appeal of *The Last Wave* (1977), *Once Were Warriors* (1994), and the *Ginger Snaps* trilogy (2000–4) lies there?

Similarly, some territories' cinema, like Cuba, Africa, Iran or Mongolia, is so poorly distributed that any film from there is an international cult phenomenon – simply by virtue of making it to festivals, videostores or cinemas at all. Among them are the Cuban revolution's satires of sex rituals *Lucía* (1968) and *Culpa* (1993), the slapstick ridicule of anthropology *The Gods Must Be Crazy* (1980) from Botswana, the comedic comment on Arabic rituals of education and routine *Where is My Friend's Home* (1987), the Russian-Mongolian Western *Urga* (1991), and the poetic exploration of girls' rituals in an Islamic culture, *Sib* (1998).

Finally, some obscure cult films originate (and thrive) in cultures recurrent across territories (rural, urban, ghetto, suburban), or are not bound by geography at all. Queer and lesbian festival culture often celebrates liberation through rituals of international carnival (like *It's in the Water*, 1997). Even less limited to physical borders is 'corporate brand territory'. Whenever filmmakers expose the rituals or taboos of capitalist corporations, and (as happens frequently) find their films cloaked in controversy, the insights they produce guarantee global cult status – ironically enough, exactly the kind of consumer loyalty brands desire. *The Coca-Cola Kid* (1985), *Superstar, the Karen Carpenter Story* (1987), *Wall Street* (1987) and *American Psycho* (2000), and several infamous Disney spoofs are good examples.[18] But perhaps the most striking exemplar, by dint of its relentless inclusiveness, is Turkish trash cinema, which mixes local rituals and western popular culture iconography, ambiguous sexual rituals, and a disregard of any copyright laws concerning brands and franchises. For that reason we have devoted an essay to it in this section.[19]

The cult of exoticism: culture shocks and shocking cultures

The international traffic in cult cinema does not always generate an appreciation of cultural belonging that everyone agrees with. Sometimes the rituals and taboos in cult films offend sensitivities – creating opposition rather than mutual understanding.

At its most implicit, this is simply a cinematic device: a character from abroad (usually from a western country) visits an exotic culture and is fascinated but also repelled by its rituals and traditions. Edward Said has shown the intricate link between such characterizations and the actual attitude of 'the West' towards anything outside its realm of immediate comprehension, and dubbed it 'Orientalism'.[20] Probably the most famous example of this is the *Emmanuelle* series, and its *Black Emanuelle* spin-offs: each film uses the exoticism of the oriental location as an explanation why a 'normal' western woman would break taboos and experiment with sexual rituals. It exposes the limits of the culture within which the film is received. Because cultists are not as easily fazed as mainstream viewers they are more likely to condone rituals unfamiliar to their own, but their curiosity can easily become condescending.[21]

The inability to separate a film's representation from its cultural surroundings has determined the cult receptions of many films, especially when their culture of origin can be linked to a 'tainted' reputation. After some infamous sex scandals, Belgian realist horror cinema gained a cult reputation as 'guerilla cinema' for its depictions of politicized sexual violence (*Man Bites Dog*, 1992); during the post-communist social chaos in Russia a small wave of 'necrorealist' films became fêted for their nihilist portrayal of atrocities (*Place on Earth*, 2001); a series of French existentialist feminist films from the late 1990s onward was seen as symptomatic of French culture's obsession with 'l'amour fou' (*Romance*, 1999). Explicit taboo-breaking scenes were at the core of each of these connections: gang rape and child killings in *Man Bites Dog*, self-castration and child torture in *Place on Earth*, non-simulated fellatio and child birth in *Romance*. Beyond generating cult curiosity and insights into local culture through rituals, these films also raised eyebrows – what kind of culture would produce such films?[22]

Often, the main reason for unease and rejection is the films' use of graphic imagery of cultural taboos, especially those of sex and violence – as the examples above testify. And in the eyes of viewers this can sometimes implicate an entire culture, without the need for a 'topical' excuse. East Asian horror films have often been derided for their inclusion of explicit torture and sexualized violence (especially against women and children).[23] Even though cultists are known to seek out such extremes, their own cultural roots seem to give them some instinctive reaction against some types of graphic situations – or rituals – characters are 'put in' (and we mean this in the most neutral possible way).[24] The acceptance of the aesthetic achievements of, for instance, Korean and Japanese neo-horror of the late 1990s onwards (*Ringu*, 1999; *Dark Water*, 2001), has not lifted that unease – in fact in some cases it has only intensified the debate, as this section's essay on Takashi Miike's notorious *Ichi the Killer* (2001) demonstrates.[25]

Global cult

Still, if one of us hadn't accepted the videotape of 'that movie' from that wild-eyed, tense shop clerk, we would never have become soul mates, and a world of cult cinema would never have opened. Every story about a cult favourite begins with such humble, local details – therefore, global cults never exist without local ones.

Notes

1 Hoberman, J. and Jonathan Rosenbaum (1983) *Midnight Movies*, New York: Da Capo Press; Triana-Toribio, Núria (2003) *Spanish National Cinema*, New York: Routledge; Eaton, Michael (2000) 'Vanishing Americans', *Sight and Sound*, 10(6), 30–2.

2 See Douglas, Mary (1966) *Purity and Danger*, New York: Routledge.

3 Hunt, Leon (2000) 'Han's Island revisited: *Enter the Dragon* as a transnational cult film', in Xavier Mendik and Graeme Harper (eds) *Unruly Pleasures: The Cult Film and Its Critics*, Guilford: FAB Press, 75–85; Newitz, Annalee (1995) 'Magical girls and atomic bomb sperm: Japanese animation in America', *Film Quarterly*, 49(1), 2–11; An, Jinsoo (2001) '*The Killer:* Cult film and transcultural (mis)reading'; in Esther Yau (ed.) *At Full Speed: Hong Kong Cinema in a Borderless World*, University of Minnesota Press, 95–113; Nayar, Sheila J. (2004) 'Invisible representation: The oral contours of a national popular cinema', *Film Quarterly*, 57(3), 13–23.

4 It also helps understand the 'respect' western martial arts stars like Chuck Norris and Jean-Claude Van Damme enjoy (they went to the origin to experience the rituals in their proper cultural environment) as well as the 'kiss controversy' surrounding Richard Gere and Bollywood icon Shilpa Shetty.

5 There are numerous other examples we do not have the space to explore: the rituals of French méridional, Breton and beur cinema, Philippino religious horror cinema, the crude Uuno comedies of Finland, classical British heritage cinema, or rituals of class, family and feminism in Irish and Northern-Irish cinema as captured in Anne Crilly's films. See selected chapters in Dyer, Richard and Ginette Vincendeau (eds) (1992) *Popular*

European Cinema, London: Routledge; and Tombs, Pete (1997) *Mondo Macabro: Weird and Wonderful Cinema Around the World,* New York: St Martin's Griffin; also see McIlroy, Brian (2001) *Shooting to Kill: Filmmaking and the 'Troubles' in Northern Ireland*, Richmond, BC: Steveston Press; McIlroy, Brian (ed.) (2007) *Genre and Cinema: Ireland and Transnationalism*, New York: Routledge.

6 Richie, Donald (1999) *Akira Kurosawa*, Berkeley, CA: University of California Press; Kapur, Jyotsna (2005) 'The return of history as horror: Onibaba and the atomic bomb', in Steven Jay Schneider and Tony Williams (eds) *Horror International*, Detroit, MI: Wayne State University Press, 83–98; Yang, Manuel (2002) 'Japanese monster movies, Ultraman, and the structure of cultural relations and forces of production in postwar nuclear imagination', in *Hihan kukan* (*Critical Space*) (in Japanese); Napier, Susan (2001) *Anime from Akira to Princess Mononoke*, London: Palgrave; McCarthy, Helen (1999) *Hayao Miyazaki: Master of Japanese Animation*, Berkeley, CA: Stone Bridge Press; Davis, Darrell William (2001) 'Reigniting Japanese tradition with Hana-Bi', *Cinema Journal*, 40(4), 55–80; Varese, Federico (2006) 'The secret history of Japanese cinema: the Yakuza movies', *Global Crime*, 7(1), 10–24. *Japan Forum*, 14(2), the official journal of the British Association for Japanese Studies, is completely devoted to anime.

7 At the tail end of the spaghetti Western cycle Terence Hill became a cult favourite for his parts in comedic Westerns like *My Name is Trinity* (1970) and *My Name is Nobody* (1973, written by Leone, with again Fonda deconstructing his Western persona – another indication of the international connection of the genre). With muscle man Bud Spencer, Hill continued to receive cult credit in hilarious but carefully choreographed buddy fistfight movies. See also Wagstaff, Christopher (1992) 'A forkful of Westerns: industry, audiences and the Italian Western', in Richard Dyer and Ginette Vincendeau (eds) *Popular European Cinema*, London: Routledge, 245–61; Newman, Kim (1986) 'Thirty years in another town: The history of Italian exploitation', *Monthly Film Bulletin*, 624–6, 20–4, 51–5 and 88–91.

8 See the entries on Lucio Fulci and Dario Argento in the bibliography, and also Jenks, Carol (1992) 'The other face of death: Barbara Steele and La maschera del demonio', in Richard Dyer and Ginette Vincendeau (eds) *Popular European Cinema*, London: Routledge, 149–62; Guins, Raiford (2005) 'Blood and black gloves on shiny discs: New media, old tastes, and the remediation of Italian horror films in the United States', in Steven Jay Schneider and Tony Williams (eds) *Horror International*, Detroit, MI: Wayne State University Press, 15–32; Barry, Christopher (2004) 'Violent justice: Italian crime/cop films of the 1970s', in Ernest Mathijs and Xavier Mendik (eds) *Alternative Europe: European Exploitation and Underground Cinema*, London: Wallflower Press, 77–89; Koven, Mikel (2006) *La Dolce Morta: The Italian Giallo Film*, Metuchen: Scarecrow Press; Greene, Naomi (1990) *Pier Paolo Pasolini: Cinema as Heresy*, Princeton, NJ: Princeton University Press.

9 See Salles, Walter (2003) 'Preface', in Alberto Elena and Maria Díaz López (eds) *The Cinema of Latin America*, London: Wallflower Press, xiii–xv.

10 See Rhodes, Gary (2003) 'Fantasmas de cine Mexicano: The 1930s horror cycle of Mexico', in Steven Schneider (ed.) *Fear Without Frontiers: Horror Cinema Across the Globe*, Guilford: FAB Press, 93–104.

11 See, Syder, Andrew and Dolores Tierney (2005) 'Importation/Mexploitation, or how a crime-fighting, vampire-slaying Mexican wrestler almost found himself in an Italian sword-and-sandals epic', in Steven Jay Schneider and Tony Williams (eds) *Horror International*, Detroit, MI: Wayne State University Press, 33–55.

12 The topic of revolution and rebellion is most notably observed by Shaw, Deborah (2003) *Contemporary Cinema of Latin America*, New York: Continuum, 180–1; and Elena, Alberto

and Maria Díaz López (eds) (2003) *The Cinema of Latin America*, London: Wallflower Press, 9; and that of violence is highlighted by Willis, Andrew (2005) 'The Spanish horror film as subversive text', in Steven Jay Schneider and Tony Williams (eds) *Horror International*, Detroit, MI: Wayne State University Press, 163–79; and Stone, Rob (2002) *Spanish Cinema*, Harlow: Longman.

13 See the discussion of *Labyrinth of Passions* in Arroyo, José (1992) '*La ley del deseo*: a gay seduction', in Richard Dyer and Ginette Vincendeau (eds) *Popular European Cinema*, London: Routledge, 31–46; Kercher, Dona (2004) 'Violence, timing, and the comedy team in Alex De La Iglesia's *Muertos De Risa*', in Ernest Mathijs and Xavier Mendik (eds) *Alternative Europe: European Exploitation and Underground Cinema*, London: Wallflower Press, 53–63.

14 Joan Hawkins' essay on Franco in Section two discusses this sensibility in more detail, and demonstrates, once more, the international trajectory of Spanish cult. Check the entry on Jesus Franco in the bibliography for more details.

15 Recently, Brian Yuzna's Fantastic Factory in Spain has managed a mix of local cult(ure) and international attraction with films such as *Rottweiler* (2004), a film aptly picking up on the theme of immigration. The entries on Yuzna in the bibliography carry several references to this effort.

16 Wu, Harmony (2003) 'Trading in horror, cult, and matricide: Peter Jackson's phenomenal bad taste and New Zealand fantasies of inter/national cinematic success', in Mark Jancovich, Antonio Lazaro-Reboll, Julian Stringer and Andy Willis (eds) *Defining Cult Movies: The Cultural Politics of Oppositional Taste*, Manchester: Manchester University Press, 84–108.

17 See, Pevere, Geoff and Greg Dymond (1996) *Mondo Canuck*, Scarborough, ONT: Prentice-Hall.

18 See Davis, Glyn (forthcoming) *Superstar: The Karen Carpenter Story*, London: Wallflower Press; Mathijs, Ernest (2001) Deconstructing or reconstructing? Disney criticism and interduck', *Plateau: International Quarterly Bulletin on Animated Film*, 21(4), 16–20.

19 Erdogan, Nezih (2002) 'Mute bodies, disembodied voices: Notes on sound in Turkish popular cinema', *Screen*, 43(3), 233–49; Arslan, Savas (2003) 'Turkish trash: Popular film in Turkey, 1960–1980', conference paper, Born to be Bad 2 Trash Cinema Conference, University of California, Berkeley, May 2003.

20 Said, Edward (1978) *Orientalism*, New York: Vintage Books.

21 See the chapters on *Emmanuelle* and *Black Emanuelle* in Mathijs, Ernest and Xavier Mendik (eds) (2004) *Alternative Europe: European Exploitation and Underground Cinema*, London: Wallflower Press.

22 See, Mathijs, Ernest (2005) 'Man bites dog and the critical reception of Belgian horror (in) cinema', in Steven Jay Schneider and Tony Williams (eds) *Horror International*, Detroit, MI: Wayne State University Press, 315–35; Stojanova, Christina (2004) 'Mise-en-scènes of the impossible: Soviet and Russian horror films', in Ernest Mathijs and Xavier Mendik (eds) *Alternative Europe: European Exploitation and Underground Cinema*, London: Wallflower Press, 90–105; Phillips, John (2001) 'Catherine Breillat's *Romance*: Hard core and the female gaze', *Studies in French Cinema*, 1(3), 133–40; Hantke, Steffen (2005) 'The dialogue with American popular culture in two German films about the serial killer', in Steven Jay Schneider and Tony Williams (eds) *Horror International*, Detroit, MI: Wayne State University Press, 56–79.

23 See: Macias, Patrick (2002) *Tokyscope: The Japanese Cult Film Companion*, Viz Media LCC; Weisser, Thomas (1997) *Asian Cult Cinema*, New York: Boulevard Books.

24 As always, every excess has its defenders. See: Hunter, Jack (1998) *Eros in Hell: Sex, Blood and Madness in Japanese Cinema*, London: Creation Books, for an overview of

some of the most extreme cinema from Asia. Etienne Barral gives a lively account of some of the more extreme aspects of the '*otaku*' cult of fandom in, Barrall, Etienne (1999) *Otaku, les enfants du virtuel*, Paris: Denoel, 239–50.

25 Mes, Tom (2003) *Agitator: The Cinema of Miike Takashi*, London: FAB Press.

3.1

El Topo: Through the wasteland of the counterculture

by J. Hoberman and Jonathan Rosenbaum

Occupying a unique space between cult figure and countercultural icon, the work of Alejandro Jodorowsky retains the status of genuine cinematic oddity. At once both macabre and mystical, erotic and esoteric, productions such as *El Topo* (1970), *Holy Mountain* (1973) and *Santa Sangre* (1989) have continually blurred the boundaries between art house and atrocity. *El Topo* is the primary subject of Hoberman and Rosenbaum's chapter, which situates Jodorowsky's breakthrough movie in terms of the countercultural aesthetic that was sweeping Europe and the USA at the time. At once a textual reading of the film, as well as a fascinating study of its American reception, the authors consider the extent to which counter-cultural politics and pulp narrative had effectively been co-opted by mainstream Hollywood by the time of *El Topo*'s release. As Hoberman and Rosenbaum suggest, the film's narrative remains essentially complex and convoluted, consisting of a three act structure which shifts from gunslinger western to mythical resurrection metaphor before concluding as a revenge narrative. If this description makes this Jodorowsky production appear essentially contradictory, it is because the director's background is equally as confused and diverse, taking in a number of Central American, European and eastern influences that would strain any concept of 'national' cult cinema. While this degree of contradiction marks both the creator of *El Topo*, as well as his creation, it is also mirrored by the film's American reception by countercultural and mainstream audiences that this chapter outlines. Hoberman and Rosenbaum also offer a fascinating account of how mainstream distribution by Allen Klein altered audience and critical reaction to both the film and its follow-up production, *Holy Mountain*.

A note on the extract: this chapter first appeared in J. Hoberman and Jonathan Rosenbaum's seminal book *Midnight Movies*, published in 1983. The original version of the chapter contains a longer consideration of the narrative of *El Topo* (and later works such as *Holy Mountain*), as well as detailing the American critical reception of Jodorowsky's film in more depth.

> I ask of film what most North Americans ask of psychedelic drugs.
> —Alexandro Jodorowsky

As the Vietnam War expanded and America's "baby-boom" generation came of age, the underground was superseded by the "counterculture"—a youthful amalgam of radical politics, oriental (or occult) mysticism, "liberated" sexuality, hallucinogenic drugs, communal life-styles, and rock 'n' roll that was sufficiently widespread (and even organized) to see itself as a movement.

From the onset, the counterculture was a powerful force in the marketplace. Beginning with independent rock documentaries (*Don't Look Back, You Are What You Eat, Monterey Pop*), post-*Blow Up* evocations of "swinging" London, and— appropriately, as we will see—American-International drive-in flicks (*The Trip, Wild in the Streets, Psych-Out*), youth-oriented films flooded the market. Within two years, *The Graduate* had been followed by *I Love You, Alice B. Toklas, Three in the Attic, Skidoo, Last Summer, Easy Rider, Chastity, Alice's Restaurant, Hail, Hero!*, and countless others. Mainstream releases (*Chappaqua, 2001, Head, Yellow Submarine, Midnight Cowboy, Medium Cool*) assimilated the techniques and themes of avant-garde films, while quasi-underground comedies like Brian De Palma's *Greetings* and Robert Downey's *Putney Swope* were considerable commercial hits. Among the counterculture intelligentsia, the fragmented pop-political meditations of Jean-Luc Godard reached the acme of their prestige. Meanwhile, ever-inventive Hollywood was experimenting with suburban wife-swapping sitcoms, homosexual comedies of manners, and even an elaborate bio-pic of Latin American revolutionary Che Guevara.

[. . .]

In December 1970, Jonas Mekas was organizing one of his periodic festivals of avant-garde films at the Elgin, a rundown six-hundred-seat theater, not unlike the Charles, on Eighth Avenue just north of Greenwich Village. Although the program was laden with major avant-garde figures, the most widely attended screenings were those on the three nights devoted to the films of John Lennon and Yoko Ono. The Elgin management took advantage of the hippie crowds to announce an added feature—Alexandro Jodorowsky's *El Topo*—to be shown at midnight because, as the first ad announced, it was "a film too heavy to be shown any other way."

El Topo (*The Mole*) was a trip, but whose and how "heavy" are open to interpretation. Jodorowsky not only wrote, directed, and scored the film, but appears on screen in virtually every scene as its eponymous hero, a character none too subtly identified with Moses, Buddha, and Jesus Christ. "*El Topo* is a quest for sainthood," he would later explain.

Stage director, cartoonist, esthetic provocateur, professional avant-gardist, guru, mime, and "maker of the *Topo*," Alexandro Jodorowsky constituted something of a counterculture unto himself. He was born in 1929 or 1930 to Russian-Jewish parents in Iquique, a small copper and nitrate port on the northern coast of Chile. "All four of my grandparents are Russian. They took a ship and tried to escape from Russia to the end of the world. . . . The Cossacks made me a Chilean." By his own account, Iquique was a tough town, filled with sailors and whores. "I lived a very sexual childhood," Jodorowsky told *Penthouse*. "We started to masturbate ourselves at four or five years. All together." His playmates, who routinely "violated" cats and drank dogs' milk, rejected him because he was Russian and circumcised: "My sex had the form of a mushroom."

Jodorowsky's immigrant father owned nothing more spectacular than a dry-goods store, perhaps precluding his son's easy identification with Iquique's other foreign-ers—the North American and British mine owners: "One of the first things I remem-ber is that we could not walk in certain areas because they were forbidden to Chileans. It was the beautiful side of the *gringo* colonies." Still, the boy's life was filled with miracles: "One day we found a great stone, an enormous stone, floating in the sea. . . . [Later] I was followed by a bee, a golden bee. For three years, every day, the golden bee follow me." Once, he claimed, the other children tied him to a giant kite and lofted him into the sky. "It was terrible. Inside the clouds I saw a cemetery of airplanes from the 1914 war. And in the airplanes was the corpse of the aviators. And inside the corpse was white vampires. And when I came in close, the white vampires began to move. . . . This was my childhood."

Later, the Jodorowsky family moved to Santiago, where Alexandro attended the university and became involved with theater. "I am called the new Rimbaud when I am 15. There was in this circle all queers and women who want young boys. I became interested in puppets and attach strings to actors and make them into human mario-nettes." Depending on the interview, Jodorowsky studied philosophy, psychology, mathematics, physics, or medicine at the University of Santiago, before dropping out to become a circus clown, act on the stage, or create his own troupe. "By the time I was 23, I have a company of 50 people." This precocious success notwithstanding, Jodorowsky left Chile in 1953, never to return. "It was a paradise, a crazy paradise. Incredible," he nostalgically recalled in 1980. "But I needed to cut with that. . . ."

Hopping a freighter to Barcelona, he made his way to Paris, where he worked for six years with Marcel Marceau, directed Maurice Chevalier's music-hall comeback (which coincided with the star's Hollywood rehabilitation, after he'd been accused of collaborating during World War II), and filmed a mime version of Thomas Mann's *The Transposed Heads*. On a world tour with Marceau, Jodorowsky stayed behind in Mexico City and spent the next few years introducing the locals to European avant-garde theater (Strindberg, Beckett, Ionesco). With several Mexican writers he founded a "surrealist" review, *S.NOB*, and went on to direct several surrealist plays. Then, back in Paris, Jodorowsky teamed up with Spanish playwright Fernando Arrabal and artist Roland Topor to form the Panic Movement (named for the Greek god Pan). Both Arrabal—the enfant terrible of the so-called Theater of the Absurd—and Jodorowsky consorted with those venerable surrealists who remained in Paris and were heavily influenced by their notions of theater.

The most important of these were the theories of the French poet/actor/madman/ seer Antonin Artaud, published in a 1938 collection of manifestos, *The Theater and Its Double*. Although Artaud was an official surrealist for only three years—quarreling with the movement's leader, André Breton, in 1927—he embodied many of surreal-ism's most radical impulses. Artaud totally rejected Western theater in favor of some-thing that "must make itself the equal of life. . . . Themes will be cosmic, universal, and interpreted according to the most ancient texts." Artaud's proposed "Theater of Cruelty" was to be a "bloody and inhuman" spectacle, a kind of ritual *cum* shock therapy that would enact and exorcize the spectator's repressed criminal and erotic obsessions. *The Theater and Its Double*, Jodorowsky would admit in 1980, "was my bible" (he needn't have added that it would be the first of many).

[. . .]

By 1967, Jodorowsky was back in Mexico City, where he started a weekly comic strip, *"Fábulas Pánicas,"* for a major newspaper, wrote three books, and established himself as one of the country's leading stage directors. (He also accumulated what various accounts describe as the largest comic-book collection in Mexico, or even South America.) Nevertheless, Jodorowsky was dissatisfied. "The theater in Mexico is definitely dead," he told an interviewer in 1968. "The only way to revive it would be for theater people to let themselves be jailed, to provoke scandals as I did six years ago." He inveighed against the timidity of Spanish literature, called again for a theater that would directly change people's lives, and dismissed his current productions as hack work. "I have directed many plays simply for clothing and food, while I am filming a movie in which I am totally involved. . . . Better to put your efforts into a film, so that if it is censored, it can be stored in cans. It may sit for 20 years, but one day it is screened."

The film to which he referred was *Fando and Lis*, an adaptation of an Arrabal play that he had first directed in Paris. For the movie, Jodorowsky kept only Arrabal's basic situation—the journey of Fando and his paralytic girl friend, Lis, through trash heap and desert to the unreachable city of Tar—and added his own specifics. Childhood flashbacks were interspersed with bizarrely sadistic vignettes. At one point a blind old man drew blood from Lis's arm, poured it into a wine glass, and drank it down. "Everything was real," Jodorowsky later asserted. "The physical violence, each drop of blood." (Well, perhaps not *everything*—when Lis died at the end of the film, her body was devoured by her mourners.) The movie, which cost some $300,000, was largely underwritten by the wealthy father of one of Jodorowsky's students. According to Juan Lopez Moctezuma, another Mexico City avant-gardist involved in the project (and the future director of such cheap horror films as *Mary, Mary, Bloody Mary* and *Dr. Tarr's Torture Garden*), *Fando and Lis* was "made at a killing pace," mainly on weekends.

In Mexico, as elsewhere, 1968 was a year of violent—albeit short-lived—political turmoil. Police and students clashed all that summer in confrontations that left hundreds dead and received worldwide media attention, amplified by the near-simultaneous Olympic Games in Mexico City. *Fando and Lis* premiered at the 1968 Acapulco Film Festival shortly after the Mexican army crushed the student movement with a bloody, unprovoked massacre in downtown Mexico City. In the tense atmosphere, the film became a *cause celebre* and even provoked a riot. ("The army had to intervene to protect us," Moctezuma remembered.) The scandal contributed to the suspension of the festival itself.

Although banned in Mexico, *Fando and Lis* was cut by thirteen minutes and released in New York in early 1970 to mainly negative reviews. (More than a few critics compared the film unfavorably to *Fellini Satyricon*, which had also recently opened.) Nevertheless, *Fando and Lis* proved to be Jodorowsky's entry ticket into the Mexican film industry. The film's local notoriety enabled him to raise the $400,000 he needed to make a second, even more provocative, movie. But this time his distribution strategy was different. There was no immediate attempt to open the film in Mexico. Instead, in the fall of 1970, Jodorowsky arrived in New York, carrying a print of *El Topo* under his arm.

*   *   *

Ben Barenholtz, the owner of the Elgin, first saw *El Topo* at a private screening at the Museum of Modern Art. "Half the audience walked out, but I was fascinated by it," he recalls. "I thought it was a film of its time." Barenholtz attempted to purchase the American rights and, failing that, persuaded *El Topo*'s novice distributor, music producer Alan Douglas, to begin previewing the film midnights at the Elgin.

As the onetime manager of the Village Theater (a sort of bargain-basement counterculture Carnegie Hall which later became the Fillmore East), Barenholtz knew his audience. He figured that the midnight showings during the week— 1:00 a.m. on Fridays and Saturdays—would attract hipsters, encourage a sense of "personal discovery," and stimulate word of mouth. On all three counts, his instincts were sensationally correct. *El Topo* premiered on the night of December 18, 1970, and ran continuously, seven nights a week, through the end of June 1971. There was practically no advertising—not even a poster, aside from an usher's crudely drawn sign outside the theater—and, for most of the run, no mention of the film in the daily press. Nevertheless, from January on, the Elgin's phone never stopped ringing. *El Topo* was doing turnaway business ($4,000 a week, *Variety* reported on March 10) and virtually subsidizing the entire theater. "Within two months, the limos lined up every night," Barenholtz remembers. "It became a must-see item."

The burgeoning cult (which was abetted by the Elgin management's canny refusal to clear the house after the premidnight show and resigned tolerance of marijuana consumption in the balcony) finally went public in late March when Glenn O'Brien published an ecstatic report in the *Village Voice*. "It's midnight mass at the Elgin," the O'Brien piece began.

> Cocteau's *Blood of a Poet* has just ended and the wait for *El Topo* is a brief grope for comfort before sinking back into fantastic stillness. The audience is young. It applauded Cocteau's sanguine dream as though he were in the theatre, but as credits appear on the screen, it settles again into rapt attention. They've come to see the light—and the screen before them is illumined by an abstract landscape of desert and sky—and the ritual begins again. . . . Jodorowsky is here to confess; the young audience is here for communion.

By this time, *El Topo* had begun to garner the prestige of such hippie texts as J. R. R. Tolkien's *The Lord of the Rings*, Robert Heinlein's *Stranger in a Strange Land*, Herman Hesse's *Steppenwolf*, R. Crumb's "Mr. Natural," and Carlos Castaneda's *The Teachings of Don Juan*. More profound than Marshall McLuhan's *Understanding Media*, *El Topo* captured the countercultural imagination like no movie since Stanley Kubrick's *2001*. The *Los Angeles Free Press* called it "the greatest film ever made," *Changes* found it "a work of incomprehensible depth." Dennis Hopper was said to be studying *El Topo* as he edited his follow-up to *Easy Rider, The Last Movie*. Indeed, both he and Peter Fonda had offered to appear in Jodorowsky's next film.

[. . .]

Among the Elgin regulars that spring was John Lennon, whom Barenholtz recalls seeing at three or four screenings. Lennon had just returned from the Cannes Film Festival, where he and Yoko Ono had exhibited their films and been knocked out by

Arrabal's first feature, *Viva la Muerte*. The ex-Beatle wanted his manager, Allen Klein, to purchase the rights to Arrabal's film but, after he saw *El Topo*, Lennon changed his mind. In June, Klein's Abkco Films bought *El Topo* and immediately withdrew the film from the Elgin, where it was still selling out seven nights a week. Klein had big plans for Jodoroswky: "My whole idea was to build him up as an international director." At the same time that he acquired *El Topo*, Klein signed Jodorowsky to an exclusive contract.

"We must forget the idea of making it with Broadway cinemas," Jodorowsky had declaimed a few months earlier. "In five years, those theaters will be used exclusively for showing erotic film pamphlets to propagandize war." Nevertheless, in November 1971, while Jodorowsky was working on the script of *The Holy Mountain*, Klein rented a block-long billboard off Times Square at $60,000 a month, plastered it with Jodorowsky's name, leased a Broadway theater, and gave *El Topo* its belated, official New York premiere.

The film received mixed notices from New York's mainstream reviewers (one of whom noted a number of "kids in capes and wide-brimmed hats, the '*El Topo* freaks,' " at the Broadway premiere). A few critics were disturbed by the idea that some of *El Topo*'s gaudy carnage and display of physical deformity was meant to be taken humorously. This mixture of horror and comedy was part of Jodorowsky's surrealism-derived Panic esthetic, but it had its equivalent elsewhere in the counterculture. By titling her *New Yorker* review "El Topo—Head Comics," Pauline Kael linked *El Topo* to both drug consumption and the "head" or "underground" comics of R. Crumb, S. Clay Wilson, and others. Rock aside, these comics were the purest (and most scurrilous) expression of the counterculture: availing themselves of the freedom their medium allowed, as well as the ready connection between "doodling" and unconscious desire, underground cartoonists routinely trafficked in grotesque violence, baroque sexual transgression, and freakish deformity (albeit with less metaphysical pretension than Jodorowsky). Head comics existed to violate all American taboos; as Leslie Fiedler later observed, they "made everything the 1950s found monstrous the norm." Five years a professional cartoonist, Jodorowsky was neither unaware nor unappreciative of their existence: indeed, he told one interviewer that he would like to collaborate with Crumb.

[. . .]

But for Kael, who, four years earlier, had made her national reputation in her first *New Yorker* piece by defending Arthur Penn's *Bonnie and Clyde* against the charge of excessive violence, Jodorowsky was simply pandering to his youthful audience, a view that many of the director's numerous pronouncements do nothing to assuage. (Asked if he would want spectators to be high while watching the film, Jodorowsky—who had more than once made his disdain for marijuana known—replied, "Yes, yes, yes, yes. I'd demand them to be.") Kael felt that Jodorowsky's "fundamental amorality" wasn't even an "honest amorality."

> He's an exploitation filmmaker, but he glazes everything with a useful piety. It's the violence plus the unctuous prophetic tone that makes *El Topo* a *heavy* trip. . . . Jodorowsky has come up with something new: exploitation filmmaking joined to sentimentality—the sentimentality of the counter-culture.

[. . .]

Although hip film buffs objected to *El Topo*'s graceless amalgam of Luis Buñuel, Federico Fellini, Sergio Leone, Sam Peckinpah, and Jean-Luc Godard, the movie bypassed cinematic sophistication to address the counterculture directly. More than any other film, *El Topo* presented itself as a spiritual initiation (if not a kind of Dionysian bloodbath), speaking at once to the counterculture's love of the arcane and its collective paranoia. By 1971, the counterculture had lost the euphoria of the late sixties and was beginning to experience a dissolution into the sullen privatism of the 1970s. In this light, the messianic revenge fantasy that *El Topo* offered was a complex one—directed against both an evil social order and a faltering spiritual authority.

Rather remarkably, none of *El Topo*'s American exegetes seem to have made the connection between the film's title and Karl Marx's celebrated image of the revolution as a "red mole." Even more surprisingly, no one appears to have linked the figure of El Topo to that of his contemporary near-look-alike, Charles Manson. Manson's 1970 arrest for the previous summer's Tate–La Bianca murders presented the counterculture with a thorny ideological problem. Not everyone in the Movement was as eager to embrace Manson as were the ultraleft Weathermen who declared 1970 "The Year of the Fork," in reference to the kitchen implement that the killers of Leo La Bianca plunged into his stomach. As David Felton and David Dalton observed in a lengthy piece on the Manson "family," first published in *Rolling Stone* in June 1970:

> The underground press in general has assumed kind of a paranoid-schizo attitude toward Manson, undoubtedly hypersensitive to the relentless gloating of the cops who, after a five-year-search, finally found a longhaired devil you could love to hate. . . . The question that seemed to split underground editorial minds more than any other was simply: Is Manson a hippie or isn't he?

El Topo was conceived and scripted before the world had ever heard of Manson, but the film appeared less than six months after the specter of his LSD-commune-run-amok began to haunt the counterculture. Thus, Jodorowsky's movie served to comfort its original audience by investing hippie violence with a religious aura.

If the film's devotees identified with the "holy killer" in the first and second sections of the movie, by the third he presented himself as their savior—the champion, quite literally, of the *freaks*. *Freak*, after all, had enjoyed universal currency as a self-descriptive countercultural term since at least 1967. ("That's what we call ourselves," says one of the first longhairs interviewed in the counterculture's *Triumph of the Will*, the three-hour *Woodstock*.) What other way to take *El Topo*'s penultimate massacre—in which the innocent freaks are destroyed by degenerate frontier capitalists—than as an apocalyptic vision of the end of the counterculture?

[. . .]

Recognizing *El Topo*'s "commercialized surrealism," Kael observed that "the avant-garde devices that once fascinated a small bohemian group because they seemed a direct pipeline to the occult and 'the marvelous' now reach the mass bohemianism of youth." Actually, the counterculture was in many respects popularized, updated, mass-produced surrealism. Where the surrealists had prized dreams, trance states and automatic writing as paths to the unconscious, the counterculture substituted psychedelic drugs and various modes of meditation. Indeed, surrealists like René Daumal, a poet who left the movement to experiment with hashish, study Gurdjieff, and learn Sanskrit (and whose novel *Mount Analogue* was an obvious model for Jodorowsky's *The Holy Mountain*), or even Artaud, who became immersed in Tarot, alchemy, Rosicrucianism, and peyote, were virtual proto-hippies. The more politically, esthetically, and pharmaceutically radical elements of the counterculture shared the surrealists' belief that the transcendence of ego functions, the blurring of binary opposites—dream/daily life, work/leisure, social/political—and the valorization of taboo practices could combine to change reality itself.

If rock had superseded movies as the privileged form of popular art, the lyrics of Bob Dylan and Jim Morrison bore more than a passing resemblance to the poetry of such teen-aged proto-surrealists as Arthur Rimbaud and Lautréamont. (The first album released by the Jefferson Airplane was titled *Surrealistic Pillow*, while the cover art of innumerable rock records were blatant pastiches of Salvador Dali and René Magritte.) Both the counterculture and the surrealists repudiated Western rationality, exalting Asia and the cult of the self-destructive adolescent. Their two great values were Love and Revolution, what Susan Sontag called "the politics of joy." The call of the first surrealist manifesto to "open the prisons, disband the army" could just as well have been issued by the counterculture. On the other hand, such counterculture media-manipulations as the 1967 attempt to exorcise and levitate the Pentagon and the showering of the New York Stock Exchange with dollar bills, would surely have met with the surrealists' approval.

[. . .]

The success of *El Topo* did nothing to diminish Jodorowksy's ego. "I want to be the Cecil B. De Mille of the Underground," he told the *Los Angeles Free Press*. "This I really want. I like Cecil B. De Mille. Fantastic!" Elsewhere, he confided that he expected to become enlightened while making *The Holy Mountain* for producer Allen Klein, adding, "Maybe I am a prophet. I really hope one day there will come Confucius, Mohammed, Buddha, and Christ to see *me*. And we will sit at a table, taking tea and eating some brownies."

Before beginning *The Holy Mountain*, Jodorowsky and his wife, Valerie, went a week without sleep under the direction of a Japanese Zen master. Then they took the Arica training developed by Oscar Ichazo. The son of a Bolivian general, Ichazo was no less eclectic than Jodorowsky—his system was an amalgam of Zen, Sufi, and yoga exercises with a theoretical overlay derived from alchemy, the *Kabala*, the *I Ching*, the teachings of Gurdjieff, and other esoteric doctrines. Ichazo was a year younger than Jodorowsky and their careers had some interesting parallels. At the same time that Jodorowsky was filming *El Topo*, Ichazo established his first institute in Arica, Chile, 150 miles up the coast from Jodorowsky's birthplace. Shortly after *El Topo* made Jodorowsky a counterculture superstar, Ichazo moved his Arica Institute to New York, where he attracted numerous acolytes among the hipper show-biz intelligentsia. The main actors for *The Holy Mountain* (among whom Jodorowsky had hoped to include John Lennon) were required to take three months of Arica training, after which they spent a month living communally in Jodorowsky's home. Only then, in the spring of 1972, was the film ready to start shooting.

Budgeted at $750,000, *The Holy Mountain* was filmed entirely in Mexico. As with

El Topo, the scenes were shot in consecutive order. Jodorowsky, his hair dyed platinum blond and bound back in a long braid, starred as well as directed. The cast and crew seemed inspired by a mystical sense of purpose. "You know, I think this is the most important thing going on in the world today," one bearded production assistant told the *Rolling Stone* reporter who visited the set. "At least, it's the most far out." Ichazo frequently dropped in on the shooting and two Arica group leaders were assigned to the project, standing by to provide any necessary "Mongolian massages" with a wooden spoon.

Despite Jodorowsky's inability to get everything he wanted (including a real corpse to hack apart during the opening credits), the first hour of *The Holy Mountain* is arguably the best moviemaking of his career. Thereafter—despite the canny recycling of his elaborate studio set—the film becomes increasingly schematic and dull.

[. . .]

The Holy Mountain was finished in the nick of time for the 1973 Cannes Film Festival, where it was eagerly anticipated but, for the most part, coolly received. Marco Ferreri's *La Grande Bouffe*—a grotesque comedy in which a segment of the bourgeoisie literally eats itself to death—was the festival's *succès de scandale*, and Klein picked up its American rights. Meanwhile, Jodorowsky trimmed twenty minutes from *The Holy Mountain* (eliminating as much dialogue as he could) and both films were scheduled to open in New York that fall. Klein was uncertain about *The Holy Mountain*'s prospects, but he had great hopes for *La Grande Bouffe*. Burned by its subsequent failure and determined, he says, to "protect" Jodorowsky from the critics, Klein restricted *The Holy Mountain*'s New York run to Friday and Saturday midnights at the Waverly Theater. (Elsewhere, the film was released as a double bill with *El Topo*. In a few key markets, notably Los Angeles, it was not released at all.) But, despite Klein's disappointment, *The Holy Mountain* cannot be considered a failure— at least as a midnight movie. After premiering at the Waverly on November 29, 1973, it played the theater continuously for the next sixteen months, through the first week of April 1975.

In a sense, the final scene of *The Holy Mountain*, which evidently disconcerted many of Jodorowsky's followers with its mixture of "Mr. Natural" and Marcel Duchamp, proved prophetic of his subsequent career. However unwillingly, the director did pass from cinema back into life. After finishing *The Holy Mountain*, Jodorowsky had hoped to make *Mr. Blood and Miss Bones*, a "pirate film" for children. But Klein was not interested in bankrolling a PG-rated film and instead proposed that Jodorowsky adapt Pauline Réage's notorious paean to female masochism, *The Story of O*. The project (which Kenneth Anger had unsuccessfully hoped to realize in Paris a decade and a half before) was ultimately rejected by Jodorowsky because—according to Klein—the director felt it was too commercial.

[. . .]

Jodorowsky did complete one other film during the 1970s, a French production, *Tusk*, described in a *Variety* item as "a G-rated epic about the entwined fate of an English girl and a rogue elephant born in India on the same day." Shot completely in the south Indian state of Karnataka at a cost of $5 million, the movie featured 110 pachyderms. India reminded Jodorowsky of Mexico: "Almost the same climate, almost the same food. . . . I ate only elephant food for four months." *Tusk* was scheduled to open in the United States during the summer of 1980. It never has. *Variety* reviewed it that year at Filmex, the Los Angeles film festival, as "a two-ton turkey . . . grandiose, pretentiously simple, tonally inconsistent"—and warned that "turgid b.o. looms." Allen Klein, who had no more than a friendly interest in the film, considers it "unreleasable."

As of this writing, Jodorowsky's American reputation has evaporated along with the counterculture that nourished it. Even *El Topo* has lapsed into obscurity—in part because of Klein's stipulation that the film be booked with *The Holy Mountain*. According to Jodorowsky's first American prophet, Ben Barenholtz, *El Topo* "was strictly a product of the '60s. It wouldn't make a dime today." But Klein is not so sure. More than eleven years after *El Topo* first emptied Elaine's, he is still toying with the idea of rereleasing it in a dubbed English version: "I might go back to the Waverly yet," he muses, raising the spectre of midnight nostalgia.

3.2

Playing with genre: An introduction to the Italian *giallo*

by Gary Needham

Over the last decade, Italian splatter cinema has become a favoured object of study for cult film scholars, with a number of prominent accounts detailing its deviant deviations in film style and gender representation. However, these accounts have largely been restricted to the study of specific cult auteurs (such as Dario Argento or Lucio Fulci) or trash icons (such as Barbara Steele or Giovanni Lombardo Radice). In his article, Gary Needham considers one of the most influential genres of Italian cult film: the *giallo*. The format (developed from Italian derivations of imported classical detective fictions) is discussed by the author in both its literary and cinematic versions before considering a number of key features behind this influential Italian cycle. For instance, Needham situates the two specific periods of the cinematic *giallo* (1962–6, 1970–7) alongside postwar changes in Italian culture, where mobility, emancipation and urban enfranchisement were often coded through the cinematic signifiers of travel and transcultural exploration. However, the author also suggests that the motif of travel in the cycle not only reflects seventies' signs of sophistication, but also reflects back upon Italy's colonial past, by fusing a duel investigative/tourist gaze at the non-European locales that are often featured in the *gialli*'s transatlantic drive. Noting the *gialli*'s emphasis on sadosexual motifs of mayhem, the author also identifies a psychoanalytic dimension to the format, with the return of repressed desires being consistently evidenced as motivations for the killer's quest, while the format frequently features psychoanalysts as either heroes or aides to the investigation under review. In so doing, this article offers a long overdue consideration of this key national tradition of cult cinematic splatter.

A note on the extract: this article was first published in the online journal *Kinoeye* 2(11). The original article included an additional brief section on literary antecedents of the *giallo*.

Genre issues

In 1929, the Milanese Publishing giant Mondadori launched a line of books in yellow covers, hence *giallo*—the Italian word for yellow—as part of a large campaign to promote, specifically, tales of mystery and detection. These works consisted primarily of imported translations of British "rational-deduction" fictions of the Sherlock Holmes variety and the early twentieth century American quasi-fantastic murder mysteries built on the Edgar Allan Poe model.

Before 1929, the notion of the detective was something unknown to the Italians, but that isn't to say that works of detection, mystery and investigation were not in circulation; rather those sorts of fictions were to be found under the banner of adventure. The publication of *gialli* increased throughout the 1930s and 40s, however the importation and translation of the 1940s "hard-boiled" detective fictions from the US were prohibited from publication outright by Mussolini on the grounds that their corrupting influence and glamorisation of crime would negatively influence "weak-minded" Italians.

It wasn't long before Italian authors began writing under anglicised pseudonyms their own *gialli* based on the early British and American models of rational thought and logical deduction. Only after the war did a truly Italian form of the fiction began to emerge, principally in the work of Leonardo Sciascia. Not only did Sciascia write his own important *gialli* (including *Il giorno della civetta* [*The Day of the Crow*] and *A ciascuno il suo* [*To Each His Own*]); he also published two polemical articles in the 1950s on the specificity of the Italian *giallo* and its need to be taken seriously by Italian intellectuals, particularly those on the left influenced by Gramsci. Today, *gialli* continue to be written by Italians, Umberto Eco's *Il nome della rosa* (*The Name of the Rose*) in 1984 being the most famous and prestigious outside of Italy. There are also numerous translations into Italian of novelists such as Thomas Harris, Patricia Cornwell, et al.

However, it is the cinematic *giallo* that concerns us here and it emerges during the "Golden Age" of Italian cinema in the early 1960s. One interesting point about the *giallo* in its cinematic form is that it appears to be less fixed as a genre than its written counterpart. The term itself doesn't indicate, as genres often do, an essence, a description or a feeling. It functions in a more peculiar and flexible manner as a conceptual category with highly moveable and permeable boundaries that shift around from year to year to include outright gothic horror (*La lama nel corpo* [*The Murder Clinic*, Emilio Scardimaglia, 1966]), police procedurals (*Milano, morte sospetta di una minorenne* [Sergio Martino, 1975]), crime melodrama (*Così dolce, così perversa* [*So Sweet So Perverse*, Umberto Lenzi, 1969]) and conspiracy films (*Terza ipotesi su un casa di perfetta strategia criminale* [*Who Killed the Prosecutor and Why?*, Giuseppe Vari, 1972]).

It should be understood then that the *giallo* is something different to that which is conventionally analysed as a genre. The Italians have the word *filone*, which is often used to refer to both genres and cycles as well as to currents and trends. This points to the limitations of genre theory built primarily on American film genres but also to the need for redefinition concerning how other popular film-producing nations understand and relate to their products. This introduction to the *giallo*, therefore, begins from the assumption that the *giallo* is not so much a genre, as its literary history might indicate, but a body of films that resists generic definition. In this respect it is unlike the Italian horror and *poliziotto* (police) genres yet, at the same time, the *giallo* can be understood as an object to be promoted, criticised, studied, etc.

By its very nature the *giallo* challenges our assumptions about how non-Hollywood films should be classified, going beyond the sort of Anglo-American taxonomic imaginary that "fixes" genre both in film criticism and the film industry in order to designate something specific. As alluded to above, however, despite the *giallo*'s resistance to clear definition there are nevertheless identifiable thematic and stylistic tropes. There is a stereotypical *giallo* and the *giallo*-fan has his or her idea of what constitutes the *giallo* canon. The following points therefore, are an attempt to clarify and define familiar aspects of this "canon."

Early efforts

In 1963, Mario Bava directed the first true Italian *giallo: La ragazza che sapeva troppo* (*The Girl Who Knew Too Much*). It can be argued that the Italian *giallo* pre-dates Bava's film, as the term has frequently been used to associate Luchino Visconti's *Ossessione* (1943) with the tradition. However, the reason why Bava's film is the "true" starting point of the *giallo* is its explicit and successful attempt to say to the spectator, in effect, "The Italian *giallo* has arrived."

The opening sequence has Nora Davis (Letícia Roman) reading a *giallo* novel on an airplane. The entire scene is essentially a foundational gesture that brings together several elements all at once: the staging of the *giallo*'s literary origins through *mise-en-abîme* (also central to Dario Argento's *Tenebre* [*Unsane*, 1982]); the foreigner coming to/ being in Italy; the obsession with travel and tourism not only as a mark of the newly emerging European jet-set (consider how many *gialli* begin or end in airports), but representative of Italian cinema's selling of its own "Italian-ness" through tourist hotspots (initiated by the murder on the Spanish Steps in Bava's film as well as countless deaths in or around famous squares, fountains and monuments throughout the *giallo*); and of course fashion and style.

I am confident in suggesting that the familiar black raincoat associated with the *giallo* killer stems from continental fashion trends in the 1960s and has since shifted its meaning over the decades to become the *couture* choice of the assassin by default in addition to serving as one of the *giallo*'s most identifiable visual tropes. Bava's *Sei donne per l'assassino* (*Blood and Black Lace*, 1964), set in a fashion house, confirms this observation as the use of a black Macintosh for disguise purposes potentially means it could be any number of the models and, at the same time, situate itself on the pulse of fashion.

Returning to *La ragazza che sapeva troppo*, the American title of the film is *The Evil Eye*, illustrating the *giallo*'s obsession with vision and the *testimone oculare*, or eye-witness. *La ragazza che sapeva troppo* (*The Girl Who Knew Too Much*) might have been called *The Girl Who Saw Too Much*, but that would have betrayed the allusion to Hitchcock in the title. Nora questions the authority of her own witnessing of a murder on the Spanish Steps in Rome. She ends up unconscious and delirious in a hospital, and is subjected to scrutiny by both the police inspector and her doctor—the twin agents of naming sickness and of doubting female testimony.

The hybrid medico-detective discourse is a popular one in the *giallo*. Hallucinations and subjective "visions" are central both to the protagonists and the narrative enigma in *Una lucertola con la pelle di donne* (*Lizard in a Woman's Skin*, Lucio Fulci, 1971) and *Lo strano vizio della signora Wardh* (*Next!*, Sergio Martino, 1971) and are part of the *giallo*'s inherent pathologising of femininity and fascination with "sick" women. Hysterics are in abundance here: films such as *Il coltello di ghiaccio* (*Knife of Ice*, Umberto Lenzi, 1972) and *Tutti i colori del buio* (*They're coming to get you*, Sergio

Martino, 1972) anchor their narratives around the collapse of the "sickness" and mystery, albeit through the conduit of femininity.

The 1960s made a slow but sure inroad for the *giallo* in Italian cinema. The period following 1963's *The Evil Eye* was clearly a mapping out of new territory for Italian directors, not only for the *giallo* but also for the Italian horror film. The early- to mid-60s *giallo* didn't exhibit the strength of other genres of the period such as the western, the horror and the *peplum* ("sword-and-sandal" movie). However, one remarkable thing about the *giallo* is its longevity; even if its presence has been slight at times, it has still spanned over four decades of Italian cinema with the latest Dario Argento film, *Non ho sonno* (*Sleepless*, 2001). Not only does *Sleepless* constitute a return to form for the director, but it signals a revisting of his own debut, *L'Uccello dale piume di cristallo* (*The Bird with the Crystal Plumage*, 1969). Perhaps again the *giallo*'s staying power can be reduced to a resistance of the homogenising constraints that traditional genre membership often imposes on bodies of films by making them fit particular historical and critical categories.

Instead of defining the *giallo* in generic and historical terms, I would like to suggest that we understand it in a more "discusive" fashion, as something constructed out of the various associations, networks, tensions and articulations of Italian cinema's textual and industrial specificity in the post-war period. It happens that the *giallo* revolves around murder, mystery, detection, psychoanalysis, tourism, alienation and investigation. Therefore, I would like to tentatively flag the following issues as a starting point for future study.

Psychoanalysis

The *giallo* literally begs for psychoanalytic inquiry and at the same time stages both the "analytical scene" and the "classic symptoms." As usual, this staging occurs through the conduit of femininity but in some cases—as in (almost) every Dario Argento film—masculinity becomes the focal point. The typical Argento protagonist is the victim/witness of trauma who must keep returning to the scene of the crime (the Freudian "*nachtraglichkeit*" or retranscription of memory; popularly represented via flashback sequences), often committed by a killer who just can't resist serial murder (the psychoanalytic "compulsion to repeat").

L'occhio nel labirinto (*The Eye in the Labyrinth*, Mario Caiano, 1972) is about the murder of a male psychoanalyst by his female patient who confuses him as lover, doctor and father. *L'occhio nel laberinto* also goes so far as to open with a cryptic quote from Borges, from which the film constructs the triple analogy of labyrinth:mind: narrative before structuring the old Freudian war-horse of "woman as mystery." Many of the *giallo*'s female protagonists are either in therapy, have had therapy or are told that they *need* therapy. (The *giallo* queen of psychic discontent has to be Edwige Fenech, whose performances confirm that hysteria is always histrionic when it comes to Italian cinema.)

The *giallo* is a paradigm case in defence of psychoanalysis. It solicits psychoanalytic interpretation and stages every oedipal scenario literally and spectacularly.

Testimone oculare

The Italian term for the eye-witness of a crime. Those who watch their *gialli* in Italian will hear these two words frequently. The *giallo* makes a point about the failings of vision as a source of authority and knowledge. *Il gatto a nove code* (*The Cat O'Nine Tails*, Dario Argento, 1971) goes as far as to create an "aural mystery," a restaging of Alfred Hitchcock's *Rear Window* (1954), including a blind crossword-puzzle maker as one of its detectives.

All sorts of vision/knowledge dynamics are explored in the *giallo*, but never to such great effect as in *L'Uccello dale piume di cristallo*, whose foreigner abroad, *flaneur* Sam Dalmas (Tony Musante), is eye-witness to a knife assault in a chic Roman art gallery. The gallery is explicitly concerned with maximising clarity and vision: the space is minimal so there are no distractions for the gaze other than that of the crime; the doors/façade are enormous glass panels; nothing is obscured; the entire area is brightly lit. However, despite all of these supports aiding Dalmas's vision, he fails to see (or in psychoanalytic terms, he *misrecognises*) the truth of his gaze. Other *gialli* which foreground the eye-witness narrative strand are >Passi di danza su una lama di rasoio (*Death Carries a Cane*, Maurizio Pradeaux, 1972) and, of course, *La ragazza che sapeva troppo*.

Quite related to the theme of eye-witnesses and unreliable sight—and in the spirit of Carol Clover—are the numerous incidents of violence done to the eyes (including those in *Gatti rossi in un labirinto di vetro* [*Eyeball*, Umberto Lenzi 1974] and *Opera* [Dario Argento, 1988]) and the generous amount of titles with "*gli occhi*" in them, whether this refers to the eyes of detectives, victims, killers or cats (eg, *I gatto dagli occhi di giada* [*The Cat's Victim*, Antonio Bido, 1977] and *Gli occhi freddi della paura* [*Cold Eyes of Fear*, Enzo Girolami Castellari, 1971]). The *giallo* eye is both penetrating and penetrated.

[. . .]

Camp

While many *giallo* viewers await the ubiquitous Susan Scott's next undressing scene, many many others are waiting to see her next fabulous outfit. Such is the *giallo* that it panders to both readings: erotic anticipation and camp sensibility. The *giallo* is a document of 60s and 70s style that years later can be seen as utterly camp. Even the most tired of *gialli* is capable of being resurrected as a "masterpiece," thanks to Alexander Doty's example of making things queer and wardrobe departments whose creativity and expression at times exceeds that of the director.

How many *gialli* are set in and around fashion houses and photographers' studios? *Sei donne per l'assassino, Nude per l'assassino* (*Strip Nude for your Killer*, Andrea Bianchi, 1975) and *La dama rosa uccide a sette volte* (*The Red Queen Kills Seven Times*, Emilio P Miraglia, 1972), just to name a few. How many of the *gialli*'s victims are fashion models?

The literary

Referring back to the *giallo*'s origins in the 1930s with the translations of British and early American murder mysteries, it appears that the cinematic *giallo* has never quite forgotten its debt to the literary. The most explicit examples include the staging of the *giallo* book as an object in *La ragazza che sapeva troppo* and the author/reader of the *giallo* as central to the narrative in *Unsane*. In the latter film, Peter Neal (Antonio Franciosca) is an American *gialli* author, and Giuliano Gemma's detective is an avid reader of Sherlock Holmes stories who even quotes what is perhaps the mantra of the *giallo*'s dénouement: "Whatever remains, however improbable, must be truth" (from Arthur Conan Doyle's *The Hound of the Baskervilles*).

Although uncredited, Agatha Christie is the main source of inspiration and imitation for *Concerto per un pistola* (*The Weekend Murders*, Michele Lupo, 1970) and *Cinque bambole per la luna d'agostso* (*Five Dolls for an August Moon*, Mario Bava, 1970). Edgar Allan Poe is also represented in *gialli* such as *Sette note in nero* (*The Psychic*, Lucio Fulci, 1977), not to mention Argento's ineffectual cut-and-paste of Poe's world in the "black cat" episode of *Due occhi diabolici* (*Two Evil Eyes*, Dario Argento and George Romero, 1990).

The postcolonial question

Travel, tourism, exoticism, hybridity and foreignness are all familiar features of the *giallo*. The textuality of Italian cinema after the 1950s has many features that seem to open up queries problematising the concept of a national film movement and a national identity. The main protagonist of the *giallo* is often the foreigner in Italy or the Italian on holiday. "Exotic locations" include Scotland (*L'iguana dalla lingue di fuoco* [*The Iguana with a Tongue of Fire*, Riccardo Freda, 1971]), Haiti (*Al tropico del cancro* [*Death in Haiti*, Edoardo Mulargia, 1972]) and Africa (*L'uomo più velonosa del cobra* [*Human Cobras*, Bitto Albertini, 1971]). Characters don't seem fixed to a home or location; they are always (in) between different places. This justifies the advertisements for various transatlantic airlines that bookend the *giallo*, not to mention the promos for every traveller's favourite drink—a J&B whisky. This must be the most plugged product in the history of European Cinema. Look out for it.

When the *giallo* is set in Italy it typically takes one of three different routes. Sometimes it promotes "Italian-ness" through a foregrounding of identifiable tourist spots that often halt the narrative and serve as sheer spectacle. Other times it strives to erase Italian-ness by establishing the setting as an (other) anonymous European city, avoiding distinctive signifiers of Italy altogether. And still other times it constructs a "rural-historical" locale as a place of the uncanny, as in *La casa dale finestre che ridono* (*The House with the Windows that Laugh*, Pupi Avati, 1976).

Italian popular cinema tends to promote the non-national, and this variably results in a tendency to exaggerate and exploit the "foreign" through the tropes of travel and the tourist's gaze. Ugo Liberatore's *Incontro d'amore a Bali* (1969) and the *Black Emanuelle* series (1975–83) instigated a whole *filone* of soft-porn desert island and globe-trotting adventure films, fueling what Anne McClintock calls the "porno-tropics", and which in turn influenced the direction of the *giallo* towards a more pan-exotic exploration of mystery, detection and murder to sustain the public's interest and changing tastes.

Conclusion

The *giallo* is quite difficult to pin down as a body of films. Criticism tends to gather around auteur directors or singular examples. However, if we can understand the *giallo* discursively, we may begin to make interesting connections between its textual, industrial and cultural features. Such a strategy would allow us to open the *giallo* up rather than close it down. One final note specifies the *giallo*'s discursive potential in everyday criticism. A recent Japanese animated feature, *Perfect Blue* (Satoshi Kon, 1997) was referred to as an animated Japanese *giallo*. There is also a frequent and longstanding tradition of appropriating Spanish (*Una libelua para cada muerto* [*A Dragonfly for Each Corpse*, Leon Klimovsky, 1974]), Belgian (*Die Potloodmoorden* [*The Pencil Murders*, Guy Lee Thys, 1982]), Japanese, French and Dutch films for inclusion in the *gialli* tradition.

3.3

Han's Island revisited: *Enter the Dragon* as transnational cult film

by Leon Hunt

Although Hong Kong cult cinema retains a contemporary international appeal, courtesy of action stars such as Jackie Chan and Jet Li, it is the transnational status of seventies Kung Fu cinema which Leon Hunt considers in his chapter 'Han's Island revisited'. Here, he offers a star study of the late cult icon Bruce Lee, as well as accounting for the contested status of his breakthrough movie *Enter the Dragon* (1973). Although this Hong Kong/US production helped high kick the kung fu craze that was sweeping the West during the early to mid 1970s, the film has often been seen as an inauthentic example of Chinese action cinema, which contains a number of cultural and racial contradictions. If *Enter the Dragon* does retain a contradictory cultural message, then these tensions seem embodied in the film's location, revealed to be an island of questionable geographical and national authenticity. Moreover, for theorists of Chinese cinema, *Enter the Dragon* actually downgrades Lee's central billing to reinforce some oriental stereotypes that exist within the colonial imagination. Indeed, the author points to a number of scenes where Lee 'performs' before an authoritative and apparently controlling Western male gaze as evidence of this perspective. While the author does concede that the film eschews much of the martial arts philosophy found in earlier incarnations of kung fu cinema, Hunt calls for a more dialogic understanding of 'colonizer and colonized' that the film seems to embody. Rather than viewing *Enter the Dragon* as a cult aberration, he notes that a transnational ethic remains a longstanding construction within Chinese cinema and that Lee's star status allows for some crucial interventions into this contested cult classic.

A note on the extract: this chapter was originally published in 2000 in the anthology *Unruly Pleasures: The Cult Film and its Critics*. The original version of the chapter contained a slightly longer account of Chinese cinema in the light of wider debates around postcolonialism and national film traditions. This original version also contained an extended account questioning *Enter the Dragon*'s ethnic representations as derived from the Sax Rohmer tradition.

"This 'unique' dragon (the Chinese, the spiritual, etc.) is not one of those Won Ton Kung Fu flicks from H.K. . . . (the title) 'Enter the Dragon' suggests the emergence (the entrance) of someone (a personality) that is of quality."

Bruce Lee

Hong Kong in action

For fans of 'Hong Kong action', 1998 was a key year. Jackie Chan, the biggest star in Asia, finally 'arrived' in Hollywood with the Top 10 hit *Rush Hour* (Brett Ratner, US 1998). Chow Yun Fat and Jet Li made Hollywood debuts in *The Replacement Killers* (Antoine Fuqua, US 1998) and *Lethal Weapon 4* (Richard Donner, US 1998), respectively; Michelle Yeoh had just beaten them to it as a 'Bond Girl' in *Tomorrow Never Dies* (Roger Spottiswoode, US/UK 1997). But for an older generation of fans, the restoration of Bruce Lee's *Enter the Dragon* (Robert Clouse, HK/US 1973) was the key event, and a reminder of an earlier 'crossover', from cult to mainstream, from East to West. While *The Replacement Killers* has been described as "a film which competently integrates the best levels of American and Hong Kong action cinema . . . an example of an original transnational film", *Enter the Dragon* was arguably the first transnational Chinese-American action film.

Enter the Dragon takes place on an island – Han's Island was mooted as a title – an island, appropriately, of uncertain nationality. At one level, this seems like a reference to Hong Kong, given that Han's Island rests partly in British waters. But what Hong Kong and *Enter the Dragon* share is a similar sense of hybridity, of uncertain owner-ship and cultural affiliation. The film is most frequently damned as inauthentic, neither one thing nor the other – too cheap and tacky for Hollywood, too cynical and prepackaged for Hong Kong. According to Stephen Teo, its "Chineseness . . . does not integrate well with the Western sense of narrative decorum", as though this hybridity was doomed from the start. Tony Rayns, meanwhile, represents the orthodox view that it attempts to "crossbreed a Sax Rohmer revival . . . with the most thoroughly discredited aspects of the James Bond ethic", later concluding that it was "better forgotten". *Enter the Dragon* has, of course, not been forgotten – it's a key reference point for kung fu/'China'/Hong Kong imprinting themselves on the western popular imaginary. Moreover, the gleeful hybridity of recent Hong Kong cinema – Kevin Costner's *The Bodyguard* (Mick Jackson, US 1992), remixed to accommodate Jet Li's kung fu skills, becomes *Bodyguard From Beijing* (Yuen Kwai, HK 1994), for example – does much to problematise these lurking implications of 'pure' national cinemas. Nevertheless, the film's enduring appeal seems a pre-dominantly Western (and Japanese) phenomenon. It was less successful in Hong Kong than early Lee films like *Fist of Fury* (Lo Wei, HK 1972) and *Way of the Dragon* (Bruce Lee, HK 1972). "Rarely, if ever," Bey Logan suggests, "has one film with one star loomed like such a colossus over a genre", but he admits that the com-parison is with other American Martial Arts films. Elsewhere, he acknowledges that Lee's long term influence on Hong Kong cinema was "negligible" and that the "big Chinese hits released the year after his death . . . look pretty much as they would had Bruce never returned to Hong Kong". I do want to suggest, however, both that there's rather more 'Hong Kong cinema' in *Enter* than tends to be acknowledged and that, in any case, Western fans (who may also include diasporic Chinese) have some right to Bruce Lee's crossover film – Lee was himself a transnational, trans-Pacific. If *Enter* is heavily contested – breakthrough or sellout? – that's because Lee is, too.

Director Robert Clouse rather notoriously claimed that he had to "kick the strut" out of Lee to make him palatable for international audiences, citing a gesture well known to fans of his Hong Kong films – "he slid his thumb across his nose like they used to do in American gangster movies of the '30s". Chow Yun Fat, too, seems to have been 'de-strutted' for *The Replacement Killers*. But when Clouse extracts his foot from his mouth – a style of kung fu much practiced by Western film-makers – he describes "the new Bruce Lee" as a "mosaic". He has clothes, in particular, in mind – a combination of "beautiful silk Chinese suits" and ('70s fashions permitting) sharp western tailoring (shades of the debonair Chow). If this suggests a rather culturally polarised wardrobe, one might also mention the tight, black jump-suit Lee wears in the underground cavern scenes which suggests a less geographically overdetermined generic space.

Blurring the boundaries of cult status

In Sheldon Hsiao-peng Lu's anthology *Transnational Chinese Cinemas*, transnationalism describes not only the way contemporary global capitalism operates, but the blurring of national cinematic boundaries through international markets, foreign investment and co-productions. Lu demonstrates that Chinese cinemas were transnational from the start – the first Chinese feature, *The Difficult Couple* (1913), was made by a US company based in China and there were abortive plans in the 1930s to build an 'Oriental Hollywood' in Shanghai. This scenario is now much more pronounced, both because of the tripartite terrain of 'Chinese cinema' (Mainland, Hong Kong, Taiwan) and because all three are part of the global market. In addition, Hong Kong and other émigrés are creating a "nascent Chinese American film . . . a transpacific, transnational Chinese film culture". The book includes persuasive accounts of both John Woo and Jackie Chan as transnational Chinese figures, but Lee is little more than a footnote, despite the fact that he anticipates both men. Like Chan, Lee was employed as a performer of action; like Woo, he was employed as an orchestrator of action – he choreographed (some might say directed) the fight scenes in *Enter the Dragon*. Like Chan (but unlike Woo), Lee brought other Chinese talent into his 'crossover' film – eagle-eyed aficionados like to spot Chan himself, Samo Hung, Yuen Biao, Yuen Wah (Lee's acrobatic stunt double) and Lam Ching-ying amongst *Enter*'s stunt team.

The film was a co-production between Warners' subsidiary Sequoia and Golden Harvest's Concorde (Lee and Raymond Chow), written and directed by Americans with a predominantly Chinese crew – it's Lee's input on script and direction which partially qualifies this distinction between primary (American) and secondary (Chinese) labour. Warner Brothers were the prime movers in the western incorporation of kung fu, and of Lee, who had already had a less than happy experience with them over what was to become *Kung Fu* (ABC 1972–5). More importantly, Warners had picked up Shaw Brothers' *King Boxer/Five Fingers of Death* (Cheng Chang-Ho, HK 1972) for distribution and had an unexpected hit with it (the film outgrossed the first two Lee films in Britain and the US). Clouse attributes this initiative to Warners' head of Asian distribution, Richard Ma, who had spotted an Orientalist fad in the making with Nixon's visit to China and the popularity of Chinese food. *Enter*, it seems, was partly a way of squeezing Run Run Shaw out of any further deals, but there's also a sense of 'conquering' the genre just as martial arts had come to the West via American excursions into South-East Asia.

Even so, the signs of caution were visible – Rayns refers sniffily to "American 'stars' of the calibre of John Saxon", and his equal billing with Lee gives us some sense of what Warners thought of their Chinese leading man. Nevertheless, Saxon is an interesting transnational figure in his own right, as fans of Italian exploitation would no doubt testify – a minor character actor at best in the US, Saxon has often shone for directors like Mario Bava, Dario Argento and Antonio Margheriti. Add a touch of blaxploitation in the irresistible figure of Jim Kelly ("I'll be too busy lookin' good!") and it's little wonder that *Enter* is one of the quintessential cult films. This second-guessing of different audiences now seems very modern and astute. Lalo Schifrin's score joins the trans-generic dots, deploying blaxploitation motifs (wah-wah guitar) alongside echoes of his own *Mission Impossible* score and the sort of 'Oriental' themes only found in the West. Hong Kong soundtracks did their 'sampling' rather more directly, mixing snatches of, say, Isaac Hayes' *Theme From Shaft* with selected Morricone or John Barry. Kung fu has remained central to the hip-hop soundscape, from Wu Tang Clan samples to the 'shapes' thrown on the dance floor.

Enter the Dragon was the most successful of Hong Kong's international co-productions, but it wasn't the only one. [. . .] *The Man From Hong Kong* (Brian Trenchard-Smith and Wang Yu, HK/Australia 1975) anticipates kung fu's Eighties excursions into gritty urban thrillers and has impressive choreography by Samo Hung. *The Legend of the Seven Golden Vampires* (Roy Ward Baker, HK/GB 1974), a co-production between Shaw Brothers and Hammer Films, also has impressive choreographic credentials – Lau Kar Leung and Tang Chia – and provides a particularly illuminating comparison with *Enter the Dragon*.

Kitsch, comics and comparisons

Enter the Dragon has Vietnam at least partly on its mind – its two American heroes are vets, the narrative 'goal' is the securing of an island of uncertain territorial ownership and neither Saxon nor Kelly fully grasp the codes or agendas underlining the struggle. *The Legend of the Seven Golden Vampires* is more overtly colonialist. The film opens with a marvellous representation of two genres merging. Kah, High Priest of the Seven Golden Vampires, travels from China to Transylvania to seek the aid of Dracula in restoring the cult to its former glory. The Count is uncooperative by nature but tired of languishing in "this miserable place", and so he 'possesses' Kah's body and leaves for China. Thereafter, Kah speaks with Dracula's voice, but a flamboyant gesture is accompanied by an unmistakable 'swish' on the soundtrack to represent these two genres inhabiting one body. Subsequently, however, the film is about two white Europeans – Dracula and Peter Cushing's Van Helsing – performing a kind of mythological colonization. We first meet Van Helsing as he delivers a lecture on ancient Chinese legends to a frankly sceptical audience at Chungking University. Naturally, the Prof knows better. As he travels into the cursed village of Ping Kwei, he experiences a "been here before feeling", an anticipation of what's around the next corner – in other words, for this colonizer of the Orient's imaginary, China's mysteries are already 'known'. Van Helsing teams up with Hsu Tien-an, his brothers and his sister (Shih Szu). "My brothers would die in your defence," Hsu Tien-an promises Van Helsing rather unwisely, because that's pretty much what transpires. Kung fu is explicitly played out as a spectacle for a (diegetic) white Western gaze – "It was the most fantastic display – I've never seen anything like it," Van Helsing tells Chiang rather condescendingly after one battle. *Enter the Dragon* seems to begin similarly – Lee 'performs' for the gaze of British emissary Braithwaite, who arrives at the Shaolin Temple to employ him. But at least Lee has his own agendas – when Braithwaite says that "we" would like him to attend Han's tournament, Lee replies sardonically, "We, Mr Braithwaite?"

Lee plays a (former?) Shaolin monk employed to take part in a martial arts tournament while gathering information on a heroin and prostitution ring on a secluded island – the island's mastermind is Mr Han (Shek Kin), a renegade Shaolin. Lee is one of three heroes, but the only one with clearly defined goals – revenge (Han is indirectly responsible for his sister's death), honour (less clear in the 'unrestored' version) and what is usually seen as a colonial/colonised policing of the 'Orient'. Roper (Saxon) is a gambler, a devil-may-care, white American smoothie – he arrives with dozens of suitcases, all of them presumably containing polo-neck sweaters. Williams's (Kelly's) hair puts the 'afro' into Afro-American – he's defined through Black Power and Hendrix posters, hassles with racist cops, an inexhaustible sexual appetite, plenty of 'strut' and most of the best lines. The tournament proceeds; Lee gathers evidence. In his first bout, he's pitted against his sister's killer, Oharra (Bob Wall, Lee's favourite punchbag), and takes the opportunity to humiliate and then kill him. Han mistakes Williams for the island prowler and kills him, using one of a selection of deadly artificial hands – he's rather more taken with Roper and offers him a job. As Roper seemingly wavers, Lee works his way through the island caverns and numerous guards before being captured. Roper refuses to fight Lee and they team up against more of Han's guards. Han tries out some more of his lethal hands – a bear claw and a hand of knives – but the wounds just make Lee more photogenic. Only a hall of mirrors delays Han's defeat and he's left impaled on a spear.

"Man, you come right out of a comic book!" Kelly says to Han – oh, how the reviewers jumped on that line! – and he's almost right. But, as most writers point out, Sax Rohmer and Ian Fleming got there first. At one level, it's almost as though the price of Lee embodying the Chinese Superman – he'd never been so invincible before – was a Yellow Peril villain. It's more likely, though, that the film had to work with some of the representations it already knew – representations which still had some mythic power. Rohmer's *Fu Manchu* novels had been reprinted by Pyramid books in the US in the 1960s, and their success was a factor in Harry Alan Towers' series of films starring Christopher Lee (1965–8). Marvel Comics had made a deal with Rohmer's estate to base a comic around the character, but were initially unable to find a suitable format. The kung fu 'craze' evidently provided the impetus for such a format, because in December 1973, *Special Marvel Edition* number 15 featured Fu Manchu's oedipally heroic son, Shang Chi, Master of Kung Fu. Shang Chi was a hit – by issue 17, the comic was retitled *Master of Kung Fu* and ran continuously until 1983. Its most immediate influences were Bond, *Nick Fury Agent of S.H.I.E.L.D.* and *Where Eagles Dare*, but by issue 31, *Enter the Dragon* was exerting a visible influence – island fortresses, international drug rackets, whirling nunchakus and a bare-chested, pouting hero. Like his TV counterpart, David Carradine's Kwai Chang Caine, Shang Chi was of mixed race – also a recurring device in American kung fu paperbacks – and portrayed as a lethal, philosophically-minded hippy (he later developed an alarming taste for Fleetwood Mac). Trained in seclusion – like an inverted Shaolin Temple – Shang Chi is initially his father's assassin. But Nayland Smith 'turns' him, and, like Lee, he defects to the British secret service.

[. . .]

Fu Manchu was already a nostalgic figure when he first appeared in 1913 – Nayland Smith first set eyes on him in 1911, the year Sun Yat Sen saw off the Quing Dynasty for good. What seems to be going on in the early '70s – against the backdrop of Nixon and Vietnam – is a renegotiation of what 'Chinese culture' signified in the west, a resetting of boundaries around who could be incorporated (martial artists, 'mystics') and who couldn't ('inscrutable' hardliners – i.e. communists). Western kung fu heroes were positioned between races, like Caine and Shang Chi, or between cultures, like Lee. But kung fu itself could easily inhabit the same cultural imaginary as the Yellow Peril – an excess of civilisation and culture, a decadent refinement of violence.

[. . .]

Eastern west

Both the '70s and the '90s Hong Kong crossovers were preceded by dubbed exports. In the '70s, such exports constituted an entire cycle, but more recently, it was New Line's unexpected success with a dubbed, re-edited *Rumble in the Bronx* (Stanley Tong, HK 1995) which created a space once more for Chinese action stars in the US. Tony Rayns has likened the film to *Way of the Dragon* (Bruce Lee, HK 1972) – "naive Hong Kong boy travels abroad to visit relatives and tangles with local gang" – while noting that Jackie Chan's "stance is far more populist and far less Chinese-chauvinist than Lee's". Chan, as both Rayns and Fore note, has for some time been an transnational figure – his characters and films favour international locales – and yet his blend of comedy and action took longer to catch on in the West than Lee's superheroic persona. Chan's low-key 'patriotism' implicitly authenticates him for Rayns as a modern Hong Kong star – someone who represents a more complex sense of belonging than simply being 'Chinese'. Yet *Enter*'s lack of Chinese-patriotism is often taken as a sign of its inauthenticity, an 'emasculation' which represents "the West's antipathy towards Lee's nationalism".

Two things happen to Lee's ethnic populism in the film. On the one hand, it is pushed down in the mix – he defends the Chinese workers against a gwailo bully on the junk to Han's island, but significantly without landing a punch ("the art of fighting without fighting"). But ethnic pride is displaced most visibly onto Williams – Hollywood had a generic model for representing black (male) pride, and Warners were shrewd in gauging the demographics of kung fu's Western audience. But as Lee's patronising reference to "Won Ton Kung Fu flicks" suggests, his sense of belonging, too, was contradictory. Even his fighting was "neither wholly foreign nor wholly Chinese . . . very international". Lee bit, scratched and grappled, combined graceful traditional moves with western boxing and street fighting. His image as

Super-Patriot rests largely on *Fist of Fury*'s Japan-bashing, although Abbas suggests that the film's anticolonialism was already slightly quaint, "as if Bruce Lee were fighting again in a new Boxer Rebellion through the medium of cinema, in much the same way that Hollywood refought the Vietnam War". *Way of the Dragon* – Lee's most popular film in Hong Kong, but the last to reach the west (comedy again?) – softens this xenophobia. Lee beats the western heavies with "Chinese boxing", but cautions his friends against dismissing "foreign fighting". It isn't Chinese boxing which defeats Chuck Norris in the Coliseum; rather, Lee's transnational Jeet Kune Do, a fighting style designed to transcend both 'style' and national-cultural tradition. Tang Lung (Lee) is "part bumpkin, part martial arts master-philosopher", and never quite coheres into a unified character. Teo is as troubled by this inconsistency as he is by *Enter*'s alleged co-opting. When he suggests that the bumpkin "is emphasised at the expense of Lee's nationalism", he seems to be longing for a fusion of the latter with the fighter-philosopher. Instead, Tang's move from parochial bumpkin to master fighter is channeled through the international language of his fighting style.

Enter the Dragon doesn't exactly back off from Lee's 'philosophy', even if it finds it equally difficult to consistently square it with generic imperatives. The 'restored' version of the film – in fact, the version originally released in Hong Kong – makes this more apparent. The additional material is a pre-credits conversation between Lee and the head monk about martial arts technique. Even Teo acknowledges that the sequence provides "(Lee's) only chance to expound on the spiritual principles of kung fu".

[. . .]

Enter does seem to have been conceived as more of a 'straight' action film – the 'monk' scene was felt to slow down the action and cut from the western print. Its restoration comes in the wake of a flood of books devoted to Lee's letters, essays, interviews and notebooks. The images of fluidity expounded by his character are familiar to anyone who's read such material: "When the opponent expands, I contract; and when he contracts, I expand. And when the time comes, I do not hit – (holds up his fist) it hits by itself."

I'm not trying to resurrect the auteur here, but authorship does complicate the idea of a western co-opting as well as suggesting that a more international production does seem to have opened a limited space for such material (even if it took twenty five years for the scene to find a Western audience). The scene has other implications, because it gives Lee a dual narrative function, falling as it does in between his opening duel with Samo Hung and his recruitment by Braithwaite. Lee first hears of Han through the head monk, and his mission to "restore the integrity of the Shaolin Temple" inscribes him into the Shaolin legends. But *Enter* is an odd Shaolin film – western representations seem to have fallen for the prelapsarian exoticism of the locale before Hong Kong cinema established its more elaborate myths in the films of Chang Cheh and Lau Kar Leung. Where is this Shaolin Temple supposed to be? China? Hong Kong? And Lee both belongs and doesn't belong there – his black gloves and trunks and '70s hairstyle contrast with the robes and shaven heads of the other monks. The spectacle offered in the opening fight is a mixture of (kick)boxing and grappling, interspersed with Peking Opera-style tumbling. Once again, Lee is a "mosaic", everywhere and nowhere, a mobile transnational signifier.

Lee's death made *Enter the Dragon* seem like a (flawed) culmination of the West's 1970s Eastern romance, rather than a transitional film, harbinger of a crossover which has only now arrived. [. . .] Watching the film with an audience recently was a revelation – the cavern fights were still impossibly thrilling, the audience gasped at the speed of the 'untelegraphed' punches meted out to Oharra and cheered the nunchaku scene usually missing from British prints. In addition, the new stereo soundtrack further amplified the sort of hyperbolic sound effects that could only emanate from a Hong Kong film. That this "*mosaic*" doesn't always hold together adds to rather than detracts from its continuing fascination. That it still retains its following suggests that it addressed its diverse audience rather better than tends to be acknowledged.

3.4

Magical girls and atomic bomb sperm: Japanese animation in America

by Annalee Newitz

While Leon Hunt's account of 1970s kung fu suggests a formative cult film format able to transcend cultural and geographical boundaries, Annalee Newitz considers a more contemporary study of oriental influences of the popular Western imagination. Her study of Japanese animation considers both the differing cycles that comprise the Manga phenomenon, as well as their reception by mixed gender American audiences. Reiterating previous accounts around the subversive nature of subcultural cult formats, Newitz concludes that the perceived male orientation of the Manga format in fact masks an intriguing number of subgenres that includes the high-school romance fantasy, the action adventure narrative as well as the pornographic body horror format. As such, these texts offer a varied range of gender messages that are received differently by Japanese and American adolescent audiences. Whereas Manga retains the status of mainstream entertainment in its domestic setting, it is more fully received as cult object by subcultural American audiences, thus establishing some interesting paradoxes around sexual and national identity. Considering Manga cycles such as the 'magical girl' format, Newitz identifies a motif of male passivity and asexuality that dominates the troubled masculine landscape of the animated texts. These works thus convey a range of contradictory gender messages, from images of female physical power (as in the *Oh! My Goddess!* series) to curious fantasies of transgendered desire (as demonstrated with the transformative hero of *Ranma 1/2*). If, as Newitz suggests, the exotic Otherness of the Manga narrative allows the adolescent American viewer a range of transgressive subject positions, then these fluid gender boundaries are confirmed by more pornographic body horror narratives that comprise other Manga cycles. Here, images of female passivity are often overshadowed by scenes of excessive male bodily transformation. While Newitz's article is relevant for opening up a debate on Manga modes of representation, it also raises the interesting status that the non-Western cult object has in an era of American global media domination, an issue which the author explores in the final sections of her article.

A note on the extract: this article was first published in 1995 in *Film Quarterly* 49(1). The original article included more examples of the 'magical girl' and body horror subgenres, which have been excised for reasons of space. The original article also included a longer consideration of Manga's reflections of US/Japanese historical relations contained in the final sections of the author's account.

In the past few years, there has been a noticeable escalation in the availability of Japanese animated films in America. At my local Blockbuster video store, a new "animation" section was created several months ago which is largely comprised of Japanese animation: one can rent everything from movies like the highly acclaimed *Akira* to a series of videos from popular animated TV shows aired in America such as *Robotech* and *Speed Racer*. Known to fans as *anime*, Japanese animation is available mostly on videocassette or laserdisc, and it is far more than just cartoons for children. Often graphically violent and sexual, *anime* range from comic romances about high school students to pornographic tales of demons whose penises are larger than sky-scrapers. *Anime* can be feature films, OVA (original video animation, or "straight to video" releases), or Japanese television series collected on video. A "Japanese anima-tion festival" on the cable "Sci Fi Channel" introduced American viewers all over the country to popular *anime* such as the satirical film *Project A-ko* and the science fiction series *Dominion: Tank Police*. Furthermore, the past seven years have seen a massive expansion and organization of American fans of Japanese animation; clubs, conven-tions, and fanzines dedicated to *anime* and its fan culture have sprung up on college campuses and in large cities all over the United States.

Small distribution companies in the United States will sometimes make *anime* available to fans who shop at specialty video stores or through catalogues. More often than not, fans get their *anime* from each other: there are networks of fans who use home multimedia technology to subtitle *anime* brought from Japan. Using a software program designed for this purpose, fans transfer *anime* from laserdisc to videotape, editing in the subtitles. Many of the *anime* contain this edited-in subtitle: "Subtitled for fans by fans. Not for sale or rent." I found this on bootlegged tapes and on tapes I rented from a local specialty video store. With a few exceptions, such as the kinds of mainstream videos one can find at Blockbuster or on American television, *anime* are circulated through fan communities, either at conventions or fan clubs. Fans of *anime* in the United States are engaging in what critics such as John Fiske or Constance Penley might call "appropriation." That is, they are transforming Japanese culture for their own uses, which are somewhat different from the uses to which it might be put in Japan. Whereas *anime* are mainstream culture in Japan, in America they are still "alternative culture," particularly when we start talking about the hard-to-find videos. For this reason, American fans enjoy *anime* partly because it allows them to feel as if they have specialized knowledge ordinary Americans do not. On another level, the fans' appropriation of *anime* involves translating and duplicating it so that it is access-ible to a wider audience in the West. This allows them to convert a Japanese product into a uniquely American one. What might be satisfying for Americans about this is that it essentially allows them to "steal" Japanese culture away from Japan. Perhaps this is some form of revenge on a consumer culture which seems to have surpassed their own in its power and complexity?

Animation could be described as just another lucrative Japanese export commod-ity—like high technology or cars—which is consumed avidly by Americans who often feel it is unlike anything available in the West. In 1980–81, exports of Japanese television shows were led by animated programs, which accounted for 56% of total television exports. But what kinds of social issues are involved in the sudden popular-ity of *anime* in America? Certainly, there is a strong possibility that this popularity might be both a result of and a cause for American anxieties about the potency of its national culture in the world. We can look at this anxiety through several critical lenses: by considering how gendered and sexual relations get represented in *anime*, by examining what it means to be a fan of another country's mass culture, and in theorizing how America understands itself in relation to Japanese cultural imperialism. Most importantly, watching *anime* gives Americans a chance to reflect on their own (national) culture in displaced form. Although *anime* does often strike us as utterly different, or "other," it also quite noticeably resembles—and is influenced by—American mass culture and generic narratives. That Americans might be interested in looking at their own culture through Japanese eyes tells us that Americans' feelings about their own culture are deeply bound up with America's evolving relationship with Japan.

Otaku in love

Otaku is the Japanese slang term for people who become particularly loyal fans of a subculture. It is somewhat insulting to be called *otaku*, and it gets translated into English as "fanboy." *Otaku* is a term often used to describe a fan of *anime* subcultures, and he is usually understood to be obsessive, socially inept, or pathetic. I use the pronoun "he" for a reason—while quite racially mixed as a group, *otaku* are overwhelmingly male, particularly in the U.S. For this reason, it is important to understand that what is at stake for Americans watching *anime* is certainly bound up with gender identity, especially masculine identity. What is striking for the scholar of gender and film in the United States, and more generally in the West, is that some genres avidly consumed by American *otaku* are often conceived of as "women's genres" in the West. For instance, one of the most popular *anime* genres is the romantic comedy, which features male point-of-view characters. Aside from the romantic comedy genre, the kinds of generic narratives popular with American fans are more in line with Western expectations about gendered taste preferences: *otaku* enjoy *mecha* (a term used to designate science-fiction or action narratives which focus mostly on technology) and various shades of fantasy-horror. Looking at these three (sometimes overlapping) genres, we can form a fairly complete analysis of gendered and sexual representations in *anime*.

The romantic comedy genre can be characterized by one of its chief subgenres: "magical girls." Magical girls appear in a number of romantic comedies such as *Video Girl Ai*, *Urusei Yatsura*, *Tenchi Muyo*, and *Oh! My Goddess!* All feature young men who have romantic, but non-sexual, relationships with women who possess superhuman powers. These powers might range from preternatural strength to psychic abilities and interdimensional traveling. Ai comes to life out of a videocassette, Lum in *Urusei Yatsura* is an alien, the women in *Tenchi Muyo* are spirits, and Belldandy in *Oh! My Goddess!* is a goddess Keiichi (the college student protagonist) accidentally orders over the phone from the "Goddess Relief Agency." Like American sitcoms of the 1960s such as *Bewitched* and *I Dream of Jeannie*, the magical girl genre features women who are simultaneously powerful and traditionally feminine. Often, jokes center around the mishaps involved in the magical girl's effort to hide her powers so that she may appear demure. The men in these *anime* are young, bewildered, and sexually inexperienced—they are, as one *anime* fan put it to me, the kind of "nice guy" we hope can win the heart of a "special girl" (or a magical girl).

Relationships between characters in the magical girl genre are characterized by slapstick-style encounters which are sexy but innocent, and realistic but fantastical. In *Oh! My Goddess!*, for example, Keiichi is a fairly "realistic" cartoon figure, drawn to appear like an ordinary college freshman. His daily experiences, as well as his friends, are also believable, intended to evoke the kinds of feelings and situations a young adult audience might encounter. Keiichi lives in his college dorm and tries desperately to fit in with a group of slightly older students who mock him about his lack of experience with women. Like an ordinary young man, he studies frantically for exams, goes to the beach, and loves to race his motorcycle. His magical girl Belldandy (the goddess) even arrives in his life in a ludicrously pedestrian manner: trying to order take-out food over the phone, Keiichi accidentally orders a gooddess instead. Belldandy is the one "fantastical" animated figure in the show. She floats; her hair is impossibly long and fluffy; her eyes sparkle constantly; and her body is so perfectly proportioned we cannot help but remember that we are, after all, watching a cartoon. When Belldandy offers Keiichi one wish, he makes the mistake of asking that she remain with him always. This magical stipulation, then, becomes the joke and the romance at the heart of *Oh! My Goddess!* Belldandy, the flagrantly magical figure, must accompany Keiichi everywhere in his incredibly normal life. After getting him kicked out of his (all male) dormitory, Belldandy must find a way to make herself a part of Keiichi's world, and he must do the same for her. Usually they do this by trying—humorously and often unsuccessfully—to hide Belldandy's true nature.

[. . .]

The TV series *Kimagure Orange Road*, which is one of the most popular romantic comedy *anime* with American fans, is a soap opera-type narrative which offers us a glimpse of masculine desire American men see very little of in their own mass culture. Its male point-of-view character wants to fall in love, rather than simply experience sex. Like the magical girl subgenre, many of its basic themes are, for an American audience, somewhat anachronistic. *Kimagure Orange Road* is the story of a "magical boy," a high-school student named Kyousuke who has telekinetic powers (he comes from a family of telekinetics). He falls in love with a young woman named Madoka, who is not magical, but nevertheless is so physically strong that she routinely beats up whole groups of men. Clearly, both characters are slightly fantastical, and this aspect of the narrative is enhanced by the fact that Kyousuke continually has fanciful romantic dreams about wooing, kissing, or simply being near Madoka. He imagines himself with her on the beach at sunset, or watching her play the saxophone. Indeed, the clichéd image of a lonely Madoka playing sad saxophone music is an important, recurring romantic motif in *Kimagure Orange Road*, and sets the tone for much of Kyousuke's romantic longings. In a scene to which fans often refer as a perfect *Kimagure Orange Road* moment, Kyousuke hides while Madoka—who is portrayed as a kind of social outcast—plays the blues on her sax in an empty classroom. It is enough for him simply to be with her, even if she does not realize he is there.

[. . .]

Like *Kimagure Orange Road*, the TV series *Ranma 1/2* is very popular with American fans. However, *Ranma 1/2* is not romantic like *Kimagure Orange Road*, and overtly treats sexual themes bound to arouse heterosexual male discomfort. It concerns another magical boy, Ranma, whose special power is actually called a "curse": when splashed with cold water, he turns into a beautiful, curvaceous girl. His father Genma suffers a similar curse which turns him into a giant panda when he is splashed with cold water. Both return to their "normal" bodies when splashed with hot water. Unlike most romantic comedy *anime*, *Ranma 1/2* features a good deal of nudity and sexualized encounters between Ranma and nearly everyone he knows. A frequent joke revolves around someone squeezing Ranma's breasts in order to "believe" that he has transformed into a female. Ultimately, there is really only one difference between Ranma-the-male and Ranma-the-female besides their gendered bodies: female Ranma has red hair, and male Ranma has black hair. Both wear the same clothes, and both are martial arts experts. But it is clear that becoming female is a problem for Ranma. He is perpetually trying to hide his female half at school; and many of the slapstick routines in the series depict his efforts to avoid being splashed with cold water in public (although at home, Genma is constantly throwing him into a handy pool of water outside).

Ranma 1/2 betrays a number of male fears at the heart of the comedy romance genre, which emerge full-blown in the *mecha* and horror-fantasy *anime* I will discuss in a moment. Quite simply, *Ranma 1/2* demonstrates to the young man who enjoys romantic comedy *anime* that he is constantly in danger of becoming a girl. Because women are associated in these *anime* with passivity, a character like Ranma stands in for male anxieties about losing power or being ridiculed. Indeed, Genma uses Ranma's transformative ability as a way of humiliating and punishing him. "I am so ashamed of you!" Genma yells at one point after turning Ranma into a girl by throwing him in the pool. Like Ranma, the male *anime* fan has a "feminine half" who enjoys passively consuming animated fantasies about love. His attachment to non-sexual romance might be said to feminize him. Especially for the heterosexual male fan who watches *anime* in an American context, this fear would be particularly acute, since American romantic comedies are aimed at a largely female audience. But the American *otaku*'s worries about gender transposition, solicited humorously in *Ranma 1/2*, go beyond a fear that he might be enjoying "women's culture" too much. He is, more importantly, enjoying this culture with other men. American fans consume and discuss *anime* in heavily male-dominated environments.

One of Ranma's biggest problems in the series is Kuno, a young man who has fallen in love with Ranma's female half and constantly asks her out on dates. Ranma-the-male has a nightmare about Kuno kissing him, and is clearly alarmed by Kuno's desire (which is not properly homosexual, since he desires Ranma-the-female, but Ranma nevertheless understands it as such). Furthermore, Ranma's only love interest is the tomboyish Akane, who can beat up all the boys in their high school without batting an eyelid. Akane is an ambiguously gendered character who seems more like a young man than anything else—in fact, Ranma jokes with her that his breasts are larger than hers when he is female. Clearly, one of the issues for young heterosexual men enjoying depictions of male sexual passivity is a fear of becoming bisexual, or even homosexual. Hence, enjoying these *anime* with other men might also be a source of discomfort. Interestingly enough, one of the most popular depictions of Ranma on fan T-shirts and posters is of Ranma-the-female being emphatically feminine in a skimpy bikini, which she rarely (if ever) wears in the show. That is, even within the straight male *otaku* culture, Ranma is consumed as a sex object. Fans are thus put into the unwanted position of identifying with the ambiguous sexual orientation of a character like Kuno, and are therefore understandably nervous about Ranma's male half—precisely because they are somehow attracted to his female half. Keeping Ranma as female as possible in fan culture would certainly help alleviate this nervousness. But however you look at him/her, Ranma represents a kink in the heterosexual *otaku*'s desire.

Multicultural sexuality

While sexuality and explicit representations of intercourse are not the focus of most romantic comedy *anime*, they are foregrounded in the *mecha* and fantasy-horror genres. Often, however, sexuality is coded in certain ways, specifically in the *mecha anime*. A perfect example of this kind of coding occurs in the highly surrealistic live-action film, *Tetsuo the Iron Man*, which has achieved cult status both in Japan and in the United States. While not specifically an *anime*, it deals with a number of *anime* themes, particularly what happens to people who enjoy fan culture too intensely. *Tetsuo the Iron Man* is the story of a *mecha otaku*, a young man named Tetsuo who is gradually converted into a heap of machine parts during the course of the film. His transformation begins when he is hit by a cab, although clearly there is supposed to be a connection between his *otaku*-style obsession with machines and his transformation. The most graphic portions of the film come when he begins turning into "iron man"—he discovers that the flesh of his leg has been torn open by a thick metal cable which originates inside his body. Later, when large portions of his body have been converted into machine parts, his penis turns into a huge industrial drill which he uses to penetrate and kill his girlfriend. Once he has done that, his transformation is complete, and the rest of the film is caught up in a final fight scene between Tetsuo and another iron man. *Tetsuo the Iron Man* is an ironic meditation on popular culture and its *otaku* which tries to make a connection between consuming popular culture and being physically transformed by it: Tetsuo the *mecha otaku* becomes *mecha*. His masculine sexuality is clearly important to this transformation, since his drill penis is nearly the last part of his body to go *mecha*, and performs quite spectacularly when it does. Looking at these images, we have to ask: What kind of sexuality is Tetsuo acting out here? There are really two answers to this question, one having to do with sexuality specifically, and another having to do with why fans consume popular culture.

In the *mecha anime*, *Guyver: Bio-Booster Armor*, we find another example of Tetsuo's form of sexuality. After encountering a piece of alien technology, the young male protagonist in *Guyver* finds himself enveloped in a huge, high-tech suit of armor. While it greatly enhances his physical strength and stature, the "guyver armor" also fuses with him at a biological level: it penetrates his face and body with metal tentacles and causes him excruciating pain. This scene is highly reminiscent of Tetsuo's discovery of the metal cable in his leg. The guyver armor helps its wearer to defeat a monstrous mutant "bionoid," then evaporates. While men who come into contact with this guyver armor experience agony as it first penetrates their bodies, the women who don guyver armor are penetrated vaginally by its metal tentacles, stripped naked, and given what appear to be orgasms as the armor envelops them. Put simply, what hurts men about this human-*mecha* fusion is a source of pleasure and gratification for women.

Furthermore, in terms of female representation, *mecha* is treading the same ground as romantic comedy. There is a subgenre of *mecha* which closely parallels the "magical girl" subgenre. These *mecha*, such as *Bubblegum Crisis, Dominion: Tank Police, Iczer-1*, and *Appleseed*, feature women or female mutants who use guyver-like armor or high-tech ships and motorcycles to fight crime, corruption, or monsters of various types (especially bionoids, which appear in *Bubblegum Crisis* and its spin-off, *AD Police*). Unlike magical girls, however, these women use their power openly, but tend to hide their gender in one way or another. Especially in the series *Bubblegum Crisis*, the team of women are so heavily armored that occasionally a character will marvel, "You're women under there?" What these *anime* demonstrate is the way male and female bodies are largely indistinguishable once wedded to *mecha* technologies.

But at the same time, the male body appears to put up more resistance to *mecha* conversion: after all, Tetsuo's penis is the last part of his body to be mechanized, and the guyver armor suits women far better than men (at least when they merge with it). This brings me back to my original question: What kind of sexuality is this? First of all, this is a kind of sexuality which allows for the creation of new beings. Tetsuo becomes the "iron man"; people in the guyver armor become half-human, half-technological; and the group of women in *Bubblegum Crisis* go from jobs as office girls, shop clerks, and singers to being vigilante cyborg cops chasing down bionoids in Mega-Tokyo. Bodies manipulated by *mecha* science are merged with pieces of technology in order to "give birth" to new creatures. In *All-Purpose Cultural Cat Girl Nuku Nuku*, for example, the main character Ryunosuke gains a "new sister" when his father, the scientist, creates Nuku Nuku out of the body of a robot and the brain of a cat. This is an instance in which childbearing is equated specifically with the merging of technology and biology. Female bodies and sexuality are therefore "best suited" to *mecha*—and male bodies and sexuality are disfigured by it—precisely because it is related to reproduction and giving birth.

Mecha reproduction also involves the co-dependence or synthesis of two radically different orders of being: human and machine. While visible gender difference in *mecha* is downplayed—men and women look the same in armor or spaceships—the differences between human bodies and *mecha* are quite stark. Clearly, these *anime* are telling a story about a very specific form of reproduction, one in which offspring are hybrid beings rather than duplicates of their "parents." This kind of reproduction, which we find in horror-fantasy *anime* as well, often ends up serving as an allegory for the horrors of miscegenation—and, implicitly, the horrors of multiculturalism. Miscegenation is, after all, one sexual corollary to American multiculturalism.

In Japan, a country with a history of isolationism and racism, miscegenation is a source of shame and anxiety. Although miscegenation is also a problem for Americans, United States history is fraught with both miscegenation and its offspring: hence, Americans are at least more familiar (and perhaps slightly more comfortable) with the idea that their culture is a "multiculture." Japanese political and cultural leaders, in general, do not wish to define their culture as "multi" in any way.

Multiculturalism is a concept quite alien to Japanese society, in which non-Japanese people—such as Koreans—face intense discrimination and contempt. Not surprisingly, then, horror-fantasy *anime* tend to represent the merging of separate cultures, realms, or species as socially disruptive. The movie *Vampire Hunter D*, for instance, centers upon a half-vampire character whose goodness is confirmed when he battles to preserve the boundaries between the supernatural and human realms. Although he is himself the product of a vampire-human union, he nevertheless proves his honor by keeping the worlds which produced him as separate as possible.

[. . .]

The OVA series *The Overfiend* offers the most coherent instance of an anti-multicultural bent in *anime*. The Overfiend is a being who has the power to unite the human world with "the demon world" and "the man-beast world," and we discover early on that this power is dangerous because it will lead to chaos, death, and—most horrifically—miscegenation between beings from each world. In fact, one character's vision of the post-Overfiend future depicts a burning city filled with humans copulating quite graphically with beasts and demons. When the Overfiend begins to manifest himself, we discover his power is directly linked to sexual reproduction. Nagumo, the Overfiend's father, first experiences his supernatural powers when engaged in intercourse. His penis becomes so large that it causes his partner's body to explode; then it grows to the point where it bursts out of the roof of the building he is in and destroys the city in a flaming blast of sperm. Watching this animated image, it is clear that his penis has become some kind of atomic bomb. This "atomic blast" sets the stage for the birth of the Overfiend, who will allow the human realm to be invaded by demons and man-beasts.

[. . .]

American *anime* fans—of all racial backgrounds—may be getting pleasure from *anime*'s negative representations of miscegenation and American multiculturalism for reasons surprisingly similar to those of the Japanese audience. That is, Americans may enjoy Japanese *anime* precisely because it criticizes American culture. A fan suggested to me that American audiences are tired of being blamed for the oppression of various minority groups and nations in the world, and respond to these *anime* as a respite from "political correctness" guilt so often talked about in United States mass media. Racist or nationalist sentiment in *anime* might seem refreshing to *anime* fans because it harks back to a less complicated (although more oppressive) series of relations in United States culture. I would also add that *mecha* and horror-fantasy *anime* are probably reassuring to American audiences precisely because they offer representations of traditional masculinity and male culture which are recognizable as such to a Western audience. In the United States, audiences are used to the idea that men enjoy—and are target markets for—movies about "action hero" men, machines, and gory special effects. This is in contrast to the romantic comedy, which is generally seen as a woman's genre in the West. That is, both the gendered and racial implications of these *anime* might elicit the approval of an American audience unhappy with contemporary progressive changes in representations of American identity. Finally, because Japanese *anime* rarely disparage American culture overtly—or unequivocally—American fans can also consume them without necessarily acknowledging their negative American stereotypes.

Textual dependence

What I have been describing, in part, is the way Japanese *anime* take issue with past and present American cultural imperialism in Japan. Allegorical representations of America, and Japanese people who consume American-influenced culture, are often frightening or heavily satiric. What is therefore ironic about Japanese animation fans in America is that they are, in many ways, the first generation of United States citizens to experience cultural imperialism in reverse: that is, they are being colonized by Japanese pop culture, rather then the other way around. One specific instance of this kind of cultural imperialist role-reversal in action came when Disney's "original story" for 1994's *The Lion King* was rumored to be a rip-off of the Japanese animated television series (shown in the U.S. during the early 1960s) called *Simba the White Lion*. Osamu Tezuka, the creator of Simba and Astroboy, is Japan's equivalent of Walt Disney, and his work was in fact inspired by Disney animation. But these days it appears that Disney is taking its inspiration from Japanese animation—certainly a sign that cultural influences are now traveling both ways (if not in a wholly opposite direction).

While we are used to understanding American media culture as imperialist, particularly through its dissemination in the Third World, Jeremy Tunstall has noted that Japan has always been an exception to the rule of what he calls American "media imperialism." Through setting up their own media monopoly and regulating American advertising and entertainment programming imports, Japanese media have remained largely insulated. Looking at the reception of Japanese animation in America, it seems possible that Japanese culture might become a "colonizing" force in other countries, particularly the United States. I make this comment strictly as an observation of what American culture seems to be experiencing, not as an attack on Japanese culture per se.

Gendered and sexual anxieties common to the romantic comedy, *mecha*, and horror-fantasy genres can tell us something about the structure of Japanese cultural imperialism—as an American fantasy and as an economic reality. I suggested before that what makes the romantic comedy *Ranma 1/2* notable is the way it deals explicitly with male fears about becoming feminized *otaku*—particularly in the United States, where romantic comedy is a "woman's genre." This anxiety, however, must be understood in the context of *The Overfiend*'s allegorical representations of miscegenation and imperialism. To explain why the *otaku* is feminized for consuming Japanese animation, and the Overfiend is hypermasculinized because he is associated with imperialism, we must deploy a widely accepted theorem of multicultural feminism: relationships in which women are subordinate to men often stand in for or mirror imperialist relationships in which one country is subordinate to the other. This theorem certainly helps to explain why Ranma is not only feminized, but also associated with China, a country invaded and occupied by Japanese imperialist forces several times during the 20th century. Ranma's "curse" is in fact a Chinese curse, which he got during martial arts training with Genma in China. Moreover, Ranma wears his hair in a queue and his clothing is Chinese; at school, the students often refer to him as "the one in Chinese clothing." Ranma's feminization, in other words, is bound up with his Chinese identification. On the other hand, the Overfiend's ability to cause separate realms to colonize one another—to be an imperialist power—is associated with the deployment of (American) atomic bombs from his penis. One might say that he literally penetrates a Japanese city with his erection, later blowing it up with his ejaculate. What matters here is that these figures bring together feminization with colonization, and masculinity with a colonizing country.

When Americans are *anime otaku*, they are, in a sense, being colonized by Japanese pop culture. Even if they are from Asian racial backgrounds, they are still Americans, and they are rejecting their national culture in favor of another national culture. Furthermore, the act of doing so seems to threaten them with feminization. Here, "feminization" is a way of figuring the kind of disempowerment and dependence a nation experiences when it is colonized. Albert Memmi, in his *The Colonizer and the Colonized*, explains that the attempt to take on or enjoy a colonizing nation's culture is one important way in which the colonized cope with their subordinate status. While he is speaking of direct and coercive forms of colonization, I think we can understand how his points might work within the context of cultural imperialism. Describing the psychology of the colonized, he writes:

> A product manufactured by the colonizer is accepted with confidence. His habits, clothing, food, architecture are closely copied, even if inappropriate. . . . This fit of passion for the colonizer's values would not be suspect, however, if it did not involve such a negative side. . . . The crushing of the colonized is included among the colonizer's values. As soon as the colonized adopts those values, he similarly adopts his own condemnation.

This description reminds us of the way fan culture works, particularly when something about the status of "fan" threatens feminization and disempowerment. The American *anime* fan is deliberately choosing to enjoy a foreign culture which—in this case—often ridicules and belittles his native culture. Elsewhere, Memmi suggests that the relationship between colonizer and colonized is one of dependence—this point goes back to Hegel's famous dialectic of master and slave. I would point out that American fans of Japanese animation are in many ways dependent upon Japan not just for material commodities, but for stories. They are, in other words, dependent upon Japanese culture itself. One might say the American fan has a kind of textual dependence on Japanese culture, the only country which has the power to give him what he wants—a good story. And often, these stories are critical of the fan's national culture as well as threatening to the fan's sense of his own (masculine) power.

[. . .]

Throughout this analysis I have been referring to "culture," and how it generates relationships between individuals and nations. One way culture does this is through ideology, which Louis Althusser has described as the "unity of the real relation and the imaginary relation between [people] and their real conditions of existence." In other words, ideology is one way that people make reality change to suit their imaginations. Let me close with a final example of the way Japanese animation works as a form of ideology specifically aimed at influencing a Western audience. *Anime* feature multiracial casts of characters, many—if not most—of whom are clearly Western. Often lead characters, especially women, have blonde hair and big blue eyes. Some *anime*, such as *Riding Bean*, take place in America—although Bean himself is supposed to be a combination of all the "best races" in the world (what this means is unclear). *Bubblegum Crisis*, with its team of Asian and Caucasian women, takes place in "Mega-Tokyo," a city of the future populated by people of all races in what appear to be equal numbers (unlike contemporary Tokyo). What these *anime* act out is a fantasy in which people of all races and Japanese people are interchangeable. They are imaginary versions of East-West relations which might exist someday, but do not exist yet. While this kind of ideology might seem satisfying and "right" to Americans raised in a multiculture, we must also remember that the Japanese are not multicultural. The ideological implications of these representations are more complex than something like "racial harmony." This multicultural fantasy takes place largely in Japan, and all the races are speaking and being Japanese. What these *anime* suggest is that a very American-looking multiculture is in fact Japanese. And it also suggests that the Japanese are quite aware that part of their target audience for this *anime* is outside Japan, in multicultural America. In a way, these *anime* want to imply that Americans are Japanese. If Americans are already Japanese, then it should be no surprise to any American that Japan, economically speaking, already owns a large portion of the United States.

However, I would not want to end here, without acknowledging that there are implications to the ideology of *anime* which go beyond national interests. In fact, the production and consumption of *anime* within Japan are dramatized in *Otaku no video*, the partly-fictionalized *anime* story of Gainax corporation, a huge *anime* producer in Japan. *Otaku no video* is the tale of two college student *otaku* who form a lucrative company which manufactures "garage kits" (a form of model) related to *anime*. Often, these characters—based on Gainax's employees—are drawn as zany superheroes who call themselves *otakings* and fly. Interspersed throughout this story are live-action "interviews" with Japanese *otaku*, supplemented with fake statistics and graphs about *otaku* culture in Japan. The *otaku* are all "nerds," or people who have no social life. They have office jobs. Often they are supposed to appear slightly crazy, obsessed as they are with taping every new animated show on TV, or dressing up like a favorite *anime* character. One "statistic," which gets elaborated upon in many interviews, claims that 100% of *otaku* are virgins. The young men who form a company to manufacture *otaku* products are animated superheroes (rather than virginal, office worker nerds) precisely because they are producers and not consumers. The Japanese *otaku* consumers here are just as feminized and disempowered as I postulate American *otaku* fear they might be. In other words, the relationship of textual dependency is not necessarily one of colonizing country to colonized country. It is also the relationship of one class to another: wealthy capitalists to lower middle-class consumers.

3.5

The Killer: Cult film and transcultural (mis)reading

by Jinsoo An

As with Newitz, it is a cross-cultural cult focus that dominates Jinsoo An's fascinating study of John Woo's 1989 film. Here, An considers multiple receptions of *The Killer* across the USA and Korea. Rather than reading John Woo's film in terms of 'anxieties' that surround the social and historical status of Hong Kong, the author considers this production as a cult phenomenon, replete with stylistic, representational and generic transgressions. Although the film uses violent action scenes as a mechanism of narrative progression, these set pieces are themselves complicated by the introspective moments of male melodrama that come to define the text. Interestingly, An notices that these elements of emotional excess were either misread or ignored upon the film's initial American release, because they failed to fit with the prevailing precepts that surround codes of behaviour within 'male' action cinema. As the author concludes, while these additional elements of masculine mediation provide *The Killer* with a camp dimension, it is precisely these deviations which have registered with cult viewers. Although An's consideration of the differing American receptions of Woo's cinema is truly interesting, what gives the article additional value to the cult film scholar is the way in which this is linked to a wider transcultural reading of the film. Here, the author considers the Korean reception of Woo's film among the 'mini-theatre', male audience used to marginal film programming. Indeed, An links the success of the film to changing definitions of cult and midnight movies within the Korean context, as well as changing social and industrial factors which provoked an increased interest in Hong Kong action cinema within this domestic context. Importantly, the author also identifies the very same issues of male melodrama that remained an undercurrent to the film's American reception as prominent to Korean viewers, who linked themes of masculine bonding to a wider appreciation of leading actor Chow Yun-fat's star persona. The fact that these fan affiliations also led to an official Korean attempt to provide nationally defined codes of action cinema and action movie star, indicates the degree of cultural exchange and contradiction inherent in this cult crime classic.

A note on the extract: this article first appeared in the anthology *At Full Speed: Hong Kong Cinema in a Borderless World*, edited by Esther C.M. Yau in 2001. The original article contained an extended narrative consideration of *The Killer* as well as a wider discussion of how its elements of excess could be theorized by film theory. Beyond its consideration of the American reception of the film, the original article also contained a longer section on Chow Yun-fat's star persona within a Korean context.

I regard The Killer *as a romantic poem.*

—JOHN WOO

It [The Killer] *is the theater of the ridiculous.*

—JAMI BERNARD, *NEW YORK POST*

Those of us who love Hong Kong action cinema think of the lousy subtitling as one of the incidental pleasures of the genre. When Chow Yun-fat voices his suspicions of a drug smuggler's underwear in Tiger on the Beat, *and it comes out as "I suspect her bra also contains cock," you can't really be irritated by it. (emphasis in original)*

—A READER'S RESPONSE TO "LOUSY SUBTITLING," *SIGHT AND SOUND*

Critical attention to John Woo's Hong Kong action films in the West has engendered inquiries about the relationship between his exuberant cinematic style and the social anxiety driven by the historical situation of Hong Kong. According to some views, these films are preoccupied with the rapidly changing geopolitics of Hong Kong and its uncertain future after the 1997 takeover. Such contextual readings locate Woo's action films ambiguously in the tropes of national cinema, which are concerned particularly with the ways in which the social anxiety attendant on impending takeover is configured in crisis and apocalyptic visions. By reading the films in close relation to their sociopolitical settings, critics have rescued the cinema of John Woo from the pejorative descriptions of exploitation action flicks or cult movies.

Yet, Woo's Hong Kong action films consistently occupy the center stage of cult cinema in the United States. More specifically, his 1989 film *The Killer [Diexue Shuangxiong]* has become one of the most celebrated cult films in recent years. To overlook the cult phenomenon of the film, it seems to me, is to leave out too many questions about the film's unique textual system and the cultural space that popular Hong Kong films occupy in the United States. In this essay, I examine *The Killer* primarily in the critical terms of the cult film phenomenon. This means that the film will be discussed, in the most literal sense, as foreign film. Consequently, my attention lies in the practice of transcultural readings of the cult film experience and what this reception indicates with respect to the exchange of films between Hong Kong and the United States. I argue that *The Killer*'s particular reception mode and formal features are of certain theoretical importance for inquiries into film culture in the transcultural age, for the film's enduring cult following not only illustrates the existence of an expanding space for popular Asian cinema in America, it also poses questions regarding the relationship between the practice of cultural misreading and the increasing dissemination of Hong Kong film images in the West. Later in this essay, I will expand my inquiry beyond cult film in the United States by examining the film's different reception and meanings in Asian transcultural settings, specifically in Korea. How Woo's films have been understood by Korean viewers, and how those viewers have engaged them, will inform a dynamic transcultural reading practice that is significantly different from the American mode.

[. . .]

In order to discuss *The Killer* in terms of cult film, I would first like to delineate its categorical boundaries. This slippery journalistic term derives from a sociological phenomenon: cult film experience refers to the feverish worshiping of privileged film by the fans, who share exclusive knowledge of it. However, this sociological account is often too broad to mark a visible boundary of cult film. Descriptions such as "it's a cult film if it has a devoted fan following" tend to be so indiscriminate in the numbers and kinds of films included that the term itself runs the risk of losing its specificity. Recently, more rigorous scholarship has modified the territory of cult film by adding the deviant and overtly disruptive nature of the film's subject into the discussion. The cultural role of cult film, namely the relationship between film text and audience, has been central to theory on cult film.

Transgression, or the violation of boundaries, is one of the most important features of cult films. Whether it is a boundary of time, style, genre, cultural convention, or aesthetic evaluation, cult films demonstrate volatile energy for crossing the constraints of these established boundaries. According to Bruce Kawin, classic cult films such as *Casablanca* (1942) provide their worshipers with a sense of deep nostalgia for the glamour of stars who transcend temporal constraints. Meanwhile, midnight movies like *The Rocky Horror Picture Show* (1975) form a subcultural terrain where urban teenagers' desire to resist mainstream conformity is expressed in a participatory viewing practice. In any case, as Telotte notes, this irrational worshiping is tied to the gestural act of transgression, which is concerned particularly with crossing formal or cultural boundaries. That is, cult film serves an arena of transgression after which one safely returns home but with the feeling of transgression intact.

In the case of *The Killer*, then, the questions we must ask are: What kind of formal and cultural boundaries does *The Killer* transgress and violate in becoming an object of popular worship in the United States? What ends do the film's unique formal and stylistic elements serve in the production of this peculiar pleasure? How does this transgressive pleasure differ from that available from other types of cult films? And, finally, what does this pleasurable effect tell us about the location of Hong Kong cinema in contemporary film culture in the United States?

[. . .]

First, a synopsis of the film is in order. Jeff (Chow Yun-fat), a professional assassin, accidentally blinds Jenny (Sally Yeh), a singer, during a shoot-out at a nightclub. Guilt-ridden, Jeff decides to follow the advice of his friend Sydney (Chu Kong) for one last job to procure the resources needed for an operation to restore Jenny's sight. This last assassination unveils the betrayal of the mob that hired him, and Jeff is chased by both the mob and Inspector Lee (Danny Lee), a chase that for the inspector has become an obsession. The two men develop a friendship, and they end up forming a partnership in the final shoot-out against the mob gunmen. In the end, Jeff and his loyal friend Sydney die, and Jenny is left blind. Lee shoots the mob boss and weeps over the loss of his friend Jeff.

[. . .]

The cinematic excess of graphic violence is the locus of the film's principal energy and attraction. Kristin Thompson's theory of cinematic excess provides critical terms for conceptualizing this distinctive filmic effect. According to Thompson, cinematic excess occurs as the materiality of images functions beyond the purpose of narrative progression. Narrative film is basically the site of tension between narrative logic and the materiality of images that often transgresses intended meanings.

Reading cinematic excess in cine-formalist terms, Thompson defines excess that "implies a gap or lag in motivation" as "counter-narrative" and "counter-unity." She attributes value to obtrusive and "strange" works like *Ivan the Terrible* (1944), as they make the audience aware of "the structure," rather than the narrative, of the film.

The strong images and forced motifs in *The Killer* certainly function beyond the narrative purpose. The recognition of these excessive elements, however, does not simply encourage intellectual contemplation, as Thompson contends. Unlike *Ivan the Terrible*, where the slow progression of the narrative forces viewers to observe or reflect on the "materiality" of the images, the rapid kinetic images in *The Killer* do not call for meditation as such. Instead, Woo's masterful manipulation of spatiotemporality through a continuous sequence of shootings in confined space shows the characteristics of exhibitionism and theatrical display often associated with what Tom Gunning calls "the cinema of attractions." According to him, the cinema of attractions refers to the early cinema in which an exciting spectacle itself is the central feature stimulating spectator attention. Unlike narrative film, with its voyeuristic nature, the cinema of attractions is an exhibitionist cinema. Woo's experiment with formal properties such as slow motion, overlapping, and shot repetition often exceeds the narrative requirement, calling attention to the film's presentational and exhibitionistic features. Instead of contemplative engagement, Woo's cinematic excess aims at a certain psychological impact on viewers through the elaborate choreographed violence.

In terms of generic affiliation, *The Killer* transgresses a boundary of the action-film genre. Its sentimentality suggests a melodramatic mode of representation operating parallel to the kinetic and sensational world of the action film. According to Julian Stringer, Woo's *A Better Tomorrow [Yingxiong Bense]* (1986) and *The Killer* present a configuration of masculinity different from the Hollywood mode in that the demarcation between the male action ("doing") genre and the female ("suffering") genre collapses in these films. The male protagonists in both films engage simultaneously in "doing," that is, in violent action and heroism, and in "suffering"—loss, sadness, and melancholy. The jarring dramatic effects I have mentioned owe a great deal to odd generic features of the "male melodrama of doing and suffering." In this context, excessive violence is a transferred figuration of the melodrama's intention to express that which is unutterable in realistic convention. Given that melodrama of excess is rare in the contemporary Hollywood filmmaking scene, the suffering yet morally authoritative male protagonists in Woo's films come to be viewed as a kind of new, odd, and fascinating cinematic representation: something that waits to be "discovered" by American audiences.

When *The Killer* was released in the United States, film critics largely failed to understand this dynamic of generic hybridity and charged that the film displayed sentimentality and emotional excess. But these affective features, which had been unavailable in the Western cinematic tradition, are precisely the lure of Hong Kong action cult films. Contrary to film critics, cult followers of these film texts find that the melodramatic ordeal and tragic fate of the male protagonists broadly speak for, in Telotte's term, their "deepfelt and perhaps unacknowledged desire." Cult audiences have been able to grip the "structure of feeling" of the text, which, beneath its incoherence and ricketiness, is truthful, sincere, and moving.

The melodramatic dimension of *The Killer* described above helps to explain how the film's campiness is registered and maintained. According to Barbara Klinger, the generic conventions of film melodramas are especially subject to mass camp appropriation. Mass camp views and evaluates old objects from contemporary realist standards and makes fun of its artifices and anachronism. In the case of classical Hollywood melodrama, Klinger notes, the subject matter and socially pertinent theme look decidedly outdated in a contemporary context because of the changed social circumstances. More importantly, the genre's expressive conventions such as intensified dramatic conflicts and emotional affect fail to register once-serious meanings to contemporary viewers.

Although Klinger's study focuses exclusively on Hollywood melodramas, her observations on the deterioration of generic integrity by mass camp can be applied to *The Killer*. Here the degradation of textual coherence appears in terms of both temporal and cultural difference. The present cultural condition of mass camp, as led by increasing mass production and dissemination of media texts, affects the ways in which the modern viewer perceives and understands film texts from other cultures. In *The Killer*, the melodramatic expression is a dominant narrative articulation in many crucial sequences. Yet, it is an outdated mode of expression that has long been swayed by a more realistic mode of representation in America. Simultaneously, the film is also a chic contemporary action genre film filled with sophisticated action sequences, far surpassing the artistry of conventional Hollywood action films. Thus, the film registers dual generic features. On the one hand, its affective design has some ties to the visible representational mode of the past, that is, melodrama. On the other hand, its dynamic configuration of kinetic activities suggests new possibilities and directions for the burgeoning contemporary genre. It is old *and* new. *The Killer*, in other words, is an accessible action film that looks decidedly foreign, with its prominent melodramatic subtext of male suffering. This dual tendency, this odd combination, is the essential fabric of *The Killer*'s cult universe.

[. . .]

Having discussed the factors that formed the cult phenomenon of *The Killer* in the United States, I now turn to a popular film exchange in an inter-Asian context. In particular, the way *The Killer* and other Hong Kong action films achieved success in the South Korea of the late 1980s illustrates a distinctive pattern of cultural dialogue and appropriations. In order to understand the dynamics between Hong Kong action films and film reception in Korea, one needs to go back to 1987, when *A Better Tomorrow* was first shown to Korean viewers. This flagship film neither received critical attention nor achieved commercial success when it was first released in Korea. Consequently, it went to "mini-theaters." In this marginal film exhibition arena, the film rapidly gained unusual popularity among local audiences. Ching Siu-tung's *A Chinese Ghost Story [Qiannu Youhun]* (1987) followed a similar trajectory of cult following in Korea: the film did not do well initially but was accepted by the same audiences upon repeated viewing. This quiet cult film phenomenon has largely been ignored by the mainstream media. Yet, the growing interest in cult film has transformed Korean film culture in subsequent years, particularly in the area of fan culture, where Hong Kong film stars like Chow Yun-fat and Joey Wong became symbols of masculine and feminine ideals, respectively. This scattered cult following entered into mainstream culture in following years, and *A Better Tomorrow II [Yingxiong Bense Xuji]* became the ninth largest box office draw in the following year. The trend continued in 1989 as *The Killer* and Wong Jing's *Casino Raiders [Zhizhuan Wuxiang]* (1989) took the seventh and eighth places in the year's box office receipts, respectively.

[. . .]

The term "cult film" requires some retooling when one examines Korean film culture, where it has a different set of implications and followed a different trajectory of development. After first entering cultural discourse in South Korea during the late 1980s, it was widely embraced by film buffs and journalists alike. The term "cult film" in South Korea usually refers to a group of Western "midnight movies" that generally feature grotesque themes and a peculiar style and formal design. Rather than being an indigenous subcultural phenomenon, "cult film" is understood more in terms of genre. Such titles as David Lynch's *Eraserhead* (1978) and *Blue Velvet* (1986) and Alexandro Jodorowsky's *El Topo* (1971) appear regularly on the list, while popular Hong Kong films rarely appear on the same list, despite their cultish followings. This is because Hong Kong films have a long-established, solid generic and (trans)national identity of their own and do not blend easily with other kinds of genre or national cinema. Despite this categorical difference, I argue that the Korean mass interest in cult film and the spectacular success of Hong Kong films are historically linked cultural phenomena. That is, the atypical success of Hong Kong films, more specifically Woo's films, and the growing demand for cult film share some common ground that are shaped and developed by complex industrial, social, and cultural factors in Korea.

The success of *The Killer* in South Korea owed a great deal, to be sure, to the textual appeal and ingenuity of Woo's filmmaking. Woo's films, starting with *A Better Tomorrow*, signaled what to Korean viewers seemed to be a new departure in Hong Kong cinema. Korean journalists and critics discovered something very different in new Hong Kong gangster and action films and coined the term "Hong Kong noir" to conceptualize the peculiarly pessimistic energy and allegorical implications. The films' success also depended upon the translatability of their common themes, such as loyalty and male bonding, which were very accessible to Korean viewers, especially a male audience. This is partly owing to the fact that virtues such as loyalty are still powerful social mores in the Confucian tradition in South Korea. Furthermore, Korean subtitles conveyed the subtleties of the films' original dialogues more faithfully than English ones, shielding the films from the accidental and campy misreadings that are central to cult pleasure in the United States.

There are, however, more important social factors that played a significant role in shaping the growth of Hong Kong cinema into the Korean film vocabulary. As I mentioned above, in the 1980s Korea saw drastic changes in film exhibition; the number of mini-theaters and video rentals increased rapidly, and there was a greater diversification of film preferences and exhibition practices. In 1987 the Korean government, pressured by U.S. government agencies, passed a law that opened the film sector up to more imports. Since the new film law allowed foreign film companies to produce and directly distribute films in Korea, the new legislation met with fierce resistance from the local film industry. The industry launched a popular campaign to protect Korean films from the aggressive cultural imperialism of the United States; it included mass demonstrations and boycotts of directly distributed foreign (mainly American) films. Theaters that showed these films were subject to fierce criticism and attack, which culminated in paint being thrown at the screen and snakes (!) and tear gas being released into the auditorium. This contentious situation also promoted an urgent need to reform and restructure the existing film industry in the areas of production, distribution, and exhibition. The biggest beneficiaries of the new law during these years of struggle for Korean cinema were, however, Hong Kong films. Because of hostility toward the cultural aggression of Hollywood and the high price of its products, many film importers in Korea turned their interest toward Hong Kong films, which already had a reputation for wide appeal. Concurrently, the unrecognized cult following of Chow and other Hong Kong film stars began to translate into box office receipts. Thus, the number of Hong Kong film imports increased strikingly during this period, from four films in 1986 to ninety-eight in 1990, close to the number of Hollywood pictures.

Central also to these films' success was the image of new masculinity that Hong Kong film stars, and Chow Yun-fat in particular, embodied. As I noted, films like *The Killer* did not generate camp appeal, but were understood in Korea as more earnest texts on masculinity. This is closely linked to the translatability of a new paradigm of Hong Kong masculinity within a Korean cultural context. The masculine ideals these films articulate hardly seem radical to Korean viewers. The notions of honor, loyalty, and male bonding are very common in masculine discourses in Korea. What these films offered, however, was a refashioning and reaffirmation of the masculine ideals with which much of the Korean male audience felt a deep affinity. Historically, the wave of Hong Kong action films thus coincided with radical changes in the structure of Korean society during and after the 1988 Seoul Olympic Games. In the midst of proliferating discourses on globalization and the formation of a new national identity lies social anxiety over how contemporary demands might be combined with old values. In this context, the Hong Kong action film's reiteration of traditional masculine values and melodramatic pathos provided an arena of fantasy where the Korean male subject was able to come to imaginary terms with these pressing anxieties.

[. . .]

Hong Kong movie stars' cult followings also raised questions about the terms of masculinity that were increasingly defined by Hong Kong models. In particular, an idealized masculinity strongly associated with Hong Kong movie stars such as Chow Yun-fat, Leslie Cheung, and Andy Lau was viewed as problematic. It was under these anxiety-ridden circumstances that Im Kwon-taek, a renowned Korean filmmaker, directed a commercial gangster film, *The General's Son [Chang'gun-ŭi Adŭl]* (1988), in an endeavor to articulate a distinct and authentic Korean masculinity. The film quickly became the biggest blockbuster of 1990, setting the model for Korean gangster films in subsequent years. Im noted later that the flood of Hong Kong action films propelled him to revive the Korean masculine image onscreen. This production shows how deeply Hong Kong action films and their masculine ideals engage with the discourse of Korean masculinity and cultural production. Korean audiences embraced a new configuration of masculine ideals that Hong Kong action films offered; yet, Hong Kong films' increasing visibility also produced anxiety over the boundaries of Korean cultural identity. While the production of *The General's Son* was an attempt to distinguish the popular cinema of Korea from Hong Kong cinema, it demonstrates the degree to which the former was influenced by the latter.

A specific set of formal, narratological, generic, extratextual, and cultural factors constitutes the cult phenomenon of *The Killer*. Its cult film aesthetics derive from particular cinematic excesses and implausibilities situated within a cultural misreading. As demonstrated above, *The Killer*'s narrative construction reveals numerous implausible turnarounds. In the United States, the film's ambiguities or organic imperfections place it in the category of camp, but this camp reading is different from the conventional ridiculing of old objects. This mass camp involves cultural distance and generic (un)familiarity. In terms of generic association, the film is a hybrid, that is, a combination of male melodrama and action film, which further complicates the viewer's perception of it. Instead of being a historical artifact that has lost its relevance to history, the film becomes culturally sanitized so that it is "outrageous" and "ridiculous." Additionally, the postmodern crisis of representation and increasing privatization of cultural artifacts has encouraged this practice of "pleasurable misreading."

Hong Kong film's immense popularity in Korea shows a different pattern of cultural exchange, however. Articulation of the affective economy works more seriously here, preventing any possibility of camp readings. Instead, the code of masculine ideals and virtues found their proper translation in a Korean context. More importantly, the expanding space for Hong Kong films in Korea resulted from various contextual factors such as changing modes of film exhibition and the introduction of new media. The phenomenon also coincides with immense anxiety caused by the cultural aggression of the United States. Consequently, Hong Kong films offered that which Korean cinema was unable to provide during this historical juncture: an imaginary and imaginative space of (male) fantasy where traditional virtues appear to be a viable option for coping with rapidly changing circumstances. Thus, while for viewers in the United States *The Killer* seems to be a fresh new film with curious and odd components, for Korean viewers it projects a deeply moving tragic vision of the world and heroic struggle.

Changing film viewing practices both in the United States and Korea have created ghettoized film viewing communities that valorize the performance of non-Hollywood texts. Audiences relate their deep-seated desire and fulfillment to the outrageousness of the performing text. Paradoxically, the cult film connotes a liberating interpretive practice where the audience constructs its own meanings regardless of the intended textual effects. This also signifies the deterioration of textual authority and serious thematic. Yet, the space that the cult film *The Killer* carved out for itself illustrates how a non-Western film text can resist being aggressively appropriated by the hegemonic West. In the case of Korea, this film facilitated the debate on the question of national cultural identity. In this way, *The Killer* occupies a smooth and fluid cultural space for Korean viewers and as such provides an alternative imaginary landscape to the hegemonic Hollywood model. Still, the overt valorization raises the question of the cultural boundaries of contemporary Korea. Meanings are always distorted and misread in cult films; yet, there is also a profound sense of distance between our projected reading, conditioned by various contextual factors, and the performance of the foreign text. The reason for feverish worship of such films may lie in this odd textual integrity, a complex aura that brings us together in shared pleasure despite (or because of) distance and differences.

3.6

Trading in horror, cult and matricide: Peter Jackson's phenomenal bad taste and New Zealand fantasies of inter/national cinematic success

by Harmony Wu

While Jinsoo An considers the cross-cultural receptions of a single cult text, Harmony H. Wu analyses the multiple cult configurations of a single director: Peter Jackson. Her article situates Jackson's high budget fantasy work with *The Lord of the Rings* trilogy, alongside earlier, low budget splatter movies such as *Bad Taste* (1987) and *Brain Dead* (1992). Drawing on the work of theorists such as Bourdieu and Sconce, Wu reiterates cult's status as 'bad', low or degraded text that sets up oppositional positions to established cultural and political hierarchies. And with their emphasis on body horror and bodily excess, dark humour and even darker maternal representations, Jackson's early works stand as a good example of the transgressive/rule-breaking features that the cult text contains. However, what is interesting about Wu's account is the way she traces this subversive stance from the low budget, gore ghetto, to Jackson's more recent blockbuster fantasy productions, drawing on some interesting fan website data as part of her study. Moreover, the author notes the extent to which Jackson's transition from 'low' to 'high' cultural capital has carried with it some interesting issues of national cinema and its reception in a wider international domain. Thus, while his early splatter productions were received by international sources such as *Variety* as 'Kiwi' horror movies, thus confirming existing North American presumptions around the 'outback otherness' of such regions, this also assisted in formulating domestic definitions of how such films related to other marginal texts being produced in New Zealand at the time. Moreover, later productions, such as *Heavenly Creatures* (1994), were marketed internationally under the more legitimate tag of 'foreign' art-house movie (to fit with the new trend of serious New Zealand productions such as *The Piano* [1991]), offering interesting examples of how this new Jackson label occurred via the suppression of his association with earlier gross-out productions. As Wu concedes in her lengthy analysis of *Heavenly Creatures*, the film does offer a different degree of characterization and complexity to previous Jackson works as indicated by the distinct modes of identification and investment undertaken by fan communities for these products. However, noting that the cult reputation of *Brain Dead* led to the New Zealand Film Commission's funding of more mainstream productions such as *Heavenly Creatures*, Wu's study points to the crucial role that national identity has in the domestic and international receptions of cult texts that span the low/high cultural divide.

A note on the extract: this article first appeared in the volume *Defining Cult Movies: The Politics of Popular Taste* (2003). The original article contained a slightly longer introduction which contextualizes Jackson's recent *Lord of the Rings* work alongside early gore productions such as *Brain Dead*. The original version of the article also contains an additional section which considers fan responses to *Heavenly Creatures* in more detail.

Once and future cults

Three of the most anticipated Hollywood-style blockbuster 'event' pictures at the beginning of the new millenium were made far from Hollywood, on New Zealand soil, by New Zealander Peter Jackson. J. R. R. Tolkien's beloved fantasy trilogy *The Lord of the Rings* has been translated to the big screen, the first live action rendering of the epic tale of the battle of good against evil waged by Hobbits, elves, goblins and dwarves in the fantasy realm of Middle-earth. It is also the first time Tolkien's tale has been told in three parts (one film released in 2001, 2002, 2003). [. . .]

Despite the big production gloss and mainstream respectability of *The Lord of the Rings*, before this Peter Jackson was mostly known to cult audiences, at first for his 'low' splatter horror and gore films, and then for his 'high' art house film *Heavenly Creatures*. The *Rings* films are by far Jackson's biggest, most commercially mainstream productions to date – and yet, contrary to usual oppositions of 'cult' and 'mainstream', these anticipated blockbusters, like his earlier films, are still the site of cult desire, as illustrated by the examples of fan behaviour above. This intersection of 'cult' with both 'low' and 'high' texts as well as with 'mainstream' in Jackson's films is a useful reminder of the need to be attentive to the nuanced articulations of cultism in a variety of locations; an underlying goal of this essay, then, is to dislodge the marginalization of cult as perpetually 'Othered' by the 'center'. Through Jackson's films, I will attempt to trace the currency of cinema, genre, horror and cult aesthetics and cult reception across international borders and hierarchies of taste, and examine how this currency trades in tropes of the nation. A central focus will also be how with Jackson, 'horror' – the usually debased genre – becomes embedded at the centre of cinematic constructions of New Zealand nationality, symbolically and materially, for Jackson has been uniquely successful in parlaying genre and cult 'capital' into international success, and simultaneously using generic and cult idioms to formulate texts of national identity.

High and low horror

Recent critical work in media studies on taste hierarchies has obvious resonance here and informs my thinking about Jackson's cult films. As these arguments are treated elsewhere in this collection, I will only briefly indicate facets of the taste discourse particularly relevant to my discussion. Drawing Pierre Bourdieu's conclusions on taste and class, Jeffrey Sconce has argued that the mainstream's designation of certain cinematic texts as 'aberrant' or 'bad' is part of larger political structures working to reify patterns of cultural power and authority (1995). He concludes, then, that cult (or to use his term, 'paracinematic') fan activity – specifically those cases where reading groups use 'high' cultural capital to read 'low' texts with sophistication – is ultimately an act of resistance against received power hierarchies. Like in Sconce's paracinema, high and low are also mixed in the figure of Jackson as 'cult auteur', with his cinematic roots in bad taste horror and gore, his critically acclaimed art house success, and his current role as architect of international blockbusters – but in this case the mixing of high/slow is across the filmography of one filmmaker, raising further questions about the way good and bad taste, high and low aesthetics circulate and intersect. This suggests that cultural legitimacy and illegitimacy can be mutually constitutive and, materially and economically speaking, less hegemonic than might otherwise be presupposed.

Also of importance is horror's special relation to bad taste. Scholars such as Linda Williams (1995), Carol Clover (1992) and William Paul (1994) have argued that, in the hierarchy of genre legitimacy, horror is at the bottom, above only pornography. Bourdieu's important work on taste and class provides insights here, too. Describing the formations of taste, Bourdieu points to a certain corporeal essentialism that is quite suggestive *vis-à-vis* film aesthetics, the horror genre and cinematic hierarchies of taste: 'Tastes are perhaps first and foremost distastes, disgust provoked by horror or visceral intolerance ("sick-making") of the tastes of others' (1986: 192). With 'good taste' located in the act of rejecting that which produces corporeal sensations of disgust and precisely *horror*, it becomes clear why the horror genre is always-already 'low'. The genre that takes its name from the bodily affect has an especially intimate relationship to the substance of bad taste, for its very generic imperatives are to produce exactly the kind of 'visceral intolerance' in which reviled distaste is firmly rooted. It would also seem that horrific forms thus are intractably stuck at the bottom, the 'lowbrow' end, of the hierarchy of genres.

These cult and taste discourses surrounding horror, with their implications of power, centre and margins, inevitably circle back to issues of the nation. If a national cinema comes to be known for 'low' texts with cult value, how does this affect the nation, its representation, its cultural image and its political position?

The international currency of bad taste

Peter Jackson's first features – *Bad Taste* (1987), *Meet the Feebles* (1989) and *Braindead* (also known as *Dead Alive*, 1992) – illustrate a particular obsession with the absurd, the comically grotesque and the splatter and gore strains of horror. *Bad Taste* is an alien/zombie film; *Meet the Feebles*, a backstage musical with X-rated puppets; *Braindead*, a zombie film with a staggeringly high body count. All share a comedic sensibility, and all are determined to push the limits of the body, probing the meaty and fluid excesses of corporeal form with a combination of fear and delight. These films, which can be called the 'gross-out trilogy', were all eventually picked up for international distribution, and, though none played in mainstream venues, the gross-out films generated a dedicated, cult audience of gore and splatter fans who were impressed by the extremes to which Jackson decimated, erupted, destroyed and drained bodies of various forms (puppets, zombies, aliens). Each of the films has become a video and midnight movie cult favourite.

Bad Taste has aliens vomit copious amounts of chunky blue spew, which is then consumed by a sickened human. In the film's climax, Derek, played by Peter Jackson himself, slices off an alien's head, dives into its body through the bloody cavity and slices his way out at the other end, declaring, beneath thick layer of sticky ooze and blood, 'I'm born again!' *Meet the Feebles* features a fly tabloid reporter, who gets the sexual scoop on the celebrity rabbit (who hosts the variety television programme 'Meet the Feebles') by rooting around in his fetid toilet and snacking on the contents, while the rabbit's fast-acting venereal disease causes his body to decompose rapidly in dripping wounds and explosions of vomit and pus. *Braindead* also features pus and rotting flesh, and takes the destructive body logic of *Bad Taste* to extremes, depicting a hundred ways to dispatch zombies and abuse the human form – legs are ripped off, a human head is puréed in a blender, a zombie baby burrows through a woman's face from the back of her head. *Braindead*'s *pièce de resistance* is the thirty-minute non-stop parade of zombie dismemberment, culminating in the spectacle of hero Lionel strapping on a lawnmower to pulverize a host of oncoming zombies, until nothing but pulpy bloody flesh remains.

Braindead, *Feebles* and *Bad Taste*'s stock in trade is clearly 'bad taste'. Through the degradation of the screen bodies, the films explicitly traffic in 'sick-making', deliberately seeking viewers' 'visceral intolerance'. These films do not court audiences that would see Merchant Ivory's *The Remains of the Day*; rather, they cultivate the very specific cult horror viewing aesthetic, specializing in extremes defined explicitly in contrast to mainstream aesthetics and good taste. Still, even while cult, paracinematic and horror texts are generally debased for their 'bad taste' and loved only by a narrow group of fans, these marginalized texts can also simultaneously translate into very material audiences and financial substance, as indicated by *Variety*'s review: 'This is one of the bloodiest horror comedies ever made, and that will be enough to ensure cult success in cinemas and especially on video. Kiwi gore specialist Peter Jackson goes for broke with an orgy of bad taste and splatter humor. Some will recoil, but "Braindead" wasn't made for them' (1992: 51). Though maligned by arbiters of cultural legitimacy, bad taste films are at the same time potentially valuable to producers, distributors and exhibitors for their niche dollars, especially as cult fans of bad taste and horror are given to serial viewings. This places cult texts and audiences in the possibly conflicted space of being, on the one hand, vilified by the cultural mainstream and, on the other, financially exploitable by the corporations that produce and distribute the dominant media comprising the mainstream that shuns bad taste texts in the first place.

When the bad taste films in question are made outside of the dominant US/ Hollywood film industry, 'taste' and 'cult' gather connotations in a larger web of cultural 'value' expressed specifically along terms of national identity. When the squarely Hollywood-centric trade paper *Variety* explicitly labels Jackson 'kiwi', the rhetorical gesture brands not only the director but also New Zealand itself as 'goremeisters' in the imaginations of industry insiders, critics and consumers. This elision of an entire national identity with the vocabulary of cult aesthetics and genre can be found across a variety of publications: *Onfilm* called Jackson a 'Kiwi sicko' (Doole 1993: 4), *British Modern Review* claimed that, for grossness, 'nobody does it better than the antipodeans' ('BFI Praise' 1994: 12), and a cult film website asserts, 'Peter Jackson has put New Zealand firmly on the map as far as Cult cinema is concerned . . . [*Braindead* is] the best thing that has come from New Zealand since good ol' kiwi lamb chops' (*The Hot Spot*). With these low texts' international cult success, the New

Zealand nation itself is mapped and becomes synonymous with cult, horror and bad taste.

This simultaneous inscription of Jackson and New Zealand as purveyors of horror, splatter, bad taste and gore develops out of and reinforces an international perception of New Zealand as an off-kilter land with strange and dark obsessions, an idea explicitly articulated in *Cinema of Unease*, the 1995 documentary on New Zealand cinema (written and directed by Sam Neill and Judy Rymer), which takes the 'off-kilter Kiwi' point of view as its primary thesis. As presumed by *Cinema of Unease* and illustrated in global critical and fan consumption of Jackson's gross-out films, genre, taste and a strange world-view *become* 'nation' – New Zealand itself is genrified, figured as cult object, a site where kooky perspectives and horrific bad taste can be reliably found. In the case of non-dominant, non-Hollywood cinema industries, 'cult' success ultimately can become a question of how the nation is represented on the international stage.

The larger political ramifications of occupying the subordinate positions of these binaries (good/bad taste, high/low culture, mainstream/cult audiences, Hollywood/ national cinema) were made visible in a minor scandal after the New Zealand Film & Television Awards bestowed the 'Best Film' honours on *Braindead* in 1993. Awards juror John Cranna, author of short stories and then budding screenwriter, went public with his opposition to the selection of Jackson's film, criticizing *Braindead* as 'a crude horror that makes a mockery of serious film making in New Zealand' ('Integrity and the B.O.' 1993: 8). In Cranna's reading of *Braindead*, the discourses of taste, genre and nation are again implicated in one another, reproducing the international critical conflation of New Zealand with horror and bad taste: the 'bad taste' of *Braindead*'s 'crude' execution of the horror genre, then, reflected *New Zealand*'s own 'bad taste', reaffirming New Zealand's status as second-tier filmmakers on the world stage, and undermining any pretences to cultural legitimacy. Too much revelling in horrific bad taste condemns New Zealand culture industries to perpetual performance of its marginality.

Cranna's is not the only way of looking at the intersection of these hierarchies of taste, power and cinemas, however; 'borders' can be less a rigid wall and more of a permeable membrane, a model which allows for greater moments of exchange between the two sides of a binary. Jackson's gross-out horror films *can* be seen, as in Cranna's view, as ritual exercises in bad taste, repeatedly performing its status as marginalized, an act that only reaffirms the immutability of 'good taste's' position as 'centre'. But alternatively, the films' unapologetic entrenchment in 'gross-out' can be seen also as an exploration of the boundaries of taste in a more active manner (much as Sconce's paracinematic reading practices purposely explore bad taste as a protest against repressive power structures filtered through aesthetic hierarchies of taste).

Instead of conceiving of the hierarchies as fixed, we might see the repeated exercises of 'sick-making' in splatter and gore films as working to deconstruct the very demarcations of 'good taste'. The border thus is not so much a hegemonic barrier as it is a site of renegotiation, a site where new relationships of centre and margin can potentially be re-drafted. And in so far as discourses of national/international cinema are implicated in the discourse of taste, these aggressively horrific cult films from New

Zealand and their transgressions of good taste can be read as laying bare, and possibly reconstituting, the centre/margin dialectic that holds other national cinemas – New Zealand national cinema – perpetually subordinate to US/Hollywood hegemony. When a national cinema producing specialized niche titles claims the allegiance of audiences and becomes branded as a reliable source of a particular kind of film, Hollywood's fiercely protected position as centre becomes somewhat denaturalized and the inevitability of Hollywood's dominance less apparent.

That Cranna's dismal view of Jackson's horrific bad taste was not widely shared by members of the New Zealand film industry might have had as much to do with *Braindead*'s attention from international cult fans as with the film's cinematic merits, indicating yet another way of understanding the margin/centre dialectic *vis-à-vis* genre, national cinema and taste. By doggedly pursuing the niche cult market by pushing the limits of taste and working squarely within genre pleasures, Peter Jackson's gross-out films, it might be argued, afforded him the capital (both economic and cinematic) to transcend the limitations of working in a tiny national cinema in Hollywood's shadow and to reap success that would be otherwise unavailable; Jackson's current role as director of *The Lord of the Rings* suggests that this is indeed the case. First revelling in bad taste to court the marginal audiences, then exploiting the niche dollars of cult cinema, and finally using cult success to vault into 'legitimacy' with big budget, good taste projects, however, is a paradigm that in the end still reaffirms the power dynamics inherent in the good/bad taste discourse. After *Braindead*, Jackson claimed that he would not abandon the horror genre, saying, 'I'm definitely not one of those guys who says they want to stop making horror movies to become a serious filmmaker. I fully intend to remain working in the genre' (Helms 1993: 33). Yet, his claims to generic fealty and his implication that 'serious' filmmaking is the 'Other' of horror filmmaking echoes Cranna's statement that *Braindead* 'makes a mockery of serious film making in New Zealand'. All of this suggests that, while Jackson has made an impressive shift from poverty auteurism in lowly horror to Hollywood-style epic filmmaking with staggering budgets, the dialectic of good/bad taste, high/low culture and Hollywood/national cinema is, while not entirely stable, stubbornly resistant to change. And as far as the taste and the national discourses are intertwined, Jackson's trading in of lowbrow horror for mainstream big-budget fantasy spectacle reiterates a dynamic where the Hollywood model of filmmaking (and its good taste, polished aesthetics and bourgeois ideologies) remains on top.

In exploring the various ways of seeing the dialectics of genre, taste and national cinema, I do not hope to suggest pejoratively that Jackson has 'sold out' to bigger Hollywood budgets. Indeed, Jackson, ostensibly abandoning horror genre filmmaking, at the same time remains decidely committed to the promotion of New Zealand national cinema, and landing *The Lord of the Rings* on New Zealand shores is the biggest thing to have ever happened to the local film industry. Jackson's follow-up to *Braindead* was *Heavenly Creatures*, his film that is most engaged with issues of New Zealandness and at first glance seems a departure from the horror, gore, splatter and bad taste that marked Jackson's first films. The next section examines *Heavenly Creatures* and its connection to Jackson's gross-out films *vis-à-vis* the emergence of a cult dynamic that still surrounds the film years after its initial release. Discourses of horror and art, cult and mainstream, auteur and genre, national and international cinema, usually conceived in contradiction, intersect in Jackson's films, making it inadequate to consider any one of these paradigms individually; each problematizes the other and must be considered dialogically.

The art of cult

Heavenly Creatures dramatizes the real-life 1954 murder in Christchurch, New Zealand, of Honora Parker, whose life was bludgeoned out of her by forty-seven blows to the head, neck, face and shoulders with a half brick in a stocking wielded by her teen daughter, Pauline, and Pauline's friend Juliet Hulme. Despite the grisly nature of the subject, *Heavenly Creatures* is no grim or gritty 'true crime' flick. Though bookended with the murder, the film is more concerned with the girls' strong personalities and intense pre-crime friendship, their flights of fancy in which they invent complex fantasy worlds (brilliantly rendered with morphing and other computer-generated scenes), their homoerotic explorations, their often vexed family relationships and their class differences. It is a virtuosic film, coursing with visual power and irrepressible kineticism (giddy, gliding camerawork, impeccable production design and imaginative use of computer-generation technology) and driven by stunning debut performances by Kate Winslet and Melanie Lynskey, putting contemporaneous Hollywood films to shame in comparison.

Released internationally in 1994 by Miramax, in the USA the film played on independent and art house screens, accumulating word-of-mouth and critical praise. *Heavenly Creatures* even garnered an Academy Award nomination for 'best screenplay'. The film's emergence as a legitimate, critically acclaimed 'quality' film must be understood as coming out at a time when New Zealand cinema was causing a ripple with more 'highbrow' US viewers as a site of provocative fare associated with the 'art' film, in direct contrast to marginalized cult audiences' perception of Jackson and New Zealand as sites of gross-out horror and gore. New Zealander Jane Campion's international reputation as 'art house' feminist filmmaker had jelled with *The Piano*'s release the year before, with its moody evocations of a woman's patriarchal repression and sexual reawakening. And another New Zealand film, *Once Were Warriors*, directed by Lee Tamahori, was also released to critical acclaim in 1994. The adaptation of Alan Duff's tremendously well-received novel explored domestic abuse and urban poverty through a portrait of a Maori family, with particular focus on the point of view of the adolescent daughter.

At this moment, then, as far as it registered on so-called *legitimate* US film-going consciousness, New Zealand signified smart, challenging, edgy and beautiful 'art' films committed to exploring a feminine perspective. *Heavenly Creatures* was promoted and received in the vernacular of 'art film'; Miramax sold it as a prestige production and a cinematic achievement – a marketing strategy that was then becoming Miramax's signature in distributing and marketing 'foreign' films (where 'foreignness' itself coupled with exploration of eroticism – especially homoeroticism – is apparently sufficient to signify 'arty' difference from Hollywood). Peter Jackson's gross-out cult success was suppressed; most film-goers had no idea that the director of this 'quality' art film was known to cult audiences as the 'Orson Welles of gore'.

When critics acknowledged Jackson's earlier films, it was only to remark with surprise how much the director had matured, dismissing the gross-out trilogy as an unfortunate detour to Jackson's newfound artistry, re-articulating the diametric opposition of the disdained 'lowbrow' of the gross-out films and the 'legitimacy' of *Heavenly Creatures*, with its artfulness and sheen of quality.

Heavenly Creatures, with its structurally and thematically sophisticated narrative, fully realized character development, first-rate performances, and highly developed visual and aural sensibility, does indeed seem a radical departure for Jackson. While these accomplishments were not absent in Jackson's earlier films (and are perhaps most notable in *Braindead*), the overwhelming presence of 'bad taste' in the other films shifts focus away from more conventionally lauded narrative and formal achievements toward the spectacles of ruined bodies. But one of the interesting facets of the film's reception in light of the prior gross-out and forthcoming *Lord of the Rings* trilogies is that *Heavenly Creatures*'s art house success and nods from 'legitimate' critics eventually morphed, like the computer-generated images in the film itself, into an internet-based fan community with cult-like devotion.

One important difference, however, is that fan communities around the *Rings* and gross-out trilogies fit into pre-existing categories of cultism – fandom for the horror genre and for Tolkien's Middle-earth fantasies precedes and exceeds Jackson's films. Alternatively, *Heavenly Creatures*'s cult fan base seems to have grown out of ardent love for the film itself: *Heavenly Creatures* fandom is not part of a larger cult community. That is, for example, one does not come to a cult appreciation of *Heavenly Creatures* because one is a fan of the coming-of-age genre. At the same time, *Heavenly Creatures*'s cultism does fit some discernible features of cult fandom generally.

Jeffrey Sconce (1992) has described two distinct kinds of cult cinephilia, the archaeological and the diegetic: the archaeological cinephile is obsessed with 'collection' and 'artefacts' of cinema, while the diegetic cinephile is invested in a particular universe, an encompassing mise-en-scène offered by a genre (such as the urban landscapes of film noir) or, sometimes, a single cinematic text (such as *Titanic* or *The Wizard of Oz*). *Heavenly Creatures* seems to foster this latter 'diegetic' form of cult cinephilia, wherein fans seek aesthetic delight in the beauty of the girls' friendship and the fantasy-scapes of their books and play-acting. The diegetic cinephile's effort to relive and extend the story universe can take expression as original artwork and creative writing 'inspired' by the film, acts of creation through which the film's story is integrated into the fan's or artist's life.

[. . .]

In contrast, cult allegiance to Jackson's gross-out films seems to cleave to the archaeological impulse. In this paradigm, fans of gore and splatter seek to 'collect' and add to their viewing repertoire (what Sconce terms a 'mental checklist') as many severed body parts and buckets of blood as possible; the films and their fetishized body spectacles are part of a larger corpus of related films – they are endowed with cult value only in relation to the larger list of cult films. An expression of the imperatives of this 'checklist logic' is found on web pages for Jackson's gross-out films, where filmographies of other horror, splatter and gore films are frequently posted – panegyrics to horrific bad taste following the 'if you liked *Braindead*, then you'll love –'

algebra. Conversely, while fans' *Heavenly Creatures* universe is in its own right deeply intertextual, the cult object of *Heavenly Creatures* fandom ultimately is bounded by the extent of the lives, fictionalized and real, of Juliet and Pauline; there is no readily iterable filmography that can be generated from *Heavenly Creatures*. The gross-out films, in contrast, are a part of a much more expansive cinematic topos, one that includes the horror and splatter cult universe and can extend into matters of production and special effects, other films and auteurs of gore, super-specialized subgenres and the unpredictable and often strange vagaries of personal predilections.

Consistent with the larger discourses on taste and respectability surrounding the differences between the films, the differences between 'diegetic' and 'archeological' cult cinephilia seem to be a matter of form that once again circles the question of 'taste': it is the very bad taste of *Braindead, Bad Taste* and *Meet the Feebles* – their gore, their splatter, their scatology – that the cult cinephile fetishizes. On the other hand, fans of *Heavenly Creatures*, like the girls in the film itself, immerse themselves in the fictional universes offered by the film and prized for their pleasing character, complexity and hermetic completeness – features of classical aesthetic beauty, which is to say, aesthetics valued by 'good taste'.

[. . .]

Trading in horror and other film fantasies

One might argue that it is precisely in the extreme reading practices of various forms of 'cult' cinephilia that boundaries of high and low are, by turns, most visibly transgressed and insistently reinforced. The cult of *Heavenly Creatures* and the cult of the gross-out films take distinct forms, with differences boiling down to 'art' as opposed to 'splatter', 'quality' in place of 'trash', 'high culture' instead of 'low' and 'good' taste not 'bad'. A simultaneously 'high' and 'low' cult director, Jackson uniquely embodies the construct of the 'cult auteur', revealing how the high modernist conceit of the 'author' is embraced by both high and low taste communities. While the idea of 'low auteurs' is not new, what is different here is that Jackson is *one* director engaging, at different times, both ends of the high/low spectrum, putting into sharper relief the distinctions, as well as the similarities, between the distinct iterations of 'cult' and how these divergent cult practices cling to or jettison accepted notions of high and low culture and 'taste'. Yet for all of the criss-crossing of high and low in Jackson's work, it is also telling that, while the two cult communities of the gross-out trilogy and of *Heavenly Creatures* both rally around the work of one director, cult admiration for one of Jackson's films does not translate into cult fascination with his other films – with few exceptions *Heavenly Creatures* fans do not become fans of the gross-out films and vice versa. This in particular illustrates that while high and low do intermingle in the figure of Peter Jackson, in cult *practice*, there remain divisions between high and low, good taste and bad.

So far in my discussion, the movement between high and low has been on an extratextual level – across Jackson's body of films, the spanning of cultism over disparate texts. But there is one crucial *textual* commonality between the high and low films. *Braindead* and *Heavenly Creatures* are the two films that the different cult communities would claim as Jackson's masterpiece. With Academy-Award-nominated

Heavenly Creatures, Jackson seemed to have traded the lexicon of horror, gross-out, splatter and bad taste for critical acclaim, prestigious awards and the aura of quality; *Heavenly Creatures* and *Braindead* seem fundamentally at odds. Yet the thematic centres of each film are strikingly similar.

Braindead concerns the meek Lionel, who is trapped in an emasculating and infantilized role of servile care-giver to his ageing, widowed, repressive mother who, like Mrs Bates in *Psycho*, jealously limits Lionel's interaction with the rest of society, particularly young women. When 'Mum' becomes a zombie, Lionel must balance mother-love with increasingly extreme efforts necessary to keep the zombie 'infection' from spreading. Lionel's unhealthy attachment to Mum is given literal expression in the finale of *Braindead*, when the zombie Mum returns, giant-sized, with a monstrous maw and immense drooping breasts, to re-assimilate – literally – Lionel into her womb. As she stuffs him into her belly, which has opened up like a giant mouth, she growls, 'No one will ever love you like your mother!' Lionel cuts his way out of his mother's body from within, spilling out in a torrent of viscera and finally killing her in the process. The matricidal moment enables blood-drenched Lionel to be reborn, unfettered at last from the manacles of mother-love.

Heavenly Creatures opens and closes with the murder of Pauline's mother; the matricide literally frames the story as the narrative flashes back to the blossoming of the girls' friendship. The opening sequence of the film has the manic, sobbing girls running away from the body, just after the murder. When they run into the wide-screen close-up, we see blood splattered all over their faces and hair. The murder itself, shown at the end of the film, is shockingly violent and graphic, with close-ups of the dying woman shot from low perspective, blood trickling her face from her matted hair; we see each blow of the brick to her head, and the girls' wildly determined and frightened faces as they swing the brick. While the film as a whole abandons the gross-out aesthetics of his earlier films, in this crucial murder scene – the critical narrative moment from which the rest of the film unspools – *Heavenly Creatures*, like *Braindead* before it, signifies aggressively with the direct language of horror and splatter, not supposedly 'artful' restraint and veiled allusion. And, lest the point be lost beneath the buckets of blood, matricide drives both narratives and the films' most sensational moments of horrific and/or horrifying spectacle.

The international cult success of *Braindead* led to the New Zealand Film Commission's funding of *Heavenly Creatures*, which in turn was the cinematic calling card leading to Jackson's first Hollywood-funded production, *The Frighteners* (1996), which led ultimately to *The Lord of the Rings*. Jackson's film career illustrates a canny ability to parlay specialized cult films, as well as both high and low films, into mainstreamed commercial viability that does the often tricky job of crossing international borders while still working in a national cinema historically plagued by the dreaded 'brain drain', where homegrown talent seeks better prospects elsewhere. Peter Jackson illustrates that a manipulation of 'cult' and both high and low aesthetics in the intersection of national/international cinemas and audiences works, paradoxically, to make possible a broader international audience, and to engender, through the capital his cult films have secured for him, more wide-scale commercial production on New Zealand soil – as with *The Lord of the Rings*. The cultivation of cinematic expertise, the development of infrastructure, the influx of capital and the international attention

Jackson has brought to New Zealand by pulling off this mega-project will by all accounts power the engine of the still infant New Zealand film industry for decades to come. Whatever is in store for the unwritten future of New Zealand cinema, it is built on the border-crossing cult currency of bloody matricides, breathtaking fantasies and horrific bad taste.

3.7

Invisible representation: The oral contours of a national popular cinema
by Sheila J. Nayar

Many extracts in the national and international cults section outline the reception of non-Western texts by European and North American cult imagination. However, it is the cult comprehension of popular texts across Asian/African regions which dominates Sheila J. Nayar's article. In her account, Nayar considers the ways in which trans-Asian cultures 'make familiar' texts from other regions, often without the aid of cinematic anchors such as dubbing or subtitles. Using a case study of popular Hindi films, Nayar considers texts which employ a 'Masala mix' of escapism, excess and elaborate storytelling to consider their transcultural popularity among disparate developing cultures. Although these texts are frequently rejected by domestic critics, the author considers the appeal of narratives such as *Sholay* (1975), *Mother India* (1975) and *Khal Nayak* (1993) among those cultures dominated by shared extended family structures and an ambivalent relationship to Western notions of modernism. For Nayar, these texts have a strong appeal to the 'non-writing mindset' by appealing to longer-standing oral based traditions of storytelling, which she outlines by consideration of the key features of popular Hindi cinema. By identifying key characteristics such as flashbacks, formulaic characterization and narrative subplots in works such as *Sholay*, Nayar considers the extent to which popular Hindi narratives function as cinematic folk tales, which replace originality with an emphasis on orality and excessive visual performance. As a result, the author notes the extent to which these formulaic films feature an 'agonistic delivery' combining an excess of character explanation with a flamboyant mode of delivery, which clearly exceeds role and plot motivation. Via analysis of these and other key devices, Nayar makes a convincing case for these often rejected pulp postcolonial narratives.

A note on the extract: this article first appeared in *Film Quarterly* 57(3). The original article contained a longer section comparing the oral traditions of popular Hindi cinema with the more 'writerly' emphasis of western-based narratives. This version also expanded upon some of the oral-based devices used by these popular texts.

Nation-states are incomplete regions for the purposes of analyzing cinema. Neither from a production nor a consumption standpoint do political boundaries sufficiently divide, group, or structure world cinema. If global cinema is more than the sum of all the national cinemas, then the task confronting us is to develop a set of regions more meaningful and more powerful in explaining the phenomenon as a communications medium.

—Gerald M. McDonald, in *Place Power, Situation and Spectacle*

Orality invisible

The theme of social inclusion as it relates to media readily anticipates consideration of race, gender, class, and other such visible markers of identity. But what about *invisible* modes of identification and representation that link outwardly divergent cultures and groups? In other words, though film may be a visual medium, not everything that determines one's representation on screen is necessarily related to sight. Too often we limit our assessment of how viewers are being socially excluded from the media experience on the basis of physical *presence*, neglecting other seminal ways in which groups or, indeed, entire subcultures, such as that of the subaltern, may be finding representation—and not always in a manner wedded to national or linguistic boundaries.

Take, for example, the case of a Nigerian villager who has never left the confines of his or her community, yet finds an Indian popular film—seen without the benefit of subtitles or dubbing—completely comprehensible, even culturally *familiar*. Indeed, a film as "indigenous" and "nationalistic" as *Mother India* (1957) continues to be embraced by audiences of other nations and races and languages and histories, as if it were in fact recounting the story of Mother Nigeria, or Mother Egypt, or of Romany Gypsies in Eastern Europe or Swahili-speaking girls in Zanzibar.

To be sure, scholars have speculated (albeit often only in passing) as to why such disparate nations identify so intensely with these Hindi-language popular films—films which are, incidentally, frequently ridiculed by critics for their *masala* ("spice-mix") blend of tawdry escapism, formulaic storytelling, and narratively irrelevant song-and-dance numbers. Some analysts have (also in passing) attributed this peculiar transcultural identification to a parallel experience of modernization encroaching on traditional society (one of the films' common themes). Others maintain it derives from a mutual privation that privileges escapist melodrama and the presentation of a material utopia, while still others contend that it is born of shared family values, or of poorer nations' inability to afford better, more substantive entertainment. (These Bollywood films are, after all, comparatively cheap entertainment imports.) These are of course all reasonable theories and under no circumstances invalid. But is it not possible that in our commitment to that which we can readily measure with pens and computers, or support through an intellectual reasoning carefully organized and modified on paper, a much broader infrastructure of identification has been missed?

My mention of these instruments of writing and the processes that accompany them is not solely rhetorical. It relates significantly to the theory I want to suggest here. Indeed, I think one of the reasons we may have neglected this other possibility is that—by virtue of the technologies we possess—we are, in actual fact, more *same* than different. That is, one thing binds us (for, if you are reading this, you are one of "us"—irrespective of your race, your culture, your gender, or your class). This one thing fundamentally separates and distinguishes us from millions of others (from 300 million such people in India alone), and thus makes this invisible transcultural identity that much harder to conceptualize, let alone to identify. I am speaking here of literacy—of our literacy, and hence of the non-literacy of others—and of the cognitive consequences of this as they apply to an individual's comprehension, organization, and experience of the world.

Why might a Nigerian villager who has never left his or her village call a film like *Mother India* culturally familiar and completely comprehensible? Perhaps it is because such movies do not take the form of a literacy-driven object. Instead, the conventional Indian popular film possesses clear characteristics of oral performance and orally transmitted narratives, conspicuously sharing traits with, for example, Homeric epic and the Indian *Mahabharata*. It is a cultural product that has been historically circumscribed by the psychodynamics of orality—that is, by the thought processes and personality structures that distinguish a non-writing mindset, and, as such, it is a product that employs specific devices and motifs that are traditionally part of orally based storytelling.

[. . .]

I am not trying to propose that there is some distinct and definitive split between "oral" and "literate" films, nor some great fixed opposition between orality and literacy—or, worse yet, between literate and illiterate. But certainly the number of years that the average student in the United States must devote to honing a "higher order of thinking"—some 15 to 20, if one counts college—attests to the length, breadth, and complexity of acquiring a literate mindset.

Imagine, then, a film industry such as Bombay's, whose primary mission these past 50 years has been profit; to be sure, it is in such an industry's interest to reach the largest audience possible. Now, imagine that this is an audience with a historically significant percentage of non- and low-literate viewers, and also one not bound by a serviceable lingua franca. (Significantly, only one-third of Indians are native Hindi speakers.) What does an industry of this type do? If it's savvy, it shapes its product into one that satisfies the greatest numbers. And orally based characteristics of thought and storytelling would not only make a visual product accessible to the oral mindset; given that they are generally seen as more elemental, more universal, perhaps even more natural, they would also render a visual product more "readable" to those unschooled in the spoken language of the film. No wonder, then, that such films have been popular in nations with significant numbers of non- or low-literate viewers. True, India's recently expanded upper-middle class, in conjunction with a wealthier audience of Indians abroad, is starting to make subtle inroads into the Bollywood film formula landscape. But the films that succeed with *non*-elite audiences (i.e., rural, uneducated) rarely depart from the oral latticework.

So, let us examine some of these oral particulars. Their presence can be seen in some of the industry's biggest hits of the past five decades, including *Mother India*, *Sholay* (*Flames*, 1975), *Khal Nayak* (*The Villain*, 1993), *Baazigar* (*Trickster*, 1993), and *Hum Aapke Hain Kaun* (*Who Am I to You*, 1994).

The oral contours of the conventional Hindi film

I. Pastiche and preservation

One of the broadest psychodynamic characteristics of orally based thought is the tendency toward the additive rather than the subordinative. Without the ability to write, to store, and to organize information elsewhere than the brain, the possibility of developing structural cohesiveness, of manipulating a story for tight shape and flow—especially as regards lengthy narrative—is impossible. Indeed, the "analytic, reasoned subordination that characterizes writing" arises *with writing itself*. Without writing, meticulously sculpting a sentence—let alone an entire plot—is quite impossible. Oral narratives are hence, by noetic necessity, episodic, sequential, and additive in nature. Works such as the *Mahabharata* and African oral epic are not built upward into some kind of pyramidal form, but are rather constructed around techniques like the use of flashbacks, thematic recurrences, and chronological breaks. This is because these are the only ways to handle extended narrative, to keep it manageable, memorable, and uncomplicated. For this reason, orally inscribed narrative—and this includes Bombay cinema—often has the feeling of being piecemeal and disaggregative, of being coarsely stitched together. It is pastiche—but quite without the postmodern self-consciousness.

One of these oral structural devices in particular, the flashback, deserves consideration. Its prevalence in oral epic is due in large part to its facilitating a movement between data more easily transmittable in separate containers. To be sure, the oft described "boxes within boxes" feel of oral epic arises to a large degree from the repeated use of the flashback. In the Hindi film, we are constantly transported back and forth and back again in time—between various storage spaces, so to speak—to watch the playing out of this romance or that crisis. In *Sholay*, for instance, there is a police chief's story-within-story recollection of meeting two thieves whom he plans now to hire to execute his vengeance; this is followed by a protracted flashback to the chief's once idyllic family life and also its tragic ruination at the hand of the film's villain, Gabbar Singh; and finally by a third flashback portraying the once exuberant, spirited life-force of the police chief's daughter-in-law, who is now reduced to forlorn widowhood.

In the more recent *Khal Nayak*, we straggle in and out of a rough, crude underworld tale, a Rama and Sita-type love story, not to mention a mother-son melodrama, stalling on several occasions to voyage back in time and witness the childhood experiences that led to the protagonist's transformation into a heinous villain, as well as the traumatic aftermath of that particular metamorphosis on the boy's upright family.

As with lengthy oral narrative, in the typical Hindi film there are also numerous sidetracks or "parallel skits" that, unlike subplots, have little to no bearing on the major story line. These digressions may be fun, funny, maudlin, titillating, even gruesome, but they are neither particularly revealing of character nor narratively instrumental. Much like the African oral epic, where episodes of, say, horror or comedy are developed for their independent appeal, Hindi film is rife with stand-alone sketches and deviations, often of a humorous or violent nature and similarly amplified for full effect. In *Sholay*, one finds a solid 15 minutes of the first half dedicated to the two goodhearted anti-heroes' extraneous gambol through a prison sentence. In *Hum Aapke Hain Kaun*, the servants' vaudevillian mishaps take the spectator down a narrative blind alley for the sheer enjoyment of it. And certainly this collective willingness to digress is reflected in the obligatory song-and-dance numbers that punctuate, sometimes puncture, virtually every conventional Bollywood movie.

To be sure, the Hindi film is often derided by film scholars and critics for its stringy and episodic nature, for its lack of an "organic consistency." Sometimes this lack of any organizing principle, this constant detouring and often lengthy meandering, is kindly attributed to its imitating indigenous precursors like the *Mahabharata*. But, rather than paying tribute to or being modeled on ancient tales, the Hindi film and the earlier oral epics are, I believe, cognate with respect to form. (Certainly many of the characteristics of the Hindi film that have been dubbed "indigenously Indian" by critics are also common to oral performance and orally based narrative irrespective of national or cultural boundaries.) Other similarities seem to bolster this point—like a second broad psychodynamic characteristic common to orality: the commitment to a conservative-traditionalist rather than experimental mind-set.

[. . .]

Relatedly, because the fabric of oneself in oral cultures is transmitted by word of mouth, from one person to another, from the previous generation to the next, what this also implies is that self-preservation is an inherently *collective* affair, a group endeavor. As a result, communal structures of personality are fostered, with things being "we"-inflected rather than "I"-inflected. (Indeed, the assertion of *individual* rights, as Marshall McLuhan has noted, appears only with the rise of print.) Certainly this is applicable to the Bombay film industry, which specializes in "we"-inflected dramas that consistently and continuously conserve the traditional order. The movies, like the oral epics before them, ensure that the way things *are* is, in the end, restored— and triumphantly so. The emphasis is similarly on the preservation of the ordered society, which is considered in oral narrative the "highest good and goal toward which the hero's physical and intellectual development is bent." This is not to say that there cannot be all measure of disruption, disorder, and discord during the course of a story—through displays of intergenerational aggression, say, or the transgressing of civilly sanctioned boundaries. But, by the end, the existing social order must be preserved. Those who have gone amiss must be punished, banished, or destroyed, or prove themselves certifiably penitent, for only such actions can ensure that the "communal self" is not atomized.

So, in *Mother India*, we have Nargis shooting her wayward son rather than allowing him to run roughshod over the ethics of their community. In *Sholay*, it is Gabbar Singh who is eliminated, with the village returned to the good management of the police chief. In *Khal Nayak*, the villain, awash in sudden moral conviction, surrenders before the *city* is returned to the good management of the police chief. And in *Hum Aapke Hain Kaun*, where no villains exist, two families—united by a marriage that has since terminated due to a death—are wedded together again by another marriage within the same family. All ends happily because in effect all ends *just as it started*.

[. . .]

Perhaps you are here reminded of Vladimir Propp's analysis of the narrative structure of fairy tales. Indeed, analysts have often labeled Hindi films "fairy tales," or "myths," and this is largely because this kind of storytelling is, to literate minds, profoundly ahistorical, exhibiting a tendency to fly in the face of "realism," to revert to fantasy endings. But if we take into account how the oral mind-set must synthesize all experience into a present story—that is, that each tale in the telling must be a repository of the past, and "a resource for renewing awareness of present existence"—then Hindi film's sameness, its repetition, its aforementioned telescoping of temporalities, makes complete sense. In this case, the storyteller's art lies in being able to entwine the old formulas and themes with the new, in being able to "read" the audience's desire for the novel from *within* "a deep sense of tradition, which preserves the essential meaning of stories."

If we are willing to concede that the films' formulaic nature, their grand-scale redundancy, is born of their orally inscribed communal nature—of their being a public, as opposed to private, property—then another peculiar characteristic of Hindi films is explained: their proclivity for quoting one another. That is to say, there are incessant references in Hindi films to prior films, an endless borrowing-cum-stealing of previous movies' tunes, lyrics, dialogue, iconic props, whole characters, and sometimes even entire plots. In *Hum Aapke Hain Kaun*, for example, the characters assemble one evening to play an extended (in terms of screen time, at least) game in which they recite passages, sing songs, and dialogically act out complete scenes from other movies (including *Sholay*). *Hum Aapke Hain Kaun* has itself been referenced, used, and abused in at least half a dozen movies since that film's 1994 release, by way of reprised melodies, quoted lines, borrowed costumes, embezzled props heavy with sentimental weight, and even one farcical send-up of a musical number. In Hollywood, some of these strategies would indubitably result in hefty legal suits. But the concept of plagiarism, of idea-ownership, is a consequence of literacy, more specifically of print. In the oral universe, there is no such thing. One cannot steal what belongs to the collective consciousness of the group. Of course, such pilfering is not only for the purpose of repeating knowledge in order that it live on and maintain its relevancy; repetition is also "a token of the joy of recollection." The viewer, in other words, joins in a highly *participatory* event, an overtly shared memory-event that is pleasurable precisely because it is continuous with other films, not separate from them.

2. The good, the bad, and the wordy

There are other characteristics of orally inscribed narrative which may be less broad, but which play out with equal significance in the Hindi film. Their reasons for being may perhaps be evoked best in the form of a question: If one must store information exclusively in the mind, how must a story—with its transitory oral utterances—be executed so that it can be thus stored? In the Hindi film, the answers are manifested in two ways: verbally (as one might expect), and also visually.

One of the traits of oral performance, of oral cultures even, is agonistic delivery. That is, there exists the tendency to perform verbally in a manner that is, by literate turns of phrases, dynamic, thick, excessive, or flatulent. This is because knowledge in the oral world, incapable as it is of being disengaged from the act, is situated within the "context of struggle." Knowledge exists *in* the speaking—as outward display, as event; and as such, it necessarily "engage[s] others in verbal and intellectual combat."

This is certainly not hard to discern in the conventional Bollywood film, where actors do not so much talk as spout, orate, and hyperbolically perorate, and where success is wholly in the *doing* of things. Heroes and heroines have no problem talking out loud to themselves; but their discussions are neither about nor demand from an audience anything that is analytical, self-reflective, or categorizationally abstract. Talking and existing is fully tied to the operational world. As Nandy has averred, though without connecting it to orality, Hindi films are "anti-psychological"; there is no "interior" story. Nothing exists within a character that is not said. And so, when the police chief in *Sholay* wants vengeance, he expresses himself in the form of a highly dramatized oath, full of bravura and overstated spite. And when in *Hum Aapke Hain Kaun* there is a discussion of familial ethics, it is housed not in personal admittances or intimate confessions, but in publicly shared truths or memories—that is, in clichés, in proverbs, in forms of utterances that are guarded against change because they render knowledge easily transportable.

It is rare, in fact, to find a Hindi film that has not, by its denouement, skidded into language that is noticeably aphoristic. For example, in *Baazigar*, just prior to that film's violent showdown, the protagonist declares imperiously to his fiancée about her diabolical father: "You have only seen the crown on his head. Look under the thief's sleeve and you will find blood." We then witness in flashback the pitiful aftermath of her father's depravity (i.e., his father and sister are dead, his mother stricken with dementia). When we return to the present, it is to the protagonist informing his betrothed with axiomatic import: "You have only been pricked with a thorn. I have been wounded with a trident." Some literate minds may find such dialogue platitudinous, even embarrassing, but that is only because long-term exposure to print has engendered an anxious need to be original, to shun clichés.

Agonistic display in oral narrative (and cultures) manifests itself in other ways, too. Because of the give-and-take nature of oral communications—the fact that all knowledge must pass through word of mouth—interpersonal relationships are generally kept high. In order to render interaction memorable, then, physical behavior is presented in a fashion that is celebrated, exaggerated, even extreme. In Homer, for instance, one finds enthusiastic portrayals of gross physical violence: of "slaughtered corpses" and "bloody filth," and of "jaws glistening, dripping red," as "brazen spearhead[s] smash [their] way clean through below the brain in an upward stroke." As for the *Mahabharata*, who doesn't shudder at Bhima's placing his foot upon the throat of his enemy, so that he might rip open his breast and drink his warm lifeblood? The same applies to Hindi film, where, stagy as they may be, fight scenes are grisly and blood-soaked, with lurid sound effects enhancing the kung-fu kicks, snapped limbs, gruesome impalings, and glass panes literally shattering and plunging "clean through below the brain in an upward stroke." In the protracted 12-minute showdown of *Baazigar*, for instance, an already embattled, blood-soaked Shah Rukh Khan downs seven savage thugs twice his size, is choked once, thrown against a wall twice, finally is skewered (in slo-mo)—and still lives long enough to crawl into his mother's lap, where he can die in maudlin, regressed, and oratorical splendor.

But this is the case not only for antagonistic interchanges; it is equally so for approbatory ones. One finds equal cinematic energy invested in extravagant praise and an unabashed—and to literate minds, over-ripe—glorification of others: of stoic mothers and sacrificing sons, of virtuous daughters and pals-for-life. For instance, in *Sholay*, we find the two male leads racing down a rural road on a motorcycle, declaring boisterously in song, "This friendship will never be destroyed; we'd sooner die than let that occur"; and in *Khal Nayak*, the villain's "Ma," cast here as the receptacle of all goodness and the mute bearer of all ills, is exalted on several occasions—including during an argument, within a sentimental song, and even between the punches of a fistfight.

Amplification and polarization—and their inevitable by-product, melodrama—are also part and parcel of the characters who inhabit orally inscribed narrative. Colorless personalities—characters who are quiet, still, delicately nuanced—cannot survive in such a world. They must, like the mnemonic phrases of an oral epic, be organized into some kind of form that will render them permanently memorable. Hence Bollywood is populated by one-dimensional, oversized, and inflated personalities who can be classified (almost mnemonically) into stereotypes such as "wicked dacoits" and "beautiful village girls," or "victimized mothers" and "millionaire's sons." They are big, they are brash, they are epic. They stand out from the background; they cannot belong to it. (In fact, Indian movie stars—who, for many spectators, have a status akin to that of gods—themselves tend to stand out from the roles they are inhabiting, with most stars playing the same "mnemonic personality" over and over again.)

Of course, one might also say that the background itself stands out, in the sense that these stories are always enacted on sets that are optically excessive, visually voluble. The Hindi film universe is, after all, one of sprawling mansions and evildoer hideaways that smack of Disneyland, of idyllic villages inhabited by people who sport spangled costumes of crisp, clean silk. The real is discarded in favor of the grand, which is certainly more memorable. Fantasy—or, rather, the fanciful, the cinematically resplendent and utopian—though indubitably speaking to an audience's desire for escape from a much less fanciful existence, also fortifies sights and sounds, rendering them less forgettable. The same could be said for the Hindi film's propensity for amplified camerawork, such as its heavy, but never ironic, use of multiple zooms-in on a heroine's horrified look, or its rapid encirclings of the leading man in trouble. Though perhaps excessive and overwrought to the literate mind, such emphatic cinematography provides cues to the spectator that are easy to read, and so to remember—a modern-day extension, perhaps, of the oral epic's reliance on clichés.

Finally, there is the Hindi film's commitment to a Manichean world, one where a highly polarized good and evil are pitted against each other, and where good (that is, the collectively agreed-upon moral order of the world) beats out—virtually without exception—all dark, destructive forces. This should not be surprising, given the reliance on outsized characters who are themselves heavily polarized, the focus on exterior exploits rather than interior consciousness, and the inclination toward the preservation of the existing social structure. This aspect too can be explained when one looks to the structures and performative aspects of orality. For, in an oral universe, the memory cannot retain information that is not sufficiently amplified; nor can the individual afford trajectories that do not pragmatically bolster collective survival. Thus, for very good reason, the ambiguities of existence, the nuances of the psychological self, the grayness of the moral universe, the ordinariness of human life—all those characteristics to which texts circumscribed by literacy are so rigorously devoted—are here rarely to be found.

Oral cinema beyond India

If characteristics of oral performance and orally transmitted narratives were reflected more subtly or less numerously in the Hindi film, it would not be possible to argue that the industry has been largely contoured by the particular cognitive needs of its spectators. But the fact that so many appear so prominently, so resiliently, suggests theoretical legitimacy. Of course, this does not imply that there are not other historical, cultural, or aesthetic influences on the form and content of India's popular cinema and on its success outside national borders. But, certainly it seems that, up to this point, orality's contouring of the Hindi film has been fairly substantial. Further, many of the Bollywood movie's perceived inconsistencies and oft-cited contradictions as a text and practice actually make sense when examined through the prism of orality.

But what about beyond the borders of India? There are other nations that cater to audiences with large non-literate, or low-literate, or linguistically diverse populations; and wouldn't one expect to find national cinemas elsewhere that pay inadvertent heed to the noetic requirements and expectations of their audiences? Certainly. However, there is as yet no similar work on other national cinemas whose roots may have been, or whose existence continues to be, inspired or constrained by an invisibly represented body of spectators. Still, some important evidence from secondary sources seems to confirm the theoretical claim being made here. For instance, in *Planet Hong Kong*, David Bordwell commences his study of Chinese popular cinema with a detailed description of its "distinct aesthetic." Though apparently unacquainted with the movies' oral underpinnings, he describes the form and energies of that mass entertainment as being: (i) non-contemplative, (ii) non-realist, (iii) "Manichean," (iv) loosely plotted (and of "kaleidoscopic variety"), (v) kinesthetically arousing, (vi) flashback-using, (vii) tradition-refining (as opposed to originality-seeking), (viii) favoring formulas and clichés, (ix) brutal in their violence, (x) plagiaristic, and (xi) possessing a tendency to "swerve into a happy ending." I can think of no better support from an impartial outside source than this, and would propose that the common "aesthetic" shared by these two cinematic forms suggests that orality might prove a worthy departure point from which to analyze the cultural, aesthetic, and sociopolitical vicissitudes of various visual media worldwide.

In fact, witnessing orality's vivid circumscription of one nation's cinema assists in exposing its more subtle and sometimes splintered forms elsewhere: in Egyptian cinema, and in the Italian peplums (mythic "sword and sandal" movies) of the 1940s and 50s, and Hollywood blockbusters, like *Titanic, Rambo*, and *Lara Croft: Tomb Raider*; in the *Amar Chitra Katha* comic books and Japanese *manga*; in Doordarshan's *Ramayana* mini-series, Mexican *telenovelas*, and American serials like *Xena: Warrior Princess*; even in MTV and the current spate of popular video games. In other words, narrative heavily inscribed by orality still persists, even within societies that are ostensibly highly literate. It is not a disappearing phenomenon, only a migratory one.

But with regard to the primary audience with which I have been dealing, that is, those of a subaltern status, certainly the new discovery of this transcultural identity has repercussions as regards social inclusion. For programs or movies that the literate-minded tout as superior, meaningful, or original, as being about something *real*, about something that *matters*, may speak more to an individual's literate biases, of his or her literate construction of the world, than to what constitutes an authentic or valid—or even real—representation.

Once, not too long ago, a rhetorical question was formulated, one that has now grown quite famous: Who speaks for the subaltern? We might modify that question somewhat in relation to the media and this invisible marker of identity, and ask: Who speaks in the *language* of the subaltern, so that his representation can be self-accessed and her identification assured? After all, can we rightly say that a media image is "representing," if the spectator it is representing is from the outset noetically excluded from comprehending it?

Of course, with respect to Hindi popular film, one might contend that the subaltern has been speaking all along, and that perhaps it is the built-in limitation of the intellectual community, with its critical imprimatur derived exclusively from *literate* thought and perception, which has caused it to miss this fact—or, at the least, caused it to read only with ideological curiosity and stringent concern what has in fact been a form of subaltern self-constitution.

3.8

Mute bodies, disembodied voices: Notes on sound in Turkish popular cinema
by Nezih Erdoğan

Rather than focus on the visual aspects of a cult cinematic cycle, Nezih Erdoğan provides a study of the role of soundtrack in the 1970's *Yeşilçam* format of popular Turkish film. Focusing on a series of critically derided texts such as *Streetwalker* (1970) and *Goddess of Love* (1969), the author considers the extent to which dubbing inconsistencies added an additional layer of (inadvertent) comic excess to these already melodramatic and fantastical texts. Erdoğan's article takes into account both institutional and technological issues relating to these cult productions, as well as considering possible strategies of resistance that these cinematic inconsistencies achieved. In terms of the soundtrack features under review, the author analyses the limits of lipsynching, the problems of pronunciation and digressions between diegetic and non-diegetic modes of address that these works contain. While these dubbing deficiencies appear as deviations from accepted (i.e. Western) norms of filmmaking, Erdoğan actually links these trashy Turkish texts to longer-standing forms of national fiction, such as *Kardagös*, or traditional shadow play performances. Here, vocal interiority is replaced by a singular puppet master who effectively 'speaks' through all the character types being performed. It is this similar disembodied aesthetic that is produced by the dubbing facilities of the *Yeşilçam*, which Erdoğan then argues offers a resistance to westernized notions of coherent subjectivity. The author extends this analysis to cover both male and female formats of disembodied film, thus providing a necessary examination of the still undertheorized domain of Turkish cult cinema.

A note on the extract: this article first appeared in *Screen* 43:3 in autumn 2002. The original article contained an additional section on the theorization of Turkish dubbing procedures in the light of wider film studies approaches to sound/body in cinema. The original article also contained additional examples of Turkish trash cinematic subversions of accepted dubbing procedures which have been excised for reasons of space.

A paradigmatic shift

In 1997, veteran film star Tanju Gürsu won the award for best male actor at the Antalya Golden Orange Film Festival for his role in *Köpekler Adası/Isle of Dogs* (Halit Refiğ, 1997). The jury's decision provoked heated debate because Gürsu's character had been post-dubbed by another film and theatre actor, Müşfik Kenter. It was questioned whether an actor who borrowed someone else's voice should be honoured with such an award. In connection with this, a newspaper published a series of interviews with various well-known personalities, who expressed a range of opinions on the matter. Burçak Evren, film historian and critic, claimed that dubbing 'prevented film from naturalness and it became something artificial'. The young film director Mustafa Altıoklar emphasized the concept of 'credibility': 'When a film is post-dubbed it is no longer convincing – hence the lack of sincerity. When you shoot the film with sound the player feels the magic more easily.' Şener Şen, the star of Yeşilçam, the mainstream cinema of the 1960s and 1970s, and now superstar of the New Turkish Cinema, referred to the difficulties of dubbing: 'The player forgets the feelings of that particular moment of the shoot and during the dubbing he tries hard to remember them'. Altıoklar argued further that: 'Cinema is fifty per cent sight and fifty per cent sound; ignoring the sound means we start filming with only the remaining fifty per cent'. This chimes with the claim made by the television celebrity Cem Özer, that 'the Yeşilçam actor is sixty per cent absent from the cinema'.

Dubbing, which was standard practice for Yeşilçam, is central to the debates about sound in the emerging New Turkish Cinema. It is a practice which seems unlikely to survive the shift to a new paradigm in which the keywords are 'credibility', 'naturalness' and 'sincerity' – a clear break from Yeşilçam's mode of representation. Although New Turkish Cinema does not seek to disown the heritage of its predecessor entirely, Yeşilçam's conventional use of sound seems to have been abandoned.

The mid 1980s witnessed an attempt at a radical break with Yeşilçam. A number of filmmakers tried their hands at new themes and styles which, roughly speaking, reflected the changing role of women, an increasingly liberal economic policy, the growing interest in various sorts of self-reflexive fiction, and the stylistic influence of television commercials and pop videos. In the latter, I am referring particularly to a visual style which, for example, avoided the flat lighting, highly saturated colour and minimal camera movement favoured by Yeşilçam. In contrast, New Turkish Cinema tended to play on high-key and low-key lighting, chiaroscuro and use of a travelling camera. It was not until 1996, however, that the filmmakers took the final step: one by one they dropped post-dubbing and started shooting with sound. The audience thus saw for the first time the famous Dolby Digital train precede a Turkish film, *Eşkiya/ The Bandit* (Yavuz Turgul, 1995), which quickly became a blockbuster. *Eşkıya* was a Eurimages film, welcomed by the film writers for being as technically flawless as any Hollywood film. Yavuz Turgul, who used to write screenplays for the late Ertem Eğilmez (a director of stereotypical melodramas), did not try to disguise the film's Yeşilçam roots. A documentary on the making of the film shows him on set, lecturing on how Yeşilçam is too easily condemned for its limitations when it should in fact be taken seriously. Indeed, *Eşkiya* addresses issues that Yeşilçam had raised again and again: money versus love, love versus paternal responsibility, dedication versus individual freedom, all boiling down to redemption and sacrifice. Some recent popular films, for example *Ağir Roman/Cholera Street* (Mustafa Altıoklar, 1997), *Dar Alanda Kisa Paslaşmalar/Offside* (Serdar Akar, 2000), *Hemşo/Compatriot* (Ömer Uğur, 2000), and even a very successful television serial, *Ikinci Bahar/Second Spring* (dir. Türkan Derya, tx 2000–2001, designed by Turgul) seem to have taken a similar tack. However, this thematic continuity is overshadowed by some of the practices adopted by

New Turkish Cinema; in addition to shooting with sound, the tendency to construct 'genuine' characters (as against the non-psychological types of Yeşilçam) yielded an altogether different mode of representation. As I will try to demonstrate, the actor's body is the site of this difference.

The criticism levelled against dubbing overlooks the fact that auditory practices are socially constructed and their terms can be challenged by the same values they have adopted. One need only recall the account given by Michel Chion of a Frenchman who travelled to Britain in 1929 to attend the screening of a talking film for the first time. Although the film was perfectly synchronized, he wrote later, 'it was extremely annoying for it strengthened the audience's demand for credibility'. 'But we now know how the film sound developed', says Chion, 'along the lines of establishing tolerances, approximations.' Tolerances may negate and even replace each other, and what is regarded as annoying today may be tolerated tomorrow or vice versa. By tolerance I am referring to a function of the audiovisual contract mutually conceived by the cinematic institution and the viewing subject. In this essay I will discuss some aspects of this contract in its relation to the body as constituted by Yeşilçam. For the sake of convenience, I will limit my essay to two main issues: first, understanding the practice of dubbing in a framework given by the cinematic apparatus which embodies the configurations of the voice and the body; second, 'loss of sight', a recurrent theme in melodrama which becomes symptomatic in its play on characters' sensory perception. These issues demand closer analysis in relation to the development of diverse sound practices.

[. . .]

Dubbing

[. . .]

Many film scholars are surprised to learn that dubbing had not always been standard practice in Turkish Cinema. In the early 1930s Kemal Film, a pioneering film company, hired a German sound technician to build it a studio. In 1932 its contract director, Muhsin Ertuğrul, made the first commercial talking film, *Bir Millet Uyanıyor/A Nation Awakening*. However, a decade later the producers of *Dertli Pınar/ The Troubled Spring* (Faruk Kenç, 1943), who did not want to wait for the arrival of some equipment that had been sent to Germany for maintenance, started shooting without sound. Screenwriter Bülent Oran remembers:

> Silent shooting is easier and more feasible. It saves time and thus cuts down the production costs. Also, it offers the possibility of casting good-looking actors with bad diction. In addition to that, the prompter saves the players from wasting their time by memorizing their lines. That is, to cut a long story short, it offered many advantages.

Until then the existing sound studios were used for dubbing foreign-language films. Interestingly, dubbing was already recognized as part of what made foreign films enjoyable. Among the first dubbing directors were Ferdi Tayfur, who 'gave his voice to' Laurel and Hardy and The Marx Brothers, his sister Adalet Cimcoz, who ran an art gallery, and Nazim Hikmet, an internationally renowned poet who had to flee to Moscow because of his Communist leanings. Turkish audiences still have vivid memories of Tayfur's improvisations in the studio, playing not only with the characters' lines but also with their accents, creating alternative, and more familiar, identities for them than those originally conceived. To his Turkish fans, for example, Groucho Marx was known as Arşak Palabıyıkyan, an Armenian name referring to his bushy moustache. So, in its early years, dubbing did not merely serve as translation from a foreign language into Turkish; it was also the means by which adaptations and imitations were assimilated, creating identifiable characters and plots for the audience.

Obviously, conversion to post-dubbing cannot be explained solely by a studio's impatience over a faulty piece of machinery, rather it can be seen as an anticipation of the shape of things to come. The indigenous film business was given a premature spur, first by tax cuts, then by migration within Turkey from rural areas to big cities. Along with radio, cinema became the leading entertainment form in this period (television took over much later, in the 1970s), and by the early 1960s the growing demand for indigenous films caught producers off guard. The film industry made a number of hasty rearrangements in order to speed up production: flat lighting, fewer camera setups and more remakes (to save on screenwriting time), all of which gave way to a specific form of narration. Given the circumstances, it seems inevitable that Yeşilçam would have to convert to dubbing. It brought with it not only a degree of flexibility, but also a shorter production period, shifting the actors' load onto the sound studios.

There were only a few actors who dubbed themselves. Most were prevented from doing so by the unsuitability of their accent or diction, or by tight schedules. Instead, sound studios hired 'dubbing artists', mostly theatre actors. Dubbing was an extra job for which they were paid well, and a theatrical background meant they generally spoke distinctly and intelligibly. Each film was dubbed in three to five sessions, each lasting three hours. The film was divided into segments and the actors were scheduled accordingly, with the dubbers who were not voicing lead characters often taking on more than one lesser character each. Each segment was looped and played repeatedly while the actors studied the lip movements, if necessary made alterations to the dialogue, and then rehearsed the scene. When the dubbing director felt that they were ready, she/he gave a cue to start recording. During the recording, with the text in their hands, the actors gathered around the microphone and usually maintained the same distance from it regardless of how the players were positioned in relation to the camera. Thus the distance between onscreen actors and the camera and between dubbing actors and the microphone did not cohere: the former varied, while the latter usually remained unchanged; the point of audition was oblivious to both shooting scale and the positions of the actors onscreen.

This may not have been an altogether pleasant situation for the actors. In 1965 Cüneyt Arkın, at the beginning of a brilliant acting career, wrote that to rely too heavily on dubbing during the shooting ruined an actor's performance. He suggested that due to lack of rehearsal time or from carelessness, the actor would not be able to appropriate the dialogue for herself/himself and often feared that the lines would not be given in good time. However, she/he trusted that all these mistakes would be repaired in that magic place, the sound studio: 'The actor, then, trying to get rid of her/his line at once, rolls up the words and does not care to convey their meanings'. For example, we could envisage a scene in which two characters are having a conversation. Since the players would only be able to have a quick glance through the screenplay and would not know what they were supposed to say, they would need a prompt to read out their lines for them. The prompt – usually the scriptgirl – sometimes had to hide behind a couch or under a table to avoid being caught on camera. She occupied a space within the diegesis of the film, yet was always invisible. For the actors onscreen it is the prompt who initiates and controls their speech: the first player repeats to the second player what she has just heard from the prompt. The second player does not listen to her but to the prompt, who is now reading out his lines. This means that on the sonic level, the body of the Yeşilçam screen actor is a waiting body; waiting and anxious to hear what is to come from a place other than that represented visually onscreen. The discrepancy between the visual and the aural is divisive in both its reception and its delivery of speech. The film actually represents two voices which come simultaneously from different sources – one from the player in the space of the profilmic event and the other from the prompt who, whilst present, is deliberately absented from the visual field. This is further complicated by the fact that during the screening the audience hears neither of the two; it receives the voices and sounds from the sound studio.

Yeşilçam is prone to other discontinuities and failures. Lipsynch, for example, may collapse at anytime; on many occasions the audience will see the actor opening her/his mouth with no voice to accompany it, and speech will be heard after the mouth is shut. Another technical failure is the distortion of the first syllable of words. Such an error may cause an exclamation required at a climactic moment (for example, 'Hayır! Olamaz!'/'No, that's impossible!') to be unintentionally hilarious ('N'ayır! N'olamaz!'/ 'No! N'at's n'impossible!'). Another more consistent discrepancy can be observed in the process of reverberation. As I have already mentioned, the reverberation or audible placing of the actors produced in the soundtrack does not mirror the space of the imagetrack in the way we expect today. An example would be the cliche of two lovers meeting on a hill with a view of the sea and the city of Istanbul: even when the bodies are clearly placed outdoors, 'their' voices come from an interior. Ambient sound is scarcely used – no wind blowing, no waves breaking, no birds chirping – music compensates for everything. If sound-effects were used, they were mostly produced in the studio; if there was time to search the archives for suitable sources, then stock material was used. From this perspective, the soundtrack of Yeşilçam appears extremely impoverished. Take, for instance, the opening scenes of *Sürtük/Streetwalker* (Ertem Eğilmez, 1970): we see Ekrem (Ekrem Bora), a tough owner of a chain of music halls, and his men in a car on their way to bust a night club. On the soundtrack we hear jazz music which is apparently non-diegetic. On reaching the club the men beat up a bodyguard who stands in their way and enter, pushing through a crowd dancing to the same music, which has now become diegetic. Aside from music, the soundtrack contains only footsteps and the sounds of intermittent fighting between Ekrem's men and the guards. The sound-effects thus function only as 'images of sounds' and are not intended to produce a reality effect. A final significant discrepancy relates to singing, which also functions in a curious manner. This is especially important, for Yeşilçam as a genre is dominated by melodrama. Many of the films exploit singing both for its entertainment value and to enable a twist in the narrative. A common plot follows a poor female character who becomes a famous singer. In *Hayatım Sana Feda/This Life Devoted to You* (Muzaffer Aslan, 1970) – a film which I will discuss in detail later – the star, Türkan Şoray, is dubbed by Adalet Cimcoz. However, when she begins to sing, we hear the voice of Lale Belkıs, another well-known actor and singer. To us the screen actor's body, commuting between voices, is possessed twice, for narrative (speech) and for non-narrative (musical performance) purposes.

Rick Altman suggests how the image – or, to be more precise, the body – may serve as an alibi for the voice onscreen. He argues that sound in cinema is like a ventriloquist who 'uses' the body, that is, manipulating it as if it were a puppet. Trying to conceal the fact that the voice comes from the loudspeakers placed behind the screen, the players move their lips and the audience is led to – and wants to – believe that its source is someone within the diegesis of the film. Thus, an impression of reality is maintained and the audience is protected from the uncanny effect of the voice coming from a non-human source (the speakers). Altman's analogy may be extended further: the practice of dubbing as described above suggests that in Yeşil-çam, it may appear as if all the puppets are 'spoken' by the same ventriloquist. This is very much in accordance with the traditional shadow play, *Karagöz*, which was dethroned by cinema. The *Karagöz* master (*hayali*) speaks through the mouths of all the types, each with a different accent, and even produces the musical score as well as the sound effects (mostly by the help of a *def*, a kind of tambourine with cymbals). What are the implications of this?

In a discussion of what happened to the body with the coming of sound, Stephen Heath draws on the observation by Jean-Luc Godard and Jean-Pierre Gorin that when the cinema began to speak, every actor began to speak the same thing. He argues:

> Evidently there is a strong homogenization and idealization of the silent cinema here that needs resisting and analyzing, but the point remains valid that the sound cinema is the development of a powerful standard of the body and of the voice as hold of the body in image. . . . In the silent cinema, the body is always pulling towards an emphasis, an exaggeration, a burlesque (the term of an intractable existence); in the sound cinema, the body is smoothed out, given over to that contract of thought described by Godard-Gorin, with the voice as the medium, the expression, of a homogenous thinking subject – actor and spectator – of film.

Although Heath is writing of sound cinema in general, his observations are insightful. Does Yeşilçam allow for or produce a thinking subject? Do the actors all speak the same thing? I would argue that, as far as the dubbing described above is concerned, they do not speak at all. Their bodies are given over not to homogenous thinking subjects but to Logos expressing itself through voices that were only slackly attached to bodies. Hence Yeşilçam is like the shadow-play master whose voice remains the same by way of the differences it produces. It might well be suggested that the voice *in* Yeşilçam is the voice *of* Yeşilçam; the utterances are instances of Logos which dictates its moral universe and orchestrates the unfolding narrative. An analysis of the scripts may confirm this. Onat Kutlar, in his criticism of Yeşilçam screenplays, argues that speech is, in effect, mostly redundant, for it simply describes the action, and the language itself is not colloquial, ultimately producing a kind of cinema which is not 'alive'. Thus an actor in Yeşilçam, I maintain, is 'be-spoken'. This is why almost all of the dialogue, instead of functioning as the indices of a character's interior psychological situation, transform all the characters into a set of statements. Does this therefore suggest that speech in these instances takes more or less the form of a voiceover? For although bodies are seemingly assigned to speech, the soundtrack, and particularly the sound of the voice, fails to conceal the fact that it (and thus Logos) simply uses bodies as a vehicle for its mediation. The voice is thus disembodied, and this disembodied voice creates/comes from a theocentric space. In an endnote to her article on the articulation of body and sound in cinema, Mary Ann Doane points to these theological implications of the disembodied voice:

> Two kinds of 'voices without bodies' immediately suggest themselves – one theological the other scientific (two poles which, it might be added, are not ideologically unrelated): (1) the voice of God incarnated in the Word; (2) the artificial voice of a computer. Neither seems to be capable of representation outside a certain anthropomorphism, however. God is pictured, in fact, as having a quite specific body – that of a male patriarchal figure.

Whilst western culture allows for a visual representation of God, endowing Him with a male, patriarchal body, the voiceover nonetheless gains its theological status thanks to its disembodiment. Leaving aside the ambiguity that arises from the possibilities of representing God, I want to reiterate with Doane that in the classical cinema the use of voiceover can reveal the relationship between sexual difference and its theological implications.

Doane's arguments, however, are related to a specific cultural heritage and belief system. In contrast, Yeşilçam originates from a very different conception of reality and the relationship between various domains of Being. Islam, not unlike some eastern doctrines such as Tibetean Buddhism and Taoism, devised a conception of Being – Allah – which escapes any kind of figurative representation, let alone anthropomorphism. If we leave aside the symbolism of esoteric teachings (such as Sufism) which can mostly be traced in literary texts, it is clear that personification, and therefore spatio-temporalization, of Allah is strictly avoided. Seyyid Hussein Nasr argues:

> Islamic aniconism, which removes the possibility of the concretization of the Divine Presence (*hudur*) in an icon or image, is a powerful factor in intensifying the spiritual significance of the void in the Muslim mind. . . . God and His revelation are not identified with any particular place, time or object. Hence His Presence is ubiquitous. He is everywhere, in whichever direction one turns, as the Quranic verse, 'Whithersoever ye turn, there is the face of God' (II; 115), affirms.

Obviously, all this is not to say that space-time is devoid of divinity, for everything serves as a sign-vehicle of the Divine. The dichotomy of the embodied voice/ disembodied voice, in so far as it reserves a specific place for God as the disembodied voice or Logos, is based on Christian theology which, as Doane argues, eventually issued a patriarchal figure, whereas Islam strictly rejects attributing a body to Allah. Hence in Islam Logos may penetrate all bodies. I think this may provide us with clues as to how voiceover functions differently in Yeşilçam: having diffused the 'Divine Presence' throughout the soundtrack, voiceover proper and voiceover as travesty of dialogue eventually blur the border between what we may perceive as diegetic and non-diegetic, thus making it impossible to identify the male voice alone with the attributes of the apparatus.

Blind men 'seeing' the voice

The play between the voice and the body may be still more complicated, however. The voice may be seen to establish a character, but then transcend it by restoring the distance between audience and character onscreen. This may be understood through 'loss of sight', an often ridiculed theme which is very common in Turkish melodrama. I will argue that this subgenre may serve as an object-lesson for my purposes in this essay.

In his essay on Indian melodrama, a genre which heavily influenced Turkish cinema, Ravi Vasudevan argues that the man's loss of sight connotes his indifference to the woman's desire. Indeed, in *Aşk Mabudesi/Goddess of Love* (Nejat Saydam, 1969), for example, former lovers Leyla (Türkan Şoray) and Ekrem (Cüneyt Arkın) encounter each other in a music hall. Leyla does not know that Ekrem has had an accident and has lost his sight. Ekrem shivers, and when his companion asks him what happened he replies that he felt the presence of someone he knew. Leyla looks at him but he does not return her gaze. Her heart broken, she leaves. Thus it may be suggested that his loss of sight makes him indifferent to, and unaware of, her desire. However, the theme of the blind man in Turkish cinema requires a broader scope that enables a discussion of body–voice split. The incidents and coincidences – blindness being the most prominent – devised by Yeşilçam are carefully planned and controlled by the logic which also governs the construction of cinematic bodies. Sightlessness provides clues about the psychic mechanisms at work in Yeşilçam's approach to voice and body. When the characters are or become blind, desire is not only made possible but also mediated by the voice which is disembodied not for the audience but for the character in the diegesis of the film. This involves an investment in the diegetic/character and non-diegetic/audience (op)positions.

Both men and women may be subject to a deprivation of this kind, but economy of sexual difference dictates a specific plot for each sex. In *Feride* (Metin Erksan, 1971), *Aşk Mabudesi* and *Adını Anmayacağım/I Shan't Recall Your Name* (Orhan Elmas, 1971), the man, having split up with his woman, loses his sight. For instance, *Feride* tells the story of Kemal (Engin Çaglar) who sees his wife, Feride (Emel Sayin), in the arms of another man and thinks he is dishonoured. In fact, the man has set them up, but no matter how hard Feride tries to explain the situation, Kemal will not listen and sends her away in disgrace. Left in the house with a collaborator in the deception, Füruzan (Lale Belkıs, the archetypal wicked blonde), Kemal proceeds to lose all his money in a desperate card game. When Füruzan realizes that she will not now be able to enjoy his wealth she walks out. Then Kemal loses his sight as a result of heavy drinking. He retires to a modest house and lives in isolation, but one day he meets, in a nearby park, a little girl whose charm returns the joy of life to him. She is, of course, his daughter by Feride, who is now a famous singer. Feride comes to his house in search of the child and they meet again. She manages to overcome the shock of seeing him and easily convinces Kemal, who shows his horror and disgust upon hearing her voice, that she is not Feride but someone else. She begins to visit him regularly and they start an 'innocent' affair which lasts until Kemal regains his sight thanks to a successful operation. Feride disappears again but, in the end, the child reunites them.

Adını Anmayacağım follows the same plot with a slight variation: Gül (Hülya Koçyiğit) returns home as a nurse to look after Engin (Cüneyt Arkın). Neither he nor their grown-up daughter, Oya, recognize her. Engin falls in love with Gül and decides to have the operation to cure his blindness ('I want to look at you until I am gratified!'). Just as Gül is about to disappear out of the fear that Engin would expel her again if he saw her, she learns that the man who destroyed her marriage is now after their daughter. Indeed the man drugs Oya and attempts to rape her. Gül follows them and saves Oya but has to kill the man. In court she does not even defend herself but, having learned that she is sacrificing her life for the honour of the family, Engin appears as a lawyer and 'proclaims' the truth. When he tells the judge and the audience the sad story of Gül, their sympathy stands in for the verdict and the narrative jumps to her immediate release and the reunion of the family. It is significant here that the space of the Law is where all misunderstanding and conflict are resolved. As already discussed, *Aşk Mabudesi* deviates from this plot but still conforms to the same structure. Ekrem and Leyla fall in love and decide to marry. However, a jealous ex-fiancee convinces Leyla that she has caused the suicide of Ekrem's brother. She unwillingly leaves Ekrem on the pretext of her desire for a singing career. When Ekrem learns that she actually loves him, he rushes to her home but crashes his car on the way. He loses his sight but pride prevents him from letting her know this. They run into each other on a few occasions, but since Leyla does not know that he is blind she thinks Ekrem is refusing to acknowledge her presence/appearance and thus her desire. In the end, however, she learns the truth and they are reunited.

All three plots position the woman as the victim of a third party. The male protagonist's rejection of the woman is repaid by a split in his perception of the world. The disappearance of the woman coincides with the man's loss of sight and sometimes his property, thus exposing castration as a necessary ordeal. He is blinded by what he has seen (because he has believed in the truth of what he apparently 'sees') and thus fails to 'see' what the woman is really saying. The voice attached to the female body is now a waste of words and the body is established as the site which negates the desire of the man and the family that legitimates his desire. Anything that her body will now emit, vocally such as explanations and excuses, or physically such as another body (a baby), is discarded as waste, if not abject. Only then may the woman return as the voice. Her voice is thus worth listening to only when it is detached from its 'material' source, that is, her body. The proximity of the protagonists may vary: in *Feride* and *Adını Anmayacağım* they are within each other's reach, whereas in *Aşk Mabudesi*, Ekrem can hear Leyla's singing only via loud speakers placed outside the music hall. In different contexts the woman's voice represents both closure and disclosure, revealing an ambivalent attitude towards the female voice. So while Ekrem can listen to Leyla singing, which stands in for her presence, Engin cannot endure Gül's voice coming from the radio; agitated, he yells to have it turned off. Yet both types of reaction arguably derive from the same psychic structure: the mother's voice is substituted for the umbilical cord, but at the same time it evokes the painful memory of rupture.

The audience's identification with the male character is understood in narrative terms as the sharing of the same information about a given situation. At the moment of crisis this position shifts to one of empathy; the audience knows more than the character does, and does not approve of his attitude, yet will still side with him. While the audience is almost always given an omniscient view, the pathos of melodrama lies in the flaws in the distribution of information. Empathy returns to a position of identification only when the male character begins to 'see', which also returns the voice to the body of the female character. This is why the audience feels so frustrated when the character cannot see what it sees – that the voice which is divine to the male character is in fact coming from the body he condemned as disgraceful.

Blind women 'hearing' the sight

Women lose their sight, too. They are either already blind when the film opens (*Üç Arkadaş*/*Three Comrades* [Memduh Ün, 1958, 1971], *Serseri*/*The Tramp* [O. Nuri Ergün, 1959]) or lose their sight very early on (*Hayatım Sana Feda*). Therefore, unlike the men who pay for their misunderstandings, women's loss coincides only with the initial narrative thrust. And while men begin to see in the finale, women's acquisition of sight, instead of concluding the film, gives the narrative a final push: the beloved one is still to be attained. The woman has to choose the right man from several who claim the same identity, and has to return the male voice, which is the source of her desire, to the originary body. The emblematic film here is *Üç Arkadaş*. It features Muhterem Nur as a blind girl who earns a living by selling safety pins on the street. Three musicians, all male, seeing that she is vulnerable to the dangers of the big city, take her to their ramshackle house. Here they construct a make-believe world for her, convincing her that she is living with successful musicians in a luxurious villa. They find the money necessary for an operation to cure her blindness, but the moment she regains her sight they disappear. She goes on to become a famous singer and starts to search for them. On finding the house where they used to live, she realizes she had become a part of, and target for, their fiction. Even the portrait which they had told her was of an aristocratic ancestor turns out to be a kitsch painting of an ape. In the end she finds them by following the distant sound of their voices.

Hayatım Sana Feda, meanwhile, tells the story of Zeynep (Türkan Şoray), who loses her sight in a car accident. Harun (Cüneyt Arkın), who is responsible for the accident, tries to help Zeynep financially only to find that she is too proud to accept such an offer and is full of hatred for the man who caused her loss of sight. Zeynep finds a job as a singer in a music hall, whose owner agrees to employ her on the condition that the audience must not realize that she is blind. In order for her to act as if she could see, his authorial voice maps the space of her performance, with the microphone (the 'phallus') in the centre: 'First find the microphone', he instructs, 'it will be your guide on the stage. Then five steps to the right and then five to the left. That is all.' Thus Zeynep's body becomes a spectacle for the audience in reference to the microphone which mediates her voice and serves as her anchor on stage. But Zeynep's desire will jeopardize this illusion. Harun introduces himself as a blind musician and soon they fall in love. One night, after she has sung one of Harun's songs, her awareness of his presence in the audience endangers the power of the microphone (as phallus), and she fails to locate it and loses her balance. Surprisingly, Zeynep's desire is not punished and the accident does not have serious consequences. Harun provides the money for an operation and, once Zeynep can see, he disappears and then reappears in the guise of a music tycoon, Kemal, who is willing to make her a star. Kemal proposes to her and she accepts, but this fails to make him happy. Kemal feels betrayed and swears to take revenge on behalf of his 'true' self, Harun. But the day before their marriage, Zeynep, while singing, has a vision of Harun (whose face is obscured) and realizes that she is still in love with him. She confesses to Kemal that she cannot marry him, upon which he reveals his true identity.

[. . .]

Since the voice is always the medium of truth – although it reserves a right to fiction – it belongs to a higher order in the hierarchy of Being. However, as I have tried to demonstrate, this does not mean that Yeşilçam aims to establish the Cartesian body–soul duality. In connection with this, a Sufi source gives an eloquent illustration of a change in the body of the prophet Joseph, Jacob's eleventh son. Having shed all his wordly desires and personal attributes, the appearance of Joseph undergoes a radical transformation: 'His body is not wrapped around flesh but Divine Love, thus his skin becomes transparent; when he eats, one can see the colour of the food going down his throat, and when he drinks it is possible to see the flow of the drink'. Curiously, the text does not stop there: 'Looking at the soles of his feet, one can see his face. I cannot give an exhaustive account of all the implications of this story, I must be content with saying that this, obviously, does not suggest a rejection of the body in favour of spirituality, that is, a split between 'body' and 'soul'. On the contrary, Divine Love penetrates Joseph's body, releasing its parts from the hierarchy (head/feet, heaven/ earth) into which they were initially inscribed. By the same token, by giving the body to the service of Logos and frequently by denying the characters the 'look', and therefore the sight of the body (particularly the body of the other), Yeşilçam appears to have separated the two domains. Ultimately, however, the body–soul duality is resolved, since it is made clear that there has to be a body in the first place, for it is the body which makes the mediation of voice, and thus truth, possible.

3.9

Ichi the Killer
by Tom Mes

While Japanese extreme cinema has frequently been a favoured object for European and North American cult film scholars, it is the cinema of Miike Takashi that has given it renewed controversy and prominence in recent years. It was the release of Miike's *Audition* in 2000 that revealed the director to a wider international audience as a filmmaker with a cruel but creative cinematic eye. The film (depicting the downfall of a lonely widower who unwittingly chooses a manhating dominatrix as his new bride) introduced the curious concept of torture by cheesewire into the vocabulary of cult cinema. It is Miike's more recent, even more controversial film *Ichi the Killer* that is the subject of Tom Mes' chapter. This narrative (based on a Manga comic strip) features a sexually retarded adolescent hero who manages to (literally) cut a swath through local warring Yakuza gangs with a pair of razor sharp ice skates. With its emphasis on sadism, sexual torture and extreme CGI body horror effects, *Ichi the Killer* has appealed and appalled in equal measure. However, despite the labels of exploitation and misogyny frequently associated with the film, Mes argues that Miike's skill is in implicating the audience in the extreme acts of violence unfolding in this curious cult narrative. Interestingly, these transgressive acts of spectator inclusion occur along gendered lines via a distinction of the excessive and comically orientated CGI scenes of Ichi's murderous quest from the far more disturbing sequences of a Yakuza-led rape and torture of a young female prostitute. One sequence of sexual violation, which Mes discusses in some depth, uses the soundtrack to convey extremes of punishment absent from the screen and conveys Miike's ability to exploit all aspects of the cinematic medium for unsettling effect. Although this scene gives the appearance of female violation as being at the cult core of *Ichi the Killer*, Mes argues that sadomasochistic relations are ultimately played out between male characters in the text, as he exemplifies in an analysis of the relationship between Ichi and his nemesis Kakihara which closes the final article in this section.

A note on the extract: this chapter was originally published in the book *Agitator: The Cinema of Takashi Miike*, which Tom Mes published in 2003. As the first English language book-length consideration of Miike, the whole of the volume offers a fascinating study of this confrontational cult figure. Of particular merit is Chapter 2, which outlines the importance of key themes (such as the role of violence, the family unit and the geographical displacement) in the director's work. The original version of the chapter included in this volume contained a longer consideration of the narrative of *Ichi the Killer*.

If one thing stands out about *Ichi the Killer*, it's the film's extremely violent content and the strong reactions this provoked from audiences and critics alike. Based on a manga by Hideo Yamamoto (not to be confused with the cinematographer of the same name, who also worked on this film), *Ichi the Killer* has been dismissed as exploitative, misogynist, indulgent and as simply an example of pushing the envelope to see how far one film (and one filmmaker) can go in the depiction of violence.

[. . .]

It's a paradox, but *Ichi the Killer*, a film that sets new boundaries in the portrayal of violence and bloodshed, takes a strongly critical stance towards the portrayal and the consumption of the violent image. However, it does so without ever taking a moral stance towards either the portrayal or the consumption, thus circumventing any accusations of hypocrisy on the part of the director. Miike does not moralise or chastise, but provokes the audience into questioning their own attitudes towards viewing images of violence. He steers them into a direction but leaves it up to them to draw their own conclusion.

Miike's intentions pervade the film on every level, in form as much as in content. Characterisation is a crucial tool in this respect, but the characters are so well drawn, developed and motivated that for the most part even regarded purely as a character study, *Ichi the Killer* works rather well. If we look at the film in this way, we notice that the narrative again follows Miike's regular thematic process faithfully, combining two main strands from previous films: *MPD-Psycho*'s theme of mental rootlessness (in the shape of the titular killer who is the subject of mind control through hypnotic suggestion) and *Audition*'s theme of the search for happiness in an ideal partner.

Protagonist Kakihara (Tadanobu Asano) is the person doing the searching here. Like *Audition*'s Aoyama he has lost the person he loves, who in this case is the boss of the Anjo yakuza group to whom he served as main lieutenant. Instead of the homosexual relationship this would at first glance appear to be, the bond between the two men is based on pain as much as love: masochist Kakihara found in Anjo the sadist who could fulfil his every desire, as witnessed by the scars that cover his face. Their relationship was so ideal (the fact that aside from one brief glimpse from the back Anjo is never seen adds to the near-mythical status he holds in Kakihara's eyes) that Anjo's death has left Kakihara with no one to satisfy his need. As top lieutenant in one of the most powerful crime syndicates in Shinjuku, he is now a masochist with no one to hurt him.

In effect, the death of Anjo has made Kakihara rootless, unable to be what he truly is. This rootless state is expressed in two ways: first in the character's persistent belief that his boss is still alive (the culprits removed his body and cleaned up the crime scene in order to make it seem like a disappearance), leading him into a determined search for any trace of Anjo's whereabouts. Secondly it's expressed in the fact that during his search Kakihara tortures the people he even slightly suspects of being involved, something he does with glee. The displacement from his true nature has made him the opposite of what he is: he behaves as a sadist instead of a masochist.

The actions he undertakes as a result of becoming rootless inevitably force him into the position of an outcast. After receiving a tip-off, he takes to torturing Suzuki (Susumu Terajima), a lower-ranking member of an affiliate yakuza group. Kakihara suspends him on hooks through his flesh and goes to work on him with needles and boiling oil, until Suzuki's boss (Jun Kunimura) intervenes, furious at Kakihara's actions. Kakihara's method of apology makes the situation even worse. Instead of chopping off the customary pinky, he takes a blade to his own tongue and is quickly expelled from the outfit by godfather Nakazawa (Yoshiki Arizono).

[. . .]

The slicing of his tongue was also a form of masturbation, a temporary fulfilment of Kakihara's own desires. This indicates how Kakihara's only loyalty is to those desires. Later, when he finds irrefutable evidence that Anjo is indeed dead, the search for the killer is not a quest for vengeance, but a search for a replacement sadist. Especially when the assassin continues his slaughter among Kakihara's men, the masochist admires the gruesome results of the killer's handiwork in awe and realises that he has found the person who can give him the pain he longs for. The irony that Kakihara's new potential lover is the same man who killed his boss and previous lover only serves to illustrate where the protagonist's priorities lie.

There's further irony in the situation since the killer in question, the Ichi of the title (Nao Ômori), is even more of a rootless individual than Kakihara. He is the victim of mind control by his employer Jijii (Shinya Tsukamoto) and has therefore entirely lost his identity. Barely an adult, his immature sexual drives have formed the source for Jijii's manipulation. The hypnotist placed in his mind the false memory of a traumatic event he supposedly witnessed in high school, whereby several bullies raped a girl in front of him and Ichi was not only unable to intervene, he was sexually aroused by the sight of such humiliation and pain inflicted on another human being. The resulting duality between Ichi's hatred of bullies and excitement over the infliction of pain on others is what allows Jijii to manipulate him and use him as little more than a weapon. By associating Ichi's target with the high school bullies, he creates the willingness to intervene, while Ichi's sadism and the excitement it evokes make him a gruesomely effective murderer. Jijii's handling of Ichi is almost mechanical; the young man's loss of identity has gone so far as to rob him of his humanity.

An early scene in the film establishes Ichi's confused personality. After murdering Anjo, he spies on hooker Sara (Mai Gotô) as she is viciously beaten and then raped by her pimp (Hôka Kinoshita). When a sound betrays Ichi's presence, the pimp comes out to look for the intruder, only to find a fresh glob of semen where Ichi was standing just moments earlier. This scene is later reprised, this time resulting in a confrontation between Ichi and the pimp. Ichi kills the bully (he uses a razor sharp blade in the heel of his left shoe to kill), then turns to Sara and says: "I'll rape you now, if you want." Judging from these words, it's not rape in itself that upsets Ichi, but the pimp's bullying behaviour. Quite the opposite, Ichi is very happy to take the dead man's place if Sara wants him to.

[. . .]

This scene also sets up Ichi's compatibility with Kakihara, the only character who would be happy to accept Ichi's proposal of a voluntary beating. This division between sadist and masochist not only holds true for them, but also forms the most fundamental definition of all other characters, who are predominantly one or the other.

[. . .]

Kaneko in turn is an unmistakeable masochist. A retread of such earlier failed characters as *Rainy Dog*'s Yuji, *Full Metal Gokudô*'s Keisuke and *Visitor Q*'s Kiyoshi, he is a former policeman kicked off the force after losing his gun. Then his wife left him too, leaving him – in another parallel with *Rainy Dog*'s protagonist – with their 12-year old son Takeshi (Hiroyuki Kobayashi). Kaneko's failures have therefore made him an outcast, who found his group unit only through more failure, when Takayama saved him from a beating by another gangster in an alleyway. Inducted into the Anjo group at Takayama's request, he is an outcast there too, the subject of ridicule due to being an ex-cop who lost his gun but is now supposed to function as expert marksman gangster (here again we see Miike's use of irony as a tool to define characters rather than as an end unto itself).

[. . .]

The one exception to *Ichi the Killer*'s cast of clearly defined characters is Jijii. While it's clear what he wants – the total annihilation of the Anjo group in the most humiliating way possible (which in fact makes him the film's biggest sadist) – why he wants this remains an enigma. His motivation, as well as his exact function and his relation to the other characters (including Ichi) is never explained. This seeming (and seemingly blatant, since he could be considered the story's main villain) discrepancy is in fact the most crucial clue as to the film's true intent.

The function of Jijii is to be found in what he does, not in why he does it. To ask why is beside the point. He is a manipulator, the man who pulls the strings and determines the flow of the other characters' lives, either by proxy (through Ichi) or occasionally in person. He is in many ways a godlike being (his all-powerful nature is illustrated visually in the one scene in which he interferes in person: confronting Takayama, Jijii undresses to reveal the body of a champion weightlifter). In cinema however, there is only one godlike being, who controls all the characters and determines their lives, and that is the director. Jijii's function here is to serve as the director's alter ego. His manipulation of the other characters in the end serves the purpose of manipulating the audience, in other words the function of Jijii equals that of the director.

This relationship is most directly apparent in Jijii's treatment of Ichi. Ichi's costume, a padded leather suit with a large yellow '1' (pronounced *ichi* in Japanese) on the back, is reminiscent of the costume of a superhero, complete with emphasised masculine build and a logo. A hero, in its literary function, is a character who does good deeds by evil means (i.e. the use of violence) and who provides the audience with a source for (often vicarious) identification. Ichi however, uses those evil means, but does no good deeds. He looks like a hero and uses the same methods, but the hero's justification for his violence is missing. Thanks to Jijii's manipulation, he becomes a perversion of the hero figure. The first time we see him is in the scene where he spies on the beating of Sara. We see him from a distance and from the back. What catches the viewer's eye is his logo, establishing the connection with the hero figure. This set-up is further expanded by the situation, which is straight from a superhero comic book and creates the expectation that the hero will rescue the damsel in distress. But instead he is revealed as a voyeur, who gets off on seeing people hurt and humiliated. In parallel with the way Jijii has robbed him of his individuality and any semblance of heroism, with this scene Miike the director robs the audience of its identification figure. Here, the parallel between Jijii and the director is established.

But this scene is only the first step in a process aimed at making the audience question its own attitude towards the viewing of violence. By depriving them of one identification figure, Miike effectively forces them to side with the other: Kakihara. In this context, Kakihara's masochism gains a new dimension. While we've seen that most characters are masochistic in nature, none of them take pleasure in it the way Kakihara does. He undergoes pain with glee and revels in violence, making the connection between him and the audience, who consume the violence in the film not unlike he does, a suitable one. It's also an intentional one: when Ichi cuts Sara's pimp in half from head to crotch or slices up a group of gangsters, covering the room in body parts and blood, at those moments Miike wants us to laugh and go "Wow!" In fact he provokes it through the style he employs in these scenes. Their explicitness, exaggeration, and the use of CGI and special effects renders the violence in these scenes harmless. The explicitness makes them darkly comic instead of painful or offensive. When Kakihara pours hot oil over the defenceless Suzuki, it's not an act of violence but one of the director's trademark kitchen jokes, since the protagonist used that oil to fry shrimp just seconds earlier.

Unlike the dark comedy such jokes created out of violence in *Shinjuku Outlaw*, *Fudoh* and *Dead or Alive*, in *Ichi the Killer* they serve a higher purpose. Right after we laugh or let out that collective "Wow!" we are smacked square in the face for it, because Miike alternates this 'playful' violence with 'painful' violence; violence that has a much stronger and much less pleasurable impact on the viewer (the switching between these two could be seen as a variation on the juxtaposition-based style of *Dead or Alive* and *Full Metal Gokudô*). Right after we chuckle over Jijii and his men slipping on a floor covered in blood and entrails, we are forced to sit through the beating and rape of Sara, which is anything but playful. Here too it's Miike's style that forces this reaction in the viewer and interestingly the stylistic approach is the complete opposite of the comical violence. Instead of explicitness he opts for suggestion and instead of special effects he employs montage and sound to achieve the desired effect, expanding upon the work he did in this area in the finale of *Audition*.

The two scenes of beating and rape of Sara never show the physical impact of fists or feet on the woman's body, instead either letting them take place off screen or suggesting the impact through choice of camera angle or by cutting away just before the impact to its direct aftermath. In a later scene where a woman's nipples are sliced off with a small hobby knife, the blade is never seen touching flesh. This particular sequence consists of four shots:

1. The first is a close-up of the woman's breast on a metal tabletop, the nipple stretched out with a clamp.
2. The second is a close shot of the knife as it slides out of its sheathe and taps the metal surface.
3. The third shot is slightly wider, a medium close-up, seen from above, of the hand holding the knife scratching across the table towards the breast. At the moment when knife and flesh are supposedly about to touch, Miike cuts to the fourth shot.
4. A wide shot of Jirô (Suzuki Matsuo), the culprit, standing on the table, his arm

making the last movement of what is supposed to have been the cutting, away from either breast.

This montage suggests the movement of the knife across the table and through the flesh but never shows it. The sound effects of the knife scraping across the metal surface of the table helps the audience fill in the blanks.

By using suggestion, Miike implicates the audience in the violence. The violence the viewer purports to have seen took place not on the screen but in his or her own head. The viewer creates and decides for himself the intensity of the violence in these scenes. If it shocks the viewer, then to all intents and purposes the viewer is shocked by his own imagination. The viewer fills in the blanks and is provoked into finding violence inside himself, violence that is more painful and disturbing than anything Miike explicitly shows in the film, because each individual viewer decides the intensity of it for himself.

It's not a coincidence that many of the victims in these 'painfully' violent scenes are women. The use of female characters in these scenes forms part of the provocation of the audience. Since women are regarded as weaker, more fragile and less able to defend themselves than men, their presence as victims adds to the impact the scene makes on the audience. This is a matter of filmmaking technique, it has nothing whatsoever to do with ideology and can therefore not be considered misogynist. Particularly when the filmmaker's intention is to make the viewer question the uncritical consumption of violent images. This leaves no room for misogyny, since it would contradict the intent.

The director's intentions and the role of Jijii as his alter ego therein come to a head in the film's finale. The film builds up to this scene with the promise of a showdown between Kakihara and Ichi. Although it whets the audience's appetite for more violence, what it delivers is something else entirely. Set on a rooftop, the scene does indeed pitch Ichi against Kakihara, but the showdown Kakihara and the audience hope for doesn't come. This is the final provocation on the part of the director (towards the audience) as well as Jijii (towards Kakihara). Just as the confrontation starts, it's interrupted by Kaneko, who with Kakihara is the last surviving member of the Anjo gang. Learning from his son that the man his group had been looking for is the same who taught Takeshi to fight, and misunderstanding Kakihara's wish to be killed by Ichi as the ultimate masochistic kick, he interferes and points his gun at Ichi. Hypnotised by Jijii into believing that Kaneko is his older brother who bullied him as a child, Ichi confronts Kaneko instead, leaving Kakihara behind, alone and jealous.

Ichi slashes Kaneko's throat and receives a bullet in the foot from the ex-cop in return. Now Ichi is down on the ground, unable to use his leg to kick or even walk. Takeshi starts kicking him as he lies there helpless and crying. Ichi has become the opposite of Kakihara's ideal sadist, and the protagonist watches the scene in despair, yelling: "There's nobody left to kill me." To get rid of the symbol of his disillusionment – the sound of Ichi's crying – Kakihara sticks the needles he was fighting Ichi with into his own ears. A CGI shot shows the needles entering, piercing his ear drums and moving even further inside: there's no one left to hurt him, so he does it himself. Like the cutting of his own tongue, the piercing of his eardrums is masturbation, which here underlines his disappointment.

The sound of Ichi's cries fades and disappears over a close-up of Kakihara's face, from which the frustration disappears at the same time. The next shot is of extreme importance in the context of the finale: we suddenly see Ichi standing upright, with Takeshi's decapitated head in his hand. This is a very unexpected turn of events, almost a rupture, given what has gone on just seconds before. But the shot of Ichi holding Takeshi's head is subjective, it's a point-of-view shot through the eyes of Kakihara, and therefore the degree of narrative 'truth' is dubious. This shot and the ones that follow are in fact visions of Kakihara's own imagination, the masturbation fantasy he wishes would come true: Ichi comes up to him despite a wounded foot, swings up his leg and buries his blade in Kakihara's forehead. Kakihara falls back, onto the ledge and after swinging precariously back and forth he loses his balance and plummets to his death, yelling "Wow, this is great!" before crashing to the ground below.

The point-of-view shot is not the only indication that what we see is in fact the product of Kakihara's imagination. Right after he hits the ground, Jijii appears from the shadows to inspect Kakihara's body and we see that the cut of the blade in the protagonist's forehead is no longer there. Next, Miike cuts to a shot of Takeshi, still very much alive and kicking the stuffing out of the wounded Ichi on the roof. Also, the movement of Kakihara falling back from the impact of Ichi's kick and his position on the ledge don't gel. The position of the body in the first shot is incompatible with that in the second. Although he imagined Ichi overcoming his own pain to give him the death he so desired, the visual information we are given suggests that Kakihara in fact climbed onto the ledge and jumped off the roof himself, committing suicide (or in his case masturbating, like the needles in the ears and the knife through the tongue) out of frustration and loneliness. His ideal sadist partner lay on the ground crying and unable to defend himself against a child; the finale is a complete deception for Kakihara, who gets nothing he wanted or hoped for. This is illustrated by the shot that ends the sequence: a flashback to the aftermath of his equally disappointing coupling with Karen, in which we see him sitting amidst his hooks and chains, isolated, a vision of utter loneliness.

This disillusionment is of course exactly what Jijii wanted. Not only is the Anjo group destroyed, each of its members died a miserable death. Even his greatest challenge, Kakihara, a man who *wanted* to die painfully, didn't get the satisfaction he wanted from his demise.

This is where the parallel between Jijii and the director (and between Kakihara and the audience) is most apparent: like Kakihara, its identification figure, the audience did not get what it wanted from the finale. Miike frustrates them the way Jijii frustrates Kakihara. There was no big showdown, no ultimate act of exciting violence. Instead there was disillusionment. But for the viewer to feel disillusioned over the finale is for him or her to acknowledge the wish to consume violence. In his game of chess with the audience, this is Miike's checkmate: just like Kakihara's craving for pain ended up self-destructive, so did the viewer's wish for violence turn against himself.

[. . .]

Ichi the Killer shows us Takashi Miike as a master of his own art. The film is not only an exploration into the possibilities of cinema, both on the level of form and content, but it's also a critical examination of the medium and of the interaction between the moving image and the spectator. The film as a whole is a completely cohesive unity, in that all of its parts are absolutely crucial to the functioning of the whole. Any attempt at censorship or toning down the violence will have the opposite effect and will in fact make the film *more* exploitative and thereby undermine its critical stance. Excising scenes of violence, particularly the 'painful' scenes, will harm the symbiosis between the 'playful' and the 'painful' violence, which forms the basis for Miike's critical approach. One forms the context in which the other can function. In the version of the film that was released in Hong Kong, both scenes of the rape and beating of Sara and the cutting of the woman's nipples were taken out by the censor. These are three crucial scenes, without which the entire effect the film has on the audience changes drastically: because it leaves only the 'playful' violence intact, the film now only lets the audience indulge itself in consuming violence, with no moment left for critical reflection.

SECTION 4
Cult consumption

Introduction

Audiences are at the core of the study of cult cinema. Given the current acceptance of considerations and configurations of the audience in film research, this seems like an evident statement to make. But it is worth bearing in mind that the degree and intensity of audience involvement in cult cinema has always been one of its essential characteristics. Therefore audiences are *really* at the core of the study of cult cinema.

When discussing audiences and cult cinema, however, it is necessary to recognize the 'double bind' of the discussion. On the one hand, there are audiences of cult cinema, and on the other there are cult audiences of cinema. The first refers to textual properties of a certain kind that any kind of audience can pick up on; and the second to particular kinds of audiences who will apply certain viewing strategies to any kind of cinema. In theory, such a double bind may pose a terminal loop, preventing research. In practice, the semantics of such a philosophical distinction are less of an obstacle. It turns out that in most cases cult audiences watch cult films – the one attracting the other as it were, in an endless dance of courtship and rejection.

Most cult consumption revolves around three major constellations of spectatorship: problematic audiences, fandom and critics. Each of these represents a particular sensibility of the activity of cult viewing: the category of problematic audiences contains viewing modes with moral ambiguities, often in the margin of legality, challenging mainstream attitudes; the category of fandom contains viewing modes with excessive affiliation, often recognized by extreme attachment and involvement, and thus challenging 'proper' taste patterns; and the category of critics contains viewing modes of extraordinary scrutiny and detailed expertise, often characterized by meticulous research, and as such a challenge to the dictate of 'mass appeal' and generalizations so typical for mainstream cinema. Each of these sensibilities has received academic attention, especially in the last few decades. Before that, the study of cult cinema was a 'freelancing' interest. Most theoretical concepts were developed by critics who were keen observers of the practices of cult cinema, and its audiences, but who were seldom inclined to hard-data collecting. For example, Siegfried Kracauer's apt remarks about mass audiences and 'cults of distraction' (which we reprint here) are based on one person's perceptiveness, not on a systematic method of research. That changed in the wake of the influence of the writings of Pierre Bourdieu on the academic study of cult, especially his paradigmatic, groundbreaking *Distinction*, a meticulously rigorous, methodical cultural mapping of French audiences of culture, mapped according to their tastes (and their tastes mapped according to their economic and cultural 'capital'). No study of cult audiences can ignore Bourdieu and therefore his work is at the centre of cult consumption (which is why we reprint it here). Since then, empirically gathered data about the viewers and users have found their way into virtually all considerations of cult cinema.

Problematic audiences: violence

A fairly substantial body of research on cult cinema audiences presupposes a culturally 'problematic' status for cult films and, hence, their audiences. The presupposition goes more or less like this: cult cinema includes imagery that 'normal' culture deems offensive, outrageous or deviant. This is because certain tropes inside films, most particularly 'violence' and 'sex', cause harm to weak, impressionable viewers, either directly, or in the long term.

Let us start with 'violence'. The most notorious or alarming research in this respect (depending on your point of view) was conducted by Albert Bandura, Philip Zimbardo, George Gerbner and Dolf Zillmann – mind you, it is the reputation and (ab)use of the research by opinion-makers more than its original merit that often caused outrage towards cult cinema. Albert Bandura's belief that behaviour, including aggression, was part of a learning process (the so-called 'social learning theory') led him to conduct experiments, the most famous of which was the Bobo-doll experiment, in which children imitated aggressive behaviour they were exposed to because of the 'rewards' they perceived to be involved (they beat the Bobo-doll). Bandura, and others, usually included media and violent cinema in their lists of instruments that could reinforce aggression with children.[1] One film they named was *Born Innocent* (1974), a film since considered a cult by all measures. Philip Zimbardo's infamous Stanford Prison Experiment of the early 1970s, though abruptly terminated before it could reach its conclusion, seemed to demonstrate the willingness of 'torturers' to exceed their peers' and superiors' commands and see incitement where there was none. Moral advocates (lawyers, preachers, local school boards) connected it to the 'appeal' of on-screen torture to claim a causal effect.[2] (We cannot forego on the coincidence – the pun of destiny – that Zimbardo's experiment has itself become a cult movie project, acquired by Madonna's Maverick films.)[3] George Gerbner's cultural indicators research, often labelled 'cultivation analysis', focused on the longer-term effects of media violence on viewers, claiming that the accumulation over time of exposure to certain imagery to 'heavy viewers' makes the medium itself become a 'socializing agent', potentially leading to actions that could be seen as invited/incited by it. Substitute 'heavy viewers' for 'cult fans' and 'medium' for 'cult film', and it is clear that cult movies became, again, a target for moral concern.[4] Finally, Dolf Zillmann and his associates' research tried to measure the degree to which viewers get 'worked up', 'aroused' or 'infected' by exposure to 'violent' pornographic and horrific images and scenes. While most of Zillmann's research concerned films that fell well outside the boundaries of the cult film, some, especially that involving porn and horror cinema, which was directed by his students Tamborini and Weaver (but to which his contribution was instrumental), does bear direct relevance on cult consumption.[5]

It is by no means a coincidence that three of the four theories about audiences' behaviour as a result of their exposure to 'uncomfortable' imagery occurred in the early 1970s. As Martin Barker has pointed out, the early seventies become, quite suddenly, preoccupied with 'cinematic violence'.[6] Until then, it was a part of film style, present in many genres, including avant-garde and art-house cinema. Since then, and via films like *A Clockwork Orange* (1971), *Straw Dogs* (1971) and *Last House on the Left* (1972), it became a contested motif of which the origin was located in an uncomfortable mélange of political malaise, cultural unease and social change (Watergate, the Middle East, Northern Ireland, the Vietnam war, the Munich Olympics hostage takings, left-wing terrorism in Germany and Italy, plane hijackings, the Stonewall riots, the Kent State University shootings, the women's and gay rights movements, sexual liberation, *Roe* vs. *Wade*, Black Panthers, decolonization etc.), and a boost of independent and exploitation cinema across the world – from Cinema Novo and New German cinema to blaxploitation and porn chique. This curious intertwining of cinema and cultural unsettlement equipped films with a sudden relevance and, hence, with a dedication, but it also set them up to be blamed for fuelling discomfort and change. Many of the cult films of the period, like the ones mentioned above, but also midnight movies like *El Topo*, *Night of the Living Dead*, *The Rocky Horror Picture Show*, *The Texas Chain Saw Massacre*, *Shivers*, *Shaft* and the films of Larry Cohen, John Waters or Paul Morrissey, became cult phenomena because of the way critics and audiences started using them in their political position-taking, and the 'violence' depicted in them became a key element in that move. No wonder then that cult films were singled out as corrupting society and messing up people's minds – conservatives still hold that view.

Problematic audiences: subculture and censorship

The mass communications tradition aside, research into cult audiences is mostly conducted from a cultural studies perspective, slowly garnering momentum from the 1970s onwards, throughout the 1980s, into the 1990s, in each step demanding more attention to the active roles audiences play in making sense of cult films. The influence of the British school of cultural studies has also played an important part in the development of a sensitivity for audiences of cult (and cult-related) film. British cultural studies scholars did not really write about film much, but rather researched cults and subcultures within popular culture, often from a perspective that emphasized class relationships (like Pierre Bourdieu), but also gender, ethnicity and regional origins (urban versus countryside for instance). Dick Hebdige's study of the subculture of punk and reggae as a form of stylistic resistance against hegemonic culture in inner-city London, Stanley Cohen's research into the moral panics surrounding the mod and rocker subcultures (and their legendary 'Brighton' clashes), and Martin Barker's investigation of comic book readers as a self-sustaining subculture in a 'power-struggle' relationship with 'official culture', for instance, are frequently cited as sources of inspiration for the study of cult audiences (cult activities and self-positioning one could say in this case).[7] British cultural studies scholars also stressed the significance of perception and reception, bringing attention to the way in which subcultures, cults and the like were portrayed within mass media as 'deviant' (Cohen's term) or 'dangerous' (Barker's term).[8]

One particular way in which British cultural studies approached cult films and their audiences was through research into censorship of films. Usually, the elements singled out for censorship were 'violent imagery' and 'sexual imagery' – in this sense the foci are not that different from those of the 'effects research'. But the approach is distinctly different. Let us deal with 'violence' research first. In the 1980s Martin Barker's research into the 'video nasties' uproar (in which dozens of horror and exploitation films were denied a British video release because of an orchestrated press campaign claiming they incited violence) revealed how mechanisms of censorship, the state's struggle to control popular culture, and concepts such as 'harm', 'vulnerable audiences' and 'media consumption' were mixed together to create the impression that cult movies could actually harm society.[9] As Barker, and Julian Petley's research into censorship, demonstrates, anxieties over cult movies' 'powers' to corrupt audiences hid concerns about lower-class audiences using film for their own, potentially revolutionary, needs.[10] Needless to say the movies implicated in the video nasties scandal, like *Last House on the Left*, *Cannibal Holocaust*, *Tenebrae*, *House on the Edge of the Park*, *I Spit on Your Grave* and *Driller Killer* soon became even more sought after, de facto creating a cult of video nasties, seen as decorated veterans in the war against dictated taste.

Further moral panics around 'violence' in cinema throughout the 1980s and 1990s, and ever since, complicated much of the assumed connection between filmic violence and progressive cinema or cult cinema. Controversial examples included *Taxi Driver* (said to have inspired the 1981 assassination attempt on Ronald Reagan), *Alien* (mentioned in the 1996 Dunblane primary school shootings), *First Blood* and *Rambo* (linked to a series of shootings), *Terminator* (simply because of the sheer number of on-screen killings, but later the film also became implicated in the Dunblane primary school shootings), *Child's Play III* (the 1993 Jamie Bulger case in which two children abducted and murdered a toddler) and *Natural Born Killers* (again a film linked to shootings). Most of these films are not considered cult cinema at all, and have no cult audience or following attached to them and their political make-up covers the entire spectrum. Their public presence however, by implication or by proxy, has given them a 'public cult' reputation. Cynically, by the end of the 1990s, there had been so many 'links' between violence and violent cinema that movies themselves began to take it as their subjects – with *Donnie Darko*'s allusions to the 1999 Columbine High School shootings as an example in which the cult of the film derived, partly, from its clever inferences of links between violence and cinema.

Barker and Petley's efforts have spawned a mini-tradition of (anti-)censorship research and investigations of audiences of 'problematic' cinema, with notable studies of audiences of shocking entertainment by Annette Hill (which concentrated on so-called 'nouvelle violence' cult films such as *Man Bites Dog* or *Reservoir Dogs*), Brigid Cherry's research into female horror audiences, Mark Kermode's self-reflexive investigation of horror fandom, Barker and Brooks' study of disappointed fans of the comic book adaptation *Judge Dredd*, Barker, Arthurs and Harindranath's research into the *Crash* controversy (excerpts of which we reprint here), Kate Egan's study of video nasty fandom, and studies of trash aesthetics, horror fans and 'fringe' arthouse audiences.[11]

Problematic audiences: sex

Compared to the attention 'violence' and censorship have received in cult audience research, sex and porn might seem a bit under-researched. Much of that has to do with sensitivities around researching sex and cinema audiences. While there is a genuine arena for debates on 'violence', with all kinds of stances, representations of sex draw less diverse opinions. Until the 1980s, and mostly not until the 1990s, there was no real research into audiences of sexual imagery because no one dared to ask the question as to who would 'enjoy' such films. Because of that avoidance, two orthodox views have been allowed to dominate the debate around pornography for decades. The first is again the 'effects' tradition, where Dolf Zillman (the same as in the 'violence' research) and Jennings Bryant executed much-quoted research into pornography for policy purposes, which claims causal connections between viewing pornography and shifts in acceptance of 'deviant' behaviour. In this view, audience desensitization is key – basically, the more you watch the more likely you are to condone sexual aggression.[12] The second is the feminist attack on pornography, in which the economic exploitation and physical and moral degrading of the female body stands central. In this view, civil rights issues are at the core of the argument.[13]

In essence, these views were concerned more with hardcore pornography and the sex industry than with cult films containing sexual imagery. But in their actual examples they often stuck to products far from hardcore to which then extreme implications were attached. In one example 'violent pornography's degrading of and violence against women' was illustrated by a cover from a *Rolling Stones* album. Similarly, many softcore films, or lesbian and queer cinema, often found themselves in the line of fire of attacks against illegal produce with which they had no connection whatsoever. Through this practice cult cinema, again, became a scapegoat for symptoms of cultural unease. Journalists usually also threw viewing porn chique, soft-porn and sexploitation of the 1970s (*Emmanuelle*, *Deep Throat*, *Caligula*, the films of Tinto Brass or Radley Metzger/ Henry Paris) into the equation. It wasn't until the 1990s, when rating systems found themselves unable to separate art house and exploitation, and the actual nature, 'enjoyment' and 'relevance' of films like *Atame!*, *The Cook, the Thief, his Wife and her Lover*, *Henry and June*, *American Psycho*, *The Idiots*, *The Annabelle Chong Story*, *Romance*, *Baise-moi*, or Shannon Tweed's erotic thrillers, the erotic spoofs of seduction cinema, or Nigel Wingrove 'sleaze' productions of salvation/redemption (*Visions of Ecstasy* and *Sacred Flesh*), became a matter of wider debate, that the cult consumption of sexual imagery attracted more nuanced attention.[14]

Spearheading the debate as far as hardcore pornography is concerned are Linda Williams' groundbreaking study of the aesthetics of pornography, and Richard Dyer's discussions of gay pornography.[15] With regard to non-hardcore cult cinema, much of the debate is crystallized by Paul Verhoeven's *Showgirls*, a film so ostensibly offending morals and mores it is still unsure whether it is intentionally 'bad to the bone' or just, well, bad (that is the reason why we reprint here the essay that started the debate about the film's status, and its spectatorship). Since 2000, several more attempts have been made to investigate cult audiences for films containing sexual imagery, and gradually a small tradition is establishing itself, in which especially female and new-feminist research has been calling attention to alternative viewing modes, as well as to cults and fandoms of sexploitation, Doris Wishman, Russ Meyer's films or audiences of cult pornography.[16]

Cult audiences: fans

If we take exception of 'sex' and 'violence', and the ways in which these two tropes have dominated discussions on cult cinema audiences, only two more 'types' of audiences have received attention: fans and critics. Nowadays, fandom seems like a well-embedded subdivision of film and media studies, but it wasn't until the early 1990s that fan consumption of cinema became a topic of study. Cult cinema led the way. The first forms of fandom to be investigated were cult fans of television series like *Star Trek*, *Cagney and Lacey*, and *Beauty and the Beast*, films like *The Rocky Horror Picture Show* and *The Blues Brothers*, and icons like Judy Garland, Rock Hudson or Madonna. Most of the research in this area situated itself within media studies as much as film studies, with American scholars like John Fiske, Henry Jenkins (both of whose works we reprint here) and Janet Staiger, and British cultural studies scholars like Camille Bacon-Smith, Janice Radway and Lisa Lewis paving the way for what quickly became one of the fastest growing subdivisions of audience studies.[17] The key elements in early fandom studies involved cultural capital (following Bourdieu), appropriation and textual poaching (a concept originating with Michel De Certeau), 'interpretive communities' (a concept originating with Stanley Fish), and oppositional readings and resistance against dominant readings (a concept originating with Stuart Hall), and focused on easily identifiable, self-declared fan groupings, often subculturally delineated as 'queer', 'camp' or 'geeky'. Today, studies of fans cover all areas of the spectrum of film, with gradually more attention being devoted to less visible fans, slowly uncovering the interests and involvements of more mute, less outspoken fandoms buried deep into underground subcultures (shy Goths, for instance, or vampire fans), or middle-of-the-road occasional blockbuster fans.[18]

Cult audiences: critics

Critics are usually placed against fans. They have long played a dubious role in the traffics and tensions between high and low culture. Traditionally, criticism functions as the forum of discussion par excellence of aesthetics and arts. It is a form of writing dedicated to close examination of cultural products, the relationship of products to their contexts, and their social roles. Terry Eagleton places criticism firmly within the bourgeois public sphere, as a tool through which communication on the topics of society, its culture, its values and its arts can be facilitated.[19] But Eagleton also makes note of the pressures that criticism is subject to. Among the many he and others note, two stand out as most significant.[20]

First, there is pressure to set a tone: whoever makes the first argument, whoever scores the first point, has an advantage. In terms of cult cinema, this is easily translated as a pressure to identify a 'deviant opinion' (a sometimes less than honourable one), and the subculture that goes with it. For much criticism this means declaring a sort of 'alignment', a preference for a certain sort of film. It is an attitude that goes directly against the 'disinterestedness' of traditional criticism. Second, and partly subsequently, there is a pressure on the critic to submit to the lures and appeals of either the product or the cultural context it attains to. All products, and their makers, presenters and beneficiaries, have an interest in receiving the best possible criticism, as it will (they hope) increase the relevance of the product. Similarly, forces within cultural contexts will try their best to accommodate or oppose certain products – will try to force or prevent connections with certain values and tastes. They see the critic and his or her judgement as one that must be influenced in order to attain a desired outcome. Editorial policies and formats, personal egos, partisan alignments and restricted access are recent examples of these pressures.[21]

In the case of cult cinema, such alignments are usually seen as advantages, allowing the critics to become an active force in the championing of alternative tastes, especially in the forms of aesthetes of the 1930s to 1960s, the fan-critics of the 1970s to 1990s, and the citizen reviewers of the twenty-first century. Fanzine critics are a crucial part of this, and that is the reason why we reprint in this section David Sanjek's study of horror fanzine criticism. As an audience, critics have only recently been scrutinized, and their practices and influences upon wider audiences are still under-theorized. But since the 1990s, work into the 'critical reception' of cult cinema has blossomed, uncovering mechanisms such as 'auteurship', 'topicality', 'diachronic and synchronic reception trajectories' and 'schools' ('esoteric networks' and 'invisible colleges') of interpretation as significant forces in the consumption of cult cinema.[22]

Fans and critics: smart and queer audiences

Finally, right on the intersection between fans and critics, a new category of cult consumption emerges, that of 'smart' or 'avid' audiences. Typified by their familiarity with generic conventions, equipped with an academic understanding of film narratives, and encyclopaedic knowledge of film-related facts, such audiences 'read into' films as a matter of routine, instantly connecting tropes, motives and metaphors regardless of the film's intentions – often deliberately opposing any prescriptions on how to 'understand' cinema. While still a tradition of investigation on the rise, we include it here because of the way it allows us to uncover fanlike and critical attitudes within the same audience cohort.

One of the most visible instances of smart audiences is the queer reading. The term 'queer' usually refers to the playing out of homosexual (and lesbian) predispositions – it denotes the performance of homosexuality. The term has, since the 1980s, frequently been used to describe an attitude of viewing in which audiences approach films as containing 'implicit' and 'covered up' homosexual tendencies and preferences. *The Rocky Horror Picture Show*, *Hedwig and the Angry Inch* and *Showgirls* are excellent examples of such 'cover ups' – in fact they hardly cover up anything. Their audiences highlight the gay and lesbian overtones and celebrate these as the 'true' essence of the films. Because of the highly stylized way in which these films seem to invite such queer readings, they are often connected with camp (see Section one). But queer readings of less suggestive films are equally capable of drawing cult audiences. The essential example here is *Top Gun*, an at face-value super-macho film about navy jet pilots. The queering of *Top Gun* exists in the wilful, premeditated 'misreading' of the film as filled with gay imagery (locker room scenes, references to anal and oral sex, jets as phallic symbols, the male nickname of a female instructor, the mobilization of all associations of the navy as gay boot camp). In the case of *Top Gun* such a reading remains largely playful, but in the case of other films it allows the unmasking of potentially homophobic attitudes. Queer readings of *The Silence of the Lambs* even led to targeted protests,[23] and with regard to *Thelma and Louise* it led to a surge in interest in on-screen lesbian sexuality (and fan fiction). In such contexts, queer readings, and audiences' employment of queer reading strategies, need to be seen as political as well as cultish – a relation amplified by the rise of queer and independent cinema.

Next to queer audiences, film festivals play a unique role in the reading and reception of cult cinema. While the widespread presence of festivals caters to all kinds of cinema (and queer and gay and lesbian festivals are prominent among them), cult cinema festivals distinguish themselves by their audiences, cultural placing, programming and long-term reputation. A lot of festivals found their origin in the early 1980s, at a time when midnight cult screenings evolved into festivals. Cult festivals display unusually high degrees of audience involvement, encapsulated by subscriptions (annual reservations guaranteeing access to all screenings, creating de facto in-crowd elites), dressing-up, fringe activity attendance (press conferences, signings), 'communal preparing' for midnight screenings, and more spontaneous behaviour like shouting and waving during screenings. Cult festival audiences make their delights or disappointments clearly audible in front of guests. All of these practices often take on a ritualistic character (with levels of initiation and expertise), and display a near religious function (albeit often of a boisterous nature), close to those of cults in prehistoric rites. Festival audiences facilitate debate about the tensions between local and global concerns of taste and cultural value. As rallies for or against ideologies, they have instigated campaigns for the recognition of (problems in) the representation of sensitive cultural issues (a good example is the issue of censorship). Specializing in 'genres' or 'attitudes' they battle for a better understanding of the aesthetic celebration of (highly problematic) movie fare. And as public events they have helped develop ideas about critical values in alternatives to mainstream cinema (creating esoteric networks of meaning and competing canons). Festival audience research is still a nascent tradition, and we reprint research into the smart audience of the *Ginger Snaps* films – films which also drew a significant number of queer readings – as an example in this section.[24]

Conclusion

Whether they are slaves of the effects of sexual and violent imagery, seekers for cheap thrills, critics of censorship, devoted fans, queer 'unmaskers' or clever detectors, audiences of cult cinema, and cult audiences of cinema, deserve much more scrutiny. They need to be seen not just as parts of other research programmes but as subjects deserving of their own approaches, methodologies and research plans.

Notes

1   Bandura, Albert and Ribes-Inesta, Emilio (1976) *Analysis of Delinquency and Aggression*, Mahwah, NJ: Lawrence Erlbaum Associates.
2   Milgram, Stanley (1974) *Obedience to Authority,* New York: Harper & Row; Zimbardo,

Philip (1971) 'The power and pathology of imprisonment', *Congressional Record* (Serial No. 15, 25 October), hearings before subcommittee No. 3 of the Committee on the Judiciary, House of Representatives, Ninety-Second Congress, *First Session on Corrections, Part II, Prisons, Prison Reform and Prisoner's Rights: California*, Washington, DC: US Government Printing Office; Zimbardo, Philip, C. Haney, W.C. Banks, and D. Jaffe (1973, 8 April) The mind is a formidable jailer: A Pirandellian prison, *The New York Times Magazine*, Section 6, 38 ff; Zimbardo, Philip (1985) *Cults Go to High School: A Theoretical and Empirical Analysis of the Initial Stage in the Recruitment Process*, American Family Foundation.

3   see www.tmz.com/category/the-biz/page/2/.

4   Gerbner, George, *et al.* (1973) *Communications Technology and Social Policy: Understanding the New 'Cultural Revolution'*, New York: Interscience Publication.

5   Weaver, James B. and Ron Tamborini (eds) (1996) *Horror Films: Current Research on Audience Preferences and Reactions*, Mahwah, NJ: Lawrence Erlbaum.

6   Barker, Martin (2004) 'Violence redux', in Steven Jay Schneider (ed.) *New Hollywood Violence*, Manchester: Manchester University Press, 57–79.

7   Hebdige, Dick (1979) *Subculture: The Meaning of Style*, London: Routledge; Cohen, Stanley ([1972, 1980] 2003) *Folk Devils and Moral Panics*, London: Routledge; Barker, Martin (1983) *A Haunt of Fears: The Strange History of the British Horror Comics Campaign*, London: Pluto Press.

8   Barker, Martin (2005, 2006) 'Loving and hating *Straw Dogs*: The meanings of audience responses to a controversial film', *Particip@tions*, 2(2) (December 2005) and 3(1) (May 2006), online via www.participations.org.

9   Barker, Martin (ed.) (1984) *The Video Nasties: Freedom and Censorship in the Media*, London: Pluto Press.

10   Petley, Julian (2000) ' "Snuffed out": Nightmares in a trading standards officer's brain', in Xavier Mendik and Graeme Harper (eds) *Unruly Pleasures: the Cult Film and its Critics*, Guilford: FAB Press, 205–19; Barker, Martin and Julian Petley (eds) (1997) *Ill Effects: the Media/Violence Debate*, London: Routledge.

11   Hill, Annette (1997) *Shocking Entertainment: Viewer Responses to Violent Movies*, Luton: University of Luton Press; Cherry, Brigid (1999) 'Refusing to refuse to look: Female viewers of the horror film', in Melvyn Stokes and Richard Maltby (eds) *Identifying Hollywood's Audiences*, London: BFI; Barker, Martin and Kate Brooks (1997) *Knowing Audiences: Friends, Fans and Foes of Judge Dredd*, Luton: University of Luton Press; Barker, Martin (1997) 'Taking the extreme case: understanding a fascist fan of Judge Dredd', in Deborah Cartmell, I.Q. Hunter, Heidi Kaye and Imelda Whelehan (eds) *Trash Aesthetics: Popular Culture and its Audiences*, London: Routledge, 14–30; Egan, Kate (forthcoming) *Trash or Treasure? Censorship and the Changing Meanings of the Video Nasties*, Manchester: Manchester University Press; Barker, Martin, Ernest Mathijs, Jamie Sexton, Kate Egan, Melanie Selfe and Kate Egan (forthcoming) *Audiences and Receptions of Sexual Violence in Contemporary Cinema*, London: British Board of Film Classification.

12   Zillmann, Dolf and Jennings Bryant (eds) (1989) *Pornography: Research Advances and Policy Considerations*, New York: Lawrence Erlbaum.

13   Dworkin, Andrea (1981) *Pornography: Men Possessing Women*, New York: Putnam; Dworkin, Andrea and Patricia A. MacKinnon (1988) *Pornography and Civil Rights*, Minneapolis, MN: Organizing Against Pornography.

14   See, Eberwein, Robert (1998) 'The erotic thriller', *Post Script*, 17(3), 25–33; Petley, Julian and Mark Kermode (1998) 'The censor and the state: The distributor's tale', *Sight and Sound*, 8(5), 14–18; Hunter, I.Q. (2006) 'Tolkien dirty', in Ernest Mathijs (ed.) *The Lord of the Rings: Popular Culture in Global Context*, London: Wallflower Press, 317–33; Smith,

Iain Robert (2008) 'When Spiderman became Spider Babe', in Ernest Mathijs and Xavier Mendik (eds) *Peepshows*, London: Wallflower Press.

15 Williams, Linda (1999) *Hard Core: Power, Pleasure, and the Frenzy of the Visible*, Berkeley, CA: University of California Press; Dyer, Richard (2004) 'Idol thoughts: Orgasm and self-reflexivity in gay pornography', in Pamela Church Gibson (ed.) *More Dirty Looks: Gender, Pornography and Power,* London: British Film Institute.

16 See selected chapters in Mendik, Xavier and Graeme Harper (eds) (2000) *Unruly Pleasures: The Cult Film and its Critics,* Guilford: FAB Press; Mathijs, Ernest and Xavier Mendik (eds) (forthcoming) *Peepshows*, London: Wallflower Press; Smith, Clarissa (2007) *Women and Porn: Readers, Texts and Production,* Bristol: Intellect Books; Sigel, Lyn (ed.) (2005) *International Exposure: Perspectives on Modern European Pornography 1800–2000*, New Brunswick, NJ: University of Rutgers Press; Krzywinska, Tanya (2006) *Sex and the Cinema*, London: Wallflower Press; Hawkins, Joan (2003) 'Midnight sex horror movies and the downtown avant-garde', in Mark Jancovich, *et al.* (eds) *Defining Cult Movies*, Manchester: Manchester University Press, 223–34; Avedon, Carol and Alison Assiter (1993) *Bad Girls & Dirty Pictures*, London: Pluto Press.

17 Bacon-Smith, Camille (1992) *Enterprising Women: Television Fandom and the Creation of Popular Culture*, Philadelphia, PA: University of Pennsylvania Press; Radway, Janice (1991) *Reading the Romance: Women, Patriarchy and Popular Literature,* Chapel Hill, NC: University of North Carolina Press; Lewis, Lisa (ed.) (1992) *The Adoring Audience*, London: Routledge; Staiger, Janet (1992) 'The logic of alternative readings: *A Star is Born*', in *Interpreting Films*, Princeton, NJ: Princeton University Press, 154–77; Jenkins, Henry (2000) 'Reception theory and audience research: The mystery of the vampire's kiss', in Christine Gledhill and Linda Williams (eds) *Reinventing Film Studies*, London: Arnold.

18 Williamson, Milly (2005) *The Lure of the Vampire from Bram Stoker to Buffy*, London: Wallflower Press; Mathijs, Ernest (2005) 'Bad reputations: The reception of trash cinema', *Screen*, 46(4), 451–72; Pullen, Kirsten (2006) '*The Lord of the Rings* online blockbuster fandom: pleasure and commerce', in Ernest Mathijs (ed.) *The Lord of the Rings: Popular Culture in Global Context*, London: Wallflower Press; Hills, Matt (2006) 'Realising the cult blockbuster: *Lord of the Rings* fandom and residual/emergent cult status in "the mainstream" ', in Ernest Mathijs (ed.) *The Lord of the Rings: Popular Culture in Global Context*, London: Wallflower Press; Barker, Martin and Ernest Mathijs (eds) (2007) *Watching the Lord of the Rings,* New York: Peter Lang.

19 Eagleton, Terry (1984) *The Function of Criticism,* London: Verso.

20 Ciment, Michel (1998) 'The function and the state of film criticism', in J. Boorman and W. Donahue (eds) *Projections 8: Film-makers on Film-making*. Londen: Faber & Faber, 35–43; Taylor, Greg (1999) *Artists in the Audience: Cult, Camp and American Film Criticism*, Princeton, NJ: Princeton University Press; Mathijs, Ernest (2003a) 'AIDS references in the critical reception of David Cronenberg: It may not be such a bad disease after all', *Cinema Journal*, 42(4), 29–45; Mathijs, Ernest (2003b) 'The making of a cult reputation: Topicality and controversy in the critical reception of shivers', in Mark Jancovich, Antonio Lazaro-Reboll, Julian Stringer and Andrew Willis (eds) *Defining Cult Movies: The Cultural Politics of Oppositional Taste*, Manchester: Manchester University Press, 109–26.

21 Corliss, Richard (1990) 'All thumbs or, is there a future for film criticism?', *Film Comment*, 26(2), 14–18; Ebert, Roger (1990) 'All stars or, is there a cure for criticism of film criticism?', *Film Comment*, 26(3), 45–51; Cook, David (1993) 'Making sense', *Film Criticism*, 17(2–3), 31–9; Wood, Robin (1993) 'Critical positions and the end of civilization; or, a refusal to join the club', *Film Criticism*, 17 (2–3), 79–92.

22 Shrum, William (1991) 'Critics and publics: Cultural mediation in highbrow and popular performing arts', *American Journal of Sociology*, 97(2), 347–75; Klinger, Barbara (1997)

'Film history terminable and interminable: Recovering the past in reception studies', *Screen*, 38(2), 107–28; Staiger, Janet (2000) *Perverse Spectators: The Practices of Film Reception*, New York: New York University Press; Staiger, Janet (2005) *Media Reception Studies*, New York: NYU Press; Erb, Cynthia (1998) *Tracking King Kong: A Hollywood Icon in World Culture*, Detroit, MI: Wayne State University Press; Guins, Raiford (2005) 'Blood and black gloves on shiny discs: New media, old tastes, and the remediation of Italian horror films in the United States', in Steven Jay Schneider and Tony Williams (eds) *Horror International,* Detroit, MI: Wayne State University Press; Newitz, Annalee (2000) What makes things cheesy? Satire, multinationalism, and B-Movies', *Social Text*, 18(2), 59–82.

23 See Staiger, Janet (1993) 'Taboos and totems: Cultural meanings of *The Silence of the Lambs*', in Jim Collins, Hilary Radner and Ava Preacher Collins (eds) *Film Theory Goes to the Movies,* London: Routledge, 142–54.

24 Mendik, Xavier and Graeme Harper (2000) 'The chaotic text and the sadean audience: Narrative transgressions of a contemporary cult film', in Xavier Mendik and Graeme Harper (eds) *Unruly Pleasures: The Cult Film and its Critics*, Guilford: FAB Press, 237–49; Sconce, Jeffrey (2002), 'Irony, nihilism and the new American "smart" film', *Screen*, 43, 349–69; Van Extergem, Dirk (2004) 'A report on the Brussels International Festival of Fantastic Film', in Ernest Mathijs and Xavier Mendik (eds) *Alternative Europe*, London: Wallflower Press, 216–28.

4.1

Cult of distraction: On Berlin's picture palaces

by Siegfried Kracauer

This is the oldest essay in this reader, published before cinema entered the sound era. Playing its role as grumpy old senior to the fullest, it does not really carry cult audiences in its heart – they are described as part of 'the *masses*'. The term 'masses' is a qualifier, not a quantifier: it refers to viewers from a certain social stratosphere, not to the numbers in which they turn up. It also refers to audiences without much, shall we say, 'sophistication' in their consumption of cinema. And in making that inference, *The Cult of Distraction* corrects, actually predates, an impression of cinema cultism as a uniquely 'cool' attitude. Critics like Harry Allan Potamkin, aesthetes like Ivor Montagu, or historians like Georges Sadoul were creating the impression that cult audiences were audiences of progressive taste: discerning, elitist, vanguard, and attacking the petty bourgeoisie's middle class tastes. But German critic and sociologist of culture Siegfried Kracauer shows that there is a cult of the mass. It is lower class, disenfranchised, non-discerning, populist, and it attacks nothing – it only defends its insistence that it is interested in nothing else but basic (some say debased) entertainment. It wants sex, violence, and repetition. As such, Kracauer's view is very similar to those warning us of 1950s drive-in audiences, 1980s home-video viewers, and contemporary multimedia addicts. And it is that resemblance which makes it fascinating reading. There is a stunning topicality to Kracauer's description of the lush picture palaces he calls 'optical fairylands', like the UFA Palaces or the Gloria Palast. They remind us of more recent comments on multiplexes and home-viewing environments: they create distraction, with their 'elegant surface splendor' and 'total artwork of effects', bombarding the spectator. They prevent, or so it is inferred, in-depth connoisseurship because they dominate lowest common denominator demand. Kracauer writes: 'the masses are no longer left to their own devices [. . .] they demand to be served [. . .]. There is little room left for the so-called educated classes [and] their snobbish aloofness'. The 'community of worshipers', as Kracauer calls the attendants, are the ones Walter Benjamin would later invoke to argue that the star status of film actors was replacing the 'aura' of uniqueness of a work of art (see Section one). Kracauer links the cult of the mass audience to several social developments: rapid urbanization (and its creation of inner city niches), and the increased inclusion of the masses in the circuit of culture. And Kracauer may not like it, but at least he is willing to describe it. In that respect it should not be overlooked that the essay was one of many Kracauer wrote for the *Frankfurt Zeitung*. It reflects a climate in which intellectuals like him, but also his Frankfurt School companions Walter Benjamin, Theodor Adorno, and Max Horkheimer, saw themselves compelled to study popular art forms, film a prime one among them. Kracauer fled

Germany from the Nazis, and in the United States his work at the Museum of Modern Art and, later, Columbia University, led to insightful historical and theoretical work, with publications like *From Caligari to Hitler* and *Theory of Film* making him one of the most respected film scholars. If one bears in mind that cult audiences have often been ostracized for their lack of discrimination (movie buffs do watch everything) then Kracauer's 'community of worshipers' may well have been Weimar Berlin's true cinema cultists.

A note on extracting: *The Cult of Distraction: on Berlin's Picture Palaces* was first published as *Kult der Zerstreuung: über die Berliner Lichtspielhäuser*, in Frankfurter Zeitung 70, issue 167 of 4 March 1926. In English it was first published as *The Cult of Distraction: on Berlin's Picture Palaces*, translated by Thomas Y. Levin, in New German Critique, volume 14, issue 40, in 1987. The version we have reprinted here is from *The Mass Ornament: Weimar Essays*, a collection of writings by Siegfried Kracauer, edited by Thomas Y. Levin, and published by Harvard University Press in 1995, pages 323–328.

The large picture houses in Berlin are palaces of distraction; to call them *movie theaters [Kinos]* would be disrespectful. The latter are still abundant only in Old Berlin and in the suburbs, where they serve neighborhood audiences, and even there they are declining in number. Much more than such movie houses or even the ordinary theaters, it is the picture palaces, those optical fairylands, that are shaping the face of Berlin. The *UFA palaces* (above all, the one at the Zoo), the *Capitol* built by Poelzig, the *Marmorhaus*, and whatever their names may be, enjoy sellouts day after day. The newly built *Gloria-Palast* proves that the style these palaces have initiated is still developing in the same direction.

Elegant *surface splendor* is the hallmark of these mass theaters. Like hotel lobbies, they are shrines to the cultivation of pleasure; their glamor aims at edification. But while the architecture does perhaps bombard the patrons in its attempt to create an atmosphere, it in no way relapses into the barbaric pomposity of Wilhelminian secular churches—like the Rhinegold, for example, which seeks to give the impression that it harbors the Wagnerian Nibelungen treasure. Instead, the architecture of the film palaces has evolved into a form that avoids stylistic excesses. Taste has presided over the dimensions and, in conjunction with a refined artisanal fantasy, has spawned the costly interior furnishings. The *Gloria-Palast* presents itself as a baroque theater. The community of worshipers, numbering in the thousands, can be content, for its gathering places are a worthy abode.

The programs, too, display a well-wrought grandiosity. Gone are the days when films were allowed to run one after another, each with a corresponding musical accompaniment. The major theaters, at least, have adopted the American style of a self-contained show, which integrates the film into a larger whole. Like the program sheets which have expanded into fan magazines, the shows have grown into a structured profusion of production numbers and presentations. A glittering, revuelike creature has crawled out of the movies: *the total artwork [Gesamtkunstwerk] of effects.*

This total artwork of effects assaults all the senses using every possible means. Spotlights shower their beams into the auditorium, sprinkling across festive drapes or rippling through colorful, organic-looking glass fixtures. The orchestra asserts itself as an independent power, its acoustic production buttressed by the responsory of the lighting. Every emotion is accorded its own acoustic expression and its color value in the spectrum—a visual and acoustic kaleidoscope that provides the setting for the physical activity on stage: pantomime and ballet. Until finally the white surface descends and the events of the three-dimensional stage blend imperceptibly into two-dimensional illusions.

Alongside the legitimate revues, such shows are the leading attraction in Berlin today. They raise distraction to the level of culture; they are aimed at the *masses*.

The masses also gather in the *provinces*, but there they are subjected to a pressure that does not allow them the spiritual and cultural *[geistig]* fulfillment appropriate to their number and real social significance. In the industrial centers where they appear in great numbers, they are so overburdened as workers that they are unable to realize their own way of life. They are handed down the rubbish and outdated entertainment of the upper class, which, despite its repeated claims to social superiority, has only limited cultural ambitions. In contrast, in the larger provincial towns not dominated primarily by industry, the traditional forces are so powerful that the masses are unable to shape the cultural and spiritual *[geistig]* structure on their own. The bourgeois middle classes remain segregated from them, as if the growth of this human reservoir meant nothing, and thus they maintain the illusory claim that they are still the guardians of culture and education. Their arrogance, which creates sham oases for itself, weighs down upon the masses and denigrates their amusements.

It cannot be overlooked that there are *four million* people in Berlin. The sheer necessity of their circulation transforms the life of the street into the ineluctable street of life, giving rise to configurations that invade even domestic space. The more people perceive themselves as a mass, however, the sooner the masses will also develop productive powers in the spiritual and cultural domain that are worth financing. The masses are no longer left to their own devices; rather, they prevail in their very abandonment. Refusing to be thrown scraps, they demand instead to be served at laid-out tables. There is little room left for the so-called educated classes, who must either join in the repast or maintain their snobbish aloofness. Their provincial isolation is, in any case, at an end. They are being absorbed by the masses, a process that creates the *homogeneous cosmopolitan audience* in which everyone has the *same* responses, from the bank director to the sales clerk, from the diva to the stenographer. Self-pitying complaints about this turn toward mass taste are belated; the cultural heritage that the masses refuse to accept has become to some extent merely a historical property, since the economic and social reality to which it corresponded has changed.

Critics chide Berliners for being *addicted to distraction*, but this is a petit bourgeois reproach. Certainly, the addiction to distraction is greater in Berlin than in the provinces, but the tension to which the working masses are subjected is also greater and more tangible; it is an essentially formal tension, which fills their day fully without making it fulfilling. Such a lack demands to be compensated, but this need can be articulated only in terms of the same surface sphere that imposed the lack in the first place. The form of free-time busy-ness necessarily corresponds to the form of business.

A correct instinct will see to it that the need for entertainment is satisfied. The

interior design of movie theaters serves one sole purpose: to rivet the viewers' attention to the peripheral, so that they will not sink into the abyss. The stimulations of the
senses succeed one another with such rapidity that there is no room left between them
for even the slightest contemplation. Like *life buoys*, the refractions of the spotlights
and the musical accompaniment keep the spectator above water. The penchant for
distraction demands and finds an answer in the display of pure externality; hence the
irrefutable tendency, particularly in Berlin, to turn all forms of entertainment into
revues and, parallel with this tendency, the increasing number of illustrations in the
daily press and in periodical publications.

This emphasis on the external has the advantage of being *sincere*. It is not
externality that poses a threat to truth. Truth is threatened only by the naïve affirmation of cultural values that have become unreal and by the careless misuse of concepts such as personality, inwardness, tragedy, and so on—terms that in themselves
certainly refer to lofty ideas but that have lost much of their scope along with their
supporting foundations, due to social changes. Furthermore, many of these concepts
have acquired a bad aftertaste today, because they unjustifiably deflect an inordinate
amount of attention from the external damages of society onto the private individual.
Instances of such repression are common enough in the fields of literature, drama,
and music. They claim the status of high art while actually rehearsing anachronistic
forms that evade the pressing needs of our time—a fact that is indirectly confirmed by
the artistically derivative quality of the respective works. In a profound sense, Berlin
audiences act truthfully when they increasingly shun these art events (which, for
good reason, remain caught in mere pretense), preferring instead the surface glamor
of the stars, films, revues, and spectacular shows. Here, in pure externality, the audience encounters itself; its own reality is revealed in the fragmented sequence of
splendid sense impressions. Were this reality to remain hidden from the viewers, they
could neither attack nor change it; its disclosure in distraction is therefore of *moral*
significance.

But this is the case only if distraction is not an end in itself. Indeed, the very fact
that the shows aiming at distraction are composed of the same mixture of externalities
as the world of the urban masses; the fact that these shows lack any authentic and
materially motivated coherence, except possibly the glue of sentimentality, which
covers up this lack but only in order to make it all the more visible; the fact that these
shows convey precisely and openly to thousands of eyes and ears the *disorder* of society—this is precisely what would enable them to evoke and maintain the tension that
must precede the inevitable and radical change. In the streets of Berlin, one is often
struck by the momentary insight that someday all this will suddenly burst apart. The
entertainment to which the general public throngs ought to produce the same effect.

Most of the time it does not, as is demonstrated in exemplary fashion by the programs
of the large movie theaters. For even as they summon to distraction, they immediately
rob distraction of its meaning by amalgamating the wide range of effects—which by
their nature demand to be isolated from one another—into an "artistic" unity. These
shows strive to coerce the motley sequence of externalities into an organic whole. To
begin with, the architectural setting tends to emphasize a dignity that used to inhabit
the institutions of high culture. It favors the lofty and the *sacred* as if designed to

accommodate works of eternal significance—just one step short of burning votive candles. The show itself aspires to the same exalted level, claiming to be a finely turned organism, an aesthetic totality as only an artwork can be. The film alone would be too paltry an offering, not primarily because one would want to increase the sheer quantity of distractions but because the show has pretensions to artistic form. The cinema has secured a standing independent of the theatrical stage, yet the leading movie theaters are once again longing to return to that stage.

This thespian objective of the movie theaters—an objective that may be considered symptomatic of Berlin social life as well—displays *reactionary* tendencies. The laws and forms of the idealist culture that haunts us today only as a specter may have lost their legitimacy in these movie theaters; nonetheless, out of the very elements of externality into which they have happily advanced, they are attempting to create a new idealist culture. Distraction—which is meaningful only as improvisation, as a reflection of the uncontrolled anarchy of our world—is festooned with drapery and forced back into a unity that no longer exists. Rather than acknowledging the actual state of disintegration that such shows ought to represent, the movie theaters glue the pieces back together after the fact and present them as organic creations.

This practice takes its revenge in purely artistic terms: the integration of film into a self-contained program deprives it of any effect it might have had. It no longer stands on its own, but appears as the crowning event of a type of revue that does not take into account its particular conditions of existence. The *two-dimensionality* of film produces the illusion of the physical world without any need for supplementation. But if scenes of real physicality are nevertheless displayed alongside the movie, the latter recedes into the flat surface and the deception is exposed. The proximity of action that has spatial depth destroys the spatiality of what is shown on the screen. By its very existence, film demands that the world it reflects be the only one; it should be wrested from every three-dimensional surrounding, or it will fail as an illusion. A painting, too, loses its power when it appears alongside living images. Nor should one fail to mention that the artistic ambitions behind the move to incorporate film into the pseudo-totality of a program are inappropriate, and hence remain unsuccessful. The result is at best *applied art [Kunstgewerbe]*.

But the movie theaters are faced with more urgent tasks than refining applied art. They will not fulfill their vocation—which is an aesthetic vocation only to the extent that it is in tune with its social vocation—until they cease to flirt with the theater and renounce their anxious efforts to restore a bygone culture. Rather, they should rid their offerings of all trappings that deprive film of its rights and must aim radically toward a kind of distraction that exposes disintegration instead of masking it. It could be done in Berlin, home of the masses—who so easily allow themselves to be stupefied only because they are so close to the truth.

4.2

Introduction to Distinction
by Pierre Bourdieu

Distinction, written by French sociologist Pierre Bourdieu, compiled into one argument nearly a decade of empirical data about audiences of art, and the consumption of culture. It has a paradigmatic reputation in the sociological study of art. Roughly, *Distinction* argues that taste cultures are predetermined by one's economic position and cultural capital (one's 'training' into appreciation of 'proper' taste), which happens through education, experience and social exposure – the result of a bourgeois upbringing. Bourdieu argues that such predispositions are harder to overcome than generally thought because of the robustness of the structure they create (he uses the term 'habitus' to refer to this): 'taste classifies, and it classifies the classifier', Bourdieu writes. For a field of study as obsessed with taste as cult cinema, Bourdieu's research, and his concepts, have become an essential point of reference, especially in the study of cult audiences. The fit is not always that tight though. For one, cult cinema presupposes a (relative) freedom to apply taste, and Bourdieu's argument leaves little room for movement outside the fixed confinements of one's cultural or economic capital-position. But we have to bear in mind that Bourdieu's map is a snapshot. While it considers data accumulated over time, it is in essence a view *of* a time (the fifties, sixties and early seventies in France), and as such it is unable to indicate any movement – say from popular towards elitist (a movement that would not be untypical for cult appreciations). *Distinction* is hesitant in its claims about cinema appreciation, and downright elusive about popular cinema, but one can see how cult appreciations, or cult appropriations of popular texts would occur at the high cultural capital/lower economic capital end of the diagram. It fits observations about the role of college crowd audiences and campus cults in the advancement of cult cinema (see Mark Jancovich, section 1; Noel Carroll and Lawrence O'Toole, section 2). No surprise then that virtually all subsequent work on cult audiences, and fandom, refers to Bourdieu.

A note on extracting: *Distinction: a Social Critique of the Judgment of Taste* was first published in French, under the title, *Distinction, critique social du jugement*, by Editions du Minuit. Its English translation was published in 1984, by Routledge, from which our excerpts are taken. One of the reasons why Pierre Bourdieu's *Distinction* is only seldom excerpted in readers is because of the intricate connectedness of its argument. Its flow, across data, theories, and observations makes for a tight, and coherent, but also slightly insular rhetoric, from which parts cannot be extracted without compromising its understanding. We reprint here the introduction to the volume (pp 1–7).

Introduction

There is an economy of cultural goods, but it has a specific logic. Sociology endeavours to establish the conditions in which the consumers of cultural goods, and their taste for them, are produced, and at the same time to describe the different ways of appropriating such of these objects as are regarded at a particular moment as works of art, and the social conditions of the constitution of the mode of appropriation that is considered legitimate. But one cannot fully understand cultural practices unless 'culture', in the restricted, normative sense of ordinary usage, is brought back into 'culture' in the anthropological sense, and the elaborated taste for the most refined objects is reconnected with the elementary taste for the flavours of food.

Whereas the ideology of charisma regards taste in legitimate culture as a gift of nature, scientific observation shows that cultural needs are the product of upbringing and education: surveys establish that all cultural practices (museum visits, concert-going, reading etc.), and preferences in literature, painting or music, are closely linked to educational level (measured by qualifications or length of schooling) and secondarily to social origin. The relative weight of home background and of formal education (the effectiveness and duration of which are closely dependent on social origin) varies according to the extent to which the different cultural practices are recognized and taught by the educational system, and the influence of social origin is strongest—other things being equal—in 'extra-curricular' and avant-garde culture. To the socially recognized hierarchy of the arts, and within each of them, of genres, schools or periods, corresponds a social hierarchy of the consumers. This predisposes tastes to function as markers of 'class'. The manner in which culture has been acquired lives on in the manner of using it: the importance attached to manners can be understood once it is seen that it is these imponderables of practice which distinguish the different—and ranked—modes of culture acquisition, early or late, domestic or scholastic, and the classes of individuals which they characterize (such as 'pedants' and *mondains*). Culture also has its titles of nobility—awarded by the educational system—and its pedigrees, measured by seniority in admission to the nobility.

The definition of cultural nobility is the stake in a struggle which has gone on unceasingly, from the seventeenth century to the present day, between groups differing in their ideas of culture and of the legitimate relation to culture and to works of art, and therefore differing in the conditions of acquisition of which these dispositions are the product. Even in the classroom, the dominant definition of the legitimate way of appropriating culture and works of art favours those who have had early access to legitimate culture, in a cultured household, outside of scholastic disciplines, since even within the educational system it devalues scholarly knowledge and interpretation as 'scholastic' or even 'pedantic' in favour of direct experience and simple delight.

The logic of what is sometimes called, in typically 'pedantic' language, the 'reading' of a work of art, offers an objective basis for this opposition. Consumption is, in this case, a stage in a process of communication, that is, an act of deciphering, decoding, which presupposes practical or explicit mastery of a cipher or code. In a sense, one can say that the capacity to see (*voir*) is a function of the knowledge (*savoir*), or concepts, that is, the words, that are available to name visible things, and which are, as it were, programmes for perception. A work of art has meaning and interest only for someone who possesses the cultural competence, that is, the code, into which it is encoded. The conscious or unconscious implementation of explicit or implicit schemes of perception and appreciation which constitutes pictorial or musical culture is the hidden condition for recognizing the styles characteristic of a period, a school or an author, and, more generally, for the familiarity with the internal logic of works that aesthetic enjoyment presupposes. A beholder who lacks the specific code feels lost in a chaos of sounds and rhythms, colours and lines, without rhyme or reason. Not having learnt to adopt the adequate disposition, he stops short at what Erwin Panofsky calls the 'sensible properties', perceiving a skin as downy or lace-work as delicate, or at the emotional resonances aroused by these properties, referring to 'austere' colours or a 'joyful' melody. He cannot move from the 'primary stratum of the meaning we can grasp on the basis of our ordinary experience' to the 'stratum of secondary meanings', i.e., the 'level of the meaning of what is signified', unless he possesses the concepts which go beyond the sensible properties and which identify the specifically stylistic properties of the work. Thus the encounter with a work of art is not 'love at first sight' as is generally supposed, and the act of empathy, *Einfühlung*, which is the art-lover's pleasure, presupposes an act of cognition, a decoding operation, which implies the implementation of a cognitive acquirement, a cultural code.

This typically intellectualist theory of artistic perception directly contradicts the experience of the art-lovers closest to the legitimate definition; acquisition of legitimate culture by insensible familiarization within the family circle tends to favour an enchanted experience of culture which implies forgetting the acquisition. The 'eye' is a product of history reproduced by education. This is true of the mode of artistic perception now accepted as legitimate, that is, the aesthetic disposition, the capacity to consider in and for themselves, as form rather than function, not only the works designated for such apprehension, i.e., legitimate works of art, but everything in the world, including cultural objects which are not yet consecrated—such as, at one time, primitive arts, or, nowadays, popular photography or kitsch—and natural objects. The 'pure' gaze is a historical invention linked to the emergence of an autonomous field of artistic production, that is, a field capable of imposing its own norms on both the production and the consumption of its products. An art which, like all Post-Impressionist painting, is the product of an artistic intention which asserts the primacy of the mode of representation over the object of representation demands categorically an attention to form which previous art only demanded conditionally.

The pure intention of the artist is that of a producer who aims to be autonomous, that is, entirely the master of his product, who tends to reject not only the 'programmes' imposed a priori by scholars and scribes, but also—following the old hierarchy of doing and saying—the interpretations superimposed a posteriori on his work. The production of an 'open work', intrinsically and deliberately polysemic, can thus be understood as the final stage in the conquest of artistic autonomy by poets and, following in their footsteps, by painters, who had long been reliant on writers and their work of 'showing' and 'illustrating'. To assert the autonomy of production is to give primacy to that of which the artist is master, i.e., form, manner, style, rather than the 'subject', the external referent, which involves subordination to functions—even if only the most elementary one, that of representing, signifying, saying something. It also means a refusal to recognize any necessity other than that inscribed in the specific tradition of the artistic discipline in question: the shift from an art which imitates nature to an art which imitates art, deriving from its own history the exclusive source of its experiments and even of its breaks with tradition. An art which ever increasingly contains reference to its own history demands to be perceived historically; it asks to be referred not to an external referent, the represented or designated 'reality', but to the universe of past and present works of art. Like artistic production, in that it is generated in a field, aesthetic perception is necessarily historical, inasmuch as it is differential, relational, attentive to the deviations (*écarts*) which make styles. Like the so-called naive painter who, operating outside the field and its specific traditions, remains external to the history of the art, the 'naive' spectator cannot attain a specific grasp of works of art which only have meaning—or value—in relation to the specific history of an artistic tradition. The aesthetic disposition demanded by the products of a highly autonomous field of production is inseparable from a specific cultural competence. This historical culture functions as a principle of pertinence which enables one to identify, among the elements offered to the gaze, all the distinctive features and only these, by referring them, consciously or unconsciously, to the universe of possible alternatives. This mastery is, for the most part, acquired simply by contact with works of art—that is, through an implicit learning analogous to that which makes it possible to recognize familiar faces without explicit rules or criteria—and it generally remains at a practical level; it is what makes it possible to identify styles, i.e., modes of expression characteristic of a period, a civilization or a school, without having to distinguish clearly, or state explicitly, the features which constitute their originality. Everything seems to suggest that even among professional valuers, the criteria which define the stylistic properties of the 'typical works' on which all their judgements are based usually remain implicit.

The pure gaze implies a break with the ordinary attitude towards the world, which, given the conditions in which it is performed, is also a social separation. Ortega y Gasset can be believed when he attributes to modern art a systematic refusal of all that is 'human', i.e., generic, common—as opposed to distinctive, or distinguished— namely, the passions, emotions and feelings which 'ordinary' people invest in their 'ordinary' lives. It is as if the 'popular aesthetic' (the quotation marks are there to indicate that this is an aesthetic 'in itself' not 'for itself') were based on the affirmation of the continuity between art and life, which implies the subordination of form to function. This is seen clearly in the case of the novel and especially the theatre, where the working-class audience refuses any sort of formal experimentation and all the effects which, by introducing a distance from the accepted conventions (as regards scenery, plot etc.), tend to distance the spectator, preventing him from getting involved and fully identifying with the characters (I am thinking of Brechtian 'alienation' or the disruption of plot in the *nouveau roman*). In contrast to the detachment and disinterestedness which aesthetic theory regards as the only way of recognizing the work of art for what it is, i.e., autonomous, *selbständig*, the 'popular aesthetic' ignores or refuses the refusal of 'facile' involvement and 'vulgar' enjoyment, a refusal which is the basis of the taste for formal experiment. And popular judgements of paintings or photographs spring from an 'aesthetic' (in fact it is an ethos) which is the exact opposite of the Kantian aesthetic. Whereas, in order to grasp the specificity of the aesthetic judgement, Kant strove to distinguish that which pleases from that which gratifies and, more generally, to distinguish disinterestedness, the sole guarantor of the specifically aesthetic quality of contemplation, from the interest of reason which defines the Good, working-class people expect every image to explicitly perform a function, if only that of a sign, and their judgements make reference, often explicitly, to the norms of morality or agreeableness. Whether rejecting or praising, their appreciation always has an ethical basis.

Popular taste applies the schemes of the ethos, which pertain in the ordinary circumstances of life, to legitimate works of art, and so performs a systematic reduction of the things of art to the things of life. The very seriousness (or naivety) which this taste invests in fictions and representations demonstrates a contrario that pure taste performs a suspension of 'naive' involvement which is one dimension of a 'quasi-ludic' relationship with the necessities of the world. Intellectuals could be said to believe in the representation—literature, theatre, painting—more than in the things represented, whereas the people chiefly expect representations and the conventions which govern them to allow them to believe 'naively' in the things represented. The pure aesthetic is rooted in an ethic, or rather, an ethos of elective distance from the necessities of the natural and social world, which may take the form of moral agnosticism (visible when ethical transgression becomes an artistic *parti pris*) or of an aestheticism which presents the aesthetic disposition as a universally valid principle and takes the bourgeois denial of the social world to its limit. The detachment of the pure gaze cannot be dissociated from a general disposition towards the world which is the paradoxical product of conditioning by negative economic necessities—a life of ease—that tends to induce an active distance from necessity.

Although art obviously offers the greatest scope to the aesthetic disposition, there is no area of practice in which the aim of purifying, refining and sublimating primary needs and impulses cannot assert itself, no area in which the stylization of life, that is, the primacy of forms over function, of manner over matter, does not produce the same effects. And nothing is more distinctive, more distinguished, than the capacity to confer aesthetic status on objects that are banal or even 'common' (because the 'common' people make them their own, especially for aesthetic purposes), or the ability to apply the principles of a 'pure' aesthetic to the most everyday choices of everyday life, e.g., in cooking, clothing or decoration, completely reversing the popular disposition which annexes aesthetics to ethics.

In fact, through the economic and social conditions which they presuppose, the different ways of relating to realities and fictions, of believing in fictions and the realities they simulate, with more or less distance and detachment, are very closely linked to the different possible positions in social space and, consequently, bound up with the systems of dispositions (habitus) characteristic of the different classes and class fractions. Taste classifies, and it classifies the classifier. Social subjects, classified by their classifications, distinguish themselves by the distinctions they make, between the beautiful and the ugly, the distinguished and the vulgar, in which their position in the objective classifications is expressed or betrayed. And statistical analysis does indeed show that oppositions similar in structure to those found in cultural practices also appear in eating habits. The antithesis between quantity and quality, substance and form, corresponds to the opposition—linked to different distances from necessity—between the taste of necessity, which favours the most 'filling' and most economical foods, and the taste of liberty—or luxury—which shifts the emphasis to the manner (of presenting, serving, eating etc.) and tends to use stylized forms to deny function.

The science of taste and of cultural consumption begins with a transgression that is in no way aesthetic: it has to abolish the sacred frontier which makes legitimate culture a separate universe, in order to discover the intelligible relations which unite apparently incommensurable 'choices', such as preferences in music and food, painting and sport, literature and hairstyle. This barbarous reintegration of aesthetic consumption into the world of ordinary consumption abolishes the opposition, which has been the basis of high aesthetics since Kant, between the 'taste of sense' and the 'taste of reflection', and between facile pleasure, pleasure reduced to a pleasure of the senses, and pure pleasure, pleasure purified of pleasure, which is predisposed to become a symbol of moral excellence and a measure of the capacity for sublimation which defines the truly human man. The culture which results from this magical division is sacred. Cultural consecration does indeed confer on the objects, persons and situations it touches, a sort of ontological promotion akin to a transubstantiation. Proof enough of this is found in the two following quotations, which might almost have been written for the delight of the sociologist:

'What struck me most is this: nothing could be obscene on the stage of our premier theatre, and the ballerinas of the Opera, even as naked dancers, sylphs, sprites or Bacchae, retain an inviolable purity.'

'There are obscene postures: the stimulated intercourse which offends the eye. Clearly, it is impossible to approve, although the interpolation of such gestures in dance routines does give them a symbolic and aesthetic quality which is absent from the intimate scenes the cinema daily flaunts before its spectators' eyes . . . As for the nude scene, what can one say, except that it is brief and theatrically not very effective? I will not say it is chaste or innocent, for nothing commercial can be so described. Let us say it is not shocking, and that the chief objection is that it serves as a box-office gimmick. . . . In *Hair*, the nakedness fails to be symbolic.'

The denial of lower, coarse, vulgar, venal, servile—in a word, natural—enjoyment, which constitutes the sacred sphere of culture, implies an affirmation of the superiority of those who can be satisfied with the sublimated, refined, disinterested, gratuitous, distinguished pleasures forever closed to the profane. That is why art and cultural consumption are predisposed, consciously and deliberately or not, to fulfil a social function of legitimating social differences.

4.3

Portrait of a cult film audience: *The Rocky Horror Picture Show*
by Bruce A. Austin

Only rarely does cult cinema receive attention from scholars of the empirical study of mass communication. It appears the ambiguities of cult films do not lend themselves easily to the necessarily reductionist procedures and methodologies of quantitative research. As such, Bruce Austin's charting of the audience of *The Rocky Horror Picture Show* in the *Journal of Communication* is an anomaly – but a fascinating one. Austin foregoes the usual theoretical obstacles by looking at the audience afresh, as its own constitution, and not as a deviation of 'normal' or 'normative' film going. In fact, by doing this, Austin's essay is the first to give a basic description of any actual midnight movie audience, the phenomenon which arose during the 1970s, spearheaded by *The Rocky Horror Picture Show*, *Eraserhead*, *Night of the Living Dead*, and *The Texas Chain Saw Massacre*, which altered the conditions for cult movie appreciation forever, pulling it out of the regular art-house environment, into the grindhouse, student-theatre, special-screening, and festival circuit. And Austin's essay was also the first to empirically testify of the participatory behaviours and rituals so often associated with attending *The Rocky Horror Picture Show*: dressing up, queuing, shouting, throwing at the screen. Researched, and published, when the original *Rocky Horror* cult was at its peak and screenings of the film were abundant across the US, it is very much a 'live slice' piece of research. Since 1981, there have been several additional attempts to quantify and measure cult film audiences in action. Austin executed similar research, contained in his *Immediate Seating* book of 1989, he published several cult-related essays in *Current Research in Film*, a journal he edited in the 1980s (on teenpics and subcultural audiences, for instance – one of which is the next entry in this Reader), and he also developed a more complicated hypothesis concerning elitism and taste cultures (published in the *Journal of Popular Film* in 1983). But besides Austin, empirical, quantitative research into cult audiences is still a nascent endeavour. Only very recently have his significant initiatives been followed up by projects with similar empirical and quantitative clout (see further in this Reader).

A note on extracting: this paper first appeared in the *Journal of Communication*, volume 31, issue 2 (Spring), pages 43–54. We are printing this version in full.

The preparation, the waiting, and the active participation in the viewing of the film itself appear to be part of a group ritual which characterizes the cult film as an event.

The Rocky Horror Picture Show and its generation of a cult phenomenon have received attention in the national popular press, but its particular characteristics and components have not been studied in detail. Because of the continuing popularity of the film and especially because of the participation of the audience in the "event," the film provides a unique opportunity for a case-study investigation of the cult phenomenon.

Cult films are the "private genre" of "the privileged children of the middle class," according to Monaco. He traces the beginning of the cult film phenomenon to "the late sixties as camp interest developed in Roger Corman's various monster and motorcycle movies." He cursorily identifies several attributes as constituent elements of the cult film. The films are "generally offered at Friday and Saturday midnight screenings in college towns across the U.S." to a young audience. A "general trend [of the film content] has been toward what we might call a trash esthetic in cult" laced with a "vivid element" of sadomasochism. The films also are populated by "egregiously eccentric characters," are inexpensively produced using on-location settings, and are given poor ("dumped") distribution by their studios. Monaco is probably correct, although this cannot be readily verified, in stating that the cult film phenomenon began in the 1960s. Distribution and exhibition practices (e.g., vertical integration) prior to this time would most likely not have permitted the occurrence of what will be defined here as a cult film. (Of course, this does not necessarily preclude pre-1960 films from becoming cult films.)

Two items which tend *not* to define the cult film are the intent of the filmmaker and the film's content. Cult films are not *made* (as, for example, one sets out to make a musical, western, etc.) as much as they *happen* or *become*.

Conceivably, however, the actual content of the film that later becomes a cult film might very well have something—or a great deal—to do with its later status. For instance, cult films such as *Rocky Horror* appear to have a close affinity with the elements of Sontag's definition of "Camp" (and, more specifically, what she terms "deliberate Camp"). Sontag states that ". . . the essence of Camp is its love of the unnatural: of artifice and exaggeration. And Camp is esoteric—something of a private code, a badge of identity even, among small urban cliques". Thus in Sontag's terms *Rocky Horror* and its audience clearly qualify as Camp. However, this cannot be said to be true of all cult films.

What can be said of all cult films is that it is the audience which identifies them as such

The nature of its audience and the nature of its exhibition qualify the showing of a film as part of the cult film phenomenon. First, the film must be screened at irregular hours (usually around midnight, as Monaco mentions) and these screenings must play on a regular and continuing (minimally once a month) basis. Thus the occasional re-release (e.g., *Fiddler on the Roof, Gone with the Wind,* and most of the Disney catalogue) and films that are not shown in movie theaters (e.g., television broadcasts such as the annual presentation of *The Wizard of Oz*) are excluded. Further, this definition allows us to differentiate between the true cult movie and the popular one-shot revival film so often presented at film festivals (i.e., "classic" films at retrospectives).

Exactly *how* a film comes to this exhibition arrangement (and others do not) cannot, at this point, be empirically demonstrated. It seems reasonable to suggest, however, that the determinants of exhibition as specified above are probably partly fortuitous and partly the outcome of an exhibitor's or film company marketing researcher's lucky hunch or casual observation.

The second defining aspect of the cult film is the audience, which is the subject of this study. Cult films may be uniquely characterized by the repeated attendance of a group of certain individuals. The cult film recidivist (or veteran) is typically young, single, and a high school or college student. Cult films found an audience, for one reason or another, in the 16 mm. college circuit and in repertory theater houses, whose audiences are heavily populated with students. By employing the concept of repeated attendance, coupled with the above discussion of exhibition, we can exclude from the cult category—at least for the present—such films as *Star Wars*. Similarly, the definition prohibits us from discussing television programs such as "Monty Python's Flying Circus," Groucho Marx's "You Bet Your Life," and "Star Trek" as cult films, even though all of the above examples (at least reputedly) meet the repeat viewing requirement. And while a number of Marx Brothers films, for instance, are clearly popular, they cannot be included in the cult definition since in most cases they do not meet the continuing exhibition criterion.

Finally, it is important to distinguish between those films which have a cult following and cult films in terms of their audience. A movie such as Lumet's *Bye Bye Braverman* (1968) might very well have a cult following but cannot be classified as a cult film due to its infrequent exhibition.

In summary, the cult film may be defined as a motion picture which is exhibited on a continuing basis, usually at midnight, and gathers a sizeable repeat audience. This working definition of cult films emphasizes the importance of the repeated regular screenings for the build-up of a regular, returning audience which characterizes the cult film phenomenon.

The film history and audience activity surrounding *The Rocky Horror Picture Show* provide an excellent case study of the intensity and variety of the cult film phenomenon

The film itself may be characterized as both a parody and a metamovie. In a burlesque fashion, the film details the overnight experiences of a stereotypical middle-American couple, Brad and Janet, who innocently seek help from the inhabitants of a nearby castle after their car breaks down and encounter an odd assortment of earthly and extraterrestrial characters. Through them the film effectively parodies conventional mores, values, and attitudes. As a metamovie *Rocky Horror* follows the tradition of Godard, Truffaut, Chabrol, and Rivette, "the first [filmmakers] to turn movies in on themselves." The film blends science fiction, horror, and both rock and roll and traditional musical genres, and the picture's characters act as referents to characters in other, older films. Sight gags and song lyrics also draw on other movies. In sum, the film presents a clever synthesis of thematic, visual, and verbal elements which, with a good deal of panache, parody and satirize accepted cinematic and societal conventions.

During the preparation and early marketing of *Rocky Horror* in 1975 "the word 'cult' reportedly never came up." The film was shot in eight weeks in England at an approximate cost of $1 million. Except for brisk business in Los Angeles, response to its 1975 release was unenthusiastic. The picture was subsequently poorly distributed and unenthusiastically promoted, and very few reviews, outside of industry publications, appeared.

Rocky Horror "officially broke into the midnight circuit at the Waverly Theater in New York City on April 1, 1976." Around Halloween of the same year, "an anonymous group of people, largely unknown to each other, began to dress up" when they went to the midnight screenings. In 1977 a National Rocky Horror Fan Club was formed and is merging with the International Fan Club, which will have combined membership of 5000. A national newspaper, *The Transylvanian*, is published on a semi-regular basis by the national fan club and many locales issue their own 8½ × 14″ newsheets (e.g., the weekly *Rochester* [N.Y.] *Rocky Regular*) which feature personals, *Rocky Horror* trivia, and assorted *Rocky*-related news items. Other publications include an irregularly issued *Rocky Horror Official Poster Book* and the annual *Rocky Horror Picture Show Official Magazine*. In November 1979 the Third Annual *Rocky* Convention was held in New York City.

The fans of *Rocky Horror* not only participate in organizations and publications, but actually participate in the screenings as well. Throughout the showing of the film fans call for camera cuts and character actions. They ask questions of the characters, respond to the characters' comments, and add lines to the film's dialogue. The fans also "help" the characters—by providing flashlights to show the way to Brad and Janet as they trudge through the dark, rainy night, for example. In addition, the audience adds its own special effects, such as hurling toast when a toast is proposed in the film, and squirting one another with water pistols in the rain sequence.

The audience members for *Rocky Horror* interact as much with each other as they do with the characters and action on the screen. To pin down the precise reason(s) for the behavior demonstrated at *Rocky Horror* screenings is beyond the scope of this study. Nonetheless, whatever the reason, audience participation appears to be a key variable which explains not only first-time *Rocky Horror* attendance but repeat attendance as well.

Who are the audience members for *Rocky Horror*, why do they attend, and what can they tell us about cult films in general?

For this study, 562 patrons of the theater where *Rocky Horror* was playing in Rochester, New York were interviewed while waiting in line for the movie. (A strict probability sample for this field study was neither possible nor practicable.) The interviews took place on Friday and Saturday evening one weekend in October 1979 and one in November 1979. Patrons were interviewed only once even if they attended on subsequent evenings. Fewer than 30 patrons refused to be interviewed. For the four evenings when interviews were conducted, nearly half (45 percent) of those attending *Rocky Horror* were surveyed.

The interviewers were college juniors and seniors enrolled in a mass communications course who had been trained in interview techniques. The interview consisted of

34 open- and closed-ended questions. Responses to open-ended questions were later subjected to content analysis.

Based upon the data gathered in this study and the resulting frequency distribution, the audience can be divided into three groups: "first-timers," individuals who had not seen *Rocky Horror* before; "veterans," individuals who had seen *Rocky Horror* one to twelve times; and "regulars," individuals who had seen *Rocky Horror* thirteen or more times. Nearly two-thirds (61.7 percent) of those interviewed had seen *Rocky Horror* at least once. The number of times the respondents had seen *Rocky Horror* ranged from 0 to 200. The overall mean number of attendances was 7.03 and the median was 1.22. Excluding the first-timers, the mean number of times *Rocky Horror* had been seen was 11.39 and the median was 2.98. By way of comparison, Earnest's national telephone survey for 20th Century-Fox of "about 750 people" in the top 30 film markets found the mean *Rocky Horror* attendance to be 2.37 and the median 5.48.

To check for differential attendance patterns between veterans and regulars as well as the meaningfulness of the categories, these individuals were asked, "In the past four weeks, how many times have you seen *The Rocky Horror Picture Show?*" Table 1 clearly indicates that regulars were significantly more likely ($p < .001$) to have greater recent repeat attendance than veterans. Thus, not only is there a substantial repeat audience for *Rocky Horror*, but there is a small group of extremely devoted *Rocky Horror* regulars.

Participants were also asked whether or not they had attended by themselves. Only two first-timers, four veterans, and four regulars reported attending alone. Individuals who indicated that they were not attending alone were asked with whom and how many others they were attending. The size of the attendance unit (excluding the person questioned) ranged from one to 60. No significant difference ($\chi^2 = 45.15$, df = 46, p = .507) was found between audience aggregates for the size of the attendance group. Overall, the mean size of the attendance unit was 4.67 and the median 3.15.

Table 1 Number of times veterans and regulars had seen *Rocky Horror* in the past four weeks

	Veterans (n = 283) %	Regulars (n = 58) %
None	43.5	8.6
Once	23.3	8.6
Twice	17.0	17.2
Three times	8.8	12.1
Four times	3.6	12.1
Five times	2.5	8.6
Six times	0.7	5.2
Seven times	0.3	3.5
Eight times	0.3	24.1
	$\bar{X} = 2.19$	$\bar{X} = 5.18$

$\chi^2 = 44.81$, df = 8, p < .001, C = .34

Table 2 Who attended *Rocky Horror* with whom

	First-timers (n = 213) %	Veterans (n = 285) %	Regulars (n = 56) %	Total (n = 554) %
Alone	0.6	1.4	7.1	1.6
Opposite-sex friend	9.9	11.2	19.6	11.6
Same-sex friend	7.0	6.7	8.9	7.0
Spouse	2.3	0.0	5.4	1.5
Male group	17.8	21.0	16.1	19.3
Female group	10.3	11.6	1.8	10.1
Mixed-sex group	52.1	48.1	41.1	48.9

$\chi^2 = 34.73$, df = 12, p < .001, C = .24

Table 2 shows that the most common attendance unit was the mixed-sex group (more than two persons), followed by the all-male group, with an opposite-sex friend, the all-female group, and attendance with a spouse. Regulars were more likely than both first-timers and veterans to attend alone, or with one other person of the same or opposite sex. Veterans were more likely than the other two aggregates to attend in groups, either all male or all female. First-timers, more so than veterans or regulars, attended with mixed-sex groups.

As shown in Table 3, males made up a greater proportion of the *Rocky Horror* audience than did females. Only within the first-timers group did females outnumber males, and then by just a few. Significantly more males than females were regulars. Further, when veterans and regulars were combined and compared with first-timers we find that, among the former, significantly more males than females were repeat attenders ($\chi^2 = 4.06$, df = 1, p < .05, C = .08). Thus, the data suggest that the repeat audience to *Rocky Horror* becomes increasingly male. Earnest also found that more males than females had seen *Rocky Horror*, although he did not segment his sample as was done here.

Table 3 Social characteristics of the *Rocky Horror* audience

	First-timers %	Veterans %	Regulars %	Total %
Sex	(n = 214)	(n = 285)	(n = 58)	(n = 557)
Male	48.6	56.1	65.5	54.2
Female	51.4	43.9	34.5	45.8

$\chi^2 = 6.13$, df = 2, p < .05, C = .10

	First-timers %	Veterans %	Regulars %	Total %
Age	(n = 213)	(n = 283)	(n = 57)	(n = 553)
13–16	20.3	17.3	7.2	17.4
17–22	63.4	73.6	65.0	68.4
Over 22	16.3	9.1	27.8	13.9
	$\bar{X} = 19.5$	$\bar{X} = 18.7$	$\bar{X} = 22.0$	$\bar{X} = 19.3$

$\chi^2 = 20.23$, df = 4, p < .001, C = .18

While the range of ages reported was from 13 to 50, generally the *Rocky Horror* audience was a relatively young one. Most individuals were between 17 and 22. Overall, veterans tended to be the youngest and regulars the oldest audience groups. Further, an analysis of variance showed that each of the three groups differed significantly in age. Interestingly, 17 percent of the audience was under 17 years old even though *Rocky Horror* is rated R (restricted for such individuals without accompanying parent or guardian).

Given the youthfulness of the audience, it is not surprising to find that few (6.3 percent) were married. Nor is it surprising that more than half of the audience (61.9 percent) reported their occupation as either high school or college students. For those not enrolled in school, the largest segment were blue-collar workers. Within this category were twice as many regulars as first-timers or veterans. Regulars were also more likely than either of the other two groups to report white-collar or professional employment.

The *Rocky Horror* audience was virtually all white (98.7 percent); no blacks were audience members. Catholics comprised half (50.2 percent) and Protestants nearly one quarter (21.2 percent) of the audience. These religious characteristics reflect the population of the area in which the study was conducted. Most of the audience reported being politically independent and middle-of-the-road on political issues.

In relation to media habits, overall movie attendance (*Rocky Horror* was not included) tended to increase slightly in a linear fashion from first-timers to regulars, although no significant difference ($p = .354$) was found between the three groups, using a one-way analysis of variance test. Regulars also tended to watch the most television and veterans the least; again, no significant difference ($p = .101$) between the three groups was found. Thus it may be concluded that while regulars were higher consumers of visual media, overall the three *Rocky Horror* audience aggregates did not differ significantly in their use of such media.

Newspaper reading among all three groups was found to be very high (overall, four times weekly on the average). Regulars reported reading most frequently and first-timers read least often, although the differences among all three groups were nonsignificant ($p = .130$). The number of magazines read monthly also increased in a linear manner from first-timers to regulars, with regulars reporting reading significantly more ($p = .015$) magazines per month than both first-timers and veterans. In summary, regulars were found to be the heaviest media consumers for the four media examined. However, only for magazine reading was there a significant difference between the three audience groups.

How did these audience members learn about *The Rocky Horror Picture Show* and what prompted them to attend?

Respondents were asked to recall where or from whom they first heard of *Rocky Horror*, and how they found out *Rocky Horror* was playing at this particular theater. It is worth noting that 20th Century-Fox's current marketing strategy for the movie has been purposefully low-key, on the assumption that the audience needs to feel it is creating an event rather than responding to media hype.

Table 4 Initial source of information about *Rocky Horror*

	First-timers (n = 215) %	Veterans (n = 288) %	Regulars (n = 58) %	Total (n = 561) %
Personal				
Friends	74.0	69.4	58.6	70.1
Relatives	9.3	9.4	15.5	10.0
Other word-of-mouth	3.7	3.1	0.0	3.0
Total	87.0	81.9	74.1	83.1
Media				
Newspaper	4.6	4.2	1.7	4.1
TV	2.3	2.4	0.0	2.1
Radio	1.9	0.4	0.0	0.9
Total	8.8	7.0	1.7	7.1
Marquee	0.5	0.3	1.7	0.5
Other	2.3	7.3	19.0	6.6
Don't recall	1.4	3.5	3.5	2.7

As Table 4 indicates, word-of-mouth was by far the largest initial source of information about *Rocky Horror*. Nearly three-quarters of the sample reported learning about the film from various personal contacts. For all three audience aggregates, "friends" was the most commonly named source of information. The mass media (newspapers, television, and radio) were mentioned by slightly more than five percent of the total sample as their initial source of information.

While personal contact was clearly the predominant way that most individuals learned about the film, newspapers and personal contact shared approximately equal roles in providing more specific knowledge about *Rocky Horror*. Newspapers accounted for 43.6 percent and personal sources 44 percent of the total sample's source of information about where the film was being screened.

Is attendance at *Rocky Horror* a planned or a spontaneous behavior? More than three-fourths of the respondents stated that their attendance had been planned. The percentage of attendance that was intended increases in a linear fashion from first-timers to regulars, as would be expected if one assumes that the more ardent *Rocky Horror* fans have established an habitual pattern of attendance. First-timers, on the other hand, might attend out of curiosity and thus may wait for an opportunity (perhaps fortuitous) to satisfy this feeling.

A distinguishing feature of the audience members for *Rocky Horror* is their level and frequency of interaction with both the movie and each other

Although actual audience participation could not be measured by a questionnaire prior to viewing, two measures of *preparation* for such participation could be readily assessed: bringing "props" and dressing like one of the film's characters. Overall, slightly more than half (51 percent) of the respondents brought some form of prop with them. No significant difference in who brought props was found between first-timers, veterans, and regulars (p = .078), or by sex (χ^2 = 1.12, df = 1, p = .289), although regulars were far more likely than the veterans to report having done so in the past.

By far the most popular prop, as Table 5 shows, is rice (to be thrown at the wedding scene early in the picture). A variety of water sprayers (for the rain sequence) and newspapers were also popular items. Newspapers are used to imitate Janet as she walks through the rain holding one over her (they may also offer protection from the other audience members' water spraying and rice throwing). Less frequently mentioned props include marshmallows, eggs, potatoes, balloons, bird seed, noisemakers, teddy bears, and ears and nose masks. Thus, while not everyone brings a prop to the theater, those who do come well prepared.

Table 5 Number of times a prop was mentioned

	n
Rice	195
Watergun/sprayer/squirtgun	155
Newspaper	152
Toilet paper	135
Toast	110
Flashlight	33
Playing cards	26
Candle	6
Hot dogs	6
Total	818

Note: Multiple responses were permitted.

Costuming oneself like one of the film's characters is a more extreme form of participation, a form of public commitment. Overall, relatively few (8.6 percent) in this sample indicated that they had ever dressed up. Nearly half (41.4 percent) of the regulars, though, reported such behavior. No significant difference ($\chi^2 = 1.92$, df = 1, p = .165) between the sexes was found. Among those audience members who had dressed up, *Rocky Horror*'s leading character, Frank N. Furter, was the most popular model. No significant difference (p = .766) between veterans and regulars as to character copied was found. In summary, persons who have dressed like one of the film's characters make up only a tiny minority of the *Rocky Horror* audience and are largely regulars. This finding tends to contradict the implication by Shah and others that dressing up is a widespread and popular phenomenon.

As Table 6 shows, the most common reason for first-timers' attendance to *Rocky Horror* is the reputed unique nature of the film and the audience. Word-of-mouth "advertising" plays a large part in their attendance decision. Few first-timers mention quality of the film as the factor which attracted them. (In fact, respondents in Earnest's study reported "a very average rating" for the film; people generally thought it was "not a terrific film.") The social experience promised by *Rocky Horror*'s reputation and satisfaction of one's curiosity are potent drawing cards for first-time viewers.

To attempt to discern the most important elements in *Rocky Horror*'s attraction to

Table 6 First reason given by first-timers for attending *Rocky Horror* (n = 214)

	%
Heard the film was fun/good	14.0
Recommended by friends	13.6
Heard the film was different	10.8
Nothing else to do	9.3
Novelty	8.9
Came along with friends	7.0
Heard the audience was fun	5.6
Other	30.8

Table 7 Veterans' and regulars' reasons for repeat attendance

	Veterans (n = 289) %	*Regulars (n = 58)* %	*Total (n = 347)* %
Like the film	21.8	22.4	21.9
To have a fun time	22.2	13.8	20.8
Like the audience participation	10.4	8.6	10.1
"Craziness"	10.0	6.9	9.5
Social event	9.3	5.2	8.6
Like one (or more) star	2.1	12.0	3.8
Like the music	3.1	0.0	2.6
Like to participate	1.4	5.2	2.0
Other	19.7	25.9	20.7

$\chi^2 = 22.24$, df = 8, p < .005, C = .24

first-timers, respondents were asked, "What about this film appealed to you most?" Almost half (47.2 percent) reported having no one reason that rose above the others for their attendance and 8.9 percent responded that they did not know. Virtually all of the remaining responses point to the expectation of participating in a unique experience and, by inference, satisfaction of curiosity.

Table 7 presents the reasons offered by the veterans and regulars for their repeated attendance. Slightly more than one-fifth of each group mentioned the film itself as a reason. The remaining motives, with the exception of enjoying the film's music and liking a particular actor, all encompass the social experience and event status offered by the film. In considering the most important reason for repeat attendance, enjoyment of the film decreases in importance and the social aspects (audience participation and having a "fun time") increase in importance. Veterans and regulars tended to agree to a considerable extent on their most important reasons for repeat attendance.

Attendance for veterans and regulars clearly means more than simply going to *a* film or even *Rocky Horror*. On the evenings when the interviews were conducted for this study, the ticket line would begin to form as early as 10 p.m., a full two hours before the show. A good deal of socializing took place while waiting in line. In fact, the queuing behavior appeared to be less of a wait and more of an opportunity to meet one another, talk with friends, and re-establish acquaintances. From casual observation, much of the in-line activity seemed to be an important prelude to the more intense activity which was to occur later on in the theater.

What this study suggests, then, about the cult film phenomenon as a whole is that it is the event that attracts and continues to support the popularity of a cult film. The preparation, the waiting, and finally the active participation in the viewing of the film itself appear to be part of a group ritual which characterizes the audience of the cult film.

Further examination of the audiences for cult films is clearly warranted. The cult film has existed for more than a decade and, as Earnest states, the midnight movie audience is a "market that has a slow build, but there is a definite market there." Many questions remain to be answered. Why does audience participation occur? What are the social and psychological needs of the audience that are being met and presumably gratified by the *Rocky Horror* experience? How are these needs met? What factors can be identified that determine the process of how and why one individual becomes a *Rocky Horror* regular and others do not? Why don't all veterans go on to become regulars? To what extent is the content of the cult film an important element in drawing repeat attendance and what are the most salient components? Finally, why are these components important to the audience?

4.4

Subcultural studies and the film audience: Rethinking the film viewing context
by Gina Marchetti

By the mid-1980s it had become clear that the physical and cultural context within which audiences encountered films, including alternative and underground films, was changing. The midnight movies phenomenon, the advent of video, the rise in genre festivals, and a general deployment of tastes and attitudes across a range of subcultures, made the idea of a single dichotomy between 'normal' audiences and 'underground' patrons untenable. Taking its cues from Dick Hebdige's study of music subcultures in the UK (punk and reggae in particular), and to some extent mixing a British and American Cultural Studies approaches. There are traces of Martin Barker's and Stanley Cohen's concern for, and preoccupation with, ideology and power, for instance, and of Howard Becker's and Erving Goffman's ethnographies of 'deviancy' and everyday life experience. Marchetti proposes to use a distinction between subcultures and 'parent cultures' (official culture in Bourdieu's terminology) to sketch the space within which cult audiences express their affiliations to films. The social context of this positioning is essential. Marchetti calls attention to film studies' ignorance of film audiences' viewing contexts, something which becomes clear when she states that 'the fact that the viewing experience goes beyond an individual viewer's relationship to the screen still seems to elude film theorists', and goes on to call for more sociologically and anthropologically inspired research to investigate the actual environments within which audiences view cult movies. Marchetti uses *The Rocky Horror Picture Show*, *Now Voyager*'s gay audience, Beth and Scott B's *The Offenders*, Andy Warhol's *Vinyl*, and *Personal Best*'s lesbian/feminist audiences, to demonstrate how audiences' cult appreciations of these films exist not just in the interaction between text and spectator, but also in the wider framework of cultural trends and reputations (fuelled by, among others, the press, policies, and the state). Marchetti proposes an ethnographic method of participant observation ('hanging out'), and a 'good grasp of the workings of ideology within a culture' to enable a true understanding of subcultural, alternative viewing practices. It is a pity that Marchetti's essay was largely overlooked by film audience researchers, as it predates methodological practices of high relevance in subsequent studies. We hope that by reprinting it here it will regain some of its significance.

A note on extracting: 'Subcultural Studies and the Film Audience: Rethinking the Film Viewing Context' first appeared on pages 61–79 in volume two of Bruce Austin's *Current Research in Film*, an annual journal, and was published by Ablex (Norwood, NJ). We reprint it here in full.

"Who is out there?" and "Why are they sitting there paying money to watch this?" are two crucial questions that have puzzled film financiers, producers, distributors, and exhibitors as well as film scholars ever since Lumière put up a bed sheet in a cafe and charged admission. Certainly, the reasons for asking those questions have varied over time, but the nagging issues of audience motivation, participation, and pleasure remain.

Why should the audience continue to be a theoretical thorn after decades of scholarly and entrepreneurial probes? Library shelves are crammed with books and journals, industry tabloids and doctoral dissertations containing graphs, tables, lists, and figures on audience size, composition by race, ethnic group and gender, frequency of attendance, and so on. Demographers quantify viewers. Behavioral psychologists observe behavior and measure physiological responses. Sociologists count up the hours of leisure time spent in front of the screens and chart film's impact on changing attitudes toward nuclear war or race relations. Industry plots marketing strategy. Although dwarfed by the piles of research devoted to television audiences (who are, after all, "sold" to advertisers based on that sort of data), empirical studies of film audiences have amassed their share of statistical information.

However, beyond quantification lies the *quality* of the viewing experience—its specificity. Why does the viewer find looking at a film pleasurable and exciting or boring and intolerable? Psychoanalysts and various other types of psychologists have stood up to claim this question as their territory. Films have been laid out on the couch, dissected like dreams, and treated like symptoms of a diseased collective mind. With this came an assumption that viewers must be responding to films like social daydreams, group fantasies which key into the structure of the individual's psyche. From this point of view, the audience looks like a collection of identically like-minded individuals who respond to the screen fantasy according to the determinations of the psychological model favored at the moment—Jungian, Freudian, and so on.

With the translation of Christian Metz's work on film semiotics into English in the early 1970s, the determining paradigm for the film viewing experience changed from psychology to linguistics—temporarily. As Metz himself, along with such scholars as Raymond Bellour in Paris and Stephen Heath in London, began to rethink liguistic structures in psychological terms, the image of the film as a dream or symptom reemerged. In the wake of French psychoanalyst Jacques Lacan's work on the way in which language determines ego structure and gender identification and Roland Barthes' application of psychoanalysis, linguistics, and a Marxist critique of ideology to literary theory, film theorists became much more sensitive to the intricacies of the film-viewer relationship. The study of the film-text (fine points of editing, mise-en-scene, sound, and narrative structure) overshadowed historical, cultural, and sociological considerations. Lacan saw language as creating and determining individual psychological make-up and his patient, Marxist theorist Louis Althusser, viewed language, psychology, and ideology as molding and structuring the individual "subject" within the strictures of a class-stratified society. Following their lead, film scholars began to see the film-text as creating its "subject," structuring and determining the viewer's relationship to the screen.

In fact, according to this view, the viewer's position is so textually predetermined that he/she is "sutured" into a place created by the film. Hence, differences among viewers vanish as they struggle to fit into the mold fashioned by the text. Recently, this view of the spectator as a projection or creation of the film text has been amended somewhat by its early advocates to include the possibility of gender and other differences in viewing practices. However, the fact that the viewing experience goes beyond an individual viewer's relationship to the screen still seems to elude film theorists. After all, the viewer goes to the cinema as a member of various social institutions—families, schools, governments, churches, businesses—as a creature of a particular historical moment. So the question remains: as film scholars, how do we look at the interaction between the screen and the social and cultural forces which forge the viewer's relationship to that screen fantasy?

By using methods developed by urban anthropologists, film audience researchers can begin to get at the dynamics of the group experience. Coupling these methods with the current work being done on the composition, self-expression, and collective identity of subcultural groups on the edges of the dominant culture, film theory can move even closer to pinpointing how social class, race, gender, or age identity can shape the viewing experience at a specific moment in history.

Subcultural studies: a link in a missing chain?

With the question of the social position of the viewer, the issue of audience research comes full circle and lands once again in the domain of the sociologist. In a field dominated in the United States for the last several years by statisticians and behaviorists, there seems to be a dearth of methods available to the film audience researcher who does not want to ignore the importance of the film text itself, but who wants to keep close tabs on the viewer's situation as an audience member, as a part of a specific community.

A possible approach to this problem comes from what at first may seem to be a completely unrelated area of sociology—deviance theory. Although the word "deviance" may conjure up images of criminals, jails, and the moral niceties of the science of penology, deviance theory, in certain circles, has also been wedded to the study of social group formations and the development of group and individual identities. Using many of the methodological tools of the anthropologist (particularly the urban anthropologist), sociologists like Howard Becker, for example, look at "deviants" as members of cultural formations with distinctive argot, dress, art forms, institutions, and forms of social interaction. In *Outsiders: Studies in the Sociology of Deviance*, Becker looks at deviant groups as "subcultures":

> Members of organized deviant groups have one thing in common: their deviance. It gives them a sense of common fate, of being in the same boat. From a sense of common fate, from having to face the same problems, grows a deviant subculture: a set of perspectives and understandings about what the world is like and how to deal with it, and a set of routine activities based on those perspectives. Membership in such a group solidifies a deviant identity.

Certainly, the concept of "subculture" has been batted around in sociological circles for some time. In *Keywords: A Vocabulary of Culture and Society*, Raymond

Williams notes that the term evolved organically out of the way in which the word "culture" has been used in the anthropological sense of human social formations and ways of life (rather than the more arcane, but still common, meaning of the cultivation of the arts and intellectual pursuits). Williams defines "subculture" as "the culture of a distinguishable smaller group". Thus, as a category, the concept of "subculture" can cover quite a bit of territory.

However, as a working concept, "subculture" has been increasingly identified with deviance theory of one sort or another. In other words, the subculture is "distinguishable" precisely because it deviates from the norms set by the larger culture. In most current usage, the concept of "subculture" refers to any identifiable and cohesive group which is outside the dominant culture and its ideological norms because of differences of race, age, gender, sexual orientation, lifestyle or outlook. Thus, although subcultures share many common characteristics with the larger cultural formations of which they are a part, they have their own patterns of thought and behavior which are obscure, if not completely incomprehensible, to outsiders.

Like all social formations, subcultures are in a constant state of growth, transformation, and decay. In fact, the term has both structural and historical implications. For example, black subcultures have always existed in American culture; however, dress, argot, language, and so on, associated with various black subcultures have changed over time (from slavery to urban black life today) and are also characterized by geographical, class, age, and other variables within a given historical period (e.g., note the differences between rural and urban black life). Similar observations can be made about youth, gay, and other subcultures.

To assume that every film viewer is a member of an identifiable subculture would be ludicrous. However, the importance of this concept to a study of film audiences cannot be denied. A close examination of one specific type of audience identified with a particular subculture enables the concrete discussion of a viewer who is a member of a specific group with a set of shared economic, social, and cultural circumstances at a specific point in history. This provides an alternative to looking at the audience as merely a dry list of demographic statistics unrelated to the film image. Rather, a study of subculture allows for an examination of the interaction between viewers' cultural circumstances and their perception of, or possible distortion or transformation of, the film's message or presentation of experience. Viewers' relationships with a given film (whether it is a Hollywood feature about a subculture, a feature having nothing to do with the subculture, or a documentary about a certain aspect of the subcultural group) may be completely changed by their identification (or lack of identification) with a subculture.

Perhaps the area of recent subcultural work which will prove to be the most fecund for film audience researchers will be youth subcultural studies. In general, film audiences have become younger. Films that have done well at the box office—from *Star Wars* to *Gremlins*—have been openly directed to this market. Many adolescents become involved in some kind of subcultural activity—ranging from gang deliquency to wearing a spangled glove à la Michael Jackson—in the course of growing up. The interrelationship of youth subcultural activity and film viewership needs to be examined more closely. The ways in which subcultural activities find their way to the cinema screen, as well as the way in which screen fantasies mold and direct subcultural identity and behavior need to be looked at carefully. Specific youth sub-cultures react to films in very specific, visible ways. For example, youth involved in the punk subculture can enjoy a film which actually condemns their subcultural identity by simply turning up in the theater as a group and vocally cheering on the "villains" while hissing at the "heroes." A film like *Blade Runner* can be enjoyed in this fashion by siding with the punked-out androids against the "straight" humans.

Using youth subcultures as a starting point also makes quite a bit of sense when the existing research on the subject is taken into account. An important body of work already exists in the area of subcultural studies of youth. Since World War II, a number of sociologists, psychologists, and other cultural analysts have devoted a great deal of their attention to the study of youth subcultures. Primarily concerned with working-class youth, these researchers are part of an important tradition within British cultural studies. Like the work of Richard Hoggart, Stuart Hall, Paddy Whan-nel, Raymond Williams, and E.P. Thompson, among others, this research draws a direct link between working-class life and many aspects of popular culture which could be defined as exclusive to that class.

The focus on youth of this research is not surprising given the visibility of youth subcultural activity—primarily in Britain, but also in the United States—after the war. In the early 1950s, youth in Britain and America had more disposable income available to them to spend on leisure pursuits. These leisure activities developed into a number of distinctive youth subcultures. Highly visible youth subcultures have con-tinued to flourish since. In the case of youth subcultures, group identity is expressed in the form of a distinctive style—in, for example, music, fashion, argot. Although the nature and extent of their critique of the dominant culture and its norms vary, virtu-ally all youth subcultures have seen themselves, and have been seen by the dominant culture, as opposed to aesthetic, economic, religious, legal, sexual, familial, or edu-cational institutions which structure the social system. Even though subcultural styles are adopted by and adapted to mass commercial culture, youth subcultures still manage—if only briefly—to convey a sense of opposition and rebellion, though this critique usually remains in the realm of style.

When sociologists first began to consider seriously the phenomenon of youth and other types of subcultures, the discipline of sociology was dominated by Emile Durk-heim's views on group dynamics and the importance of "outsiders" or "deviants" to the maintenance of the dominant group's own sense of cohesiveness, common iden-tity, and social order. Most of the earliest research into subcultures, in fact, fell into this tradition. What became known as the "transactional" approach developed out of this and focused primarily on juvenile delinquents and petty criminal groups. The social fact of deviancy came to be thought of as a labeling system whereby the domin-ant culture had the prerogative to set limits and define itself in opposition to an outside other. In *Subculture: The Meaning of Style*, Dick Hebdige points to Howard Becker's *The Outsiders* as a classic study of this type:

> One of the best examples of the transactional method in which the construction of deviant groups is interpreted as the result of a dynamic process whereby those in power define the limits of acceptable and unacceptable behavior through *label-ing* (e.g. marijuana smoker = lazy, long-haired, potentially violent malcontent, etc.)

Becker summarizes his view as follows:

> Deviance or delinquency are . . . seen, not as arising naturally from the world of the "outsider," but as part of an ascribed social identity, arising in the interaction between groups which are unequal in the distribution of power. The "deviance" of a group is not "natural" but the result of a specific kind of social construction: and one of the key mechanisms of this process is the power to define situations *for* others, and the power to label others—and make those labels stick.
>
> [emphasis in original.]

In "Naturalistic Research into Subcultures and Deviance," Brian Roberts explicates this type of analysis further:

> *Social groups create deviance by making the rules whose infraction constitutes deviance*, and by applying those rules to particular people and labeling them as outsiders. From this point of view, deviance is *not* a quality of the act the person commits, but rather a consequence of the application by others of rules and sanctions to an "offender." The deviant is one to whom that label has successfully been applied; deviant behavior is behavior people so label.
>
> [emphasis in original.]

Although Becker's work on deviance focuses equally on the way in which the society labels deviant behavior and the way in which the individual subcultural member constructs his/her identity vis-à-vis the dominant culture, other sociologists working within the transactional approach have tended to concentrate on the dominant culture's power to define and label deviations from what it considers the social norm. Erving Goffman, for example, concentrates his attention on how the dominant culture takes some characteristic of an individual outside the norm and elaborates on this in order to create a stereotypic pattern of *stigma* to label that individual as "deviant." Goffman states:

> While the stranger is present before us, evidence can arise of his possessing an attribute that makes him different from others in the category of persons available for him to be, and of a less desirable kind—in the extreme, a person who is quite thoroughly bad, or dangerous, or weak. He is thus reduced in our minds from a whole and usual person to a tainted, discounted one. Such an attribute is a stigma, especially when its discrediting effect is very extensive; sometimes it is also called a failing, a shortcoming, a handicap.

For Goffman, deviancy is almost always a fact of outside labeling rather than individual construction of an identity that differs from the norm.

Although this type of research has contributed a number of important concepts to the field of subcultural studies by underscoring the importance of the power struggle existing between subcultures and the dominant culture for control over group identity, this approach also has a number of severe limitations. As Roberts points out:

This now locates deviance *too* much in terms of rule-breaking, too much in terms of the "reaction" of social control agencies, and gives too little to the way the controlled subject or group sees the world from its point of view.

[emphasis in original.]

In order to counter this presentation of subcultural identity as something primarily attributed to a group by a more powerful agency of social control, a number of cultural analysts have attempted to place subcultural theory within the broader context of general cultural relationships. To this end, Stuart Hall and his colleagues formed an association at the University of Birmingham in England to study post-World War II British youth subcultures. First published as a special issue of *Working Papers in Cultural Studies*, a collection of essays summarizing their research was later brought out under the title *Resistance Through Rituals: Youth Subcultures in Post-War Britain*. In order to elaborate on the work begun by the transactionalists in subcultural theory, these researchers draw on Marxist conceptions of class, ideology, hegemony, and cultural struggle in order to situate the subcultural member in a broader social framework. As stated in the introduction:

Our aim . . . remains . . . to explain *both* social action *and* social reaction, structurally and historically in a way which attempts to do justice to all the levels of analysis: from the dynamism of "face to face" interactions between delinquents and control agents to the wider, more mediated, questions—largely ignored by "pure" transactionalists—of the relation of these activities to shifts in class and power relations, consciousness, ideology and hegemony.

[emphasis in original]

By placing subcultural study within a Marxist framework, the members of the Birmingham School are able to highlight the importance of looking at subcultural activity within the context of a larger whole. This emphasis on a cultural totality underscores the interconnectedness of the economic base, class stratifications, social institutions, and the realm of ideas and aesthetics. With economic change comes changes in the social fabric. This historical dynamic arises out of the contradictions inherent in this cultural whole—between those who control the economic base and those who do not, between those in political power and those outside the power structure, hence among members of various class strata. In "Subcultures, Cultures and Class: a Theoretical Overview," John Clarke, Stuart Hall, Tony Jefferson and Brian Roberts paint a picture of culture as a site of both structural consistencies and constant struggle and change:

The "culture" of a group or class is the peculiar and distinctive "way of life" of the group or class, the meanings, values and ideas embodied in institutions, in social relations, in systems of beliefs, in mores and customs, in the uses of objects and material life . . . cultures are differently ranked, and stand in opposition to one another, in relations of domination and subordination, along the scale of "cultural power" . . . it is crucial to replace the notion of "culture" with the more concrete, historical concept of "cultures"; a redefinition which brings out more clearly the fact that cultures always stand in relations of domination—and subordination—to one another, are always, in some sense, in struggle with one another.

Various cultures arise out of certain class ties. These relatively large cultural structures, however, also give rise to a number of smaller cultural units, "subcultures," which are both like and different from their larger "parent" cultures. Thus, these subcultures bear a certain relationship to both the dominant culture and their parent cultures. Youth, sexual orientation, race, lifestyle, and so on set the subcultural member apart from both the parent and the dominant culture.

Structurally, the dominant culture, parent culture, and subculture are in conflict. However, the nature of the antagonism among these structures varies. For example, the working class may deny its differences from the dominant culture, because it may be economically advantageous to identify as much as possible with the aims and goals of one's corporation, for example, in order to obtain a promotion or salary increase. Similarly, a subculture may identify very strongly with its parent culture—as in the case of the British Skinheads who vehemently espouse what they perceive to be "working-class" values (which often leads them to assault "decadent" nonconformists such as hippies or punks). However, for the most part, the parent culture remains quite distinct from the dominant culture, and the relationship between a parent culture and a youth subculture is, more often than not, antagonistic.

Although the apparent difference of age or skin color, for example, is usually perceived by the dominant culture as a negative characteristic, the subcultural member, instead of trying to efface the difference and blend in as well as possible with the dominant ideology's picture of "normal," transforms this difference into a strength, the foundation of individual identity.

All class cultures have, at one point in time or another, been parent cultures for oppositional subcultures. As a parent culture, for example, the bourgeois elite has given rise to the youthful "jet set" or "beautiful people" subculture, reported in the press as the latest exploits of the "Kennedy Kids." Taking the professional middle classes (petite-bourgeoisie) as the example, the hippies, the beats, the bohemian art circles and much of the illegal drug culture can be pointed out as subcultures arising principally from this class. Mods, skinheads, and rockers (duppers, bikers, and greasers in the United States) are usually cited as examples of youth subcultures principally arising out of the working class.

Thus, affiliation with a particular youth subculture generally does not change an individual's class affiliation. For example, although hippies claim to "drop out" of the petite-bourgeois culture of their parents, many still retain that class affiliation by becoming small business entrepreneurs, for example, running health food stores or head shops, becoming skilled artisans or craftspeople. All of these occupations essentially keep them within the same class position as their parents, although they are quite definitely outside the mainstream of occupations generally considered acceptable by other members of their class.

However, although the class affiliations of these subcultures are undeniable, it must be remembered that the subculture is a relatively autonomous structure, with many characteristics which contradict the values and beliefs of the parent culture. Moreover, shared experiences often erode class boundaries. The relationships between a subculture and its parent culture, the subculture and the dominant culture, and between one subculture and another are always in a constant state of change and contradiction.

To cite only one example, Andy Warhol's Factory, a thriving avant-garde institution of the 1960s which still exists today, brought together members of various subcultural groups with diverse class backgrounds to form an important part of the New York Underground—a new bohemianism. In *Stargazer: Andy Warhol's World and His Films*, Stephen Koch somewhat histrionically describes this subcultural meeting ground as follows:

> One senses that, in those days, a thrilling complicity united the artistic and sexual and drug subcultures, that some kind of shared refusal threw together mute *seriosos* like the composer LaMonte Young with the hardened, quick-witted, druggy street performers with names like Rotter Rita, Narsissy, and Ondine, people living on drugs and their wits, doing their numbers in bars and apartment lofts, of the existence of which the straight world had only the merest dreadful intimations. Men for whom the flamboyant pose and a tongue like lightning were the only life found themselves in a department of limbo adjacent to middle-class artists.

Of course, this is only one very limited historical instance—a time and a place in which various subcultures met and pooled their stylistic resources, magnifying their opposition to the dominant culture. These periods and places of subcultural intermingling are somewhat rare. There are often as many barriers between subcultures as there are points of association. Even among subcultures arising out of the same parent culture, there are antagonisms: Mods despised rockers; skinheads hated punks, gays, and blacks. It is also important to keep in mind that subcultures are fleeting phenomena. Although subcultures are a fact of our social structure, specific subcultural groups form, come to prominence, and suddenly disappear. As Albert K. Cohen notes in his study of subcultures and deviancy, *Delinquent Boys:*

> Culture is continually being created, recreated, and modified wherever individuals sense in each other like needs, generated by like circumstances, not shared generally in the larger social system. Once established, such a subcultural system may persist, but not by sheer inertia. It may achieve a life which outlasts that of the individuals who participated in its creation, but only so long as it continues to serve the needs of those who succeed its creators.

Subcultural identification, however, while it does last, serves a very important function for its adherents. As Hall, Clarke, Jefferson, and Roberts observe, subcultures

> win *space* for the young: cultural space in the neighborhood and institutions, real time for leisure and recreation, actual room on the street or street-corner. They serve to mark out and appropriate "territory" in the localities. They focus around key occasions of social interaction: the week-end, the disco ... They cluster

around particular locations. They develop specific rhythms of interchange, structural relations between members: younger to older, experienced to novice, stylish to square. They explore "focal concerns" central to the inner life of the group: things "done" or "never done," a set of social rituals which underpin their collective identity and define them as a "group" instead of a mere collection of individuals. They adopt and adapt material objects—goods and possessions—and reorganize them into distinctive "styles" which express the collectivity of their being-as-a-group. These concerns, activities, relationships, materials become embodied in rituals of relationship and occasion and movement. Sometimes, the world is marked out, linguistically, by names or an *argot* which classifies the social world exterior to them in terms meaningful only within their group perspective, and maintains its boundaries.

[emphasis in original.]

One of the more important places in which subcultures have managed to "win space" for themselves is the cinema. Although they often sensationalize and exploit subcultures, films have also helped validate subcultural identity by graphically representing, and often tacitly accepting, subcultural lifestyles and experiences.

Subcultures and film audiences

Many subcultures have had complex and diverse relationships with the institution of the cinema. At the most basic level, the local cinema has provided a meeting ground for a number of subcultural groups. As a dark, but public, place outside the realm of parental and social authority operating in the home and at the workplace, the cinema is a place to gather and meet like-minded fellows during leisure time. This use of the cinema as a meeting ground can range from the Friday and Saturday night "takeover" of many neighborhood movie theaters by *Rocky Horror Picture Show* fans to the proliferation of all-male pornography cinemas frequented by gay men to find available lovers. In one sense, no matter what may or may not be on the screen, the movie theater has consistently been an important aspect of the lives of many subcultural members.

However, for most subcultures, the cinema remains a comparatively peripheral forum of stylistic expression. *The Rocky Horror Picture Show* phenomenon is the rare exception. Originally produced as a play to exploit the popularity of London's glam subculture (known as "glitter" in the United States) of the early 1970s, the film adaptation surprisingly revived glitter clothing, music, humor, and street theatricality long after the subculture itself had virtually sunk into obscurity. *The Rocky Horror Picture Show* created a subcultural pocket around screenings of this film in major cities. Although this remains a rather unusual offshoot of a once-popular subcultural style, in and of itself, the *Rocky Horror* audience does not constitute a separate subculture. Rather, it is a "sub-" subculture, a variant of the glitter subculture, firmly within the style and issues foregrounded by glitter.

The cinema is also an important site for the formation of group identity and feelings of comradeship with subcultural members from other places. In fact, films provide an important channel for the diffusion of subcultural style. For example, the

Hollywood film industry will note a new fashion, musical trend, or subcultural style. Small studios like New World Pictures or American International will take a chance on a low budget film exploiting the newly visible subculture; larger studios may also invest money in a feature on the subculture. By making a film about a subcultural group, the studio can profit from two potential audiences. Ostensibly, these "exploitation" films are exposés of juvenile delinquency, the pitfalls of loose sexuality, or the horrors of drug abuse and a life of crime on the fringes of urban society. These activities are condemned as criminal, perverse, or deviant, and the offenders in the films either die, are jailed, or reform. The status quo is affirmed after a journey through this "deviant" underworld, most clearly identified as such by the trappings of a well-publicized subculture, for example, leather jackets and motorcycles in the 1950s, flowered shirts, beads, and long hair in the 1960s, and shaved heads and safety pins in the 1970s.

Of course underneath this apparent condemnation, there is an unmistakable element of titillation for the nonsubcultural audience member. Forbidden desires are indulged by the "naughty" members of the subculture who freely spit on figures of authority, indulge in taboo sexual activities, thumb their noses at conventional morality, and basically have a good time before their inevitable downfall. The viewer's voyeuristic desires are catered to—a well-known subculture provides the perfect vehicle for the expression of socially forbidden wishes. Thus, the general audience indulges in a simultaneous sanctimonious condemnation and vicarious identification with the Hollywood fantasy of the subculture's activities. The forbidden is projected onto the outsiders, the subcultural members.

By comparing themselves with "deviants," members of the dominant culture also solidify their own ranks. Their sense of group cohesiveness is strengthened by opposition to the threat of those who represent alien values. The subculture may represent a fantasy of being free from the constraints of the nuclear family, the work ethic, or the legitimacy of capitalism. This fantasy of freedom, however, co-exists with a reaffirmation of the dominant culture's principal values.

On the other hand, the same "exploitation" films can have a radically different significance for another segment of the audience. Although these films ostensibly condemn any type of behavior which goes against the mores of the dominant culture, they can also be looked at and interpreted in radically different ways by members of the subculture represented or by those outside the dominant culture, who may be sympathetic to the position of the characters identified with a subculture in the film. As John Clarke points out, the media's presentation of subcultural activities is subject to "deviant readings" by those outside the dominant culture. Hence, subcultural members can still enjoy a film in which their activities are condemned by assuming an ironic position vis-à-vis the film's narrative. Removed from a fantasy identification with the negation of the subculture or punishment of its activities by this ironic detachment, the subcultural viewer enjoys variations on style, new music, and interesting "villains" who may fulfill a viewer's secret wishes with impunity. By its very presentation on the screen, the subculture is displayed and tacitly affirmed.

In fact, it is in that way that subcultural styles spread. Although these films ostensibly condemn the subculture and strip it of any real significance other than that necessary to conform to the label of "deviancy" or "villainy" which enables the subculture to fit into the standard exploitation plot, these films also help to popularize the style. Clarke's comments on the presentation of subcultures in the news media are equally applicable to the presentation of subcultural activities in Hollywood films:

> Where the news-media strip down and dislocate the indigenous style, in order to make their own symbolic (and derogatory) communication, they may actually widen the "cultural space" which permits the selective re-working and re-appropriation of the style by geographically-dispersed groups. Similarly, the motivations of marketing prompt a generalization and stripping-down of the original sub-cultural style; symbolic elements lose their first, integral relation to a specific life-context, and become thus more open to variation in the precise structuring of their reappropriation by others, whose activities, self-images, and focal concerns are not precisely the same.

Thus, according to Clarke, the subculture is simultaneously "diffused" and "defused" through the media.

The dominant cinema's exploitation of a subculture can extend far beyond these titillating exposes of "deviancy," however. This originally minor, sensationalized "fringe element" may eventually grow into a rather substantial audience in its own right. Eventually, low-budget features made especially for the subcultural market find their way to the local cinema. If popular, a studio may then decide to create bigger budget films about the subculture, hoping for larger profits.

Hollywood films also affect subcultural identity in another important way. Many films, having absolutely nothing to do with subcultures or their activities, find a special place within the subculture's pantheon of valued objects appropriated from the dominant culture. Looked at in a radically different way, these films are transformed by the subcultural viewer's active and deliberate misreading into something of peculiar significance to those involved in the group. Like other objects of mass culture appropriated by the subcultural style makers, these films are not arbitrarily selected but have a particular aspect—or subtext—which allows them to be read in an originally unintended way.

Camp is perhaps the best documented example of this phenomenon. Camp transforms a classic Hollywood film, through a sense of ironic humor, into an object with a totally different significance. In "Rehearsal for a Theory of Subtextual Readings," for example, Chuck Kleinhans notes the way in which the Warner Brothers melodrama *Now Voyager* is transformed by the gay audience into a text with a radically different significance:

> Consider *Now Voyager*. The plot portrays the gradual emergence of a repressed, mousy spinster (Bette Davis) into a sexually active mature woman under the tutelage of a wise older man (Claude Rains). This emergent butterfly metaphor, while certainly being a universally understood pattern within our culture, has a special resonance for many gay men who themselves have experienced or who are experiencing the conditions of discovering and exploring one's sexuality which has been repressed within the family and other institutions. In other words, identification with the character and situation is very strong. This is visually enhanced

because the changes in the Davis character are signalled in changing dress, hair, style, and physical bearing—precisely those areas which gay men often first publically present their resistance to dominant heterosexual norms.

Thus, a film considered quite straightforward by most members of the audience takes on a special significance for the members of a subcultural group. *Mommie Dearest* provides another example. Marketed as a biographical melodrama which exposes the sadistic underbelly of Joan Crawford's relationship with her adopted daughter, the film was quickly taken up as a camp classic of histrionic dominance fantasies. Mops and wire hangers in hand, the subcultural audience has transformed the film into the "Mommie Horror Show."

Of course, Hollywood features are not the only films to portray or have an impact on subcultures. As an adjunct of the news media, documentaries have also capitalized on and sensationalized subcultural activity. Most often, like their fictional counterparts, these documentaries ostensibly condemn the subculture while titillating the audience with a voyeuristic journey into taboo territory. However, perhaps because of lower costs or a desire to be journalistically "objective" about the phenomenon presented, many of these documentaries have had considerable success with the members of the subcultures presented by the film. Cinéma-vérité documentaries like *Woodstock, Monterey Pop*, and *Gimme Shelter* have been quite successful, providing the subcultural audience with a chance to see their favorite rock group on the big screen.

The large budget commercial documentaries with wide theatrical distribution are, of course, only one end of the spectrum of nonfiction films made about subcultures. With the increased availability of small gauge film and video equipment, many members of subcultural groups are eager to make their own films and videotapes. Occasionally, these "home movies" become parts of feature length documentary films. Others remain private, in-home, personal records. Still others, however, become part of a circuit of avant-garde filmmaking distribution and exhibition.

A cultural space often forms somewhere between the world of the subculture and the institution of independent filmmaking. An audience may be comprised of subcultural members, the local literati, and the curious. Although subcultural members may venture into an avant-garde theater to see a film about a favorite band or even themselves depicted on film, more often new venues are organized to screen these experimental film-subcultural coproductions. Bars, clubs, or local auditoriums may host a band or a dance and show a film as part of the performance. Perhaps the most notorious showcase for this type of activity during the 1960s was Warhol's Exploding Plastic Inevitable. As described by Stephen Koch, it was a bar, a disco, a meeting place, a continuous Op Art light show, a showcase for new talent including the rock group The Velvet Underground, as well as a screening room for Warhol's film productions. Koch describes the way in which Warhol exhibited his film *Vinyl* as follows:

Part of the environment, the film was projected on a screen high above the stage amid five or six other films, light shows, and bursting and sliding abstract images all over the walls. Silently running up there on the wall, *Vinyl* seemed to drown in rampagant [*sic*] sound and overwhelming blaring fantasy of that first light-blasted multimedia discotheque. And yet, in that ear-splitting, wall-shaking music box, as deafening recorded rock alternated with the utterly deadening music of the Velvet Underground, the Warhol rock group, *Vinyl's* remote, silenced vision of sexual violence assumed a strange admonitory authority over the hall . . . The Plastic Inevitable seemed at first a merely barnlike, faintly tacky discotheque. There were tables placed around the place, and various things were served. There was a dance floor. High on the walls, high above the immense floor-throbbing woofers and merciless tweeters, the films and light shows poured like an endless, drenching visual rain. But as the music alternated between cacophony and the hideous "acid" maundering of the Velvet Underground's insufferable navel-gazing guitars, the effort to create an exploding . . . environment capable of shattering any conceivable focus on the senses was all too successful. It became virtually impossible even to dance, or for that matter to do anything else but sit and be bombarded—stoned, as it were—cursing that six-dollar admission fee . . . the environment became a chamber of sensual assault, its aesthetic battery.

The Exploding Plastic Inevitable was really the rough equivalent of DADA's infamous Cabaret Voltaire, a meeting place of popular entertainment, subcultural style, and avant-garde experimentation.

The punk subculture has also given rise to similarly unusual types of film viewing venues. Even before video monitors became standard fixtures in most youth-oriented bars and clubs, punk discos featured televisions or film screens. Many bands included visual materials as part of their performances. Filmmakers found themselves attracted to punk clubs as exhibition outlets with particularly receptive audiences.

Beth B and Scott B's film *The Offenders* offers an interesting case in point. Originally *The Offenders* was shown as a serial at New York's well-known cabaret and showcase for punk artists and musicians, Max's Kansas City. Each episode of the film was, in part, financed from profits of the preceeding week. A great deal of the film was written, performed, and filmed just in time for each week's screening. As a result, *The Offenders* has a rather loose, lumbering, "home-movie" structure. Many scenes were improvised, and the film projects this sense of spontaneity and immediacy.

Rather than disguising the passage of time, for example, the Bs self-consciously foreground it. Process becomes part of the film text. Posters for the various episodes of the film appear at some of the locations used to film the following week's episode. The characters act out this week's action in front of the posters advertising the previous week's events.

In addition, the savvy viewer is brought into the filmmaking process in another important respect. The Bs use very familiar local punk haunts as locations in the film. The viewer's own neighborhood is transformed each week into the fantasy of *The Offenders*. In addition, bits of topical material are woven into the film fantasy. The "crime wave" depicted in the film occurred simultaneously with an actual "crime wave" in New York. The Bs exploit this topical goldmine by intercutting sensational headlines from the New York *Post* with the fictional events, for example, bank robberies, murders, and so on, depicted in the film. The gulf between fiction and reality collapses. The viewer recognizes the similarities between current events, actual happenings, and the film's fictional ones. The assumed passivity of the

Hollywood spectator is called into question. Viewer participation in the form of retorts to the film, vocal recognition of fellow subcultural members on screen, dancing, drinking, and other active responses to the screen fantasy are expected and encouraged. Cliff-hangers at the end of each week's episode invited the audience to come back next time for the resolution of the crisis. *The Offenders* became a punk version of *The Perils of Pauline*.

Thus, from the perspective of subcultural studies, specific film audiences become active, creative forces. The subculture opens up the possibility for the viewer to look at a film in a particular way, often actively misreading an apparently straightforward fantasy. Moreover, the subculture may give rise to unique film exhibition environments in which film viewing behavior may differ radically from more common behavior at local suburban multiplexes.

A note on method

The question of how the film researcher goes about the task of investigating a particular subculture's film-viewing activities remains. An especially fruitful possibility comes from the discipline of urban anthropology. Like an anthropologist, the subcultural analyst not only observes and records the behavior of the group under study, but also participates in the community. Although the degree of the researcher's participation within the subculture varies (from being openly identified with the group to acting as an outside advocate or simply an interested nonmember), this type of "participant-observer" research avoids many of the pitfalls of statistical studies. For example, the observer's own effects on the phenomenon are taken into account; the researcher becomes, at least to a degree, part of the event analyzed. Also, the analyst develops a sympathy or insider's feeling for the group because of his/her intimate relationships with the subculture. Informal conversations, close observations, and actual participation in group activities reveal a type of information and insight that often substantially differs from findings gleaned from more traditional quantitative methods.

Although the "objectivity" of the results of these urban-anthropological methodologies has been questioned, this issue can also be turned around to expose the falacious "objectivity" of many researchers who ask certain types of questions, in often leading ways, and who are seldom surprised by the results. These methods seldom question the researcher's own prejudices in wording a survey, choosing participants, or analyzing and interpreting data. On the other hand, years of field work and critiques of the anthropologist's methods have brought a certain self-awareness to many working within the discipline and related fields. Personal expectations and prejudices do play their roles, but these biases are offset by self-examination, analysis, and an awareness of the important dialectical relation between sciences and personal commitment. In fact, this self-consciousness has become an indispensable component of the method itself.

"Hanging out" with a particular subculture may strike those who have never attempted this type of work as a rather haphazard method of collecting data. However, close observation of audiences can yield a wealth of information. When do group members attend film performances? How do they dress? What cinemas do they frequent? How do they speak to each other and to outsiders (both verbally and nonverbally)? How do they relate to the screen fantasy—that is, verbal comments, laughter, snickers, quiet talking to one another? With whom do they attend the performance—dates, children, parents, and so on? What kinds of activities go on before, during, and after the screening? What is the physical venue like? How does the viewing environment mold group behavior?

With a solid grounding in participant-observation, most current studies of subcultures (particularly those done under the auspices of Birmingham and Open University in England) have been characterized by a lively eclecticism. Film audience studies inspired by this research likewise tend to draw on several types of information in order to draw as complete a picture as possible of the subculture's peculiar interaction with the screen. This material can range from secondary sociological, anthropological, or historical studies to film reviews or other records about film viewing made by those within the subculture to oral histories and interviews. All of these materials become particularly useful when this information is wedded to a close analysis of a specific film text.

Chris Straayer's "*Personal Best*: Lesbian/Feminist Audience" provides a good example of the fecundity of this openly eclectic type of research method. In this article, Straayer reports the results of a survey conducted with a number of women who identify themselves as either "feminist" or "lesbian" or both. Beyond a simple survey of data, however, Straayer's study places this information within a clear context. Her analysis shows a historical and cultural understanding of the lesbian/feminist community in the United States and a recognition of the importance of a close reading of the text which exposes the ways in which a film can be open to a number of readings.

In fact, a sensitivity to the complexities of the film text itself is crucial to an understanding of audience response. Assuming that a researcher can get at the intricacies of the film-viewer relationship by simply observing the audience or asking questions about a viewer's reaction to a film or viewing habits is naive. A viewer can never be looked at as a completely self-conscious, self-critical, and scrupulously honest source of information. Rather, a film audience researcher must have a good grasp of the workings of ideology within a culture, of the ways fantasies are molded by but also react against the dominant powers, and of the means by which a film text may give pleasure to both those within and those hostile to a subculture.

The potential importance of subcultural film audience studies cannot be overemphasized. Within a culture which is so often perceived as being almost completely homogeneous, subcultures point to important social, economic, political, class, gender, racial, and other differences. Subcultural study takes the diversity of our culture into account. With this diversity comes an implied opposition to—and occasionally a stated criticism of—the status quo. Although primarily through fantasy and the superficial trappings of style, change is still conceived of, and more importantly, acted upon. The dominant culture does not remain an immutable given, but becomes a structure subject to change, an order which can be opposed.

4.5

Fans' notes: The horror film fanzine
by David Sanjek

The fanzine is a major marker of subculture and cult fandom, in the time before the advent of the internet perhaps its most visible representation in the public sphere. While it exists in the margins of official culture, and its varying print-runs, irregularity of publication, and eclectic contents may not fully fit the framework of what one would call 'the press', they are the closest possible example of cult viewing's press representation. American popular culture scholar David Sanjek acknowledges the long existence of fan publications on stardom and genre, with those concentrating on the horror genre as the most prolific (*Famous Monsters of Filmland* and *Castle of Frankenstein* are the key examples). But it is since the 1970s that horror fanzines have come to occupy a pivotal position in expressing the jocular tone, the contrarist politics, an archivist obsession with breadth, completeness and correct facts, a uniqueness of aesthetic vision, and the liberation of imagination so typical for cult-viewing – the kind of characteristics essential to 'paracinema' (see Jeffrey Sconce's chapter in Section one). Sanjek mentions *Cinefantastique* and *Fangoria* as crucial examples, and analyses editorials and reviews from *Sleazoid Express* and *Gore Gazette*. His analysis explains why directors like David Cronenberg, David Lynch, and Dario Argento have established such firm subcultural fanbases. Since Sanjek's work, analyses of fan-criticism have strayed away from considerations of fanzines as 'audiences', investigating them through institutional and political-economy approaches instead – emphasizing the reviews rather than the reviewers (Ian Conrich's work on *Fangoria*'s influence on the neo-horror culture of the 1980s is one example; Mark Kermode's autobiographical account of horror viewing another – see bibliography). Sanjek's study reminds us that all fanzines are, in essence, public expressions of private pleasures, and as such they allow a glimpse into the minds of cult audiences and fans.

A note on extracting: Fans' notes: the Horror Film Fanzine, first appeared in *Literature/Film Quarterly*, in 1990, volume 18, issue 3, pages 150–160. It has since been reprinted in Gelder, Ken (2000), *The Horror Reader*, London: Routledge, 314–324. We reprint here the original version.

The man who insists on high and serious pleasures is depriving himself of pleasure; he continually restricts what he can enjoy: in the constant exercise of his good taste he will eventually price himself out of the market, so to speak.

—Susan Sontag

"film buff": that species who collect movies the way others collect stamps or butterflies, thereby depriving them of their contextual significance.

—Robin Wood

Slimetime, Grind, Trashola, The Gore Gazette. The titles reflect an unseemly juvenile fascination with unrespectable and illicit imagery, the domain of the horror film. For most adults horror films are the junk food of the imagination, trivially dispensable cultural artifacts undeserving of critical attention and devoid of artistic or intellectual sophistication. Even defenders of the genre, like Stephen King, admit that "good horror movies operate most powerfully on this 'wanna-look-at-my-chewed-up-food?' level," a primitively childish consciousness "sometimes also known as the 'Oh my God, was that gross!' factor." Sophisticated critics may speak of a typology of the monstrous or the genre's reflection of personal, social or mythic structures, but it is some undeniable, primitive, precritical instinct that compels successive generations willingly to pay good money to be made extremely uncomfortable and thereby answer "an invitation to indulge in deviant, antisocial behavior by proxy—to commit gratuitous acts of violence, indulge our puerile dreams of power, to give in to our most craven fears."

Among the willing participants in this sometimes unsavory process are the editors of horror film and video fanzines: independent, non-commercial, amateur publications compulsively produced by individuals who have fallen prey to what Stephen King call "the siren song of crap." Either mimeographed or off-set printed, available only by mail and unpredictable in their publication, the fanzines are suffused with that juvenile fascination with grue and gore, most evident in their frequent inclusion of illustrations appealing to the lowest kind of prurient interest and guaranteed to offend: a policeman's severed head laid out on a kitchen table like some grisly hors d'oeuvre; ravenous zombies about to satisfy their appetites upon an unwilling victim.

Connoisseurs of the badfilm, trash, and gore, the fanzine editors insist upon the pleasures to be found in the consumption of such raw, undiluted imagery. Their enthusiasm may seem to lack irony or finesse; however, at its source the fanzine perspective is "such a deadly serious undertaking that its seriousness can never be openly acknowledged. The gross-out afficionado savors his sense of complicity when the values of a smug social stratum, from which he feels himself excluded, are systematically trashed and ridiculed." What may seem to some a sophomoric interest in putatively indefensible outrage for outrage's sake is to the fanzine editor a healthy interest in forms of expression that call into question social and cultural norms. This perspective is best summarized by V. Vale and Andrea Juno in the introduction to their seminal publication *Research #10: Incredibly Strange Films:*

> This is a functional guide to territory largely neglected by the film-criticism establishment—encompassing tens of thousands of films. Most of the films discussed test the limits of contemporary [middle-class] cultural acceptability, mainly because they don't meet certain "standards" utilized in evaluating direction, cinematography, etc. Many of the films are overtly "lower-class" or "low-brow" in content and art direction. However, a high percentage of these works disdained

by the would-be dictators of public opinion are sources of pure enjoyment and delight, despite improbable plots, "bad" acting, or ragged film technique. At issue is the notion of "good taste," which functions as a filter to block out entire areas of experience judged—and damned—as unworthy of investigation.

The concepts of "good taste" are intricately woven into society's control process and class structure. Aesthetics are not an objective body of laws suspended above us like Plato's supreme "Ideas"; they are rooted in the fundamental mechanics of how to control the population and control the status quo.

Clearly, these publications cannot be dismissed in the pejorative tone employed by Robin Wood as merely the sophomoric ramblings of overgrown adolescents, cinephiliacs who lack the skill or the desire to distinguish between the work of Edward D. Wood Jr. and David Cronenberg. Instead, their editors are acutely in touch with what David Chute has called those "rock-bottom truths about movies [which] precede the operation of criticism," including "the plain fact that some of the things movies do for us can easily be done without finesse or imagination or wit." The fanzines constitute an alternative brand of film criticism, a school with its own set of values and virtues. They aim not only to *épater le bourgeois* but also to root out obscure marginalia of the horror genre and revel in the private consumption of outrage for outrage's sake.

What values, then, do these publications hold and what use can they be to the film scholar? Once the reader gets beyond the often alienating nature of their format, the fanzines provide a valuable resource for examination of the horror and other genres, albeit at times in a sophomoric manner, as well as embody a distinct though disturbing element of the contemporary sensibility: that which identifies with the monstrous in a nihilistic manner.

Fanzines typically are amateur publications, which by form and content distinguish themselves from "prozines": the commercial, mainstream magazine, typified in the horror field by *Cinefantastique* (1970–) and *Fangoria* (1979–). Both widely distributed publications focus almost exclusively on current films, previewing them before release in a sycophantic manner fanzine editors condemn as little more than unpaid publicity. Too often the articles resemble press kits, replete with interviews of cast and crew and premature praise of the unfinished product. True, both prozines have incorporated retrospective analyses of major figures and films in the genre or coverage of the European horror market, but for the most part their emphases are exclusively Anglo-American and predictable in the attention paid to the "hot" figures in the genre Craig Ledbetter, editor of *Hi-Tech Terror*, caused a sympathetic stir in fanzine circles when he wrote:

I don't give a shit A) What Larry Cohen is doing. B) How Sam Raimi plans on remaking *Evil Dead* for the rest of his life, or C) The fact there are hundreds of straight-to-video American made Junk waiting to find a home in someone's VCR. *I JUST DON'T CARE*. We Americans refuse to recognize the tremendous amount of superlative work taking place overseas. We'd rather fawn over Tobe Hooper Abortions from Cannon (next up is Empire), thank Charles Band for resurrecting the drive-in double-bill so we can see two turds for the price of one and interview Hershel Gordon Lewis for the 50th time. C'mon folks, show some originality.

Furthermore, if the fanzines can be accused of indulging in an auteurist cult of the director, the prozines are dedicated to a cult of the technician. They often discuss the construction and execution of special effects and makeup artists such as Ray Harryhausen, Tom Savini, or Rick Baker to the point of idolatry. A case in point is the July-August 1982 issue of *Cinefantastique*, which devotes more than twenty-five pages to Ridley Scott's *Blade Runner*, yet for all the discussion of production design little mention is made of how Scott's mise en scène visualizes Philip K. Dick's post-nuclear anomie. At the same time, it must be said that even creditable analyses of the horror genre too often emphasize thematic content but ignore stylistic inadequacies. A case in point is Robin Wood's excessively sophisticated reading of the apocalyptic imagery in Larry Cohen's films. "World of Gods and Monsters." Wood's acknowledgement of Cohen's "frequent refusal to underline effects or insist on points" neglects Cohen's all too often slapdash technique.

The fanzines' point of view, on the other hand, owes a great deal to two defunct prozines: Forest J. Ackerman's *Famous Monsters of Filmland* and Calvin Beck's *Castle of Frankenstein*. *Famous Monsters of Filmland*, which began publishing in the 1950s, projected a jocular tone, indulging at times in wearisome punning, and a predilection for the horror classics of Karloff, Lugosi, and the Chaneys Jr. and Sr. as well as the archetypical horror figures, particularly the vampire and Frankenstein's monster. For all its affability and good humor, *Famous Monsters of Filmland* seemed singularly devoted to what James Twitchell calls "artificial horror": "what an audience searches for in a verbal or visual text when it wants a particular kind of frisson without much intellectual explanation or sophistication." *Castle of Frankenstein*, on the other hand, displayed a greater affinity for "real horror," those images which often are repellent in actuality and deliberately violate our sensibilities. Beck's prozine, which was published twenty-five times between 1962 and 1975, furthermore avoided *Famous Monsters of Filmland*'s Anglo-American exclusivity by covering European and Asian efforts in the genre as well as horror and fantasy literature, art, and theatre. It also provided valuable research materials, as one of *Castle of Frankenstein*'s editors, director Joe Dante, then only a teenager, contributed an astute and extensive capsule dictionary of film reviews, thereby introducing many readers to the wealth of material in the genre. Fanzines ever since have incorporated both publications' perspectives, treating the horror genre in a jocular or synoptic manner.

As a result of their independent, amateur status, fanzine editors feel obliged to no one, save, perhaps, their subscribers. They lack the indiscriminate, slavish devotion of prozine editors, who bow to commercial producers for interviews, access to sets, and provocative and grotesque publicity photos to attract or offend their readers. If anything, fanzines seem most attracted to uniqueness of vision. Their editors have so immersed themselves in the genre about which they write that they have little interest in and no patience for the slavish devotion to accepted formulae and conventions of the mainstream Hollywood product. Few fanzines therefore praise the ritualized carnage of the recent installments of the *Friday the 13th* or *Nightmare on Elm Street* series, for, as a reviewer in *Samhain* asks, "how can anything like *Friday the 13th Part 7* be original in *any* aspect?" The degree to which these films now border on self-parody is underscored by their exploitation as syndicated television series which bowdlerize whatever frisson they may once have possessed. Therefore, if to the outsider fanzines appear to be obsessed with the most turgid forms of exploitation fodder, it must be remembered that "Bad films may sometimes be amusing, sometimes even successful, but their only real usefulness is to form that basis of comparison: to define positive values in terms of their own negative charm." At the same time, the fanzines' exhaustive research often uncovers "the sort of interesting, untouted, 'discovery' movies that crop up whenever devotees of the genre write." Fanzine editors and writers may well be drawn by "the siren song of crap," but they just as well know crap when they see it.

This devotion to uniqueness of vision has led the fanzines to value most works which bear the mark of an uninhibited visionary sensibility, one which pushes the boundaries of social, sexual, and aesthetic assumptions. The fanzine writers were among the first to praise the work of such now mainstream directors as George Romero, David Lynch, Wes Craven and David Cronenberg. It has also led them to be attentive to censorship of the genre, practiced in the United States by the MPAA ratings board and abroad by state bodies of social control, such as those in England which in the early 1980s legislated against "video nasties." The British fanzines in particular regularly editorialize against the powers of the state: *Samhain* has included a column, "Police 55: Banned!," which describes in detail those films the law has made unavailable to the public, while *Cold Sweat* discusses the effect of censorship laws upon the availability of films in European markets. In an environment where the censor's band has been so indiscriminate, even summarizing a restricted film's plot can be a subversive action.

Furthermore, those fanzines which have begun to market videotapes, including not only titles in the public domain but also others sometimes surreptitiously obtained from foreign sources, underscore their devotion to authenticity of expression by emphasizing that their copies are *uncut* or recorded in the proper letterboxed, widescreen format. Such factors are of particular importance in the case of foreign films, as students of the genre are aware of the extent to which non-domestic horror films are routinely released in any number of versions, their continuity undermined by unconscionable tampering. For example, Dario Argento's *Phenomena* (1985) was domestically released by New Line Cinema with twenty-two minutes excised; the fanzines alone carry a complete print, taken from a Japanese laser disk. The perplexing proliferation of running times listed for many films in Phil Hardy's *Encyclopedia of Horror Films* underscores this point. Fanzines have rectified the dilemma by obtaining the most complete prints by legal or clandestine means.

While many fanzines employ a studious tone, others revel in a smart aleck, supercilious approach to the genre, best typified by John Bloom a.k.a. Joe Bob Briggs's 1982–85 columns in the "Dallas Times Herald." Adopting the persona of a redneck drive-in afficionado, Bloom sarcastically covered such fare as *The Grim Reaper* and *Pieces* until his journalistic tenure was terminated by the publication of a facetiously offensive parody of the popular anthem against world hunger "We Are the World." The final paragraphs of Joe Bob's reviews always enumerated how much blood was spilled, how many breasts were bared and beasts were featured in the given film, ending more often than not with the admonition, "Joe Bob says check it out." His analysis of Tobe Hooper's *Texas Chain Saw Massacre* aptly represents Bloom's style:

> But, of course, the most brilliant thing about *Chain Saw* is that it can scare the bejabbers out of you to the point where you think it was made by a cannibal. A lot of people say *Psycho* is the scariest movie ever made. Bullstuff. *Chainsaw* is the only movie ever made in which anybody can die at any moment. It's also the only movie with *three* psychos who are buddies working shifts, so as soon as Sally and Franklyn veer off that main highway, they're potential meals. Think about *that* the next time you stop for gas in a strange place.

Any number of fanzines feature a similar sarcastic perspective, including *Temple of Schlock*, *Exploitation Retrospect*, and *Gore Gazette*, which featured the following review in issue 93.

> *Feel the Heat*—Another example of a "free" feature being offered to theatres to satisfy a video presale, this wacky exploitationer features sultry slopehead kara-tress Tianna Alexandra as an LA narcotics detective sent to Buenos Aires to break up has-been Rod Steiger's international heroin ring. It seems that the old Rodster is posing as a South American talent agent scouting for dancers to come to New York. When he finds prospective bimbo candidates, he gets them to submit to silicone beef-ups, and unbeknownst to the girls he fills up their hooters with heroin instead of silicone and subsequently offs them by having goons tear off their tits when they reach the U.S. This radical plot premise could have been handled a lot grislier by restrained director Joel Silberg as its blood count is quite anemic, but *Feel the Heat* still packs enough double-entendres, killings, assorted vulgarities and groin crunchings by Alexandra to elicit a bunch of chuckles from fans of Grade B depravity. Well worth a look!

As is evident in this review, the sarcastic fanzines' jocular tone is often laced with self-conscious misogyny, racism and sexism, the very qualities which led Bloom to lose his newspaper column. The editors of the *Gore Gazette* explain their irreverence as "meant merely to inform, entertain and expose those wormbags who may be trying to take advantage of genre fans' hardearned greenbacks and nothing more." A recent *Washington Times* article on fanzines written by David Mills stressed this perspective, much to defensive dismay of a number of editors who felt the author missed the point that this intentionally juvenile hard-boiled tone goes hand in hand with the fanzines' belief that only the most hardened sensibilities can bear the assault of offensive imagery. Charles Kilgore, editor of *Ecco*, provided one of the most intelligent responses to the controversy:

> Though they vary somewhat in content, the angry editorials both employ a "fuck 'em if they can't take a joke" rationale. Both suggest that Mills didn't "get" the gag: that only his hyper-sensitivity, and not his color (yes, Mills is Black), excludes him from appreciating their ethnic humor. One even tries the long-dead "But some of my best friends are . . ." routine. When Mills interviewed me by

phone, the subject of racism in one of the 'zines was inadvertently raised. I defended the fanzine explaining that what he found offensive was not racism but rather a nihilistic form of humor based on sarcasm and irony.

I should have also reminded him of Jonathon Swift's essay "A Modest Proposal," in which Swift outlines the absurdity of a position by pretending to adopt it. Or pointed to the independent music scene of the late seventies, when bands tired of baiting born-again conservatives turned on their aim on fresh quarry: complacent liberals. *Kill The Poor, Crippled Children Such, Holiday in Cambodia.* Titles designed to make fair-minded people squirm . . . if they don't get it.

The trouble is, what if they don't? Mills apparently didn't. What about the reader who misunderstands, nodding in agreement instead of laughing? In case you haven't noticed, racism is back with a vengence. Some of its newest manifestations, such as the skinhead branch of the Aryan Nation, veer uncomfortably close to idealogical home. If Morton Downey Jr. lied about his attack by young neo-Nazis, his populists grandstanding will have trivialized a serious issue.

For the most part, fanzine editors lack Kilgore's deliberate and thoughtful consideration of this issue, and their frat-boy sensibility proves wearisome unless taken in small doses.

On the other hand, a number of fanzine editors are anything but facetious in their interest in exploitation films and use their fanzines as a forum to fill black holes in the analysis of commercial cinema by their encyclopedic knowledge of internationally produced exploitation material. Steve Puchalski, editor of *Slimetime*, has published exhaustive overviews of the blaxploitation and biker genres in the British fanzine *Shock Express*, while Craig Ledbetter contributed a lengthy study of the Italian zombie and cannibal cycles that followed the release of George Romero's *Dawn of the Dead* to the fanzine *Wet Paint*. However, most studies, serious and otherwise, of the horror genre are unashamedly Anglo-American in their bias and rarely consider non-English material. Many fanzines form an exception to this rule, Bill Connolly's *Spaghetti Cinema* being the work of a capable archivist of Italian commercial film, having included analyses of the peplum, giallo, spaghetti western and other genres. His conclusive legwork helps illuminate the hazy material conditions in which international exploitation filmmaking is conducted. Such work can only help answer questions of production and consumption, thereby adding to the "transdisciplinary" approach to the analysis of "formula cinema" proposed by Christopher Frayling in his study *Spaghetti Westerns*. As Frayling indicates, adequate assessment of "formula cinema" must not be reduced to any simple ideological or theoretic grid which excludes "questions about production ('How did this film come to be made?', 'What process did the film go through, to become the finished product?') or about reception ('Why did audiences choose this film or this genre as opposed to that one?', 'What was particularly exciting about this director's work?')." The work of archivists like Connolly help to "incorporate the act of film-making [and] the act of looking at films into [our] theoretical model, factors which are typically unexamined in analyses of foreign commercial film."

Other fanzines also have taken on the role of archivist. There has been of late considerable reevaluation of the British Gothic horror film, particularly the work of the Hammer Studio; Dick Klemenson's *Little Shoppe of Horrors* devotes itself exclusively to that studio, and other zines, *Samhain* in particular, have assessed the virtues of Hammer's premiere director, Terence Fisher, both adding to the landmark study of the English horror film, David Pirie's *A Heritage of Horror*. However, it is the work of certain Italian horror stylists which has received the most considerable and detailed attention and begun to indicate the degree of European influence upon Anglo-American filmmakers. Three directors in particular—Riccardo Freda, Mario Bava, and Dario Argento—appropriately have been singled out for attention.

Freda, whose two delirious, Gothic melodramas starring horror icon Barbara Steele, *The Horrible Doctor Hitchcock* (1962) and *The Ghost* (1963), have been praised by Phil Hardy as deploying "perfect control of colour, rhythm, and atmosphere," receives extensive analysis in issues of *Shock Express* and *Spaghetti Cinema*. The dark, exotic romanticism of his visually lush style reanimated the gothic stereotypes of the Hammer films by underscoring the form's sexual morbidity while engaging in a obsessive fascination with Steele's physically striking features.

Of even greater importance and influence is the work of Mario Bava, originally a cinematographer, whose work in the horror genre stretches from 1956, when he photographed Freda's *I Vampiri*, to 1977's *Shock* a.k.a. *Beyond the Door II*. Even those critics conscious of his faults—indifferent scripting and acting as well as a tendency to overuse shock cuts and zoom lenses—readily admit "Bava is a superb painter on celluloid, electrifying otherwise routine films by his color and compositions." More specifically, a number of Bava's films initiated stylistic and thematic trends in the genre: *Black Sunday* (1960), his first and in the mind of many critics best film, starring Barbara Steele, stylishly combined elegant and loathsome imagery while reinvigorating, like Freda, gothic stereotypes; *Blood and Black Lace* (1964) initiated the giallo genre as well as laid the visual and thematic seeds for the slasher film, albeit with greater style and psychological complexity than any of its successors; *Planet of the Vampires* (1965) integrated the science fiction and horror genres and incorporated imagery foreshadowing later similar works, including *Alien* (1979); and *Kill Baby Kill* (1966), a film of genuine poetic power and visual ingenuity, successfully inverted gothic stereotypes of good and evil by having the power of good embodied by a dark-haired witch while evil is represented by a angelic, blonde young girl. Bava's erratic but fascinating work has been discussed by any number of fanzines, including *Shock Express, Ecco,* and *Spaghetti Cinema*, which has helped increase interest in and awareness of his influential landmark films.

Finally, the fanzines have been instrumental in seriously analyzing the visually excessive, rhapsodically violent giallo thrillers of Dario Argento, whose work is critically and commercially honored in Europe and dismissed as grindhouse fodder in the United States. Save for Maitland McDonagh's recent *Film Quarterly* article, the fanzines alone have accorded the Italian director the attention he deserves for "eight horror films whose visual density is extraordinary; their intricate storylines— improbable and deceptive—are systematically sublimated to a mise en scène whose escalating complexity ... [conspires] to delineate a diegetic world gone mad." Appraisal of Argento's work has appeared in *Wet Paint, Photon, Blood Times,* and *Samhain*, which published John Martin's three-part "Magic All Around Us," the only analysis of substance other than McDonagh's.

In addition to these sarcastic or archivist fanzines, others, including *Subhuman,*

Trash Compactor, Cold Sweat, and *Sheer Filth,* nihilistically identify with repulsive imagery. They propose that good taste acts as a repressive safety valve, filtering out entire areas of experience and expression, and relish the deliberate breaking of social and aesthetic taboos. The structural principle of the films they most appreciate seems to be one of deliberate visual and thematic aggression whereby "an almost musical interaction [exists] between moments of tension and moments of respite, in the form of more or less closely spaced and more or less pronounced crossings of the pain threshold." And yet, these fanzines all too infrequently raise or address questions proposed by *Ecco* editor Charles Kilgore: "Where in the nether-world of exploitation does freedom of expression end and the necessity for social responsibility begin . . . is it possible to advocate cinematic celebrations of human depravity and cruelty in a socially responsible manner?"

Liberation of the unfettered imagination and the crossing of social taboos can result in films imbued with frightening negativity, such as Tobe Hooper's *Texas Chainsaw Massacre,* which redeem their unrelenting horror through a "degraded but impressive creativity . . . a kind of hideous aesthetic beauty." A striking, though less well-known example of this phenomenon is Michael Reeves' *The Conquerer Worm* a.k.a. *The Witchfinder General* (1968). In this film, detailing the horrendous behavior of a putative hunter of witches (Vincent Price) during Cromwell's struggle for power, "evil is inextricably intertwined with good, the [characters'] violence is circular, and ambiguous." No one escapes the taint of inherent depravity, yet while Reeves never minimizes the narrative's brutality, he refuses to titillate the audience or allow them respite from the "theme of the morally outraged seeking a revenge that ultimately degrades them to the level of their quarry." Clearly, our empathy for the film's hero must acknowledge his sadistic extermination of Price's character and therefore force us to question our voyeuristic involvement with the narrative.

However, Reeves' film is an exception, and all too often liberation of the unfettered imagination gives birth to grisly works of art which transgress the "greyland between art and porno-exhibitionism." Many filmmakers have descended to the base level of unredeemable splatter and gore typified by the cycle of Italian cannibal and zombie films, the spawn of directors like Lucio Fulci and Ruggere Deodato, which followed in the wake of George Romero's infinitely superior *Dawn of the Dead.* Films such as Fulci's *The Gates of Hell* (1980) and Deodato's *Cannibal Holocaust* (1979) not only deny us any protection or distance from their effects but endorse a kind of obscene literalism, defying their audiences to dismiss the undeniable gruesomeness of their imagery.

The nihilistic fanzines fecklessly address this sub-aesthetic realm, seemingly oblivious to its unregenerate nihilism. What is even more disturbing is that the films' conservative point of view, particularly their misogynistic dismissal of female sexuality, is believed to undermine the status quo. The editors of these zines rarely address the reactionary elements of the splatter genre or the disturbing assertion made by Robin Wood: "One important aspect of what the horror film has come to signify [is] the sense of a civilization condemning itself, through its popular culture, to ultimate disintegration, and ambivalently (with the simultaneous horror/wish-fulfillment of nightmare) celebrating the fact."

One fanzine, Bill Landis's *Sleazoid Express,* faced this dilemma and as a result ruled itself out of existence. Its five-year run (1980–85) began typically, as Landis staked out 42nd Street and its environs as his territory. He reviewed the requisite exploitation fare, albeit with a discriminating eye that took in the work of underground filmmakers, including Kenneth Anger, Curt McDowell, and Stan Brakhage. Quite quickly, however, Landis's tone grew more acerbic and biting; much of the exploitation fare now seemed to him witless and indefensible. His comments in the April 1983 issue on films he selected for a Sleaze Festival are instructive. He points to the "emotional brutality" pervading the work of Andy Milligan, a New York splatter filmmaker. All his characters, Landis states, are "completely hateful," providing us with "the most unflattering portraits of humanity ever to reach a movie screen."

Increasingly, Landis had little patience with commercial exploitation films, including those often praised by the mass of fanzine editors. In an article titled "Exploitation Cancer" in the March 1983 issue, he lambasts Sam Raimi's *Evil Dead* as

> just the latest model in the invasion of exploitation by a nerd brained, stamp collector mentality which has particularly involved itself in gore. Obsession with special effects, blockheadedly judging laughability without comprehending its aesthetic basis, and praising gore for gore's sake are all examples of this. It's just these type of fans are now picking up cameras.

Bored and angered by such triviality, Landis turns his attention to the consumers of sleaze, for whom he has even more considerable contempt. To Landis, they are self-indulgent voyeurs, living out repressed, juvenile fantasies, using the stock phrase "so bad it's good" to rationalize their debased appetites. He designates the habitues of adult theaters "popeyes" and those muscle-bound pontificators over the virtues of sleaze "blockheads." Landis's loathing for both groups is obvious and unremitting.

In the end, Landis leaves commercial exploitation movies behind, and the final issues of *Sleazoid Express* anatomize the culture and preoccupations of the denizens of 42nd Street, most memorably, as Jack Barth has said, "an entire Summer 1984 issue sketching the ambience of The Deuce that comes across like Joyce describing Dublin." As virtually all films, exploitation and otherwise, bore Landis, he increasingly turns his attention to hard core pornography, which he feels at least has the honesty to lack any pretense of social redemption or pseudo-artistic self-consciousness. *Sleazoid Express* holds a mirror up to an element of the audience that the fanzines represents and illustrates that, as Roland Barthes has written, "What's terrible about the cinema is that it makes the monstrous viable." If Landis has given attraction to the monstrous a human face, few of us would wish to share its features.

The range of fanzines is wide, from the sophomoric to the archival to the nihilistic. They define and dissect a territory of expression that can fascinate as easily as it can repulse. Furthermore, they widen our knowledge of the range of human expression and reanimate those primal urges which drew us in the dark to the screen. Much as we do not wish to admit, to deny the pleasures they address will only price us out of the market.

4.6

"Get a life!": Fans, poachers, nomads
by Henry Jenkins

The work of American scholar Henry Jenkins is widely credited as pivotal in the legitimizing of fandom as a valid topic of academic investigation. Arguing against popular perceptions of fans as 'sad', 'without a life', 'lost', and geeks without a sense of reality (prejudices also often encountered by cult audiences), Jenkins describes a wide variety of fandoms, and their visible appearances at conventions, in fanzines, at reunions, in their fan productions (be it 'fan-fiction' or 'filk') and through real and imaginary communities, as equally discriminate, sophisticated, and 'in charge' of their own tastes as any other audience, be they critics or accidental spectators. A self-confessed fan of the cult television series *Star Trek* himself, Jenkins used his first-hand experiences to map fandoms' socio-cultural and aesthetic viewings as operations that allow fans to position themselves against, or in relation to, judgments of evaluation. But instead of relying, as John Fiske does (see below), on a concept of fandom as 'compensating' a 'lack' in other forms of cultural capital, Jenkins sees fandom as a part of everyday life (a semi-ethnographic approach he borrows from French philosopher Michel De Certeau). Among the most important of De Certeau's concepts Jenkins applies are ironic viewing, appropriation, bricolage, and 'textual poaching' (his best-known short-hand reference point): four ways in which fans can 'use' their viewing activities for cultural gain, often against the commercial intentions of the industry (for instance by actively engaging in copying, sharing, and alternative distribution of self-produced fan materials). For Jenkins, fandom encapsulates a cultural 'surplus', in that it allows audiences to play out their intellectual skills, which remain unchallenged by their professional occupations, and aim for 'utopian' values, such as community and friendship. While the chapter we reprint comes from a book whose subtitle emphasizes television, Jenkins draws examples from serialized films like *Star Wars*, *Indiana Jones*, and *Batman*, as well as crossover television series with a large 'cinematic' cult legacy (*Doctor Who*, *Star Trek*, *Robin of Sherwood*, *The Prisoner*).

A note on extracting: 'Get a Life: Fans, Poachers, Nomads' was first published in 1992, as the first chapter in Henry Jenkins' *Textual Poachers: Television Fandom and Participatory Culture*, published by Routledge, pages 9–49. It has since been extracted and reprinted a few times. Our extract stresses those elements of Jenkins' exploration of fandom which come closest to 'cult viewing' instances, like 'ironic' viewing, 'nomadism', or 'textual poaching'. In addition to reading the entire chapter in Jenkins' book, we also recommend the last chapter 'In My Weekend-Only World . . . Reconsidering Fandom' as reading relevant to the study of cult cinema audiences.

[. . .]

"Fan" is an abbreviated form of the word "fanatic," which has its roots in the Latin word "fanaticus." In its most literal sense, "fanaticus" simply meant "Of or belonging to the temple, a temple servant, a devotee" but it quickly assumed more negative connotations, "Of persons inspired by orgiastic rites and enthusiastic frenzy" (*Oxford Latin Dictionary*). As it evolved, the term "fanatic" moved from a reference to certain excessive forms of religious belief and worship to any "excessive and mistaken enthusiasm," often evoked in criticism to opposing political beliefs, and then, more generally, to madness "such as might result from possession by a deity or demon" (*Oxford English Dictionary*). Its abbreviated form, "fan," first appeared in the late 19th century in journalistic accounts describing followers of professional sports teams (especially in baseball) at a time when the sport moved from a predominantly participant activity to a spectator event, but soon was expanded to incorporate any faithful "devotee" of sports or commercial entertainment. One of its earliest uses was in reference to women theater-goers, "Matinee Girls," who male critics claimed had come to admire the actors rather than the plays (Auster, 1989). If the term "fan" was originally evoked in a somewhat playful fashion and was often used sympathetically by sports writers, it never fully escaped its earlier connotations of religious and political zealotry, false beliefs, orgiastic excess, possession, and madness, connotations that seem to be at the heart of many of the representations of fans in contemporary discourse.

Robert Jewett and John Shelton Lawrence (1977), for example, come close to the original meaning of the word, "fanaticus," in their absurdly literal account of the mythic aspects of *Star Trek* and of "Trekkie Religion." Drawing on the work of Joseph Campbell, Jewett and Lawrence claim that science fiction television and its fans constitute a kind of secular faith, "a strange, electronic religion . . . in the making" (24). The hyperbolic rhetoric of fan writing is read literally as "written in the spirit of . . . religious devotion" (26); Kirk and Spock are understood as "redeemers," fans as their "disciples," and fanzines as "apocryphal literature" forming the basis for a new "theology" (27–31). Jewett and Lawrence are particularly concerned with the program's female devotees, whose erotic fantasies about the characters are likened to the "temple rites" of vestal virgins. The writers both celebrate and distrust this zealous relationship to fictional texts, seeing it as evidence supporting their own claims about the mythic possibilities of *Star Trek*, yet also comparing it to the obsessiveness of the Manson family and the suicidal Werther cult of 19th-century Germany. In the end, Jewett and Lawrence are unable to understand how a television program could produce this extreme response, a confusion they pass onto the fans who are characterized as inarticulate about the series' popularity.

Building on the word's traditional links to madness and demonic possession, news reports frequently characterize fans as psychopaths whose frustrated fantasies of intimate relationships with stars or unsatisfied desires to achieve their own stardom take violent and antisocial forms. The murderous actions of Charles Manson (a Beatles fan), John Hinkley (a Jodie Foster fan), and Dwight Chapman (a John Lennon fan), as well as less-publicized incidents like the attack on *Cagney and Lacey*'s Sharon Gless by a "lesbian loony" as one tabloid described it, are explained according to a stereotypical conception of the fan as emotionally unstable, socially maladjusted, and dangerously out of sync with reality. Julie Burchill (1986) evokes this same myth of the "unbalanced" fan in her account of the destructive quality of celebrity culture:

A harmless crush can become a clinical obsession when held a beat too long. The fan has no power over the performer but to destroy. . . . The thin line between love and hate, between free will and fate, gradually disappears for the fan in the attic, lumping around his unacknowledged, unwanted love like an embarrassing erection all stressed up with nowhere to go; and the love turns into a weapon as he realizes he can never touch the one he wants, except with a bullet.

(143)

What Burchill describes as "the fan in the attic" is a stock figure in suspense films, detective novels, and television cop shows, one of the "usual suspects" for the commission of crimes and a source of almost instantaneous threat.

[. . .]

The myth of the "orgiastic" fan, the groupie, survives as a staple fantasy of rock music reporting and criticism, exemplified perhaps most vividly by the lurid promotion of Fred and Judy Vermorel's *Starlust* (1985). That book promises its readers "the secret fantasies of fans," fantasies largely erotic in nature (such as the confessions of a woman who thinks about Barry Manilow while making love to her husband). The book's editors claim their project was initiated by a desire to offer a sympathetic treatment of fans "not [as] passive victims of showbiz exploitation, but real and socially functioning people working through and acting out the consequences of fandom for all of us" (247). However, their presentation of this material, from the image of a screaming woman on the cover to chapters with titles like "Possession," "Obsession," "Ecstasy," and "Delirium," confirms traditional stereotypes. The Vermorels' fans speak endlessly of their desire to possess and be possessed by their favorite celebrities.

Significantly, if the comic fan and the psychotic fan are usually portrayed as masculine, although frequently as de-gendered, asexual, or impotent, the eroticized fan is almost always female (the shrieking woman on the cover of the Vermorels' book); the feminine side of fandom is manifested in the images of screaming teenage girls who try to tear the clothes off the Beatles or who faint at the touch of one of Elvis's sweat-drenched scarfs, or the groupie servicing the stars backstage after the concert in rockamentaries and porn videos. Not only are these women unable to maintain critical distance from the image, they want to take it inside themselves, to obtain "total intimacy" with it. Yet, these representations push this process one step further: the female spectator herself becomes an erotic spectacle for mundane male spectators while her abandonment of any distance from the image becomes an invitation for the viewer's own erotic fantasies.

[. . .]

To understand the logic behind these particular discursive constructions of fans, we must reconsider what we mean by taste. Concepts of "good taste," appropriate conduct, or aesthetic merit are not natural or universal; rather, they are rooted in social experience and reflect particular class interests. As Pierre Bourdieu (1979) notes, these tastes often seem "natural" to those who share them precisely because they are shaped by our earliest experiences as members of a particular cultural group, reinforced by social exchanges, and rationalized through encounters with higher education and other basic institutions that reward appropriate conduct and proper tastes. Taste becomes one of the important means by which social distinctions are maintained and class identities are forged. Those who "naturally" possess appropriate tastes "deserve" a privileged position within the institutional hierarchy and reap the greatest benefits from the educational system, while the tastes of others are seen as "uncouth" and underdeveloped.

[. . .]

Though the enculturation of particular tastes is so powerful that we are often inclined to describe our cultural preferences not simply as natural but as universal and eternal, taste is always in crisis; taste can never remain stable, because it is challenged by the existence of other tastes that often seem just as "natural" to their proponents. The boundaries of "good taste," then, must constantly be policed; proper tastes must be separated from improper tastes; those who possess the wrong tastes must be distinguished from those whose tastes conform more closely to our own expectations. Because one's taste is so interwoven with all other aspects of social and cultural experience, aesthetic distaste brings with it the full force of moral excommunication and social rejection. "Bad taste" is not simply undesirable; it is unacceptable. Debates about aesthetic choices or interpretive practices, then, necessarily have an important social dimension and often draw upon social or psychological categories as a source of justification. Materials viewed as undesirable within a particular aesthetic are often accused of harmful social effects or negative influences upon their consumers. Aesthetic preferences are imposed through legislation and public pressure; for example, in the cause of protecting children from the "corrupting" influence of undesired cultural materials. Those who enjoy such texts are seen as intellectually debased, psychologically suspect, or emotionally immature.

The stereotypical conception of the fan, while not without a limited factual basis, amounts to a projection of anxieties about the violation of dominant cultural hierarchies. The fans' transgression of bourgeois taste and disruption of dominant cultural hierarchies insures that their preferences are seen as abnormal and threatening by those who have a vested interest in the maintenance of these standards (even by those who may share similar tastes but express them in fundamentally different ways). As Bourdieu (1980) suggests, "The most intolerable thing for those who regard themselves as the possessors of legitimate culture is the sacrilegious reuniting of tastes which taste dictates shall be separated" (253). Fan culture muddies those boundaries, treating popular texts as if they merited the same degree of attention and appreciation as canonical texts. Reading practices (close scrutiny, elaborate exegesis, repeated and prolonged rereading, etc.) acceptable in confronting a work of "serious merit" seem perversely misapplied to the more "disposable" texts of mass culture. Fans speak of "artists" where others can see only commercial hacks, of transcendent meanings where others find only banalities, of "quality and innovation" where others see only formula and convention.

[. . .]

Yet the fans' resistance to the cultural hierarchy goes beyond simply the inappropriateness of their textual selections and often cuts to the very logic by which fans make sense of cultural experiences. Fan interpretive practice differs from that fostered by the educational system and preferred by bourgeois culture not simply in its object choices or in the degree of its intensity, but often in the types of reading skills it employs, in the ways that fans approach texts. From the perspective of dominant taste, fans appear to be frighteningly out of control, undisciplined and unrepentant, rogue readers. Rejecting the aesthetic distance Bourdieu suggests is a cornerstone of bourgeois aesthetics, fans enthusiastically embrace favored texts and attempt to integrate media representations into their own social experience. Unimpressed by institutional authority and expertise, the fans assert their own right to form interpretations, to offer evaluations, and to construct cultural canons. Undaunted by traditional conceptions of literary and intellectual property, fans raid mass culture, claiming its materials for their own use, reworking them as the basis for their own cultural creations and social interactions. Fans seemingly blur the boundaries between fact and fiction, speaking of characters as if they had an existence apart from their textual manifestations, entering into the realm of the fiction as if it were a tangible place they can inhabit and explore. Fan culture stands as an open challenge to the "naturalness" and desirability of dominant cultural hierarchies, a refusal of authorial authority and a violation of intellectual property. What may make all of this particularly damning is that fans cannot as a group be dismissed as intellectually inferior; they often are highly educated, articulate people who come from the middle classes, people who "should know better" than to spend their time constructing elaborate interpretations of television programs. The popular embrace of television can thus be read as a conscious repudiation of high culture or at least of the traditional boundaries between high culture and popular culture. What cannot easily be dismissed as ignorance must be read as aesthetic perversion. It is telling, of course, that sports fans (who are mostly male and who attach great significance to "real" events rather than fictions) enjoy very different status than media fans (who are mostly female and who attach great interest in debased forms of fiction); the authority to sanction taste, then, does not rest exclusively on issues of class but also encompasses issues of gender, which may account for why popular publications like *Newsweek* or programs like *Saturday Night Live* find themselves aligned with the academy in their distaste for media fans as well as why stereotypes portray fans either as overweight women (see *Misery*) or nerdy, degendered men (see *Fade to Black*).

The fan, whose cultural preferences and interpretive practices seem so antithetical to dominant aesthetic logic, must be represented as "other," must be held at a distance so that fannish taste does not pollute sanctioned culture. Public attacks on media fans keep other viewers in line, making it uncomfortable for readers to adapt such "inappropriate" strategies of making sense of popular texts or to embrace so passionately materials of such dubious aesthetic merit. Such representations isolate potential fans from others who share common interests and reading practices, marginalize fan activities as beyond the mainstream. These representations make it highly uncomfortable to speak publicly as a fan or to identify yourself even privately with fan cultural practices.

[. . .]

Rejecting media-fostered stereotypes of fans as cultural dupes, social misfits, and mindless consumers, this book perceives fans as active producers and manipulators of meanings. Drawing on the work of Michel de Certeau, it proposes an alternative conception of fans as readers who appropriate popular texts and reread them in a fashion that serves different interests, as spectators who transform the experience of watching television into a rich and complex participatory culture. Viewed in this fashion, fans become a model of the type of textual "poaching" de Certeau associates with popular reading. Their activities pose important questions about the ability of media producers to constrain the creation and circulation of meanings. Fans construct their cultural and social identity through borrowing and inflecting mass culture images, articulating concerns which often go unvoiced within the dominant media.

The fans' response typically involves not simply fascination or adoration but also frustration and antagonism, and it is the combination of the two responses which motivates their active engagement with the media. Because popular narratives often fail to satisfy, fans must struggle with them, to try to articulate to themselves and others unrealized possibilities within the original works. Because the texts continue to fascinate, fans cannot dismiss them from their attention but rather must try to find ways to salvage them for their interests. Far from syncopathic, fans actively assert their mastery over the mass-produced texts which provide the raw materials for their own cultural productions and the basis for their social interactions. In the process, fans cease to be simply an audience for popular texts; instead, they become active participants in the construction and circulation of textual meanings.

Fans recognize that their relationship to the text remains a tentative one, that their pleasures often exist on the margins of the original text and in the face of the producer's own efforts to regulate its meanings. While fans display a particularly strong attachment to popular narratives, act upon them in ways which make them their own property in some senses, they are also acutely and painfully aware that those fictions do not belong to them and that someone else has the power to do things to those characters that are in direct contradiction to the fans' own cultural interests. Sometimes, fans respond to this situation with a worshipful deference to media producers, yet, often they respond with hostility and anger against those who have the power to "retool" their narratives into something radically different from that which the audience desires.

Michel de Certeau (1984) has characterized such active reading as "poaching," an impertinent raid on the literary preserve that takes away only those things that are useful or pleasurable to the reader: "Far from being writers . . . readers are travellers; they move across lands belonging to someone else, like nomads poaching their way across fields they did not write, despoiling the wealth of Egypt to enjoy it themselves" (174). De Certeau's "poaching" analogy characterizes the relationship between readers and writers as an ongoing struggle for possession of the text and for control over its meanings. De Certeau speaks of a "scriptural economy" dominated by textual producers and institutionally sanctioned interpreters and working to restrain the "multiple voices" of popular orality, to regulate the production and circulation of meanings. The "mastery of language" becomes, for de Certeau, emblematic of the cultural authority and social power exercised by the dominant classes within the social formation. School children are taught to read for authorial meaning, to consume the narrative without leaving their own marks upon it: "This fiction condemns consumers to subjection because they are always going to be guilty of infidelity or ignorance. . . . The text becomes a cultural weapon, a private hunting reserve" (171).

Under this familiar model, the reader is supposed to serve as the more-or-less passive recipient of authorial meaning while any deviation from meanings clearly marked forth within the text is viewed negatively, as a failure to successfully understand what the author was trying to say. The teacher's red pen rewards those who "correctly" decipher the text and penalizes those who "get it wrong," while the student's personal feelings and associations are rated "irrelevant" to the task of literary analysis (according to the "affective fallacy").

[. . .]

All too often, teachers promote their own authority at the expense of their students' ability to form alternative interpretations. De Certeau invites us to reconsider the place of popular response, of personal speculations and nonauthorized meanings in the reception of artworks and to overcome professional training that prepares us to reject meanings falling outside our frame of reference and interpretive practice.

De Certeau (1984) acknowledges the economic and social barriers that block popular access to the means of cultural production, speaking of a culture in which "marginality is becoming universal" and most segments of the population remain "unsigned, unreadable and unsymbolized" within dominant forms of representation (xvii). Yet de Certeau seeks to document not the strategies employed by this hegemonic power to restrict the circulation of popular meaning or to marginalize oppositional voices but rather to theorize the various tactics of popular resistance. De Certeau gives us terms for discussing ways that the subordinate classes elude or escape institutional control, for analyzing locations where popular meanings are produced outside of official interpretive practice. De Certeau perceives popular reading as a series of "advances and retreats, tactics and games played with the text," as a type of cultural bricolage through which readers fragment texts and reassemble the broken shards according to their own blueprints, salvaging bits and pieces of the found material in making sense of their own social experience (175).

Like the poachers of old, fans operate from a position of cultural marginality and social weakness. Like other popular readers, fans lack direct access to the means of commercial cultural production and have only the most limited resources with which to influence entertainment industry's decisions. Fans must beg with the networks to keep their favorite shows on the air, must lobby producers to provide desired plot developments or to protect the integrity of favorite characters. Within the cultural economy, fans are peasants, not proprietors, a recognition which must contextualize our celebration of strategies of popular resistance. As Michael Budd, Robert Entman, and Clay Steinman (1990) note, nomadic readers "may actually be powerless and dependent" rather than "uncontainable, restless and free." They continue, "People who are nomads cannot settle down; they are at the mercy of natural forces they cannot control" (176). As these writers are quick to note, controlling the means of cultural reception, while an important step, does not provide an adequate substitute for access to the means of cultural production and distribution. In one sense, then, that of economic control over the means of production, these nomadic viewers truly are "powerless and dependent" in their relationship to the culture industries. Yet, on another level, that of symbolic interpretation and appropriation, de Certeau would suggest they still retain a degree of autonomy. Their economic dependence may not be linked directly to notions of passive acceptance of ideological messages, as these critical writers might suggest; consumers are not governed by "a subjectivity that must, perforce, wander here, then wander there, as the media spotlight beckons," as these writers characterize them (Budd, Entman, Steinman 1990, 176). Rather, consumers are selective users of a vast media culture whose treasures, though corrupt, hold wealth that can be minded and refined for alternative uses. Some of the strategies fans adopt in response to this situation are open to all popular readers, others are specific to fandom as a particular subcultural community. What is significant about fans in relation to de Certeau's model is that they constitute a particularly active and vocal community of consumers whose activities direct attention onto this process of cultural appropriation. As such, they enjoy a contemporary status not unlike the members of the "pit" in 19th-century theatre who asserted their authority over the performance, not unlike the readers of Dickens and other serial writers who wrote their own suggestions for possible plot developments, not unlike the fans of Sherlock Holmes who demanded the character's return even when the author sought to retire him. Fans are not unique in their status as textual poachers, yet, they have developed poaching to an art form.

The history of media fandom is at least in part the history of a series of organized efforts to influence programing decisions—some successful, most ending in failure. Many have traced the emergence of an organized media fan culture to late 1960s efforts to pressure NBC into returning *Star Trek* to the air, a movement which has provided a model for more recent attempts to reverse network decisions, such as the highly publicized efforts to save *Beauty and the Beast* or *Cagney and Lacey* (D'acci, 1988). Local *Blake's 7* clubs emerged in many American cities throughout the 1980s, with their early focus on convincing local PBS stations to buy the rights to this British science fiction program. American *Doctor Who* supporters volunteer their time at PBS stations across the country, trying to translate their passion for the program into pledge drive contributions that will ensure its continued airing. *War of the Worlds* devotees directed pressure against its producers trying to convince the studio not to kill some of their favorite characters, playfully suggesting that the only rationale for such a decision could be that "aliens have infiltrated Paramount studios!!!!!" (flier distributed at Media West, 1989). COOP, a national *Twin Peaks* fan organization, employed local rallies and computer networking to try to keep that doomed series on the air ("All we are saying is give *Peaks* a chance!")

[. . .]

Many program producers are sympathetic to such campaigns and have shrewdly employed them as a base of support in their own power struggles with the network executives. Others, however, have responded to such fan initiatives with contempt, suggesting that fan efforts to protect favorite aspects of fictional texts infringe upon the producer's creative freedom and restrict their ability to negotiate for a larger audience. Confronted with a letter campaign by *Batman* comic book fans angry about the casting of Michael Keaton as the Dark Knight, *Batman* director Tim Burton responded: "There might be something that's sacrilege in the movie. . . . But I can't care about it. . . . This is too big a budget movie to worry about what a fan of a comic would say" (Uricchio and Pearson 1991, 184). William Shatner adopts a similar position in his characterization of *Star Trek* fans: "People read into it [the series] things that were not intended. In *Star Trek*'s case, in many instances, things were done just for entertainment purposes" (Spelling, Lofficier, and Lofficier 1987, 40). Here, Shatner takes on himself the right to judge what meanings can be legitimately linked to the program and which are arbitrary and false.

In extreme cases, producers try to bring fan activities under their supervision. Lucasfilm initially sought to control *Star Wars* fan publications, seeing them as rivals to their officially sponsored and corporately run fan organization. Lucas later threatened to prosecute editors who published works that violated the "family values" associated with the original films. A letter circulated by Maureen Garrett (1981), director of the official *Star Wars* fan club, summarized the corporation's position:

> Lucasfilm Ltd. does own all rights to the Star Wars characters and we are going to insist upon no pornography. This may mean no fanzines if that measure is what is necessary to stop the few from darkening the reputation our company is so proud of. . . . Since all of the *Star Wars* Saga is PG rated, any story those publishers print should also be PG. Lucasfilm does not produce any X-rated *Star Wars* episodes, so why should we be placed in a light where people think we do?. . . . You don't own these characters and can't *publish* anything about them without permission.

This scheme met considerable resistance from the fan-writing community, which generally regarded Lucas's actions as unwarranted interference in their own creative activity. Several fanzine editors continued to distribute adult-oriented *Star Wars* stories through an underground network of "special friends," even though such works were no longer publicly advertised or sold. A heated editorial in *Slaysu*, a fanzine that routinely published feminist-inflected erotica set in various media universes, reflects these writers' opinions:

> Lucasfilm is saying, "you must enjoy the characters of the *Star Wars* universe for male reasons. Your sexuality must be correct and proper by my (male) definition." I am not male. I do not want to be. I refuse to be a poor imitation, or worse, of someone's idiotic ideal of femininity. Lucasfilm has said, in essence, "This is what we see in the *Star Wars* films and we are telling you that this is what you will see."
> (Siebert 1982, 44)

C.A. Siebert's editorial asserts the rights of fan writers to revise the character of the original films, to draw on elements from dominant culture in order to produce underground art that explicitly challenges patriarchal assumptions. Siebert and other editors deny the traditional property rights of producers in favor of a readers' right of free play with the program materials.

[. . .]

De Certeau's term, "poaching," forcefully reminds us of the potentially conflicting interests of producers and consumers, writers and readers. It recognizes the power differential between the "land-owners" and the "poachers"; yet it also acknowledges ways fans may resist legal constraints on their pleasure and challenge attempts to regulate the production and circulation of popular meanings. And, what is often missed, de Certeau's concept of "poaching" promises no easy victory for either party. Fans must actively struggle with and against the meanings imposed upon them by their borrowed materials; fans must confront media representations on an unequal terrain.

A few clarifications need to be introduced at this time. First, de Certeau's notion of "poaching" is a theory of appropriation, not of "misreading." The term "misreading" is necessarily evaluative and preserves the traditional hierarchy bestowing privileged status to authorial meanings over reader's meanings. A conception of "misreading" also implies that there are proper strategies of reading (i.e., those taught by the academy) which if followed produce legitimate meanings and that there are improper strategies (i.e., those of popular interpretation) which, even in the most charitable version of this formulation, produce less worthy results. Finally, a notion of "misreading" implies that the scholar, not the popular reader, is in the position to adjudicate claims about textual meanings and suggests that academic interpretation is somehow more "objective," made outside of a historical and social context that shapes our own sense of what a text means. (This problem remains, for example, in David Morley's *Nationwide* study (1980) which constructs a scholarly reading of the program against which to understand the deviations of various groups of popular readers.) De Certeau's model remains agnostic about the nature of textual meaning, allows for the validity of competing and contradictory interpretations. De Certeau's formulation does not necessarily reject the value of authorial meaning or academic interpretive strategies; such approaches offer their own pleasures and rewards which cannot easily be dismissed. A model of reading derived from de Certeau would simply include these interpretive goals and strategies within a broader range of more-or-less equally acceptable ways of making meaning and finding pleasure within popular texts; it questions the institutional power that values one type of meaning over all others.

Secondly, de Certeau's notion of "poaching" differs in important ways from Stuart Hall's more widely known "Encoding and Decoding" formulation (1980). First, as it has been applied, Hall's model of dominant, negotiated, and oppositional readings tends to imply that each reader has a stable position from which to make sense of a text rather than having access to multiple sets of discursive competencies by virtue of more complex and contradictory place within the social formation. Hall's model, at least as it has been applied, suggests that popular meanings are fixed and classifiable, while de Certeau's "poaching" model emphasizes the process of making meaning and the fluidity of popular interpretation. To say that fans promote their own meanings over those of producers is not to suggest that the meanings fans produce are always oppositional ones or that those meanings are made in isolation from other social factors. Fans have chosen these media products from the total range of available texts precisely because they seem to hold special potential as vehicles for expressing the fans' pre-existing social commitments and cultural interests; there is already some degree of compatibility between the ideological construction of the text and the ideological commitments of the fans and therefore, some degree of affinity will exist between the meanings fans produce and those which might be located through a critical analysis of the original story.

[. . .]

Such a situation should warn us against absolute statements of the type that appear all too frequently within the polemical rhetoric of cultural studies. Readers are not *always* resistant; *all* resistant readings are not necessarily progressive readings; the "people" do not *always* recognize their conditions of alienation and subordination. As Stuart Hall (1981) has noted, popular culture is "neither wholly corrupt [n]or wholly authentic" but rather "deeply contradictory," characterized by "the double movement of containment and resistance, which is always inevitably inside it" (228). Similarly, Hall suggests, popular reception is also "full of very contradictory elements—progressive elements and stone-age elements." Such claims argue against a world of dominant, negotiating, and oppositional readers in favor of one where each reader is continuously re-evaluating his or her relationship to the fiction and reconstructing its meanings according to more immediate interests.

[. . .]

De Certeau offers us another key insight into fan culture: readers are not simply poachers; they are also "nomads," always in movement, "not here or there," not constrained by permanent property ownership but rather constantly advancing upon another text, appropriating new materials, making new meanings (174). Drawing on de Certeau, Janice Radway (1988) has criticized the tendency of academies to regard audiences as constituted by a particular text or genre rather than as "free-floating" agents who "fashion narratives, stories, objects and practices from myriad bits and pieces of prior cultural productions" (363). While acknowledging the methodological advantages and institutional pressures that promote localized research, Radway wants to resist the urge to "cordon" viewers for study, to isolate one particular set of reader-text relationships from its larger cultural context. Instead, she calls for investigations of "the multitude of concrete connections which ever-changing, fluid subjects forge between ideological fragments, discourses, and practices" (365).

Both academic and popular discourse adopt labels for fans—"Trekkies," "Beastie Girls," "Deadheads"—that identify them through their association with particular programs or stars. Such identifications, while not totally inaccurate, are often highly misleading. Media fan culture, like other forms of popular reading, may be understood not in terms of an exclusive interest in any one series or genre; rather, media fans take pleasure in making intertextual connections across a broad range of media texts. The female *Star Trek* fans discussed earlier understood the show not simply within its own terms but in relationship to a variety of other texts circulated at the time (*Lost in Space*, say, or NASA footage on television) and since (the feminist science fiction novels of Ursula LeGuin, Joanna Russ, Marion Zimmer Bradley, and others). Moreover, their participation within fandom often extends beyond an interest in any single text to encompass many others within the same genre—other science fiction texts, other stories of male bonding, other narratives which explore the relationship of the outsider to the community. The *Batman* fans Spigel and I interviewed likewise found that they could not remain focused on a single television series but persistently fit it within a broader intertextual grid, linking the Catwoman across program boundaries to figures like *The Avengers*' Emma Peel or the *Girl from UNCLE*, comparing the campy pop-art look of the series to *Mad* or *Laugh In*. Fans, like other consumers of popular culture, read intertextually as well as textually and their pleasure comes through the particular juxtapositions that they create between specific program content and other cultural materials.

[. . .]

Approaching fans as cultural nomads would potentially draw scholars back toward some of the earliest work to emerge from the British cultural studies tradition. As Stuart Hall and Tony Jefferson's *Resistance through Rituals* (1976) or Dick Hebdidge's *Subculture: The Meaning of Style* (1979) document, British youth groups formed an alternative culture not simply through their relationship to specific musical texts but also through a broader range of goods appropriated from the dominant culture and assigned new meanings within this oppositional context. The essays assembled by Hall and Jefferson recorded ways symbolic objects—dress, appearance, language, ritual occasions, styles of interaction, music—formed a unified signifying system in which borrowed materials were made to reflect, express, and resonate aspects of group life. Examining the stylistic bricolage of punk culture, Hebdidge concluded that the meaning of appropriated symbols, such as the swastika or the safety pin, lay not in their inherent meanings but rather in the logic of their use, in the ways they expressed opposition to the dominant culture.

Feminist writers, such as Angela McRobbie (1980, 1976), [. . .], criticized these initial studies for their silence about the misogynistic quality of such youth cultures and their exclusive focus on the masculine public sphere rather than on the domestic sphere which was a primary locus for feminine cultural experience. Yet their own work continued to focus on subcultural appropriation and cultural use. Their research emphasized ways women define their identities through their association with a range of media texts. McRobbie's "Dance and Social Fantasy," (1984) for example, offers a far reaching analysis of the roles dance plays in the life of young women, discussing cultural materials ranging from a children's book about Anna Pavlova to films like *Fame* and *Flashdance* and fashion magazines. Like Hebdidge, McRobbie is less interested in individual texts than in the contexts in which they are inserted; McRobbie shows how those texts are fit into the total social experience of their consumers, are discussed at work or consumed in the home, and provide models for social behavior and personal identity.

These British feminist writers provide useful models for recent work by younger feminists (on both sides of the Atlantic) who are attempting to understand the place of media texts in women's cultural experiences. Drawing on McRobbie's research, Lisa Lewis (1987), for example, has explored what she describes as "consumer girl culture," a culture which converges around the shopping mall as a specifically female sphere. Lewis links the "woman-identified" music videos of Cyndi Lauper and Madonna to the concerns of this "consumer girl culture," suggesting that these pop stars provide symbolic materials expressing the pleasure female adolescents take in entering male domains of activity. The young women, in turn, adapt these symbolic materials and weave them back into their everyday lives, imitating the performers' idiosyncratic styles, and postering their walls with their images. Images appropriated from MTV are linked to images drawn from elsewhere in consumer culture and form the basis for communication among female fans about topics common to their social experience as young women.

Following in this same tradition, I want to focus on media fandom as a discursive logic that knits together interests across textual and generic boundaries. While some fans remain exclusively committed to a single show or star, many others use individual series as points of entry into a broader fan community, linking to an intertextual network composed of many programs, films, books, comics, and other popular materials.

[. . .]

Fans often form uneasy alliances with others who have related but superficially distinctive commitments, finding their overlapping interests in the media a basis for discussion and fellowship. Panels at MediaWest, an important media fan convention held each year in Lansing, Michigan, combine speakers from different fandoms to address topics of common interest, such as "series romances," "disguised romantic heroes," "heroes outside the law," or "Harrison Ford and his roles." [. . .] *Walkabout* centers around the film roles of Mel Gibson including stories based on his characters in *Lethal Weapon, Year of Living Dangerously, Tim, Tequila Sunrise*, and *The Road Warrior. Faded Roses* focuses on the unlikely combination of *Beauty and the Beast, Phantom of the Opera*, and *Amadeus*, "three of the most romantic universes of all time." *Animazine* centers on children's cartoons, *The Temporal Times* on time-travel series, *The Cannell Files* on the series of a particular producer, *Tuesday Night* on two shows (*Remington Steele* and *Riptide*) which were once part of NBC's Tuesday night line-up, and *Nightbeat* on stories in which the primary narrative action occurs at night, "anything from vampires to detectives."

[. . .]

De Certeau draws a sharp separation between writers and readers: "Writing accumulates, stocks up, resists time by the establishment of a place and multiplies its production through the expansionism of reproduction. Reading takes no measures against the erosion of time (one forgets oneself *and* also forgets), it does not keep what it acquires, or it does so poorly" (174). Writing, for de Certeau, has a materiality and permanence which the poached culture of the reader is unable to match; the reader's meaning-production remains temporary and transient, made on the run, as the reader moves nomadically from place to place; the reader's meanings originate in response to immediate concerns and are discarded when they are no longer useful. De Certeau draws a useful distinction between strategies and tactics: strategies are operations performed from a position of strength, employing the property and authority that belong exclusively to literary "landowners," while tactics belong to the mobile population of the dispossessed and the powerless, gaining in speed and mobility what they lack in stability. The tactical strength and the strategic vulnerability of reading, he contends, lies in its inability to form the basis for a stable or permanent culture; readers maintain a freedom of movement at the expense of acquiring resources which might allow them to fight from a position of power and authority. Tactics can never fully overcome strategy; yet, the strategist cannot prevent the tactician from striking again.

While this claim may be broadly applicable to the transient meaning-production which generally characterizes popular reading, it seems false to the specific phenomenon of media fandom for two reasons. First, de Certeau describes readers who are essentially isolated from each other; the meanings they "poach" from the primary text serve only their own interests and are the object of only limited intellectual investment. They are meanings made for the moment and discarded as soon as they are no longer desirable or useful. Fan reading, however, is a social process through which individual interpretations are shaped and reinforced through ongoing discussions with other readers. Such discussions expand the experience of the text beyond its initial consumption. The produced meanings are thus more fully integrated into the readers' lives and are of a fundamentally different character from meanings generated through a casual and fleeting encounter with an otherwise unremarkable (and unremarked upon) text. For the fan, these previously "poached" meanings provide a foundation for future encounters with the fiction, shaping how it will be perceived, defining how it will be used.

Second, fandom does not preserve a radical separation between readers and writers. Fans do not simply consume preproduced stories; they manufacture their own fanzine stories and novels, art prints, songs, videos, performances, etc. In fan writer Jean Lorrah's words (1984), "Trekfandom . . . . is friends and letters and crafts and fanzines and trivia and costumes and artwork and filksongs and buttons and film clips and conventions—something for everybody who has in common the inspiration of a television show which grew far beyond its TV and film incarnations to become a living part of world culture." (N.P.) Lorrah's description blurs the boundaries between producers and consumers, spectators and participants, the commercial and the homecrafted, to construct an image of fandom as a cultural and social network that spans the globe. Fandom here becomes a participatory culture which transforms the experience of media consumption into the production of new texts, indeed of a new culture and a new community.

Howard Becker (1982) has adopted the term "Art World" to describe "an established network of cooperative links" (34) between institutions of artistic production, distribution, consumption, interpretation, and evaluation: "Art Worlds produce works and also give them aesthetic values" (39). An expansive term, "Art World" refers to systems of aesthetic norms and generic conventions, systems of professional training and reputation building, systems for the circulation, exhibition, sale, and critical evaluation of artworks. In one sense, fandom constitutes one component of the mass media Art World, something like the "serious audience" which Becker locates around the symphony, the ballet, or the art gallery. Not only do "serious audience members" provide a stable base of support for artistic creation, Becker suggests, they also function as arbiters of potential change and development. Their knowledge of and commitment to the art insures that they "can collaborate more fully with artists in the joint effort which produces the work" (48). Historically, science fiction fandom may be traced back to the letter columns of Hugo Gernsbeck's *Amazing Stories*, which provided a public forum by which fans could communicate with each other and with the writers their reactions to published stories. [. . .] Fans, under the approving eye of Gernsbeck and the other pulp editors, organized local clubs and later, regional science fiction conventions to provide an arena where they could exchange their ideas about their favorite genre. By 1939, fandom had grown to such a scale that it could ambitiously host a world science fiction convention, a tradition which has continued to the present day.

So, from its initiation, science fiction fandom has maintained close ties to the professional science fiction writing community and has provided intelligent user criticism of published narratives. Fan conventions play a central role in the distribution of knowledge about new releases and in the promotion of comic books, science fiction novels, and new media productions. They offer a space where writers and producers may speak directly with readers and develop a firmer sense of audience expectations. Fan awards, such as the Hugo, presented each year at the World Science Fiction Convention, play a key role in building the reputations of emerging writers and in recognizing outstanding accomplishment by established figures. Fan publishing has represented an important training ground for professional writers and editors, a nurturing space in which to develop skills, styles, themes, and perhaps most importantly, self confidence before entering the commercial marketplace. Marion Zimmer Bradley (1985) has noted especially the importance of fandom in the development of female science fiction writers at a time when professional science fiction was still male-dominated and male-oriented; fanzines, she suggests, were a supportive environment within which women writers could establish and polish their skills.

Yet media fandom constitutes as well its own distinctive Art World, operating beyond direct control by media producers, founded less upon the consumption of pre-existing texts than on the production of fan texts. Much as science fiction conventions provide a market for commercially produced goods associated with media stories and as a showcase for professional writers, illustrators, and performers, the conventions are also a marketplace for fan-produced artworks and a showcase for fan artists. Fan paintings are auctioned, zines are sold, performances staged, videos screened, and awards are given in recognition of outstanding accomplishments. Semiprofessional companies are emerging to assist in the production and distribution of fan goods—song tapes, zines, etc.—and publications are appearing whose primary function is to provide technical information and commentary on fan art (*Apa-Filk* for fan music, *Art Forum* for fan artists, *Treklink* and *On the Double* for fan writers, etc.) or to publicize and market fan writing (*Datazine*). Convention panels discuss zine publishing, art materials, or costume design, focusing entirely on information needed by fan artists rather than by fan consumers. MediaWest, in particular, has prided itself on being fan-run and fan-centered with no celebrity guests and prograraming; its activites range from fan video screenings and fanzine reading rooms to workshops with noted fan artists, focused around providing support for the emergence of fan culture. These institutions are the infrastructure for a self-sufficient fan culture.

[. . .]

Media fandom gives every sign of becoming a permanent culture, one which has survived and evolved for more than twenty-five years and has produced material artifacts of enduring interest to that community. Unlike the readers de Certeau describes, fans get to keep what they produce from the materials they "poach" from mass culture, and these materials sometimes become a limited source of economic profit for them as well. Few fans earn enough through the sale of their artworks to see fandom as a primary source of personal income, yet, many earn enough to pay for their expenses and to finance their fan activities. This materiality makes fan culture a fruitful site for studying the tactics of popular appropriation and textual poaching. Yet, it must be acknowledged that the material goods produced by fans are not simply the tangible traces of transient meanings produced by other reading practices. To read them in such a fashion is to offer an impoverished account of fan cultural production. Fan texts, be they fan writing, art, song, or video, are shaped through the social norms, aesthetic conventions, interpretive protocols, technological resources, and technical competence of the larger fan community. Fans possess not simply borrowed remnants snatched from mass culture, but their own culture built from the semiotic raw materials the media provides.

4.7

The cultural economy of fandom
by John Fiske

Communications and media scholar John Fiske is, with Jenkins, one of the first American academics to devote attention to fandom. Like Jenkins, Fiske departs from the observation that all fandom exists in a social context, and is para-social in nature. Whereas Jenkins treats fan communities solely on their own terms, Fiske keeps the framework of non-fandom in mind, as a point of reference or comparison. In an approach not dissimilar to that of David Horton and Richard Wohl (two researchers who discuss fandom as a pathology of psychological communication between a media text and its audiences), he sees fandom as an activity that might fill a 'cultural lack' – it does not 'replace' or 'substitute' other communicative acts, but it does compensate for a perceived shortfall of cultural capital. In this sense, Fiske's approach is very similar to Bourdieu's. But, whereas Bourdieu's arguments about the economic and social stratification of audiences of art (including audiences of popular and generic culture) are tied to a perspective that assumes 'class' to be an all-pervasive factor in the appreciation of any cultural artifacts, Fiske also sees gender, race, and age as 'axes of discrimination'. Fiske isolates three major groups of characteristics of the cultural economy of fandom. The first is distinction: fandom discriminates fiercely, Fiske argues, operating with value systems that are either the same, or at least very similar to, the ones operating in official culture (with similar degrees of complexity and sophistication). The second characteristic involves productivity and participation: fans produce cultural discourse, contribute to, and create, popular culture through 'carnivals of fan participation', gatherings and festivals at weekends or midnights (Fiske specifically mentions cult films such as *The Blues Brothers* and *The Rocky Horror Picture Show* as examples here). The third characteristic is accumulation: through their acts of collecting signatures, first editions, scarce fan art, and objects of visible fandom, fans participate in, and help sustain, a cultural economy in which the 'role of the insurance assessor becomes indistinguishable from that of the critic'. Together, the three characteristics make fans among the most visible and complex cultural formations in the economy of popular culture.

A note on extracting: 'The Cultural economy of Fandom' was written for *Adoring Audiences: Fan Culture and Popular Media*, an edited collection of Lisa A. Lewis, published by Routledge, pages 30–49. Our extract concentrates on the more theoretical considerations on fan audiences as 'cultish', and on the examples of film, and, to some extent, television Fiske refers to in his essay.

Fandom is a common feature of popular culture in industrial societies. It selects from the repertoire of mass-produced and mass-distributed entertainment certain performers, narratives or genres and takes them into the culture of a self-selected fraction of the people. They are then reworked into an intensely pleasurable, intensely signifying popular culture that is both similar to, yet significantly different from, the culture of more 'normal' popular audiences. Fandom is typically associated with cultural forms that the dominant value system denigrates – pop music, romance novels, comics, Hollywood mass-appeal stars (sport, probably because of its appeal to masculinity, is an exception). It is thus associated with the cultural tastes of subordinated formations of the people, particularly with those disempowered by any combination of gender, age, class and race.

All popular audiences engage in varying degrees of semiotic productivity, producing meanings and pleasures that pertain to their social situation out of the products of the culture industries. But fans often turn this semiotic productivity into some form of textual production that can circulate among – and thus help to define – the fan community. Fans create a fan culture with its own systems of production and distribution that forms what I shall call a 'shadow cultural economy' that lies outside that of the cultural industries yet shares features with them which more normal popular culture lacks.

In this essay I wish to use and develop Bourdieu's metaphor of describing culture as an economy in which people invest and accumulate capital. The cultural system works like the economic system to distribute its resources unequally and thus to distinguish between the privileged and the deprived. This cultural system promotes and privileges certain cultural tastes and competences, particularly through the educational system, but also through other institutions such as art galleries, concert halls, museums, and state subsidies to the arts, which taken together constitute a 'high' culture (ranging from the traditional to the avant-garde). This culture is socially and institutionally legitimated, and I shall refer to it as official culture, in distinction from popular culture which receives no social legitimation or institutional support. Official culture, like money, distinguishes between those who possess it, and those who do not. 'Investing' in education, in acquiring certain cultural tastes and competences, will produce a social 'return' in terms of better job prospects, of enhanced social prestige and thus of a higher socio-economic position. Cultural capital thus works hand in hand with economic capital to produce social privilege and distinction.

[. . .]

Both forms of capital are complicated further by whether they have been inherited or acquired. The difference between old and new money is a crucial distinction for the 'northerners' though ludicrous to the poor; similarly the distinction between acquired and inherited cultural capital becomes more important as we move northwards in the social space. Briefly, acquired cultural capital is that produced by the educational system and consists of the knowledge and critical appreciation of a particular set of texts, 'the canon,' in literature, art, music and now, increasingly, film. Inherited cultural capital is manifest in lifestyle rather than in textual preference – in fashion, furnishings, manners, in choice of restaurant or club, in sport or vacation preferences.

This is a productive model, but it has two main weaknesses. The first is its emphasis on economics and class as the major (if not the only) dimension of social discrimination. We need to add to Bourdieu's model gender, race and age as axes of discrimination, and thus to read his account of how culture works to underwrite class differences as symptomatic of its function in other axes of social difference. In this essay I wish to focus on class, gender and age as axes of subordination. I regret being unable to devote the attention to race which it deserves, but I have not found studies of non-white fandom. Most of the studies so far undertaken highlight class, gender and age as the key axes of discrimination.

Bourdieu's other weakness, for my particular purposes, is his failure to accord the culture of the subordinate the same sophisticated analysis as that of the dominant. He subdivides dominant culture into a number of competing categories, each characteristic of socially distinguished groups within the bourgeoisie. But he leaves proletarian culture and the proletariat as an undistinguished homogeneity. This leads him seriously to underestimate the creativity of popular culture and its role in distinguishing between different social formations within the subordinated. He does not allow that there are forms of popular cultural capital produced outside and often against official cultural capital.

These two weaknesses can be compensated for, and should not blind us to the value of his work. A concept of his which I find particularly useful is that of the *habitus*. The habitus includes the notion of a habitat, the habitants and the processes of inhabiting it, and the habituated ways of thinking that go with it. It encompasses our position within the social space, the ways of living that go with it and what Bourdieu calls the associated 'dispositions' of mind, cultural tastes and ways of thinking and feeling. The habitus refuses the traditional distinction between the social and the individual, and it reformulates the relationship between domination and subjectivity.

One final point to make about Bourdieu's model is that the idea of a map includes that of movement. Social space is that through which both class or social groups and individuals move through time. Acquiring or losing capital of either sort changes one's position on the map and thus one's habitus. In this essay I shall base my argument upon Bourdieu's model, modified to take account of gender and age as axes of subordination, and extended to include forms of 'popular cultural capital' produced by subordinate social formations (Fiske 1989a), which can serve, in the subordinate, similar functions to those of official cultural capital in the dominant context. Fans, in particular, are active producers and users of such cultural capital and, at the level of fan organization, begin to reproduce equivalents of the formal institutions of official culture. By the conclusion of this essay I hope to have shown that fan culture is a form of popular culture that echoes many of the institutions of official culture, although in popular form and under popular control. It may be thought of as a sort of 'moonlighting' in the cultural rather than the economic sphere, a form of cultural labor to fill the gaps left by legitimate culture. Fandom offers ways of filling cultural lack and provides the social prestige and self-esteem that go with cultural capital. As with economic capital, lack cannot be measured by objective means alone, for lack arises when the amount of capital possessed falls short of that which is desired or felt to be merited. Thus a low achiever at school will lack official cultural capital and the social, and therefore self-esteem that it brings. Some may well become fans, often of a musician or sports star, and through fan knowledge and appreciation acquire an unofficial cultural capital that is a major source of self-esteem among the peer group. While fandom may be typical of the socially and culturally deprived, it is not confined to them. Many young fans are successful at school and are steadily accumulating official cultural capital, but wish still to differentiate themselves, along the axis of age at least, from the social values and cultural tastes (or habitus) of those who currently possess the cultural and economic capital they are still working to acquire. Such social distinction, defined by age rather than class or gender, is often expressed by their fandom and by accumulation of unofficial or popular cultural capital whose politics lie in its opposition to the official, dominant one.

Such popular cultural capital, unlike official cultural capital, is not typically convertible into economic capital, though, as will be argued below, there are exceptions. Acquiring it will not enhance one's career, nor will it produce upward class mobility as its investment payoffs. Its dividends lie in the pleasures and esteem of one's peers in a community of taste rather than those of one's social betters. Fans, then, are a good example of Bourdieu's 'autodidacts' – the self-taught who often use their self-acquired knowledge and taste to compensate for the perceived gap between their actual (or official) cultural capital, as expressed in educational qualifications and the socio-economic rewards they bring, and what they feel are their true desserts.

Fandom, then, is a peculiar mix of cultural determinations. On the one hand it is an intensification of popular culture which is formed outside and often against official culture, on the other it expropriates and reworks certain values and characteristics of that official culture to which it is opposed.

I propose to discuss the main characteristics of fandom under three headings: Discrimination and Distinction, Productivity and Participation, and Capital Accumulation. These are characteristics of fandom in general rather than of any one fan or group of fans in particular. No one fan or fan community will exhibit all of them equally, but will differ considerably among themselves in emphasis.

Discrimination and distinction

Fans discriminate fiercely: the boundaries between what falls within their fandom and what does not are sharply drawn. And this discrimination in the cultural sphere is mapped into distinctions in the social – the boundaries between the community of fans and the rest of the world are just as strongly marked and patrolled. Both sides of the boundary invest in the difference; mundane viewers often wish to avoid what they see as the taint of fandom – 'I'm not really a fan, of course, but . . .' On the other side of the line, fans may argue about what characteristics allow someone to cross it and become a true fan, but they are clearly agreed on the existence of the line. Textual and social discrimination are part and parcel of the same cultural activity.

Fan discrimination has affinities to both the socially relevant discrimination of popular culture and the aesthetic discrimination of the dominant (Fiske 1989a). Bourdieu argues that one of the key differences between the culture of the subordinate and that of the dominant is that subordinate culture is functional, it must be *for* something. D'Acci's (1988) study of 'Cagney & Lacey' fans shows how they used the show and its stars to enhance their self-esteem which in turn enabled them to perform more powerfully in their social world. Fans reported that the show gave them the confidence to stand up for themselves better in a variety of social situations – a school girl said that her fandom had made her realize that she could perform as well as boys at school, and an adult woman attributed her decision to risk starting her own business directly to the self-confidence she generated from watching the show.

[. . .]

Other forms of fan discrimination approach the aesthetic discrimination of official culture. Kiste's (1989) study of comic book fans shows how acutely they can discriminate between various artists and storyliners, and how important it is to be able to rank them in a hierarchy – particularly to 'canonize' some and exclude others. Tulloch and Alvarado (1983) recount how some 'Dr Who' fans canonize the early series and specifically exclude the more widely popular later series in which Tom Baker played the lead. Their criteria were essentially ones of authenticity and as such were not dissimilar to those of the literary scholars who try to uncover what Shakespeare really wrote in preference to that which has been widely performed. Authenticity, particularly when validated as the production of an artistic individual (writer, painter, performer), is a criterion of discrimination normally used to accumulate official cultural capital but which is readily appropriated by fans in their moonlighting cultural economy.

[. . .]

In the comparatively few studies of fans available to us, it is possible to trace social factors within the modes of discrimination. They show a slight but regular tendency for the more official or aesthetic criteria to be used by older, male fans rather than by younger, female ones. If further studies reveal this tendency to be structural (as I suspect it is), the explanation may well lie in differential relationships to the structures of power. Those who are subordinated (by gender, age or class) are more likely to have developed a habitus typical of proletarian culture (that is, one without economic or cultural capital): the less a fan suffers from these structures of domination and subordination, the more likely he or she is to have developed a habitus that accords in some respects with that developed by the official culture, and which will therefore incline to use official criteria on its unofficial texts. It would not be surprising in such a case to find that older fans, male fans, and more highly educated fans tend to use official criteria, whereas younger, female and the less educated ones tend towards popular criteria. Cultural tastes and practices are produced by social rather than by individual differences, and so textual discrimination and social distinction are part of the same cultural process within and between fans just as much as between fans and other popular audiences.

Productivity and participation

Popular culture is produced by the people out of the products of the cultural industries: it must be understood, therefore, in terms of productivity, not of reception. Fans are particularly productive, and I wish to categorize their productions into three areas, while recognizing that any example of fan productivity may well span all categories and refuse any clear distinctions among them. Categories are produced by the analyst for analytical purposes and do not exist in the world being analyzed but they do have analytical value. The ones I propose to use may be called semiotic productivity, enunciative productivity, and textual productivity. All such productivity occurs at the interface between the industrially-produced cultural commodity (narrative, music, star, etc.) and the everyday life of the fan.

Semiotic productivity is characteristic of popular culture as a whole rather than of fan culture specifically. It consists of the making of meanings of social identity and of social experience from the semiotic resources of the cultural commodity. The Madonna fans who made their own meanings of their sexuality rather than patriarchal ones (Fiske 1989b) or the romance fans who legitimated their own feminine values against patriarchal ones (Radway 1984) were engaging in semiotic productivity. Recent ethnographies of audiences have produced numerous examples of this form of productivity, and we need not spend any longer on it here. (See, for example, Cho and Cho 1990, Dawson 1990, Jones 1990, Leal 1990, Lipsitz 1989.)

Semiotic productivity, then, is essentially interior; when the meanings made are spoken and are shared within a face-to-face or oral culture they take a public form that may be called *enunciative productivity*. An enunciation is the use of a semiotic system (typically, but not exclusively, verbal language) which is specific to its speaker and its social and temporal context. Fan talk is the generation and circulation of certain meanings of the object of fandom within a local community. The talk of women soap-opera fans has been widely studied (see for example, Brown 1987, Hobson 1989 and 1990, Seiter *et al.* 1989) to show how the meanings and evaluations of characters and their behavior in the soap opera are related more or less directly to the everyday lives of the fans. Indeed, much of the pleasure of fandom lies in the fan talk that it produces, and many fans report that their choice of their object of fandom was determined at least as much by the oral community they wished to join as by any of its inherent characteristics. If colleagues at work or at school are constantly talking about a particular program, band, team or performer, many people become drawn into fandom as a means of joining that particular social group. This is not to suggest that the acquired taste is in any way unauthentic, but rather to point again to the close interrelations between textual and social preferences.

[. . .]

There is, however, another category of fan productivity that approximates much more closely the artistic productions validated by the official culture, that of *textual productivity*. Fans produce and circulate among themselves texts which are often crafted with production values as high as any in the official culture. The key differences between the two are economic rather than ones of competence, for fans do not write or produce their texts for money; indeed, their productivity typically costs them money. Economics, too, limits the equipment to which fans have access for the production of their texts, which may therefore often lack the technical smoothness of professionally-produced ones. There is also a difference in circulation; because fan texts are not produced for profit, they do not need to be mass-marketed, so unlike official culture, fan culture makes no attempt to circulate its texts outside its own community. They are 'narrowcast,' not broadcast, texts.

[. . .]

More typical are the 'Star Trek' fans (Jenkins 1989, Penley 1990) who write full-length novels filling in the syntagmatic gaps in the original narrative, and circulate these novels, and other writings, among themselves through an extensive distribution network. So, too, Bacon-Smith (1988) has shown the productivity of other TV science fiction fans who produce their own music videos by editing shots from their favorite episodes onto the soundtrack of a popular song. While these fan-artists gain considerable prestige within the fan community, with few exceptions they earn no money for their labor.

[. . .]

Fan productivity is not limited to the production of new texts: it also participates in the construction of the original text and thus turns the commercial narrative or performance into popular culture. Fans are very participatory. Sports crowds wearing their teams' colors or rock audiences dressing and behaving like the bands become part of the performance.

[. . .]

Fan magazines often play up to and encourage this sense of possession, the idea that stars are constructed by their fans and owe their stardom entirely to them. Fandom typically lacks the deference to the artist and text that characterizes the bourgeois habitus: so soap opera fans often feel that they could write better storylines than the scriptwriters and know the characters better (Fiske 1987) and sports fans are frequently at odds with the owner's policies for their teams. The industry takes seriously letters from fans who try to participate in and thus influence the production of the text (Tulloch and Moran 1986) or its distribution (D'Acci 1989).

When this industrial text meets its fans, their participation reunites and reworks it, so that its moment of reception becomes the moment of production in fan culture.

[. . .]

More traditional texts, such as films, can also be participated in communally and publicly by their fans. This makes public and visible the widespread but more private involvement of, for instance, soap opera fans in 'sharing' the lives of their favorite characters by writing and rewriting their narratives in talk and imagination. Cult films such as *The Blues Brothers* or *The Rocky Horror Picture Show* have regular fan screenings (typically at midnight on weekends) that are carnivals of fan participation. Not only do fans take part in and *with* the original industrial text (by dressing like its characters, joining in favorite lines of dialogue, throwing rice during wedding scenes or shooting water pistols in thunderstorms) but they exceed and rework it by inserting fan-written lines of dialogue that change the meaning of the original. When, for instance the straight-faced narrator in *The Rocky Horror Picture Show* describes the storm clouds as 'heavy, black and pendulous,' the pause before his line is filled by the audience shouting 'describe your testicles' (Hoberman and Rosenbaum 1981). As Heffernan (1989) argues, such rewriting can, for a particular fan group, change much of the film's heterosexual cliches into more subversive homoerotic meanings.

Fan texts, then, have to be 'producerly' (Fiske 1987, 1989a), in that they have to be open, to contain gaps, irresolutions, contradictions, which both allow and invite fan productivity. They are insufficient texts that are inadequate to their cultural function of circulating meanings and pleasure until they are worked upon and activated by their fans, who by such activity produce their own popular cultural capital.

Capital accumulation

There is a complex, often contradictory relationship of similarities and differences between fan and official cultural capital: at times fans wish to distance themselves from the official culture, at other times, to align themselves with it. Fan cultural capital, like the official, lies in the appreciation and knowledge of texts, performers and events, yet the fan's objects of fandom are, by definition, excluded from official cultural capital and its convertibility, via education and career opportunity, into economic capital. In this section I wish to trace some of the more significant of these similarities and differences.

In fandom as in the official culture, the accumulation of knowledge is fundamental to the accumulation of cultural capital. The cultural industries have, of course, recognized this and produce an enormous range of material designed to give the fan access to information about the object of fandom. These vary from the statistics that fill the sports pages of our newspapers to gossipy speculations about the private lives of stars. This commercially produced and distributed information is supported, and sometimes subverted, by that produced by and circulated among the fans themselves. The gay community, for instance, circulates the knowledge of which apparently straight stars are actually gay, and thus knew, long before the general public, for instance, that Rock Hudson was gay and Marilyn Monroe was bisexual. Such fan knowledge helps to distinguish a particular fan community (those who possess it) from others (those who do not): like the official culture, its work is finally one of social distinction. It also serves to distinguish within the fan community. The experts – those who have accumulated the most knowledge – gain prestige within the group and act as opinion leaders. Knowledge, like money, is always a source of power.

But fan cultural knowledge differs from official cultural knowledge in that it is used to enhance the fan's power over, and participation in, the original, industrial text. The *Rocky Horror* fans who know every line of dialogue in the film use that knowledge to participate in and even rewrite the text in a way that is quite different from the way the Shakespeare buff, for instance, might use his or her intimate knowledge of the text. This dominant habitus would enable the buff not to participate in the performance, but to discriminate critically between it and other performances or between it and the 'ideal' performance in the buff's own mind. Textual knowledge is used for discrimination in the dominant habitus but for participation in the popular.

In the same way, the dominant habitus uses information about the artist to enhance or enrich the appreciation of the work, whereas in the popular habitus such knowledge increases the power of the fan to 'see through' to the production processes normally hidden by the text and thus inaccessible to the non-fan ('he had to be sent to South America on business because they couldn't agree on the terms to renew his contract'). This knowledge diminishes the distance between text and everyday life ('I know that she's not just "acting" here, she "really" knows what it's like to have a marriage collapse around her'), or between star and fan ('If he can come from a black depressed neighbourhood and win a gold medal and a fortune so can I'). The popular habitus makes such knowledge functional and potentially empowering in the everyday life of the fan.

The accumulation of both popular and official cultural capital is signaled materially by collections of objects – artworks, books, records, memorabilia, ephemera. Fans, like buffs, are often avid collectors, and the cultural collection is a point where cultural and economic capital come together.

The 'northerners' in Bourdieu's social space – those high in both economic and cultural capital – will often conflate the aesthetic and economic value of, for instance, a collection of paintings, of first editions or of antique furniture, so that the role of the insurance assessor becomes indistinguishable from that of the critic. The 'north-westerners,' however, who have greater cultural than economic capital are more likely to collect cheaper lithographs or prints rather than original paintings, and to have a library of 'ordinary' books rather than first editions, because such collections allow them to invest culturally rather than economically.

Collecting is also important in fan culture, but it tends to be inclusive rather than exclusive: the emphasis is not so much upon acquiring a few good (and thus expensive) objects as upon accumulating as many as possible. The individual objects are therefore often cheap, devalued by the official culture, and mass-produced. The distinctiveness lies in the extent of the collection rather than in their uniqueness or authenticity as cultural objects. There are, of course, exceptions to this: fans with high economic capital will often use it, in a non-aesthetic parallel of the official cultural capitalist, to accumulate unique and authentic objects – a guitar, an autographed piece of sporting equipment, an article of clothing 'genuinely' worn by the star, or an object once possessed by him or her.

[. . .]

Capitalist societies are built upon accumulation and investment, and this is as true of their cultural as well as financial economies. The shadow economy of fan culture in many ways parallels the workings of the official culture, but it adapts them to the habitus of the subordinate. A habitus involves not only the cultural dimension of taste, discrimination, and attitude towards the cultural objects or events, but also the social dimension of economics (and education) upon which those tastes are mapped: a habitus is thus both a mental disposition and a 'geographical' disposition in the social space. So the differences between fan collections and art collections are socio-economic. Fan collections tend to be of cheap, mass-produced objects, and stress quantity and all-inclusiveness over quality or exclusivity. Some fans, whose economic status allows them to discriminate between the authentic and the mass-produced, the original and the reproduction, approximate much more closely to the official cultural capitalist, and their collections can be more readily turned into economic capital.

While fan and official culture are similar in at least some respects in their material versions of accumulated cultural capital and its convertibility to the economic, they differ widely in the convertibility of their non-material capital. The knowledge and discrimination that comprise official cultural capital are institutionalized in the educational system, and thus can be readily converted into career opportunities and earning power. In Bourdieu's map of the social space education plays a key role, for it is related both to class on the vertical axis and to cultural and economic capital on the horizontal. It is the exclusion of popular or fan cultural capital from the educational system that excludes it from the official and disconnects it from the economic. This, of course, makes it an appropriate culture for those in subordinated formations of the people who feel themselves to be unfairly excluded from the socio-economic or status-enhancing rewards that the official culture can offer because of its direct interconnections, via the educational system, with the social order.

Fans and commercial (popular) culture

Fans make their culture out of the commercial commodities (texts, stars, perform-ances) of the cultural industries. Fandom thus has dual relationships to what is often, if wrongly, called mass culture, and by way of conclusion I would like to raise some of the central issues within them.

First there is the relationship of fandom to popular culture generally, of the fan to the more 'normal' audience member. Elsewhere (Fiske 1989a) I have argued that fandom is a heightened form of popular culture in industrial societies and that the fan is an 'excessive reader' who differs from the 'ordinary' one in degree rather than kind. The romantic and pornographic novels written by 'Star Trek' fans to fill the gaps in the original text would therefore be understood as elaborated and public versions of the interior, semiotic productions of more normal viewers, many of whom might imagine for themselves similar 'extra-textual' relationships among the crew of the *SS Enterprise*.

[. . .]

Fan culture is also related to the commercial interests of the culture industries. For the industries fans are an additional market that not only buys 'spin-off' products, often in huge quantities, but also provides valuable free feedback on market trends and preferences. There are thus contradictory functions performed by cultural com-modities which on the one hand serve the economic interests of the industry and on the other the cultural interests of the fans. There is a constant struggle between fans and the industry, in which the industry attempts to incorporate the tastes of the fans, and the fans to 'excorporate' the products of the industry.

Official culture likes to see its texts (or commodities) as the creations of special individuals or artists: such a reverence for the artist and, therefore, the text necessarily places its readers in a subordinate relationship to them. Popular culture, however, is well aware that its commodities are industrially produced and thus do not have the status of a uniquely crafted art-object. They are thus open to the productive reworking, rewriting, completing and to participation in the way that a completed art-object is not. It is not surprising then that the dominant habitus, with its taste for official culture, denigrates and misunderstands both the production and reception of popular culture. It fails to realize that many industrially-produced texts have pro-ducerly characteristics that stimulate popular productivity in a way that official art-works cannot. It fails to realize, too, that such popular productivity works better on industrial texts with their contradictions, inadequacies and superficialities, because it is these very qualities that make the text open and provocative rather than completed and satisfying. Because the industrial text is not an art-object to be preserved, its ephemerality is not an issue; indeed its disposability and constant, anxious search for that which is new, stimulating and yet acceptable to the people are among its most valuable characteristics.

It may be ironic or regrettable that the economic imperative has brought capitalist industries closer to the culture of the people than the purer motives of those within official culture. But it should not surprise us. Official cultural capital, like economic capital, is systematically denied to the people and their lack then functions to distinguish them from those that possess it. In capitalist societies popular culture is necessarily produced from the products of capitalism, for that is all the people have to work with. The relationship of popular culture to the culture industries is therefore complex and fascinating, sometimes conflictive, sometimes complicitous or co-operative, but the people are never at the mercy of the industries – they choose to make some of their commodities into popular culture, but reject many more than they adopt. Fans are among the most discriminating and selective of all formations of the people and the cultural capital they produce is the most highly developed and visible of all.

Author's note: I would like to thank Lynn Spigel and Henry Jenkins for their helpful comments on early drafts of this essay.

4.8

The *Crash* controversy: Reviewing the press

by Martin Barker, Jane Arthurs and Ramaswami Harindranath

The films of David Cronenberg have often attracted censorship, and they are among the most noted cult films of recent decades. Yet research into audiences and receptions of his films has only recently garnered momentum. Martin Barker and his colleagues used the opportunity of the long-awaited UK release of the J.G. Ballard adaptation *Crash* (1996) to investigate what audiences value in Cronenberg's films. *Crash* had been notoriously vilified by the British press as a film 'beyond the bounds of depravity' when it was shown in Cannes, and a press campaign was mounted to have it banned (in a move similar to that of the 'video nasties' scandal). Though no ban ensued, by the time UK audiences got to see the film they had been bombarded with a relentless anti-*Crash* campaign of British tabloids and conservative media, only slightly balanced by fierce defending of the film's premises and tactics in the liberal press. *Crash* was eventually released, uncut, almost a year after the original Cannes screening to lukewarm acclaim. Barker, Arthurs and Harindranath's research included a comparison between viewing tactics used by reviewers and critics, on the one hand, and 'regular' audiences on the other hand (not so much containing fans, but admirers of Cronenberg). We reprint here the part of the research that analyses the discourses used during the instigation of the controversy (the initial 'moral panic'), and the comparison of the critical reception of *Crash* in the UK to the US and France. They come to the conclusion that art-house and cult cinema pose to a serious difficulty to the act of 'homing in' a film into a cultural framework, resisting ready-made categories of moral value and aesthetic valour. Instead, Barker, Arthurs and Harindranath isolate philosophical and critical categories such as 'coldness', 'detachment', and 'alienation' in the response to the film. Not only are these categories essential to many cult films, though often ignored because of their all too theoretical connotations, they also show the 'audacity' (a made-up rubric in which *Crash* won a Cannes award) of cult cinema in relation to its zeitgeist.

A note on extracting: 'The Crash Controversy: Reviewing the Press' was first published as a chapter in the book *The Crash Controversy: Censorship Campaigns and Film Reception* (London: Wallflower Press), pages 11–25.

The *Crash* controversy featured in just about all broadcast media: newspapers, television, radio, magazines. But it was first and foremost a creature of the Press. Here, the story was told that *Crash* was coming, and was dangerous. Here, the foundations and main shapes of 'public opinion' were laid down. In this chapter we review the nature of Press responses to *Crash*.

Ordinarily, when journalists write reviews of films, they do so with two things balanced in their minds: their personal opinion on the film, and their sense of who the readers of their publication are. From our interviews with journalists, we learnt a good deal of the normal dynamics here. Readers do not want to be told too much, so a self-denying ordinance operates on 'giving away' too much of a film. But they do like, in general, to gain a sense of the reviewer's opinion. Yet that only works if they feel that the reviewer belongs broadly to the same cultural universe as they do. So journalists told us that they work with a general sense of the kinds of readers they are speaking to. Personal preferences therefore are moulded, either by not reviewing films that would be a long way out of the register of likely readers, or by writing in the guise of 'if this is the kind of thing you like . . .'.

However, *Crash* was anything but ordinary, and therefore reviewing it took on other purposes; and of course a very large proportion of the coverage was not in the form of reviews – *Crash* passed over into the sphere of 'news' (important events, controversies, public policy issues). Knowing how to write about it became a matter of more than personal opinion. For a few people writing reviews, there were editorial requirements. It is rarely the case, we sense, that journalists are expected to take a 'party-line' on a film, but with *Crash* this clearly happened in some cases. More significantly, we believe, reviewers felt the need to write about the film by reference to the controversy. Repeatedly we were told that it was difficult not to write about *Crash*, even if the film was almost certainly outside their readers' likely viewing, or even if it was not being shown in the immediate area, but also difficult to write about it without making reference to the claims and language of the *Mail*. This did not at all mean that reviewers felt that they had to *agree* with the *Mail*, but as we will see, it did in significant ways shape the way the film was dealt with.

This might seem a very obvious point to make, but in fact it has quite wide ramifications, once carefully considered. To feel constrained to write about *Crash*, and to write about it by reference to the *Mail*'s account, is to agree to a certain definition of the 'terrain of debate'. What do we intend by this idea of a 'terrain of debate'? This concept invites an examination of the relations among different responses to, for example, a film. It invites questions such as: how far are individual responses shaped by their acknowledgement of other, perhaps different ones? Is there a hierarchy of responses, such that one, perhaps, sets the terms of reference which the others, in being formulated into words, have to take account of (by agreement, qualification, circumvention, or direct disagreement, for instance)? We aim to show that the *Mail*'s account of the film became the dominant and defining account in the British debate, to the extent that those seeking to defend the film – even if they were writing for audiences who would not normally encounter, let alone agree with, the *Mail*'s version – still wrote with an eye to that account. The effect of this was that the British terrain of debate over *Crash* was markedly different from that which we found when we compared British responses with those in France and the USA. With caution because of the limits to our evidence, we suggest that there were, in effect, distinct national terrains of response – an idea we explore later.

The *Mail*'s account, first. We saw in Chapter 1 the general character of its campaign against *Crash*, but here it is necessary to go deeper: what language was used, what assumptions were made, and what broader ideological positions were being invoked?

Walker, Tookey and the *Daily Mail*

We begin with Alexander Walker's original article, as this became the touchstone for many – partly, of course, because of Walker's own status as an elder statesman of film reviewing and author of several highly regarded books on Hollywood cinema. Walker opened his long (around 1,000 word) review with a prediction that *Crash* was going to test Britain's censors, and public tolerance, to the limit. He queries how it is possible for people with the pedigree of Cronenberg, and his cast, to have become involved in such a monstrous film:

> To explain why means describing some of the most perverted acts and theories of sexual deviance I have ever seen propagated in main-line cinema. *Crash* takes place among a group of people, urban sophisticates, so morally exhausted, so remote from reality, that they need to invent a series of sexual perversions merely to keep their feelings alive. The form this takes is bizarre. It involves deliberate participation in car crashes, all engineered to top up their libido by courting injury, mutilation, sometimes death.

Walker dismisses any defence that this is a 'cautionary tale', pressing the case that even to conceive such characters and tell such a story is 'immoral by any reasonable standard'.

As already noted, Walker was not responsible for the headline with which his account became associated. The text of the original article, though, is hardly less forthright. *Crash* is described as 'in effect, if not in intention, movie pornography' which 'left many hardened film-goers at the Cannes preview feeling debased and degraded'. There had been many challenging and difficult films before, but this one was different. It crossed a line, for Walker, because the characters in the film 'push the envelope of sexual encounter farther than I can remember seeing or hearing in a film intended for public screening'. Walker seems to have been particularly disturbed by the rear-entry sex.

Yet all this, although important, does not quite explain his vehemence, sufficient for him to name *Crash* as possibly the most corrupt movie ever made. Something in the nature of the film hit Walker, a filmically highly experienced person, very hard. It is only possible to guess in part what this was, but there are two clues, one of which is important in light of the subsequent career of his claims. Walker hints at a parallel between the characters and the likely viewers: 'The characters are defined solely in terms of their sexual obsessions. The normal world outside is simply used for the fetishistic opportunities it offers.' As the characters, perhaps so the audience. He talks of the film delivering a 'sensory overload'. Walker is claiming, in effect, that the film had moved out of the realm of the representational. It – and its potential audience – were positively drowning in excess. He shows no interest in the usual claims of possible copycatting which would feature in the articles by Christopher Tookey in the *Mail*. For Walker, the problem of *Crash* is its proximity to an amoral intelligentsia.

How any of this might be true is unexplained, but we get a tiny indication in something he says, which in subsequent repeats gets slightly edited. Aside from the headline, the most quoted sentence from his article was the claim that '*Crash* contains some of the most perverted acts and theories of sexual deviance I have ever seen propagated in mainline cinema'. From almost all subsequent uses of this, two words disappear: ' . . . and theories'. What might those two words mean, given the context of the rest of his argument? A number of possibilities suggest themselves. He might most obviously be referring to the moments in the film where particular characters talk about the potency of sex – Vaughan's assertion, for instance, that car crashes should be thought of as 'fertilising' rather than destructive; or perhaps the talk-dirty scene, in which Catherine, being made love to by her husband James, arouses herself by fantasising out loud about what sex with Vaughan would be like. He might, at a next level of generalisation, be drawing from *Crash* a proposition that the central characters are just driven by desire, but see the pursuit of sexual pleasure as the *point* of their lives. In either case, in those two small words is an admission that *Crash* is a film, and that is not a trivial statement. Walker understands that narrative film works in particular ways. To be the vehicle for a theory of sexual deviation, a film must either place it in the hands of one or more of its favoured characters, or else embody such an idea through an act of filmic enunciation (through practices of camerawork, editing, point of view, *et cetera*). Yet this suggests a primarily *cognitive* evaluation of the film, which is flatly contradicted by the unavoidable sense that Walker was *deeply disturbed* by *Crash*. He does not just disagree with a message he sees the film as promulgating; he hates what he feels it does to him, personally. This is an unresolved mix of disagreement and dislike. Whether because a review does not have the length to allow its full expression, or because Walker could not have done so (his subsequent contributions add nothing to this), we cannot say.

In the hands of Christopher Tookey and the *Daily Mail*, this relative complexity, along with those two words, all but vanishes. The series of lead articles by Tookey and others descend to adjectival disgust. *Crash* is now simply 'offensive', 'sick', 'perverted', 'filth'. Using the full might of the random hypothetical, Tookey stormed at *The Telegraph*'s Barbara Amiel, who had advised Virginia Bottomley not to get so heated over *Crash*. Tookey listed a series of (supposed) copycat crimes of various natures and then added: 'joy-riding, ram-raiding and reckless driving by the young are already social problems. Cronenberg's reputation as a cult horror director might tempt many more to seek out this movie than would normally be attracted to a boring, repetitive art-house film'. The poverty of this kind of argument is astonishing. And it is worth noting the difference from Walker, for whom *Crash* was definitely not boring – it was overwhelming.

Beyond these kinds of specious claims and adjectival sermonisings, the *Mail*'s arguments are conspicuously thin. Like an exhausted general rallying troops, a great deal of its case depends on quoting yet another person saying how 'perverted', 'filthy' and 'obscene' the film is, and that now is the time to 'draw the line'. If only they shout long enough, surely our side will see the need to fight on! Two premises underpin the rallying call.

First, without one step that is as common as it is illogical, none of their claims could stand up for one instant. It is the claim that what to 'us' is bizarre, revolting, disgusting and depraved might be to 'them' a turn-on to something they would never have dreamed of on their own; and the worse it seems to 'us', the greater the danger it might get to 'them'. Indeed, the *Daily Mail* even delighted in its refusal to give any further arguments. In response to the BBFC's arguments when announcing its classification decision, an editorial declared: 'All the psycho-babble in the world cannot refute the simple fact: The film is sick. It should not be shown.'

The second step is to treat *Crash* as a symptom of a universal moral decline. One article by Bel Mooney, who wrote specially for the *Mail* on this issue, particularly illustrates this. In a full-page assault, Mooney takes as given that *Crash* is an agreed problem – her comments on the film are limited to two paragraphs out of fifty-six. Instead, she issues a challenge to 'liberals'. Once upon a time it was possible, if not necessary, to stand up for total 'freedom of expression'. But now, the world has become such an unpleasant place that it is time to make a different stand:

> In recent years I have felt myself to be increasingly at odds with many of my peers over an issue of huge importance – one of the most vital issues we have to confront today. I am talking about the limits of freedom of expression. About whether we shall allow our society to be corrupted by a handful of people who believe that there are no boundaries to what the screen should show or the writer describe. Over many a dinner table I have argued that unless people like myself take a stand against the seemingly endless downward spiral of sex and violence in books, film and on television, the world that I was born into will disappear forever, and we shall allow our children to inherit a moral vacuum, not a civilised community.

This style of argument takes the film as a symptom of something much larger. It fits the attack on *Crash* into a much wider ideological project. The enemy now is 'liberalism', an 'anything goes' society. It also points the finger – it is time for former liberals to stand up and be counted. Not to do so is to condone evil. It reads the world as a whole in one mode: the 'endless downward spiral', the 'end of civilisation as I have known it'. And most importantly, it has an enemy: the 'intellectual establishment'. The article marked a meeting point between a certain style of liberal, anti-porn feminism and the populist conservatism of the *Mail*. The result is a general charge laid against the middle-class establishment. At their door lies the blame for this general decline of standards.

The most striking thing in all the *Mail*'s articles about *Crash* is the virtual absence of argument. Repeated tirades are packed with adjectives, and warnings of doom. Given this, we must ask how the *Daily Mail* could have such an impact. This is a serious, not a rhetorical question. There is a total absence of evidence or argument in the *Mail*'s coverage, a wholesale presence of moral screaming. Why didn't others, including other journalists, just mock? In the next section we examine how other newspapers dealt with the film.

The *Crash* debate in the British press

Among the more than 400 articles about *Crash* which we examined from national and local press and magazines, there are substantial differences. Yet in one respect there is virtual unanimity: *Crash* is marked as 'controversial'. News coverage in local papers often turns on whether there might be a local authority ban the film. National news coverage spotlighted various results of the *Mail*'s campaign, such as the many assertions of its harmfulness, the challenges to the BBFC, and in particular the actions of the few local authorities who banned the film for a time. The question which underpins news coverage is: how much of a danger is *Crash*? But what kind of danger? How is the film perceived and understood?

A useful way in is to look at the criteria through which reviews were organised. Reviews are, of course, a special kind of writing. They are places within a newspaper where opinion is often allowed free run. There is less likely to be editorial pressure to express a particular view. But reviewers do more than give personal responses to a film. They also generally write with an eye to the kind of reader they are addressing. For example, how knowledgeable about films in general are they? What interests in film and cinema are they likely to have? What kinds of discussions and debates might they have been privy to? While these considerations tend to make the character of much film reviewing more 'local', there are factors which tend in other directions. Films reach localities on the back of national distribution systems, and national marketing and publicity. These intrude very directly into the routines of reviewing journalists, in the form of Press Packs and Electronic Press Kits, screenings for journalists, director and star interviews, and other means by which distributors try to drum up interest in their films. Reviews are also constrained by many other factors. Most newspapers have very limited space allowed for reviews overall, and there may be competition from other new releases. In some cases, films are absorbed within a general category of 'Leisure and Entertainment', a siting which may press reviewers to measure films against a 'popcorn' criterion – is this a good 'Friday Night Out' experience?

However, other things also become relevant on those occasions when films become the subject of debate outside the arena of films, stars and cinema. Most commonly, perhaps, this is where films are judged to offend against morality. Yet there are other possibilities. *Schindler's List* (1993), for instance, occasioned a good deal of discussion which entered the fields of historical memory, of education, of racism and anti-semitism, and so on. *U571* (2000) produced furious arguments about Hollywood's rewriting of history. At such moments, reviews are very likely to carry traces of the terms of reference of these broader debates. These are our interest here, inasmuch as they can reveal the broad character of the British debate about *Crash*.

An important clue emerges when we examine how different reviews in Britain presented the narrative of *Crash*. Take, first, Nigel Reynolds in the *Telegraph*. Reynolds disliked the film intensely, but did not want it banned – that would be to give it an undeserved importance:

> *Crash*, the movie, has no plot. It has an idea, or possibly several. Central is a group of emotionally dysfunctional adults who are so bored by normal sex that they seek

their thrills by crashing cars and watching people being maimed. After a crash, they have sex.

This is the sum total of the narrative for him. There is no need to say more:

> The film is morally vacuous, nasty, violent and little more than an excuse to string together one scene after another of sexual intercourse. I totted up 16 such scenes – on the back seat of cars, on the front seat, in wrecks of cars, in a car wash – before I stopped counting.

Crash is thereby reduced to a list of its incidents, each counted and given a mark for level of disgust. But Reynolds' denial that there is a 'plot' does not mean that events do not have a cause-effect sequence – clearly they do for him. 'Plot' has to be more than a list of linked events. A film must have a moral point. Notice the interesting elision in one sentence: 'The film has so little merit, so little reason, it adds so little to the sum of human knowledge, condition or entertainment . . .' From 'merit' to 'reason': Reynolds makes an argument that *Crash* does something worse than failing. It *pretends* to morality. Therefore the film was a test-case for Parliament:

> Time and again Parliament and Mr Ferman have made it clear that while it is difficult to stem Hollywood's daily diet of sleaze, porn and punch-ups they will not tolerate scenes promulgating the idea that violence can lead to sexual pleasure.

'A daily diet of sleaze, porn and punch-ups': this is markedly tabloid writing, and very readily connects with the *Mail*'s complaint that *Crash* is a symptom of overall moral decline. Yet Reynolds shows no sign of taking the *Mail*'s route towards demanding a ban on the film. The reason for this perhaps emerges four months later in a *Daily Telegraph* editorial. Commenting on the BBFC's eventual decision to classify *Crash*, the editorial restated Reynolds' dislike: 'The film *is* disgusting, depraved and debauched. But it has an 18 certificate and most adults . . . will decide it looks repulsive. Parents should ensure that their children do not sneak past the ushers. Those drawn to the film: sexual voyeurs, sado-masochists or people looking for the thrill of the new, will know what they are in for'. *Crash* thus dismissed, the *Telegraph* declares its real film fear: *The English Patient*. Precisely *because* it is 'cinematically wonderful', 'likely to become a classic' and makes audiences cry, 'it could therefore do more damage to the nation's moral health than *Crash*'. The list of crimes the *Telegraph* attributes to *The English Patient* is long: immoral, implicitly condoning euthanasia, treachery and adultery, setting the shallow demands of the individual above the greater good, and more. But the difference clearly is that *Crash* will be seen as perverse, according to the *Telegraph*, while *The English Patient* looks beautiful and makes people feel good. It is a difference in broader ideological frames which leads to the difference in the two papers' conclusions.

The manner in which the film's narrative is retold gives pretty immediate access to the judgements that will ensue. Take this review from a local newspaper, by Maria Croce:

James Ballard and his wife Catherine are already leading pretty unhappy lives, having affairs, chasing fulfilment. Then James crashes his car and feels drawn to the widow of the other driver who dies in the smash. They meet weirdo Vaughan who introduces them to a strange group. This obsessed bunch have waved good-bye to their no claims bonuses as they embark on a rather bizarre and dangerous quest for sexual kicks. They're either having sex in cars, watching re-enactments of famous crashes like the one that finished off James Dean or they're glued to videos of dummy test smashes.

Croce did not much like *Crash*, but equally did not like the campaign against it. Her way of riding these twin responses is to re-present the film in terms of its *outlandishness*. The characters, their motives and their actions are all too weird to be taken seriously! From this position the judgement about this film is one of *disappointment*: 'After such a battle against censorship it's a shame the film isn't a bit more interesting.' She thereby locks together her general anti-censorship feelings with a dismissal of the film.

Strongly positive reviews were few and far between in Britain. One of the strongest was Lesley Dick's in the film magazine *Sight and Sound*. Written from America, the review does nonetheless directly address the British context of reactions. Right from the outset, Dick posits a series of negative judgements, each of which is something which critics such as the *Mail* have claimed as its dangers:

> This film turns its medical gaze on an obsession, and it does not seduce us into partaking in this obsession, it does not invite us to identify with the obsessed, indeed it refuses to provide us with those narrative trappings like motivation or personality which would allow us to identify in any conventional sense. Not a pornographic text . . . *Crash* is rather a text on pornography, a cool, detached look at sexual obsession itself.

This strong use of negatives is a rebuff to already circulating claims. Dick then retells *Crash* in a way that allows it to express symbols:

> The opening of *Crash*, in a light aircraft hanger, sets the terms of the film's proposal of sexuality as an encounter of bodies and technology. Catherine, in high heels and straight skirt, presses her magnificent breast up against a plane, before being fucked from behind by some anonymous man. I was irritated by the Victoria's Secret-style satin bras that kept appearing until I got the technological parallel: the gleam on the protuberant satin like the skin on the bulging wing of a car or nose of a jet.

Crash has a 'proposal' which she had to 'get' by catching hold of its 'parallel' – her personal reaction, with all its ambiguities (unproblematic acceptance of 'anonymous fucking', aesthetic admiration of her 'magnificent breast', knowing irritation at the 'Victoria's Secret satin bras') had to be superseded once its overall import was reached. The narrative is incomplete until a viewer reaches the plane of metaphoric readings. This allows Dick to come to a very positive reading of the film which in the end integrates those many personal reactions: 'The sexual obsession in this movie is idea-driven, and while it presents an unutterably bleak and dark view, it also allows for a vein of wit that occasionally comes forward into outright comedy.' From this basis, she can conclude that the film is brilliant and 'brave', precisely *because* it allows its audience no hiding place – it confronts them with the very things that make them uncomfortable.

In these three (we believe, typical) cases we can see that narrative or 'plot' means incompatible things, and associates with very different judgements on the film. This is surely interesting in itself, but given the dispute of *Crash* we are particularly interested in the relation between the three interviews. The central connection is via something almost taken-for-granted in the *Mail*'s attacks, and which is then acknowledged in other reviews by their feeling the need to say the opposite. Again and again in reviews that distance themselves from the *Mail*'s position, we find the proposition that *Crash* was 'too cold' to be influential. Croce: 'The sex scenes are cold and the crashes are brutally realistic and not glamorised. [. . .] This is just a clinical study of sexual obsession.' These very qualities make it end up 'dull', and therefore incapable of influencing anyone. This is the position taken by the President of the BBFC, explaining the Board's judgement on the film:

> *Crash* . . . had been condemned in advance, because of excessive violence. Actually, there was little violence in the film. It was also diagnosed as glorifying depravity – a depravity where sexual excitement was linked to car crashes and the pain and injury resulting from them. In this case, the description of the depravity was accurate enough, but so far from glorifying it, the film stood back in icy astonishment at the desperation of a tiny minority who needed such stimuli to generate even a spark of human, sexual warmth.

Lesley Dick takes this one step further by *celebrating* the coldness. She variously called the film 'cool', 'detached', with a 'medical gaze':

> *Crash* is a brilliant, brave film – non-narrative, anti-realist, cool as a cucumber, it sticks to its conceptual guns, refusing to situate the audience comfortably, calmly bringing forward a celebration of sex and death, as if for our consideration. It is this very calm – the stylisation, the use of tableaux, the emptiness of the characters – that makes the film so disturbing, witty, and dispassionate, as it studies an obsession that is itself shocking and necessarily as obsession must be, a little dull.

This style of defence is to be found very widely in reviews, often in association with the slight sense of irritation which Croce evinced. As one further illustration, consider the *Scotsman*'s review, headlined: 'Crashing bore is all talk, no action.' This already suggests a sense of let-down, a disappointment verging on blame that *Crash* ought to have been more troubling, more 'action'. The first sentence confirms this: 'Without the hype, *Crash* would be a low-key art-house film that few people would recommend to their friends.' Dalton calls the film 'cold', 'emotionless', and 'stilted'. There was 'nothing attractive about the characters', and their coming together is 'bizarre and unbelievable'. He concludes with the following series of negatives:

> The film appeared to make no big statement about society's obsession with sex and car crashes. It certainly will not entice people to go out crashing cars for sexual gratification. I don't think audiences will empathise with the characters – or want to go out and emulate them.

This effectively refuses both the *Mail*'s propositions and what it conceives as the alternative: a 'message-driven' film verging on documentary.

As a rhetorical trope these kinds of response may have been fairly effective, but an important consequence needs noting. By insisting that *Crash* is 'cold, therefore safe', these retorts were implicitly allowing the counter-proposition that if the film *had* been arousing, it would have been dangerous. Much can be packed into the terms 'cold', of course. Among our audience it was sometimes used as a term of criticism, that the sex in the film lacked emotional involvement, and was therefore 'cold'. But that is to make coldness a criticism. When it functions as a *defence* of the film against the *Mail*'s claims, its opposite is an implied but never-stated 'heat' of arousal. The terrain of debate, thus, was set from elsewhere. The status of this claim is curious: it is so deeply embedded in British filmic culture that the *Mail* never needed to say it directly – it did not need saying that arousing an audience's senses and emotions is 'obviously' risky. We will see in a moment that the French reviewers, at least, will have no truck with that notion. And in Chapters 5 and 6, we will see that the notion of *Crash* as a cold, unemotional film found no favour with its greatest enthusiasts among our audience.

More than 400 articles appeared; a mix of news, reviews and editorials. In the vast majority of them, the terms of reference through which the film is debated are those proposed by the *Mail*: this film is controversial in the extreme; have film-makers gone too far this time, in proposing an association between sexual arousal and mayhem on the roads?; is 'art' just an excuse?; don't we all know that films can be particularly dangerous? Politicians from both main parties colluded in accepting this agenda, often accepting even the *Mail*'s conclusions. Film professionals and academics were astonishingly quiet in the main. A quite specific way of talking about *Crash* predominated in Britain, whose power very much lies in its ability to seem the *only* and the *obvious* way to discuss it.

The *Crash* debate in the French press

How unique to Britain was this controversy and the associated terrain of debate? Cronenberg himself often commented that he found the British hostility towards *Crash* a 'peculiar' phenomenon, not repeated elsewhere. We were unable to study the reaction right across the world, but we did compare in detail the reactions in Britain with those in France and the USA. Consider France, first. Here, too, there were positive, ambivalent and negative responses, but they were framed quite differently. For a highly positive review (and there were many more than in Britain), consider Gérard Lefort's. Here is his account of the narrative:

> Through the lens of a story of a troubled couple, the film lulls us with a moral tale: once upon a time there was desire. James Ballard and his wife Catherine are seeking an identity they can no longer find in an unbridled sex life in which the

pleasures of adultery, secretive outings for a furtive screw, nevertheless leaves them imprisoned in the sadness of the flesh. Only a massive accident can reorient their disoriented lives. On the road, this happens physically when James' car collides with another, driven by Dr Helen Remington. As Cronenberg films it, in slow motion, the time of the accident is a kind of extra time, which becomes an important event in James' life (and contaminates his loved ones) precisely because in this time, nothing moves any more, as if turned to stone by the atomic explosion of the event.

From the outset this account of the narrative is permeated with philosophical language: 'desire', 'identity', the 'sadness of the flesh'. To Lefort, and to a good number of other French critics, *Crash* was exciting precisely because it combined the heights of philosophy with the 'baseness' of sexual arousal: 'You come away from this film with your head filled with mad ideas and your pants filled with extraordinary itches'. But this review goes one stage further, and articulates an idea about *films in general*. Films are not mere shadows on the screen. They are like difficult friends, who will insist on asking awkward questions of us. Lefort parallels the 'orgies in the head' with the 'genital orgies', calls *Crash* a 'magnificent inquest on our desires and the abysses they open beneath us', and ends with this remarkable panegyric:

> *Crash* looks at us as we, disturbed and excited at the same time, perceive its extraordinary images. But it also happens that, as we are watching it, we attract its attention, so that it turns its beautiful eyes towards us and considers us. *Crash* is a chat-up film that chats itself up, which is to say that you have to struggle to deserve it.

This kind of language for discussing film is almost incomprehensible in a British context. It is to treat films as live entities, capable of challenging and provoking. We owe them something, and they repay by making us look at ourselves in dark but necessary ways. They achieve this by doing exactly that which British film culture cannot conceive: working on us simultaneously hotly and coldly, appealing both to mind and body, to erotic, emotional and imaginative impulses. For French enthusiasts, *Crash* was one hot movie.

Revealingly, hostile French critics accept large parts of this philosophy of film, but just see *Crash* as not meeting these criteria adequately. Here is the narrative account of one of the strongest critics, Marie Queva:

> In *Crash*, then, everything begins with an accident. A car, belonging to a producer of commercials with a pressing but exhausted sexuality, crashes headlong into a couple's car. The producer is seriously injured. The husband dies from the impact. His wife is in shock, but seeks consolation in the arms of her husband's killer. From this, the producer rekindles his love life with his own wife, who is left out of the complex and futile games in which her husband is embroiled. Henceforth, their three lives will be tuned to the frequency of automobile accidents, in a whirlwind of new sensations tied to the violence of the traumatic shocks suffered by the road's victims. The more violent the crash, the more desire is intensified;

the more conspicuous a victim's scars, the more excitement rises. Mutilated flesh becomes an object of pleasure, while the automobile chromes and leathers are promises of thrills to come. Bumper to bumper, driving at insane speeds, the protagonists flirt with death to the point of orgasm.

Unlike the hostile British critics' claims that there is 'no plot', this review recognises a powerful narrative thrust. Indeed it seems a quite positive acknowledgement. What, then, does Queva dislike or disapprove of in the film? She concludes her quite short review by damning *Crash* as 'a rather dismal little porno flick'. But this is not because of some dislike of explicit sex – it is because, in her view, *Crash* never quite lifted itself into the sphere of the metaphysical: 'The love scenes between Rosanna Arquette and James Spader cannot be taken seriously as they grow ecstatic over each others' scars. It is impossible to forget this and become involved in a metaphysical reading of the story.' It is because it is 'flat' and *not* titillating that the film fails. In a sentence that bears setting alongside British reviews, she concludes that Ballard's novel has thus become 'no more than a succession of cool and pretentious scenes'. Here 'cool' has become a term of abuse!

The majority of French reviews were enthusiastic about *Crash*; a few were condemnatory. We did find a few which neither praised nor damned *Crash*, but one notable feature of them is that, unlike the clearly positive and negative reviews, they are very short. This makes analysis a little difficult – unless brevity was simply a function of space constraints, it is as if the reviewers really see it as not worth the trouble. They are like a brief note so you can know the film is there if you like that sort of thing. Even in these, there are marks of the difference with the French. One is that, in the midst of damning, there is the faint praise for the potential of the 'auteur' film-maker. Auteurs pursue visions, even if they may be strange:

> Obsessions, phobias, metamorphoses, ambiguous parapsychological phenomena and sexual violence, identity crises, drug hallucinations, biological deformities, transformations of living beings into machines; ask Dr Cronenberg for what you have not imagined.

Cronenberg, for his French critics, has to be reclassified as the *wrong kind* of auteur, as in this one-paragraph snort of dismissal:

> The Festival finally has its controversy. David Cronenberg's *Crash*, presented to the competition on Wednesday, was profusely booed. Unjustly. *Crash* inspires more laughter than outrage. What's it about? The injured only come when they're driving and crashing into other cars; naturally, in this play of car crashes and tampons [*auto-tampons*], they are covered in pink scars and metallic prostheses. *Crash* is not a case for the vice-squad, but it is about screws. Seeing Rosanna Arquette with both legs cramped in metal frames trying to get under the steering wheel so as to be better able to make love is a perfect moment. It whines, grates and bursts with the heady vapours of *meaning*. Cronenberg, once a cult director (*The Fly, Rabid*), is now just an ass of a film-maker, and a maker of ass films.

Crash is not meaningful enough, and its effort to achieve meaning produces the 'whining' and 'grating' which marks the film for this reviewer. As a result, Cronenberg is no longer a proper auteur, he is an 'ass'. But even so, no case emerges from this that would help the moral vice-squad in Britain who pursued the film – the judgement must still be an *aesthetic* one.

The *Crash* debate in the American press

In the United States, the response to *Crash* was different again. If in Britain the hub around which reviews of all shades turned was the shared proposition that if the film aroused, it was dangerous; if in France that hub was the proposition that cinema's job is to arouse us at simultaneous sensuous and metaphysical levels; in America the shared terrain was differently defined. It appears to have turned around the category-proposition of 'art-house'. 'Art-house' designates a *kind* of film, with its own circuits of production and distribution, and its own audiences. Originating in the late 1960s to accommodate European films gaining an increasing audience, especially among students, the category combines two things in particular: an expectation of riskier (especially sexual) content; and a more philosophical approach to film-making. The third element, a feeling that there is an 'author' speaking through the film, preceded the effective growth of this market, with its origins in the film-theoretic work of Andrew Sarris, among others.

How is this tendency displayed within American reviews? The signs can be detected within this narrative summary in the *Miami Herald*:

> Based on J G Ballard's quasi-science fiction novel, it's a story about people who like to re-create famous automobile accidents and have sex in cars. They think of screeching brakes and metal tearing into metal as a 'liberation of sexual energy'. They get turned on by the idea of dying 'with a force that's unavailable in any other manner'. And they love to ogle snazzy motor vehicles: for them, a trip to a Mercedes-Benz dealership is the equivalent of Spanish Fly. OK, so on premise alone, it sounds pretty ridiculous. But the movie is something else, strange and disturbing and obscenely beautiful. It's hot, too: here, for a change, is a movie about sex that is really, truly erotic. It's just not the kind of sex you'd describe as 'normal' – which is what gives *Crash* its subversive edge.

Rene Rodriguez's review nicely acknowledges that there are two distinct ways in which *Crash* can be understood. If you are within the first mode of response, *Crash* will seem ridiculous. What makes the difference is to perceive *Crash* filmically – in which case it turns from 'cold' to 'hot' ('it radiates a cold heat') and becomes 'subversive'. And this is precisely *through* being that combination of 'strange' and 'disturbing' and 'beautiful': 'it's frightening . . . because it gets so deep under your skin'. This is a quality Rodriguez is happy to choose for himself, although he recognises that this may not be the case for others, more content with mainstream or 'traditional movies':

> *Crash* doesn't work like a traditional movie: It's practically plotless, and its characters remain as impenetrable to us as they do to each other. The film is more of a

mood piece, and what tone that mood takes depends greatly on the viewer's own sensibilities. Some will find the film repetitious and pointless; others will find it weirdly beguiling, a cerebral film about sex on wheels. Count me among the latter. [. . .] *Crash* is some kind of freaky classic. Fans of the offbeat, start your engines.

This is a particularly clear expression, it seems to us, of the characteristics that art-house films are supposed to offer, and the status that this kind of cinema has – a matter of choice and sensibility, off-beat, provocative. The absence of 'plot' is not a barrier to the film's meaningfulness, it merely requires that it be approached differently. Heat (erotic pleasure, emotional involvement) is produced by the (cold) distancing that is achieved by focusing on its filmic qualities. These allow it to interrogate us and our world, to be 'subversive'. It is against just such claims that those who disliked *Crash* in the US also measured it. For instance, here Stephen Hunter. Seen on its own, the following narrative summary might sound similar to, say, Nigel Reynolds:

Derived from a 1973 novel by British sci-fi bad boy J G Ballard, it basically watches as an upscale Toronto couple, used to life in the sexual fast lane, allows itself to be seduced by the force's darkest side. The Ballards, James and Catherine, drift into a culture that finds sexual stimulation among the smeared flesh, bent metal, shattered glass and bones and stench of octane and blood that attend an automobile catastrophe. That's it: car crash = sex. Duh.

Hunter definitely loathed *Crash*, calling it 'rancid, putrid, offensive'. His long review explores the narrative of the film in some detail, describing it as an induction into a 'wacky world of crash fetishists, a small band of mutants, most of them crash survivors, who appear to worship at the altar of crippled flesh and crumpled steel' (something he is positively unwilling to attempt, having recently survived a major crash). All this could have appeared in any hostile British review. But there is another current, one which allows (even in the middle of intense dislike) that there might be another way of watching, in which the film is a 'troubling threnody' – not the kind of language the *Mail* will be likely to allow to sully its critique of the film! To watch it this way, 'it's definitely for graduate students in this area'. And Hunter is able to deal with *Crash* in these terms. His critique of the film is not just that it is horrible, but that it is not as subversive as it seems:

Yet the secret arc under all this voluptuous carnage happens to be an arc of healing. Cronenberg isn't really as brave as he thinks, even if he never averts his gaze from suffering. Slice away the bent metal, and the movie is about a marriage repairing itself. Despite the proclamations of radical avant-gardism and sexual outréness, underneath one discovers a tepid little bourgeois feel-good drama about a Mr. and Mrs. re-inventing their sex life.

In America we find, as this example suggests, the continuous presence of a way of thinking about films which is hardly available in Britain, and here only within a self-enclosed academic world of film analysis. In small but effective ways, 'art-house' cinema has carved for itself a right to its own language and criteria, in parallel with its small but significant successes in gaining and holding on to specialist cinemas or even dedicated screens within multiplexes.

Conclusion

This suggests three quite different terrains of debate: each of the three countries whose reviews we examined appears to have had a different set of parameters within which evaluations of *Crash* were made. In all three, we found examples of positive, ambivalent and negative reviews, but *why* and *how* they are so judged significantly varies. Yet to people in each terrain these seem just the obvious way to talk about *Crash*.

This fact, in turn, suggests the possibility of a new approach to the idea of a 'national film culture'. In current literature, this has been used largely as a way of thinking about characteristic traditions of film production, and about the ways in which films in different countries provide a commentary on the nature, and even a resource for the formation, of 'national identity'. Our research suggests that a fruitful line of enquiry could take researchers in a rather different direction: to ask whether there may be characteristic ways of understanding and responding to films within different countries. Such an enquiry might ask, for example: What are films allowed to be and to do? What role are they perceived to fulfil within different national cultures? What relations are they conceived to have with other parts of people's lives, as individuals and as members of their community? How are films conceived to touch and affect people? Many of these questions will be explored in the final chapter.

We must be cautious about what this chapter can claim to have achieved. Space limits have restricted the amount of detailed analysis we could give even to the materials where we can be sure we have a large proportion: the British press coverage. In the cases of France and America, we know that we have only a selection of the press coverage, and even of published reviews. There may still be a virtue in making quite a strong claim which can then be critically examined by other people.

Our claims here further depend on the concept we have deployed, of a 'terrain of debate'. This concept owes a good deal to two sets of ideas. It grows in part from Michel Foucault's notion of a discourse as a field of knowledge and power which, in the very act of 'knowing' its object, creates the space for counter-knowledges. This important idea has been widely used in an indicative way, for example in showing how the category 'homosexual' produced by medicalising knowledge simultaneously produced a ground from which those so named could demonstrate the 'naturalness' of their state. But to our knowledge, it has not been much used as the basis for systematic study of other cultural fields. The second source is the idea of a 'discursive repertoire' developed by discourse researchers. There, it refers to the resources which speakers draw upon which they do not originate, but which provide them with the bases for making culturally valid argumentative moves. But researchers such as Michael Billig have largely used this idea as a means of investigating particular contexts of talk. They have not in the main sought to determine, within a field of talk, what are the limits, hierarchies, dependences and conflicts that speakers observe and acknowledge.

It is not difficult to see why people might shy away from this. To make this move, a number of conditions would need to be met. In the first place, it depends on having good reason to suppose that one has a sufficiently enclosed body of materials, a distinct field. Otherwise, the materials would constitute simply a collection, rather than a linked body. Then, one has to be confident that one has access to a secure sample across that field. If not, one would be trying illegitimately to draw conclusions from an unreliable range. Finally, one has to be sure that analysis reveals sufficiently strong traces of these relationships to be able to 'map' the discursive state of this field. For these traces mark the ways each piece is responding to others around it. With all the caveats that this generates, in the case of our British materials we believe that our analysis does genuinely point to some significant findings. Our French and American materials are less sure on all three grounds. Their main function, therefore, is to help by comparison to point up how very particular and peculiar the British response was to *Crash*.

In Britain, it seems, we still have the narrowest and most morally-restrictive view of films and what they may do, of many countries. This is not simply a matter of (as has often been commented on by critics) Britain having the strictest and most invasive forms of film censorship in Europe. It also has to do with the terms within which people feel able to debate films, their meanings, their pleasures and their roles in people's lives in the public domain. What is particularly perturbing is the ease with which and the extent to which, in this recent period, the numbing commonplaces of the *Mail* have been able to dominate any situation where a film became a topic of public debate.

4.9

Beaver Las Vegas! A fan-boy's defence of *Showgirls*
by I.Q. Hunter

At the end of the 1990s, after nearly a decade of fan studies, a new category of fandom was added to fans of science-fiction, violent movies, horror, and female fans, scholars like I.Q. Hunter, Matt Hills, and Mark Jancovich (work of the last two is reprinted in Section one) started devoting attention to fan-boys, fan-critics or fan-scholars, a rubric of viewers with the emotional and cultural investment typical for fans, but equipped with the analytical and critical skills that degrees, and professions, in higher education had given them. These fans distinguish themselves through their privileged positions, with high cultural and considerable economic capital, *and* their refusal to adhere to the aesthetic tastes associated with that position. Instead of adopting the 'proper' tastes their social positions dictate they display lowbrow and populist aesthetic preferences, which they provide with cultural weight through detailed, complicated appreciations – often not just in private but in public as well. In a sense, they are the unapologetic equivalent of 'guilty pleasures'. Key examples are television series like *The X-Files*, *Dr. Who*, and *Buffy the Vampire Slayer*, and films like *Mandingo*, *Repo Man*, *Bad Taste*, *Mars Attacks*, and the films of Paul Verhoeven (*Turkish Delight, Robocop, Basic Instinct, Showgirls, Starship Troopers*). I.Q. Hunter's first-person essay defending the cult-appreciation of *Showgirls* became a prime example of the fanboy/fan-scholar audience. Hunter takes the audiences of cult cinema to task: if their self-declared camp reading, ironic positioning, and re-evaluation of 'bad' movies is part of their cultist approach, if it is indeed what makes films cults, then why didn't this happen with *Showgirls*, and why isn't *Showgirls* celebrated as a film whose uses of exploitation transgress the boundaries between progressive and conservative? Hunter's essay became the subject of a controversy at the first cult cinema conference in Nottingham in 2000, where it was attacked for its perceived misogyny. For Joanne Hollows and Jacinda Read Hunter's treatment of *Showgirls* is typical of that of a laddish approach to cinema (they refer to the British 1990s phenomenon of the 'lad', the mature male adult continuing to revel in pubertal attitudes towards representations of sexuality, on which an entire industry of exploitation magazines is built), inherently connected with the 'old chaps' culture of male dominated academia. And as such it tends to favour only 'masculine' preferences: sleaze, nudity, submission, . . . Subsequent considerations of *Showgirls*, and its overall presence as a topic of cult contention, vindicated Hunter's defence (though not maybe his *means* of defence). In 2003 the American journal *Film Quarterly* devoted a roundtable discussion to the 'phenomenon' of *Showgirls*, asking Akira Mizura Lippit, Noel Burch, Chon Noriega, Ara Osterweil, Linda Williams, Eric Schaefer, and Jeffrey Sconce their views on the film. Next to that the film has attracted an avalanche of academic attention, appearing in courses around the globe, ironically fuelling its cult status.

A note on extracting: this essay first appeared as *Beaver Las Vegas! A Fan-Boy's Defence of Showgirls* as a chapter in Xavier Mendik and Graeme Harper's edited collection *Unruly Pleasures: the Cult Film and its Critics*, published by FABPress, Guilford, pages 187–201. It was accompanied by a half-page preface in which the author took a personal position towards 'cult cinema', and by nine revealing illustrations (which were an integral part of the controversy that surrounded it). We publish it here without the preface and illustrations.

"Andrew Sarris once began an interview with a sustained defence in intellectual depth of his auteur theory, and concluded by confessing that what really kept him coming to the cinema was its girls. Here is the beginning of wisdom."

Raymond Durgnat

'The worst Hollywood film ever made'

Showgirls (1995), Paul Verhoeven's lap-dance musical, is that rare object in cultural life: a film universally derided as 'bad'. *No one* seems to like it. At a time of alleged cultural relativism and collapsing standards of aesthetic judgement *Showgirls* has emerged as a welcome gold standard of poor taste and world-class incompetence.

From the start, critical reaction to the film was numbingly hostile. According to *Halliwell's Film and Video Guide*, only one of the 14 leading British critics and two out of 34 critics in Chicago, New York and Los Angeles ventured so much as a good word for it. The rest teetered on hysterical loathing. Mocking the film's brashness, over-blown dialogue and the acting deficiencies of its young star Elizabeth Berkley, critics deplored above all Verhoeven's hypocrisy in exploiting the very sleaze and voyeurism that his film purported to expose. Gina Gershon alone escaped general censure, if only because her arch performance as Cristal, an omnisexual dancer, appeared to send up everything around her. Not surprisingly, despite being the most hyped film of the year, *Showgirls* was a commercial disaster. Costing $40 million it took no more than $25 million in domestic theatres, and although video sales and overseas revenue meant that it eventually turned a profit, it was still the second most costly write-off of 1995.

Since the film was released, few, even among hardcore aficionados of trash, have bothered to come to its defence. An exception was the director Quentin Tarantino. "The thing that's great about *Showgirls*", he enthused, "and I mean great with a capital great, is that only one other time in the last 20 years has a major studio made a full-on, gigantic, big-budget exploitation movie [*Mandingo* (1975)]. *Showgirls* is the *Mandingo* of the '90s."

But even as an exploitation film *Showgirls* came dreadfully unstuck. It not only missed but also alienated its core audience of overheated heterosexual males. Seeming to address only straight men probably didn't help its chances. (That *Showgirls* is a campy musical suggests that an address to gay audiences, or at least a space for gay appropriation, was built into it as a possibility. This ambiguity wasn't stressed in the promotional material.) Other single-mindedly male-oriented films of the period such as *Striptease* (1996) and *Barb Wire* (1996), whose appeal rested on the exposure of celebrity silicone, also flopped badly in spite of aggressive publicity campaigns. Like *Showgirls* they were too tame to attract the porn trade, but neither romantic nor arty enough to break into the couples market for erotica.

Showgirls did, however, very briefly attract a cult following. In 1996 gays in New York and LA set up special *Rocky Horror Picture Show*-style screenings to celebrate it as "the camp classic of the decade". Emboldened by this 'resurrection', as Verhoeven called it, and eager to re-launch the film by any means, MGM/UA edited the video release version to emphasise what the reviewers had managed to overlook: the deliberate tone of mocking self-parody inspired by the tastelessness of its setting. As such *Showgirls* was redesignated as a pre-fabricated cult film, an exercise in heterosexual camp like *Repo Man* (1984) and *Mars Attacks!* (1996), whose in-jokes, rarefied irony and fondling delight in kitsch nourish cult viewing. What is so unsettling about *Showgirls* is that lines like "I've a problem with pussy", "It must be strange not to have people come on you" and "The show goes on" are not bracketed off as inappropriate or deliberately funny comic effects.

As with *Blue Velvet* (1986) the audience doesn't immediately know whether to laugh at or with the film. Should we, as most people ended up doing, regard its zingy clichés as evidence of naivety and bad writing or should we instead give Verhoeven the benefit of the doubt and conclude that they are integral to a meticulous spoof? Either way, the original negative critical judgement has become the definitive one, which the ironic 'so bad it's good' interpretations confirm rather than subvert. When a character in *Scream 2* (1998) is asked to name his favourite scary movie and smugly replies "*Showgirls*, definitely", he acknowledges not only industry lore but a truth universally recognised. *Showgirls* is *Plan Nine from Las Vegas*.

So why do I like the film? How could I be so wrong? Five years after it slunked off the screen, trying to defend *Showgirls* might seem either perverse or uninterestingly weird. But film criticism has always 'advanced' by the aggressive re-evaluation of 'bad' movies. What passes for a canon is little more than a quirky makeshift record of the enthusiasms of cultists, auteurist romantics and off-duty academics (categories at best blurred and overlapping). In this spirit, through an account of one fan's subjective discursive practices, I offer an interpretative defence of *Showgirls*, vaguely hoping thereby to re-appropriate a much-loved film from its camp detractors. At the very least it's a chance for scornful readers to find out what it's like passionately to admire the worst Hollywood film ever made.

A sort of interpretation

Briefly, it goes something like this: *Showgirls* is a coherent, self-reflexive and stylistically dynamic send up of consumerism, Hollywood and the mechanics of the star system. Incidentally, I don't just mean that the film is 'interestingly' symptomatic of its period, whose discourses it happens to articulate more openly than most other texts. Nor do I claim that it is politically transgressive (the standard line nowadays for revisionist appropriations). *Showgirls* strikes me as being very far from progressive. It is an anti-humanist, even dehumanising, film and like all exploitation movies entirely in love with its debased subject matter.

My interpretation is necessarily a very partial one, leaving out much that many critics would consider central to the film. I should say more about its sardonic plagiarism of other movies, such as Busby Berkeley musicals, *All About Eve* (1950), *The Lonely Lady* (1983), Verhoeven's own *Keetje Tippel* (1975) and the contribution of the screenwriter Joe Eszterhas, who seems to have taken the film more seriously than Verhoeven ever did. I'd also like to explore how *Showgirls* represents Las Vegas in comparison with the numerous other recent films set there, such as *Bugsy* (1991), *Casino* (1995), *Leaving Las Vegas* (1995) and *Mars Attacks!* (1997). Two key aspects of the film, its relation to erotic thrillers and its depiction of predatory lesbians, are covered elsewhere in an excellent discussion by Yvonne Tasker. I'll restrict myself, then, to a couple of ideas and move swiftly on to the main theme of this chapter, which is how the film works as the object of private cult fandom.

What is striking about *Showgirls* is not so much its sexual content as the possibilities for sexual display that it does *not* exploit. There are no romantic sex scenes, no soft lights, soft focus and jazz music. There are no extraneous sequences in showers, no female masturbation or lesbian scenes; in short none of the staple turn-ons of softcore porn. The film records public performances with sexual content (lap-dances, the stage show) rather than a succession of private sexual encounters. The forceful sweeping Steadicam presents sharp-edged action movie images of bodies in movement and hard at work.

Besides a rape, the only sex scene – between Nomi (Berkley) and Zack (Kyle MacLachlan), her boss – is presented as a very obviously simulated performance, with much flailing about in a swimming pool. There are no intimate close-ups of the female body like the conversation piece pussy-shot of Sharon Stone in Verhoeven's *Basic Instinct* (1992). The emphasis is strictly on breasts, augmented or otherwise. The emotional implications of sex and the subtleties of sexual pleasure are unimportant. What matters is sex as performance, sex as work, sex as commodity and commercial transaction. Instead of adventurous, intimate explorations of 'sexuality', the film distributes quantities of choreographed flesh, nude 'stuff', across the widescreen.

This matter of fact crudity of exposure (landscaping by nudity, if you like) is matched by the dialogue's hyperbolic obscenity. From mere exclamations ("Fuck! Fuck! Fuck!") to scatological jokes ("What do you call the useless piece of skin around a twat? A woman!"), the film boorishly insists on a vulgar anti-romantic 'realism' that identifies sex with the body. Yet for all its shamelessness the film frustratingly declines to offer any release into authentic inner emotions. Far from being distinctive to character, sex in the film is a means by which bodies manipulate other bodies on their way to meeting career goals. As Claire Monk remarked in her criticism of the film: "the message we gain [is that] valuing the authentic self over the commodified self and of erotic self-expression over commodified sexual display is to be despised."

Sexuality as consumption: the 'performance' of desire in *Showgirls*

Nomi, with her multiply punning name ('No me', 'No! *Me!*') highlights the film's existential ethic in her solitary and narcissistic trajectory towards gleeful self-abasement. The film suggests that under consumerism, there are no authentic identities but merely a series of performances. Throughout the film names are exchanged (at the Cheetah lap-dancing club everyone has a fantasy pseudonym). In the film's logic, bodies that are shaped to conform to standardised ideals matter more than 'real' selves. At the Stardust club the performers are interchangeable, functions of the corporate necessity to keep the show going. In this environment anyone could be the next 'Goddess'.

The film deliberately eliminates psychological depth by reliance on stereotypes and by ambiguity of motivation. Who is exploiting whom when Nomi performs sex with Zack? Who knows whether her orgasm is real or cunningly faked? The acting is so exaggerated and histrionic that we get little sense of true emotion or uncalculated response. In keeping with this functional thinness of characterisation, the film outrageously foregrounds its own glaring artificiality, from the numerous absurd coincidences (Nomi meets the same guy when she arrives in and leaves the city: she's Marilyn, he's Elvis) to the joltingly crude dialogue. Above all it revels in Las Vegas's abolition of nature, the perfect setting in which to define the self as an empty denatured signifier.

The overriding theme of the film is sex as the performance of power, sex as a route to advancement within a corporate system founded on exploitation. Buying and selling is the business of Las Vegas, and no relationship in the film is uncontaminated by commerce. Nomi moves from prostitute to lap-dancer and then to showgirl, not to exorcise personal trauma or as means to self-expression but in order more perfectly to achieve independence through self-commodification. She wants to become a complete material girl. Although she resists actual prostitution in the course of the film (in the back story she is a crack-addicted call girl in New York), it is made clear that little real difference exists between the apparently discrete 'levels' of her career.

What becomes noticeable throughout, is the relentlessness with which the film works through its metaphor of capitalism as prostitution. This motif is cinematically familiar in productions as diverse as *Vivre Sa Vie* (1963), *American Gigolo* (1980) and even *Pretty Woman* (1990), which normalised prostitution as a career move. In Verhoeven's film the theme is used systematically to emphasise that, as one character says, "Someday you're going to have to sell it". People are just exploitable flesh, whores in all but name. No less than *Casino*, in which Las Vegas symbolises America's economic history from gangsterism to Disneyfication, no less even than Pasolini's *Salò* (1975), *Showgirls* is about how a totalising system of exploitation can be made to work.

This exploitation is of course inescapably gendered, so the film tries to universalise from the specific oppression of woman. The aim is misanthropy rather than misogyny: as one critic said, "Reality, for Verhoeven, is that most people are nasty shits". The men are entirely unsympathetic, their expressions of power ranging from harassment at auditions to its logical conclusion in rape. The women, who are only marginally less vile, have power only so long as they are willing to be objects of consumption. Their complicity in exploitation is not only useful to them but also essential to their fantasies of self-creation. Specifically, complicity alone enables them to maximise consumption. The only hint of escape from *huis clos* is the friendship between Nomi and her housemate Molly. But even this transcendent interracial sisterhood is ambiguous; at best it is a way of sticking together to work the system more effectively.

The metaphor of prostitution is crude and cartoonish, as befits the reductive cynicism of an exploitation film. Far from stirring itself to denounce capitalist consumerism, the film merely lays bare how it functions in a "life-mostly-sucks, people-are-mostly-shitheads" kinds of way. That America, let alone Las Vegas, is about consumerism; that sex is power; that we are all commodified now – these gems of T-shirt philosophy do not require scandalised exposure. They are common knowledge, as obvious to us in life as they are to the showgirls (Cristal, for example, doesn't resent Nomi sabotaging her career, rather seeing it as the way of things). Hard-bitten Gumpisms of cynical postmodern reason are spat out all through the film: "Life sucks", "Shit happens". But the revelation of basic economic instincts can offer nothing new about human nature and social reality. The naked truth is on the surface: the system has nothing to hide because it is complete, perfect, and impregnable.

Nomi's experiences are therefore a fable of that most open of secrets: the dark side of the American Dream. She leaves Las Vegas at the end of the film, disgusted by the city's values and having, she says, gambled and won herself. But she is heading off for Los Angeles – in other words, for Hollywood, where the same system of exploitation is played out on a larger budget. *Showgirls* itself – and this is the film's sickest joke – only proves the point. Remorselessly exposing its actresses' bodies, it blurs the distinction between sexual performance in sleazy strip-clubs and bidding for stardom in Hollywood movies. Berkley, churning eagerly over MacLachlan's crotch, is just one more hungry wanna-be lap-dancing her way to the big time.

Showgirls mocks distinctions between good/bad, authentic/inauthentic, art/trash, those aesthetic and ethical ideas trashed by the logic of consumption. Although judgements about aesthetics and talent are made throughout the film, it is unclear how seriously we should take them. Nomi's skill as a dancer is much discussed, but she employs it in an apparently worthless context. At the sex club, James's dance routine, which is meant to be arty self-expression but looks suspiciously like pretentious nonsense, is booed off stage. Should we applaud the audience's good taste or condemn it as stifling 'genuine' artistry? Nomi is commended for her good taste when she buys a Versace dress (she pronounces it 'Ver-saze'). Yet Versace is the Verhoeven of high-fashion, an ironic *pasticheur* of trash for whom unembarrassed *bad* taste is a mark of true style. In *Showgirls* trash is indistinguishable from art; stripping from dancing; self-expression from pretentiousness; low-budget filth from expensive porn; Vegas from Hollywood; Hollywood from America. It's all grist for the mill of exploitation, the closed unbeatable system of consumer capitalism.

Memo from boysville

"The only thing I could imagine with regard to *Showgirls* is that part of the audience will go home in a state of excitement and, thinking of the film, make love or masturbate. That's not so bad." Paul Verhoeven

To me as a fan of *Showgirls*, for whom it is *the* key cult film, a legitimate, correct and persuasive interpretation of its meaning is not especially important. I can imagine that people might be cautiously intrigued by my brief interpretation of the film without caring to revise their appalled opinion of it. 'OK,' they might respond, 'the film is a satire, but it's not a very good one. You're right about its intentions – but it botched them.' Still, why I like the film has little bearing on whether I get the meaning of it right *in public*, although as an academic I am obliged (i.e. paid) to pretend that this matters very much indeed.

So what does it mean to be a fan or cultist of *Showgirls*? Being a fan of a canonical cult text like *Star Trek* seems relatively straightforward, at least if fannishness is identified with its more spectacular and productive manifestations. 'Trekkies' watch *Star Trek* 'obsessively'. Fandom is still widely perceived as 'sad' and inappropriate enthusiasm: populated by those who turn up at SF Cons with phasers and pointy ears, and identify with a supportive community of like-minded enthusiasts who also 'get' the point of *Star Trek*. Trekkies, though, are an unusually active and self-conscious species of fan. Most cult viewing is considerably less public, organised and socially useful. For many of us it is a private, even hermetic, activity enjoyed at home in front of the video recorder. As Steve Chibnall notes, "video transformed films from collective experiences to privatised commodities which may be used (like any others) in the process of individual identity formation and communication."

By Star Trek standards I'm not a proper fan at all; at any rate not an especially flamboyant, productive or sociable one. A description of what I actually do as a cult viewer would, I suspect, bore ethnographers of oddball tastes in movies. They'd be more interested in the dissident gay cultists at midnight screenings who performed along with the film, called out favourite lines ("You *are* a whore, darlin'!") and imitated the Busby Berkeley dance routines. Unfortunately, I can't claim to appropriate the film on behalf of subversive reading practices. Indeed by trying to reclaim *Showgirls* for myself, in the po-faced belief that it is really a good film, I risk seeming to want to 'straighten out' the camp interpretation and dismiss gay fans as delinquent misreaders.

Academia as fandom: the cult movie and 'rhetorical performance'

What I do as a cult-fan is this. I watch *Showgirls* on video, mostly by myself, and remind myself why I like it. Every time I see the film my interpretation is mysteriously reaffirmed. Fast-forwarding to keynote scenes: the 'Goddess' number, sex in the pool, the 'Ver-saze' dress. In such scenes I am diverted, amused and interpellated by the tone of heterosexual camp. Today as I write, the clippings file on my desk bulges inches thick with newspaper and internet reports, press packs, interviews with the cast (Berkley gauche and nervous, Gershon breezily unembarrassed), and off-prints on Verhoeven. I trawl the Net again for *Showgirls* links (the official and fan sites closed years ago; now you mostly get Las Vegas porn). Lurking in public I talk about the film, bore my friends with opinions about it, use it as a sign (or warning) of my unreliability in matters of aesthetic value. Now and then I lecture on its merits to disbelieving students (an activity which, if critical orthodoxy is any guide, uniquely couples sexual harassment with time wasting). And, of course, vacillating between fandom and academia, I turn out chapters like this.

In other words, my sedentary behaviour as a cultist isn't that much different from my usual life of academic research. I watch the film, go on about it, collect secondary material, and now and then jot down a few ideas. The only significant difference between *Showgirls* and the other films I research is that I rarely come across anyone who agrees with me about it – which only spurs on my mission to explain. In fact, the distinction between being a fan, an idiosyncratic partisan of texts and readings, and being a 'serious' academic is not always very clear. Joli Jensen has pointed out that academic research has much in common with fandom: *we* produce articles and attend conferences, *they* write slash-fiction and go to conventions, but a "system of bias . . . debases fans and elevates scholars even though they engage in virtually the same kinds of activities". That's why it's hard for me to distinguish between the cultural production of this chapter on *Showgirls* and the sort of thing I might write for a fanzine. At most, they're just two kinds of rhetorical performance, which seek access to nominally different but equally valid interpretative communities.

Since I'm interested in Verhoeven generally: ("he has his followers, alas", David Thomson remarked), liking *Showgirls* gears smoothly into an overall fondness for the director's work. What I like most about his films is that their facetious sarcasm and excess seem to speak directly to me. The elitist thrill of secretly shared irony, of exclusive access to double coding, encourages my belief that, like Sirk's admirers in the 1970s, I comprehend his films in ways unavailable to ordinary punters. This empowers me to construct around Verhoeven a personalised but sociologically explicable cult as 'my favourite director'.

For this fan, therefore, the point of identification in *Showgirls* was not with any of the characters but rather with the director himself: the unapologetic 'bad-boy' of flash-trash cinema, the intellectual Dutchman who frolics among the clichés of Hollywood blockbusters. A bewitched tourist in American excess, Verhoeven embodies an ideal of aroused, vicarious but wholly optional cultural slumming. Since I am captivated not only by Hollywood movies but also by the easy cultural capital I can make by 'seeing through' them, I recognise in Verhoeven my own (European?) ambivalence towards disreputable material which I both love and am culturally obliged to rise above.

This kind of postmodern irony can be seen as the 'habitus', the last refuge, of middle-class white male intellectuals. It helps to explain why I might invest so heavily in (and be so wrong about) a 'bad' film like *Showgirls*. For as Chibnall writes, "Paracinema ['bad' cinema] has provided opportunities for (predominantly) young straight white male academics to reclaim marginalised areas of cinema's history and to resist the dominant paradigms of film theory which have tended to problematise and pathologise male heterosexual pleasure in the text." A perverse liking for an 'obviously' bad film is a strategy for carving out some interpretative space and ensuring distanciation from an earlier generation of academics. Liking *Showgirls* is a special kind of cultural capital by which I signify both an independence of taste ('It's *my* film. No one else understands it') and my identification with the growing number of academic connoisseurs of trash cinema. Although few of them have much time for *Showgirls*, they certainly understand the sensibility that led to my over-investment in the film.

Of course, describing the socio-cultural background of my taste for *Showgirls* neither undercuts not legitimises my opinion of the film. To know *why* I read it in certain ways is not a prescription for how anyone, including myself, *should* read or judge it. Naturally, it dismays me to think that my interpretation of *Showgirls* is merely symptomatic of my position in the academic field. Rather than being an engaged, active and freethinking cultist, I am cruelly re-described as a case study in cultural negotiation. Exhibit One: the postmodern white male academic.

On the other hand if movies are really nothing else than discourses knitted together by History, and if my skills of understanding and evaluation are merely functions of my social position and store of cultural capital, then I might as well relax into being a fan-boy and a one-man cult audience. What else can I do? Society, history and habitus have rigidly shaped my tastes and sensibility, even down to my fondness for a trashy sex film. Liking *Showgirls* is the pathological response of a dubious social type.

The philosopher Richard Rorty offers an account of interpretation that might be relevant here in two ways. First, he suggests how we can get beyond the 'genetic fallacy': confusing the merits of an interpretation or value judgement with the psychological or social factors that gave rise to it. Second, his pragmatist take on interpretation enables us to resolve a few of the tensions between academic work and cult fandom, between reading as a contribution to knowledge and reading as a private act of self-creation.

Rorty invites us to give up trying to discover the right as opposed to the most useful personal framework for interpreting texts. We should forget about processing texts through the grid of theory in the belief that we will uncover their true objective meaning:

"One learns to 'deconstruct texts' in the same way in which one learns to detect sexual imagery, or bourgeois ideology, or seven types of ambiguity in texts; it is like learning how to ride a bicycle or play the flute. Some people have a knack for it, and others will always be rather clumsy at it."

Proving that a text is merely a disguised ideological formation is a trick, a nifty party-piece, simply another way of putting it to work. Rorty wants to blur the difference between interpreting a text (i.e. like an academic) and playfully using it (i.e. like a cult fan) as a resource for idiosyncratic negotiations of cultural space. We should "just distinguish between uses by different people for different purposes". He has a thoroughly laid back approach to interpretation:

"I should think that a text just has whatever coherence it happened to acquire during the last roll of the hermeneutic wheel, just as a lump of clay only has whatever coherence it happened to pick up at the last turn of the potter's wheel . . . Its coherence is no more than the fact that somebody has found something interesting to say about a group of marks or noises which relates them to some of the other things we are interested in talking about . . . As we move from relatively uncontroversial literary history and literary criticism, what we say must have some reasonably systematic inferential connections with what we or others have previously said – with previous descriptions of these same marks. But there is no point at which we can draw a line between what we are talking about and what we are saying about it, except by reference to some particular purpose, some particular intention which we happen, at the moment, to have."

What is appealing about this is the element of romantic voluntarism, the assumption that we choose to read texts in whatever ways suit our own purpose. Rorty takes the standard post-structuralist notion of the open text and pushes it to its limit, towards an irresponsible free-for-all aestheticism. Critics otherwise sympathetic to talk of open texts and active readers might still prefer to cling on to some notion of interpretative authority. Rather than privileging specific hermeneutic strategies, they may wish to invest that authority in the discourse of certain types of readers (expert and productive fans, for example, or those who speak from the experience of oppression). Rorty, however, recommends only that we strive for and value criticism that is:

"... the result of an encounter with an author, character, plot, stanza, line or archaic torso which has made a difference to the critic's conception of who she is, what she is good for, what she wants to do with herself: an encounter which has rearranged her priorities and purposes."

That critic's (or fan's) vivid description of such an encounter may in turn inspire other readers (or fans) to yet more vivid descriptions of their encounters with beloved and life-changing texts.

There are problems with Rorty's non-theory of interpretation. If you read with the narcissistic monomania he describes, then it is hard to see how any text could ever succeed in challenging you and altering your self-image. An honest encounter with texts and authors whose purposes are radically different from your own would be impossible by definition. Rather as paranoid Leftist critics manage to find traces of ideology in every text they read, so free-wheeling Rortyians find yet another excuse to ventilate their private obsessions, and the result is potentially as boring as other peoples' recounted dreams. Nevertheless, it is not hard to see in Rorty's defence of " 'unmethodical interpretation' of the sort that one occasionally wants to call 'inspired' " an aestheticist manifesto for cult reading. This type of activity discards for good the line between academic interpretation and the unruly pleasures of fan activity. Interpretation under this description is a series of quirky, unpredictable, self-pleasuring experiments in disguised autobiography. *Legitimate* interpretation is simply what you can get away with in public: the rare experiments for which other fans and critics happen to find a use.

For me, as an unmethodical (if not very inspired) fan, *Showgirls* has been an invaluable cultural resource. As I thought, talked and wrote about it I worked through whatever obsessed me at the time: the double life of the academic fan; the sexual thrills of consumer culture; the inevitable triumph of capitalism; the agreeable way that irony legitimises an addiction to trash culture; and so on. It was a means of revising what Rorty calls one's 'final vocabulary': "the words in which we tell, sometimes prospectively and sometimes retrospectively, the story of our lives". Verhoeven's bitter, sexy, uncaring, stupidly ambiguous film lent itself perfectly to my intellectual fantasies and aesthetic needs. Now that this chapter is done and *Showgirls* is finally out of my system, I hope other fans and critics will be able to salvage something useful from my strange interlude in Vegas. Above all I hope they'll be inspired to look again at *Showgirls* and then, goaded by the error of my interpretation, start beavering away on their own.

4.10

Menstrual monsters: The reception of the *Ginger Snaps* cult horror franchise
by Martin Barker, Ernest Mathijs and Xavier Mendik

Investigations of films that combine empirical analysis of the production, reception analysis (of critics and reviews), and audience research into a rounded view on how cult audiences engage with films, films' intentions, and critical frameworks are still rare, probably because they demand a combination of methods, but their numbers are increasing. Martin Barker, Ernest Mathijs and Xavier Mendik's research into the cult following of the Canadian feminist teenage werewolf film *Ginger Snaps* (and its two sequels: *Ginger Snaps Unleashed* and *Ginger Snaps Back*) bridged separate investigations of the films' auteurist intentions, the critical reception of the film, and different stages of audience research, with women-only accidental audiences, with selected mixed audiences, and at festivals around the world. While each step unveiled slightly different characteristics, two remarkable constants appeared: the film's appeal with 'smart audiences', and the consistency of interpretation of its feminist traits. It seemed the makers' nuances in script, direction and acting carried over to audiences who used it to mark the film as 'clever', and position themselves as separate from 'regular' genre fans. *Ginger Snaps*' attraction of cultish viewing modes, then, lies in its allowance of audiences to demand a film to work on several subtextual levels – not an ironic viewing strategy but one which expects films to be robust and complex if they want to qualify as cult. It puts the cult audience in the position of the 'citizen reviewer'; one which, with the omnipresence of online discussion groups, has a far reaching impact on the public presence and reputation of films as 'living up' to scrutiny.

A note on extracting: *Menstrual Monsters: the Reception of the Ginger Snaps Cult Horror Franchise* first appeared in *Film International*, issue 21, volume 4 number 3, pages 68–77. A longer version of the essay is planned for publication.

How quick can a scary movie establish a devoted fan following that turns a desired cinematic object into a contemporary cult classic? Pretty quickly, judging by the reception trajectory of *Ginger Snaps*. Less than five years after the release of the offbeat Canadian low-budget horror gem, *Ginger Snaps* (Fawcett, 2000), and hardly a year after the sequel and prequel, *Ginger Snaps: Unleashed* (Sullivan, 2004) and *Ginger Snaps Back: The Beginning* (Harvey, 2004), the series has become a B-movie buzz word for horror reviewers and fan communities alike. Critics have been quick to note the cycle's atypical traits, claiming that the film's focus on two teen sisters fighting off fur-lined infection represents a 'genre-busting sensation' (Vatnsdal 2004: 216) that extends horror mythologies to a new range of viewing groups.

It is more than just a shake of the hips that make the *Ginger Snaps* films different. It seems that the horror genre is unable to contain them. In 2004, the UK distributors Mosaic Entertainment commissioned an audience research project (originally intended for the DVD box set of the trilogy) meant to confirm the series as an extension of existing horror traditions. However, the resulting findings highlighted a range of unexpected responses that surprised even the commissioning agencies behind the study. Rather than reading the trilogy as unproblematic horror texts, audience responses revealed a markedly different set of concerns than those associated with traditional readings of the genre. Central to these fan engagements were the processes of 'gender' and 'identity', which became a constant focal point for fans of the franchise.

We would like to suggest that these tools give the answer as to why the *Ginger Snaps* franchise has become such a cult/fan phenomenon. They account for much of the 'weirdness' associated with the trilogy and its public appeal, in its content and tone. They also account for peculiarities associated with its production process, its critical reception and in the various audience reactions. This essay will address the various conflations of gender and identity in the production concerns, critical reception and actual audiences' responses of the *Ginger Snaps* trilogy to demonstrate how the complications these instigate invites a cult reputation. At the same time, we will also suggest that gender and identity become tools that both critics and audiences use to decode cultural meanings of such texts.

Menstrual monsters: issues of gender and identity

A quick look at the content of the *Ginger Snaps* films confirms the centrality of the themes of gender and identity to the series as a whole. The original film focuses on the close bond between two marginal and macabre heroines: Ginger and Brigitte Fitzgerald, played with deadly enthusiasm by Katharine Isabelle and Emily Perkins. The sisters' obsession with all things deathly not only marks them as a cause for parental concern, it also ensures their status as the untouchable geeks within the all too cool teen community of Bailey Downs. The opening of the film depicts the pair staging a variety of *verité*-style mock deaths for a high-school project on teenage life in the region. This montage of murder and mayhem not only demonstrates the duo's disgust at the banality of their suburban surroundings, it also proclaims their self-styled exclusion from the heterosexually fuelled dynamics of the teen scene.

However, when the pair are attacked by the wild wolf that has been terrorizing locals, Ginger is bitten by the beast on the eve of her first menstrual cycle. Not only does this assault construct Ginger as a source of threat to the rest of the teen prom-scene populous, it also comes to define a horrific point in the development of her sexual identity. Reviewers such as Bianca Nielsen (2004) have noted the connection between *Ginger Snaps* and previous horror classics such as *Carrie* (Brian de Palma, 1977), arguing that both use imagery of menstrual change to highlight monstrous connotations of female sexual development within the genre. However, while *Carrie* limits the 'unsettling' imagery associated with female cycles to its opening shower-room sequence, Fawcett expands such references to *Ginger Snaps* as a whole.

These representations of the female 'curse' centre on scenes of Ginger's loss of blood in locker-room retreats, as well as motivating extended discussions of menstrual change between the Fitzgerald sisters and other characters in the text. What is important about the film's treatment of sexual identity is the degree of disgust that characters associate with female physiological change. Not only does Mr Fitzgerald express 'his revulsion at overhearing a discussion to do with female reproductive processes at his dinner table' (Nielsen 2004: 59), but even the female school nurse offers a verbal exercise in body horror when questioned for an explanation of what is happening to Ginger's body. As Nielsen (2004: 62) notes: 'Where the school nurse in *Ginger Snaps* refers to a "discharge" which is "squeezed out like a pump", she likens the blood to a kind of "garbage". She further accentuates this by calling the "discharge" a "brownish blackish sludge".'

It is the emergence of this 'monstrous' sexual identity that brings Ginger to the attention of high-school jocks such as Jason McCarty (whom the heroine infects in a violent erotic encounter after the character unwisely questions 'Who is the guy here?') For Nielsen, 'The interest that Ginger arouses in her male classmates disgusts her younger sister Brigitte because it represents her entry into a sexualized world that they had vowed to avoid in a pact to never be "average"' (Nielsen 2004: 56). The resulting transformation in Ginger's behaviour tests the endurance and loyalty of the two sisters. This is confirmed in the film's finale, when the younger and more passive Brigitte is forced to destroy her older, more dominant sister in order to quell the infection that is spreading through the Canadian suburbs.

With its emphasis on the close bonds between females undergoing 'monstrous' transformations in sexuality, it seems unsurprising that the theme of gender was so pronounced in Fawcett's original film. While acknowledging that *Ginger Snaps* resides within the existing generic template of 'hormonal teen-horrors', Bianca Nielsen has recognized the film's atypical qualities, concluding that the film even demonstrates 'a kind of feminist solidarity experienced by two teenaged girls' (Nielsen 2004: 55). Moreover, she extends possible themes of identity to include a national perspective:

> The deviancy of Ginger's sexuality is potently contrasted with the banality of the sisters' Canadian neighbourhood. The difference between Ginger's sexuality and the town's moral position highlights the repression that underpins the female experience of adolescence in general. The opening shots of the film depict a dull and pristine suburban landscape. The camera passes over streets full of identical houses, coming to linger on a brown tussock field where many more such houses are planned. A real estate sign reads, 'Bailey Downs: A Safe and Caring Community'. The ensuing scene is juxtaposed with this image of the safe and boring Bailey Downs. A woman emerges from her garden screaming having discovered her son playing with the severed paw of their family pet, which she then finds massacred in a quaint doghouse. Children playing hockey on the street turn and stare at the hysterical mother, shrug, and resume play. The violence perpetuated

by 'The Beast of Bailey Downs' has become commonplace, an uninteresting daily reality.

(Nielsen 2004: 58)

While the issues of gender and identity came to dominate the original, it is interesting to see the ways in which they are expanded and elaborated upon by later films in the *Ginger Snaps* cycle. In terms of gender, the menstruation-werewolf-monster metaphor remains at the heart of the franchise, while wider themes of Canadian suburban isolation referenced in the original's bleak depiction of the location Bailey Downs are backtracked and backdated in the gory prequel *Ginger Snaps Back*. For many critics writing around the time of the films' releases, the gender trope seems the most salient: the emphasis on the explosive expression of repressed female rage evidenced in the original *Ginger Snaps* can even claim to have rewritten the rules of what the contemporary horror film can offer women. In particular, the film's conflation of menstruation with monstrosity has led many reviewers to argue that *Ginger Snaps* contains feminist and even lesbian subtexts (Nielsen 2004; Briefel 2005). But the theme of Canadian identity also seems to be regarded as important as well. Caelum Vatnsdal applauds *Ginger Snaps Back* for using the history of Canada as a backdrop to a horror story, one in which 'werewolves and voyagers' appear next to each other (Vatnsdal 2004: 229), and one which might lead the way into combining attention for representations of national identity with quality.

We would argue that it is the conflation of these themes that gives *Ginger Snaps* a specific appeal to multiple fan groupings, thus giving these audiences something to chew on actively in an actively 'cultish' manner. Each elaboration of gender or identity seems to pivot around another, and together they outline and relay numerous links between the original and the sequels in ways that invite a degree of audience investment atypical of the horror genre. For instance, while the original film used the metaphor of monstrous transformation to convey the potential horror of teenage transformations in female sexuality, the sequel *Ginger Snaps: Unleashed* uses the imagery of emerging monstrosity to explore female teen maladies such as self-harming, drug abuse and anorexia, in a setting few would confuse with anything but Canada. And while Grant Harvey's prequel *Ginger Snaps Back* shifts the emphasis to highlight issues of Canadian identity within a horror framework, its relocation of the two heroines to a hostile, all male, nineteenth-century outpost also allows for the extension of gender themes familiar to the series. (Here, a prototype of Victorian feminism sees the pair embrace monstrosity and infection rather than sacrifice their unity to male oppression.)

They don't call it a cult for nothing: the production concerns of *Ginger Snaps*

If issues of gender and identity are central to a range of readings and interpretations of the *Ginger Snaps* films, then their importance is identifiable at the three key levels of production, reception and audience interpretation. Indeed an analysis of the background to the original film confirms that the first level where gender and identity are issues of importance is that of the production. At the origins of the *Ginger Snaps* films are director John Fawcett and screenwriter Karen Walton. Their contributions shaped the original's main themes of gender representation and cultural identity within a horror framework. Fawcett and Walton collaborated very closely on the story, as a team and as a couple. Fawcett's experience in directing episodes of *Xena: Warrior Princess*, *La Femme Nikita* and *Queer as Folk*, the first two with female protagonists (and with close links to the horror genre), and all three pregnant with lesbian and gay overtones, mixed well with Walton's experience in the horror genre (she collaborated on *Cube* and *Prom Night II*), and her own writing for *Queer as Folk*. The atypical fusion of fright and feminist tactics that Fawcett and Walton's collaboration provided was confirmed by the overlap of other creative personnel who contributed to both the original *Ginger Snaps* and the two subsequent sequels. As Paula Devonshire, the producer of both *Ginger Snaps: Unleashed* and *Ginger Snaps Back* has explained:

> The whole *Ginger Snaps* cycle is based around an incredibly close, incredibly creative team. The first film was based around the collaboration between John Fawcett's concept and Karen Walton's script. Steve Holbert was onboard from an early stage as the producer and Brett Sullivan was the editor, before going on to direct *Ginger Snaps: Unleashed*, while Grant Harvey was the second unit director before going on to direct *Ginger Snaps Back*. We also had the same camera operator, production designer and so on. So not only was there a lot of continuity between the original and the sequels, but there was a real understanding of the characters and the female issues that all three films raise.
>
> (Devonshire, in Mendik 2004b)

At the level of casting, the trilogy benefited from the stellar pairing of Katharine Isabelle and Emily Perkins, who portrayed the outcast and outlandish Fitzgerald sisters with an awareness of the wider debates that the text was engaging on. In the case of Emily Perkins, an educational background in psychoanalysis and gender studies ensured that her performance actively drew on theoretical conceptions of female performance and feminist rhetoric.

Undoubtedly, the tight-teamed yet competitive presence (they auditioned for the sister parts together) of Isabelle and Perkins added the misunderstood girl/teenager tension to the text. This proved a key ingredient for linking the gender and identity issues to the wider references of puberty anxieties, sibling rivalry, suburban boredom, sexual awakenings and the search for gender belonging essential to giving the narrative both a cultural relevance and a feminist pertinence. At the same time, Perkins and Isabelle's prior experiences as youthful horror performers in *Stephen King's It* (Wallace, 1990), *The X-Files* (1998) and in *Disturbing Behaviour* (Nutter, 1998) respectively, helped reinforce the gender/genre prominence. According to stories surrounding the shooting and production of all three films, the gender and national identity themes later to be picked up by critics were put at the centre of the production.

With these production roots, it is easy to identify the blend of genre and gender that makes *Ginger Snaps* stand out from other horror movies. Indeed, while it is true that the *Ginger Snaps* films feed upon established folk and cinematic myths that link the werewolf to scenes of unrestrained violence and sexual excess, Fawcett and Walton's focus on female teen transformations undercut many of the gender presumptions associated with 'wolfdom'. It is not merely the fact that budgetary restrictions demarcated Fawcett's rendition from the visceral visualization of werewolf transformations evidenced in 1980s films such as *An American Werewolf in London* (1981) and *The Howling* (1981). Rather, it is the fact that while these earlier films used extended and excessive scenes of transformation as metaphors for masculine change, the body horror of the *Ginger Snaps* trilogy is closely connected to menstrual cycles and uncontrollable changes in female sexuality. As Fawcett commented:

> As soon as we found that whole lunar cycles, menstrual cycles theme and put them together in a werewolf movie, that is when this whole thing came together. The weirdest thing is that I don't know if I could defend *Ginger Snaps*' connection between menstrual blood and infection or not. I actually thought that women would be very offended by this film. I was worried that what we were saying thematically was that to go through adolescence and become a woman was like becoming a monster.
>
> (Fawcett, in Mendik 2004b)

Fawcett's concern is simultaneously confirmed and countered by Devonshire, who sees the monstrous/menstrual link as a sign of the films' message that even in apparent monstrosity, women need to demonstrate their independence:

> To the extent that there are central male characters in these films, they only really exist as a point of contrast to the two female characters. Although these male leads may desire or even wish to help the Fitzgerald sisters, the idea of these two young women having to save themselves is the abiding theme of the *Ginger Snaps* films. These movies are all about women helping themselves, they don't need men to come and rescue them, these girls contain an inner strength that the male characters could never possess.
>
> (Devonshire, in Mendik 2004b)

Devonshire also links the gender theme to issues of identity, in insistently linking the body politic to national politics, in particular to the creation of a specifically Canadian horror film aesthetic in which to situate the werewolf trilogy. As she commented:

> I would definitely argue that the *Ginger Snaps* films express a Canadian horror film aesthetic. Being that all the people on our team are all Canadian filmmakers, all Canadian crew, all Canadian locations, this very clearly signals the national roots of the *Ginger Snaps* films. *Ginger Snaps* is based on the Canadian suburb where John Fawcett was raised. In fact, I think the Canadian emphasis of the films has increased as the cycle has progressed.
>
> (Devonshire, in Mendik 2004b)

Indeed, it is interesting to note that the original's focus on the potential violence lurking behind the apparent banality of the Canadian suburban landscape is extended in the desolate sequel *Ginger Snaps: Unleashed*. This situates its surviving heroine in a range of austere, isolated institutional buildings which are largely cut off from the rest of civilization by extreme weather conditions and open to potential attack from the wolves stalking Brigitte. Once again, the connection between monstrous transformation and wider Canadian identity proves to be a theme that dominated the production processes of both *Unleashed* and *Back*. As Devonshire has commented:

> There's even a line in *Ginger Snaps: Unleashed* where Ghost says 'Has the monster come from the infinite darkness?' and Brigitte replies 'No, it's come from the suburbs,' which once again links the series to a uniquely Canadian experience. Canada is such a nation of kids growing up in suburbs, so when I look at Bailey Downs I can totally recognize where I grew up. More over, in *Ginger Snaps Back*, we go for the themes of the voyagers and French Canadian accents to make clear the film's identity, while the fort depicted in the film is clearly modelled on a Hudson's Bay Trading Fort. None of the films have any American identity to them, they are all clearly Canadian, and we are proud of these films for precisely that reason.
>
> (Devonshire, in Mendik 2004b)

Every cult film needs its production legend. It seems that, thanks to the very intimate conflations *within* the crew, the loci of gender and identity have given the production process a sort of internal rationale. It does not really matter whether or not this focus is derived from personal backgrounds or from bigger, intellectual concerns, it is the fact they are presented as relevant that counts. It always remains precarious to see these stories as 'true', but at the very least it means 'gender' and 'identity' have had a central place in 'talk' about *Ginger Snaps* from the very word 'action'.

The release and critical reception of *Ginger Snaps*

As well as motivating the production concerns of its original creators, the key variables of gender and identity are also crucial to the reception of the *Ginger Snaps* films. They were released, in typical cultish fashion, in scattered stages and on an *ad hoc* basis, without an overall strategy, generating much, unstructured, ambiguous attention: a 'noise' more than a hype, in which thematic connections become more important than narrative or chronological ones.

Waves of festival releases were followed by theatrical releases for selected territories, in turn followed by general video and DVD releases, but several of the release stages overlapped significantly. For the first film, the first wave of festival releases stretched from September 2000, when the film premiered at the Toronto Film Festival, to Spring 2001 with screenings at festivals in Amsterdam, Los Angeles and Philadelphia. A second wave carried on well into 2002, with mostly genre festival screenings. It was intersected by a wave of theatrical releases, from May 2001 (Canada) to the Fall of that year (United States and Peru). With video premieres cushioned in between, most of the world got to know *Ginger Snaps* within twelve months, but in decidedly different ways and through various formats. With the releases of the second and third films only half a year apart such overlaps and variations became more common. With the video rentals and sales massively outnumbering any theatrical returns, the impression of the three films actually forming a coherent trilogy is most emphasized by the video and DVD presentations. For instance, the Dutch distributors of the sequel, linked *Ginger Snaps* to *Ginger Snaps: Unleashed* by offering rental customers the opportunity to keep Part I when renting both, while the UK three-film box set (released 2005) actually puts *Ginger Snaps Back* as the first film in the series. Needless to say, such presentations add to the confusion of the narrative order and stylistic coherence.

At the level of critical reception, it is hard to find any bad reviews of *Ginger Snaps*. Overall, the forms that the appraisals took are more or less uniform. One striking characteristic is the need reviewers feel to demonstrate, in an almost academic fashion, how *Ginger Snaps* perfectly ticks all boxes associated with contemporary horror-film motives and motifs. The lavish *Sight and Sound* reviews, for instance, or the *Kamera.co.uk* one, mention the suburban high-school setting, the gothic style of the sisters, their repressed anger, feminism and folklore (the werewolf theme) (Williams 2001: 36; Patterson 2001) and in namedropping *Halloween, Buffy the Vampire Slayer, Friday the 13th, Carrie, The Exorcist, An American Werewolf in London* and even *Jaws* (we think it must have been the size of the fangs). Williams, like so many other reviewers, seems to suggest *Ginger Snaps* is a good candidate for canonization in the genre.

Throughout all reviews, issues of gender and identity receive by far the most attention as key points for reviewers. The most common critical argument seems to be that, by equating menstruation with monstrosity, the *Ginger Snaps* films extend the impetus of previous classics such as *Carrie*, putting the horrific potential of female sexuality at the forefront (see Nielson 2004). Furthermore, the films' transgressions and recuperations of dominant conceptions of the female body clearly signal evidence of contradictory appreciation and celebration of an alternative take on the subgenre's foundations without being all too sure where it would end up. In fact, the positive reception even surprised its creators. As Fawcett has commented:

> I thought that women were really going to hate this movie. In fact, the reverse was true. Women loved it! I had more criticism of this movie from men who felt very uncomfortable with some of the themes that we raised. This is quite a unique thing, because women largely don't watch horror films. I know that is to generalize, but it is still largely considered as a male genre. So to create a movie that was effectively a horror film with all the blood, special effects and very 'male' stuff that I wanted to do coupled with very female themes turned it into something special that women really responded to.
>
> (Fawcett, in Mendik 2004b)

It usually took critics only one or two lines to identify the film's unusual representations of gender and link this to a wider consideration of identity. Suzie Young, for instance, swiftly shifts from an acknowledgement of the gendered body identities towards a consideration of political identities, developing a crude allegory in which Isabelle equates to the United States and Perkins represents Canada, to hammer home an argument about border identities (Young 2005). Vatnsdal's review of the series also situates it within a national tradition of terror, noting that 'the words "Canadian horror movies" were given some twenty-first-century relevance, and it was badly needed' (Vatnsdal 2004: 222). Similarly, Dominic Marceau, in an interview with Perkins, Devonshire and Director of Photography Michael Marshall employs a reference to the appearance of the quintessentially quaint Canadian hard-rock band *April Wine* on the soundtrack of *Ginger Snaps: Unleashed* to progress from gender to national identity issues, ending with an unabashed celebration of the 'Great White North', against current American ignorance (Marceau 2004).

Fur and fandom: the *Ginger Snaps* audience project

As the comments of makers, reviewers and critics confirm, concerns of gender representation/national identity were very much on the agenda during the production of *Ginger Snaps* as well as its reception. Therefore, it is only logical they are similarly received by the attuned audiences that make up the fan base for the franchise. In order to assess such activities and detect the possible sexual/national positions underpinning such activity, we conducted the first ever audience analysis of fans of the franchise. During this project we surveyed different audiences' responses to the films across a number of different test sites. A first run of the audience research (with a screening of the first film to an all-female audience) was staged in Northampton in November 2004. A second run (screening the first film to a mixed-gender audience) took place in Aberystwyth in February 2005. A third run (with an international audience watching the premiere of the third film) and an intermediate panel on results, happened at the Brussels International Fantasy Film Festival in March 2005. A DVD documentary of the first results, *Menstrual Monsters: The Ginger Snaps Trilogy* (Mendik 2005) was premiered at this festival. A fourth run (of the second and third films, with a mixed-gender audience) took place in Aberystwyth again, in May 2005. A second intermediate panel was organized at the Puchon International Fantastic Film Festival, in Korea, July 2005, against a screening of all three films and the documentary. The first final results were presented at the Society for Cinema and Media Studies Conference in Vancouver, March 2006.

From the different audience formations we researched (gender-specific, mixed, national, international) it quickly became clear that there was indeed a strong will to see the clues towards gender and identity as key tools for making sense of the films. The ability to read these clues was in part due to the fact that our respondents positioned themselves as what we would like to call 'critical fans'. By this we mean fans whose dedication and appreciation has to be 'won over' by the films, and whose criticism is less concerned with petty preferences and objections about characters and narrative logic (such as Ginger's manifestation as a ghost in *Ginger Snaps: Unleashed* or the historical leap in *Ginger Snaps Back* as part of the game). However, these critical fans could get quite worked up over thematic coherence, and a definite source for their overall approval of the films is the trilogy's care for such coherence, especially in its explorations of gender and identity, set up through the intimate collaborations during production.

The identification of gender and identity issues in the films usually happens through the characters. Obviously audiences care a lot about the two Fitzgerald sisters, in differing ways. It matters to them that Emily Perkin's Brigitte wears a gothic outfit (though they have reservations about whether she actually 'is' a goth) and that she is the intellectual of the two sisters, well-read and emotionally sensitive but also psychologically shrewd, the same way it matters to them that Katharine Isabelle's Ginger is powerful, emancipated and intimidating.

It is not surprising that the way into a lot of appreciation of subtexts goes via the characters and, together with the audiences' awareness of how preciously rare genuinely strong female characters are in horror films. What is significant, however, is that an appreciation of the issues of gender and identity raised in the *Ginger Snaps* series assisted a decoding of its subtexts that clearly exceeds a knowledge of genre codes.

This is borne out by data gathered from the study sample conducted in May 2005. Here, we asked audiences first about their experience of watching horror films. It turned out that only 27% of respondents saw themselves as experienced horror viewers (though no one actually saw themselves as 'very experienced'). A total of 33% of the audience sample saw themselves as inexperienced (with 13% as very inexperienced) and the remaining 40% (almost half of them) saw themselves as neutral, neither experienced nor inexperienced.

We also asked audiences about their enjoyment of watching the *Ginger Snaps* films. A total of 80% of viewers said that they enjoyed watching it, with 27% stating they enjoyed it very much; 13% were neutral (or ambivalent) and 7% did not enjoy watching it (with none not enjoying it very much). Correlating these two dimensions we found that only a quarter of viewers enjoying watching *Ginger Snaps* counted themselves as experienced horror viewers and the remaining three-quarters who enjoyed it claimed no particular affiliation with the genre. This means that in order to enjoy watching the *Ginger Snaps* films one does not really have to be a fan of the genre.

Subtexts for smart people: activating the active audience of *Ginger Snaps*

A narrative twist late on in *Ginger Snaps: Unleashed* poses a very interesting test case of how such generically unaware or neutral audiences are still actively engaging and adapting their expectations around gender and identity to fit with subtexts present in the series. When we interviewed and surveyed audiences, *Ginger Snaps: Unleashed* was seen by most of our respondents as the best of the three (results from May 2005). Not only as Matthew Leyland describes a 'worthy follow-up' but also one that uses and expands the themes set in motion in the first film (Leyland 2005: 77).

Having killed her sister at the end of the original, an already infected Brigitte finds herself incarcerated in a drug-rehabilitation facility. Without access to her Monkshood (a herbal remedy poisonous to werewolves), Brigitte's own monstrous transformation garners speed. Here, the heroine has to fight off her own growing infection as well as the advances of abusive male staff such as Tyler (Eric Johnson), who are preying on female patients. Her only ally at the institution is Ghost (Tatiana Maslany), an immature, insecure girl effectively stranded at the institution after an apparent accident befalls her only guardian. Everything about Ghost speaks childlike, insecure and naïve. She cannot even write properly – in her comic book we see that she has made a mistake, captioning her story about a vampire as a 'reign of moral terror', instead of the expected 'mortal'.

Brigitte befriends Ghost, especially when she is picked on by some of the older girls in the facility – Brigitte almost literally 'shows her teeth' at one point, and the relationship between the pair comes to reproduce the issues of close female bonding identified in the first film (with Ghost becoming the younger sister figure to Brigitte). And when Brigitte decides that she must escape or die (by becoming a werewolf), Ghost begs to go with her. After the pair escape from the facility, one of the female therapists finds them hiding out in Ghost's grandmother's house. And all together, from a vantage point in the attic, they wait to confront the werewolf that has penetrated the location. Brigitte, herself half-transformed, kills the beast in a scene that is largely unsurprising. Ghost herself then strikes what seems like a final blow for their freedom, by suddenly shooting and then killing the therapist with a hammer in an act of unmotivated murderous mayhem. But, when Brigitte – weak and now almost completely lupined – begs for death, Ghost, with a look of cool deliberation pushes her into the cellar and drops the trap door on her. As the final shots roll, her voice-over narrates the end of the film: this will be the beginning of her own 'reign of moral terror'.

This is a demanding ending to the film, because it asks from audiences an alertness that goes well beyond generic appreciation. It requires attention to the subtexts of gender, identity and reflexivity through a range of clues. Up until the ending, Ghost has been presented as very innocent, soliciting audiences' involvement, caring for her. She is presented as definitely pre-sexual and, unlike the rest of the girls in the facility, is not subject to Tyler's advances. She dresses differently, and more child-like. Her love of comics, albeit with some very gothic stories, has a childlike edge to it. Not only these, but *we* see her make what seem like childlike mistakes – there is a clear temptation to read her 'reign of moral terror' as evidence of her incompetence. We, as audience, are entitled to 'read' her as a little girl in need of care and protection. In which case, the ending is a very particular shock.

Yet at the same time, a particular species of alertness to gender and identity issues could suggest a different set of personal qualities in Ghost. Her grandmother is fully swathed in bandages (itself suggestive of monstrosity and a play on the term 'mummy'), and at the outset we see Ghost reading to her thus helpless relative. But as the film progresses, she appears, curiously, to bump into and move her grandmother's bed, especially when she is restless and might seem to be reaching for a button to call for attention from the staff. Added to this is Ghost's curious interest in sexual voyeurism, referenced in the scene where climbing to her escape through the ducts, she pauses to watch Tyler having sex with one of the other girls in the facility.

Now imagine a subtextually alert audience watching the film, an audience 'knowing' something completely unexpected has to happen – and an audience frantically searching for clues towards that. A first rule of such a mode of attending might be: if this is to be any good as a horror film, then something completely unexpected has to happen. What might it be? By the time Brigitte and Ghost are in the grandmother's house, everything is indicating that there is not long to go. The pace of events is speeding up; Brigitte is struggling to contain her transformation; editing is becoming faster; and the whole thing is approaching the typical length of a horror film. What characters are left who might be the locus of the surprise, and who could emerge holding the narrative reins? Brigitte had already had a surprise moment at the end of the first film – killing her sister, after all her pledges to her that they would be 'together, forever', but then hugging the corpse, had turned the film quite unexpectedly. Tyler *might* be the source of it, but the odds would be against that. First, in the main, werewolves here are being associated with the female line. Not only this, but his sexual predations had clearly marked him as someone deserving a bad death. It would be hard for an audience to plan ahead for him to survive and emerge as any kind of victor. (This is confirmed in the finale when he is fatally rejected from the all-female location after Ghost falsely accuses him of trying to molest her.)

The therapist is another possibility, except she has had a very small narrative role, and one of adult incompetence in a film where (like its original predecessor) adults are presented as essentially uncomprehending and irrelevant, except in as much as they constrain and make problems. This leaves Ghost – too innocent by half, whether or not the particular moments identified above have been noticed, and always managing to turn up, knowingly, at the 'right time' – managing, for instance, to find Brigitte in the complex basement of the facility when Brigitte had apparently left her behind in her escape attempt. Ghost, then, is an anomaly awaiting exposure, a reversal needing to happen, a revelation in waiting. But of what kind? If the film is a 'classic werewolf story', she surely should turn out to be a werewolf. But if the generically altert watcher has seen the first film, then foreknowledge from that could well indicate that this is precisely *not* going to be a standard tale. So, what might Ghost be? A ghost unleashed, like Ginger's appearance in the film?

These modes of encountering the narrative twist depend upon building frames of interpretation from a set of available clues within the film, upon a *will* to find a coherent interpretive position, and upon the *kind of orientation* that audiences have taken up towards the film. When talking about these issues, the audiences we surveyed appeared to be very ingenious in discovering and constructing such subtexts. We also found them able to move beyond the creation of these fictional subjects in an appreciation of the wider issues raised by the franchise. These included their ability to praise the trilogy for its feminist (or 'feminist-like') stance through an incredibly wide variety of gender references (ranging from family bonding to lesbian subthemes). Similarly, they see issues of identity in the Canadian locations, the suburban surroundings, but also in age and in more abstract loci such as 'home' and 'school'. As tools, 'gender' and 'identity' can, then, mean a lot of things to audiences. But their significance in *coming* to that meaning is undeniable.

There was also a difference in how audiences use 'gender' and 'identity' for the individual films. For *Ginger Snaps* and *Ginger Snaps: Unleashed*, 'gender' issues seem more important, while for *Ginger Snaps Back* identity issues are considered more crucial. But, interestingly, both are used as tools for analysis across all of the films. It rather looks as if audiences are using a sliding scale from gender to identity when moving from the first, over the second, to the third film, but are prepared to return to any of the two when a particular cue in the film demands it. For instance, in *Ginger Snaps Back*, the entrance of the sisters in the all-male settlers' dining room reminds audiences suddenly of the gender issue, in the same way the Bailey Downs neighbourhood reinforces the Canadian stamp on Fawcett's original when we see a neighbourhood child in full ice-hockey gear looking for his dog.

Finally, and surprisingly, 'gender' and 'identity' also break open the genre shackles. References to puberty, growing up, menstruation and bonding were seen as signs to take the viewing of these films beyond the boundaries of the horror genre, into a not really well-defined category of 'coming of age' metaphors. But, it also transpired that the liking of the film (and roughly 75% of the audience liked it a lot) was less a matter of being a fan of the genre than of an appreciation of the themes (about one out of five respondents declared themselves not to be experienced horror viewers). So, at the end, the themes/tools even outclass the very scope within which the trilogy was set up; a sign for us that when Fawcett and Walton declared that they wanted to make a 'smart horror film' in order to get a little 'broader audience' they got exactly what they wanted, smartness included (*Rue Morgue*, 2000).

Conclusion

By fusing issues of gender and identity alongside traditional shock tactics and genre imagery, the *Ginger Snaps* series has provided an interesting set of meanings and associations for both fans and non-fans of the horror film. In the context of such images, fans are often seen as overly subjective audiences, uncritically buying into whatever aspect of the fan-object is being pushed down their throat. Not so our fake fur and fang loving *Ginger Snaps* fans. Our research has shown that they are clever, critical and caring. It matters to them that films make sense, and when they discover this, in a film, they are prepared to lift it out of its generic constraints, onto a cult status.

The *Ginger Snaps* trilogy owes its cult reputation partly to the smart way in which it updates established myths around the werewolf to include female concerns, extending the popularity of the horror genre to a wider range of viewing groups. And while the discussion of key sexual and cultural issues raised in the cycle may remain of interest to critics and theorists, the *Ginger Snaps* films also reveal the pivotal role that film fans have in snapping back the meaning created by the contemporary terror text.

Cult bibliography

This bibliography presents an overview of sources on cult cinema, and on the biographical, encyclopedic, theoretical and methodological materials that have been a significant inspiration for its study. It includes most of the works cited from the articles excerpted (which we have, where possible, updated and completed). We have also included some sources on individual films and territories where such sources have had a marked impact on the overall study of cult film. In a few cases this means we have included sources that are not straightforwardly academic, but whose reputation and wide use have given them prominence in the field.

A selective bibliography of sources related to directors with particular cult reputations is included at the end of the general bibliography. This selection guides readers to analyses and studies of some of cult cinema's most renowned figures – and we have listed them alphabetically per director's name. The selection is based on the applicability for classroom use, and for case studies of cult directors, so we have emphasized general overviews, accessible journal articles and sample analyses. Where appropriate, we have included approaches that contain insightful and clarifying (and occasionally demystifying) investigations that inform theory.

Comprehensive cult concepts bibliography

Aden, Roger (1999) *Popular Stories and Promised Lands: Fan Cultures and Symbolic Pilgrimages.* Tuscaloosa, AL: University of Alabama Press.

Adorno, Theodor (2001) *The Culture Industry.* London: Routledge.

Agee, James (1949) 'Comedy's greatest era', *Life Magazine*, 3 September, reprinted in Gerald Mast and Marshall Cohen (eds) (1974) *Film Theory and Criticism* (1st edn). Oxford: Oxford University Press, 439.

Allen, Robert and Douglas Gomery (1985) *Film History: Theory and Practice.* New York: Knopf.

An, Jinsoo (2001) '*The Killer*: cult Film and transcultural (mis)reading', in Esther Yau (ed.) *At Full Speed; Hong Kong Cinema in a Borderless World.* Minneapolis, MN: University of Minnesota Press, 95–113.

Anderson, Chris (2006) 'The new tastemakers' and 'Niche culture', in *The Long Tail: Why the Future of Business is Selling Less of More.* New York: Hyperion, 98–124, 177–91.

Andrews, David (2006) 'Sex is dangerous, so satisfy your wife: the softcore thriller in its contexts', *Cinema Journal*, 45(3), 59–89.

Anger, Kenneth ([1974] 1957) *Hollywood Babylon*. London: Arrow Books.

Anger, Kenneth (1984) *Hollywood Babylon II*. London: Arrow Books.

Anger, Kenneth (2000) 'A vivianne romance: ode to a French screen legend', in Jack Stevenson (ed.) *Fleshpot: Cinema's Sexual Myth Makers and Taboo Breakers*. Manchester: Headpress, 91–100.

Arroyo, José (1992) '*La ley del deseo*: a gay seduction', in Richard Dyer and Ginette Vincendeau (eds) *Popular European Cinema*. London: Routledge, 31–46.

Arslan, Savas (2003) 'Turkish Trash: Popular film in Turkey, 1960–1980', conference paper, Born to be Bad 2 Trash Cinema Conference, University of California, Berkeley, May.

Auslander, Philip (1997) 'Tryin' to make it real: Live performance, simulation and the discourse of authenticity in rock culture', in *Liveness*. New York: Routledge, 61–72.

Auslander, Philip (2006) *Performing Glam Rock: Gender and Theatricality in Popular Music*. Ann Arbor, MI: University of Michigan Press.

Auster, Albert (1989) *Actresses and Suffragists: Women in the American Theatre, 1890–1920*. New York: Praeger.

Austin, Bruce (1981) 'Film attendance: why college students chose to see their most recent film', *Journal of Popular Film and Television*, 9 (spring), 43–9.

Austin, Bruce (1981) 'Portrait of a cult film audience', *Journal of Communication*, 31 (spring), 43–54.

Austin, Bruce (1983) 'Critics' and consumers' evaluations of motion pictures: A longitudinal test of the taste culture and elitist hypotheses', *Journal of Popular Film*, 10(4), 156–67.

Austin, Bruce (1984) 'Portrait of an art film audience', *Journal of Communication*, 34 (winter), 74–87.

Austin, Thomas (1999) '*Gone With the Wind* plus fangs: the assembly, marketing and reception of Bram Stoker's *Dracula*', *Framework: The Journal of Cinema and Media*, 41 (autumn).

Austin, Thomas (1999) 'Desperate to see it: straight men watching *Basic Instinct*', in Melvyn Stokes and Richard Maltby (eds) *Identifying Hollywood's Audiences: Cultural Identity and the Movies*. London: British Film Institute, 147–61.

Austin, Thomas (2002) '*Natural Born Killers*: a film for hooligans', in *Hollywood, Hype, and Audiences: Selling and Watching Popular Film in the 1990s*. Manchester: Manchester University Press, 152–94.

Avedon, Carol and Alison Assiter (1993) *Bad Girls & Dirty Pictures*. London: Pluto Press.

Bacon-Smith, Camille (1988) 'Acquisition and transformation of popular culture: the international video circuit and the fanzine community', paper presented at the International Communications Association Conference, New Orleans, 1988.

Bacon-Smith, Camille (1992) *Enterprising Women: Television Fandom and the Creation of Popular Culture*. Philadelphia, PA: University of Pennsylvania Press.

Bakhtin, Mikhail (1981) *The Dialogical Imagination*. Austin, TX: University of Texas Press.

Bakhtin, Mikhail (1984) *Rabelais and his World*. Bloomington, IN: Indiana University Press.

Bakhtin, Mikhail and Pavel Medvedev ([1928] 1985) *The Formal Method in Literary Scholarship: a Critical Introduction to Sociological Poetics*. Cambridge, MA: Harvard University Press.

Bandura, Albert and Emilio Ribes-Inesta (1976) *Analysis of Delinquency and Aggression*. Mahwah, NJ: Lawrence Erlbaum Associates.

Bangs, Lester (1988) *Psychotic Reactions and Carburetor Dung*. New York: Vintage Books.

Barker, Martin (1983) *A Haunt of Fears: The Strange History of the British Horror Comics Campaign*. London: Pluto Press.

Barker, Martin (ed.) (1984) *The Video Nasties: Freedom and Censorship in the Media*. London: Pluto Press.

Barker, Martin (1997) 'Taking the extreme case: Understanding a fascist Fan of Judge Dredd', in Deborah Cartmell, I.Q. Hunter, Heidi Kaye and Imelda Whelehan (eds) *Trash Aesthetics: Popular Culture and its Audiences*. London: Routledge, 14–30.

Barker, Martin and Kate Brooks (1997) *Knowing Audiences: Friends, Fans and Foes of Judge Dredd*. Luton: University of Luton Press.

Barker, Martin and Julian Petley (eds) (1997) *Ill Effects; the Media/Violence Debate*. London: Routledge.

Barker, Martin, Jane Arthurs and Ramaswami Harindranath (2001) *The Crash Controversy: Censorship Campaigns and Film Reception*. London: Wallflower Press.

Barker, Martin (2004) 'Violence redux', in Steven Jay Schneider (ed.) *New Hollywood Violence*. Manchester: Manchester University Press, 57–79.

Barker, Martin and Ernest Mathijs (2005) 'Understanding vernacular experiences of film in an academic environment', *ADCHE – Arts, Design and Communication in Higher Education*, 4(1), 49–71.

Barker, Martin (2005, 2006) 'Loving and hating *Straw Dogs*: The meanings of audience responses to a controversial film', *Particip@tions*, 2(2) (December 2005) and 3(1) (May 2006). Online via: www.participations.org.

Barker, Martin (2006), 'On being a 1960s Tolkien reader', in Ernest Mathijs and Murray Pomerance (eds) *From Hobbits to Hollywood: Essays on Peter Jackson's Lord of the Rings*. New York: Rodopi, 81–100.

Barker, Martin, Ernest Mathijs and Xavier Mendik (2006) 'Menstrual monsters: the reception of the *Ginger Snaps* cult horror franchise', *Film International*, 4(3), 68–77.

Barker, Martin and Ernest Mathijs (eds) (2007) *Watching The Lord of the Rings*. New York: Peter Lang.

Barral, Etienne (1999) *Otaku: Les enfants du virtuel*. Paris: Denoel.

Barry, Christopher (2004) 'Violent justice: Italian crime/cop films of the 1970s', in Ernest Mathijs and Xavier Mendik (eds) *Alternative Europe: European Exploitation and Underground Cinema*. London: Wallflower Press, 77–89.

Barthes, Roland (1966) *Critique et vérité*, Paris: Seuil.

Barthes, Roland (1974) *S/Z*, New York: Hill & Wang.

Barthes, Roland (1977) 'Myth today', in *Mythologies*. New York: Hill & Wang, 109–59.

Barthes, Roland (1977) *Image/Music/Text*. New York: Hill & Wang.

Baudrillard, Jean (1995) *Simulacra and Simulation*. Ann Arbor, MI: Michigan University Press.

Baudrillard, Jean (1996) *The System of Objects*. New York: Verso.

Becker, Howard (1963) *Outsiders: Study in the Sociology of Deviance*. New York: The Free Press.

Becker, Howard (1984) *Art Worlds*. Berkeley, CA: University of California Press.

Behlil, Melis (2005) 'Cinephilia, internet and online film communities', in Marijke De Valck and Malte Hagener (eds) (2005) *Cinephilia: Movies, Love and Memory*. Amsterdam: Amsterdam University Press, 111–24.

Benjamin, Walter ([1969] 1935) 'The work of art in the age of mechanical reproduction', in Hannah Arendt (ed.) *Illuminations*. New York: Pimlico, 217–51.

Bennett, Tony (1979) *Formalism and Marxism*. London: Methuen.

Benshoff, Harry (2000) 'Blaxploitation horror films: generic reappropriation or reinscription', *Cinema Journal*, 39(2), 31–50.

Berger, John (1972) *Ways of Seeing*. Harmondsworth: Penguin.

Betz, Mark (2003) 'Art, exploitation, underground', in Mark Jancovich, Antonio Lazaro-Reboll, Julian Stringer and Andy Willis (eds) *Defining Cult Movies: The Cultural Politics of Oppositional Taste*. Manchester: Manchester University Press, 202–22.

BIFFF (2001) *Le Cinéma peut-il engendrer la violence?* Brussels: Pey Mey Diffusion.

Biskind, Peter (1983) *Seeing is Believing: How Hollywood Taught Us to Stop Worrying and Love the Fifties*. New York: Pantheon.

Biskind, Peter (1999) *Easy Riders, Raging Bulls: How the Sex 'n' Drugs 'n' Rock 'n' Roll Generation Saved Hollywood*. New York: Simon & Shuster.

Black, Andy (ed.) (1996) *Necronomicon: Book One: The Journal of Horror and Erotic Cinema*. London: Creation Books (there have since been several more editions of *Necronomicon*).

Bonila, Paul (2005) 'Is there more to Hollywood lowbrow than meets the eye?' *Quarterly Review of Film and Video*, 22, 17–24.

Bordwell, David (1989) *Making Meaning; Inference and Rhetoric in the Interpretation of Cinema*. Cambridge, MA: Harvard University Press.

Bordwell, David and Kristin Thompson (1994) 'History, historiography, and film history', in *Film History, an Introduction* (1st edn). New York: McGraw-Hill, xxxi–xlii.

Bordwell, David (1997) *On the History of Film Style*. Cambridge, MA: Harvard University Press.

Bourdieu, Pierre (1980) 'The aristocracy of culture', *Media, Culture and Society*, 2(3), 225–54.

Bourdieu, Pierre (1984) *Distinction: A Social Critique of the Judgment of Taste*. London: Routledge.

Bouyxou, Jean-Pierre (1980) 'Le cinéma et la presse (VII): les revues du cinéma érotique', *Image et Son/ la revue du cinéma*, 348, 87–96.

Briefel, Aviva (2005) Monster pains: masochism, menstruation, and identification in the horror film, *Film Quarterly*, 58(3), 16–27.

Britton, Andrew, Robin Wood, Richard Lippe and Tony Williams (eds) (1979) *The American Nightmare: Essays on the Horror Film*. Toronto: Festival of Festivals.

Brophy, Philip (1984) 'Tales of terror: the horror films you think you know', *Cinema Papers*, 49, 400–7.

Brophy, Philip (1986) 'Horrality: the textuality of contemporary horror films', *Screen*, 27(1), 2–13.

Brophy, Philip (1987) 'Violence on the screen: this isn't a film, it's a disease', *Cinema Papers*, 62, 18–22.

Brottman, Mikita (1997) *Offensive Films: Toward an Anthropology of Cinéma Vomitif*. Westport, CT: Greenwood Press.

Brottman, Mikita (1997) 'Faecal phantoms: oral and anal tensions in the tingler', in Deborah Cartmell, I.Q. Hunter, Heidi Kaye and Imelda Whelehan (eds) *Thrash Aesthetics: Popular Culture and its Audience*. London: Pluto Press, 103–17.

Brottman, Mikita (1999) *Hollywood Hex*. London: Creation Books.

Budd, Mike (1984) 'Authorship as commodity: The art cinema and *The Cabinet of Dr. Caligari*', *Wide Angle*, 6(1), 12–19.

Budd, Mike, Robert Entman and Clay Steinman (1990) 'The affirmative character of US cultural studies, *Critical Studies in Mass Communication*, 7, 169–84.

Burchill, Julie (1986) *Damaged Gods: Cults and Heroes Reappraised*. London: Century.

Burgin, Victor (1986) *The End of Art Theory: Criticism and Postmodernity*. Basingstoke: Macmillan.

Card, James (1991) 'Confessions of a Casablanca cultist: An enthusiast meets the myth and its flaws', in J.P. Telotte (ed.) *The Cult Film Experience*. Austin, TX: University of Texas Press, 66–78.

Carey, Peter (2006) *Wrong About Japan*. Toronto: Random House.

Carroll, Noel (1981) 'Nightmare and the horror film: the symbolic biology of fantastic beings', *Film Quarterly*, 34(3), 16–25.

Carroll, Noel (1998) *Interpreting the Moving Image*. Cambridge: Cambridge University Press.

Cartmell, Deborah, I.Q. Hunter, Heidi Kaye and Imelda Whelehan (eds) (1996) *Pulping Fictions*. London: Pluto Press.

Cartmell, Deborah, I.Q. Hunter, Heidi Kaye and Imelda Whelehan (eds) (1997) *Trash Aesthetics: Popular Culture and its Audience*. London: Pluto Press.

Chamberlin, Philip (1960) 'Allies, not enemies: commercial and nontheatrical experience on the West Coast', *Film Quarterly*, 14 (winter), 36–9.

Cherry, Brigid (1999) 'Refusing to refuse to look: female viewers of the horror film', in Melvyn Stokes and Richard Maltby (eds) *Identifying Hollywood's Audiences*. London: BFI, 169–78.

Chibnall, Steve (2003) *Get Carter*. London: IB Tauris.

Chin, Bertha and Jonathan Gray (2001) 'One ring to rule them all': Pre-viewers and pre-texts of the *Lord of the Rings* films', *Intensities: The Journal of Cult Media*, 2, autumn/winter.

Chriss, James J. (1993) 'Durkheim's cult of the individual as civil religion: Its appropriation by Erving Goffman', *Sociological Spectrum*, 13(2), 251.

Church, David (2007) 'Notes toward a masochizing of cult cinema: The painful pleasures of the cult film fan', *Offscreen*, 11(4), online at: www.offscreen.com/biblio/pages/essays/masochizing_of_cult_cinema/P1/ (accessed 1 July 2007).

Ciment, Michel (1998) 'The function and the state of film criticism', in John Boorman and Walter Donahue (eds) *Projections 8: Film-makers on Film-making*. Londen: Faber & Faber, 35–43.

Clover, Carol (1992) *Men, Women, and Chainsaws: Gender in the Modern Horror Film*. Princeton, NJ: Princeton University Press.

Cohen, Albert (1955) 'A theory of subculture', in Ronald Farrell and Victoria Lynn Swigert (eds) *Social Deviance*. Philadelphia, PA: Lippincott, 179–82.

Cohen, Stanley ([1972, 1980] 2003) *Folk Devils and Moral Panics*. London: Routledge.

Conrich, Ian (1997) 'Seducing the subject: Freddy Krueger, popular culture and the *Nightmare on Elm Street* films', in Deborah Cartmell, I.Q. Hunter, Heidi Kaye and Imelda Whelehan (eds) *Thrash Aesthetics: Popular Culture and its Audience*. London: Pluto Press, 118–31.

Cook, David (1993) 'Making sense', *Film Criticism*, 17(2–3), 31–9.

Cook, Pam (1976) 'Exploitation films and feminism', *Screen*, 17(2), 122–7.

Cook, Pam (2005) 'The pleasures and perils of exploitation films', in *Screening the Past: Memory and Nostalgia in Cinema*. London: Routledge, 52–64.

Cooper, Ian (2008) *Bring me the Head of Alfredo Garcia*. London: Wallflower Press.

Corliss, Richard (ed.) (1973) 'Cinema and sex', *Film Comment*, 9(1), 4–64.

Corliss, Richard (1990) 'All thumbs or, is there a future for film criticism?' *Film Comment*, 26(2), 14–18.

Corrigan, Timothy (1986) 'Film and the culture of cult', *Wide Angle*, 8(3–4), 91–9.

Couldry, Nick (2002) *Media Rituals: A Critical Approach*. New York: Routledge.

Curci, Loris (1996) *Shock Masters of the Cinema*. Key West, FL: Fantasma Books.

D'Acci, Julie (1994) *Defining Women: The Case of Cagney and Lacey*. Chapel Hill, NC: North Carolina University Press.

Darius, James (1995) *That's Blaxploitation! Roots of the Baadasssss 'Tude (Rated X by an All-Whyte Jury)*. New York: St Martin's Griffin.

Davies, Steven Paul (2003) *A–Z of Cult Film and Filmmakers*. London: Batsford.

Davis, Darrell William (2001) 'Reigniting Japanese tradition with Hana-Bi', *Cinema Journal*, 40(4), 55–80.

Davis, Glyn (forthcoming) *Superstar: The Karen Carpenter Story*. London: Wallflower Press.

De Certeau, Michel (1984) *The Practice of Everyday Life*. Berkeley, CA: University of California Press.

De Seife, Ethan (2007) *This Is Spinal Tap*. London: Wallflower Press.

Diawara, Manthia (1994) 'On tracking world cinema: African cinema at film festivals', *Public Culture*, 6(2), 385–96.

Doherty, Thomas (1984) 'The exploitation film as history: wild in the streets', *Literature/Film Quarterly*, 12(3), 186–94.

Doherty, Thomas (1988) *Teenagers and Teenpics: The Juvenilization of American Movies in the 1950s*. London: Unwin Hyman.

Doherty, Thomas (1999) *Pre-Code Hollywood: Sex, Immorality and Insurrection in American Cinema 1930–1934*. New York: Columbia University Press.

Donner, Marc (2004) 'Cult classics', *IEEE Security and Privacy*, 2(3), 66–8.

Douglas, Mary (1966) *Purity and Danger*. New York: Routledge.

Dowler, Kevin (2001) In the bedrooms of the nation: State scrutiny and the funding of dirty art, in Sally McKay and Andrew Paterson (eds) *Money Value Art: State Funding, Free Markets, Big Pictures*. Toronto: YYZ Books.

Durkheim, Émile ([1915] 1995) *The Elementary Forms of Religious Life*. New York: Free Press.

Dworkin, Andrea (1981) *Pornography: Men Possessing Women*. New York: Putnam.

Dworkin, Andrea and Patricia A. MacKinnon (1988) *Pornography and Civil Rights*. Minneapolis, MN: Organizing Against Pornography.

Dyer, Richard (1986) *Heavenly Bodies: Film Stars and Society*. London: Macmillan.

Dyer, Richard and Ginette Vincendeau (eds) (1992) *Popular European Cinema*. London: Routledge.

Dyer, Richard (2004) 'Idol thoughts: orgasm and self-reflexivity in gay pornography', in Pamela Church Gibson (ed.) *More Dirty Looks: Gender, Pornography and Power*. London: British Film Institute.

Eagleton, Terry (1984) *The Function of Criticism*. London: Verso.

Eaton, Michael (2000) 'Vanishing Americans', *Sight and Sound*, 10(6), 30–2.

Ebert, Roger (1990) 'All stars or, is there a cure for criticism of film criticism?', *Film Comment*, 26(3), 45–51.

Eberwein, Robert (1998) 'The erotic thriller', *Post Script*, 17(3), 25–33.

Eco, Umberto (1986) 'Cult movies and intertextual collage', in *Travels in Hyperreality*. London: Picador, 197–211.

Eco, Umberto (1989) *Open Work*. Cambridge, MA: Harvard University Press.

Eco, Umberto (1990) *The Limits of Interpretation*. Bloomington & Indianapolis, IN: Indiana University Press.

Egan, Kate (2008) *Trash or Treasure?: Censorship and the Changing Meanings of the Video Nasties*. Manchester: Manchester University Press.

Elena, Alberto and Maria Díaz López (eds) (2003) *The Cinema of Latin America*. London: Wallflower Press.

Ellis, John (1982) *Visible Fictions*. London: Routledge.

Erb, Cynthia (1998) *Tracking King Kong: A Hollywood Icon in World Culture*. Detroit, MI: Wayne State University Press.

Erdogan, Nezih (2002) 'Mute bodies, disembodied voices: notes on sound in Turkish popular cinema', *Screen*, 43(3), 233–49.

Everman, Welch (1993) *Cult Horror Films*. New York: Citadel Press/Virgin Books.

Farber, Stephen (1981) 'Why do critics love trashy movies?', *American Film*, 6(6), 65–8.

Fenton, Harvey (ed.) (2003) *The Flesh and Blood Compendium*. Godalming: FAB Press.

Fiedler, Leslie (1984) *Freaks*. New York: Touchstone.

Fiedler, Leslie (1985) '*Beyond Beyond the Valley of the Dolls*', *American Journal*, 1(5), 5.

Fiske, John (1989) *Understanding Popular Culture*. Boston, MA: Unwin Hyman.

Fiske, John (1989) *Reading the Popular*. Boston, MA: Unwin Hyman.

Fiske, John (1992) 'The cultural economy of fandom', in Lisa A. Lewis (ed.) *The Adoring Audience: Fan Culture and Popular Media*. New York: Routledge, 30–49.

Foucault, Michel (1971) *The Order of Things*. New York: Pantheon Books.

Foucault, Michel (1972) *Archaeology of Knowledge*. New York: Pantheon Books.

Foucault, Michel (1979) *Discipline and Punish*. New York: Vintage Books.

Foucault, Michel (1988) *Madness and Civilisation*. New York: Vintage Books.

Freeland, Cynthia (1996) 'Feminist frameworks for horror film', in David Bordwell and Noel Carroll (eds) *Post-Theory: Reconstructing Film Studies*. Madison, WI: University of Wisconsin Press, 195–218.

French, Karl and Philip French (2000) *Cult Movies*. London: Billboard Books.

Friedman, David (with Don DeNevi) (1990) *A Youth in Babylon Confessions of a Trash-Film King*. Buffalo (NY): Prometheus Books.

Frow, John (1998) 'Is Elvis a god? Cult, culture, questions of method', *International Journal of Cultural Studies*, 1(1), 197–210.

Fuller, Kathryn (1996) *At the Picture Show: Small-Town Audiences and the Creation of Movie Fan Culture*. Washington: Smithsonian Press.

Fung, Richard (1999) Programming the public, *GLQ*, 5(1), 89–93.

Gabbard, Krin (1999) *Jammin' at the Margins: Jazz and the American Cinema*. Chicago: University of Chicago Press.

Gamson, Joshua (1997) 'The organizational shaping of collective identity: the case of lesbian and gay film festivals in New York', in Martin Duberman (ed.) *A Queer World*. New York: New York University Press, 526–43.

Gans, Herbert (1974) *Popular Culture and High Culture*. New York: Basic Books.

Gerbner, George, Larry Gross and William Melody (eds) (1973) *Communications Technology and Social Policy: Understanding the New 'Cultural Revolution'*. New York: Interscience Publications.

Gever, Martha (1990) 'The names we give ourselves', in Russell Ferguson, *et al.* (eds) *Out There: Maginalization and Contemporary Culture*. New York: New Museum of Contemporary Art.

Grant, Barry Keith (1991) 'Science fiction double feature: ideology in the cult film', in J.P. Telotte (ed.) *The Cult Movie Experience*. Austin, TX: University of Texas Press, 122–37.

Grant, Barry Keith and Jeanette Solniowski (eds) (2002) *Documenting the Documentary*. Detroit. MI: Wayne State University Press.

Graver, Gary (1993) *Working With Orson Welles* (DVD, Image Entertainment).

Greene, Naomi (1990) *Pier Paolo Pasolini: Cinema as Heresy*. Princeton, NJ: Princeton University Press.

Gripsrud, Jostein (1989) 'High Culture Revisited', *Cultural Studies*, 3(2), 194–207.

Grossberg, Lawrence (1992) 'Is there a fan in the house? The affective sensibility of fandom', in Lisa A. Lewis (ed.) *The Adoring Audience*. London: Routledge, 50–65.

Guins, Raiford (2005) 'Blood and black gloves on shiny discs: New media, old tastes, and the remediation of Italian horror films in the United States', in Steven Jay Schneider and Tony Williams (eds) *Horror International*. Detroit, MI: Wayne State University Press, 15–32.

Gwenllian-Jones, Sara and Roberta Pearson (eds) (2004) *Cult Television*. Minneapolis, MN: University of Minnesota Press.

Gwenllian-Jones, Sara (2007) *Cult-TV: Television, Cult, and the Fantastic*. Oxford: Oxford University Press.

Hall, Stuart and Tony Jefferson (eds) (1976) *Resistance Through Rituals: Youth Subculture in Post-War Britain*. London: Hutchinson.

Hall, Stuart (1980) 'Encoding/decoding', in Stuart Hall, Dorothy Hobson, Andrew Lowe and Paul Willis (eds) *Culture, Media, Language*. London: Hutchinson.

Hammond, Paul (ed.) (1991) *The Shadow and its Shadow: Surrealist Writings on the Cinema*. Edinburgh: Polygon.

Hansen, Miriam (1995) Early cinema, late Cinema: transformations of the public sphere, in Linda Williams (ed.) *Viewing Positions: Ways of Seeing Films*. New Brunswick: Rutgers University Press, 134–54.

Hantke, Steffen (ed.) *Caligari's Grandchildren: German Cinema of Fear Since 1945*. New York: Scarecrow Press.

Hantke, Steffen (2005) 'The dialogue with American popular culture in two German films about the serial killer', in Steven Jay Schneider and Tony Williams (eds) *Horror International*. Detroit, MI: Wayne State University Press, 56–79.

Harbord, Janet (2002) *Film Cultures*. London: Sage.

Harrington, Curtis (1952) 'Ghoulies and ghosties', *The Quarterly of Film Radio and Television*, 7(2), 191–202.

Harris, Cheryl and Alison Alexander (eds) (1998) *Theorizing Fandom: Fans, Subculture and Identity*. Creskill, NJ: Hampton Press.

Harvey, David (1989) *The Condition of Postmodernity*. London: Blackwell.

Hawkins, Joan (2000) *Cutting Edge: Art Horror and the Horrific Avant-Garde*. Minneapolis, MN: University of Minnesota Press.

Hawkins, Joan (2000) 'Sleaze mania, Euro-trash and high art: the place of European art films in American low culture', *Film Quarterly*, 53(2), 14–29.

Hawkins, Joan (2003) 'Midnight sex horror movies and the downtown avant-garde, in Mark Jancovich, Antonio Lazaro-Reboll, Julian Stringer and Andy Willis (eds) (2003) *Defining Cult Movies: the Cultural Politics of Oppositional Taste*. Manchester: Manchester University Press, 223–34.

Hebdige, Dick (1979) *Subculture and the Meaning of Style*. London: Routledge.

Hebdige, Dick (1988) 'In poor taste: Notes on pop', in *Hiding in the Light*. London: Routledge, 116–43.

Heffernan, Kevin (1989) Heterotextuality, unpublished paper, University of Wisconsin-Madison.

Heffernan, Kevin (2002) 'Inner-city exhibition and the genre film: Distributing *Night of the Living Dead* (1968), *Cinema Journal*, 41(3), 59–77.

Heffernan, Kevin (2004) *Ghouls, Gimmicks, and Gold: Horror Films and the American Movie Business, 1953–1968*. Durham, NC: Duke University Press.

Hentzi, Gary (1993) 'Little cinema of horrors', *Film Quarterly*, 46(3), 22–7.

Hill, Annette (1997) *Shocking Entertainment: Viewer Responses to Violent Movies*. Luton: University of Luton Press.

Hills, Matt (2000) 'Media fandom, neo-religiosity and cult(ural) studies', *The Velvet Light Trap*, 46, 73–84.

Hills, Matt (2002) *Fan Cultures*. London: Routledge.

Hills, Matt (2005) *The Pleasures of Horror*. London: Continuum.

Hills, Matt (2006) 'Realising the cult blockbuster: *Lord of the Rings* fandom and residual/emergent cult status in 'the mainstream', in Ernest Mathijs (ed.) *The Lord of the Rings: Popular Culture in Global Context*. London: Wallflower Press, 160–71.

Hoberman, J. and Jonathan Rosenbaum (1983) *Midnight Movies*. New York: Da Capo Press.

Hollows, Joanne (2003) 'The masculinity of cult' in Mark Jancovich, Antonio Lazaro-Reboll, Julian Stringer and Andy Willis (eds) *Defining Cult Movies: the Cultural Politics of Oppositional Taste*. Manchester: Manchester University Press, 35–53.

hooks, bell (1993) 'The oppositonal gaze: black female spectators', in Manthia Diawara (ed.) *Black American Cinema*. New York: Routledge, 288–302.

Horkheimer, Max and Theodor Adorno (1976) *Dialectic of the Enlightenment*. London: Continuum.

Hunt, Leon (2000) 'Han's Island revisited: *Enter the Dragon* as a transnational cult film', in

Xavier Mendik and Graeme Harper (eds) *Unruly Pleasures: The Cult Film and its Critics.* Guilford: FAB Press, 75–85.

Hunter, Jack (1998) *Eros in Hell: Sex, Blood and Madness in Japanese Cinema.* London: Creation Books.

Hunter, I.Q. (2000) 'Beaver Las Vegas: A fan boy's defence of *Showgirls*', in Xavier Mendik and Graeme Harper (eds) *Unruly Pleasures: The Cult Film and its Critics.* Guilford: FAB Press, 189–201.

Hunter, I.Q. (2006) 'Tolkien dirty', in Ernest Mathijs (ed.) *The Lord of the Rings: Popular Culture in Global Context.* London: Wallflower Press, 317–33.

Hunter, Jack (ed.) (2002) *The Bad Mirror: Cult Exploitation, and Underground Cinema.* London: Creation Books.

Huyssen, Andreas (1986) *After the Great Divide: Modernism, Mass Culture, Postmodernism.* Bloomington & Indianapolis, IN: Indiana University Press.

Jacobs, Lea (1992) 'The B film and the problem of cultural distinction', *Screen*, 33(1), 1–13.

Jakobson, Roman (1963) *Essais de linguistique générale.* Paris: Editions de Minuit.

Jameson, Fredric (1992) *The Geopolitical Aesthetic: Cinema and Space in the World System.* London: British Film Institute.

Jameson, Fredric (1992) *Signatures of the Visible.* New York: Routledge.

Jancovich, Mark (2002) 'Cult fictions: Cult movies, subcultural capital and the production of cultural distinctions', *Cultural Studies*, 16(2), 306–22.

Jancovich, Mark, Antonio Lazaro-Reboll, Julian Stringer and Andy Willis (eds) (2003) *Defining Cult Movies: the Cultural Politics of Oppositional Taste.* Manchester: Manchester University Press.

Jenkins, Henry (1989) '*Star Trek*: Rerun, reread, rewritten: fan writing as textual poaching', *Critical Studies in Mass Communication*, 5(2), 85–107.

Jenkins, Henry (1992) *Textual Poachers.* London: Routledge.

Jenkins, Henry (2000) 'Reception theory and audience research: The mystery of the vampire's kiss', in Christine Gledhill and Linda Williams (eds) *Reinventing Film Studies.* London: Arnold, 165–82.

Jenks, Carol (1992) 'The other face of death: Barbara Steele and La maschera del demonio', in Richard Dyer and Ginette Vincendeau (eds) *Popular European Cinema.* London: Routledge, 149–62.

Jensen, Joli (1992) 'Fandom as pathology: The consequences of characterization', in Lisa Lewis (ed.) *The Adoring Audience: Fan Culture and Popular Media.* London: Routledge, 9–29.

Jerslev, Anne (1992) 'Semiotics by instinct: "Cult film" as a signifying practice between film and audience', in Michael Skovmond and Kim Schroder (eds) *Media Cultures: Reappraising Transnational Media.* London: Routledge, 181–98.

Jerslev, Anne (1993) *Kultfilm & Filmkultur.* Copenhagen: Amanda.

Kadrey, Richard (1993) *Covert Culture Sourcebook.* New York: St Martin's Press.

Kael, Pauline (1960) 'Fantasies of the art-house audience', *Sight and Sound*, 31(1), 4–9, reprinted in 1965 in *I Lost it at the Movies.* Boston, MA: Little, Brown, 31–44.

Kant, Immanuel ([1788] 1997) *Critique of Practical Reason.* Cambridge: Cambridge University Press.

Kant, Immanuel ([1981] 1998) *Critique of Pure Reason.* London: Macmillan.

Kant, Immanuel ([1790] 2000) *Critique of the Power of Judgment.* Cambridge: Cambridge University Press.

Kapur, Jyotsna (2005) 'The return of history as horror: Onibaba and the atomic bomb', in Steven Jay Schneider and Tony Williams (eds) *Horror International.* Detroit, MI: Wayne State University Press, 83–98.

Kelly, Richard (2003) *The Donnie Darko Book*. London: Faber & Faber.

Kercher, Dona (2004) 'Violence, timing, and the comedy team in Alex De La Iglesia's *Muertos De Risa*', in Ernest Mathijs and Xavier Mendik (eds) *Alternative Europe: European Exploitation and Underground Cinema*. London: Wallflower Press, 53–63.

Kerekes, David and David Slater (1993) *Killing for Culture: An Illustrated History of Death Film from Mondo to Snuff*. London: Creation Books.

Kermode, Mark (2001) 'I was a teenage horror fan': Or, 'How I learned To stop worrying and love Linda Blair', in Martin Barker and Julian Petley (eds) *Ill Effects: The Media/Violence Debate* (2nd edn). London: Routledge, 126–34.

Kermode, Mark (2001) '. . . It was you and me; *Gimme Shelter*', *Sight and Sound*, 11(3), (March), 66.

Kilgore, John (1986) 'Sexuality and identity in *The Rocky Horror Picture Show*', in Donald Palumbo (ed.) *Eros in the Mind's Eye*. New York: Greenwood Press, 151–9.

King, Geoff (2007) *Donnie Darko*. London: Wallflower Press.

King, Steven (1982) *Danse Macabre*. New York: TimeWarner Books.

Kinkade, Patrick and Michael A. Katovich (1992) 'Toward a sociology of cult films: Reading *Rocky Horror*', *Sociological Quarterly*, 33(2), 191–209.

Kiste Nyberg, Amy (1998) *Seal of Approval: The History of the Comics Code*. Jackson, MS: University Press of Mississippi.

Klinger, Barbara (1997) 'Film history terminable and interminable: Recovering the past in reception studies', *Screen*, 38(2), 107–28.

Knee, Adam (1986) '*Liquid Sky, Repo Man*, and genre', *Wide Angle*, 8(3–4), 101–13.

Koven, Mikel (1999) 'You don't have to be filmish: The Toronto Jewish Film Festival', *Ethnologies*, 21(1), 115–32.

Koven, Mikel (2003) 'The terror tale: Urban legends and the slasher film', *Scope: An on-line journal of film studies*, available via: www.scope.nottingham.ac.uk/.

Koven, Mikel (2006) *La Dolce Morta: The Italian Giallo Film*. Metuchen: Scarecrow Press.

Kracauer, Siegfried (1926) 'The cult of distraction', in *The Mass Ornament*. Cambridge, MA: Harvard University Press, 323–8.

Kraszewski, Jon (2002) 'Recontextualizing the historical reception of Blaxploitation: articulations of class, black nationalism, and anxiety in the genre's advertisements', *The Velvet Light Trap*, 50, 48–61.

Krzywinska, Tanya (2006) *Sex and the Cinema*. London: Wallflower Press.

Kuchar, George (2000) 'Lips on latex: How to make a sex symbol', in Jack Stevenson (ed.) *Fleshpot: Cinema's Sexual Myth Makers and Taboo Breakers*. Manchester: Headpress, 205–14.

Kyrou, Ado (2005) [1952] *Le surréalisme au cinéma*. Paris: Editions Ramsay.

Lastra, James (1999) 'Why is this absurd picture here? Ethnology/equivocation/Buñuel', *October*, 89 (summer), 51–68.

Lavery, David (1991) 'Gnosticism and the cult film'; in J.P. Telotte (ed.) *The Cult Film Experience: Beyond All Reason*. Austin, TX: University of Texas Press, 187–200.

Levi, Heather (2001) 'Masked media: The adventures of Lucha Libre on the small screen', in Gilbert Joseph, Anne Rubenstein and Eric Zolov (eds) *Fragments of a Golden Age: The Politics of Culture in Mexico Since 1940*. Durham, NC: Duke University Press.

Levine, Lawrence (1988) *Highbrow Lowbrow: the Emergence of Cultural Hierarchy in America*. Cambridge (MA): Harvard University Press.

Lewis, Lisa (ed.) (1992) *The Adoring Audience*. London: Routledge.

Lippit, Akira Mizuta, Noel Burch, Chon Noriega, Ara Osterweil, Linda Williams, Eric Shaefer and Jeffrey Sconce (2003) 'Round table: Showgirls', *Film Quarterly*, 56(3), 32–46.

Lipsitz, George (1990) *Time Passages: Collective Memory and American Popular Culture*. Minneapolis, MN: University of Minneapolis Press.

Macdonald, Dwight (1960) 'Masscult and midcult', *Partisan Review* (spring), reprinted in Dwight Macdonald (1962) *Against the American Grain*. New York: Random House, 3–75.

MacDonald, Scott (1993) *Avant-Garde Film*. Cambridge: Cambridge University Press.

Macias, Patrick (2002) *Tokyscope: The Japanese Cult Film Companion*. San Francisco: Viz Media LCC.

Marchetti, Gina (1986) 'Subcultural studies and the film audience: Rethinking the film viewing context', in Bruce Austin (ed.) *Current Research in Film* (Vol. 2). Norwood, NJ: Ablex, 61–79.

Marx, Karl (1976) 'The fetishism of the commodity and its secret', in *Capital*(Vol. 1). London: Penguin, 163–77.

Mathijs, Ernest (2001) Deconstructing or reconstructing? Disney criticism and interduck', *Plateau: International Quarterly Bulletin on Animated Film*, 21(4), 16–20.

Mathijs, Ernest (2003) 'AIDS references in the critical reception of David Cronenberg: It may not be such a bad disease after all', *Cinema Journal*, 42(4), 29–45.

Mathijs, Ernest (2003) 'The making of a cult reputation: Topicality and controversy in the critical reception of shivers', in Mark Jancovich, Antonio Lazaro-Reboll, Julian Stringer and Andy Willis (eds) *Defining Cult Movies: the Cultural Politics of Oppositional Taste*. Manchester: Manchester University Press, 109–26.

Mathijs, Ernest (2004) 'Nobody is innocent: Cinema and sexuality in contemporary Belgian culture', *Social Semiotics*, 14(1), 85–101.

Mathijs, Ernest and Xavier Mendik (eds) (2004) *Alternative Europe: European Exploitation and Underground Cinema*. London: Wallflower Press.

Mathijs, Ernest (2005) 'Man bites dog and the critical reception of Belgian horror (in) cinema', in Steven Jay Schneider and Tony Williams (eds) *Horror International*. Detroit, MI: Wayne State University Press, 315–35.

Mathijs, Ernest (2005) 'Bad Reputations: The reception of trash cinema', *Screen*, 46(4), 451–72.

Mathijs, Ernest (ed.) (2006) *The Lord of the Rings: Popular Culture in Global Context*. London: Wallflower Press.

Mathijs, Ernest (2006) 'To die for: *Der Fan* and the reception of sexuality and horror in early 1980s Germany', in Steffen Hantke (ed.) *Caligari's Grandchildren: German Cinema of Fear Since 1945*. New York: Scarecrow Press, 129–43.

Mathijs, Ernest and Murray Pomerance (eds) (2006) *From Hobbits to Hollywood: Essays on Peter Jackson's Lord of the Rings*. New York/Amsterdam: Rodopi Press.

Mathijs, Ernest (2007) *The Cinema of David Cronenberg: From Baron of Gore to Cultural Hero*. London: Wallflower Press.

Mathijs, Ernest (2007) 'Benjamin Christensen', in Steven Jay Schneider (ed.), *501 Movie Directors*. New York: Quintet Books.

Mathijs, Ernest (2007) 'They're here! Special effects in the horror cinema of the 1970s and 80s', in Ian Conrich (ed.) *Horrorzone: The Cultural History of the Horror Film*. London: Verso.

Mathijs, Ernest and Xavier Mendik (eds) (forthcoming) *Peepshows*. London: Wallflower Press.

McCarthy, John (1984) *Splatter Movies*. New York: St Martin's Press.

McCarthy, Helen (1999) *Hayao Miyazaki: Master of Japanese Animation*. Berkeley, CA: Stone Bridge Press.

McCarthy, Soren (2003) *Cult Movies in Sixty Seconds*. London: Fusion Press.

McGilligan, Patrick (2000) 'Introduction', in *Film Crazy*. New York: St Martin's Griffin, 1–8.

McIlroy, Brian (2001) *Shooting to Kill: Filmmaking and the 'Troubles' in Northern Ireland*. Richmond, BC: Steveston Press.

McIlroy, Brian (2005) 'Irish horror: Neil Jordan and the Anglo-Irish gothic', in Steven Jay Schneider and Tony Williams (eds) *Horror International*. Detroit, MI: Wayne State University Press, 128–40.

McIlroy, Brian (ed.) (2007) *Genre and Cinema: Ireland and Transnationalism*. New York: Routledge.

McRobbie, Angela (1980) 'Settling accounts with subcultures: A feminist critique', *Screen*, 34 (spring), 37–49.

Medved, Michael and Harry Medved (1980) *The Golden Turkey Awards*. New York: Putnam.

Mendik, Xavier and Graeme Harper (eds) (2000) *Unruly Pleasures: The Cult Film and its Critics*. Guilford: FAB Press.

Mendik, Xavier and Graeme Harper (2000) The chaotic text and the sadean audience: Narrative transgressions of a contemporary cult film', in Xavier Mendik and Graeme Harper (eds) *Unruly Pleasures: The Cult Film and its Critics*. Guilford: FAB Press, 237–49.

Mendik, Xavier (ed.) (2002) *Shocking Cinema of the Seventies*. Hereford: Noir Publishing.

Mendik, Xavier and Steven Jay Schneider (eds) (2002) *Underground USA: Filmmaking Beyond the Hollywood Canon*. London: Wallflower Press.

Mendik Xavier (2004) *Menstrual Monsters: The Ginger Snaps Trilogy* (documentary, Hem Productions).

Merlock, Kathy (2000) 'Introduction: *Casablanca*: Popular film of the century', *Journal of Popular Film and Television*, 27(4), 2–4.

Merrick, Helen (1997) 'The readers feminism doesn't see: Feminist fans, critics, and science-fiction', in Deborah Cartmel, I.Q. Hunter, Heidi Kaye and Imelda Whelehan (eds) *Trash Aesthetics: Popular Culture and its Audience*. London: Pluto Press, 48–65.

Mes, Tom (2003) '*Agitator: The Cinema of Miike Takashi*. London: FAB Press.

Michaels, Scott and David Evans (2002) *Rocky Horror: From Concept to Cult*. London: Sanctuary Publishing Limited.

Milgram, Stanley (1974) *Obedience to Authority*. New York: Harper & Row.

Monaco, James (1979) *American Film Now*. New York: New American Library.

Morris, Gary (2000) 'Raging and flaming: Jack Smith in retrospect', *Bright Lights Film Journal*, 29 (July), www.brightlightsfilm.com/29/jacksmith.html.

Morton, Jim (ed.) (1986) *Incredibly Strange Movies*. San Francisco: Re/Search Press.

Napier, Susan (2001) *Anime from Akira to Princess Mononoke*. London: Palgrave.

Nayar, Sheila J. (2004) 'Invisible representation: The oral contours of a national popular cinema', *Film Quarterly*, 57(3), 13–23.

Needham, Gary (2002) 'Playing with genre: An introduction to the Italian *giall*', 2(11), 10, www.kinoeye.org.

Nelson, Alondra (ed.) (2005) Afrofuturism: *A Special Issue of Social Text*, 20(2).

Newitz, Annalee (1995) 'Magical girls and atomic bomb sperm: Japanese animation in America', *Film Quarterly*, 49(1).

Newitz, Annalee (2000) 'What makes things cheesy? Satire, multinationalism, and B-movies', *Social Text*, 18(2), 59–82.

Newman, Kim (1986) 'Thirty years in another town: The history of Italian exploitation', *Monthly Film Bulletin*, 624–6, 20–4, 51–5, 88–91.

Ng, Jenna (2005) 'Love in the time of transcultural fusion: Cinephilia, homage and *Kill Bill*', in Marijke De Valck and Malte Hagener (eds) *Cinephilia: Movies, Love and Memory*. Amsterdam: Amsterdam University Press, 65–81.

Nielsen, Bianca (2004) 'Something's wrong, like more than you being female: Transgressive sexuality and discourses of reproduction in *Ginger Snaps*', *Thirdspace*, 3(2), 55–69.

Orgeron, Marsha (2003) 'Making *It* in Hollywood: Clara Bow, fandom and consumer culture', *Cinema Journal*, 42(4), 76–97.

Osgerby, Bill (2003) 'Sleazy riders: Exploitation, "otherness", and transgression in the 1960s biker movie', *Journal of Popular Film & TV*, 31(3), 98–108.

O'Toole, Lawrence (1979) 'The cult of horror', *Maclean's*, 16 July, 46–7, 49–50.

Peary, Danny (1981) *Cult Movies*. New York: Delta Books.

Peary, Danny (1983) *Cult Movies 2*. New York: Delta Books.

Peary, Danny (1989) *Cult Movies 3*. London: Sidgwick & Jackson.

Peary, Danny (1991) *Cult Movie Stars*. New York: Simon & Schuster.

Penley, Constance (1986) 'Time travel, primal scene and the critical dystopia (on *Terminator* and *La Jetee*)', *Camera Obscura*, 15, 67–86.

Penley, Constance (1992) 'Feminism, psychoanalysis, and the study of popular culture', in Lawrence Grossberg, Cary Nelson and Paula Treichler (eds) *Cultural Studies*. New York: Routledge.

Peterson, Richard A. and Roger M. Kern (1996) 'Changing highbrow taste: From snob to omnivore', *American Sociological Review*, 61(5), 900–7.

Petley, Julian and Mark Kermode (1998) 'The censor and the state: The distributor's tale', *Sight and Sound*, 8(5), 14–18.

Petley, Julian (2000) ' "Snuffed Out": Nightmares in a trading standards officer's brain', in Xavier Mendik and Graeme Harper (eds) *Unruly Pleasures: The Cult Film and its Critics*. Guilford: FAB Press, 205–19.

Pevere, Geoff and Greg Dymond (1996) *Mondo Canuck*. Scarborough, ONT: Prentice-Hall.

Phillips, John (2001) 'Catherine Breillat's *Romance*: Hard core and the female gaze', *Studies in French Cinema*, 1(3), 133–40.

Pomerance, Murray (ed.) 2003 *Bad: Infamy, Darkness, Evil, and Slime on Screen*. New York: SUNYPress.

Pomerance, Murray (2005) *Johnny Depp Starts Here*. New Brunswick: Rutgers University Press.

Potamkin, Harry Allan (1977) 'Film cults' and 'Ritual of the movies', in Lewis Jacobs (ed.) *The Compound Cinema*. New York: Columbia University Press, 227–31.

Prawer, S.S. (1980) *Caligari's Children: the Film as Tale of Terror*. New York: Da Capo Books.

Puchalski, Steven (2002) *Slimetime: A Guide to Sleazy, Mindless Movies*. Manchester: Headpress.

Pullen, Kirsten (2006) '*The Lord of the Rings* online blockbuster fandom: Pleasure and commerce', in Ernest Mathijs (ed.) *The Lord of the Rings: Popular Culture in Global Context*. London: Wallflower Press, 172–88.

Radway, Janice (1984) *Reading the Romance: Women, Patriarchy and Popular Literature*. Chapel Hill, NC: University of North Carolina Press.

Ragas, Matthew and Bolivar Bueno (2002) *The Power of Cult Branding*. New York: Prima Venture/Random House.

Ray, Robert B. (1985) 'The culmination of classic Hollywood: *Casablanca*', in *A Certain Tendency of the Hollywood Cinema, 1930–1980*. Princeton, NJ: Princeton University Press, 89–112.

Ray, Robert B. (1985) 'The dissolution of the homogenous audience and Hollywood's response: Cult films, problem pictures, and inflation', in *A Certain Tendency of the Hollywood Cinema, 1930–1980*. Princeton, NJ: Princeton University Press, 129–52.

Ray, Robert B. (1993) 'Film studies/crisis/experimentation', *Film Criticism*, 17(2–3), 56–78.

Ray, Robert B. (2001) *How a Film Theory Got Lost and Other Mysteries in Cultural Studies*. Bloomington, IN: Indiana University Press.

Read, Jacinda (2003) 'The cult of masculinity', in Mark Jancovich, Antonio Lazaro-Reboll, Julian Stringer and Andy Willis (eds) *Defining Cult Movies: The Cultural Politics of Oppositional Taste*. Manchester: Manchester University Press, 54–70.

Rhodes, Gary (2003) 'Fantasmas de cine Mexicano: The 1930s Horror Cycle of Mexico', in Steven Schneider (ed.) *Fear Without Frontiers: Horror Cinema Across the Globe*. Guilford: FAB Press, 93–104.

Rich, B. Ruby (1999) 'Collision, catastrophe, celebration: The relationship between gay and lesbian film festivals and their publics', *GLQ*, 5(1), 79–84.

Richie, Donald (1999) *Akira Kurosawa*. Berkeley, CA: University of California Press.

Robbe-Grillet, Alain, Anthony Fragola and Roch C. Smith (1992) *The Erotic Dream Machine: Interviews with Alain Robbe-Grillet on His Films*. Carbondale, IL: Southern Illinois University Press.

Rosenbaum, Jonathan (1980) The *Rocky Horror* picture cult, *Sight and Sound*, 49(2), 79–80.

Ross, Andrew (1989) 'The uses of camp', in *No Respect: Intellectuals and Popular Culture*. New York: Routledge, 135–70.

Said, Edward (1978) *Orientalism*. New York: Vintage Books.

Salles, Walter (2003) 'Preface', in Alberto Elena and Maria Díaz López (eds) *The Cinema of Latin America*. London: Wallflower Press, xiii–xv.

Samuels, Stuart (1983) *Midnight Movies*. New York: Macmillan.

Sandler, Kevin (2001) 'The naked truth: *Showgirls* and the fate of the X/NC-17 rating', *Cinema Journal*, 40(3), 69–93.

Sanjek, David (1990) 'Fans' notes: The horror film fanzine', *Literature/Film Quarterly*, 18(3), 150–60.

Sargeant, Jack (1995) *Deathtripping: The Cinema of Transgression*. London: Creation Books.

Sarris, Andrew (1964) 'The farthest-out moviegoers', *Saturday Review*, 26 (December), 14–15.

Sarris, Andrew (1970) *Confessions of a Cultist: On the Cinema (1955–1969)*. New York: Simon & Schuster.

Saunders, Michael William (1998) 'Queer views from the outside: Damned and damned proud of it', in *Imps of the Perverse: Gay Monsters in Film*. Westport, CT: Praeger, 90–1.

Sayre, Nora (1979) 'Cult films', *Horizon*, September, 64–9.

Schaefer, Eric (1997) 'The obscene seen: Spectacle and transgression in postwar burlesque film', *Cinema Journal*, 36(2), 41–66.

Schaefer, Eric (1999) *Bold! Daring! Shocking! True! A History of Exploitation Films, 1919–1959*. Durham, NC: Duke University Press.

Schaefer, Eric (2002) 'Gauging a revolution: 16mm film and the rise of the pornographic feature', *Cinema Journal*, 41(3), 3–26.

Schneider, Steven (ed.) (2003) *Fear Without Frontiers: Horror Cinema Across the Globe*. Guilford: FAB Press.

Schneider, Steven (ed.) (2004) *New Hollywood Violence*. Manchester: Manchester University Press.

Schneider, Steven Jay (2004) 'The essential evil in/of *Eraserhead*', in Erica Sheen and Annette Davison (eds) *The Cinema of David Lynch: American Dreams, Nightmare Visions*. London: Wallflower Press, 5–18.

Schneider, Steven Jay and Tony Williams (eds) (2005) *Horror International*. Detroit, MI: Wayne State University Press.

Schonner, Johannes (2002) *Trashfilm Roadshows: Off the Beaten Track with Subversive Movies*. London: Headpress.

Sconce, Jeffrey (1989) Colonizing cinematic history: The cult of 'bad' cinema and the textuality of the bad film', masters thesis, University of Texas, Austin.

Sconce, Jeffrey (1993) 'Spectacles of death: Identification, reflexivity, and contemporary horror', in Jim Collins, Hilary Radner and Ava Preacher Collins (eds) *Film Theory Goes to the Movies*. New York: Routledge, 103–19.

Sconce, Jeffrey (1995) 'Trashing the academy: Taste, excess and an emerging politics of cinematic style', *Screen*, 36(4), 371–93.

Sconce, Jeffrey (2002) 'Irony, nihilism and the new American "smart" film', *Screen*, 43: 349–69.

Sexton, Jamie (2005) 'Alchemical transformations: The abstract visions of Harry Smith', *Senses of Cinema*, 36 (July–September), www.sensesofcinema.com.

Sexton, Jamie (2006) 'A cult film by proxy: *Space is the Place* and the Sun Ra mythos', *New Review of Film and Television Studies*, 4(3), 197–215.

Shaw, Deborah (2003) *Contemporary Cinema of Latin America*. New York: Continuum.

Shrum, Wesley (1991) 'Critics and publics: Cultural mediation in highbrow and popular performing arts', *American Journal of Sociology*, 97(2), 347–75.

Shrum, Wesley (1996) *Fringe and Fortune. Princeton: the Role of Critics in High and Popular Art*. Princeton, NJ: Princeton University Press.

Siegel, Mark (1980) '*The Rocky Horror Picture Show:* More than a lip service', *Science-Fiction Studies*, 7, 305–12.

Sigel, Lyn (ed.) (2005) *International Exposure: Perspectives on Modern European Pornography 1800–2000*. New Brunswick, NJ: University of Rutgers Press.

Simpson, Paul (2002) *The Rough Guide to Cult Television*. London: Rough Guide.

Simpson, Paul, Helen Rodiss and Michaela Bushell (eds) (2004) *The Rough Guide to Cult Movies*. London: Rough Guide.

Sitney, P. Adams (ed.) (1970) *The Film Culture Reader*. New York: Praeger.

Skal, David (1993) *The Monster Show: A Cultural History of Horror*. New York: W.W. Norton.

Smith, Clarissa (2007) *Women and Porn: Readers, Texts and Production*. Bristol: Intellect Books.

Smith, Iain Robert (2008) 'When Spiderman became Spider Babe', in Ernest Mathijs and Xavier Mendik (eds) *Peepshows*. London: Wallflower Press.

Smith, Jack (1963) 'The perfect filmic appositeness of Maria Montez', *Film Culture*, 27 (winter), 28–36.

Smythe, Dallas, Parker B. Lusk and Charles A. Lewis (1953) 'Portrait of an art-theater audience', *The Quarterly of Film, Radio, and Television*, 8 (fall), 28–50.

Sontag, Susan (1964) 'Notes on camp', in *Against Interpretation and Other Essays*. New York: Farrar, Strauss & Giroux, 275–92.

Sontag, Susan (1996) The Decay of Cinema', *New York Times Magazine* (25 February), 60–61.

Staiger, Janet (1985) 'The politics of film canons', *Cinema Journal*, 24(3), 4–23.

Staiger, Janet (1992) 'The logic of alternative readings: *A Star is Born*', in *Interpreting Films*. Princeton, NJ: Princeton University Press, 154–77.

Staiger, Janet (1992) 'With the compliments of the auteur: Art cinema and the complexities of its reading strategies', in *Interpreting Films*. Princeton, NJ: Princeton University Press, 178–95.

Staiger, Janet (1993) 'Taboos and totems: Cultural meanings of *The Silence of the Lambs*', in Jim Collins, Hilary Radner and Ava Preacher Collins (eds) *Film Theory Goes to the Movies*. London: Routledge, 142–54.

Staiger, Janet (2000) *Perverse Spectators: The Practices of Film Reception*. New York: New York University Press.

Staiger, Janet (2000) 'Hitchcock in Texas: Intertextuality in the face of blood and gore', in *Perverse Spectators: the Practices of Film Reception*. New York: New York University Press, 179–87.

Staiger, Janet (2000) 'Finding community in the early 1960s: Underground cinema and sexual politics', in *Perverse Spectators: The Practices of Film Reception*. New York: New York University Press, 125–60.

Staiger, Janet (2005) 'Viewers of stars, cult media, and avant-garde', in *Media Reception Studies*. New York: New York University Press, 129.

Stevenson, Jack (ed.) (2000) *Fleshpot: Cinema's Sexual Myth Makers and Taboo Breakers*. Manchester: Headpress.

Stevenson, Jack (2003) *Land of a Thousand Balconies: Discoveries and Confessions of a B-Movie Archaeologist*. Manchester: Critical Vision/Headpress.

Stojanova, Christina (2004) 'Mise-en-scènes of the impossible: Soviet and Russian horror films', in Ernest Mathijs and Xavier Mendik (eds) *Alternative Europe: European Exploitation and Underground Cinema*. London: Wallflower Press, 90–105.

Stolnitz, Jerome (1960) *Aesthetics and Philosophy of Art Criticism: a Critical Introduction*. Boston, MA: Riverside Press.

Stone, Rob (2002) *Spanish Cinema*. Harlow: Longman.

Stringer, Julian (2001) 'Global cities and the international film festival economy', in Mark Shiel and Tony Fitzmaurice (eds) *Cinema and the City: Film and Urban Societies in a Global Context*. London: Blackwell, 134–44.

Strout, Andrea (1981) 'In the midnight hour', *Film Comment*, 6(4), 34–7.

Studlar, Gaylin (1991) 'Midnight s/excess: Cult figurations of femininity and the perverse', *Journal of Popular Film and Television*, 17(1), 2–14.

Syder, Andrew and Dolores Tierney (2005) 'Importation/mexploitation, or how a crime-fighting, vampire-slaying Mexican wrestler almost found himself in an Italian sword-and-sandals epic', in Steven Jay Schneider and Tony Williams (eds) *Horror International*. Detroit, MI: Wayne State University Press, 33–55.

Szwed, John F. (1998) *Space is the Place: A Biography of Sun Ra*. New York: Da Capo Press.

Taylor, Greg (1999) *Artists in the Audience: Cults, Camp, and American Film Criticism*. Princeton, NJ: Princeton University Press.

Taylor, Helen (1989) *Scarlett's Women: Gone with the Wind and its Female Fans*. New Brunswick, NJ: Rutgers University Press.

Telotte, J.P. (1991) 'Beyond all reason: The nature of the cult', in J.P. Telotte (ed.) *The Cult Film Experience: Beyond All Reason*. Austin, TX: University of Texas Press, 5–17.

Telotte, J.P. (ed.) (1991) *The Cult Film Experience: Beyond All Reason*. Austin, TX: University of Texas Press.

Telotte, J.P. (2001) '*The Blair Witch Project*: Film and the internet', *Film Quarterly*, 54(3), 32–9.

Thompson, Kristin (1977) 'The concept of cinematic excess', *Ciné-Tracts*, 1(2), 54–63, reprinted in Leo Braudy and Marshall Cohen (eds) (2004) *Film Theory and Criticism* (6th edn). Oxford: Oxford University Press, 513–24.

Thompson, Kristin (1990) 'Dr. Caligari at the Folies-Bergere', in Mike Budd (ed.) *The Cabinet of Dr Caligari: Texts, Contexts, Histories*. New Brunswick, NJ: Rutgers University Press, 121–69.

Thompson, Stacy (2004) 'Punk cinema', *Cinema Journal*, 43(2), 47–66.

Tierney, Dolores and Andrew Syder (2004) 'José Mojica Marins and the cultural politics of marginality in Third World film criticism', *Journal of Latin American Cultural Studies*, 13(1), 63–78.

Tohill, Cathal and Pete Tombs (1995) *Immoral Tales: European Sex and Horror Movies 1956–1984*. New York: St Martin's Press.

Tombs, Pete (1997) *Mondo Macabro: Weird and Wonderful Cinema Around the World*. New York: St Martin's Griffin.

Triana-Toribio, Núria (2003) *Spanish National Cinema*. New York: Routledge.

Tulloch, John and Manuel Alvarado (1983) *Dr Who: The Unfolding Text*. London: Macmillan.

Twitchell, James (1983) '*Frankenstein* and the anatomy of horror', *Georgia Review*, 37(1), 41–78.

Tyler, Parker (1969) *Underground Film*. London: Pelican Books.

Tyler, Parker (1970) 'Orson Welles, and the big experimental film cult, in P. Adams Sitney (ed.) *The Film Culture Reader*. New York: Open Square Press, 376–86.

Vale, V., Andrea Juno and Jim Morton (eds) (1986) *Incredibly Strange Films*. San Francisco: RE/search Publications.

Van Extergem, Dirk (2004) 'A report on the Brussels International Festival of Fantastic Film', in Ernest Mathijs and Xavier Mendik (eds) *Alternative Europe: Eurotrash and Exploitation Cinema Since 1945*. London: Wallflower Press, 216–27.

Varese, Federico (2006) 'The secret history of Japanese cinema: The Yakuza movies', *Global Crime*, 7(1), 105–24.

Vatnsdal, Caelum (2004) *They Came from Within: A History of Canadian Horror Cinema*. Winnipeg: Arbeiter Ring Publishing.

Vogel, Amos (1974) *Film as a Subversive Art*. New York: Random House.

Voloshinov, V.N. (1973) *Marxism and the Philosophy of Language*. New York: Seminar Press.

Wagstaff, Christopher (1992) 'A forkful of Westerns: Industry, audiences and the Italian Western', in Richard Dyer and Ginette Vincendeau (eds) *Popular European Cinema*. London: Routledge, 245–61.

Waller, Gregory, A. (1991) 'Midnight movies, 1980–1985: A market study', in J.P. Telotte (ed.) *The Cult Film Experience*. Austin, TX: University of Texas Press, 167–86.

Wander, Brandon (1975) 'Black dreams: The fantasy and ritual of black films', *Film Quarterly*, 29(1), 2–11.

Warner, Michael (2002) *Publics and Counterpublics*. New York: Zone Books.

Watson, Ben (1998) *Art, Class and Cleavage*. London: Interlink.

Watson, Paul (1997) 'There's no accounting for taste: Exploitation cinema and the limits of theory', in Deborah Cartmell, I.Q. Hunter, Heidi Kaye and Imelda Whelehan (eds) *Trash Aesthetics: Popular Culture and its Audience*. London: Pluto Press, 66–83.

Weaver, James B. III and Ron Tamborini (eds) (1996) *Horror Films: Current Research on Audience Preferences and Reactions*. Mahwah, NJ: Lawrence Erlbaum Associates.

Weinstock, Jeffrey (2007) *The Rocky Horror Picture Show*. London: Wallflower Press.

Weisser, Thomas (1997) *Asian Cult Cinema*. New York: Boulevard Books.

Weldon, Michael (1983) *The Psychotronic Encyclopedia of Film*. New York: Ballantine.

White, Patricia (1999) 'On exhibitionism – queer publicity: A dossier on lesbian and gay film festivals', *GLQ*, 5(1), 73–8.

Wilensky, Harold (1964) 'Mass society and mass culture: Interdependence or independence?' *American Sociological Review*, 29, 173–97.

Williams, Linda (1994) 'Learning to scream', *Sight and Sound*, 4(12), 14–17.

Williams, Linda (1999) *Hard Core: Power, Pleasure, and the Frenzy of the Visible*. Berkeley, CA: University of California Press.

Williamson, Milly (2005) *The Lure of the Vampire from Bram Stoker to Buffy*. London: Wallflower Press.

Willis, Andrew (2005) 'The Spanish horror film as subversive text', in Steven Jay Schneider and Tony Williams (eds) *Horror International*. Detroit, MI: Wayne State University Press, 163–79.

Wood, Robin (1979) 'An introduction to the American horror film', in Andrew Britton, Robin Wood, Richard Lippe and Tony Williams (eds) *The American Nightmare*, reprinted in Bill Nichols (ed.) (1985) *Movies and Methods, Vol. II*. Berkeley, CA: University of California Press, 195–220.

Wood, Robin (1986) *Hollywood from Vietnam to Reagan*. New York: Columbia University Press.

Wood, Robin (1993) 'Critical positions and the end of civilization; or, a refusal to join the club', *Film Criticism*, 17(2–3), 79–92.

Wu, Harmony (2003) 'Trading in horror, cult, and matricide: Peter Jackson's phenomenal bad taste and New Zealand fantasies of inter/national cinematic success', in Mark Jancovich, Antonio Lazaro-Reboll, Julian Stringer and Andy Willis (eds) *Defining Cult Movies: the Cultural Politics of Oppositional Taste*. Manchester: Manchester University Press, 84–108.

Young, Suzie (2005) 'Snapping up schoolgirls: Legitimation crisis in recent Canadian horror', in Steven Jay Schneider and Tony Williams (eds) *Horror International*. Detroit, MI: Wayne State University Press, 235–56.

Zillmann, Dolf and Jennings Bryant (eds) (1989) *Pornography: Research Advances and Policy Considerations*. New York: Lawrence Erlbaum.

Zilzer, Gyula (1947) 'Remembrances of Jean Vigo', *Hollywood Quarterly*, 3(2), 125–8.

Zimbardo, Philip (1971) 'The power and pathology of imprisonment', *Congressional Record* (Serial No. 15, 25 October), hearings before subcommittee No. 3 of the Committee on the Judiciary, House of Representatives, Ninety-Second Congress, *First Session on Corrections, Part II, Prisons, Prison Reform and Prisoner's Rights: California*. Washington, DC: US Government Printing Office.

Zimbardo, Philip (1985) *Cults Go to High School: A Theoretical and Empirical Analysis of the Initial Stage in the Recruitment Process*. Washington: American Family Foundation.

Zimmer, Jacques (ed.) (2002) *Le Cinema X*. Paris: La Muscardine.

Zizek, Slavoj (1991) *Lookin Awry: An Introduction to Jacques Lacan through Popular Culture*. Cambridge, MA: MIT Press.

Selective cult directors bibliography

Kenneth Anger

Brook, Vincent (2006) 'Puce modern moment: camp, postmodernism and the films of Kenneth Anger', *Journal of Film and Video*, 58(4), 3–15.

Brottman, Mikita, Carel Rowe and Anna Powell (2001) 'Moonchild: The films of Kenneth Anger', in Jack Hunter (ed.) *Persistence of Vision*, Vol. 1. London: Creation Books.

Frumkes, Roy (1997) 'Look back with Kenneth Anger', *Films in Review*, 48(1/2), 16–25.

Huag, Kate (1996) 'An interview with Kenneth Anger', *Wide Angle*, 18(4), 74–92.

Hutchison, A.L. (2004) *Kenneth Anger: A Demonic Visionary*. London: Black Dog Publishing.

Rowe, Carel (1974) 'Illuminating Lucifer', *Film Quarterly*, 27(4), 24–33.

Dario Argento

Cooper, L.A. (2005) 'The indulgence of critique: relocating the sadistic voyeur in Dario Argento's *Opera*', *Quarterly Review of Film and Video*, 22(1), 63–72.

Gallant, Chris (ed.) (2001) *Art of Darkness: The Cinema of Dario Argento*. London: FAB Press.

Hunt, Leon (2000) 'A (sadistic) night at the opera', in Ken Gelder (ed.) *The Horror Reader*. London: Routledge.

Hutchings, Peter (2003) 'The Argento effect', in Mark Jancovich, Antonio Lazaro Reboll, Julian Stringer and Andy Willis (eds) *Defining Cult Movies: The Cultural Politics of Oppositional taste*. Manchester: Manchester University Press, 127–41.

Jones, Alan (1982) 'Cinema profile: Dario Argento', *Cinema*, 5 (September), 36–42.

Jones, Alan (2004) *Profondo Argento*. London: FAB Press.

Kitson, N. (2003) 'Silver and red: the films of Dario Argento', *Film Ireland*, 94 (September/October), 16–18.

Knee, Adam (1996) 'Gender, genre, Argento', in Barry Keith Grant (ed.) *The Dread of Difference: Gender and The Horror Film*, Austin, TX: University of Texas Press.

McDonagh, Maitland (1987) 'Broken mirrors/broken minds: The dark dreams of Dario Argento', *Film Quarterly*, 41(2), 2–13.

McDonagh, Maitland (1991) *Broken Mirrors/Broken Minds: The Dark Dreams of Dario Argento*. London: Sun Tavern Fields.

Mendik, Xavier (2001) *Tenebrae*. Trowbridge: Flicks Books.

Kathryn Bigelow

Jermyn, Deborah and Sean Redmond (eds) (2002) *The Cinema of Kathryn Bigelow: Hollywood Transgressor*. London: Wallflower Press.

Karnicky, Jeff (1998) 'Georges Bataille and the visceral cinema of Kathryn Bigelow', *Enculturation*, 2(1), online at http://enculturation.gmu.edu/2_1/karnicky.html.

Lane, Christina (1998) 'From *The Loveless* to *Point Break*: Kathryn Bigelow's trajectory in action', *Cinema Journal*, 37(4), 59–81.

Rascaroli, Laura (1997) 'Steel in the gaze: On POV and the discourse of vision in Kathryn Bigelow's Cinema', *Screen*, 38(3).

Tod Browning

Brottman, Mikita (1997) '*Freaks*', in *Offensive Films: Towards an Anthropology of Cinema Vomitif*. Westport, CT: Greenwood Press.

Hawkins, Joan (1996) ' "One of us": Tod Browning's *Freaks*', in Rosemarie Garland Thomson (ed.) *Freakery: Cultural Spectacles of the Extraordinary Body*. New York: New York University Press, 265–76.

Herzogenrath, Bernd (2002) 'Join the United Mutations: Tod Browning's Freaks', *Post Script: Essays in Film & the Humanities*, 21(3), 8–19.

Herzogenrath, Bernd (ed.) (2006) *The Films of Tod Browning*. London: Black Dog Publishing.

Skal, David J. and Elias Savada (1995) *Dark Carnival: The Secret World of Tod Browning, Hollywood's Master of the Macabre*. New York: Doubleday.

Luis Buñuel

Abel, Richard (1984) '*Un chien andalou*', in *French Cinema: The First Wave*. Princeton, NJ: Princeton University Press, 480–5.

Buñuel, Luis (1984) *My Last Sigh*. New York: Vintage Books.

Edwards, Gwynne (1982) *The Discreet Art of Luis Buñuel: A Reading of His Films*. London: Boyars.

Evans, Peter W. (1995) *The Films of Luis Buñuel: Subjectivity & Desire*. New York: Clarendon Press.

Jones, Julie (2003) 'Long live death! The end of revolution in Luis Buñuel's *The Phantom of Liberty*', *Cinema Journal*, 42(4), 63–75.

Lyon, Elisabeth, H. (1973) 'Luis Bunuel: The process of dissociation in three films', *Cinema Journal*, 13(1), 45–8.

Mellen, Joan (ed.) (1978) *The World of Luis Buñuel: Essays in Criticism*. Oxford: Oxford University Press.

Vigo, Jean (1932) '*Un chien andalou*', in Luis Bunuel and Salvador Dali, *Un Chien Andalou*. London: Faber & Faber, xxv–xxvi.

Tim Burton

Hanke, Ken (1992) 'Tim Burton' [part one of two], *Films in Review*, 43(11/12), 374–81.
Hanke, Ken (1993) 'Tim Burton' [part two of two], *Films in Review*, 44(1/2), 40–8.
Newman, Kim (2000) 'The cage of reason', *Sight and Sound*, 10(1), 14–16.
Salisbury, Mark (ed.) (2006) *Burton on Burton* (2nd edn). London: Faber & Faber.
Woods, Paula (ed.) (2002) *Tim Burton: A Child's Garden of Nightmares*. London: Plexus.
Woof, William (1998) 'In praise of Tim Burton: finding the masterpiece in *Mars Attacks*', *Kinema*, 9 (spring), 57–72.

Donald Cammell

Chang, Chris (1996) 'Cinema, sex, magick: The films of Donald Cammell', *Film Comment*, 32(4), 14–19, 83.
Le Cain, Maximilian (2001) 'Donald Cammell's *Wild Side*', *Film West*, 44 (1 July), 46–7.
Libin, R.J. (1972) 'Don Cammell: Performance pluperfect', *Interview*, 23 (1 July), 10–12, 43.
Rigby, J. (2000) 'Demon seeds: The haunted screen of Donald Cammell', *StarBurst*, 265 (1 September), 60–3.
Umland, Rebecca and Sam Umland (2006) *Donald Cammell: A Life on the Wild Side*. Godalming: FAB Press.

Larry Cohen

Mac Cárthaig, L. (2002) 'Cohen underground', *Film Ireland*, 88 (September/October), 36–8.
Williams, Tony (1983) 'Cohen on Cohen', *Sight and Sound*, 53(1), 21–5.
Williams, Tony (1997) *Larry Cohen: The Radical Allegories of an Independent Filmmaker*. London: McFarland.
Wood, Robin (1978) 'Gods and monsters', *Film Comment*, 14(5), 19–25.

Roger Corman

Corman, Roger, with Jim Jerome (2000) *How I Made a Hundred Movies in Hollywood and Never Lost a Dime*. New York: Random House.
Gray, Beverly (2000) *Roger Corman: An Unauthorized Life*. New York: Thunder's Mouth Press.
Hillier, Jim and A. Lipstadt (eds) (1981) *Roger Corman's New World*. London: BFI.
Hillier, Jim and A. Lipstadt (1986) 'The economics of independence: Roger Corman and New World Pictures 1970–1980', *Movie*, 31/2 (winter), 43–53.
Naha, Ed (1982) *The Films of Roger Corman: Brilliance on a Budget*. New York: Arco Publishing.
Rayner, Jonathan (2000) 'The cult film, Roger Corman, and *The Cars That Ate Paris*', in Xavier Mendik and Graeme Harper (eds) *Unruly Pleasures: The Cult Film and its Critics*. Guilford: FAB Press, 221–33.

Wes Craven

Karlyn, Kathleen Rowe (2003) '*Scream*, popular culture, and feminism's third wave: "I'm not my mother" ', *Genders*, 38, online via www.genders.org.

Lowenstein, Adam (2005) *Shocking Representation: Historical Trauma, National Cinema and the Modern Horror Film*. New York: Columbia University Press.

Robb, B.J. (1998) *Screams and Nightmares: The Films of Wes Craven*. London: Titan Books.

Rockoff, Adam (2002) *Going to Pieces: The Rise and Fall of the Slasher Film, 1978–1986*. Jefferson, NC: McFarland & Company.

David Cronenberg

Beard, William (1994) 'The Canadianess of David Cronenberg', *Mosaic*, 27(2), 113–33.

Beard, William (2006) *The Artist as Monster: The Cinema of David Cronenberg*. Toronto: University of Toronto Press.

Conrich, Ian (2000) 'An aesthetic sense: Cronenberg and neo-horror film culture', in Michael Grant (ed.) *The Modern Fantastic: The Films of David Cronenberg*. Trowbridge: Flicks Books, 35–49.

Handling, Piers (ed.) (1983) *The Shape of Rage: the Films of David Cronenberg*. Toronto, Academy of Canadian Cinema- General Publishing Co.

Hantke, Steffen (2004) 'Spectacular optics: The deployment of special effects in David Cronenberg's films', *Film Criticism*, 29(2), 34–52.

Mathijs, Ernest (2008) *The Cinema of David Cronenberg: From Baron of Gore to Cultural Hero*. London: Wallflower Press.

Mathijs, Ernest (2003) 'AIDS references in the critical reception of David Cronenberg: it may not be such a bad disease after all', *Cinema Journal*, 42(4), 29–45.

Rodley, Chris (ed.) (1997) *Cronenberg on Cronenberg* (2nd edn). London: Faber & Faber.

Jesús Franco

De Mendoza, Javier and Javiera Figueroa (1998) 'Expressionist by vocation: An interview with Jesús Franco', *Filmfax*, 67 (1 June), 96–9.

Mendik, Xavier (1997) 'Perverse bodies and profane texts: Processes of sadean "mixture" in the films of Jesús Franco', in Andy Black (ed.) *Necronomicon: Book Two*. London: Creation Books.

Pavlovic, Tatjana (2003) 'Transgressive bodies of the other Franco', in Tatjana Pavlovic (ed.) *Despotic Bodies and Transgressive Bodies: Spanish Culture from Francisco Franco to Jesús Franco*. New York: State University of New York Press.

Tohill, Cathall and Pete Tombs (1995) 'The labyrinth of sex: The films of Jesús Franco', in Cathall Tohill and Pete Tombs, *Immoral Tales: Sex and Horror Cinema in Europe 1956–1984* (2nd edn). London: Titan Books.

Lucio Fulci

Connolly, William (1996) 'Two more departed: Lucio Fulci', *Spaghetti Cinema*, 65 (August), 26–47.

Grant, Michael (2004) 'Fulci's waste land: Cinema, horror and the abominations of Hell', *Film Studies*, 5 (winter), 30–8, online via http://journals.mup.man.ac.uk/cgi-bin/pdfdisp/MUPpdf/FSS/V5I0/050030.pdf.

McCloy, S. (1999) 'Don't torture a film director', *Film Ireland*, 73 (October/November), 42.

Schlockoff, Rob (1982) 'Lucio Fulci', interviews translated from the French by Frederic Levy, *Starburst*, 48 (August): 51–5.

Thrower, Stephen (1999) *Beyond Terror: The Films of Lucio Fulci*. Godalming: FAB Press.

Terry Gilliam

Christie, Ian (ed.) (1999) *Gilliam On Gilliam*. London: Faber & Faber.

Cohen, Alain, J.J. (2003) '*12 Monkeys, Vertigo* and *La Jetée*: Postmodern mythologies and cult films', *New Review of Film and Television*, 1(1), 149–64.

Sterritt, David and Lucille Rhodes (2004) *Terry Gilliam: Interviews*. Jackson, MS: University of Mississippi Press.

Taylor, Rumsey (2003) 'Terry Gilliam', *Senses of Cinema*, online via www.sensesofcinema.com/contents/directors/03/gilliam.html .

Wheeler, Ben (2005) 'Reality is what you can get away with: Fantastic imaginings, rebellion and control in Terry Gilliam's *Brazil*', *Critical Survey*, 17(1).

Werner Herzog

Bachmann, Gideon (1977) 'The man on the volcano: A portrait of Werner Herzog', *Film Quarterly*, 31(1), 2–10.

Bissell, Tom (2006) 'The secret mainstream: Contemplating the mirages of Werner Herzog', *Harper's Magazine*, 313(1879), 69–78.

Carroll, Noel (1998) 'Herzog, presence and paradox', in *Interpreting the Moving Image*. Cambridge: Cambridge University Press, 284–99.

Corrigan, Timothy (1990) *The Films of Werner Herzog*. New York: Routledge.

Cronin, Paul (ed.) (2003) *Herzog on Herzog*. London: Faber & Faber.

Peter Jackson

Alemany-Galway, Mary (2006) 'Peter Jackson as a postcolonial filmmaker: National cinema and Hollywood genres', *Post Script*, 25(2), 31–3.

Pryor, Ian (2003) *Peter Jackson: From Prince of Splatter to Lord of the Rings*. Auckland: Random House.

Watson, Chris (1994) 'If Michel Foucault had seen Peter Jackson's *Heavenly Creatures*', *New Zealand Journal of Media Studies*, 1(2), 14–27.

Woods, Paul (ed.) (2005) *Peter Jackson: From Gore to Mordor*. London: Plexus.

Alejandro Jodorowsky

Cobb, Ben (2007) *Anarchy and Alchemy: The Films of Alejandro Jodorowsky*. New York: Creation Books.

Jodorowsky, Alejandro, Sergio Guzik, Joanne Pottlitzer and Sandy MacDonald (1970) 'A Mass changes me more: An interview with Alexandro Jodorowsky', *The Drama Review: TDR*, 14(2), 70–6.

Keesey, Pam (2003) 'Madmen, visionaries and freaks: The films of Alejandro Jodorowsky', in Steven Schneider (ed.) *Fear Without Frontiers: Horror Cinema Across the Globe*. Godalming: FAB Press.

Trevino, Jesus Salvador (1979) 'The new Mexican cinema', *Film Quarterly*, 32(3), 26–37.

Harry Kümel

Kümel, Harry (2004) 'Preface: Interview with Harry Kümel', in Ernest Mathijs (ed.) *The Cinema of the Low Countries*. London: Wallflower Press, xiii–xviii.

Mathijs, Ernest (2004) '*Les lèvres rouges/Daughters of Darkness*', in Ernest Mathijs (ed.) *The Cinema of the Low Countries*. London: Wallflower Press, 1–13.

Mathijs, Ernest (2005) 'Bad reputations: The reception of trash cinema', *Screen*, 46(4), 451–72.

Silver, Anthony and James Ursini (2004) *The Vampire Film: From Nosferatu to Interview with the Vampire* (3rd edn). Pompton Plains, NY: Limelight Editions.

Soren, David (1979) *Unreal Reality: The Cinema of Harry Kümel*. Columbia, MO: Lucas Brothers.

Zimmerman, Bonnie (1996) '*Daughters of Darkness*: The lesbian vampire on film', in B.K. Grant (ed.) *The Dread of Difference: Gender and the Horror Film*. Austin, TX: University of Texas Press.

David Lynch

Chion, Michel (2006) *David Lynch* (2nd edn), translated from the French by Robert Julian. London: BFI Publishing.

Clarke, Roger (2007) 'Daydream believer: David Lynch', *Sight and Sound*, 17(3), 16–20.

French, Sean (1987) 'The heart of the cavern', *Sight and Sound*, 56(2), 101–4.

McGowan, Todd (2004) 'Lost on Mulholland Drive: navigating David Lynch's panegyric to Hollywood', *Cinema Journal*, 43(2), 67–89.

Rodley, Chris (ed.) (2005) *Lynch on Lynch* (2nd edn). London: Faber & Faber.

Sheen, Erica and Annette Davison (eds) (2003) *The Cinema of David Lynch: American Dreams, Nightmare Visions*. London: Wallflower Press.

Radley Metzger

Corliss, Richard (1973) 'Radley Metzger: aristocrat of the erotic', *Film Comment*, 9(1), 18–29.

Morris, Gary (1998) 'Seduction: thoughts on Radley Metzger', *Bright Lights Film Journal*, 21, online via www/brightlightsfilm.com.

Turan, Kenneth and Stephen Zito (1974) 'An interview with Radley Metzger', in K. Turan and S.F. Zito, *Sinema: American Pornographic Films and the People Who Make Them*. New York: Praeger.

Williams, Linda (1999) *Hard Core: Power, Pleasure, and the 'Frenzy of the Visible'* (2nd edn). Berkeley, CA: California University Press.

Russ Meyer

Crane, Jonathan (2000) 'A lust for life: The cult film of Russ Meyer', in Xavier Mendik and Graeme Harper (eds) *Unruly Pleasures: The Cult Film and its Critics*. Guilford: FAB Press, 87–101.

Fischer, Craig (1992) '*Beyond The Valley of the Dolls* and the exploitation genre', *Velvet Light Trap*, 30 (fall), 18–33.

Frasier, David K. (1997) *Russ Meyer: The Life and Films – A Biography and a Comprehensive Illustrated and Annotated Filmography and Bibliography* (2nd edn). Jefferson, NC: McFarland & Company.

McDonough, Jimmy (2006) *Big Bosoms and Square Jaws: The Biography of Russ Meyer* (2nd edn). London: Vintage.

Stringer, Julian (1997) 'Exposing intimacy in Russ Meyer's *Motorpsycho!* and *Faster Pussycat! Kill! Kill!*', in S. Cohan and I.R. Hark (eds) *The Road Movie Book*. London: Routledge.

Woods, Paula (ed.) (2004) *The Very Breast of Russ Meyer*. London: Plexus.

Takashi Miike

Daniel, Rob, Dave Wood and Julien Fronfrède (2003) 'Pain threshold: The cinema of Takashi Miike, in S.J. Schneider (ed.) *Fear Without Frontiers: Horror Cinema Across the Globe.* Godalming: FAB Press.

Ko, Mika (2006) 'The break-up of the national body: Cosmetic multiculturalism and the films of Miike Takashi', in Valentina Vitali and Paul Willemen (eds) *Theorising National Cinema.* London: BFI Publishing.

Rayns, Tony (2000) 'This gun for hire', *Sight and Sound,* 10(5), 30–2.

Williams, Tony (2004) 'Takashi Miike's cinema of outrage', *CineAction!,* 64 (1 October), 54–62.

Paul Morrissey

Hawkins, Joan (2000) *Cutting Edge: Art-Horror and the Horrific Avant-Garde.* Minneapolis, MN: Minnesota University Press.

MacCormack, Patricia (2003) 'Italian peversions', *Kinoeye,* 3(8), online via www.kinoeye.org.

Tyler, Parker (1995) *Underground Film: A Critical History* (2nd edn). Cambridge, MA: Da Capo Books.

Yacowar, Maurice (1993) *The Films of Paul Morrissey.* Cambridge: Cambridge University Press.

Vincenzo Natali

Kunkle, Shelia (2000) 'Lacan's life, the universe, and Vincenzo Natali's *Cube',* *American Imago,* 57(3), 281–97.

Monk, Katherine (2002) *Weird Sex and Snowshoes, and Other Canadian Film Phenomena.* Vancouver: Raincoast Books, 223–4.

Young, Suzie (2005) 'Snapping up schoolgirls: Legitimation crisis in recent Canadian horror', in Steven Jay Schneider and Tony Williams (eds) *Horror International.* Detroit, MI: Wayne State University Press, 235–256.

Jean Rollin

Bird, Daniel (1996) 'Fascination – Jean Rollin: cinematic poet', in A. Black (ed.) *Necronomicon: Book One.* London: Creation Books.

Black, Andy (1996) 'Clocks, seagulls, Romeo & Juliet – surrealism Rollin style', in Andy Black (ed.) *Necronomicon: Book One.* London: Creation Books.

Odell, Colin and Mitch Le Blanc (2004) 'Jean Rollin: le sang d'un poète du cinema', in E. Mathijs and X. Mendik (eds) *Alternative Europe: Eurotrash and Exploitation Cinema Since 1945.* London: Wallflower Press.

Tohill, Cathall and Pete Tombs (1995) 'Back to the beach: The films of Jean Rollin', in C. Tohill and P. Tombs, *Immoral Tales: European Sex and Horror Movies 1956–1984.* New York: St Martin's Press.

George Romero

Dillard, R.H.W. (1988) '*Night of the Living Dead*: it's not like just a wind that's passing through', in Gregory A. Waller (ed.) *American Horrors: Essays on the Modern American Horror Film.* Champaign, IL: Illinois University Press.

Grant, Barry Keith (1996) 'Taking back the *Night of the Living Dead*: George Romero, feminism, and the horror film', in B.K. Grant (ed.) *The Dread of Difference: Gender and the Horror Film*. Austin, TX: University of Texas Press.

Harper, Sue (2002) 'Zombies, malls, and the consumerism debate: George Romero's *Dawn of the Dead, Americana: The Journal of American Popular Culture (1900–present)*, 1(2), online via www.americanpopularculture.com.

Williams, Tony (2003) *The Cinema of George A. Romero: Knight of the Living Dead*. London: Wallflower Press.

Wood, Robin (2003) *Hollywood from Vietnam to Reagan . . . And Beyond* (2nd edn). New York: Columbia University Press.

Eli Roth

Carolyn, Axelle (2006) '*Hostel* territory', *Fangoria*, 250 (1 February), 62–5.

Crawford, Travis (2003) 'Saturday night *Cabin Fever*', *Fangoria*, 224 (1 July), 40–4.

Jones, Alan (2006) Director's chair: Eli Roth', *Film Review*, 669 (1 May), 76–80.

Quentin Tarantino

De Palma, Brian and Quentin Tarantino (1996) 'Brian De Palma talks to Quentin Tarantino', in John Boorman and Walter Donohue (eds) *Film-makers on Film-making*. London: Faber & Faber.

Gallafent, Ed (2006) *Quentin Tarantino*. London: Longman.

Giroux, Henry, A. (1995) 'Pulp Fiction and the culture of violence', *Harvard Educational Review*, 65(2), 299–315.

Hill, Annette (1997) *Shocking Entertainment: Viewer Responses to Violent Films*. Luton: University of Luton Press.

Mills, Jane (2002) 'Catch me if you can: The Tarantino legacy', *Bright Lights Film Journal*, 36 (April), online via www.brightlightsfilm.com.

Ng, Jenna (2005) 'Love in the time of transcultural fusion: Cinephilia, homage and *Kill Bill*', in Marijke de Valck and Malte Hagener (eds) *Cinephilia: Movies, Love and Memory*. Amsterdam: Amsterdam University Press.

Peary, Gerald (1997) *Quentin Tarantino Interviews*. Jackson, MS: University Press of Mississippi.

Poleg, Dror (2004) 'The unbearable lightness of being cool: Appropriation and prospects of subversion in the works of Quentin Tarantino', *Bright Lights Film Journal*, 45 (August), online via www.brightlightsfilm.com.

Willis, Sharon (2000) 'Style, posture, and idiom: Tarantino's figures of masculinity', in Christine Gledhill and Linda Williams (eds) *Reinventing Film Studies*. London: Arnold, 279–95.

Paul Verhoeven

Bouineau, Jean-Marc (2001) *Paul Verhoeven: Beyond Flesh and Blood*. Paris: Cinéditions.

Hunter, I.Q. (2000) 'Beaver Las Vegas: A fan Boy's defence of *Showgirls*', in Xavier Mendik and Graeme Harper (eds) *Unruly Pleasures: the Cult Film and Its Critics*. Guilford: FAB Press, 189–201.

Shea, Chris, Wade Jennings, Linda Mizejewski, Johanna Schmertz and R.E. Wood (1993) *Special issue, Post Script*, 12(3).

Telotte, J.P. (1999) 'Verhoeven, Virilio and "cinematic derealization" ', *Film Quarterly*, 53(2), 30–8.

Van Scheers, Rob (1997) *Paul Verhoeven*, translated from the Dutch by Aletta Stevens. London: Faber & Faber.
Williams, Linda Ruth (2007) 'Sleeping with the enemy', *Sight and Sound*, 17(2), 18–20.

Jean Vigo

Baldwin, David (1985) '*L'Atalante* and the maturing of Jean Vigo', *Film Quarterly*, 39(1), 21–7.
Johnson, Morgan (2001) 'School's out: celebration and elegy in Jean Vigo's *Zéro de conduite*', *Film Comment*, 37(6), 49–52.
Temple, Michael (1998) 'Dreaming of Vigo', *Sight and Sound*, 8(11), 14–16.
Temple, Michael (2005) *Jean Vigo*. Manchester: Manchester University Press.
Teush, B. (1973) 'The playground of Jean Vigo', *Film Heritage*, 9(1), 11–22.
Vigo, Jean (1932) '*Un chien andalou*', in Luis Bunuel and Salvador Dali, *Un Chien Andalou*. London: Faber & Faber, xxv–xvi.
Zilzer, Gyula (1947) 'Remembrances of Jean Vigo', *Hollywood Quarterly*, 3(2) (winter), 125–8.

John Waters

Chang, Chris (2003) 'John Waters', *Film Comment*, May–June.
Chute, David (1981) 'Still Waters', *Film Comment*, 17(3), 26–32.
Hoberman, J. (2004) 'Back at the raunch', *Sight and Sound*, 14(12), 24–7.
Ives, John G. (1992) *John Waters*. New York: Thunder's Mouth Press.
Waters, John (1981) *Shock Value: A Tasteful Book about Bad Taste*. New York: Dell.
Waters, John (1983) 'John Waters: guilty pleasures', *Film Comment*, 19(4), 20–3.
Waters, John (1984) 'Guilty pleasures', in *Crackpot: the Obsessions of John Waters*. New York: Vintage, 108–15.

James Whale

Curtis, James (2003) *James Whale: A New World of Gods and Monsters*. Minneapolis, MN: University of Minnesota Press.
Gattiss, Mark (1995) *James Whale, a Biography*, London: Cassell.
Heffernan, James A.W. (1997) 'Looking at the monster: "Frankenstein" and Film', *Critical Inquiry*, 24(1), 133–58.
Picart, Caroline Joan (1998) 'Re-birthing the monstrous: James Whale's (mis)reading of Mary Shelley's *Frankenstein*, *Critical Studies in Mass Communication*, 15(4), 382–404.

Ed Wood

Benshoff, Harry (1997) *Monsters in the Closet: Homosexuality in the Horror Film*. Manchester: Manchester University Press.
Bruzzi, Stella (1998) *Undressing Cinema: Clothing and Identities in the Movies*. London: Routledge.
Cooling, Chris (2003) 'Ed Wood, *Glen or Glenda* and the limits of Foucauldian discourse', in Gary D. Rhodes (ed.) *Horror at the Drive-in: Essays in Popular Americana*. Jefferson, NC: McFarland & Company.
Hoberman, J. (1995) 'Ed Wood . . . not', *Sight and Sound*, 5(5), 10–12.

Brian Yuzna

Farren, Paul (2002) 'Producing horror', *Film Base News* [now *Film Ireland*], 84 (1 January), 24–5.

Ferrante, Anthony C. (2003) 'Brian Yuzna looks beyond', *Fangoria*, 255 (1 August), 24–8.

Jones, Alan (1990) 'Brian Yuzna's *Society, StarBurst*', 140 (1 April), 9–12.

Nutman, Philip (1986) '*Re-Animator!*: An interview with Producer Brian Yuzna', *StarBurst*, 91(1 March), 26–9.

Index of film titles

General index

CONTEMPORARY AMERICAN CINEMA

Linda Ruth Williams and Michael Hammond (eds)
Both at University of Southampton, UK

Contemporary American Cinema is the first comprehensive introduction to post-classical American film. Covering American cinema since 1960, the book is unique in its treatment of both Hollywood and non-mainstream cinema. Critical essays from leading film scholars are supplemented by boxed profiles of key directors, producers and actors; key films and key genres; statistics from the cinema industry.

Lavishly illustrated with over fifty film stills in black and white, and colour, the book has two tables of contents allowing students to use the book chronologically, decade-by-decade, or thematically by subject. Designed especially for courses in film, cultural studies and American studies, *Contemporary American Cinema* features a glossary of key terms, fully referenced resources and suggestions for further reading, sample essay questions, suggestions for class work and a filmography.

Contents
The Sixties: *1: Introduction: Endgames and Challenges: Key movements in American Cinema in the 1960s – 2: Debts, disasters and mega-musicals: The decline of the studio system – 3: The American New Wave, Part 1: 1967–1970 – 4. Popular Mainstream Films,1967–1970 – 5: Other Americas: The underground, exploitation and the avant garde – 6: Documentary Cinema in the 1960s –* **The Seventies:** *1: Introduction: Key Movements in 1970s Cinema – 2: The American New Wave, Part 2: 1970–1975 – 3. Popular Mainstream Films, 1970–1975 – 4: New Hollywood and the Rise of the Blockbuster – 5: Blaxploitation –* **The Eighties:** *1: Introduction: Key Movements in 1980s Cinema – 2: Film in the age of Reagan: action cinema and reactionary politics – 3: The Rise of Independent Cinema – 4: Disney and the Family Adventure movie since the 1970s – 5: Vietnam at the movies – 6: New Queer Cinema –* **The Nineties:** *1: Introduction: Key Movements in 1990s Cinema – 2: Cameron and Co.: The Nineties Blockbuster – 3: New Black Cinema – 4: Female Directors and Women in Production – 5: Action Women and Muscle Men – 6: Home Viewing: Video and DVD – Suggested Further Reading – Essay Questions – Bibliography – Filmography – Index*

Contributors include:
Michele Aaron, Jose Arroyo, Tim Bergfelder, Leslie Felperin, Lee Grieveson, Sheldon Hall, Michael Hammond, Jim Hillier, Susan Jeffords, Barbara Klinger, Peter Kramer, Richard Maltby, Jonathan Munby, Steve Neale, Stephen Prince, Eithne Quinn, Mark Shiel, Yvonne Tasker, Linda Ruth Williams, Jim Russell, Mark Jancovich, Cathy Fowler, Brian Winston, Patricia Zimmerman, Carl Plantinga, Geoff King, Jeffrey Sconce.

440pp   0 335 21831 8 (Paperback)   0 335 21832 6 (Hardback)